±10

The Stars of
Robert Burns

by

Catherine Smith PhD

Published by

Masonic Publishing, 30 Loanbank Quadrant, Glasgow, Scotland.

Designed from typeset copy supplied and Printed by
William Anderson and Sons Ltd, Commercial and Colour Printers, Glasgow, Scotland.

The Stars of Robert Burns

ISBN 10: 0-9544268-8-6
ISBN 13: 978-0-9544268-8-0

Contents

Foreword *by John Cairney PhD*

'I disapprove of what you say but I will defend to the death your right to say it.'

So said Voltaire, philosopher, poet, wit and an outstanding figure of the French Enlightenment. He also said, 'Faith consists in believing what reason does not believe.' Both remarks must be borne in mind when considering Dr Smith's redoubtable work, The Stars of Robert Burns. It is hard to describe simply, yet it has a simple aim: to bring to the general reader an aspect of Scotland's National Bard which has hitherto been overlooked. She explores the influence of astrology particularly in the early years of his life, when he was exposed to the old peasant knowledge and practices still current in southwest Scotland. This is a view that does not fall lightly on many ears but I could not fail to be impressed by the weight and breadth of scholarship applied to it.

The book emanates from a lifelong fascination with the poet. As Dr Smith has said herself, she has not written the book as a science text. The author has built up a case for astronomy also being a factor in the poet's development. She looks to discover why he took such a determined stance over the dignity of man, not only in the political and social sense, but in its hidden essence, where the spiritual exists at the heart of the mystery we call life.

It is now universally agreed that Robert Burns was a genius. Dr Smith recognises that it was this faculty that allowed him to span the two disciplines, arts and science, thus allowing mankind to gain the greater benefit of his developing knowledge as his exploration of the mind continued on both fronts. The artist part of Burns looked out from a farm cottage up to the stars, and his astrological and astronomical fascination helped him to understand an older and deeper knowledge that underpinned what he wrote. By dint of a reading obsession he had known since early childhood he sought to improve what was already a keen and curious mind so that he emerged a rounded and learned man. Catherine Smith posits the view that he was a man who looked both ways, one eye turned back to the ancients and the inner sight (sometimes called insight) and the other looking forward (with foresight) to posterity.

Dr Smith has beaten an idiosyncratic pathway to Burns that is all her own and carried the reader with her on a positive tsunami of ideas, propositions, suppositions and conjectures, based nonetheless on exhaustive research and objective selection. This field ranges from Freemasonry to Chinese fireworks taking in the Venerable Bede, Adam Smith and astronomical events en route. Everything is grist to her mill. She has ground out a novel view of Scotland's National Bard. After 250 years of often dogged bardolatry from all sides, that is saying something. Her argument has to be respected because her heart is in every word she writes. As Burns himself said:

> It's no in makin muckle mair:
> It's no in books, it's no in lear,
> To make us truly blest:
> If happiness has not her seat
> An centre in the breast,
> We may be wise, or rich, or great,
> But never can be blest!
> Nae treasures nor pleasures can make us happy lang.
> The heart's ay the part ay that makes us right or wrang.

Acknowledgements

In preparing this book I have studied the complete writings of Burns from facsimiles, early editions or validated transcription, and travelled back to sites connected with his life. I have studied not a few textbooks whose influences on him appear to have been underrated by previous writers. I have studied a wide range of other material extant in his time.

I have collated general data from a wide range of public sources and purported facts have where possible been validated. I have identified when I have taken material from publications. All quotations are from texts out of copyright. When I have learned from specific modern researchers, this is acknowledged. It may be that some reader feels that I have replicated his idea without acknowledgement. If I have done so, it has not been deliberate. Reflect that ideas, once released into open discussion, can very quickly lose their umbilical cord to their originator. Also, an idea can arise, as crystals do, in more than one place in the fluid of human intellect. Reflect too that I have been musing on Burns for fifty years. It may be that the offended reader gained his idea by osmosis from that great human database of circulating thought into which I, after giving birth to it in one of my many jottings, had placed it through speech or writing. I have no wish to deprive anyone of the credit for his idea; I have suffered financially too much myself from my ideas being stolen to wish to hurt another by theft.

I have for my research used my own extensive library and drawn on the resources of other libraries. In childhood, when I began study, I had the benefit of Clydebank Public Library, which was then excellent. In the 1970s, I was given considerable access to books through the libraries in Crieff and Dunblane. I have used the library of the Borthwick Institute of the University of York and numerous local libraries in the British Isles, and a few in the United States. My most recent researches have benefited from the interlibrary service provided through Stirling District Library and have used the National Library of Scotland, whose on-line services have also proved useful. I spent some days reading 18th century texts in Innerpeffray Library. From NASA's site I extracted data on solar and lunar eclipses. I have tapped a range of websites as well as using a disparate range of other sources.

I thank my mother for introducing me as a child to Robert Burns. I thank Cairns Mason for permission to extract data and quote conclusions from his unpublished work on the usage of Innerpeffray Library in the second half of the 18th century. I also thank him for assisting in validating the general data I have used, and for other research support. I thank Bernadette Cahill for her input and guidance on astrological matters and for assisting in analysing the horoscope of Burns. I thank Graham Smith for permission to include his commentary 'Mind and the Internet', which remains his copyright with all rights reserved. I thank Dr John Cairney for agreeing to read my draft and for responding with encouragement and with practical guidance on how I might make my book more focused and accessible.

For all that, this is my personal view of Robert Burns, but I hope you will come to share it with me.

From the hill of Grianne,
Midsummer, 2008

Prologue   *On Some Eccentric Planet*

Herein is related how Burns was born into a theocratic Scotland when people feared natural omens, why Burns believed himself a man of Destiny, and the consequent best way to understand his life.

Thought evolves. Old mindsets fade. Robert Burns, born in 1759 and dying in 1796, lived his life with one foot in the old world of wonder and the other in the world of Enlightenment science. The Enlightenment is considered to have initiated the technological era. Modern science tells us that Mankind is merely microbes living on crusts of aqueous scum formed on the surface of a hot globule that whirls with a multitude of others in the space-time continuum, round a plug-hole temporarily blocked by a much bigger and hotter globule, but that before we are inexorably flushed down the drain, science will cleverly transport Mankind, in a space-age Noah's Ark, to another hot globule with aqueous scum whirling round another blocked plughole, somewhere in a galaxy far far away. Modern science has no place for superstition. Many think it has no awe, has no place for religion, offers us no childlike wonder. That is why, more than perhaps we have ever needed them, we now need people like Robert Burns. For he was a poet.

Works of this poet are known globally if only through the singing of his 'Auld Lang Syne' at party celebrations every time an old year gives way to new. Burns never lost that awe that made his life worthwhile. He feared science was beginning to undermine humankind's childlike wish to hold the universe in awe. Fighting to the death to defend this fundamental human right, he left us wonderful poems and a large legacy of songs.

The modern world thinks of poets as airy-fairy people who, as often as not with assistance of hallucinogens, spontaneously form quirky strings of words. Robert Burns was not like this. In his eyes, drugs were for mugs, and poetry, though inspired, was worthless unless thoroughly crafted. He released nothing until its words, content, structure and meaning were polished to his highest achievable degree. He put his name to nothing unless he believed he had, as input to its creation, done his utmost to understand its matter. He immersed himself in study to achieve his understanding. This is very different from what the modern world thinks is involved in the creation of poetry.

So, to understand Burns fully, and gain the modern very real benefit of his legacy to us, not only do we need to expand our sense of wonder, but we also must experience what it means to get understanding as intense as his. He was born under a periodic comet – one of those that orbit around our Sun rather than merely making a single appearance before disappearing into the depths of the universe. Such comet orbits are very different from the familiar neat tight elliptical orbits of the planets: they are extremely elongated ellipses. But they are ellipses, none the less, returning to the position at which they were first observed. In childhood, Burns studied all he could about comets. His science school books told him the known facts and current theories. His history books told him when comets had been seen and the amazing things that happened at those times. Comets amazed him, for what science knew of them, and for the imagination they inspired.

To understand the man Burns was, we need to learn the pattern of his mind. In childhood his analytic but poetic mind learned to race like a comet, tearing deep into unknown thoughts, each trajectory reaching far, far beyond the tight orbit of the farmyards of his youth, but always each returning to the now and the everyday. Traces of his trajectories lie in what he read. The earliest far-flung orbit of his imagination and enquiry began in fascination with religious intensity around him. To get true value from his legacy, we too must trace immensely elongated elliptical trajectories like those that made him the man he was. His first great trajectory followed comets. We must plunge after him into that enquiry.

Halley's Comet, the same that some theologians have suggested heralded the birth of Jesus Christ, in one of its periodic returns, became visible to the naked eye in late January 1759. The German farmer and amateur astronomer Johann Georg Palitzsh was the first to note its return to Earth, though many were watching for it. Charles Messier was on 21st January 1759 the first professional astronomer to observe the predicted return of Halley's Comet. Until it was confirmed that this was actually Comet Halley, the 'new' comet, that scientists were observing growing brighter in the sky as Robert Burns grew in strength, was named after Messier. Observations of Comet Halley's path then enabled the verification of Newton's recently proposed laws of motion of heavenly bodies.

Being born under this comet caused Burns to have an intense sense of destiny.

Robert Burns left a legacy to the modern world in his poems and songs. His contemporary audiences enjoyed his work not just for its poetic excellence but for its human empathy. They could relate intensely to his works because they shared with him a way of understanding. A quarter of a millennium since his birth, we do not share that culture. Valuable meaning in his legacy is hidden to us. That meaning has important consequences for Mankind. It is worth decoding. To do this requires learning what and how Burns thought. Stage one is to explore modern knowledge of comets, and compare this with how people have reacted to them in the past. By looking at what contemporaries of Burns thought comets meant, we start to appreciate how they would have understood other references in the poet's works. This is the beginning of transporting our minds back in time to enable us to understand this poet's legacy to the modern world.

We don't need to explore comets from the scientific ignorance of the 18th century. But if we explore them intensely we get the feeling of how Burns felt whenever he explored things intensely.

Science has examined and explained comets. Saying it like it is, it makes them unremarkable. But human beings are perverse. Something in us makes us look away from all our modernity and irrationally gaze at the darkness of the night sky if a big one comes by. We don't know what makes us look. If we could understand, we could enrich our modern lives. That understanding would unlock a hidden wealth within that legacy. So let's reflect on comets, such as Comet Halley. Let's reflect on how Burns thought of comets. This gives us a new way of listening to the words of a wonder-inspired poor man, who came into the world a quarter of a millennium before our modern times, his birth announced by a comet.

Burns lived in the 18th century. Then, the written word – and probably speech too – was much more flowery and mellifluous than what is normal in our world. That too makes him a bit more difficult to understand. Unlike us, he didn't 'say it like it is'. But some modern poets say that our down-to-earth blunt speech actually does not 'say it like it is'. They claim we miss out on life because our world doesn't have poetic speech and writing.

Sure, it is true to say that lots of books have been written, lots of serious stuff produced and lots of professors got jobs because of Burns. But it gives a different feel, when we read: many are the books that have been written, uncountable the academic employment and multitudinous the professorial publications that have been created in the name of Robert Burns. It sounds splendid to retail that without measure is the effort that has been expended in generating Burns Suppers and without count the joy and sorrow they have produced. Despite the general sobriety of Robert Burns himself (no good entertainer dare get drunk as it spoils his act) in men-only Burns Suppers heavy drinking has traditionally been non-optional. Vegetarian and alcohol-free Burns Suppers are now becoming quite fashionable.

Numerous are stock phrases in modern English that first saw the light through his pen. These include 'of mice and men'; 'a man's a man for a' that'; 'auld lang syne' and 'cutty sark', the last to some a tall ship, to others a whisky, and to Burns lovers the nickname of a witch. (It actually is the 18th century name for a mini-skirt. Burns was quite Sixties.) Of course, far more quotations from Shakespeare are in general usage. In the general scheme of things Burns is surely merely a poet, and by many thought not a major one. But how many flock to annual Shakespeare Suppers? Yet many celebrate the life of Robert Burns and the man whom he was. People know of works of his principal artistic contemporaries, such as Schiller, Blake, Katsushika Hokusai and Mozart. Yet apart from the last, who was the focus of a controversial biographical film, few could tell you what the man stood for as they can of Robert Burns.

The spirit of this man has some power that survived his early death and lives on now a quarter of a millennium since he was born. Nothing so far generally available that has been written or said about him explains to me this amazing survivability. The feelings in his soul have somehow so far transcended death, partly encoded in his writing, despite the attempts of his first biographers to distort his memory. Somehow it defiantly has grown more powerful as time has passed. Some say it survives in what in his day would have been called the ether. But that is no explanation to the rational mind. The question is unanswered: why does Robert Burns continue to be loved and admired by so many?

It is the source of these feelings of love and admiration that I explore in this study. I hope that through seeking a greater understanding of the survivability of his memory, I might be able to give insight into the meaning that those feelings have for our modern world of increasing fragmentation and conflict. Here was a man who wrote that the most important Good that Humanity could achieve was to act with love for fellow men – true empathetic love totally free from all prejudice, whether of disability, age, race or gender and dissociated from any trace of sectarianism. But such a statement is a commonplace. The life of Burns given down to us does not quite tally with this creed. Why should Burns be remembered when we don't remember others who similarly canted?

There are few facts about Burns. One was that he was born under Halley's Comet. We take comets for granted. We also tend to take for granted that the pre-modern world was awash with childish superstition. Our education has taught us to believe so. It is commonly held that fundamental shifts in attitude took place abruptly in Isaac Newton's era, the late 17th and early 18th century. The emerging Age of Enlightenment left, by the late 18th century, only ignorant country bumpkins in awe at the arrival of such ordinary things as comets. Robert Burns was born at that time amongst such country bumpkins. He lived on that cusp of immense change of attitude, looking back to ancient beliefs, and looking forward to science.

In our modern sophisticated Western world, only children readily believe that elemental Nature sympathises with enmotioned Powers of Good or Evil that permeate a Universe that acts out the unfathomable Mind of some all powerful Creator. We respond with adult laughter at the country bumpkin simplicity implied in 'Tam o' Shanter':

> The wind blew as 'twad blawn its last;
> The rattling showers rose on the blast;
> The speedy gleams the darkness swallow'd;
> Loud, deep, and lang, the thunder bellow'd;
> That night, a child might understand,
> The Deil had business on his hand.

Today, only a child would understand a violent storm as heralding the works of the devil. But that final couplet is ambiguous: it could mean that *even* a child might take warning from such a violent storm that the Devil was at work. Robert Burns challenged the 18th century sophisticate's scientific confidence. Even as he amused his audience deliciously with his rip-roaring ghost story, he made them feel a tiny bit uncomfortable.

The world became more than a tiny bit uncomfortable as the 250th anniversary of his birth approached. With stockmarkets tumbling around the world and banks crashing, taking the life savings of hard-working small business owners with them, some even wondered whether those astrologers had a point when they said that the malefic influences of Saturn and Uranus were slogging it out, with mischief-making Pluto coming to the fore and demanding inexorable transformation. Such thinking is totally irrational – but the global economy seemed to have stopped behaving rationally. Everything seemed dependant on feelings, particularly the feeling of shaken trust in the global financial and economic system.

Feelings are, I believe, at the root of the Burns paradox. Exploring feelings is the route to understanding him. To comprehend the feelings of Robert Burns, this book aims to set out how people of his time might have formed their thoughts. In particular, it seeks to elucidate what was in his mind and influenced his own thoughts. I start with the belief that embryonic thought born into the innocent child moulds round evolving experience and education. Those who have before me written of Burns have of course explored what they considered the important aspects of both these external influences. They have failed to explain to me why Burns is loved. The explanation might lie amongst the 'trace element' influences that have been set aside as essentially irrelevant. I re-examine those, and so look at Burns from an unusual perspective.

It turns out that considering these other influences causes a big change in perspective. For example, the typical modern western reader will neither accuse me of blasphemy in my way of telling the birth-story of Robert Burns, nor take seriously a modern old-wife's prophecy. But in Scotland in 1759 neither the coming of a comet nor the utterance of an old witch over a new-born child would have gone without at least an eyebrow raised. Alongside comets in potency as portents in olden times were eclipses of the Sun and, to a lesser degree, the Moon. For 1715 Edmund Halley predicted the path of a total solar eclipse across Britain to a high degree of accuracy – and its arrival in the face of a Jacobite uprising caused panic in the London financial markets. With the Jacobite insurgence defeated, the concerned Hanoverian powers caused in June 1718 the mother Grand Lodge of English Freemasonry to be established in London, to create an indigenous English antidote to subversive Scottish-centred Jacobite philosophies within secret or secretive societies. Halley had his birth horoscope drawn up. It is kept now in the Bodleian Library, Oxford. Despite their precautions, the Hanoverian regime and London financial markets got a real fright when in 1745 Bonnie Prince Charlie landed in Scotland and successfully marched south. In 1744 there had appeared a comet so bright that it could be seen in daylight – and it had six tails. Hanoverians had, after all, come with a comet; they would surely go with another. Yet this is considered by historians to have been the Age of Reason. There is some mismatch here. So let's get back to comets to begin to understand what is behind it.

By the end of the 19th century education had been fully industrialised. The tumbling wild waters of youthful minds were divided into two mill races, one called Arts or Humanities and the other called Science. Each stream, passing through its particular processes, emerged polluted. Within their processes, each of the races, rat-ridden, has further divided into specialisation. Tumbled back into the common sea of Humankind, where the thick streams chance to mix, their waters froth and hiss with angry animosity. The sea grows covered with encrustation of preconception and its darkened depths are denied fecundity.

In other words, we are all so caught up in our own little world that we can't easily find a shared view on those really big issues whose solution would enrich all our lives with peace and prosperity. Instead, our energies go to getting and spending, wasting our power, as a different poet observed.

Scientists have created much of the fabric of our modern world. So science gets a lot of the blame. Scientists also use words that those who studied Humanities don't relate to. So they are dismissed as living on another planet. They are dismissed as boring – not the kind you want to get stuck with at a party. They've got no fun in them. It is often difficult in the modern world to remember that even the most boring dour modern scientist was once a little girl or boy wowed by the wonder of the universe. But it isn't just scientists who are stuffy. It is difficult to believe that the most narrowly focused professor of literature, supercilious of the glory and wonder of the science of comets, was once a little girl or boy with an open mind no different from all others in the playgroup.

The wonder of Burns is that he never lost the ability to wonder. That ability enriched him. If we could relearn the ability to wonder that we each once had, we would be enriched. We can relearn by asking why, and not stop asking till we get answers. That's what infants do: "why? why? why?", till even parents answer the blunt cut-off: "because". Childminders tend to be even quicker to silence whys. Each time a why is silenced a bit of the magic of the universe is dimmed to us. Mass education makes us look at life through a glass darkly.

Burns was substantially self-educated, and lived in the days before specialisation had matured to its modern granularity. So he escaped the destruction of his sense of wonder. He was interested in everything, and wanted to know the technical details. So to understand the mind of Burns, we must try to return our own minds to their state of infancy and be open to the detail of everything that confronts us. In particular, Burns was very interested in science. Specifically, as a very young child he was enthralled by astronomy. Because of his own birth time, he would have wanted to learn all there was to know about comets. In his day, that was not a lot – but to feel how he would have felt in our day, we should seek to know all he would have got to know had he had the opportunity to live in our time.

His language shows that he was constantly aware of the world around him and its place in the universe. To James Smith, he confirmed a fact by swearing,

> by sun an' moon,
> And ev'ry star that blinks aboon.

He went on to lament his own fate in terms that make sense only to the modern casual reader of newspaper horoscopes:

> The star that rules my luckless lot,
> Has fated me the russet coat,
> An' damn'd my fortune to the groat.

He included in the first edition of his poems a long description of his encounter with Coila, his poetic Muse. This 'Vision' is what modern artists would call a manifesto. Burns made Coila remark:

> I mark'd thy embryo-tuneful flame,
> Thy natal hour.

That natal hour was under a louring stormy sky, behind which lurked that comet.

Burns learned of that comet, and in his early school days was asking the why of comets. Reaching the best answer available at the time led him to lots of other reflections. To follow the path of his thought, and experience wonder such as he felt, what better first step than to explore comets. So, let's begin.

Comets are visually very interesting things. Some give spectacular tail shows, like the one in 1744. Their tails confuse perception: they suggest fast movement to human brains familiar with such tails only in thrown firebrands. Yet on any one night a comet appears stationary. In Chinese calligraphy they are broom-stars. They are also cloud-banners and blue flags. In China on the first moon of each summer, special rice is thrown into rivers to persuade fish not to devour the soul of poet Chu Yuan. In 278 BC he threw himself into the sorry waters in the face of the devastation of humankind by the comet spirit. He prayed that love could climb to the ninth heaven and soothe the comet. By 1540 it had been observed that as comets spin round the Sun their tails turn to remain pointed away from the Sun.

Burns used a secret mark, chosen when he became a Freemason. There is only one extant example of this mark in his hand. There are different views of whether it has some meaning or is purely abstract lines. I have come to the conclusion that it represents a comet – and I have concluded that this was understood by the Masonic Brotherhood in his time. The Brotherhood, steeped in the ancient art of understanding the heavens, taught him that the sign of the comet represented the beginning of a new era. In childhood, he had already learned that comets were messengers from the great Power in whose universe lived Mankind.

Halley predicted periodicity in one comet, and it was the one that reappeared in January 1759. He did not observe this return, for he died in 1742. But in any case, the comet was late – nearly two years late – its journey through the outer solar system having taken 618 days longer than expected. This was because of the gravitational attractions of Jupiter and Saturn. Or so said the three French mathematicians, Alexis Clairault, Joseph Lalande and Nicole-Reine Lapaute. Others insisted that it was because God decided when comets would be seen on Earth. Even the discovery of periodicity in certain comets had not shaken this firmly-held belief amongst the old school. Rather they said their brightness as seen on Earth and their continuing unpredictability, even if more limited, demonstrated the Almighty's power to use His creations to effect His ends. They came too as omens: when the cannon exploded that killed King James II in 1460 it was remarked that only the previous night had a great comet been seen in the sky.

We don't think that way these days. In the 18th century, people were not as certain as we are. When his neighbour at Ellisland Farm outside Dumfries allowed Burns to use a little hermitage he had built, the poet repaid in philosophical verse advising the wayfarer to enjoy his youth 'beneath thy morning star', and not let ambition distract

> As the day grows warm and high,
> Life's meridian flaming nigh.

Burns watched the planets as they wheeled across the night sky. Early in childhood he became aware of their romance, when the nightless Scottish summer days gave away again to evening, and he could enjoy that magic that still lingered round the ancient Sun festival of Lammas, at the start of August. Then,

> When corn rigs are bonie,
> Beneath the moon's unclouded light,
> [He] held awa to Annie.

Love talk then embraced the constellations he had learned to name, the meteors that flashed and were gone, and the planets that looked down inscrutable, unblinking, in the infinitely sparkled darkness behind the clearly shining Moon. Here Mars, there Saturn, that great one Jupiter.

At the start of the 21st century scientists are again regarding Jupiter as an important factor not only in affecting the trajectories of comets but also in diverting comets and major inter-planetary objects from heading directly towards Earth. Jupiter is the largest object that orbits our Sun and is three hundred times more massive than Earth. In the 1990s scientists were able to use their latest telescopes and satellites to observe the impact of a comet onto Jupiter. First of all the comet broke into pieces which then fell through Jupiter's swirling surface leaving a series of enormous storm vortices.

Comets are also very fashionable in science fiction and near-science commentary. One proposal is that human civilisations became increasingly warlike after Earth in 1500 BC passed through the tail of comet 12P/Pons-Brocks that is due to pass near Earth again on its return to the Sun in 2024. The close encounter three and a half millennia ago was around the time that the stone circle was installed at the Stonehenge complex. Around the world is geological and other evidence said to demonstrate the violent and traumatic effect of Earth's atmosphere interfacing with that comet's tail debris. The theme makes for dramatic scenes in blockbuster movies.

We moderners invoke suspension of disbelief to enable us to wonder at all the drama of science fiction. We maintain cold prosaic detachment to scientific fact. Many of us are never awed by the universe and all it contains, because we have explanations and descriptions that bring it all down to too sober earth. But hidden behind detached objective science is a reality of immense wonder. As a poet, Burns never allowed his awe to be stolen from him. He never ceased to marvel, as he did in his 'Cottar's Saturday Night', that

Circling Time moves round in an eternal sphere.

Thus too do dark distant embryo comets move. When they fall towards the Sun, in the eyes of a poet they fall like angels falling from heaven, and bode ill and evil as they fall.

Halley's Comet is the most famous of all the periodic comets. Officially known to astronomers as 1P/Halley, it has in the past been seen around every seventy six years. It is expected again in 2061. But who knows what close encounter it might have between now and then in the outer solar system, to where it returned after its last approach to the Sun in 1986. Then *Challenger* Space Shuttle Mission STS-51-L set out on 28th January to observe Halley's Comet from low Earth orbit. The seven people on board included schoolteacher Christa McAuliffe intended to be the first civilian in space. *Challenger* exploded when only ten miles up in the atmosphere, a mere 74 seconds after an apparently successful lift-off from Cape Canaveral in Florida, USA. The thousands who watched on the ground and the millions who later observed it on world-wide television screens were horrified. The Space Shuttle was grounded. Mission STS-61-E, scheduled to set off in March 1986 to carry the ASTRO-1 platform into space to study the comet, never got off the ground. ASTRO-1 did not fly until late in 1990 on STS-35.

There had been much demurring about whether the *Challenger* flight should go ahead. Its launch was delayed for three days because of bad weather. Actual countdown was stalled for two hours because of freezing on the shuttle itself and its ground support structure. There has since been intensive and wide-ranging enquiry into what caused the disaster. This concluded it was caused by a combination of technical weaknesses, weather extremes, and human hubris. But an increasingly vocal modern lobby, new-age astrologers, said that it was ill-fated from its inception. Halley's Comet is bad luck, and always has been, some say. Others say, bad luck for some is good luck for others. There can be few who saw good luck in the *Challenger* episode.

Other disasters were to follow. Direst warnings of astrologers seemed borne out. They predicted the 'passing of great men'. Popular Swedish Social Democrat Prime Minister, Olaf Palme, strolling home through Stockholm, unguarded, as he so often had done before, was assassinated on 28th February. On 31st March, a mere two weeks after the announcement of the happy event that Prince Andrew was engaged to be married to Sarah Ferguson, a great fire irreplaceably destroyed part of iconic British tourist attraction, Hampton Court Palace.

Meanwhile, the Soviet unmanned spacecraft *Vega I* successfully flew within 5,500 miles of Halley's Comet. It succeeded in sending back scientifically meaningful television pictures. It was soon possible to declare that the core at the head of the comet was at least three miles wide, that the comet consisted mainly of ice and that the gas forming the tail was emitted several times faster than had been supposed. (More accurate analysis, involving other input from the *Giotto* spacecraft, corrected the measurement of core diameter to nine miles.) In deep space a comet would be a black invisible lump, but as it approaches the Sun, the warming nucleus emits gases that become the visible tail. Stardust such as this is gathered up in our atmosphere whenever Earth moves through a comet's tail. As the tail trails and scatters, a comet must therefore shrink and change.

Prologue *On Some Eccentric Planet*

The greatest disaster in the wake of Halley's Comet in 1986 was to happen in late April. On 30th April the Soviet Union admitted the truth of Western claims that there had been a major accident at a nuclear power station. (Monitoring stations in Sweden, Finland and Denmark had reported abnormally high radioactivity levels in the atmosphere.) The scars of that accident mark a whole generation of those who lived in its vicinity; they die, some very slowly, but all horribly, from radiation poisoning. In the Ukraine, at Chernobyl, sixty miles north of Kiev, Number Four reactor exploded. This is the worst accident in the history of the development of nuclear power. The heat of the explosion took radioactive dust high into the atmosphere. The prevailing April winds carried it north and west over the shoulder of the Earth. In due course, those winds met the Atlantic winds, and the dust came down as rain. Onto the Atlantic shores of north Ireland and the west of Scotland fell radioactive dust, clearly measurable, polluting grass, and emerging in the milk of the cows. Parents of infants were warned to avoid feeding them fresh milk from these western herds. Any traces of stardust that fell from Halley's Comet were swamped by this poison of radioactivity.

That same meeting of air movements in the upper atmosphere undoubtedly over millennia has caused stardust to fall with the rains. So some say there is truth in the ancient myths that the Ayrshire coast and Scotland's western isles are indeed, like Ireland, sprinkled with stardust. So in 1759, with a comet overhead, and a child newly born, perhaps it was not unreasonable for an old woman to prophesy that this child would be different.

Horrors like Chernobyl so overshadowed the year that little global attention was given to celebrations in New York on 4th July of the hundredth birthday of the Statue of Liberty. The marriage of 'Andy and Fergie' on July 23rd, watched by 300 million television viewers, did not lift the gloom of the year when spring never came. On August 25th a volcano in northeastern Cameroon, thought extinct, suddenly emitted a cloud of toxic gas that spurted up through Lake Nios in its caldera. Over a thousand people who had lived nearby choked to death. And, by the way, by the end of 1986 insider dealing was proven indeed to be rife on Wall Street. Also that year, top people in the US government were shown to be having secret diplomatic dealings with Iran, involving the supply of weapons.

Science has told us that the human brain works in part by finding patterns and making a meaning out of those patterns. When it recognises correlations, the brain has a tendency to attribute causality. So, when there are lots of coincidences of unpleasant things, and the one common feature is that there is a comet in the sky, unless they take the detached scientific view, human communities are apt to blame the comet for the disasters. Before science, comets got a lot of blame. The general mass of people thought of them as bad omens.

Aware of the dire omen of his own entry into the world, in 1788 Burns could, in his goodwill poem to Miss Cruickshank, a friend's musical young daughter who helped him with his song writing, pen astrological blessing:

> Never baleful stellar lights,
>
> Taint thee with untimely blights.

Traditionally, the arrival of a comet above all heralded great change. Those early months of 1986 there was rapprochement between the United States and the USSR. While not giving any formal recognition to the State of Israel, Pope John Paul II visited and spoke within Rome's central synagogue. On May 14th the Soviet leader Mikhail Gorbachev spoke publicly about the Chernobyl disaster, reiterating his earlier overtures for an ending of nuclear armaments by the end of the year 2000. By then, the city of Pripyat, next to Chernobyl, was a ghost town. But the same harsh weather that weakened *Challenger*'s plumbing and perhaps destroyed Chernobyl, that year that spring never came, also worsened the effects of famine in the Soviet Union. Within four years the Berlin Wall had fallen. Soon the USSR was history.

Of course, few people in the modern world attribute the timing of any of these unconnected events with the return of a periodic comet; that would smack too much of predestination and make a mockery of such modern sciences as Chaos Theory. For those of religious leaning, it would suggest that God denied human beings true free will. At least it would suggest He is arbitrary, if He must scourge Mankind at pre-defined intervals and predictable times. Such arguments have been touted for many centuries, and have achieved almost universal acceptance – in so far as people even think about the question, nowadays. Things were not so clear cut in 1759.

Robert Burns was born into the era that academics now designate as the Enlightenment. Academics tell us that the 18th century, particularly its latter half, is the time when modern thought, based on Reason, firmly took control. It overcame, indeed ousted, the last vestiges of mediaeval unscientific irrational superstition and unfounded beliefs of old wives' tales. In 1759 in Dublin, Arthur Guinness opened a brewery that in due course became the largest in the world. The Duke of Bridgewater commissioned a canal with innovative tunnels and aqueducts. The British Museum was opened. The first blast furnace became fully operational, installed by John Wilkinson at Bilston in Staffordshire, England. This was the true beginning of the Modern Era. In this era, industrialisation, materialism and consumerism took firm root. This era saw the emergence of our wonderful modern world.

There were other infants who, like Robert Burns, were touched with some fallout from this auspicious far wandered star that reappeared to light the night sky of early 1759. On 6th May 1758 in Arras in France was born Maximilien François Robespierre. He became the Jacobin leader during the French Revolution. On 27th April 1759, Mary Wollstonecraft was born in London. She was a vocal advocate for equality for women. William Pitt the Younger, twice Prime Minister of Britain, was born on May 28th 1759. On August 24th 1759, William Wilberforce, antislavery advocate, was born in Hull. On November 10th 1759 at Marbach, Wurttemberg, in Germany, was born poet and dramatist Johann Christoph Friedrich von Schiller. Each of these, in infancy, was sprinkled with the stardust of the comet's tail.

In early September, fighting what historians call the Seven Years War, died James Wolfe, British commander who captured Quebec in Canada. The city's French defender, Louis Joseph de Montcalm-Gozon de Saint-Véran, Marquis de Montcalm, also died. Their souls, in the allegory of some contemporaries, were carried to the heavens by the comet as it sped off into the darkness.

The first to be identified as periodic, Halley's Comet became the most famous periodic comet. It is visible without the aid of a telescope. Its period is such that it might be seen twice in one human lifetime.

It was in 1705 that Halley identified the comet of 1682 with that seen in 1607 and 1531, and thus predicted its return around 1758. He had examined how close each recorded comet came towards the Sun before it turned. He noted the inclination of each comet path to the plane of the planets. He noted at what longitude each comet turned – it is approximately 302 degrees. With other significant astronomical data also constant, he claimed these three supposedly different comets must be one and the same. Its three measured appearances were also almost equally spaced in time. Thus this was probably a periodic comet. He then calculated an orbit for his proposed periodic comet. He was the first person to base such predictive astronomical work on Isaac Newton's recent concept of gravity.

All comets have orbits that are what are known as conic sections. Take an ice cream cone. Cut it in two. Lay it so that you can see all the ice cream within the cone. The cut wafer around the ice cream is a conic section. This section is the shape of a comet's path around the Sun. Probably your cut divided the ice cream at the top of the cone. If so, you have produced a typical comet orbit, that is open ended; the comet goes round the Sun once and never comes back. If you've cut the cone with all the top ice cream allocated to one part, your section is oval. This is the orbit of a periodic comet.

Teachers in ancient Greece expected all their pupils to understand conic sections. These days such matters are the preserve of those social outcasts, mathematics scholars. Amongst the wealthy musically inclined acquaintances of Burns was a man called Charles Sharpe. Burns sent him a ballad in April 1791, enclosing it in a humorous letter, posing as a near-naked beggarly itinerant versifier. Burns described each piece of the fictitious vagrant's clothing, ending with the hat:

> "My hat indeed is an old favourite; & though I got it literally for 'an old song', I would not exchange it for the best beaver in Britain. I was for several of my earlier years a kind of factotum servant to a country Clergyman, where I pickt up, among other scraps of learning, a smattering in some branches of the mathematicks. Whenever I feel inclined to rest myself on my way, I take my seat under a hedge, & laying my wallet of ballads on the one side, & my fiddle-case on the other, I place my hat between my legs, & can by means of its brim, or rather brims, go through the whole doctrine of the Conic Sections."

Conic sections are beautifully simple to demonstrate accurately, yet underlie all the fundamental movements of the universe. Mathematician Graham Smith finds this a refreshingly satisfactory elegance amidst the brain-daunting modern mania for hyper-number-crunching exotic algorithmic models of the advanced computer age in which we now live.

Halley's Comet is not generally the brightest or most spectacular comet. Likewise, Burns did not consider himself to be the brightest light in the Edinburgh in which he spent so short a part of his life. Indeed, his own period of acclaim was so short that he typically used the analogy not of a comet, but of a meteor. Using metaphor he often repeated, he wrote to his correspondent Dr Moore on 23rd April 1787 about his temporary socially important acquaintances in Edinburgh:

> "To the rich, the great, the fashionable, the polite, I have no equivalent to offer; and I am afraid my meteor appearance will by no means entitle me to a settled correspondence with any of you, who are the permanent lights of genius and literature."

But it was a comet that he used in his allegory a week later in the parting letter of thanks he wrote to William Dunbar. Dunbar was then Senior Warden at Canongate Kilwinning Lodge. In that role, he played a key part in having Burns acclaimed as Poet Laureate of Freemasonry. There is dispute whether any formal inauguration in that role took place, but there is no dispute that Brother Burns was acclaimed Scotland's Bard.

Burns seemed a mere passing fad to most of his Edinburgh audiences, fading like so many who enjoy a moment of celebrity, a fifteen minutes of fame. In the same way, in every century many comets appear that are more impressive than Halley but those that are periodic have periods much longer that Halley's. At the very end of the 20th century very many people saw the periodic Comet Hale-Bopp. Discovered independently by two American observers, Alan Hale and Thomas Bopp, it is officially known as C/1995 O1. It was visible to the naked eye for eighteen months.

Having been spotted when it was still a long way from the Sun, viewers hoped that Hale-Bopp would be spectacular. It was. The nucleus of this comet has been measured as twenty five miles wide. Close to Earth, it nearly challenged Dog Star Sirius for brightness. Its long double visible tail was an attention-grabber. Scientists were even more delighted to find it had another tail too. It was of nearly invisible sodium. This was a very attenuated pillar of salt. Hale-Bopp was found to have an unexpectedly large amount of heavy hydrogen or deuterium in its composition. This was within what scientists call heavy water. This suggested that, contrary to some opinion, the life-giving water on Earth is unlikely all to have arrived via impacting comets.

Burns knew the scientific explanation of the origins of life. So, in a letter from Edinburgh to James Dalrymple of Orangefield, in February 1787, remarking in passing

> "I am naturally of a superstitious cast",

he went on to describe the excellent reception that the Earl of Glencairn had given him. He then contrasted that man's true nobility with two self-important persons:

> "At best, they are but ill-digested lumps of Chaos, only one of them strongly tinged with bituminous particles and sulphureous effluvia."

Hale-Bopp passed closest to the Sun on 1st April 1997, and got nicknamed the Great Comet of 1997. I then lived in Wapping, east of the City of London. I saw it clearly in the evenings in the western sky through all the city haze and diesel dust.

On 11th March 1997, as the comet approached, Japan suffered its worst ever nuclear reactor problem, with one at Tokaimura discharging radiation into the atmosphere. On 15th April, fire swept through a tent city near Mecca in Saudi Arabia, killing over 200 pilgrims and injuring many others. In May, the British general election overturned many years of Conservative control by giving a handsome majority to the New Labour Party. Tony Blair became Prime Minister. On 10th May an earthquake shook northern Iran, making over 50,000 homeless. In June in Indonesia began the worst forest fires in Southeast Asian history. Millions suffered respiratory effects from the pollution. Then central Europe suffered its worst flooding in two centuries. Up in space, the Russian space station *Mir* collided with its unmanned cargo supply vessel. The space station lost oxygen and tumbled out of control, requiring urgent help. On 1st July, in accordance with an agreement made with the Chinese government of 156 years previously, Hong Kong reverted from being a British Crown Colony and returned to Chinese control. Days later, the Southeast Asian economic crisis began. Within months, began in earnest the melt-down of Japanese financial institutions. This plunged Japan into more than a decade of economic recession. At the start of August, Soufrière Hills volcano on the island of Montserrat, which had been grumbling for some time, erupted and destroyed the city of Plymouth. In a car crash in Paris on 31st August Diana, Princess of Wales, died along with her boyfriend Dodi Fayed and their driver. Mother Teresa, Nobel Peace Prize winner, died in Calcutta, but the media attention was still on Diana. On 26th September, the worst earthquakes in Italy since 1980 caused major damage to the Giotto and other frescoes at the Basilica of St Francis of Assisi. In early October Hurricane Pauline caused extensive damage in Southern Mexico leaving over 20,000 homeless. On October 27th the Dow Jones index took its then biggest fall in history. This triggered computer systems to go automatically into 'sell' mode, worsening the impact. In November, excessive rain caused severe flooding in Somalia; a quarter of a million people were made homeless and cholera soon began to grip and kill.

Tom Bopp's brother and sister-in-law, out photographing his comet as it approached its most spectacular showing, were killed in a late night car crash.

There are those who refuse to take the objective view and accept that all of this was just coincidence. Even in the modern world there are some people who believe that comets are bad luck. But going through any period of any year we can construct a catalogue of disasters and great changes. The fact is that, with modern equipment, a dozen or so comets are discovered every year. But astronomers had to go back through their records to 1811 to identify any comet that had been seen easily for anything near that length of time as Hale-Bopp; and that Great Comet had been visible only for about nine months. Its date happens to have been around the time of the retreat of Napoleon from Moscow. Once coincidences are noted, the nature of the human mind causes them to be instinctively attributed with some kind of causal relationship.

Those who want to infer them can attach a lot of causal relationships to Comet Hale-Bopp. Just as it reached its closest to the Sun, zoologists correlated death of fish to a growing hole in the ozone layer above Antarctica. Astronomers announced they had found a huge stream of antimatter at the heart of the Milky Way. They also decided there existed clouds of invisible dark matter whose presence around the universe could only be detected through examining gravitational distortions of light from distant stars. The planet Venus had been known since the 1970s to trail behind her dress of unrevealing atmosphere a long fine gauze train of ions. The SOHO satellite (Solar Heliospheric Observatory) reconnoitred the train that spiralled round the Sun behind her as she danced through her orbit. It found it was at least 28 million miles long. The meteorologist Alan O'Neill demonstrated there was a connection between the South American warm air system called El Niño and the collapse of anchovy fishing in Peru, drought in Australia, and late monsoons in India.

In the minds of many, to believe that the arrival of a comet causes things that happen around the time of its appearance is no more unreasonable than to accept some of the hypotheses that science puts forward to explain things. For example, it is not so silly to talk of the spirits of things natural when scientists announce that forest trees co-operate by exchanging food resources with the help of fungi amongst their roots. Canadian researchers announced this conclusion on 7th August 1997.

There is that other scientific claim, announced on 1st August 1997 by the Division of Planetary

Sciences of the American Astronomical Society in Cambridge, Massachusetts: the Moon was created early in the history of the Earth by a lump of Earth being knocked off during collision with a planet three times as large as Mars. It might seem a good explanation, but there are others equally good. And how come there was another big planet out there? How come there are no crumbs orbiting Earth?

We all now know that Chaos Theory says that the flap of a butterfly wing in a tropical rain forest can cause a hurricane in the Atlantic. So surely it is just as reasonable that a big chunky thing like a comet racing past in the night might cause a ripple in the molten centre of the Earth, and awaken a volcano. It simply happens to be substantially easier to make number-crunching computer models that test such theories as moons being created by billiard-ball impacts than it is to model the fluid dynamics of a molten sphere with a floating crust disrupted by the gravitational passing of a firefly.

Credulity may be the lot of the ignorant, but hubris founded on deification of rational number-crunching computers can be the sin of the scientist. Dullness is the curse of those who enumerate so much that they blind themselves to the universe they measure. Wonder is the gift of the poet. Two decades after young Burns first studied astronomy, he could see himself with his love,

> "making our remarks on Sirius, the nearest of the fixed stars; or surveying a Comet flaming inoxious by us . . . or in a shady bower of Mercury or Venus, dedicating the hour to love . . . while the most exalted strains of Poesy and Harmony would be the ready spontaneous language of our souls!"

These remarks were tangential ponderings written late on a Sunday night as his 29th birthday approached. He was stuck in an attic in Edinburgh, with a shattered knee. He had suffered a tangential encounter with a coach a month earlier. The injury made him a cripple for months. What a disaster for a man whose fine dancing had enhanced his attractiveness in an Edinburgh that allocated favourites fifteen minutes of fame. His leg injury gave him recurrent problems.

Tangential ponderings are not 'good style', according to modern editors of English-language writings – unless those editors happen to be Irish. It is the old Celtic way to nest idea within idea within idea, spiralling precipitate into depths of seeming irrelevant and irrecoverable exploration as into a black hole in the universe of thought, but then as deftly climbing out to return the listener safely to the original firm ground of the storyline. Burns wrote this way. It was a legacy from Celtic rootings of his lineage. I follow a similar way in this book, but I make no pretence to achieving his expertise. Plunging off into the seeming irrelevant can be disconcerting to those who like the linear predictability of 'good English' composition. But, the giddy rush of the roller-coaster is the spice and thrill of the funfair. Relax into it. You will be brought home safe, just as audiences of Burns relaxed into his vibrant style and were returned gently to satisfied rest.

His style of writing was exciting, taking his listener or his reader off on wonderful tangents that seemed nothing to do with the apparent matter of the poem or letter, but always with purpose and always reined back to full control in conclusion, giving satisfaction of a story well told.

> O, how that *Name* inspires my style!
> The words come skelpin' rank an' file,
> Amaist before I ken!

The ready measure rins as fine,
As *Phoebus* and the famous *Nine*
    Were glowrin owre my pen.
My spavet *Pegasus* will limp,
    Till ance he's fairly het;
And then he'll hilch, an' stilt, an' jimp,
    And rin an unco fit;
But least then, the beast then
        Should rue this hasty ride,
    I'll light now, and dight now
        His sweaty, wizen'd hide.

To give you some idea of that highly focused apparent lack of direction of his writing, I too intend to lead you off on many a tangent. All at first perhaps may seem irrelevant, but all have the one purpose. They have been written to explore inside the mind of a man who, in my view, has for too long been wronged in the images of him presented to the world. Here was a man of superstition and of science who became a highly accurate Exciseman and spoke in poetry and music. Part of his message to the world is that true science should be cause for wonder.

Comets are wonderful. When ubiquitous television makes some remark on the visibility of such a smudge against the darkness beyond the glitz of real life, we can be persuaded to glance up through city haze to try to see one in the night sky. But we then just get on with living, the moment of childlike awe gone like the fast burning of a meteor.

Hale-Bopp wasn't the only sign in the sky in 1996: Comet Hyakutake (C/1996 B2) came much closer to Earth. Had Hale-Bopp been as close, it would have been brighter than the full moon. Being the brighter, Hale-Bopp was a fitting comet to mark the end of the Western millennium, its visibility the most impressive of the preceding thousand years. With the aid of their equipment, observers could see that its tail stretched half across the sky.

The northern hemisphere saw Hale-Bopp on its way to the Sun and the southern hemisphere on its way out, because its orbit is almost at right angles to the plain of the solar system. Despite this orientation, the comet had a close encounter with Jupiter on its way out. Jupiter's gravity gave it a sharp tug. This has significantly shortened its periodicity; it is next due to be visible to the human eye from Earth in the year 4380, or thereabouts. It would previously have been expected around two millennia later.

It is easy to dismiss unscientific beliefs that still abounded in the second half of the 18th century. It is easy to laugh at panic reaction to natural things. Yet, all our science has not removed panic from the lives of even the most educated in the modern world, as has been shown by the response to the credit crunch that set in during 2007. Just so, some people still panic when they see a comet.

The arrival of a comet with a larger nucleus than any previously measured incited an unusually extreme comet-panic, perhaps assisted by the Internet then just becoming commonly available. A fair number of people convinced themselves Hale-Bopp was being followed by an alien spacecraft. Its arrival gave the sign for the thirty eight followers of Heaven's Gate, an American cult in San Diego, to commit mass suicide. The cult's two founders, Marshall Applewhite and

Justin Spaid, also killed themselves. They had convinced their followers that planet Earth was about to be recycled, and the only chance of survival was to rid themselves of the chains of their human bodies, and let their beings be carried away in that spaceship that travelled alongside the comet. The group had chosen an ascetic life and funded itself by offering professional website development for paying clients. The manner of the demise of these forty people indicates to some the extreme form of a sense of futility that increasing numbers of sociologists fear is endemic in the modern, so-called advanced, economies. Those who have belief in an all-powerful God of Goodness pray for their souls, and pray for the future of a world from which such cults arise.

Despite the blockbuster movies of earth-shattering disaster, and the real but tiny risk of Earth suffering devastating impact with another object in its revolution round a Sun that itself moves through a galaxy that is also moving through the unknown darkness of the universe, scientists can now confidently tell us that comets are not the God-sent harbingers of human misery that those mediaeval scaremongers suggested.

Historians too can reassure us that chroniclers often used the sighting of comets simply to enable calibration of their records against those of others. For example, Chinese astronomers may have noted the sighting of Halley's Comet in 467 BC. They did note its return in 240 BC, as did observers of Babylon, Persia and other States of Mesopotamia. In 87 BC it was adopted as the symbol of sovereignty of Tigranes the Great, identifying him as a King of Kings, endorsed by the gods. The 12 BC return is the one associated with the Star of Bethlehem, though with the timing so far out a supernova is more likely. In 66 AD the fact that the comet was periodic was noted in the Talmud, with this observation attributed to Rabbi Yehoshua ben Hananiah. This was at the time when the allotted span of man was considered to be three score years and ten. However, the allotted span of a woman, if she survived childbirth, was longer even then. So the rabbi probably got the idea from some old woman. As an infant granny took her onto the flat roof of her house and pointed to this moving tailed star. Her granny told her it would turn almost overhead and depart. When granny had been an infant, she said, her granny had taken her up, shown her the same star, and told her how it would turn and return as she approached the end of her days, and that she must tell her tiny grand-daughter of the wonderful star.

"You will not see that star again until you are as old as I am, but then you will see it", said granny. "It is a wonder that wanders through the great void, but always comes back." she added. "So, when you do see it again, you tell your grand-daughter that I showed it to you when it last came by on its wanderings."

The little girl gazed in wonder at this old wife's tale, and stored the memory of it until she was a wrinkled old woman, useless for everything but the amusement of infants. Then the night came when she did indeed see the strange star again, and knew that the old wife's tale was true. And so she passed on the story to the little infant girl in her care, and told her stories of the wandering of the star through the unknown of the great void, and the adventures, the monsters, the fears and joys, that the spirit of the comet met in its long eternal journey.

The Dark Ages of Europe are so called because of a failure of the light of knowledge. There is an absence of records for the period owing to death by famine, disease or armed aggression of those who wrote, to a dearth of education, and to destruction of writings at the hands of armed men. Thus the comet's return for the years 141, 218, 295, 374, 451, 530, 607, 684 and 760 are available for those who wish to retrofit to it great human catastrophe.

Robert Burns had a school book that gave world history in the form of a detailed chronicle. Amongst all the big political events and wars were statements of natural disasters and the sightings of comets. He was a voracious reader. As a child he read these lists of happenings, and in his mind he too could see that comets were often noted near the time of big events. He noted this in the light of another text book – this time on science – stating that comets were messengers of God.

The return of Halley in 837 really suits those who look for catastrophic associations. Calculations suggest that in that year Halley's Comet passed extremely close to Earth, and its tail may have stretched half way across the sky. This is around the time when the kings of Wessex began to throw their weight around Britain. King Alfred is the best known of this imperial dynasty. People are now beginning to question whether he was such a good guy as he alone says he was. (He is not to be confused with King Arthur, though usually is.)

In 1066 in New Mexico, Native Americans recorded their sighting of Halley's Comet in petroglyphs. The sighting is recorded in the Bayeux Tapestry. Chronicler Eilmer of Malmesbury had seen that same comet as an infant in 989. He remembered his childhood as a time of warring horror in the land now called England. He vented with his pen his hatred of this heavenly body that had brought nothing but disaster. Seeing it again in the skies even more terrible than he remembered it, he predicted the ending of the Saxon world he knew. Indeed it was. King Harold died at the Battle of Hastings. William the Conqueror blazed his burnt-earth trail as far north as Scotland in the wake of the comet.

The years 1145 and 1222 are also candidates for disaster-retrofit, but the sighting of 1301 forces a more positive view of the meaning of a return. This appears to have precipitated its putative association with the Star of Bethlehem. It was just after this time that artists, amongst them the famous Giotto di Bondone, began to picture a comet in their modernised paintings of the Nativity of Jesus.

Its return in 1378 was too late for it to be blamed for the origin of the Black Death in Europe, which began thirty years earlier in 1348. But no doubt some disaster can be found to associate with it. In 1456 Halley's Comet again came close to Earth. When its tail crossed one third of the visible sky and took the shape of a sabre, people feared for the armies of Christendom in the wars against the Ottoman Empire. On its return in 1531 Christendom itself was beginning to be convulsed by Reformation.

In 1682 there was a strong lobby still in England to believe that the sighting of Halley's Comet that year could only spell disaster. This comet was a signal to look carefully to the succession of the English monarchy. A comet had arrived little over a year earlier, around Christmas 1680, so this was clearly a double warning. In fact, the period since the Restoration in 1660, when Charles II was crowned King of England following the inter-regnum of Oliver Cromwell's Commonwealth, had been thick with comets. (This was partly, of course, because astronomers were more actively looking for them. Halley used in his analysis eleven reliable comet paths measured between 1661 and 1698, compared with thirteen available for the period from 1337 to 1652.)

Monarchy that was constrained by constitution had been a new idea for England. It had been tested in Scotland since 1568. Then Mary Queen of Scots was forced to abdicate in favour of her infant son, who was crowned James VI of Scotland. His tutor George Buchanan spelled out the nature and limits of the constitutional monarchy which recognised James as holding this crown. James in 1603 followed absolute monarch Elizabeth I as James I of England. From then on he bore two crowns, one constitutional, the other absolute. He left the civil service to manage Scotland – a satisfactory approach in a constitutional monarchy.

James was followed by his son Charles I, who was accused in Scotland of believing he also had the God-given right to absolute power like Elizabeth had exercised in England. The Bishops' War that this precipitated enabled rebellious elements in England to challenge absolute monarchy in his southern kingdom. The English executed Charles I in 1649. His son, on signing the Covenant, the central formalised agreement of Scotland's constitutional monarchy, was recognised in Scotland as King Charles II. He had to wait another decade before he could actually get any power in either of his kingdoms.

All comets were trouble: history spelled out that one appeared in the sky in 44 BC shortly after the murder of Julius Caesar. His successor, who became Emperor Augustus, first Emperor of Rome, declared that it had taken the soul of that great general to the heavens and thus he was a god. When Montezuma II saw a comet like a flaming ear of corn over his Aztec kingdom in 1517, he lost the heart to defend it against Spanish Conquistadors.

The risk of disruption gave strong motive for those of rational bent to take a more detached and scientific view of comets. Thus, Halley's claim in 1705 that the same heavenly entity kept coming back in a definitely predictable timescale was a boon to those who wished to dispel superstitious panic. But Halley himself was not one of those who went the further step of dissociating the regular appearance of comets from the power of an Almighty God. Rather, he realised and feared, like his close acquaintance and colleague Isaac Newton, that descriptions offered by science can be used not only to dispel ignorant superstition but equally to undermine religious faith.

His fear was shared by William Burness, father to that little infant born under the comet in 1759. William determined that his son would be as well educated as could be afforded by a man who had, ill-advisedly, started his own market-garden business on marginal soil on borrowed money just as Scotland was entering decades of vile weather. He wanted his son to be versed in letters and in mathematics, but to be God-fearing above all. Amongst the textbooks he bought for his son to study were William Derham's 'Physico-Theology' and 'Astro-Theology'. The first is a treatise of physics, the second a treatise on astronomy. Each puts its subject in the context of God's power, goodness and justice.

Derham's 'Astro-Theology' was first published in 1715, but Derham continued to revise it and republish it throughout his lifetime, so that the sixth edition of 1731, the last published before his death, was as fully up to date as he could make it with the advances constantly being made in the quickly developing science of observational astronomy.

Derham wrote textbooks for school-children. Robert Burns avidly studied what he wrote. The little boy learned that only recently had science given up the model of Sun, Moon and all the planets being physically fixed on spheres that determined their motion. A force called gravity acted in place of such spheres to keep their orbits fixed. The boy learned that shortly before his own birth astronomers proposed that stars were not all at the same spherical inside surface of an extremely massive sphere. The physical spheres discarded, sceptics now proposed that no heaven lay beyond that notional sphere.

When Matthew Henderson died in 1788, a man born before this new science, Burns could imagine the soul passing through each planetary sphere on its way to God.

> Mourn him, thou Sun, great source of light!
> Mourn, Empress of the silent night!
> And you, ye twinkling starnies bright,
> > My Mathew mourn;
> For through your orbs he's taen his flight,
> > Ne'er to return.

Though Derham made astronomical observations himself, and did use these in his text, he leaned heavily on the most advanced contemporary academic texts. Two years after Derham's 'Astro-Theology' was first published, William Whiston, strongly encouraged by his senior colleague Isaac Newton, published 'Astronomical Principles of Religion'. This added considerable weight to the arguments Derham put forward to see scientific understanding not as refuting the existence of an all-powerful God, but as endorsing and expanding on the wonder of God. Whiston wrote:

> The most eminent [comet] of all appear'd in the 44th Year before the Christian Aera; as also *A.D.* 531, or 532; and *A.D.* 1106; and lastly, *A.D.* 1680, 1681, when I saw it; and so has made within the Limits of our present Histories, three periodical Revolutions, in about 575 Years apiece.

Whiston was wrong in this conjecture, for the bright comet he had observed actually has a period of around nine thousand years. It was known as the Great Comet of 1680, because it was one of the brightest comets of the 17th century, reputedly even visible in daylight. It was discovered by Gottfried Kirch on November 14th, using a telescope. This was the first time a telescope helped in the formal discovery of a comet. Observers of the day remarked on the comet's particularly long tail. It was at its brightest at the end of December 1680. The course of this comet was charted by the Jesuit, Eusebio Francisco Kino (1645-1711), while journeying from Cadiz (where he began his observations) to Mexico City. There he published his 'Exposision astronomica de el cometa'. Wikipedia in February 2008 described this as 'one of the earliest scientific treatises published by a European in the New World', thus acknowledging that astronomical observations were published by Native Americans in the pre-Columbian era. Isaac Newton used the observations of this comet to test Kepler's laws of planetary motion.

While explaining comets as scientifically as was then reasonable, Whiston at the same time presupposed that any creation of God must have some purpose. Mankind could ascertain this purpose by examining the facts:

> As to the *System of the Comets*, it appears now to be very considerable, and indeed they are the most numerous Bodies of the entire *Solar System*. They appear both by their Bigness and Motions to be a sort of Planets, revolving about the Sun in Ellipses, so very oblong, that their visible Parts seem in a manner Parabolical; but have such vast Atmospheres about them, and Tails deriv'd from the same, especially after their Perihelia,

and those subject to such Mutations, pass thro' so much Cold and Darkness near the Aphelia, and so much Light and Heat near their Perihelia, as imply them design'd for very different Purposes from the Planets; and indeed, as to their outward Parts, in their present State they are plainly uninhabitable. Yet by passing through the Planetary Regions in all Plains and Directions, they fully prove those Spaces to be destitute of Resistance or Solid Matter, and seem fit to cause vast Mutations in the Planets, particularly in bringing on them Deluges and Conflagrations, according as the Planets pass through the Atmosphere, in their Descent to, or Ascent from the Sun; and so seem capable of being the Instruments of Divine Vengeance upon the wicked Inhabitants of any of those Worlds; and of burning up, or perhaps, of purging the outward Regions of them in order to achieve Renovation.

Whiston did not presume that heavenly bodies were immutable. Even comets could be transmuted from mechanical avenging angels to more 'friendly' entities, if God so willed. Their role as the bringers of punishments was merely as they appeared now:

This, I mean, seems likely to be their use in the present State; tho' indeed they do withal seem to present *Chaos's* or Worlds in Confusion, but capable of a Change to Orbits nearly Circular, and then of settling into a State of Order, and of becoming fit for Habitation like the Planets; but these Conjectures are to be left to farther Enquiry, when it pleases the Divine Providence to afford us more Light about them: However in my *Solar System* I have described the Orbits of all the Comets that *Dr. Halley* has put into his Catalogue, and that in the Order of the Nearness to the Sun, at their Perihelia, and as they are in their proper Plains, without any reduction to the Ecliptick. They are in Number 21; for tho' he has 24 there set down, (all which are accordingly numbered there) yet because he scarcely doubts that three of them are the same Comet, and guesses that two more are also the same, in both which Cases I fully agree with him; the real Number will then be but 21.

Whiston was too modest in his assessment of the greatness of the System of Comets. There are now known to be almost uncounted numbers of chunks of ice revolving in a spherical cloud around the Sun, a hundred thousand times further out than Earth. Any one of these can be disturbed by gravity, from inside or outside our solar system. It can then be either lost to the system or begin a plunge towards the Sun as an embryonic comet. These have now been found to contain in addition to significant amounts of water, quantities of unusual forms of carbon, and traces of important elements necessary to the generation of carbon-based life as we know it. Scientists lean towards the view that collision of comets onto Earth was instrumental in causing life to form on our planet. Whiston did not attribute Godly creativity to comets, but went on to state more of the then-known scientific facts.

The former of these two (which also seems to have appeared before his Catalogue begins, *Anno Domini* 1456) was seen in 1531, 1607, and 1682, whose Period therefore is 75 or 76 Years, and whose Return is to be expected in 1758. The latter of them appeared *Anno Dom.* 1532; and probably the same again in 1661, whose Period therefore being about 129 Years, it is to be expected again in 1789.

When the first of these expected comets did indeed appear, in the eyes of those who shared the views of Newton, Whiston and Derham, it was crucial witness to the theory that comets are associated with great revolutions in the affairs of men.

Derham reflected the line 'for Thine is the Kingdom, the Power and the Glory, now and forever' that the Established Churches of Britain appended to the Roman version of the 'Our Father' prayer. The universe appeared to be subject to the newly developed Newtonian mechanical laws centred on the force of Gravity. Derham hoped this new mathematical model would be everlasting like the Reformed church of which he was a member. He was emphatic nonetheless, that the glory of the universe, as seen by this English science, was truly:

> worthy of an infinite CREATOR; whose *Power* and *Wisdom* as they are without bounds and measure, so may in all probability exert themselves in the Creation of many Systems as well as one. And as Myriads of Systems are more for the *Glory* of GOD, and more demonstrate his Attributes than one, so it is no less probably than possible, there may be many besides this which we have the Privilege of living in.

Thus was the little child, Robert of the comet, taught to love his fellow man and fear God, and gaze up at the wonder of the night sky, and wonder whether he would live to see the day of the comet's return, or whether he was destined to join it in the heavens when it reached the furthest corner of the great void.

In reading the representation of Robert Burns in this book you might at first suspect me of having flown off into the void. I give a large amount of background material that many might at first sight consider padding. I believe it all necessary so as to present a view that differs considerably from the mainstream perception of this man who lived so long ago. Only the literary education Burns got is normally taken into account in assessing the meaning of what he wrote. Bear that in mind as you read this book, or you'll think I fly off on irrelevant tangents. When it seems I am leading you on some wild goose chase of history, I am actually demonstrating the considerable knowledge I have discovered would have been in his head. I found his wider study greatly influenced his writing yet has mostly been ignored. This makes a big difference to the meaning and value we can get from his legacy.

Quite a few readers will want me to explain why and how I have written this book the way it is, and I'm going to do this now. Others might hold the view that that kind of thing is boring. But if I don't explain my process, the book won't make quite the sense it should. Some may want at this point to skip the last part of this introduction and move straight on to the story. Those who do might later regret missing interesting things. If you do skip forward, don't complain about the story having too much historical background stuff. Because it isn't background really – it is knowledge that I found would have been in the mind of Robert Burns, and that he decided was central to his work. The trouble is, we don't share that background when we read his work.

To begin with, his earliest biographers, being contemporary, wasted no paper on 'common knowledge'; it wasn't necessary. Later biographers have augmented their works by presenting 'background material'. But this is not the missing 'common knowledge' as it would have been understood by contemporaries. Instead, it is how things seem to be through a lens of hindsight, the vision warped further at each generation by changes in the ways people related to the world in rapid transformation.

Burns was aware of how rapid such change in perception was in his own time. He actively enhanced his own specific observations of types of knowledge and practice that were passing away. In his childhood old bodies of knowledge had been instilled in him mainly by the women around him. This was alongside and often in contradiction to the formal education he was receiving under his father's direction. Yet he did not discard the women's tales, for he found them too exciting. He knew he lived in a world that was not just rich in story, but full of active belief in a real human relationship to the paranormal.

To understand Burns I feel it is necessary to present what we know of his life and what he might have felt about it as far as possible within the context of the thoughts that were current amongst his contemporaries. This means trying to exclude our hindsight. It also means trying to internalise what he would have considered to be 'common knowledge'. It means bringing back into focus and use ways of thinking that have been discarded over the centuries.

In adulthood Burns made active effort to understand old bodies of knowledge, often now called superstition, and their roles in intuitive understanding. To relate meaningfully to Burns we must re-evaluate how pervasive were such ways of thinking in his world.

Present persistence of old stories indicates that there was curious survival of old bodies of knowledge through that intensely rational period called the Enlightenment. These were preserved through folk memories in women's tales to infants. But they were also preserved in secret societies such as Freemasonry, in which Burns was very active, with undoubted considerable impact on his thought. Understanding that thought contemporary to Burns is surely helped by increasing our understanding of these preservers of ancient wisdom. We need to study these not through the lens of our modern era. We need to study them not with the mindset of how we would relate to them were they commonplace now, but in terms of what people thought and experienced in the 18th century. This means looking at how the poet's own awareness of old bodies of knowledge emerged along with where they fitted into the general philosophical milieu, both academic and mundane.

This exposes even amongst literati an underworld of reticence to discard continuing belief in those old bodies of knowledge still then extant. Many in the days of Burns still retained, for example, a secretive interest and half-belief in the proto-science of astrology, then transmuting into astronomy in the heated crucible of experiment and discourse. Burns met people who were active believers in astrology. Perhaps some saw, in the life of this poet sprung from the soil and nurtured by the ether, vindication of that mediaeval body of knowledge they still tried to keep alive. This needs to be and can be tested, because of the influence it would have had on the poet's belief in himself and hence his legacy.

How active, indeed, was the Enlightenment in curbing such old bodies of knowledge, irrespective of whether they were proto-science or mediaeval medicine, or mere cant? How active were the religious ministry and available libraries in suppressing old bodies of knowledge? What, then, was the strength of the forces Burns might instinctively have felt and actively seen working to change underlying culture of the world into which he was born?

Perhaps critics might in future search for more evidence of those old bodies of knowledge hidden in his prose and poetry, alongside the explicit descriptions of such festivities as Hallowe'en. There are surely sex ritual inferences in the song of the corn rigs on the fine ancient Sun festival, Lammas night. What of such references as Sundrum being the summer palace of Old King Cole?

Of course, those practices and stories had become merely folky even by his time, surely, with any real essence of true understanding long ago corrupted through the knowledge having been dissociated from mainstream education. Burns was already reporting the merely quaint, just as Sir Walter Scott would do explicitly in the decades after Burns's death.

But perhaps there was more to it than just folkiness in his true inner belief. We need to ask that question if we are to gain a true understanding of what manner of man he was, and thus the real meaning of his work. Those old bodies of knowledge, after all, have a strange persistence; there are many modern examples of the paranormal, of superstitions, of stories that are rather more than folklore. Perhaps they point to there being something more to humanity than all that is self-evident to the rational modern mind – something fundamental and important. Had Burns been merely folky he would not have made his work so accessible, even when using the languages of folk. He used English or near-English for thoughts intended for his widest audiences such as the transience of pleasures like poppies spread, the desire that some power would give us the gift to see ourselves as others see us, and the simple, perennial, so often challenged truth held by the Declaration of Independence of the United States to be self-evident – that a man's a man for a' that.

To try to see Burns as he would have liked us to see him, to gain that gift to see his meaning not through our eyes but through the eyes of a man with such a message that it is still living hundreds of years after his death, it is not sufficient to use modern academic process of analysis. Nor was Burns merely a poet, songwriter and entertainer; he was at core a natural philosopher, who was also extremely aware of the leading edge technology developing around him. Most importantly, though, he never let such 'progress' dull his imagination, but used everything he experienced to sharpen that instinctive element of his being. Burns has been remembered for his poetry. Blessed with a generous education Burns would have proved himself a polymath. No biography of Burns that I have yet read truly recognises this, nor combines these two apparently opposed aspects of his personality, the intuitive and the formally educated. But they were both essential in his being.

Misrepresentation of this man is in part a consequence of the social environment in which his early biographies were written. The first formal authorised biography of Burns was commissioned of James Currie soon after his death. Even at that date, this was composed from the standpoint of an emerging society of self-defined moral rectitude that came to characterise the Victorian era. The story has probably been further warped by the changes in presentational style of historical data that had come to fulfilment by the end of the 18th century. In 1776 Edward Gibbon published the first part of his 'Decline and Fall of the Roman Empire'. It was completed in 1788, just as Burns was discovered. Gibbon consolidated a change in the writing of history begun by such as David Hume earlier in the century. From being the presentation of chronicles with incisive commentary added, it became dominated by 'spin'. By the end of the 18th century a doctrine of 'Progress' had come to dominate historical thought: the concept of the 'Good Thing' and 'Bad Thing'. Although challenged by such thorough writers as John Lingard, this approach became established during the 19th century. Serious challenge came only during the 20th century. Initially this bipolar disorder of thought was attacked through ridicule in satire such as the mock-history, '1066 and All That'.

The 'progress' dogma is deeply embedded in the cultural psyche of the modern general reader. In contrast to a chronicle mode of presenting past events any narrative mode of presenting history, even if not explicitly in the 'progress' mindset, has the inherent weakness that there is an ongoing tendency to eliminate from the stories those things that have no role in promoting the storyline. The 'progress' school tends also to play down those elements that tend to disprove the 'progress'. Thus, for example, if superstition is prevalent in a community, as it does not assist 'progress', it is ignored if harmless to desired change, and denigrated if it prevents change. Thus such unwanted aspects of a New World Order are increasingly written out of the story.

Adherents of the 'progress' school amongst modern historians, for example, present the Enlightenment era as a golden age of progressive philosophy. Such history writers give scant space to the very real and large interest amongst Enlightenment scientists in continuing to promote the relevance of such studies as astrology. They tend to play down even more the massive ongoing awareness in general rural populations of old practices and herbal cures. I rarely see it written that superstition was widespread in the time of Burns. Yet this is so. And it was so not merely at the level in society into which he was born; the Scottish Presbyterian Church accepted the real existence of active evil beings of a supernatural or at least non-human sort. Ghoulies and ghosties and long leggedy beasties and things that go bump in the night were very real and people prayed to Dear God that from these He deliver them. The phrase 'Satan's Invisible World' was so everyday that Burns used it as a commonplace.

Alongside the advancing prevalence of self-proving history, there was at the same time during the period from the late 17th to early 20th centuries, a considerable separation of so-called 'science' from so-called 'arts'. This is generally unremarked by writers of social and political history, who pay little attention to details of technological change because of their lack of intimate understanding of machinery and science, despite such arcana often being the enabler of social and political change. It has taken modern economic historians to begin to fill this massive gap, and there is still considerable infill to be achieved.

There has not yet been successful attack to redress the degeneration of intellectual competence through its split into 'two cultures'. So there are now few in the Western World who comfortably span any true breadth in intellectual discourse. Indeed, if anything, separation of understanding is now moving to the point of granulation.

Where does understanding Burns fit in all this?

I believe that these changes mean that we now must try to look at such as Burns in a very different way from what modern academic process will allow. I suggest that a useful model for how to look at such as Burns does exist: it exists in the entertainment industry, where the most successfully uplifting entertainments of an historical sort are those in which the capability of consummate actors to 'get inside' the heads of their characters and portray their characters' personalities is actively combined with the most rigorous academic research of the factual data of the environment of the story and of contemporary technology. Of course, historical drama is still just drama; a story, no more. But the process can surely be translated to the exploration of history.

The approach I have taken spins together three main types of thread. The first is formal academic rigour to assess the correctness and relevance of fact. The first of these threads is the typical method that is normal to the best of the academic studies that have contributed to our modern understanding of Burns.

The second has some comparison with modern studies in social history. To the typical data used by biographers, I have added extensive research of wider data sources than the norm in central Enlightenment studies. I have done so to enable more objective reassessment of the intellectual and cultural milieu in which Burns existed. Amongst these extended data sources is more history than is usually considered. I have first immersed myself in the history of the previous two centuries, this being the accepted world view of a person of the time.

It is not arbitrary to consider the history of the two centuries before the poet's birth. I have done so for the same reason that modern citizens of the United States are expected to know in detail the history of their country from 1776 onwards and roughly what led up to that. The American War of Independence was where the modern United States started. Every nation likes to think its citizens know how the nation came into being. The same was true in Scotland in the 18th century. That Scotland began in 1560, at the Scottish Reformation. So an educated 18th century Scot would know in detail what had happened since 1560 and roughly what led up to that. So don't blame me for wasting your time when I later introduce events that seem to modern ideas very irrelevant. Here, they are not.

My own unique additional approach is that I have made every attempt not to view the 18th century data through the lens of modern prejudice. In the context of both of those first two types of study, I have read school text books studied by the child and adolescent poet. When doing so I have used my imagination to put myself into the mindset he possibly had, given the milieu of his time, in reading those books for the first time.

Some critics will find that this requires too much subjectivity for them to endorse it. I agree it is the most contentious of my ways of working. It requires considerable application of imagination which is necessarily subjective to make any guess at how a young mind might respond to new information.

I wish to stress an important point: modern regimented academic process is itself significantly conditioned by the all-embracing industrialisation of the 19th century. So that process is not of itself a sufficient lens through which to view a man who reacted in horror at those emerging signs around him of the socially devouring appetite of the infant industrial behemoth. So, modern formal academic method is not appropriate to understanding Burns. My method might not prove any better in the event, but it is an attempt to find a new way of understanding him.

I am of the view that no biographer of Robert Burns has adequately explained why he is still after two hundred and fifty years universally admired and loved. So, after a lifetime of waiting for someone else to do it, I wrote this book. I give a new way of reading this man's works that I believe gives a clearer understanding of why they continue to strike a chord in so many hearts. But Burns is not just a poet – indeed many know nothing of his poetry. It is the *man* whose immortal memory is annually celebrated, not his works. Why is this? I have tackled this question by completely re-evaluating how he thought within his own time and then explaining why to think in his way might be even more relevant in the modern world.

This book aims to break new ground by presenting a new view of Burns. I try to present him within the mindset of his perception of the world and against the spiritual makeup of the everyday life of himself and the people amongst whom he moved and worked. To do this I have used academic process to check facts and provide verifiable background. But I have approached the inner mind of the man as an actor would approach a new character. I have tried to get inside the character's head. I have in part done this through reading books he read after having put myself, as far as I was able, into the mental attitude of a person of his age, background and knowledge of the world, at the time at which he read them. What I present here is what I have achieved so far in generating a new angle on Robert Burns. My intention is to add to our understanding of him.

Out of this I believe there are new meanings hidden in his work that are his bequest to ourselves in the 21st century. Of course, I have had limited success. I would be a fool to claim otherwise. But I have tried, and hope that this book shows a new way for better people than myself to follow.

My book is wide-ranging. But it does not recount where Burns spent each day of his life from conception to apotheosis. It does not explore all the people of his world. Other books do that. This book is about how Burns formed his thoughts, from which were born his words and songs. Although I abhor the obfuscation of sophistry, my book is long, for the ideas in it are big. It is written for those who do not want things dumbed down.

My book is no apotheosis. Burns disliked being labelled a saint – far less the vilest of sinners. But somehow the way Robert Burns thought reaches the heart of the elemental universal human being. This is clear from the response of generations of so many different nations to his prose, poems and songs, whether in original or in translation. I explore why.

The general perception of Burns is still the one put out by his 19th century detractors: to drink he was inclined and cutty sarks ran in his mind. Another perception is that he championed human rights and fought for modern democracy – yet inspired Communism. Neither is enough to explain continuing admiration for the *man*.

What I have had to do to write this book has not been done before in any biography of Burns, for I have had to put myself into the mindset of an Enlightenment person in Scotland – a mindset far closer to Mediaeval thought than is commonly acknowledged. That mindset is surprisingly relevant to the challenges of the modern world. Born in poverty, Burns educated himself. I explore the normal thinking of contemporary privileged educated people and contrast this with how Burns thought. This brought me to a new explanation of why human beings around the world now join together so spontaneously so often in friendship and harmony to toast the immortal memory of a superficially ordinary man.

We can agree with Burns that we live in an awesome universe. We just open our eyes to the magic of a clear moonless night sky to experience that awe. We can see it all round us in wonderful technology. But we don't share a mindset that believes a man has destiny because a comet heralds his birth. That is as irrational as proposing a horde of witches cannot cross the Brig o' Doon. When a man, poet though he be, takes his Mission from an apparition, it is a bridge too far. When Coila, the Muse in his vision, is a tartan-draped long-legged beauty with pride in her eyes, there is real challenge to accept she confirmed his destiny. Yet I hope in this book to show Robert Burns indeed bequeathed a legacy that is greater than his poetry.

Chapter I   *Rantin' Rebel Rabbie*

The legend of Burns, the truth about pornography and vice in the poet's life and how he discovered the hard drinking of his country's leaders.

Watchers in the fields saw a great new star appear in the night sky, gaining in brilliance until it was visible even in the shining of the sun. Four days after it was first spotted by the long-awaiting wise men, a child was born. The father rushed the long unpaved miles to get the priest to baptise the frail infant. Reaching a swollen stream, he saw an old witch woman on the other side. Disregarding all superstitious nonsense, he stopped and, turning back on his journey, helped her cross the stream. Then he headed on through dub and mire. He and the priest on reaching the cottage found inside the old stranger woman sitting by the hearth, cradling the child before the eyes of the fearful mother. Looking up at the boy's father, with a sad smile on her face, in her queer dialect tones she prophesied: "He'll have misfortunes great and small, but his heart will always be above every single one of them. He'll be a blessing to everyone. We will all be proud of him." It was January 25th, 1759. Days later, the wild wind blew down the gable of the newly built cottage, so that in the great storm that continued to rage mother and child were forced to seek shelter amongst their cattle.

This true story of the birth of Robert Burns happened in a time when to tell it like this would in Scotland have merited legal prosecution for blasphemy, with all its dire punishments. No-one could dare begin in this manner to tell the story even of so honoured a man as the Scottish poet Robert Burns is today. This was a time when the awe of the God of Established Religion had ousted Mediaeval and Romish Superstition as the benchmark of Human Thought. Though a world in which astrology defiantly lurked, this was the world of the Scottish Enlightenment.

His zig zagging story involves duchesses and drudges, simplest fools and greatest philosophers, men of God and devil worshippers, sex, bigamy, divorce and disappointment, political intrigue, smuggling and more before finally a hideous death, against a backdrop of massive bank collapses, the American War of Independence and the French Revolution.

Robert Burns is a legend. Born three years after Mozart, his life lasting little longer, within a few months of his death there had begun to gather around the fast decaying memories of his personality a salacious encrustation of lust, licentiousness, and libertine rebellious rabble rousing. Gossip about Burns would make his character show up Mozart, as portrayed in the film 'Amadeus', to be guilty of high morality.

The first official posthumous edition of the works of Burns deliberately had anti-Establishment political views air-brushed out of it. But it had in its lengthy biography amongst the first of those 19th century do-gooder tales of a genius in whose chief personality failing was the embryo of his final immortal damnation. Here was a prodigal son unrepentant to the end. Thus was generated a 20th century proletarian reaction of mania to rehabilitate this rural poetic prodigy. He had been, they claimed, no worse in social behaviour after all and possibly a great deal better than his contemporaries of the 'better classes'. One lobby aimed to prove that even in morals few could hold a candle to him. Thus, legend has fought with counter legend, like the white and black dragons of myth, tossing between them the red, red fireball of the soul of a dead man of passion.

His loves were legion: Highland Mary, Clarinda, Annie of the rigs, Chloris, Mary Morrison, Phyllis, and nameless goddesses of lint white locks, or golden hair. Real persons are put forward as contenders, of course, for what woman, however chaste, would not want to be loved by such a man? Perhaps Annie of the rigs was his first girlfriend, Nellie Kilpatrick. For her he first committed the sin of Rhyme. About 1774 he put words – 'oh once I lov'd a bonnie lass' – to her favourite tune. He was then

"unacquainted and uncorrupted with the ways of the wicked world".

Honest bonnie Jean stood apart from all the other women: she took to her own bosom amongst her own brood the children of his mistresses. He had a muse, the airy Coila. She was half sister to that musical spirit who had in ancient times inspired Pictish Old King Cole to hire the best fiddlers of the land. This musical establishment, we learn through Burns, was at Old King Cole's castle at Sundrum, so near the poet's Mauchline home in Ayrshire.

With the highest lords and the lowest tinkers of a fast-disappearing mediaeval Scotland Burns drank his fill to match the greatest imbiber. He sang them songs that made even the tinkers blush and was rewarded with elevation to the role of Bard of the Masonic Brotherhood and Membership of the Royal Company of Archers.

He searched old wives' barrels for illicit whisky, and sent crates of confiscated brandy to the tables of his friends in the Excise service. He supplied his lady friends with contraband French gloves.

He was knighted with the sword of King Robert the Bruce himself. He rode through the wildest storms on Pegasus. From the thunder and the spirit of Scotland's hero, the Bruce, he drew the words of that great king's address in 1314 to the troops before the battle of Bannockburn, the iconic first triumph of national democratic independence. He praised rebellious slaves. He beat the martial drum for the leaders of France's Reign of Terror. Yet he wrote the patriot song for the Volunteers who swelled Prime Minister Pitt's defence against invasion by haughty Gaul. But he resoundingly declared that war with France was not in *his* name: there must be another way to resolve conflicts.

But he was a rotten farmer.

Dispute that as you may, such and more is the legend.

The high ground of the battle field to determine where truth lies is now held by authorities and experts whose occupation is dedicated to unearthing with fine-haired academic brushes and intimate trowels the tiny shreds of evidence to load those little bowls on each side of the balance to weigh the works and the soul of a humble man of proud mind.

Out of this battleground have indeed come some significant contributions to our understanding. These include definitive collections of his verse and prose. Most important remain the dedicated output in the early part of the 20th century of J C Dick and of J De Lancey Ferguson. Dick completed a massive study of Burns's main life's work – the preservation of old Scottish music through song. By 1931 De Lancey Ferguson had corrected from the nearest to the originals all then extant letters of Burns and collated them in chronological order.

Selections from letters had been edited and published by the first official biographer Dr James Currie with a little corruption of meaning in the process. So-called Clarinda also published carefully selected elements of her correspondence with Burns, out of their own context and that of the total output of Burns. Other letters, more or less mutilated, have appeared along with attributed poetry ever since his death. Many of the songs that passed through the hands of Burns were not originally properly attributed to him. He had in the manner of 'Ossian' sought to emphasise that the song collection represented the vanishing culture of Scottish music, which indeed was its basis. Many of Burns's substantial collection of Scottish songs were centred on remnants he gathered from all across Scotland just as they were vanishing in the smog of the advancing Enlightenment. Many were his originals. Each of them was deliberately designed to preserve one piece of that old music that was, when the poet came into the world, within Scottish culture the most at-risk of its ancient monuments.

On the other hand, the debris of the battle over interpretation of the poet's life and works fills libraries with mediocre books, provides tourist shops with myriad gee-gaws to sell to tourists, and has spawned transient plays and even the occasional sickly-romantic film. During the past fifty years there have been advances in our understanding of his output. But the chimneys of furnaces of academic pulp factories have also belched a smog of sophistry reeking with the oily detritus of repeatedly reprocessed contaminated fuel.

As a child, I at one stage grew tired of all the hype, and wearied of the lack of 'real things' that I found in all the Burns museums that I visited in search of his soul. So, a versifier then, I penned my own poem, which I called 'The Burns Museum'. I will share it with you.

This is the Burns Museum.

This is the bust, the plaster cast, that stands in the Burns Museum.

This is a (facsimile) chair, sat on by Burns, whose plaster cast is here in the Burns Museum.

This is a fiddle, badly tuned, made from the (facsimile) chair, sat on by Burns, whose plaster cast is here in the Burns Museum.

This is a man with a heavy tan who played the fiddle, badly tuned, made from the (facsimile) chair, sat on by Burns, whose plaster cast is here in the Burns Museum.

This is a note (all the ink is gone) read by the man with a heavy tan who played the fiddle, badly tuned, made from the (facsimile) chair, sat on by Burns, whose plaster cast is here in the Burns Museum.

This is a maid, with a bonnet on, who wrote the note (all the ink is gone) read by the man with a heavy tan who played the fiddle, badly tuned, made from the (facsimile) chair, sat on by Burns, whose plaster cast is here in the Burns Museum.

This is a paperback, tattered and torn, that tells of the maid, with a bonnet on, who wrote the note (all the ink is gone) read by the man with a heavy tan who played the fiddle, badly tuned, made from the (facsimile) chair, sat on by Burns, whose plaster cast is here in the Burns Museum.

The spirit in the poetry and song of Burns himself is too great for even the worst excesses of the tourist fashions to have put me off searching to understand his meaning to me.

The strange thing to me is that very few writers say about Burns that his live audiences found so much of his poetry extremely funny. People roared with true honest laughter. Yes, he wrote in the language of the labourers, but it wasn't only the labourers who earnestly laughed. Somehow, the laughter that was – and still is – in the works of Burns appears to have gone over the heads of most of those who study him. I don't believe it is just because his language is no longer spoken – for it is, by many yet of the ordinary people around Scotland. Some jokes are not understood because, like Gilbert and Sullivan, they referred to contemporary events. But that is not true of all of them. One problem, I guess, is that people no longer expect to find Burns funny. His work has become at best one of those things that people are forced to read in schools, and of course few teachers find any poems funny, so how can those in their charge? Some excellent modern comic writer should revitalise the funny side of Burns. Molière can be made modern and cause people laughter; so can Burns, and he deserves it. But it is not I who has that skill.

Few around the world, when at the turn of the year they hold hands, sometimes sobbing, and sing to the karaoke bouncing ball those strange words 'for auld lang syne', know that they are singing the praises not just of the wonder of another year gone and born, but also of one man who sang his heart out from infancy until he breathed his last breath.

Those who are aware of Rabbie Burns tend to know that he wrote a love song about every woman he slept with, and that he slept with a woman for every love song he wrote. They tend to know that he usually consumed considerable quantities of alcohol for every song he wrote. Others will add that no sooner had he made love the last time and composed his last song to the last of his transient goddesses, he died of drink. For this reason, all Scots – who of course all love loving and drinking, and drinking and loving – love Rabbie Burns.

Here was a man who in his day gained a reputation for his cutting wit which sliced through hypocrisy and pretension wherever he found it. He used this wit so incisively and without discrimination that even those closest few whom he had believed were his most trustworthy friends at some stage in his life abandoned him.

But this poet who gathered so many enemies during his life became a poet loved. That is surely surprising. A writer of love songs alone would not be loved as Burns is loved. Many attribute the love to the reputation he gained as poet of the underdog, of the working classes, as poet of equality, as poet of Reform, as poet of Social Democracy. Some claim he inspired the Russian Revolution – but that claim has grown unfashionable. The casual reader coming to his work afresh might wonder at this activist reputation. True, there are few pertinent verses: only 'A man's a man for a' that' really stands out for most people. Yet his contemporary reputation was an activist. He got this reputation despite keeping well out of such affrays as the Glasgow Weavers' Strike, violent election battles and the Dumfries food riots, in all of which he could have taken part. After he joined the Civil Service in 1788 as an Exciseman, he conformed to the political silence demanded by his bosses. Yet the period from then until his death was the time when he might have had the greatest impact, supporting the growing Irish protests that were given impetus by the French Revolution. They say he did write to newspapers, but examples are few. They say he wrote many a seditious message in his private letters – but Currie burned the most offensive and bowdlerised the rest. The search for evidence continues, and academic controversy smoulders and smokes.

Naturally, the real whole story is somewhat different. But since so few hard facts are actually truly documented, it is hard to say where the truth lies. So at each of those Burns Suppers, the person who has drawn the short straw and must toast the Immortal Memory has a very wide choice of what to say. Depending on audience, he (and very rarely she) can focus as controversially as they wish (rarely soberly) on any of many themes: the sublime nature of his poetic genius; the depth and purity of his devotion to God; the strength and world-changing influence of his radical politics; the personality that enabled his spirit to overcome his poverty; the romance of his loves and the songs they inspired; his commitment to the Masonic Brotherhood; the pornography that caused many a raucous laugh in that drinking den of the Crochallan Fencibles, Edinburgh's Auerbach's Keller mob.

All of what anyone says has probably a grain of truth. Much of it is inevitably exaggeration, based as so many of the stories of Burns are on mere hearsay gathered from friends, from large numbers of his enemies with vested interests of church, politics or power, and as time passed from just about anyone who was ever present anywhere near where he might have journeyed during his few but extensive tours in North Britain.

Facts about Burns are so bald that they hardly make a story. Even Burns knew this. He was, it seems to me, a born entertainer. Leaned on to provide the story of his life before his sudden appearance in Edinburgh society – according to his younger brother Gilbert many years later – he actually rearranged and even embellished details to make his narrative flow.

I have tried to use only verifiable fact on incident in the life of Burns. This makes actual content on life events of the poet rather thin. On the other hand, it emphasises how much even the academic studies rely for their extensive treatment on discussion of the correct fine detail of events and even whether or not they actually occurred. This suggests that the modern Establishment view of Burns and his life is in its own way as much a convention as was the Victorian view. Victorians held him up as an example to the unwashed multitudes of how, despite God-given genius, a man cannot permanently rise above his station when he is damned with those character flaws that are normally inherent in the natural underling. Modern perspective on his life is different. Opinion on him has changed more than once in the past. Such change of opinion shows that his life and works can be viewed from standpoints different from that of those who claim the modern intellectual high ground. In preparing this book I chose to climb a lonely crag and view his life from a different standpoint. This may merely show a silhouette against the bright reality of modern thorough research. On the other hand, it perhaps will show his meaning more clearly if only because I am looking at his life and work in a way not before considered.

For many, Burns has simply provided the sole excuse for those uncounted numbers of dinners that take place around the world, usually on or about 25th January. In these Burns Suppers men parade in kilts and women insist on wearing plaid sashes (if they are allowed in). A haggis is ritually slaughtered and eaten. Many a toast is drunk, and many a drunk is toasted. The haggis is addressed in one little extremely witty joke poem that very few people understand and fewer laugh at these days. Burns wrote it in Edinburgh in 1787 to put on an undeserved pedestal a pottage made of scraps. This dish was designed to sink the drinking excesses of that literary club of Anchor Lane, the Crochallan Fencibles, founded by printer William Smellie, progenitor of the Encyclopaedia Britannica. The haggis became the traditional Scottish dish after it was printed in a recipe book compiled after Robert Burns wrote 'Address to the Haggis'.

The poem is actually as gory as most non-Scots find the haggis.

Once long ago a colleague of mine, Alan, when he was not teaching mathematics, led for a bit of leisure time money-spinning a troupe that did Scottish traditional entertainment. Alan was the best Haggis Slasher I ever met. In the Address Burns praised as the greatest of food, thumbing his nose at high society, a fat sausage made of mutton discards. This designated a dish of offal as greater than the sophisticated nouvelle cuisine of his day.

Fair fa' thy honest, saucy face,
Great Chieftain o' the Puddin' Race.

Burns Suppers first started to be held within a few years of the poet's death. Victorians adopted the habit of addressing the haggis in their standardisation of this commemoration of the poet. After reciting the poem, it is ritually sliced open oven hot with one of those vicious Scot's army knives, the dirk, or with the tiny deadly skean dhu that a kilted Scotsman keeps in his stocking hidden for ready use. Like someone who has had an unhappy encounter with a mugger, the meat gushes out of the tight sausage skin.

After many years of not encountering Alan, I came across him again when I attended certain financial services conferences in Edinburgh. There he was 'Laird', entertaining us, reciting the Address and slashing the haggis. Decked out marvellously in his full Highland dress, he did it splendidly then. He began to do it even more splendidly after I invited him to a little Burns Supper of my own. It was not Alan whom I tasked with addressing the haggis.

My haggis slasher had, with great aplomb, begun his Address:

"Fair fa' thy honest, saucy face,
Great Puddin' o' the Chieftain Race."

The previously reverential audience fell about laughing. As host I intervened immediately, telling my audience that they were too Establishment to understand the true significance of haggis.

Robert Burns, I told my little circle of guests, always wrote two versions of every poem - the 'parlour' version for polite society, and the other version. This commonly believed untruth is based on several facts. The first is that, in his search for old Scots verse, when Burns found existing songs not suitable for young ladies to sing, he transformed them. He recognised that the originals were themselves of historic interest if only to the future generations that form our modern sociologists and anthropologists. So he did not destroy the words he gathered, but kept them in a book. Secondly, the Crochallan Fencibles was an important source of literary sponsorship. But it was one of those men-only clubs of *that* sort. When they adopted him as their poet, they expected him to write for their private meetings verses that pandered to their adolescent taste. He also used very blunt realistic language when appropriate in making a big point. He took it on himself to knock self-righteous people, even if members of the Establishment, off pedestals. He might do this by making it clear that the target was but dust of the gutter, and into dust he would return. He was always particularly pleased when bawdy proved the right weapon to achieve this, because of its power to shock and at the same time gain attention.

After his death were circulated copies of risqué verses. These included traditional verse that Burns collected but that he set aside because they were considered filth in his day. There were poems he did write, and some he didn't. All were attributed to his authorship. The collection and his known tendency to debase puffed up pride with bawdy has been used by his slanderers. They say all this proves that he had a filthier mind than that attributed to Mozart in the blockbuster movie about that musician. The 'fact' of there being two versions of *every* poem was by no means well known, I told my select audience, and very few indeed knew the alternative version of the 'Address to the Haggis' until it was recited at our sophisticated Burns Supper.

H-a-g-g-i-s, I said, is usually taken to be an acronym for 'heavy and greasy grub for ignorant Scots'. However, the slicing of the haggis is a much more meaningful ceremony than the

Establishment could possibly imagine. It is the symbol of a coming New World Order. From the time of the Hanoverian succession, I invented, this humble sheep's stomach sausage was used by Jacobites in dirk training akin to bayonet training for a 20th century dads' army home guard. It was very efficient use of resources. For once they had done with their soldierly training and disembowelled the pudding, they ate it.

Any true reading of 'Address to the Haggis' shows up the military nature of the verses, I pointed out. After he learned this story Alan became violent in his slashing, remembering that the true meaning of h-a-g-g-i-s is 'highland activist guerrilla garrison insurrection supplies'.

In the time of Burns, the old plaid of the Celtic Scottish lands was still outlawed after the Jacobite defeat of 1746. In 1822 it was resuscitated in glorious style, courtesy of Sir Walter Scott when he persuaded the new George IV to visit his Scottish kingdom. Tartan became very fashionable fabric. Full Highland dress became recognised throughout the world as exceedingly sexy getup for men.

Sir Walter Scott happened as a boy once to be in the same room as Robert Burns, and dined off that coincidence for the rest of his life. So did many another, including those who crossed to the other side of the street because they saw that dastardly man with the rapier of a wit and a weakening heart stumbling towards them. Behind his back – and sometimes to his face – they laughed at his pride in that so-called knighthood that caused him to flaunt that self-designed armorial on his watch fob. Knighted with the sword of Bruce indeed!

He let them laugh, though his heart ached with his frustrated desire for respect. That sword he had touched with love and reverence, that sword wielded by Bruce. Just as a knight's sword had gently tipped the shoulders of William Wallace after a successful battle in the war for independence, this sword of destiny had touched his own shoulders in like manner, wielded by old Lady Catherine Bruce of Clackmannan Tower. When his cruel-kind Muse Coila had settled on his brow that crown of thorny holly and pressed it into his burning temples, the spirit of Scotland reached roots into his heart. When Lady Bruce wielded her sword and raised him up as Sir Robert, through that ancient lady's hand in which ran the blood of kings ran power that set those roots more firmly in his fire, making his heart burst with unstoppable song.

Clackmannan Tower is one of the sites on the 'Robert Burns slept here' tourist trail. In fact, he did not sleep here any more than he slept at the grand homes of dukes and earls with whom he dined. True, they had had him at their tables for that short spell after he celebrated his year of triumph after winning the pop idol competition of 1786 as Edinburgh's transient fashionable favourite. He was discarded hardly less quickly than the intelligent sow which that same autumn was performing its tricks for the amusement of the curious populace in the Grassmarket.

The first twenty seven years of his thirty seven year life, until that autumn, Robert Burns never left his native Ayrshire. His life was lived in Alloway and near Mauchline, with trips to Ayr, Kirkoswald, Kilmarnock and Irvine. He spent two winter seasons in Edinburgh. In 1788 he settled near Dumfries. Only rarely was he thereafter able to visit his mother who still lived near Mauchline. So search for places with some connection with Robert Burns only in Ayrshire, Dumfriesshire and to a lesser degree Edinburgh.

Of course, the dictats of the tourist industry can't settle for just that. The Scottish Tourist Authorities must take out of all proportion the few trips he made out of the earnings from the publication of his poetry. These are known of partly from journals of varying intensity that he kept, and to some degree from his correspondence. He also stated that he had visited most of the places celebrated in old Scottish song. The story of his journeys has been filled out considerably with reminiscences of others. Many of these are hearsay extracted by journalistic researches long after the event. There is occasional external documentary evidence such as the discovery of a Burgess Ticket given to him when some burgh granted him freedom, or the rare note of his name in Masonic minutes.

On 27th November 1786 he headed off to Edinburgh and was there until 5th May 1787, when he headed off on his first tour. These trips might have been his special treat to himself out of his unexpected literary success. They also provided him with that knowledge he deemed necessary of the locations named in song. They made him very aware of the rapidly changing face of his native land. They were also necessary to advance the successful sales of the new Edinburgh edition of his poems.

On his first trip, going south, he visited Duns, Kelso, Jedburgh, Melrose and Selkirk. He took a side trip to cross and re-cross the Tweed over the grand new bridge at Coldstream. He went to Eyemouth and Berwick, and thence south to Alnwick and Newcastle, going to Carlisle via Hexham. Thence he went via Dumfries to reach Mauchline in early June 1787. He had returned home by the roundabout route of a tour of the Borders and then across the north of England from Newcastle to Carlisle. Bob Ainslie, later a successful lawyer, was a young man when Burns got to know him on arrival in Edinburgh in 1786. Ainslie was his companion for a short part of this first tour. Thence, Burns was in the company of prosperous farmers as far as Carlisle.

From Mauchline he then made a trip to Inveraray. He is known to have been to Paisley, Glasgow, Arrochar and Dumbarton, but there are few facts. He then returned to Edinburgh, whence from 24th August to 23rd September he took a trip west to Stirlingshire and Clackmannanshire, turning north via Dunblane, Comrie and Crieff to Dunkeld. On he went, his journey including Killiecrankie and Blair Atholl. He went to Aviemore, and thence to the Moray coast, turning west to visit Inverness. He then went to Aberdeen via the Bullars of Buchan, and followed the coast road back to Edinburgh. In April 1788 he finally left Edinburgh.

As an Exciseman he had to travel extensively around Dumfriesshire. But apart from this he had no further personal journeys, except for two tours of Galloway lasting five days in 1793 and two days the following year. His final trip away from home was three weeks in July 1796 sent under doctor's orders to Brow Well on the Solway whence he returned to die at home in Dumfries.

Apart from Clackmannan Tower, the sites to see that clearly relate to fact or actual incident of Robert's life are: the building in which he was born at Alloway; the old kirk in Alloway where his father is buried – the central site of the poem 'Tam o' Shanter'; the farms of Lochlie and Mossgeil near Mauchline; the building in Tarbolton in which was held the Bachelors' Club debating society that he formed in his youth; the house in Mauchline in which he lived after he was formally married to Jean Armour; the farm of Ellisland outside Dumfries; the two homes he occupied in Dumfries; the Mausoleum in Dumfries where he is buried. There are many sites listed in guidebooks that relate to places which appear in poem or song, others related to apocryphal stories of incident in his life or associations with people he knew, and various monuments to his fame.

Amongst the myths of Burns are his myriad sexual conquests and female loves. Few women are known to have been actual girlfriends and fewer proved to have been party to sexual activity. His first girlfriend, as an adolescent, was Nellie Kilpatrick. They were paired at reaping.

Chapter I   Rantin' Rebel Rabbie

She inspired his first stumbling verses, actually written to be sung to her favourite dance tune. His first sexual relationship was with Lizzie Paton, who bore him a girl. They were prevented from marrying. He married Jean Armour, but her father caused this to be considered invalid by the Kirk of Mauchline, despite the birth of twins. Citing as evidence a Bible and considerable hearsay, biographers claim that there was next a woman known to posterity as Highland Mary. Then is cited Clarinda, in real life Mrs Agnes McLehose, with whom he had no physical relationship. Then he married Jean.

During each winter in Edinburgh his name got associated with a pregnancy. A paternity writ was served on him in May 1787, raised by Meg Cameron. Ainslie told Burns, who denied the charge. But it was cheaper to pay than put up a fight.

Around the McLehose home, Burns was very much in non-physical mode. He was never inclined to take easy sex, and certainly not with a married woman. Resisting her coquettishness was made easier by a very serious coach accident within days of first meeting her. A smashed leg and knee laid him up for many weeks. This was followed by a long time on crutches. The incident was so bad that his leg never fully recovered. He wrote to his youthful friend Richard Brown shortly after that lady first imposed herself on him:

> "At this moment [I am] ready to hang myself for a young Edinburgh widow, who has wit and beauty more murderously fatal than the assassinating stiletto of the Sicilian banditti, or the poisoned arrow of the savage African. My Highland durk, that used to hang beside my crutches, I have gravely removed into a neighbouring closet, the key of which I cannot command; in case of spring-tide paroxysms."

Jenny Clow's is the second Edinburgh child attributed to Burns. In the old town the level of each apartment above road level reflected the level of respectability within societal hierarchy. Clow did not merely share the same address as Mrs McLehose, in the Edinburgh style of those old town tenements. She was her maid. She was also very familiar with the men of the Courts of Law and wealthy merchants of the teeming taverns. After Burns left town, Clow was found to be pregnant. Mrs McLehose threw her out. Clow was destitute.

Mrs McLehose accused Burns of causing the girl's desperation. Yeah! remember that leg injury. When Clarinda threw Burns off, Ainslie became Agnes's regular visitor. Ainslie wrote to Burns to say Clow claimed Burns was the father. Newly qualified in law, this fair weather friend prepared Clow's writ. Burns wrote very little on this matter. It is not proven – despite the name given to the boy – that he was the father. Perhaps Robert Ainslie was father of both this infant and that of Meg Cameron the previous year. In a note from Burns to Ainslie, asking Ainslie to pass financial support to Cameron, Burns told him not to

> "meddle with her as a piece".

As pop idol, Burns was the natural target for any paternity suit. A host of legal vultures, Ainslie included, were very ready to draw up writs against him. Burns was vulnerable. Here he was, pop idol in a city of lawyers, eager, in the search for fees and damages, to look for a man on whom to foist paternity. He took the less expensive course of action. He refused to fight. He paid the accepted fee for bringing a child unwanted into the world. Clow refused to give Burns the child. Clow was perhaps aware that it would surely soon be seen to be no son of the poet.

Years later when Clow was again destitute, onetime friend Ainslie drew up another writ to serve on Burns for maintenance. Agnes at the same time wrote to him disapprovingly, demanding he pay more. He was so far above the petty trifling of societal scandal that he again helped the young mother. He had bitter experience with his father's legal encounters. This had shown him that the rights or wrongs of a business are irrelevant. When things don't matter, it is cheaper to accept that old bit of legal advice when confronted with impossible opposition: "They're big; you're small; don't fight". Clow vanished into the obscurity of the myriad nobodies of Edinburgh's filthy dark. Had this really been the child of Robert Burns his behaviour in other situations suggests he could never have abandoned her and his child.

Biographers interpret payment to Cameron and to Clow as admission of paternity. Perhaps they have taken no account of Robert's experience of the nature of legal outcomes. In his youth Burns witnessed the grim reality of the pyrrhic nature of winning at law: the only constant truth of law is that lawyers collect their fees; award of damages is to receiving payment of damages as chalk is to cheese; fighting back even when innocent after a writ is served is a sentence condemning to a lifelong haemorrhage of legal expenses in fruitless attempt to staunch the suppurating sore of a good name wilfully blemished forever. Burns was not so stupid as to rise to the bait of fighting against a legal writ; he paid up and put up. He even offered to take the children into his care, but both Edinburgh mothers refused this offer. As such refusal was in the 18th century unusual for impoverished unmarried mothers, it questions paternity.

After the poet's death Ainslie produced, amongst other carefully selected salacious scraps of cut-up letters from Burns, a very mutilated piece of one letter. Its remaining words could be represented as tantamount to confession of some guilt with respect to Cameron. In Clow's case, evidence cited to prove his fatherhood is his giving her help and writing to Mrs McLehose taking responsibility for the child.

Undeniably a daughter of Robert is that born in Leith on 31st March 1791 to Anna Park, the barmaid at the Globe in Dumfries. She had the baby baptised and in due course handed her over to the father to be cared for. She married three years later.

Avid investigators sought to fill out details of his biography after he was dead and Currie had purged his remaining papers. It is worth noting that in the great slag heap of hearsay they collected, amongst all the detractors there is only one woman. She is Mrs McLehose, alias Clarinda, the huffy puffy sexually frustrated jealous self-styled widow of Edinburgh. Refusing him any possibility of marriage by rejecting seeking divorce, she was inflamed that he married Jean Armour. She failed to possess Burns and determined to punish him even after his death. The positive thing about their curious relationship is that, along with downright mediocre verses, it did produce a few good songs. Amongst them is what is probably the most sensitive expression of frustrated true love: 'Ae Fond Kiss'.

It is interesting that no biographer I have read cites even circumstantial evidence that Burns suffered from that very common male sexual disorder known as Desert Disease. The proper scientific name of this disorder is Wandering Palms. In my young days we girls abhorred this failure of respect for a woman's person. I don't believe, despite modern sexual freedom, that such abhorrence has abated. Women normally are disgusted by discovery of wilful incontinence and resent uninvited intimacy however slight a man may think it. Of course, the vast majority of biographers are male, and might not understand these things.

Burns respected women. But he did more than this: he actively rose to their defence as he would always rise to the defence of the weak. He wrote that amongst his earliest memories was an incident that had ingrained in his mind woman's need for a champion. On 6th April 1793 he sent his song 'Bonnie Wee Thing' to Miss Deborah Duff Davies, a young Tenby woman whom he had met at the home of his Dumfries friend Maria Riddell.

"The inequalities of life are, among Men, comparatively tolerable: but there is a delicacy, a tenderness, accompanying every view in which one can place lovely WOMAN, that are grated and shocked at the rude, capricious distinctions of Fortune. Woman is the blood-royal of life: let there be slight degrees of precedence among them, but let them all be sacred.

Whether this last sentiment be right or wrong, I am not accountable: it is an original component feature of my mind. I remember, & 'tis almost the earliest thing I do remember, when I was quite a boy, one day at church, being enraged at seeing a young creature, one of the maids of his house, rise from the mouth of the pew to give way to a bloated son of Wealth and Dullness, who waddled surlily past her. Indeed the girl was very pretty; and he was an ugly, stupid, purse-proud, money-loving, old monster, as you can imagine."

In his admitted relations with women there is no indication of unwillingness on their part, nor vindictiveness on his. After his death, many a woman of every class, because her name matched one he used in song, was found so coyly claiming that to herself could be retrofitted an intimate relationship with him. Despite all those, there was no woman other than Mrs McLehose who gave even the slightest hint that Burns behaved with anything but respect towards the Fair Sex.

All biographers take at superficial value his statement that he could not write unless he was 'heartily in love'. They presume, despite his own writings in his letters to the contrary, that this love took the nature of physical intercourse.

Apart from remarks to Clarinda, to whom he made clear that he loved personality without lusting for person, in August 1792 he wrote to Mrs Dunlop of Ayrshire on this matter. This lady had recently been widowed when the Kilmarnock edition was published. Reading 'The Cottar's Saturday Night' lifted her from the morbid depression into which she had sunk. She befriended Burns, and persuaded him to regard her as a kind of friendly old aunt to whom he could expose his intimate thoughts. Many of his letters to her survive.

That August he explained that he had not written recently because he had been, in addition to his Excise work, preparing two publications. One was for a friend, and the other was the second Edinburgh edition of his poems, soon to be available. Meanwhile, he was sending her, by way of apology for his long silence, his new song, 'The bonie Lesly Bailie'.

Mrs Dunlop knew beautiful Miss Bailie. Miss Bailie had been one of a party who had called on the poet. Burns told her he was in love with her.

"I am in love, souse! Over head & ears, deep as the most unfathomable abyss of the boundless ocean; but the word, 'Love', owing to the intermingledoms of the good & the bad, the pure

& impure, in this world, being rather an equivocal term for expressing one's sentiments & sensations, I must do justice to the sacred purity of my attachment. Know, then, that the heart-struck awe, the distant humble approach; the delight we should have in gazing upon & listening to a Messenger of Heaven, appearing in all the unspotted purity of his Celestial Home, among the coarse, polluted, far inferior sons of men, to deliver to them tidings that made their hearts swim in joy & their imaginations soar in transport – such, so delighting, & so pure, were the emotions of my soul on meeting the other day with Miss Lesley Bailie, your neighbour."

Such was the love that inspired poetry. Such love did not contradict marriage vows.

Biographers tend also to presume that his rapturous love required a real female object of love. None that I have read suggests that, despite being such an imaginative man, Burns could possibly have invented non-real women as heroines.

Yet he could invent the very real Coila. He could discuss medicine with a very real Death. He could listen to the conversation of very real spirits of two bridges, relay the words of the ghost of Robert Bruce, and state categorically that he had the Second Sight. There is many a creative person without any of those imaginative abilities who, in the absence of a soul companion, invents a very real personality. They give such companions a real name, and they can seem at times more real in the mind than any person whose real hand is shaken in real company.

The common characteristic of sane people who invent such persons is that they don't tell others about their virtual friend or friends who are very real to them. They know that to disclose their existence is likely to attract accusations that they have lost touch with reality. They might even get declared insane. Burns allowed his mind to fly free as by himself he wandered above those meanders of the streams, and released his thoughts from too intense logical patterns that prevented his Muse from letting her fingers feel so gently through all the veins and intimate sinews of his body and inside the very cells of his vibrant mind. Thus he experienced love, but not as the world knows love.

That freedom of his creativity led him to the arena that has brought on his head the accusation of being a libertine and promoter of pornography. This needs no excusing. Even greatest names amongst visual artists have produced licentious nudes for lust-ridden patrons. Such can yet be great art even if they have as their only redeeming feature that the spirit of the artist's creativity so permeated the work that it became imbued with a quality that uplifted it for the cesspit of mere sexual exploitation.

None of his poetry – nor even most of his letters – sprang full-grown like Aphrodite from the head of Jove. They were crafted. He wrote most letters in draft before he committed final copy to signature. His letters abound with comments on the processes of poetic production. He never deceived himself that art is achieved without hard work. How he found the time to do such work is one of the mysteries of the man. Certainly, he husbanded his resources and applied them frugally,

"making one guinea do the work of five",

as he would put it in the real-life work of farming. But he did not consider a verse acceptable until he had applied all possible mental effort to its refinement.

It is difficult enough for typical modern English-speaking Westerners to appreciate poetry, never mind distinguish between sheer filth and art in 18th century bawdy works. This is especially great in such poetry as that written by Robert Burns. The difficulties of understanding artistic quality alone exist even in his 'clean' works, and these make up the bulk. Most of what he wrote in verse is in an unusual variant of English and in complex forms. It ranges from the softly lyrical to the intensely satirical with unusual strength in that very difficult form of wit, the apparently innocent ironic. These difficulties make it all the more strange that he continues to be celebrated.

To achieve what he did meant he had real skill. To demonstrate to the modern reader even the application of intellect required in the creation of his extensive body of poems using such a range of forms is a daunting task. Perhaps, to begin to see, the reader should reflect just how much in everyday social circles people pride themselves when they are good at crosswords, or can solve today's Sudoku puzzles faster than their companions. Some who think themselves writers pat themselves on the back when they create a competent Haiku line. Consider this: virtually each line of Burns could pass muster in comparison with one average Haiku produced by a Westerner today; many match the best in Japanese literature. Then reflect that in any poem all his lines add together to create a whole greater than the sum of each of its individual lines. This begins to illustrate how much we in the 21st century Western world have lost the ability to appreciate excellence in poetry.

Instead, many today are content to be impressed with a line or two printed on a poster in the Underground. They call it poetry because it is printed not like a page of prose, but separated into sections on different lines. This suggests they believe that you achieve the transformation from prose to poetry by removing the punctuation marks from prose and putting in line changes.

Unfortunately, this is not so fanciful in the perception even of some modern teachers of literature. In the late 70s I first came across the works of Laurie Lee. Very shortly afterwards he was principal guest in one session at the Edinburgh Book Festival. Impressed by the enjoyment his writing gave me, I was one of an audience of less than two dozen people. The chairman for the session at one point called Lee a poet. Lee demurred at this, saying he sometimes wrote lyrically, but poet he was not. All his books clearly were prose. The chairman contradicted Lee. Searching quickly through one of Lee's books picked up from the table, he indicated he would read a section to prove Lee a poet.

Lee listened with a slight tolerant smile on his face as the chairman read a passage – yes a very lyrical passage – pausing at every punctuation mark as if moving to a new line. At the end, the chairman raised his chin with a smile of satisfaction. Most of the people in the audience applauded. I was watching Lee. He was looking down at his hands and his smile had faded. He had made his point. I detected a sadness.

With the demise of understanding of the considerable craft that is required to create excellent poetry there has grown up the myth that poetry comes entirely from inspiration. Burns would have been the first to agree with Edison that genius is mostly perspiration, with inspiration being only the one per cent. The one per cent is, albeit, the crucial factor without which the effort is merely that of a jobbing worker, doomed to be discarded as lacking that sparkle that transforms adequate quality, through some indefinable suffusion, into art. In January 1789 he wrote:

> "I have no great faith in the boastful pretensions to intuitive propriety and unlabored
> elegance. The rough material of Fine Writing is certainly the gift of Genius; but I as firmly
> believe that the workmanship is the united effort of Pains, Attention, & repeated Trial."

In a sentiment greatly expanded on later in letters to music editors and others, he had told Dr Moore a few weeks earlier that:

> "I do not look upon myself as having some pretensions from Nature to the poetic character. I have not a doubt but the knack, the aptitude to learn the Muse's trade, is a gift bestowed by Him 'who forms the secret bias of the soul'; but I as firmly believe that excellence in the profession is the fruit of industry, labor, attention and pains."

Burns was a poet – he had that ability to put words into streams that seem to float between levels of meaning, each of which is another aspect of the overall essence he aimed to encapsulate. That doesn't happen just by inspiration – it needs serious mental application. Just because he would come in from the fields, go to his desk, and write does not mean he wrote spontaneously; it means his subconscious, and possibly even his conscious mind, were actively working on the poem while he was apparently giving his full attention to doing the work that earned his keep. Sure he wasn't successful as a farmer, but it was not for want of application. He got excellent appraisals during his Excise career. He apparently was that rare thing, a true multiprocessing mind.

In considering what Burns achieved in poetry, it is worth noting that he made himself master of more varieties of form than did Shakespeare, who contented himself with blank verse (non-rhyming pentameters), sonnets, and simple song. Burns mastered a variety of very complex traditional bardic forms of Scottish verse. He also competently worked the 18th century so-called classical forms using English, when this was what needs dictated he do.

In the second phase of his creative life he chose to focus considerable attention on the collection, preservation and extension of the folk music tradition of Scotland. In making his collections he actively gathered from the memories of people of every class and background. His purpose was to ensure the survival of a threatened national culture. He thus predated by eighty years the work of the celebrated Danish 19th century scholar, poet and preacher, Nikolai Frederik Severin Grundtvig (1793-1872), whose central role in enabling national pride is considered as important in Denmark as the philosophy of Søren Kierkegaard and the writings of Hans Christian Anderson.

Burns was collecting the dying embers of an old oral tradition. In so doing he automatically found he was also collecting songs, rhymes and stories that, in the newly cultured atmosphere of the Enlightenment, were deemed obscene. Thus, though he realised these needed to be saved because they were central to the past culture, he also realised these should not be published. Thus, he kept these in a strictly controlled manuscript collection, which he also embellished and expanded. He permitted very few people to see this collection, but did admit that he enjoyed the earthy directness of these old forms. A collection claimed to be his own additions to the old oeuvre was published after his death as 'The Merry Muses of Caledonia'.

In his lifetime he circulated a number of works containing apparently risqué elements. It is my belief that on closer examination, in each of those cases, the direct nature of the work has specific literary purpose that fits his satirical norms. I have explored this in a separate work. Here I merely give the example of the phrase 'poor folk hae nothing but mowe', (sexual intercourse is the only relaxation available to the truly poor). Victorians found this directness offensive, despite its being a straightforward statement of fact. The suggestion that those who wielded power should spend their energies in the same way was a two-edged political statement, on the one hand critical of the abuses of power and on the other, daring to tell those in authority bluntly where to put their ambition.

This sentence just written has been couched euphemistically, in the manner normally accepted in academia. "Up yours" is not common parlance, in so many words, in academic wrangling, though I understand the message is fairly common. It is in brash modern novels, and in the cinema, that authors are expected to project 'normal ways of speaking', as if the constant use of old English words out of context is 'normal'. I have chosen to use the academic approach because I am not writing humour. Only within humour is the proper place, according to the best authorities, and in accordance with the writings of true artists such as Burns, for such habitual abuse.

In his little book 'How to Write', English Literature Professor Steven Leacock of McGill University in Montreal, Canada, discussed the question 'How to Swear in Print'. Having explored various avenues, he gave the ultimate absurd example of a true reading of the effect of simply replacing 'offensive' words with various print marks:

"Three asterisks!" shouted the pirate.

"Four!" shouted the next.

"I'll make it five", said the third, adding a stroke and a colon.

Burns used risqué language carefully – a fact seldom recognised by biographers. Critics comment how his use of words in satire was a series of fine rapier strokes; I propose that he used risqué language also in fine rapier strokes. Academic critics miss this careful use, because there is not in mainstream academia a well-ordained and approved mechanism to critique objectively the use of obscenity. Partly this is because obscenity is considered infra dig for mainstream academic analysis, and partly because academia is print-based, while obscenity is a matter of living culture. I would say 'oral', but that could be misinterpreted. This would suggest that sociologists and anthropologists would address it objectively, but the water has been muddied by the Freudian school of thought.

The living culture nature of risqué material is reflected in the history of pornography in print: it is only in recent years, with the rise of so-called female equality, that there has emerged a viable print market for pornography claimed to be aimed directly at women. Actual readership of such material reveals, however, that it is dominated by two main sectors: by medical women who require understanding of the way people's minds work, and by women who are so 'liberated' that they have taken on characteristics of male behaviour. There is a further very interesting subsection that was drawn to my attention by a senior Indian lady gynaecologist: in underdeveloped countries there is so little personal education available to women that the only inexpensive way of teaching them about sexual health and sickness is using illustrations from explicit male girlie magazines.

What lies behind this?

The feminist movement has emphasised that there are not one but two living culture forms in most levels of all societies: the male and the female. This reflects the 'Men are from Mars' syndrome. I propose that there are typically three culture forms: the male, the female and the mixed gender. These may appear in the child as much as in the adult sections of a society. I suggest that Burns was instinctively if not actually aware of these three forms of culture. The mixed culture was the culture he addressed in print as well as performance. That culture excludes those elements which are appropriate only to the gender-based forms.

In so far as risqué material is critiqued in academic process, no distinction is made between male and female risqué norms. This is mainly because modern printed pornography for women is produced in the male format, simply with male pictures and words replacing those in the girlie forms. This misses the point.

In my career I was from an early period an honorary man in male-only business circles. I later was typically the most senior woman amongst a few but apparently growing number of promoted females. Thus, I was from an early stage exposed to uninhibited male talk. As sole woman and honorary man I simply ignored it, and usually some man of fine mind objected to it. But man-talk is definitely inappropriate in mixed groups if only because it is bad manners as it is offensive at least to some. In any event, single-gender talk in a mixed-gender group insults the sensibilities of men and women present. As senior woman in such groups I learned how to use humour to dispel inappropriate talk.

The success of the film 'The Full Monty' has demonstrated a crucial fact: pornography aimed at men feeds a lust market; risqué material aimed at women finds a humour market. This is with good reason. The main agenda of male obscenity is to confirm to men that they are masters of the universe. In this model, women are subjugated, indeed slaves. Because in Western society men are indeed masters of the universe, exploitation of female images for the selfish titillation of male lust – the ultimate expression of the subjugation of women – was very early in the development of the mechanism of printing a core market for publishers.

Prominent members of the world feminist movement have, I believe, made a mistake in promoting 'female' versions of girlie pornography. Such merely gives the message that "women lust, subjugate and exploit just as well as men". While that message may have truth, it is not in my view healthy to promote this message.

When, with around me a number of mixed staff who truly believe in decent equality, I have found we are confronted by men more senior than myself telling obscene jokes, I never directly challenge the speakers. Instead, my own approach has been to appear to join the speakers. I involve myself in contributing to the discussion, by interposing a joke. But this is a well-chosen joke that undermines the process. This never made me popular with the perpetrators of such aural violence. I console myself that it did endear me to my staff.

The key is the kind of joke to contribute. There are not many simple ones available that quickly achieve the necessary result. But the essence is simple: the purpose of the male rude joke is to prove how virile the man is; the purpose of the undermining joke is to prove that men deceive themselves about their prowess. Male jokes are centred on men. The put-down joke is also centred on men, but on men's failings. Typically, the main tellers of rude male jokes don't find this latter type in the least bit funny. The women, the young people and the equality-minded men can find them extremely funny. What such jokes do is reverse the power structure: instead of the macho man being on top, he is toppled off his pinnacle.

Burns had in his collection of risqué material the macho sort, and the put-down female sort. No critic I have read has made this observation. I suggest Burns used his collection well. Certain of his verses would have greatly amused such down-to-earth people as the Duchess of Gordon (famed for outdoing men in being realistic about life). In her parlour he probably recited some of his extremely clever verses designed explicitly to achieve the male put-down. The ladies would have giggled profusely.

Such is his wonderful pastoral about Damon who makes love to his mistress in tune with the music of nature – except that when he really thinks he has got going and is just about to climax, he loses the timing. I can imagine the duchess rolling about in hilarious laughter; this poet was right on the money! Men just could never crack it! All their prowess, and at the end of it all, the woman was left thinking: damn he's gone and missed it. He's messed up again! Additional irony in this Damon poem would have been clear to Edinburgh's literati. Damon is one of the Platonic pastoral pair of lads in that Greek philosopher's Dialogues.

While Burns was no doubt what I have heard men call a 'red blooded man', he had from youth schooled himself in differentiating the false from the true in poetry and literature. In his own work he did not use pornography for mere titillation but for increasing his own projection of his awareness of the human soul and psyche. He appears to have had hardly a shred of discriminatory bias in his heart. His own experience of being patronised by academics and aristocrats when he was a lord amongst them endorsed his awareness of status divisions. He equally abhorred sectarianism and gender apartheid. There is, in my view, a new reading to be made of the risqué works of Burns from this perspective alone, if only because it can inform the continuing debate about the true nature of human equality.

He used what means he deemed appropriate to make his points, for example expressing the view in a letter to Robert Cleghorn in October 1793 that:

> "Well! the Law is good for Something, since we can make a bawdy song out of it. I never made anything of it in any other way."

The hypocrisy of the Holy Willies was a ready target. Thus in the 'Tale of a Wife' he has the predestination-sermonising self-righteous priest advise the self-confessed saintly and Whig old woman of virtuous public morals troubled by her continuing sexual desire:

> What signifies Morals and Works,
> > Our works are no wordy a runt!
> It's Faith that is sound, orthodox,
> > That covers the fauts o' your cunt.
>
> Were ye o' the Reprobate race,
> > Created to sin and be brunt,
> O then it would alter the case
> > If ye should gae wrang wi your cunt.
>
> But you that is Called and Free,
> > Elekit and chosen a saunt,
> Will't break the Eternal Decree
> > Whatever ye do wi your cunt.
>
> And now with a sanctify'd kiss
> > Let's kneel and renew covenant:
> It's this – and it's this – and it's this –
> > That settles the pride o' your cunt.

The priest's comforting solicitations caused devotion to fly up like a flame. The Enlightenment Establishment liked such poems to be published and widely read no more than did prudish Victorians. This is not to 'excuse' Burns for preserving and creating verse and prose that to some ears might give offence – merely to reflect the old dictum "Judge not others that ye may not be judged", which he paraphrased in words that epitomise the works of the Great Regulator of the Universe:

> Who made the heart, 'tis *He* alone
> Decidedly can try us,
> He knows each chord its various tone,
> Each spring its various bias.

In the third line of this part verse Burns showed his awareness of the Music of the Spheres, a concept drawn to his attention in his early days. The concept is at least as old as Pythagoras. In the City States of Ancient Greece, harmony amongst men was the goal. A man of elegance must be equally learned in harmonic politics, mathematics, astronomy and music. Pythagoras used a monochord – a single gut stretched above a board – to explore harmony in music. He demonstrated the rational mathematical relationships between musical sounds that together sounded sweet to the human ear. Looking up at the skies, watching the planets in their courses, he agreed with those who said that those movements, so regular and eternal, must of course be harmonious. Thus he imagined planets in their spheres, the stars beyond, and beyond that all the hierarchies of choirs of the heavens, each contributing sound in rational proportion to the great harmony of the universe.

The dull ears of the ordinary man cannot hear this music, because it is the inherent harmony of mathematical elegance. It is the music that makes the true mathematician ease a sigh of sheer pleasure when he reflects on the magnificent simplicities that are invariably found to underlie the most succinct representations of Nature. When a mathematician experiences such insights, he knows that purest joy that only the finest music in sound can even symbolise to those not granted that great intellectual gift.

When a true mathematician says that what he enjoys about his field of study is its poetry, do not laugh. He speaks only in a way that might let you feel an echo of his joy.

This is the Music of the Spheres.

Just as the musician could tune the strings on his lyre, taught the ancients, the Almighty could choose to re-tune that music of the spheres that permeated all His creation – but only He could do so. It was beyond the power of Man.

> Then at the balance let's be mute,
> We never can adjust it;
> What's *done* we partly may compute,
> But know not what's *resisted*.

We can use our imaginations to understand some of what might have been resisted by a man who was very handsome, appeared of strong build, was a professed lover of dancing and undoubtedly a good mover, who went into raptures over music, had a rapier wit, wrote fine and very clever poetry, had considerable respect for all people and particularly women, and had only one visible fault: he was very poor. Such a man might 'gar the lasses lie aspar', whether he sought it out or not.

Not a few biographers spend considerable energy extrapolating from the few known facts about the man and his life to imagine many other aspects of and incidents in his life. So I here will indulge myself too, a little, to help set the scene for my approach to gaining new understanding of this man of strangely persistent remembrance.

In an Edinburgh springtime, drivers rushing their cars through modern urbanity might, as they traverse that large swathe of insolent green parkland south of the Royal Mile, that so far defies the avarice of inner-city real estate developers, glance on to the south and enjoy the blues, whites and yellows of a thousand dancing crocuses between the roadway and the grey but now very classy tenements. Trees have not then put forth the fresh young green of spring. To the north is a vista past the decaying concrete of academe to the distant ridge of the ancient spine of Scotland's modern capital city. This area invites the dog walker and the jogger. But in our modern uncivil days, students are warned not to walk alone across this enticing land, and certainly not at night. The Meadows, as they are called, were drained and laid out as parkland in the aftermath of the 1745 Jacobite Rising, intended as a sign of increasing civic pride in a mature Hanoverian populace. There they could ride on horse and carriage, and display gentility and their growing affluence. By the way, the labour needed to transform these old grazing fields into a walled park also soaked up part of that great influx of displaced people whose livelihood had been devastated by the Rising. One such labourer was the father of Robert Burns. In gaps in his toils, he went to the seed merchants, which formed the local labour exchange for anyone with skills to offer and ambition to rise above the poorly paid digging and delving of ditches and planting of trees. "Go west, young man!" he was finally told when the seed merchant put up William Burness for the opportunity of a gardener's place in Ayrshire.

A quarter of a century later his son was now in that same city – a changed city, with the building works now established to the south, and new build now advancing in the north in the space that lay between the old city and its port, Leith. The young man no doubt had expectations based on reminiscences his father recounted of the toil and sweat of transformation and agricultural improvement. Great were the hopes, then. Great were the dreams. The young man's hopes were great when he came to Edinburgh, but he knew from his father's experience that dreams make false promises.

One evening he had walked south by the road alongside those Meadows to reach the home of Professor Adam Ferguson, on Sciennes Hill, so named from a convent of St Catherine of Siena that had once held this land. The professor held a weekly soirée, where met great minds, legal and academic. Professor Dugald Stewart, who encouraged the poet in Ayrshire, bringing him to dine with himself and Lord Daer at his estate in Catrine after the publication of the Kilmarnock edition, persuaded Ferguson to allow him to bring this unusual young man into this august company. Burns dressed in those plush blue hair breeches in which he had invested to make himself look as much a gentleman as he could afford, and tied round his neck that fine cravat of linen, of flax grown in his own fields at Lochlie, heckled himself, then spun by his mother and finally woven in Mossgeil.

Stewart had given the young man advice: they'll press you with drink, so sip slowly or they'll drown you; and you can slip under a table if you want to stop – others will be there before you; there'll maybe be a lad there, but his job is just to loosen the neckties so guests don't drown in their sick. Savage hospitality, thought the young man.

But this was the inescapable norm. In 1788 he wrote to a friend William Cruikshank:

"I have fought my way severely through the savage hospitality of this country – the object of all hosts being to send every guest to bed drunk if they can".

To his last days he reported to intimates how he had no difficulty forgoing entering any public house for strong drink. But the socialising his role of entertainer poet forced on him left him unable to escape having drink poured down his unwilling throat. This enforced hospitality even by his strongest ally in Dumfries, Robert Riddell, eventually divided him from his nearest friends but not before it had exacerbated the effects of the hidden illnesses contracted in childhood.

The flunkie who answered the door looked him up and down. He was by no means sure that this man, by the plainness of his clothes clearly no gentleman, should indeed be allowed inside. But he let him proceed. Burns mounted the stairs, his hand running on the smooth mahogany banister that curved round the tight corners. There, open before him were the doors of the piano nobile. This was already full of men. More flunkies went around with pewter flagons. They topped up with gushing claret or thick dark port goblets held cockily in the elegant cuffed hands of men, mostly wigged, a few more fashionably boasting their own tied hair, all with that lift of the self-important chin as their conversations gushed with those around them in their individual little circles. He moved uneasily into the room. He noted there were no carpets on the floor. In the salon of the Duchess of Gordon there was always an elegant patterned knotted carpet. He saw a goblet splash and drop and a man displace his wig as he stumbled to reach after it. He realised the good sense of any carpet being removed before a gathering such as this. In vino veritas, said the academics. Truth comes out of the wine bottle. After all, did not our leader William Pitt typically drink six bottles of port each day to hold in the course of truth and right the helm of our great British empire?

The poet paused. Noise of chatter. The odd raucous laugh. Men glanced round at his step and turned away after a disdainful glance down his length. Their backs firmed in their tight circles against him with their well practiced cold shoulder instinctively cutting out an outsider. Burns straightened his back, squared his shoulders, walked into the room, and began looking at the pictures. One caught his eye. A print of a soldier. The man lay dead in the snow with a dog beside him. Beneath it were a few lines of verse. Burns tried to make conversation with the group nearest to him.

"Can anyone tell me more of the poet or the poem with this print?"

An innocent question. Heads turned momentarily over shoulders; someone laughed; the insolence of this peasant throwing questions, without introduction, at such as they.

A silence settled around him like a miasma.

Then a quiet voice shrilly spoke.

"If it please, sir, the poem is 'The Justice of the Peace' by Langhorne."

Burns looked round. It was a lad by the door, a limping lad.

"You'll be a man, yet, sir", in his strong assured voice Burns replied to the boy.

There is very little known of this sole encounter of Burns and young Walter Scott. Much is made of that opportunity that Burns was given to have discussion with all the leading lights of Edinburgh thought. How many actually exchanged words with him is not recorded. My own wide experience and observation, in such so-called major networking events, is that any outsider, even as special guest, is generally of interest to those gathered only in so far as each can display his own talents to this new audience, and so promote his own interests. Of the evening, then, virtually all is conjecture except that, many years later, Sir Walter Scott made much of it.

Burns no doubt sipped his wine. Possibly he was ignored by the flunkies with the flagons. He might have mused that the wine tasted a bit odd. Then perhaps he reflected that it was because he was drinking out of pewter tumblers rented out by the wine merchant along with the supply of wine. He had become used to drinking from glass or even silver in the salon of the Duchess of Gordon. Pewter is fine for beer, he thought, but not for wine. Then he thought that, of course, this would not be the good wine that he drank at that first dinner with Lord Daer at Professor Stewart's home; he hadn't appreciated, then, that it was special. He had been spoiled at Kirkoswald, drinking best claret from barrels smuggled in from the Isle of Man. Alone with his thoughts and the continuing eyeing attention of a mere lad amongst the self-styled intelligentsia, he might have observed the odd rumpus of another man falling. Maybe he watched others guided to a room in the corner and heard the splash of piss into chamber pots. Perhaps he observed the odd incontinent accident mucking the polished wooden floor. But this was not his first exposure to the sophistication of Edinburgh. At the end of December just past he had written to William Chalmers reflecting on the grandeur of the Roman Empire, and mused how

> "the poor son of Zebedee [was banished] to a desert island in the Archipelago, where he was gifted with the Second Sight, and saw as many wild beasts as I have seen since I came to Edinburgh."

He was relieved when he was at last noticed by Stewart, who called loudly across the room and walked boldly towards him to drag him forward to introduce him to the company and to his host, Professor Ferguson.

"Scotland's bard! The young Mr Burns!" he would have called out to the crowd.

There would have been a surprised silence, irritation at conversation interrupted. There might then have been a little foot stamping, for true applause is hard when you are clutching a goblet. Someone probably called for a poem. Looking around at the drunken horde, and remembering the print of the soldier, the young man may have reflected on those nights he had slipped in to observe the beggars in Poosie Nancy's tavern in Mauchline, and heard the raucous drinking song of the maimed veteran in tattered rags of uniform. He had transformed that song into a wild patriotic chant. He burst into voice:

"I am a son of Mars who have been in many wars,
And show my cuts and scars where'r I come."

Dum, dum, dum, went the feet of the listeners, drowning out the words, until the pause before the next verse:

"My Prenticeship I past, where my LEADER breath'd his last,
When the bloody die was cast on the heights of ABRAM."

Dum, dum, dum, and a cheer, hoorah! for the conquest of Canada!

The song ended. The crowd hummed approval at the entertainment and turned back to the goblets and the talk.

"Well done, young man", might Stewart have muttered, patting Burns on the back and drawing him through to a group of men of his own circle.

"I haven't read that one", said Stewart.

"It is in a cantata I tried my hand at – 'Love and Liberty' I called the ensemble."

"Interesting," said Stewart. "You must let me have a copy."

Years later, when such a cantata in publication would have made him a man marked as seditious, he denied any memory of the work, and expressed surprise that anyone should know of it, or that any copy was in existence. It re-emerged after his death and was printed in 1799, not within the Currie edition. It shocked. The final song called the masses to rebellion.

> A fig for those by law protected!
> LIBERTY's a glorious feast.
> Courts for cowards were erected,
> Churches built to please the PRIEST.

No, he did not sing that in this polite society. But he watched, and he noted, and he slowly sipped the cheap wine through the bitter taste of its reaction with the pewter. And he met some very interesting men, who said curious things that excited his interest, his wonder and his imagination.

At last carriages had come and the men were helped their stumbling way down the stairs, and the poet escaped into a cold night, stars above him. The park beckoned. The smell of the grass and the wood of the trees attracted him after the stench of wine and urine. He found a place where the bank had been thrown up against the wall, so that he could get high enough to clamber over. He dropped down into the gardens. Inside he felt his feet on the soft earth. Far ahead was the city, a black monster, the outline of its back touched here and there with the glimmer of a night watchman's torch. By the light of the stars he picked his way along, and found a tree. Still a young tree it was, but its girth was sufficient to take his weight as he leaned against it. Perhaps his father had planted this tree, he may have mused.

Several months he had now been in this city and asking himself why he had come. It was a very different city from what he had expected. If it had been full of jobseekers when his father arrived, it was now full of the unemployable destitute – teeming with harlots and thieves, sons and daughters of desperation. Back in that gathering, when he had first been shocked to see a chamber pot crossing the room, he had then reflected that, of course, they gathered the urine and sold it to the tanners like he did at home. But then he realised, no, they didn't. It was poured away in a closet – only a bit less wasteful and disgusting than that stinking filth that was tossed out of every window of the tenements that lined the roads between the castle and the Canongate Tolbooth. It ran into the street, so that the Lawnmarket, where they sold all that fine linen, and the High Street by the Courts of Justice and St Giles, were stinking open sewers, draining into the many alleyways that reached down each side of the rock spine. Some of it never truly escaped and piled up against the town walls where it nurtured rats. Thus the city rotted like the abandoned carcass of a stripped stranded whale.

He had to write a poem in praise of this city, he had been advised. He had found inspiration hard to find. Writing to order was always such a chore. He murmured to himself another verse from that tavern collection; another he had not sung in this company:

> Sir Wisdom's a fool when he's fou;
> Sir Knave is a fool in a Session.

He let his back slip down the tree until he was seated on its slightly rising roots. The stars had wheeled round. Soon it would be morning. He closed his eyes and tried to think of some suitable poem that would entrance an audience such as he had just left, and inspire them to give him the means to use his mind as a mind like his should surely in justice be used.

Chapter I   *Rantin' Rebel Rabbie*

A bird began to sing, and then another. Dawn was approaching. He opened his eyes. A streak of light showed over the eastern horizon. The blackness of the city began to firm into a grey of high ridged castle and a lizard back of tenements with a frizz of chimneys. He noticed a wisp of smoke rise from one chimney as a fire was encouraged. Then another. As the sun began to push more light over the horizon more wisps emerged, and as the numbers grew they joined into a pall that coalesced. Driven by a slight wind, the pall seemed to move in a mass up the hill. The sun broke through and the smoke cloud seemed tinged with red as it moved, its top grey, like the garb of a law lord, he thought. Up the hill moved the pink grey-tipped cloud, like a bent giant climbing slowly, until it reached the great seat of the castle and seemed to turn and curve back and settle like a monster on a latrine. From the distance he heard adding to the cacophony of the increasingly noisy morning birds the tiniest screech of the throwing back of a shutter. Then he heard the squeal of the opening of a sash window. Then another, and then more. And another noise too, he could imagine, one that had shocked him and caused him to retch uncontrollably on that morning last November when he first walked out into the streets of Edinburgh after a fitful sleep sharing that cramped straw bed in a town that was never truly silent. He imagined a long sigh from that giant law lord relieving himself and he imagined he heard all the gardy loo chamber pots emptying into the morning streets and sloshing down the gutters. And he laughed. He chanted aloud:

"Edina, Scotia's darling seat!

All hail thy palaces and tow'rs,

Where once beneath a Monarch's feet,

Sat Legislation's sov'reign pow'rs!"

He laughed. The Muse had come to him. He laughed. He could make a poem. It would be just like their precious Augustan verse. In fine English as they wanted it. As good as anything Thomson could write. And they would never know! They would never know!

He jumped up. A spring was in his step. He went back to his lodging. He was smiling and happy, and he began to write.

Of course, this is conjecture. Of course, his 'Address to Edinburgh', printed to such applause in the Edinburgh edition, is now considered to show the total failure of this man of the streams and of the common people to find any true inspiration in the capital or to write well in English. There is no evidence that he found those evenings so unpleasant, only that he complained in his letters of the savage hospitality that had done no good to his health, his livelihood and his reputation. But it may be no less fanciful than many tales that have been woven round the bare threads of his verifiable story. He began to write profiles of the beasts of Edinburgh and their manners, but his room got rifled in April. His papers were stolen. He remarked to George Reid that he had realised he needed to take care. The consolation was that he was probably too irrelevant to be sued for libel, confiding to Rev Dr Hugh Blair on the "meteor-like novelty" of his appearance in Edinburgh in contrast to the "permanent lights". A few weeks later he received the gift of a copy of Spencer's mystical work 'The Faerie Queen'. He wrote to William Dunbar, thanking him for the volume, telling him he must leave Edinburgh. He expected to be quickly forgotten, as the

> "numerous Edinburgh friendships are of so tender a construction that they will not bear carriage with me".

Writing intimately in the language of mysticism in a city of rationality, he expressed the hope that Dunbar might remember him, though they might never again meet in this life.

> "It is indeed very probable that when I leave this City, we part never more to meet in this sublunary Sphere; but I have a strong fancy that in some future excentric Planet, the Comet of a happier System than any with which Astronomy is yet acquainted, you and I, among the harum-scarum Sons of Imagination and Whim, with a hearty shake of a hand, a Metaphor and a Laugh, shall recognise Old Acquaintance."

A month earlier he had already expressed his discomfort with scholastic rationalism to his school colleague of youth, James Candlish, who was at Glasgow University studying to be a medical doctor. Candlish had written him an impressive letter showing his erudition and command of scholastic argument. Burns responded in language redolent of familiarity with that traditional ending of a mathematical proof, 'quod erat demonstrandum': thus was requiring to be proven. Candlish's letter supported the poet's own point:

> "You have shewn me one thing which was to be demonstrated: that strong pride of reasoning, with a little affectation of singularity, may mislead the best of hearts. I likewise, since you and I were first acquainted, in the pride of despising old women's stories, ventured in 'the daring path Spinoza trod'; but experience of the weakness, not the strength, of human powers, made me glad to grasp at revealed religion."

His exposure to fame caused him to reflect on the worth of worldly praise, whose effects disgusted him. In mid June 1787 from Mauchline he wrote of his opinion to Willie Nicol, the Latin master at Edinburgh's High School with whom he formed lasting friendship.

> "I never, my friend, thought Mankind very capable of anything generous; but the stateliness of the Patricians in Edinburgh, and the servility of my plebeian brethren, who perhaps formerly eyed me askance, since I returned home, have nearly put me out of conceit altogether with my species. – I have bought a pocket Milton, which I carry perpetually about with me, in order to study the sentiments – the dauntless magnanimity; the intrepid unyielding independence; the desperate daring, and noble defiance of hardship, in that great personage, Satan. – 'Tis true, I have just now a little cash; but I am afraid the damn'd star that hitherto has shed its malignant, purpose-blasting rays full in my zenith; that noxious Planet so baneful in its influences to the rhyming tribe, I much dread it is not yet beneath my horizon."

By the time he left Edinburgh he had begun a fight that would last until he was laid in the grave: he had begun to oppose an inhuman rationalism that was already dominating the Edinburgh Enlightenment. It was a battle that he would fight hard. The weapons he used were put into his hands from infancy onwards. His first were what his parents gave him – the background of his father and mother. He added more in his early education. This was followed by his early work experiences, his loves and his friendships, his search for a means and a purpose in personal expression, and his dedication to preserving and enhancing the sung culture of his homeland. To show how all these influences worked within him, and how he used them to fight for humanity and create his legacy, means understanding his story against the background of the history not just of Britain but of Europe and America. It is a wide and wild story, with many twists and turns and unanswered questions – the tale of a man for our time whose story has never yet been fully told.

Chapter II   *In His Own Rite*

How Burns tried to tell his own story of his life and loves and why and how it was perverted.

Large numbers of Burns manuscripts have survived – and a considerable number of late 19th century forgeries too. The odd 'Burns manuscript' turns up every so often in car boot sales and auctions.

In the late 19th century an extremely good replica of the Kilmarnock edition was produced. Another was produced in the 1920s. I have seen argument over ownership of one of the latter, purported by certain persons to be an original first edition. This caused irreparable breach within one family. The war passed down through generations.

I have recently seen a replica page of the Glenriddell manuscript for sale at auction, labelled as a page of the First Commonplace Book. Many such may be the work of 'Antique' Smith, who was a clerk in a solicitor's office in Edinburgh. One day, in clearing out old documents he came across a letter from Burns. He found a ready buyer. Himself skilled in quill-pen writing, he realised he was onto something. Visiting libraries, he extracted the blank end leaves of volumes published during the lifetime of the poet. This gave him paper with contemporary watermarks on which he could generate what at best were facsimile letters or poems. And he invented more. He passed them all off as genuine. To reproduce the style of Burns's writing, he practiced copying known real manuscripts upside-down, thus eliminating the forger's own writing idiosyncrasies. He was finally convicted on 26th June 1893. By then quite a few of his works had got into circulation, thus confusing some academic researchers around the start of the 20th century. The buyers also had a vested interest in their 'original' being accepted as genuine.

A colleague of mine holds what he thought was a set of proofs of unpublished songs of Robert Burns. This had come down through one of his sisters, possibly Agnes. It might have been through Annabella. Agnes purportedly nursed Burns on his death bed and helped his wife at the birth of his last child. This is a reasonable supposition, as his mother in Mossgeil would certainly send an unmarried daughter south to help a dying brother and his family when his father-in-law had not sent Jean's mother. In the days before his death, Burns was sending letters to his father-in-law begging that he would let Jean's mother come to Dumfries. The story of Agnes has been given the further twist that she was written out of history because she married a Roman Catholic. The fact is that Agnes (1762-1834) is recorded as having married a William Galt in 1804 – a name of good solid Ayrshire Presbyterian connotations. They emigrated to Ireland, where Agnes lies buried in the Presbyterian cemetery at Dundalk. There is no record that Annabella married. Born in 1764, she died in 1832. She appears to have lived all her days with her mother and the family of Gilbert, the poet's brother. Their last home was at Grant Braes in East Lothian, where Gilbert had moved the family before his own death in 1827.

Having examined the volume, I have suggested to my colleague that what he has may have been a bound bundle of songs with music out of the vast collection that Burns had accumulated at the time of his death. On the other hand, it is predominantly English songs. In his last days he commented that there was soon to come out a London music publication to which he had contributed. The collection may be related to that work. I suspect it is unlikely the book he has contains proof copies of unpublished songs that Burns had written or reworked. More likely, it shows he was studying the kind of contemporary published music that was in competition with his Edinburgh song publishers.

Identifying what are truthful facts about Robert Burns is not easy. Those 'chiels that winna ding' can be pretty slippery creatures. Embellishment grows rampant with the passing of time, the debates of academia, and imaginings of biographers. Burns would have found this amusing, I guess, as he relished the thought of being listed in 'Poor Robin's Almanack'. By the way, in this study I trust I make it clear when I am being imaginative, but when quoting purported fact I have made every effort to verify that it is factual.

There is revisionism now being undertaken by those whose role in academia is to strip off the censorious overlay of 19th century evaluation of a poet himself without privilege of academic education. But it may not yet be going far enough. I believe that the best place to start in considering the legacy of this man to the modern world is in his own biographical letter. This was written to an entire stranger with whom he exchanged a number of other letters discussing aspects of poetry and writing. Burns came to respect him intellectually and morally. In this letter he confided details of his personal history.

The recipient was John Moore MD. Moore was a friend of Mrs Dunlop. Burns and Moore became correspondents when Mrs Dunlop mutually introduced them, albeit only in writing. Moore had written to her praising Burns's poems in the Kilmarnock edition. Burns sent Moore a long letter that outlined the story of his life up to the date of that publication.

Born in 1730, son to Reverend Charles Moore of Stirling, Dr Moore was himself father of General Sir John Moore, who died in the retreat to Corunna during the Peninsular War. That son was in my childhood celebrated in the English school curriculum through the study of the poem 'The Burial of Sir John Moore after Corunna'. This begins like a roll of drums with the words "Not a drum was heard". Dr Moore's father died when he was a child. His mother took him to Glasgow where she had inherited some property from her father, Anderson of Dowhill. That had once been an important family. It was reduced to poverty first by fines for religious nonconformity. It finally fell through significant investment in the ill-fated Darien expedition. Dr Moore in 1789 published the moralistic novel 'Zeluco'. He sent a copy to Robert Burns soon after their correspondence began. He asked Burns to give him his opinion. Burns covered the volume with his annotations. Interested in the developing affairs in France, Moore went to Paris in late summer 1792. He witnessed the rising of 10th August and the beginnings of the Reign of Terror. This gave him more good selling material which he published as 'A Journal During a Residence in France'. Burns was not impressed with this book. Moore died in February 1802.

Educated at Glasgow University, Moore was taken as a young man by the fifth Duke of Argyle to gain practical medical experience on the battlefields of Flanders. He followed this with the role of attaché to the British Embassy of Lord Albemarle in Paris. Then he went into medical partnership with Mr Hamilton, professor of anatomy at Glasgow University. After his time in Glasgow, Moore spent five years accompanying the young Douglas, Duke of Hamilton, on the Grand Tour, at the end of which he relocated to London where in 1779 he published 'View of Society and Manners in France, Switzerland and Germany', that gained instant popularity. His book on Italy was not so popular. In 1785 he published 'Medical Sketches', a book on medical matters for the layman.

Chapter II *In his own Rite*

In Glasgow, Moore had been involved in leading-edge thought. Anatomy was then becoming a science, with lectures to students carried out during dissection of a real human dead body – to the horror of many religious people who considered this an abomination. Edinburgh University in 1764 installed its first custom-built anatomy dissection theatre.

Available bodies were limited mainly to those of executed criminals. As desire for anatomy lessons increased, so did the demand for bodies. This began to be met courtesy of an inevitable consequence of the massive economic changes then sweeping populations out of rural areas in the name of agricultural improvement: cities filled with the destitute; the destitute died off; corpses accrued with nobody to pay for burial; university students and researchers soaked up the surplus. Where there were not enough bodies, the trade of body snatching emerged. Churchyards began to install heavy-duty mort chests to protect the remains of the recently dead. John Burns, the poet's cousin, who worked for a time at Ellisland, got the job of guarding Stewarton graveyard from body snatchers. By the first decade of the 19th century the trade in dead bodies had reached the stage that it was economically viable for the criminal classes not merely to collect existing dead bodies but to generate their own supply. Thus, the crowded stinking alleyways of old Edinburgh became the nightly haunt of Burke and Hare, whose dastardly deeds were not ended until 1831.

In a counterpart to writing biographies, the philosophical purpose of dissecting bodies was to gain greater understanding of the nature of Life. By understanding how a body is put together, went the argument, we can understand how to put bodies together. Thus arose such nightmare thoughts that were finally crystallised in the early 19th century in the story of Dr Frankenstein's monster. This was brought into his imaginary life by the daughter of Mary Wollstonecraft, a contemporary of Burns with whom he also exchanged letters.

Anatomy classes were a feature of the intellectual life of the Edinburgh Burns visited in 1786-8. He no doubt wondered that men might think to construct life by cutting up the dead. Experience in farming demonstrates all too clearly that cutting up the dead teaches nothing about what makes life. It might help to give more explanation of the cause of death. The study of death merely teaches about death. To learn of life requires the study of life.

Burns exclaimed in one poem that there is no science that will ever explain how life works. Why, asks a modern critic, should Burns write something so banal? Why did he waste a precious line and so spoil a poem? The answer is that in the late 18th century this was not considered a banal thought. It was considered by some to be downright reactionary – just as today in 2008 it is considered reactionary to urge caution in interfering in DNA structures and to promote regulation of laboratory propagation of and research into stem cells.

Burns, radical though he is said to have been, was uttering a very reactionary thought: life is beyond our understanding; all life should be treated with the respect owing to God.

When after the poet's death Currie began to prepare publication of Burns's 'Works', he prepared an introduction in which he dissected the poet's life. Dr Moore let him use the autobiographical letter. Currie also got new letters from Robert's brother Gilbert and his teacher Murdoch that, written without knowledge that any of the others existed, substantiated the main elements of the poet's autobiographical letter.

Several versions of Burns's own letter exist with differences, some of which I will comment on. I reproduce here the version originally published by Currie, which he based on the copy provided by Moore. We now know that Currie changed, removed and added words and phrases. His adaptation gave the first public impression of what Burns himself had meant to be read. That first public who read it unwittingly read a distorted voice, deliberately distorted by Currie. Interposed here with comments from other letters, it lets us hear a story of the poet's early days and earliest impressions and influences centred on his own words first drafted at Mauchline on 2nd August 1787.

After his winter in Edinburgh and his tour of the Borders, Burns took a trip to the West Highlands. He had a fall from his horse. Grounded in Mauchline, he had a recurrence of his invisible illness – his hypochondria. This may well have been a physical reaction to all the stress, hyped and positive though it had been, over the previous year. It was serious enough that as in previous major recurrences, he feared that he would die. Perhaps it was this fear that made him decide that he would commit to paper his story of what led up to his publishing his poems. The public knew him only through his published work, and his transient appearance in Edinburgh. That was too narrow a view, he surely felt. They could never understand the depth of feeling that lay behind his work, and thus they could not get the full meaning of his work, without having some awareness of the emotions that created it. But writing a life story is one thing. Sharing a written story of your own life with other people is quite another. Here was a man very far away who had volunteered sincere interest in him as a person. He had been introduced by a woman who alone, of all those grand folk who had lionised him, still actively wished to have him as her friend. Dr Moore was a Scot and would understand the context of the story. But he was also physically a very long way from the busy gossips of Scotland's elite. Perhaps he could and should entrust to this concerned man such personal information as his life story.

Burns did not send this letter immediately it was written. He first gave it to Mrs Dunlop for her to review. His fair copy was posted only when he had made corrections. Even then he delayed actually sending, letting Dr Moore have it after considerable hesitation, on returning from his tour to the north. To 'explain' the difference between the date on the letter and the date of sending, he added a note that it had been 'forgotten' during his travels.

I give it in full in this book not because I am lazy about summarising his early life. It is because it is so often taken for granted that readers won't want to read the version of his early life that Burns himself wrote, preferring the gloss of the biographer. Removing two centuries of soiled gloss varnish from the picture is now needed so as to see Burns clearly.

Currie even adulterated the opening sentence, omitting the explanation Burns gave for having been 'rambling': he had business to attend to. Thus, readers got the immediate impression that, with cash in his pocket, the sudden star was splashing it on a holiday.

> "For some months past I have been rambling in the country, but I am now confined with some lingering complaints, originating, as I take it, in the stomach. To divert my spirits a little in this miserable fog of *ennui*, I have taken a whim to give you a history of myself. My name had made some little noise in this country; you have done me the honour to interest yourself very warmly in my behalf; and as I think a faithful account of what character of a man I am, and how I came by that character, may perhaps amuse you in an idle moment,

I will give you an honest narrative; though I know it will be often at my own expense; - for, I assure you, Sir, I have, like Solomon, whose character, excepting in the trifling affair of *wisdom*, I sometimes think I resemble, - I have, I say, like him, *turned my eyes to behold madness and folly*, and, like him too, frequently shaken hands with their intoxicating friendship.

After you have perused these pages, should you think them trifling and impertinent, I only beg leave to tell you, that the poor author wrote them under some twitching qualms of conscience, arising from a suspicion that he was doing what he ought not to do; a predicament he has more than once been in before.

I have not the most distant pretensions to assume that character which the pye-coated guardians of escutcheons call a Gentleman. When at Edinburgh, last winter, I got acquainted in the Herald's Office; and, looking through that granary of honours, I there found almost every name in the kingdom; but for me,

> 'My ancient but ignoble blood
> Has crept thro' scoundrels ever since the flood.'

Gules, Purpure, Argent &c. quite disowned me."

Currie's concern for political correctness at this stage caused him to erase and replace. The words Moore received were:

"My fathers rented land of the noble Keiths of Marshal, and had the honor to share their fate."

Currie identified this statement as projecting dangerous anti-Hanoverian sentiment. The poet had then expressed a view that would have caused considerable offence in the political climate of the dying years of the 18th century:

"I do not use the word, Honor, with any reference to Political principles; loyal and disloyal I take to be merely relative terms in that ancient and formidable court known in this Country by the name of CLUB-LAW. – Those who dare welcome Ruin and shake hands with Infamy for what they sincerely believe to be the cause of their God or their King – 'Brutus and Cassius are honourable men'."

This would not have gone down well. So, what Currie published was:

"My father was of the north of Scotland, the son of a farmer, and was thrown by early misfortunes on the world at large; where, after many years' wanderings and sojournings, he picked up a pretty large quantity of observations and experience, to which I am indebted for most of my little pretensions to wisdom. I have met with few who understood men, their manners, and their ways, equal to him; but stubborn, ungainly integrity, and headlong, ungovernable irascibility, are disqualifying circumstances; consequently I was born a very poor man's son. For the first six or seven years of my life, my father was gardiner to a worthy gentleman of small estate in the neighbourhood of Ayr. Had he continued in that station, I must have marched off to be one of the little underlings about a farm-house; but it was his dearest wish and prayer to have it in his power to keep his children under his own eye till they could discern between good and evil; so, with the assistance of his generous master, my father ventured on a small farm [Mount Oliphant] on his estate. At those years I was by no means a favourite with any body. I was a good deal noted for a retentive memory, a stubborn sturdy something in my disposition, and an enthusiastic idiot piety. I say *idiot* piety, because I was then but a child. Though it cost the schoolmaster some thrashings, I made an excellent English scholar; and by the time I was ten or eleven years of age, I was a critic of substantives, verbs, and particles. In my infant and boyish days, too, I owed much to an old woman who resided in the family, remarkable for her ignorance, credulity and superstition. She had, I suppose, the largest collection in the country of tales and songs concerning devils, ghosts, fairies, brownies, witches, warlocks, spunkies, kelpies, elf-candles, dead-lights, wraiths, apparitions, cantraips, giants, enchanted towers, dragons, and other trumpery. This cultivated the latent seeds of poetry; but had so strong an effect on my imagination, that to this hour, in my nocturnal rambles, I sometimes keep a sharp lookout in suspicious places; and though nobody can be more sceptical than I am in such matters, yet it often takes an effort of philosophy to shake off these idle terrors. The earliest composition that I recollect taking pleasure in was *The Vision of Mirza*, and a hymn of Addison's beginning, *How are thy Servants blest, O Lord!* I particularly remember one half-stanza which was music to my boyish ear –

'*For though on dreadful whirls we hung*
High on the broken wave – '

I met with these pieces in Mason's English Collection, one of my school-books. The two first books I ever read in private, and which gave me more pleasure than any two books I have ever read since, were, *The Life of Hannibal*, and *The History of Sir William Wallace*. Hannibal gave my young ideas such a turn, that I used to strut in raptures up and down after the recruiting drum and bag-pipe, and wish myself tall enough to be a soldier; while the story of Wallace poured a Scottish prejudice into my veins, which will boil along there till the flood-gates of life shut in eternal rest.

Polemical divinity about this time was putting the country half-mad; and I, ambitious to be shining in conversation parties on Sundays, between sermons, at funerals, &c, used, a few years afterwards, to puzzle Calvinism with so much heat and indiscretion, that I raised a hue and cry of heresy against me, which has not ceased to this hour.

My vicinity to Ayr was of some advantage to me. My social disposition, when not checked by some modifications of spirited pride, was, like our catechism-definition of infinitude, *without bounds or limits.* I formed several connections with other younkers who possessed superior advantages, the *youngling* actors, who were busy in the rehearsal of parts in which they were shortly to appear on the stage of life, where, alas! I was destined to drudge behind the scenes. It is not commonly at this green age that our young gentry have a just sense of the immense distance between them and their ragged play-fellows. It takes a few dashes into the world, to give the young great man that proper, decent, unnoticing disregard for the poor insignificant, stupid devils, the mechanics and peasantry around him, who were perhaps born in the same village. My young superiors never insulted the *clouterly* appearance of my plough-boy carcase, the two extremes of which were often exposed to all the inclemencies of all the seasons. They would give me stray volumes of books: among them, even then, I could pick up some observations; and one, whose heart

Chapter II *In his own Rite*

I am sure not even the *Munny Begum* scenes have tainted, helped me to a little French. Parting with these my young friends and benefactors, as they occasionally went off for the East or West Indies, was often to me a sore affliction; but I was soon called to more serious evils. My father's generous master died; the farm proved a ruinous bargain; and, to clench the misfortune, we fell into the hands of a factor, who sat for the picture I have drawn of one in my *Tale of Twa Dogs*. My father was advanced in life when he married; I was the eldest of seven children; and he, worn out by early hardships, was unfit for labour. My father's spirit was soon irritated, but not easily broken. There was a freedom in his lease in two years more; and, to weather these two years, we retrenched our expenses. We lived very poorly: I was a dexterous ploughman, for my age: and the next eldest to me was a brother [Gilbert] who could drive a plough very well, and help me to thrash the corn. A novel writer might perhaps have viewed these scenes with some satisfaction; but so did not I; my indignation yet boils at the recollection of the scoundrel factor's insolent threatening letters, which used to set us all in tears.

This kind of life – the cheerless gloom of a hermit, with the unceasing moil of a galley-slave, brought me to my sixteenth year; a little before which period I first committed the sin of Rhyme. You know our country custom of coupling a man and woman together as partners in the labours of the harvest. In my fifteenth autumn [1773] my partner was a bewitching creature, a year younger than myself. My scarcity of English denies me the power of doing her justice in that language; but you know the Scottish idiom – she was *a bonnie, sweet, sonsie lass*. In short, she altogether, unwittingly to herself, initiated me in that delicious passion, which, in spite of acid disappointment, gin-horse prudence, and book-worm philosophy, I hold to be the first of human joys, our dearest blessing here below!"

Here, Currie made what might seem a little change, but which made a big impact. He reduced the poet's phrase, "initiated me in a certain delicious passion". This distorted the meaning of love as Burns experienced it, by making it mundane.

"How she caught the contagion, I cannot tell: you medical people talk much of infection from breathing the same air, the touch, &c.; but I never expressly said I loved her. Indeed I did not know myself why I liked so much to loiter behind with her, when returning in the evening from our labours; why the tones of her voice made my heart-strings thrill like an Aeolian harp; and particularly why my pulse beat such a furious rattan when I looked and fingered over her little hand to pick out the cruel nettle stings and thistles. Among her other love-inspiring qualities, she sung sweetly; and it was her favourite reel, to which I attempted giving an embodied vehicle in rhyme. I was not so presumptuous as to imagine that I could make verses like printed ones, composed by men who had Greek and Latin; but my girl sung a song, which was said to be composed by a small country laird's son, on one of his father's maids, with whom he was in love! and I saw no reason why I might not rhyme as well as he; for, excepting that he could smear sheep, and cast peats, his father living in the moor-lands, he had no more scholar-craft than myself.

Thus with me began Love and Poesy; which at times have been my only, and till within the last twelve months, have been my highest enjoyment. My father struggled on till he reached the freedom in his lease, when he entered on a larger farm [Lochlie], about ten miles farther in the country. The nature of the bargain he made was such as to throw a little ready money into his hands at the commencement of his lease; otherwise the affair would have been impracticable. For four years we lived comfortably here; but a difference commencing between him and his landlord as to terms, after three years tossing and whirling in the vortex of litigation, my father was just saved from the horrors of a jail by a consumption, which, after two years' promises, kindly stepped in, and carried him away, *to where the wicked cease from troubling, and the weary are at rest*."

At this point, Currie played down the impact on Burns of a crucial period by another, apparently innocent change. Currie removed "this climacterick" as describing this time. How much this period was a turning point in this life was thus for long not understood.

"It is during the time that we lived on this farm that my little story is most eventful. I was, at the beginning of this period, perhaps the most ungainly, awkward boy in the parish – no solitaire was less acquainted with the ways of the world. What I knew of ancient story was gathered from Salmon's and Guthrie's geographical grammars; and the ideas I had formed of modern manners, of literature, and criticism, I got from the *Spectator*. These, with Pope's *Works*, some plays of Shakespeare, Tull and Dickson on *Agriculture*, *The Pantheon*, Locke's *Essay on the Human Understanding*, Stackhouse's *History of the Bible*, Justice's *British Gardener's Directory*, Bayle's *Lectures*, Allan Ramsay's *Works*, Taylor's *Scripture Doctrine of Original Sin*, *A Select Collection of English Songs*, and Hervey's *Meditations*, had formed the whole of my reading. The collection of songs was my *vade mecum*. I pored over them driving my cart, or walking to labour, song by song, verse by verse, carefully noting the true tender, or sublime, from affectation and fustian. I am convinced I owe to this practice much of my critic craft, such as it is."

I will at this point be accused no doubt of even more of that academic nit-picking that I believe can so often undermine the value of academic process. But I noted that in Currie's publication of this list of reading there is a typographical error of considerable significance. By this accidental error Currie changed the general perception of Robert Burns much more severely than by his deliberate suppression of political views, or misrepresentation of general conduct. For the error made out that Robert Burns was an atheist.

There is only one vowel wrong – a instead of o. This was not corrected until De Lancey Ferguson read the actual letter received by Moore. This error has not since been taken up as a major issue by biographers. I need to take it up. Currie stated that Burns studied Bayle's Lectures. Burns wrote that he studied Boyle's Lectures. Had Burns studied Bayle instead of Boyle he would have read something quite different. Bayle's 'Dictionarie historique et critique' was written with significant spin with the aim of discrediting revealed religion. It was the foundation of that scepticism that took hold during the 18th century. By the end of the 19th century scepticism had virtually riven asunder any belief in the ancient understanding that study of Nature and her ways gives greater understanding of the Almighty forces of Creation.

Bayle's 'Dictionarie historique et critique' was well known to those who read this letter for the first time in Currie's biography. The frontispiece to the extensive 'Biographia Britannica', first published in 1747, advertised that this compilation had been 'digested in the manner of Mr Bayle's Historical and Critical Dictionary'. They would therefore automatically interpret this list as telling them that Burns studied Bayle.

What Burns actually studied as a young man was perhaps chemistry in its proto-modern form. In the late 17th century Robert Boyle was blessed with considerable advances in the accuracy of measuring equipment. He built on the work of the 16th century student of alchemist Trimethius, Abbot of Sponheim, Paracelsus, who practiced under the protection of the Archbishop of Salzburg. Predictions of Nostradamus were based on astrological data from Trimethius. Boyle linked the modern laboratory directly to the experimentation of the hermetic philosophers of alchemy. He thus became the founder of modern chemistry. On the other hand it is more likely that what Burns studied were transcripts of the annual set of sermons in defence of the Christian religion which Boyle endowed. These were directly opposed to Bayle's position. Whatever he read of these Boyle-related books, it means Burns studied scientific material. He later proved he was competent assessing geology and in writing of chemical matters. On 28th May 1789 he wrote to Willie Nicol reporting for him on the farm of Lagganpark in Glencairn parish that he later bought. Nicol wanted to buy a farm to provide retirement income. Burns gave a geologically technical report, noting rich limestone deposits. He suggested that Nicol was offered an excellent price.

Returning to continue reading the letter by Burns, we learn that,

"In my seventeenth year, to give my manners a brush, I went to a country dancing-school. My father had an unaccountable antipathy against these meetings; and my going was, what to this moment I repent, in opposition to his wishes. My father, as I said before, was subject to strong passions; from that instance of disobedience in me he took a sort of dislike to me, which I believe was one cause of the dissipation which marked my succeeding years. I say dissipation, comparatively with the strictness, and sobriety, and regularity of Presbyterian life; for though the Will-o'-Wisp meteors of thoughtless whim were almost the sole lights of my path, yet early ingrained piety and virtue kept me for several years afterwards within the line of innocence. The great misfortune of my life was to want an aim. I had felt early some stirrings of ambition, but they were the blind gropings of Homer's Cyclops around the walls of his cave. I saw my father's situation entailed on me perpetual labour. The only two openings by which I could enter the temple of Fortune, was the gate of niggardly economy, or the path of little chicaning bargain-making. The first is so contracted an aperture, I never could squeeze myself into it; the last I always hated – there was contamination in the very entrance! Thus [I was] abandoned of aim or view in life, with a strong appetite for sociability, as well from native hilarity, as from a pride of observation and remark; a constitutional melancholy or hypochondriasm that made me fly solitude."

Currie replaced the phrase "hypochondriac trait" with "melancholy or hypochondriasm". This fuelled an unfounded myth that fitted the emerging opiate-dazed Romantic period: Burns seemed a self-pitying youth. This contradicts his statement that he hated to be left alone. Some kind of 'hypochondriasm' does feature in a number of the poet's letters. The word has been pounced on increasingly in modern times as indicative of indulgence in self-pity. In his day, this word had a meaning very different from our modern implication of imaginary illness. It meant invisible illness, situated in the chest and organs, causing significant pain with no cause discernable to the limited medical science of those times. He hated to be left alone in case there was no-one near when he needed help.

During the 19th century the advance of Reason – by then limited to being defined as insistence that Effect must have Cause that can rationally be explained – increasingly claimed that unless Cause was visible, Effect was non-existent. In the absence of appropriate advances in medical technology, this word 'hypochondria' gained its modern connotations of illness necessarily purely imaginary. Even in our day, invisible and unnamed illness is commonly treated as imaginary and non-illness. The sophisticated technology of modern hospitals enables doctors to use microscopic cameras to travel inside the human passages and even more wonderfully to view images on screen of the living internal organs. Had such technology been available at the time of Burns the invisible illnesses and disabilities he suffered would have become visible. He might thus have met a more sympathetic audience than his Victorian detractors. The boy rose above his disability:

> "Add to these incentives to social life, my reputation for bookish knowledge, a certain wild logical talent, and a strength of thought, something like the rudiments of good sense; and it will not seem surprising that I was generally a welcome guest wherever I visited, or any great wonder that, always where two or three met together, there was I amongst them. But far beyond all other impulses of my heart, was *un penchant a l'adorable moitié du genre humain*. My heart was completely tinder, and was eternally lighted up by some goddess or other; and as in every other warfare in this world my fortune was various, sometimes I was received with favour, and sometimes I was mortified with a repulse. At the plough, scythe, or reap-hook, I feared no competitor; and as I never cared farther for my labours than while I was in actual exercise, I spent the evenings in this way after my own heart. A country lad seldom carries on a love-adventure without an assisting confidant."

This disclosure surely challenges the presumption that Burns always needed an object of personal desire before he could write of love. He could imagine himself in the mind of someone else enraptured by the goddess of his dreams.

> "I possessed a curiosity, zeal, and intrepid dexterity, that recommended me as a proper second on these occasions; and I dare say, I felt as much pleasure in being in the secret of half the loves of the parish of Tarbolton, as ever did statesman in knowing the intrigues of half the courts of Europe.
>
> The very goose-feather in my hand seems to know instinctively the well-worn path of my imagination, the favourite theme of my song; and is with difficulty restrained from giving you a couple of paragraphs on the love-adventure of my compeers, the humble inmates of the farm-house and cottage; but the grave sons of science, ambition, or avarice, baptize these things by the name of Follies. To the sons and daughters of labour and poverty, they are matters of the most serious nature; to them, the ardent hope, the stolen interview, the tender farewell, are the greatest and most delicious parts of their enjoyments.
>
> Another circumstance in my life which made some alteration in my mind and manners was, that I spent my nineteenth summer [1777] on a smuggling coast, a good distance from home, at a noted school, to learn mensuration, surveying, dialling, &c., in which I made

a pretty good progress. But I made a greater progress in the knowledge of mankind. The contraband trade was at that time very successful, and it sometimes happened to me to fall in with those who carried it on. Scenes of swaggering riot and roaring dissipation were till this time new to me; but I was no enemy to social life. Here, though I learnt to fill my glass, and to mix without fear in a drunken squabble, yet I went on with a high hand with my geometry, till the sun entered Virgo, a month which is always a carnival in my bosom, when a charming *filette* who lived next door to the school, overset my trigonometry, and set me off at a tangent from the sphere of my studies. I, however, struggled on with my *sines* and *co-sines* for a few days more; but, stepping into the garden one charming noon to take the sun's altitude, there I met my angel,

'. . .Like *Proserpine, gathering flowers,*
Herself a fairer flower'.

It was in vain to think of doing any more good at school. The remaining week I staid, I did nothing but craze the faculties of my soul about her, or steal out to meet her; and the last two nights of my stay in the country, had sleep been a mortal sin, the image of this modest and innocent girl had kept me guiltless."

Currie let his imagination roam at this stage. Burns never wrote anything about images of modest and innocent girls. He wrote that had sleep been sin, he was innocent.

As I will review later, Virgo, relative to the spirit of Robert Burns, reflects what Robert Burns stood for. Not a few biographers, reading this reference to Virgo, have focused on its connection with virginity. The modern mind often relates Virgo directly with rampant male desire for virgins. So they have concluded that his mind became full of female sexuality at this time of year. Astrologically Virgo does indeed relate to virginity, but only in the moral sense of undefiled, intense personal integrity and being respected by others. Contemporaries of Burns knew that the astrological significance of Virgo is very different indeed from typical modern casual presumption of its associations. Virgo is the sign of analysis, details, exactness and even nit-picking for perfection. It has nothing whatsoever to do with sex. Leave sex to the constellations associated with Venus and Mars. Those got no mention here.

Opinion now favours the view that he attended this school earlier than the move to Lochlie, and thus ahead of his attendance at Tarbolton dancing classes. This suggestion may not be correct. It is difficult to imagine how William Burness could have afforded the cost of this education in the final days at Mount Oliphant. When they moved into Lochlie, for the first year or two things were financially easier. But this too was a farm in need of improvement. The lease was taken on the basis it would be improved. This required money as much as labour. Investment in educating Robert might promise an early return through some paid clerkship or assistant gardener post. It could also bring more up to date knowledge on improvement techniques to the family at Lochlie.

Burns was at Kirkoswald probably from early July and stayed until harvest time when he was needed on the farm. The extent of the local smuggling trade meant that here he might observe luxury and refinery in homes of common people, not replicated in his normal surroundings. Through the Isle of Man came French lace and silks, tea, tobacco and brandy. It is said that when a brandy ship arrived an orgy of drinking lasted days – a 'Whisky Galore' experience on a regular basis. He was in the town ten years after the Revestment Act by which the Duke of Atholl yielded the Lordship of Man to the

Crown. What previously had been legitimate trade to Scotland had turned into a black market. Samuel Brown, uncle of Robert Burns, himself took part in the smuggling, even on Sundays. This resulted in at least one citation, in October 1764, to appear before the Kirk Session. Burns lodged at Ballochneil, where his uncle was a labourer and son-in law of smuggler-farmer Robert Niven.

The Sun entering Virgo, about 23rd August, heralds the arrival of the Scottish Indian summer – the beginning of harvest time. Burns might well have chosen to write 'harvest time'. Instead, he used an astrological description of this benevolent time of year. And he used a word that implies focus, not fertility. Focus with fun. He later explained that this was his most productive period when he could complete the best work from tough application on the creative ideas that had generated the seeds of his poetry.

This is the only time of the year in which, in the days of Burns, there might be plenty. People relaxed. They enjoyed. But though it was the anniversary of that first love with Nellie, there is more to this story than a mere hair-brained boy going demob-happy because Nature is entering her kindest month. There is, on page 202 of 'The Real Robert Burns' by J L Hughes published in 1922 by W & R Chambers, anecdotal evidence that Burns was expelled for insubordination. Hugh Rodger perhaps sent him down from his surveyor mathematics and surveying school in Kirkoswald. His leaving may not have been because he was no longer making progress.

At Kirkoswald Burns struck up a friendship with fellow schoolmate William Niven, of Maybole, a different branch of the Niven clan. In homework time, he and Niven honed their intellects by debating between themselves. Rodger found out about this and objected to energy being diverted, as he saw it, from mathematical exercises. Rodger accused Niven of wasting the boys' time debating, and demanded what was the subject of the next debate. In these early days of the American War of Independence, Niven answered that it was to be 'This house believes that a great general is of more use to the world than a good merchant'. Rodger retorted that such a debate was a waste of time, as it was a self-evident truth.

The precocious young Burns challenged Rodger to argue on the side of generals, and he would argue that the merchant was the more useful profession. Rodger accepted the challenge, but found himself confronted by a young mind well prepared to fight his corner. Soon the rest of the school was cheering Robert on, to the dismay of Rodger who saw his authority roughly undermined. He dismissed the school for the day. It is not improbable that he dismissed Robert outright. If indeed it was his desire to debate that precipitated dismissal from the opportunity to become fully qualified as a surveyor, with all that this might have opened up for him, his father must have been greatly angered at any thought of Robert continuing such wasteful activity.

Certainly a course in surveying, levelling and dialling was no mean challenge. Threlfall's 1946 'Text-book on Surveying and Levelling' runs to nearly 700 technical pages, with seven folding plates and 287 diagrams within the text. A totally separate textbook by R W Chapman was available also in 1946 on 'The Elements of Astronomy for Surveyors' running to 255 pages with 56 diagrams, covering everything from spherical geometry and astronomical co-ordinates to the determination of latitude and longitude and how to use these to calibrate timepieces. Armed with such core education in the 17th century (but without reliable way to determine longitude except by land distance measurement) Scottish gardener John Reid had risen to be one of the most wealthy and influential men in New Jersey.

Chapter II *In his own Rite*

The earliest lessons included overcoming local magnetic interference in the reading of a compass needle. The magnetic compass had been invented by Halley. It goes on to how properly to read measurements from telescope bearings. Dominie Rodger would have discussed differences between geographical and geocentric latitude, caused by the fact that the Earth is flattened at the poles. His students would have learned the names of the main stars that were circumpolar from his Scottish viewpoint. Rodger would have referred to transits of the meridian. He would have required his students to understand upper and lower culminations of a star, or when it has its greatest and its least altitude – measurements essential for determining latitude. Longitude was confirmed by the star's so-called elongation. Solstices and equinoxes would have been familiar terms from Robert's childhood study of Derham, but he would now have had it emphasised that each day differed slightly in true length. He would find out that spring equinoxes were not always exactly on 21st March. Thus he would have learned to know the First Point of Aries, the point in the heavens where the Sun is at the vernal equinox. Nor is the appearance of the Sun's 'movement' as even as clockwork. To confound all that, there are then the matters of parallax and refraction. Then he had to turn this to practical use. To apply all that merely to make a sundial the craftsman must learn various types of projection, the simplest being the orthographic. That was necessary in constructing that very fashionable cuboid sort.

Had the lad qualified in this course, even if only to become a gardener, it might have lifted the family from the poverty that reappeared not long after they moved to Lochlie in 1777. Thus Robert's creation in 1780 of his Bachelors' Club to enable debating amongst the local Tarbolton young men must indeed have riled his father, pouring salt into a wound that had never healed.

Hughes's book was, by the way, an example of the kind of hagiography written by the religious lobby who wished to bring Robert Burns 'inside the tent' by denying a lot of the more socially unacceptable stories put about particularly during the quarter century following his death. Hughes stated in his introduction that the purpose of any biography is to find moral example in the life studied. This had been the intention of the 19th century biographers, but their moral was that Burns was born flawed. Hughes took the view that he was not. Thus he set out to demonstrate that Burns was a very religious man, a democrat in the one-man-one-vote sense, a promoter of the brotherhood of man in the Christian sense, a champion of True Love in the purest sense, and a philosopher. Of those attributes, when Hughes wrote, the most contentious were the first and fourth; yet the second would probably have surprised Burns. The identification of his political position with Christianity might have worried him. The intellectual implications of the fifth would have pleased him greatly. Like many another commentator with an agenda in writing about the poet, Hughes carefully chose his quotations as evidence in support of his chosen position. But like every other commentator, much of his evidence could equally be interpreted in totally different ways.

A contemporary book on Burns had been full square in paralleling the poet's work with passages in Old and New Testaments. 'Burns and the Bible' by W D Fisher of Kilmacolm was published in 1926 for his fellow members of the Scottish Burns Club. He aimed to show how the Bible inspired Burns and how Biblical is the positive spirit in his poems. Fisher began with the 'Priest-like Father' of 'The Cottar's Saturday Night', reading aloud:

> . . how the royal Bard did groaning lie
> Beneath the stroke of Heaven's avenging ire.

Were these words written with a memory of his last few nights in Kirkoswald? Those were possibly spent wondering how he would explain to his irate domestically-almighty father that the hard-saved cost of the surveying course had not really been money ill-spent. I can hear him thinking of the consequences of his flight of rhetorical fancy. The BBC in 2007 broadcast its documentary 'MacMusical' in which modern Scottish poet-musician John Kielty graphically described the denouement of his intended plot of 'The Sundowe'.

He simply said: "You are going on as if everything is fine. Then suddenly it hits you like oh! God!"

This has added to the English language the powerful expression 'oh! God! moment'. I hear Burns muttering to himself this desperate prayer in like manner. Young Peggy Thomson probably had taken his fancy. But far from gazing at stars in contemplation of this lovely girl next door perhaps he found himself at midnight on 30th July 1776 gazing out at the deep red blood of the Moon in full eclipse, and wondered at the meaning to his own future life of this awesome message from the heavens.

Certainly, Burns's letter describing the incident to a complete stranger is more likely to make a light story of so abrupt an ending of what might have been the beginning of a promising gardening career. At that time gardeners were becoming massive landscapers with commensurate fees. Despite the glitch, as his autobiographical letter continued,

"I returned home very considerably improved. My reading was enlarged with the very important addition of Thomson's and Shenstone's Works; I had seen human nature in a new phasis; and I engaged several of my school-fellows to keep up a literary correspondence with me. This improved me in composition. I had met with a collection of letters by the wits of Queen Anne's reign, and I pored over them most devoutly; I kept copies of any of my own letters that pleased me; and a comparison between them and the composition of most of my correspondents flattered my vanity. I carried this whim so far, that though I had not three farthings' worth of business in the world, yet almost every post brought me as many letters as if I had been a broad plodding son of day-book and ledger.

My life flowed on much the same course till my twenty-third year. [1781] *Vive l'amour, et vive la bagatelle*, were my sole principles of action. The addition of two more authors to my library gave me great pleasure; Sterne and Mackenzie – *Tristram Shandy* and *The Man of Feeling* – were my bosom favourites. Poesy was still a darling walk for my mind; but it was only indulged in according to the humour of the hour. I had usually half a dozen or more pieces on hand; I took up one or other, as it suited the momentary tone of the mind, and dismissed the work as it bordered on fatigue."

In this last passing sentence – that gets little attention – he succinctly detailed the enormous intellectual exhausting effort involved in the process of creating good verse. He would repeat this in many a letter.

"My passions, when once lighted up, raged like so many devils, till they got vent in rhyme; and then the conning over my verses, like a spell, soothed all into quiet! None of the rhymes of those days are in print, except *Winter, a Dirge*, the eldest of my printed pieces; the *Death of Poor Maillie, John Barleycorn*, and songs, first, second and third. Song second was the ebullition of that passion which ended the forementioned school-business.

Chapter II   *In his own Rite*

My twenty-third year was to me an important era. Partly through whim, and partly that I wished to set about doing something in life, I joined a flax-dresser in a neighbouring town [Irvine] to learn his trade. This was an unlucky affair, and to finish the whole, as we were giving a welcome carousal to the new year, the shop took fire, and burnt to ashes; and I was left, like a true poet, not worth a sixpence.

I was obliged to give up this scheme: the clouds of misfortune were gathering thick round my father's head, and what was worst of all, he was visibly far gone in a consumption; and, to crown my distresses, a *belle fille* whom I adored, and who had pledged her soul to meet me in the field of matrimony, jilted me, with peculiar circumstances of mortification. The finishing evil that brought up the rear of this infernal file was my constitutional melancholy being increased to such a degree that for three months I was in a state of mind scarcely to be envied by the hopeless wretches who have got their mittimus – *Depart from me ye accursed!"*

Burns wrote nothing about "constitutional melancholy". He wrote that his "hypochondriac complaint" became "irritated to such a degree" that for three months he was "in a diseased state of body and mind". In recent years was found the notebook of the doctor who tended him. This proves he was extremely ill in this period. Perhaps he was jilted because he was unlikely to prove a viable husband, so poor was his physique.

The 'belle fille' was identified to subsequent biographers as being called Ellison Begbie, daughter of a small farmer in Galston parish. When Burns fell in love with her she is reputed to have been a servant in a house about two miles from Galston's Loudon Castle.

In my young years I spent a number of holidays in a two-roomed ground floor flat in a red sandstone tenement block of eight homes in Gas Lane abutting the river at Galston. There was only one other occupant of the tenement at the time – Old Aggie. She lived in what was then called a single-end that Estate Agents would now hype up as a studio apartment. The entire tenement shared one outside toilet in a hut outside our back window. Naturally, such an unsanitary tenement was condemned once Old Aggie passed away. My mother's flat was compulsorily purchased.

On the hill across the river was the alluring pile of ruined Loudon Castle, burned down in 1941. Despite prominent 'Danger Keep Out' signs, this was too great a temptation for me and my young daredevil brother to ignore. On not a few occasions we scrambled through rubble into the vaulted corridors of its basement. We climbed into the great halls of the ground floor and gazed in awe at the empty spaces of the high windows. Here, Covenanters met. The estate was one haunt of William Wallace, who might well have known the yew tree that still flourishes in the grounds. Today it is the haunt of tourists. There they can enjoy scary rides and family fun. Burns knew it first as a place of tragedy and then as the home of the daughter and son-in-law of his self-appointed 'mother confessor', Mrs Dunlop.

From Lochlie in 1781 Burns wrote to this girl asking her to marry him. He based his letters on the models in his book of sample letters suitable for exchange in polite society in Queen Anne's day. In retrospect he must have realised that they must have appeared to this very natural Scots girl the most cringingly constructed epistles. She refused him. He had genuinely believed he was doing the proper thing putting in such terms his wish that she become his wife. She must have reacted in a manner very similar to Mistress Jean on the sudden intrusion of the Laird of Cockpen. He disturbed her from making the elderflower wine. She told the unfeeling man very bluntly to get lost. Burns had not been unfeeling. He was deeply upset.

This experience confirmed in him that when you truly feel love for another person, the contrived written word is not the vehicle to express it. He would realise this even applied to poetry and song. Those are for entertainment. They are never true communication between two lovers. The language of lovers is heart rent tears, sighs and groans; no more. To paraphrase the Chinese 'Way', the love that can be written is not the true love.

Thus, when Edinburgh flirt Agnes McLehose insisted, six years later, that they begin an affair purely of intimate correspondence, the poet must have known immediately that this 'love' Agnes McLehose bore was not the true love. Her love could have no real depth if she believed it was a love that could be expressed in written words. This was safe ground for a young countryman in the big bad world of the city. Or so he perhaps innocently thought.

For their ensuing exchange of letters he had the models ready to hand. He eagerly embraced the opportunity to practice such writing. Here was a mature woman with whom there could never be any serious prospect of marital attachment or even real love. She insisted she would be more than delighted to receive such unnatural contrived love letters and respond to them in kind. Where better, in such a harmless environment, to practice that style of writing suited to the comic opera? Their exchanges could enable him to become proficient with the artificial dialogue necessary to become author of those elegant amorous comedies that filled the new late Georgian theatres with audiences eager for the latest parody of polite society. But he still had a lot to learn about human nature.

Writing to Dr Moore he stated he had learned from his unhappy youthful period, particularly the failure of the business venture in Irvine:

> "From this adventure I learned something of town life; but the principal thing which gave my mind a turn, was a friendship I formed with a young fellow, a very noble character, but a hapless son of misfortune. He was the son of a simple mechanic; but a great man in the neighbourhood taking him under his patronage, gave him a genteel education, with a view of bettering his situation in life. The patron dying just as he was ready to launch out into the world, the poor fellow in despair went to sea; where, after a variety of good and ill fortune, a little before I was acquainted with him, he had been set on shore by an American privateer, on the wild coast of Connaught, stripped of everything. I cannot quit this poor fellow's story without adding, that he is at this time master of a large West-Indiaman belonging to the Thames.
>
> His mind was fraught with independence, magnanimity, and every manly virtue. I loved and admired him to a degree of enthusiasm, and of course strove to imitate him. In some measure I succeeded; I had pride before, but he taught it to flow in proper channels. His knowledge of the world was vastly superior to mine, and I was all attention to learn. He was the only man I ever saw who was a greater fool than myself, where woman was the presiding star; but he spoke of illicit love with the levity of a sailor, which hitherto I had regarded with horror. Here his friendship did me a mischief; and the consequence was, that soon after I resumed the plough, I wrote the *Poet's Welcome*."

Chapter II *In his own Rite*

Richard Brown is the sea captain blamed for this bad influence. Here Currie did Burns a mischief. Burns did not write "illicit love". He wrote "a certain fashionable failing". This has opened up room for much dispute on interpretation.

But Burns was unfair to himself too. His baby was born to a girl whom he had hoped to marry. In Scotland trial marriage called handfasting had been commonplace. It had only recently ceased to be the norm. It was permitted by the law of the land, though condemned by the Scottish Kirk. Handfasting allowed a couple intending marriage to live together and make up their minds later. At Langholm in 1772 there was still an annual fair in which young men and women were paired off. They co-habited for a year. At the end of the year each had a once-only chance to end the marriage. Any child that came of the year's union became the responsibility of the party who insisted on separation.

Before their child was born both families prevented marriage being solemnised between Robert Burns and Lizzie Paton. Instead, it was agreed by the Kirk Session that there had not been even a Common Law marriage; Robert must only declare his sin and accept censure, pay the regulation nurse's fee, and take responsibility for the upbringing of the child when weaned. I have seen no-one remark that this occurred when Robert was technically head of the family as his father was recently dead. What would make an 18th century head of family defer to family opinion on so fundamental a question as choosing his bride? Could this 25 year old not stand up for himself? Did he regret not doing so? Was it this, and not the influence of his sailor friend that subsequently made him defiant in matters of the heart? I know no answer. Perhaps if the families had not both been so adamant, toasts at Burns Suppers might now be made not to Bonnie Jean but to Bonnie Lizzie and we would have no stories of a Highland Mary. Perhaps we would have no toasts because with Lizzie as wife he had no need to write poetry.

> "My reading was only increased, while in this town, by two stray volumes of *Pamela*, and one of *Ferdinand Count Fathom*, which gave me some idea of novels. Rhyme, except some religious pieces that are in print, I had given up; but meeting with *Fergusson's Scottish Poems*, I strung anew my wildly-sounding lyre with emulating vigour. When my father died, his all went among the hell-hounds that prowl in the kennels of justice;"

Currie toned down the poet's criticism of the legal profession. The hell hounds were rapacious.

> "but we made shift to scrape a little money in the family amongst us, with which, to keep us together, my brother and I took a neighbouring farm. My brother wanted my hair-brained imagination, as well as my social and amorous madness: but, in good sense, and every sober qualification, he was far my superior.
>
> I entered on this farm with a full resolution, *Come, go to, I will be wise!* I read farming books; I calculated crops; I attended markets; and, in short, in spite of *the devil, and the world, and the flesh*, I believe I should have been a wise man; but the first year, from unfortunately buying bad seed, the second, from a late harvest, we lost half our crops. This overset all my wisdom, and I returned, *like the dog to his vomit, and the sow that was washed, to her wallowing in the mire*."

We will see later how unfair Burns was to himself in his account of this outcome. Nature was against them in this farming venture.

"I now began to be known in the neighbourhood as a maker of rhymes. The first of my poetic offspring that saw the light, was a burlesque lamentation on a quarrel between two reverend Calvinists, both of them *dramatis personae* in my *Holy Fair*. I had a notion of myself, that the piece had some merit; but to prevent the worst, I gave a copy of it to a friend who was very fond of such things, and told him that I could not guess who was the author of it, but that I thought it pretty clever. With a certain description of the clergy, as well as laity, it met with a roar of applause. *Holy Willie's Prayer* next made its appearance, and alarmed the kirk-session so much, that they held several meetings to look over their spiritual artillery, if haply any of it might be pointed against profane rhymers. Unluckily for me, my wanderings led me on another side, within point-blank shot of their heaviest metal. This is the unfortunate story that gave rise to my printed poem, *The Lament*. This was a most melancholy affair,"

So printed Currie. Actually Burns described the affair as "shocking".

"which I cannot yet bear to reflect on, and had very nearly given me one or two of the principal qualifications for a place amongst those who have lost the chart, and mistaken the reckoning of Rationality. I gave up my part of the farm to my brother; in truth it was only nominally mine; and made what little preparation was in my power for Jamaica. But before leaving my native country for ever, I resolved to publish my poems. I weighted my productions as impartially as was in my power; I thought they had merit; and it was a delicious idea that I should be called a clever fellow even though it should never reach my own ears – a poor negro-driver – or perhaps a victim to that inhospitable clime, and gone to the world of the spirits! I can truly say, that *pauvre inconnu* as I then was, I had pretty nearly as high an idea of myself and of my works as I have at this moment, when the public has decided in their favour. It ever was my opinion, that the mistakes and blunders, both in the rational and religious point of view, of which we see thousands daily guilty, are owing to their ignorance of themselves. To know myself, had been all along my constant study. I weighed myself alone; I balanced myself with others; I watched every means of information, to see how much ground I occupied as a man and as a poet: I studied assiduously Nature's design in my formation – where the lights and shades in my character were intended."

Astrological adepts could interpret this last sentence as inferring that Burns was familiar with his horoscope, particularly as he used the word "intended". The Sun and Moon are in astrology known as "the lights" and astrology also speaks about the "shadow" side.

"I was pretty confident my poems would meet with some applause: but at the worst, the roar of the Atlantic would deafen the voice of censure, and the novelty of West-Indian scenes make me forget neglect. I threw off six hundred copies, of which I had got subscriptions for about three hundred and fifty. My vanity was highly gratified by the reception I met with from the public; and beside I pocketed, all expenses deducted, nearly twenty pounds. This sum came very seasonally, as I was thinking of indenting myself, for want of money to procure my passage. As soon as I was master of nine guineas, the price of wafting me to the torrid zone, I took a steerage-passage in the first ship that was to sail from the Clyde; for

'*Hungry ruin had me in the wind.*'

I had been for some days skulking from covert to covert, under all the terrors of a jail; as some ill-advised people had uncoupled the merciless pack of the law at my heels. I had taken the last farewell of my few friends; my chest was on the road to Greenock; I had composed the last song I should ever measure in Caledonia, *The gloomy night is gathering fast*, when a letter from Dr Blacklock, to a friend of mine, overthrew all my schemes, by opening new prospects to my poetic ambition. The doctor belonged to a set of critics, for whose applause I had not dared to hope. His opinion that I would meet with encouragement in Edinburgh for a second edition, fired me so much, that away I posted for that city, without a single acquaintance, or a single letter of introduction. The baneful star that had so long shed its blasting influence in my zenith for once made a revolution to the nadir."

No-one can tell whether Robert Burns was aware of his horoscope or was merely using astrological allegory in this climax of his autobiographical letter. He went on to praise the "providential care of a good God" for placing him under the patronage of the Earl of Glencairn – a political reference that Currie felt it advisable to leave out. Burns concluded his letter by asserting that the chief elements of his character were integrity and honour come what may, while fancy, whim, sensibility and passion determined his zig-zag life path. He then repeated his concern that his baneful star should again

"blaze in his meridian with tenfold more baneful influence."

Astrological reference recurred. In a letter written in 1786 to the otherwise virtually unknown John Arnot of Dalquhatswood, Loudon Parish, he alluded to his ill luck, this time as "baleful". Prefacing his misfortune in the process of trying to wed Jean Armour, he wrote:

"A damned Star has always kept my zenith, and shed its baleful influence, in that emphatic curse of the prophet – 'And behold, whatsoever he doeth, it shall not prosper!' I rarely hit where I aim; and if I want anything, I am almost sure never to find it where I seek it."

This same theme was repeated several more times in letters that are extant.

To Arnot he had gone on, then, in more jocular vein, indicating that he kept what I would describe as 'putting things in safe places'. The places were so safe that the thing was invariably and disturbingly lost just when most needed. But he clearly did feel some "baneful star" tossed him from heights of creativity into depths of depression. Fate seemed to promise him hope yet restrain and frustrate all his endeavours. Perhaps in his early Masonic years he had had explained to him his horoscope – its interpretation possible for some adept amongst the Brothers. The actual horoscope was not difficult to tabulate. He could have done it as homework in Hugh Rodger's classes. There he was taught to use a sextant, one of the new pieces of equipment available to the professional surveyor, invented as recently as 1757 by Captain John Campbell. He could have produced it later from interpolation of data from the nautical almanac of January 1759.

Certainly, in his lessons on dialling he was taught astronomy. There is quite a skill in designing a sundial. True sundials that reliably give the time whatever the season are rather more complicated than those brass castings on reconstituted stone plinths that are so readily bought in garden centres. The true sundial is marked for the latitude and angle of the Sun's mid-day incidence at its intended installation location. This means taking a survey of the location and then carrying out appropriate mathematical calculations.

Burns no doubt held a fine brass telescope to his eye when with sailor friend Richard Brown, if he had not done so before. He would have looked with wonder at those details of the face of the Moon that he had seen on that engraving in Derham's 'Astro-Theology'. Probably he had heard tell of the supposed dire influence of Saturn. The planet has bequeathed to the language the very word, saturnine, to describe that darkness of the soul through which Burns found himself so often travelling.

For this book I have sought advice on astrological matters. The term 'baneful star' normally epitomises Saturn. It might relate to the comet under which he was born, but the Saturn impact is worth examining. Astrology adepts regard as important what they call the secondary progression of the Sun in a person's birth chart. In this, one day represents a year of future life. A very important point for a person is when the progressed Sun conjoins, or in other words reaches the same position as, the natal Saturn. This correspondence is by astrologers considered to predict the time when the individual's sense of self should reach confidence in achievement and crystallise as something concrete in the world. For Burns the progressed Sun conjoined his natal Saturn on July 7th 1786. It was at this propitious astrological season that he had his poems printed. His fortune abruptly changed in the summer of 1786. This is a coincidence between astrological predictions and reality. In the 18th century there were many who would regard that coincidence as very significant.

Burns's fortune, though, never came in the form of wealth as the world knows it. When I was a Glasgow school child, I was fortunate to achieve a small award in the Hutcheson Bursary competition. On each of my fourth and fifth years at school, just before going to University, I queued with other young people at Hutcheson's Hall near Glasgow City Chambers to collect my money. My parents allowed me to spend this modest sum as I chose. One year I spent £3. 10/- buying the four volumes, bound as two, of the seventh edition of 'The Works of Robert Burns' edited by Currie. A previous owner annotated on 21st July 1930 (the 134th anniversary of the day of Burns's death) that he or she had read the volumes for the third time. The then owner appended a verse:

> Coila's Bard were surely mad
> Or least wise twa parts crazy
> Tae waste his time on chance's jad,
> On a moose or a mountain daisy
> When weel spun words tae kings and lords
> Wad brocht him wealth in plenty.

The verse suggests that if Burns had been less of a stickler for doing the right thing he could have made a great deal more money. Burns could never have been such a sycophant in his writing. It was as much anathema to him as that tainted fast route to wealth beckoning men of his intellect – walking over the backs of others. He had dismissed that in youth. The cost of integrity is high. But apart from not appreciating the high ethical standard that Burns set himself, the writer of this little verse in my view seriously misjudged – as many an academic does, I fear – the poet's addresses to the mouse and to the mountain daisy. I will begin to explain what I mean.

Burns wrote to Dr Moore from Ellisland on 23rd March 1789. His friend Mr Neilson carried the letter. He was

> "on his way to France to wait upon his Grace of Queensberry, on some little business of a good deal of importance to him".

The purpose of the letter was to ask Dr Moore to give travel advice to Neilson. Burns observed that it seemed there was nothing more valuable to a Scotsman in London than a letter of introduction to Dr Moore. In thanks he enclosed an "Ode to a deceased lady". The ode was "a compliment to the memory" of Mrs Oswald of Auchencruive whom Dr Moore,

> "probably knew personally, an honour of which I cannot boast; but I spent my early years in her neighbourhood, and among her servants and tenants, I know that she was detested with the most heartfelt cordiality. However, in the particular part of her conduct which roused my poetic wrath, she was much less blamable."

Almost certainly Moore knew of Mrs Oswald, if not having actually met the lady socially. Her husband Richard Oswald was the London merchant who was leader of those who represented Britain in the Paris meeting that agreed the terms of the ending of the American War of Independence. He had died in 1784 but his widow had continued to reside at Auchencruive, although it was in London that she died in December 1788.

> "In January last, on my road to Ayrshire, I had put up at Bailie Whigham's in Sanquhar, the only tolerable inn in the place. The frost was keen, and the grim evening and howling wind were ushering in a night of snow and drift. My horse and I were both much fatigued with the labours of the day; and just as my friend the Bailie and I were bidding defiance to the storm, over a smoking bowl, in wheels the funeral pageantry of the late great Mrs Oswald, and poor I am forced to brave all the horrors of the tempestuous night, and jade my horse, my young favourite horse, whom I had just christened Pegasus, twelve miles farther on, through the wildest moors and hills of Ayrshire, to New Cumnock, the next inn. The powers of poesy and prose sink under me, when I would describe what I felt. Suffice it to say, that when a good fire, at New Cumnock, had so far recovered my frozen sinews, I sat down and wrote the ode."

There are not a few who have experienced the gall of being bounced by a superior, as it is a not uncommon abuse of privilege in modern business. Usually it is not life-threatening, but merely insulting. For Robert Burns, being bounced that night caused him to have to pull on damp boots already cold, wrap round himself his woollen shawl limp with its previous soaking, and mount a horse weary of battling a wild storm that still raged. On the horse and rider forced themselves against the howling gale. At last they rounded the shoulder of the hill where at the foot of the brae he glimpsed with relief the glimmer of a candle still glancing through a tiny square window. It was not too soon that he was hammering at the door, begging to be let inside.

What a relief it must have been at last for a hand he could not quite focus on to take his horse from him and round the back to shelter. He must have sighed with relief as he himself was helped in under the low lintel and space made for him to let himself drop beside the fire in its tiny grate in the south wall. How he must have shivered even as the frozen cloak was taken from his shoulders, and the soaking boots were eased off his legs. How he must have winced as he tried to taste the gruel they thinned with a drop of whisky to give him inside heat. He found his stomach churned with nausea. How his chest must have been screaming with the exertion. How he must have feared that inner knowledge that yet another nail had been hammered into his too early coffin.

I first became aware of Robert Burns in January 1955 when I was an infant not yet four years old. For the first paid job he got after his marriage, my father moved my mother and the four of us children to New Cumnock in Ayrshire. There at first we lived in a new but damp local authority house that my mother was convinced was already falling down. It alone amongst all the others in the estate was soon after demolished. After a very short time, her misgivings caused her to relocate us all – husband and four infants – into a roadside cottage. At the time it felt derelict, despite the owner's insistence that it had been upgraded with 'all mod cons', including cold running water, electricity and 'inside' toilet in a lean-to.

The hill above New Cumnock, source of the River Nith and its tributary the Afton, Burns called his Parnassus, sacred home of his poetic muse, Coila. This house, my mother told us all, was that very howff where Robert Burns came for refuge in that wild night. Here on another occasion he wrote 'Flow Gently Sweet Afton'. No authority has demonstrated a proven location for this inn. I have searched contemporary maps. The building did not exist in 1770. Scotland's roads were thoroughly surveyed for the creation of a road map published in Edinburgh in 1776. This was in the contemporary form of strips of accurately-drawn maps of the whole length of standard routes. Thus over several pages run the strips that give the main road from Dumfries to Ayr that passes through Sanquhar, New Cumnock and Cumnock.

On this 1776 map I found symbols of small buildings, indicated at the location corresponding to my mother's long-demolished but and ben on Afton Bridgend mystically numbered 33. These symbols are not connected with any farm. There are no other viable contenders for the inn where Burns thawed out after his encounter with the Auchencruive cortège and stayed on not a few other occasions. I suggest my mother was correct in her surmise. She was the kind who studied title deeds and would have known all she could find out about the building. She certainly believed her story, and was angered that the building was bulldozed.

My extremely down-to-earth and practical mother was ever a romantic, but she was also a graduate in English Literature and Mathematics despite being second daughter of a mere shipyard riveter who did his bit in the building of the great Queens of the North Atlantic. Against all the odds she borrowed to study at Glasgow University. She subsequently became a teacher in Clydebank. She had survived the hunger of the First World War years, and supported her parents and siblings through the Great Depression. She was promoted to the post of Principal English Mistress. She was thus a young woman in a responsible position in local society at the start of the Second World War. Then Hitler's intensive bombing on two nights of 1941 obliterated her home and burned her town to ashes in a great firestorm that lasted days. This left a populace so devastated that Prime Minister and War Leader, Winston Churchill, blanked the story from the media lest it destroy all morale in England and kill the will to fight. So there is no record of it in mainstream British history. Even now, with official documents disclosed, the story of that devastation is usually absent even from Scottish history. It is part of Britain's national amnesia. But, in those nights, my mother learned bitterness and the helplessness as of a mouse when cruelly and inhumanely the plough's 'cruel coulter passed right through [its] cell', making vain mockery of all her hopes and all her efforts to create a happy home for her dependants.

The earliest poem by Robert Burns of which I was truly aware was his 'To a Mouse On Turning Her Up in Her Nest with the Plough November 1785', published in the first collection of poems that was produced in Kilmarnock, Ayrshire in 1786. Burns had just invested in one of those state-of-the-art wheel-mounted ploughs that improved labour productivity. They also greatly reduced the ability of the ploughman to make fast slight adjustments when steering the ploughshare. He found he could not avoid cutting through ground nests of birds and rodents whose modest food intake at harvest time was compensated by their airing the ground during growth and discouraging more dangerous vermin.

Though this poem is written in a manner and with occasional vocabulary reflecting the language spoken around Burns in 18th century Ayrshire, its sentiments are readily understood. English speakers need no translation to take in its meaning, if they should only read the poem aloud:

> Wee, sleekit, cowrin, tim'rous *beastie*,
> O, what a panic's in thy breastie!
> Thou need na start awa sae hasty,
>> Wi' bickering brattle!
> I wad be laith to rin an' chase thee,
>> Wi' murdering pattle!
>
> I'm truly sorry Man's dominion
> Has broken Nature's social union,
> An' justifies that ill opinion
>> Which makes thee startle
> At me, thy poor, earth-born companion
>> An' *fellow mortal*!
>
> I doubt na, whyles, but thou may thieve;
> What then? poor beastie, thou maun live!
> A daimen icker in a thrave
>> 'S a sma' request;
> I'll get a blessin wi' the lave,
>> An' never miss't!
>
> Thy wee-bit housie, too, in ruin!
> Its silly wa's the win's are strewin!
> An' naething, now, to big a new ane,
>> O' foggage green!
> An' bleak *December*'s win's ensuing,
>> Baith snell an' keen!
>
> Thou saw the fields laid bare an' waste,
> An' weary *Winter* comin fast,
> An' cozie here, beneath the blast,
>> Thou thought to dwell,
> Till crash! The cruel *coulter* past
>> Out thro' thy cell.

That wee bit heap o' leaves an' stibble,
Has cost thee monie a weary nibble!
Now thou's turned out, for a' thy trouble,
  But house or hald,
To thole the Winter's *sleety dribble*,
  An' *cranreuch* cauld!

But Mousie, thou art no thy lane,
In proving foresight may be vain:
The best laid schemes o' *Mice* an' *Men*
  Gang aft agley,
An' lea'e us nought but grief an' pain,
  For promis'd joy!

Still thou art blest, compared wi' me!
The present only toucheth thee:
But Och! I backward cast my e'e,
  On prospects drear!
An' forward, th' I canna see,
  I *guess* and *fear*!

Critics have defined this poem as 'Horatian satire'. They link it with another Burns wrote in which he describes a louse climbing up the hat of a posh lady in church. But when my mother recited this poem to me it was never satire. She squirmed with pain as she reached the fourth stanza. I could feel her horror hearing the siren bomb fall and seeing space where her own home had stood only moments before, nought left but rubble, dust and fear.

Robert Burns and his whole family faced homelessness in February 1784. Then his father's death at Lochlie Farm was all that saved this not-too-old man from the indignity of roup to pay debts. These had been ameliorated by the Court of Session granting him victory – pyrrhic as so many such victories are – in ruling that his version of his contract with his landlord was correct. It was lawyers who got any financial benefit. The family carried his corpse on poles slung on the backs of two ponies to Alloway Kirk. There they buried him. They then gathered what little they could salvage from the roup to begin life all over again at Mossgeil Farm. The cruel coulter of legal process passed through their lives in the keen cold of the worst ever winter, just as that of blitzkrieg smashed the joys of my mother's youth.

I could feel with my mother the devastation of empty fields of shattered tenements and homes. Those had been such few years earlier before the War, places of life and joy and hope for the future for oh, so many. After all their years of labour she and all a large town were turned out without house or home. I could feel her pain as she reflected on the effort she had made through the unemployment years of the Great Depression. She had been forced to maintain her parents and all her many brothers and sisters on her teacher's salary. They had been denied any government aid because there was one modest earner in the family. I could see a drop of tear at the corner of her eye as she reflected on all the dreams of her youth, gone agley. I felt her fear for the future of her little children in an increasingly uncertain world.

Chapter II *In his own Rite*

In later years my young teachers in school botched and gangled the same verses as if they were a toy baby doll in a bouncy chair. Academic apologists refer to this as a great animal poem of the sentimental sort. Contrasting it with another described as to a hyperactive louse, one modern critic politically correctly interprets the poem as naturalist sympathy with a 'hypothermic mouse, houselessly unprotected'.

In my mother's voice it was a different language. It repeated words that she had found herself reciting to maintain her calm and soothe those around her in the darkness of the homeless nights. In makeshift shelters she told poems and led songs to entertain those around her in cold homeless fields after their stunned survival from the Blitz – people who did not even have advanced education to keep them warm. In her voice I heard no sentimental silly sympathy for the collateral casualties that were a daily fact of a typical field ploughing. I heard deep allegory. In her experience she saw within this poem an empathy in Burns with the hapless unknown individual human beings and helpless families displaced in the Seven Years War that raged at his birth. It speaks his empathy for the many made destitute in the devastating upheavals that followed. Their experiences were made more immediate by remembrance, oft repeated in his own home, of the fall of the house about his infant head. The empathy was amplified by his personal experience of fighting debt and an inhumane landlord to keep a roof over the head of his dying father.

Some comfortable academic critics most certainly feel a need to apologise for this poem. It demonstrates that they have never themselves experienced or been emotionally close to the real horror of sudden violent complete loss through wilful actions of Man, of all that is owned, that had through years of personal work been gathered into a home for all loved ones. It is not for nothing that the phrase, 'of mice and men', is an everyday term in the English language. It resonates in the toughest chords of so many hearts. The poem expresses the helplessness of the ordinary individual against the churning faceless might of self-interested Establishment or vicious enemies. But it is more than an expression of the common interests of faceless individuals against tyrannical thoughtlessness. Even in translation, this poem spoke humanely and with sympathy to the displaced proletariat and peasants of Russia in the great displacements following the Revolution of 1917. People who had lost everything except life knew on hearing this poem that somehow they were not alone. Though despair might dominate, others had survived before them. There was still hope. It speaks today to the displaced wherever they are in the world.

After the end of that War, to lift herself from the despair around her, my mother married. She was forced, by the standard contract for women teachers in those days, to give up her job. But my invalid father found it impossible to get work. So she cashed in what savings she still had to pay for him to get through university. Meanwhile she persuaded the Education Authority to let her back into teaching, albeit as a junior assistant in her old school. Yet their infants came, and she cared too for all of us.

In 1955, seven years after he married, my father got his first teaching job. This was in the new primary school beside the new coal mine at Knockshinnoch. A grand old house was pulled down when the mine was sunk. This had been the home of John Logan, one of those who helped promote subscriptions to the Kilmarnock edition. He found buyers for rather more than twenty copies. Knockshinnoch was a mile up the valley from the bridge over the Afton at the mill in New

Cumnock. The Afton joined the River Nith downstream from the mill, past the ford and stepping stones near the farm. From it the road to Sanquhar followed the west bank of the Nith. This was the late 18th century post road between the bridge of the Afton and the town of Sanquhar twelve miles to the south. A few hundred yards south of Afton's bridge was a little cottage. It was an ancient two-room cottage, rubble built. By the mid 20th century, its floor was well below the surface of the road. Though its two rooms were tiny, there was good worked stone surrounding the little window on each side of the front door and the door itself.

My mother immediately identified the cottage as probably having been built to offer roadside service. She was convinced that it was on the door of this ancient cottage that on a wild and stormy night in cold midwinter, snow deep on the ground, Robert Burns hammered late at night, seeking admission, after the funeral cortège of the deceased Mrs Oswald, Mistress of Auchencruive, travelling from London to Mauchline for her interment, had pulled rank and ejected this poor farmer from his pre-booked bed in the inn at Sanquhar.

In identifying this cottage as the inn at New Cumnock, my mother might not have been wrong. Tradition in the 19th century was clear that Burns had not stayed at what was by then the Castle Inn but at what had been a small building, like a little croft house, on the south side of the Afton west of the Nith. Such a cottage would probably have been like the one in which he had been born in Alloway, with a small-holding or garden immediately attached to it. Such my mother's cottage once had, though most of this had been separately sold off before my mother owned the cottage. We moved into a rubble-built house with a chimney at each gable. The one on the north end was no longer usable being damaged by that chimney having been built round by a much more recent red sandstone two-storey building that had become derelict. The roof of the cottage was sufficiently steep to lie down in the attic space. Up there, my father put down a floor. He added two attic lights. As years passed he lined the attic roof. At the outset all six of us slept there on mattresses on the floor. Then my mother got a horrific leg injury at the miners' gala. She could never again climb the ladder.

Up in that very loft might Burns have kipped down on a blanket. Burns consoled himself with the thought in the Ode to Mrs Oswald that

> ten thousand glittering pounds a year

could not save an evil person from the torments of hell. Yet,

> The cave-lodged beggar, with a conscience clear,
> Expires in rags, unknown, and goes to heaven.

Mammon might prevail omnipotent on Earth, but not in the eyes of heaven. He got the poem published in *The London Star* under the pseudonym Tim Nettle in May 1789. His guise was thin. Small wonder, that with problems looming in France, Burns found himself identified as a potential revolutionary.

On a more congenial night perhaps it was in that loft, with the light of a taper, that he wrote down the words of 'Flow Gently Sweet Afton'. This is considered by many his most reverent love song. Perhaps it was inspired by the words of the Psalm 'I charge you, O ye daughters of Jerusalem, that ye stir not, nor awaken my love, my dove, my undefiled!' The story goes that one evening in 1791 a crowd gathered in this inn, because word had got out he was dining at one of the houses in

New Cumnock. They hoped to meet the poet. They awaited his return. They had grown respectfully silent when he distractedly walked through them all and climbed up to his allotted sleeping space. They knew that meant he had been inspired. I have my own memories of that downstairs main room, small though it was, vibrant with parties and song, crowded with visitors sharing music at New Year, shrieking with children dooking for apples at Hallowe'en after doing their obligatory party piece to the thumping of my mother on her piano.

My mother hoped to keep the house, when circumstances moved my parents' work back to Glasgow. She wanted it to become a monument to Robert Burns and the Afton he loved, though grand homes he had visited and the Afton Glen he had known be buried deep in the detritus of the new post-war coal mines. But the house, then known as Number 33 Afton Bridgend, is long gone. It fell victim in the destructive early 1960s to compulsory purchase at a derisory sum. It was replaced by a retirement cottage that itself lasted hardly three decades. The Powers That Be, the Omnipotent They, who in the 1960s seemed to have rankled envy of the little working class person made a tiny bit good, decreed that my mother's dream be denied. So there is no howff now in New Cumnock where Robert Burns could meet with Jolly Beggars the likes of us, and sleep after a night of laughter and joy on the boards of the tiny loft.

My mother's loss of that house heightened my awareness of 'cruel coulters' that passed through people's lives, leaving them like little mice scurrying beneath the trampling feet of Establishment. But it was while living there that I became aware of sweet dreams by Afton's gentle stream "amongst its green braes". I began going to school after Easter, my fourth birthday now past. Around me daily the children of the farm workers and the miners spoke the patois of Ayrshire in the classroom and in the playground, much though teachers and the system would strive to make us 'speak proper English'. As an infant I was bilingual in English and the language of Robert Burns.

In the evenings, at home, our mother would play her piano and we would sing songs. Thus I became aware of words that I now know were brought into the light by Robert Burns, written by himself, by unknown Scots of old, and by contemporaries whose work he promoted. My little voice tended to sing them in the accent of the children with whom I played by day.

Perhaps the great love of my mother for the works of Robert Burns came from affinity. Her life embraced a full return of Halley's Comet. It arrived in 1910 while she was an infant. It came again in the months before her sudden death in 1986. Of course, nothing like that would have entered her head – nor mine neither, in those days. I was a child of the second half of the 20th century, bred to rational thought, to scientific study and to thorough analysis of facts – those 'chiels that winna ding, and daurna be disputed'. But also bred to believe in a mysterious thing called Faith that seemingly contradicted Reason, but which my father insisted was merely greater than the mere reason of human science. Life, I discovered, was paradox.

At secondary school in Glasgow, when our formal study of poems focused on some by Burns, I found myself uncomfortable with teachers' diction and interpretations. But I was soon told who knew best.

Throughout the 1960s I grew aware of the academic movement to regenerate Scottish Literature. I grew uncomfortable on reading the many publications in that strange scholastic language called Lallans. This seemed to me of a type with Esperanto, eclectically picking grammar forms, vocabulary and usages from published works of Scots over many centuries. It seemed to glean and weave indiscriminately the different patois of Scotland's varied regions. The Lallans mix and match approach was fully justified, argued adepts, because Burns himself had done this. He had been so eclectic that he had even felt it necessary to add a glossary not just to the edition of his poems published to reach the Edinburgh readers and those in London; he had added a glossary to his Kilmarnock edition. This demonstrated that even his own readers didn't know the meaning of the words he was using.

The argument struck me as far fetched and made me uncomfortable; Burns used words of varied origin, yes, but always in natural setting. In those days, of course, who was I to challenge the diktat of authorities? I knew nothing – except that as an infant I had spoken fluently two very different forms of English. One was the 'proper' English at school, encouraged by parents and teachers. The other was the local English of the children in the playground, in my infancy the sons and daughters of the miners and farm labourers of south Ayrshire. I later learned to speak another variant – Glaswegian. And all of us kids spoke two forms of English. But we spoke them at different times and for different reasons.

After a lifetime of successfully working internationally in business, I am in a position to make my own strong statement about those glossaries, particularly the first one, in the Kilmarnock edition. I know – because professionally it has been vital to my success – that excellent communication is core to getting an important message through. When you have a message, and you find an audience, if you then don't communicate, you achieve nothing. Good communication is achieved only when the message is given in a language the audience understands. Excellent communication is achieved when the message is in the language that the audience is already tuned to listen to.

Robert Burns had a message – that life was for enjoying, that despite everything that Fate threw at you, life was uplifted by fun and laughter; that throughout all the cares and pressures of life, every man and woman had inner dignity that should be valued and protected by all men as brothers. Once he began moving into company, having slipped away to the dancing and then at Tarbolton found a few lads who would meet up of an evening to discuss things that mattered, by no means just girls, he began to have an audience. But the audience was, until he was invited into the circles of Freemasonry, an audience of locals, of farm workers down the pub. To get his message through, he had to make them laugh by telling them clever stories in verse in their own tongue – the patois of the smithy and farmyard.

Once he entered the Masonic Lodge he found that his wider audience did not all have fluency in this other language, yet recognised the value in his poems. I once had the privilege of reciting 'Tam o' Shanter' to an audience that was entirely Scots but for a Papal Legate who was Italian. After my recital, he came over to thank me, and said "I have never before heard the poem. I don't know the language. It is clearly not English. But you made me understand it." Thus would Masonic friends, themselves not fluent in that worker's everyday language, have understood poems Burns recited, though they were not totally familiar with the vocabulary. They understood because he was *reciting* the poems. He was giving them meaning by his actions and his facial expressions. They would not have understood them if they were simply reading them, no matter how much they might mouth the words out loud. So, having consigned the words to the printed page, that would wend its way alone, unaided by his personal presence, into alien homes where the language of the salon was a foreign tongue untainted by the patois, Burns needed to help his poems' reception by providing the reader with a list of the meanings of words. He provided a larger gloss for his second edition, thus creating the beginnings of the first dictionary of Scottish dialect.

I suggest that had his natural audience from the outset been the posh people of Edinburgh, he would have spoken with a different voice and tongue. As it was, he certainly invented words – any really creative communicator invents words, which is how language grows and evolves. (Contemporary poet William Cowper, who with John Newton of slave abolition fame published 'Olney Hymns' in 1779, complained about his word inventions.) But he never concocted a language that only he understood. He would, I fear, have scoffed at any artificially generated academic Lallans, no matter how much it was promoted by poets who could generate a cult audience in a classy literary pub, however straw-strewn.

The hold of Lallans on academic study of Scottish literature was one factor that directed me away from following my instinct and my mother into formal study of Literature along with Mathematics at University. Instead I followed the separate route of focussing on Mathematics and Natural Philosophy.

Thus it was with a sense of defiance that, in the months around the birth of my daughter in 1973, at home alone in a remote Scottish village without car of my own and no regular public transport, I determined to keep my mind active and prevent myself becoming a neurotic housewife cabbage by immersing myself deep in the study of Robert Burns, his poems, his writings and his history. By the beginning of 1975 this activity was perforce superseded by the need to augment family income, despite my remoteness from work opportunity. But already I had been given the strong message that one such as I could never contribute anything worthwhile to the general knowledge of Burns, his works and his meaning to the world. So I let it lie. But it festered. Within me, however quietly it smouldered for the intervening years, years as long altogether as the whole life of the poet, was an unstoppable belief that there was something big that was not yet said regarding Robert Burns, and that it was my duty to try to say it.

Robert Burns was born in January 1759 and died in July 1796. His life spanned less than four decades of the 18th century. In those four decades the world witnessed the emergence of the key modern conflicts between empires, and the initial successes of the modernist interpretation of democracy founded on acceptance of certain aspects of individual equality. Burns himself was seen to be and is even now considered a key champion in the cause of individual equality. Within four decades of his death democracy had taken modern form of meaning a widening of the number of people who each had equal weight in voting representation in government. Were Burns alive today he might not endorse the form to which modern democracy has evolved.

But mine is not a book about politics. That critical path is well worn. I believe there is far more to the legacy of Burns than his contribution to the emergence of modern so-called Human Right of Self-rule. I believe that in his work he built a bulwark of defiant defence of the Dignity of Man against the so-called Enlightenment's dehumanising pressure on the hidden essence of the mind and inner nature of Mankind.

Friend of the Poet, tried and leal,
Wha, wanting thee, might beg or steal;
Alake, alake! the meikle deil
    Wi' a' his witches
Are at it, skelpin jig and reel,
    In my poor pouches.

I modestly fu' fain would hint it,
That, One-pound-one, I sairly want it;
If wi' the hizzie down ye sent it,
    It would be kind;
And while my heart wi' life-blood dunted,
    I'd bear't in mind.

So may the Auld Year gang out moanin'
To see the New come laden, groanin',
Wi' double plenty o'er the loanin',
    To thee and thine,
Domestic peace and comfort crownin'
    The hale design.

Chapter III   *Beltane Babe*

How Burns in youth was surrounded by magic ritual and wisdom of other worlds, and how respect for believers freed him from religious dogma and prejudice, and inspired his art.

At the start of the 21st century, poetry is not fashionable. Even Shakespeare now gets attention outside academia principally because his plays make a useful model for film scripts. His audience is mostly so narrow that it could be described as 'cult', with the actual words that Shakespeare wrote secondary to the quality of his stories as general entertainment. So, how can Robert Burns be relevant to the modern world if he was merely a poet? To understand how this might be so, I believe it is necessary to explore the global political environment of the second half of the 18th century, and relate that to our own times. The best way to do this, I believe, is from the more fashionable angle of genealogical history. I will start with the maternal influence, though some may consider it the lesser. That influence was subtle, as maternal influence often is.

Currie presented the typical image of a man born of men, educated by male teachers. Currie wrote little about the women who influenced Burns. He gave little credit to the women in the boy's life. This was despite that very emphatic statement in the poet's autobiographical letter about the important impact of womenfolk in his infancy. Few who followed Currie thought to enquire further. We have a few names, but the women are lost. As so often is the case in the lives of great men, we have very little real knowledge about the hands that rocked his cradle and shaped his inner mind.

In preparing that first official full-length biography of Robert Burns, Currie projected a romantic failure who laughed long and sang sweetly of love until his dying day. Couthieness became quite a thing in Scotland, after the terrors and trauma of the French Revolution precipitated government subjugation of all free thought in Britain. From the start of 1793 vicious anti-terrorism laws enabled government agents to molest suspects and to imprison without trial or even proper evidence. After a 'not in my name' outbreak of popular protest, even respected academics were beaten up for uttering dissension to a regime that had against France begun a war that many thought unjust. Even the staunch *Scots Magazine*, trumpeter of Enlightenment thinking in the 18th century, survived that period through transmutation. Today it proudly presents itself in the tough modern world as what the Scots call a couthie read. Dissent went underground, seeking to become invisible, but never disappearing. Currie wished to cause the posthumous edition of Burns's collected works to generate income for the poet's widow and orphans. So he bent over backwards to ensure that nothing in his edition would attract the opprobrium of the contemporary Powers That Be. Currie focussed on the couthie side of Burns – the soft, cuddly side.

Couthie was not the word for the stories that Burns heard around the fireside when he was an infant. He learned then about another world, to most people an invisible world, that surrounded all the lives of men, women and especially children, pervading everything they did, listening to their hearts, invading their deepest private thoughts. The world of the other world was, despite the Enlightenment of the Men of Letters, a total daily reality amongst the everyday people of the world of Burns.

It is from the period of the Enlightenment that the concept of 'old wives' tales' gets its modern connotation. Then, as now, it was often grandmothers who told bedtime stories. The worn-out old woman, unable to do heavier labour, can yet knit with blind hands and spin a good yarn as well, in those days metaphysically too. Infants were clustered round them, just as young people today expect parents to act on demand the unpaid babysitter. Through this age-old process, ancient stories and songs survived, leap-frog manner, through generations, irrespective of fashion of the day in adult gatherings and carousings.

Robert's mother was Agnes Brown or Broun, born 1732 and living until 1820. The 1891 edition of the poet's works edited by Robert Chambers provides genealogical data on the ancestors of Burns. Agnes was descended of a tenant farmer family with roots in Ayrshire at least from the time of Robert the Bruce, when documents refer to at least two people of that family name. By the fifteenth century, there were in the Burgh of Ayr burgesses called Broun, in various trades.

Legal documents are often the only source of historic reference to any except gentry and aristocracy, and thus it is as criminals that Brouns have been found in 17th century records: in June 1683 two Brouns from Cumnock were sentenced to decapitation at Ayr Assizes for taking the Covenanter part in the confrontation at Bothwell. Their sentences were remitted. The earliest known Broun ancestor of Burns's mother was then eight years old. This John Broun, who lived until 1724, married local girl Jennet McGren and tenanted the farm of Craiginton near Kirkoswald. Their second son Gilbert, father of Agnes, was born there in 1708. In 1731 Gilbert married Agnes Rennie, daughter of the Ayr baker William Rennie and his wife Jean Ramsay. Jean probably came from Maybole and had in her youth been in service. Gilbert took on the tenancy of Craiginton after his father. He and Agnes had four sons and two daughters before she died in 1742. Daughter Agnes, Burns's mother, was then ten years old. Gilbert entrusted childcare to his eldest daughter before he remarried, which he did twice.

When her father remarried for the first time in 1744, Agnes was sent to live first with her maternal grandmother. There she spun, led the plough horse, and assisted with threshing corn. Subsequently she became carer for her blind widower uncle, William Broun. She had been expected to marry her grandmother's ploughman, William Nelson. This association suddenly ended after years of expectation. Some while afterwards at the Maybole Fair, she met William Burness. Previously at Alloway Mill, he had seen her and she had impressed him. After a year of courtship, William began building a two-roomed cottage on the nursery land he had leased at Alloway. On December 15th 1757 they were married.

Lacking book knowledge (though she learned to read) and never able to write her name, Agnes carried a book of lore in her head. She had been taught reading by a weaver who provided a basic school while at his loom. She had a great singing voice. Her education ended at her mother's death. From her grandmother Jean she learned a repertoire of songs and Covenanting stories. Thus she passed on to her children a martial lore of fiery religion intermingled with fairy stories of a very real and wonderful hue, many of which possibly owed their origin to the heated imagination of extreme religious intolerance.

The Covenanting story goes back to the Reformation era of John Knox. Just as 1776 dates the start of the United States of America, so the Reformation was for Burns the start of modern Scotland. Burns studied the history of what happened thereafter. This was one of the strong threads in the make-up of that interweaving of lore and book learning that underpinned how Burns thought and wrote. To follow his line of thinking and understand him, we need to understand Covenanters, and we will explore them later. Scotland's Reformation spawned them. So first we must explore that foundation of the Scotland of Robert Burns.

Burns knew Scotland's history, and we get inside his head by knowing it too.

John Knox kindled Scotland's Reformation fire. Initial conflagrations ousted Roman Catholicism. Fire did not rage wild until reforming zeal of Westminster Stuart kings seriously challenged the strict religious practices of the Scottish Presbyterian Church. There had been murmurings when in 1618 King James VI of Scotland and I of England issued a declaration permitting a range of non-violent sports to be enjoyed on Sundays. This disgusted Scottish Presbyterians and the English Puritan faction. The Pilgrim Fathers, leaving Holland for America in 1620, took passengers from England to escape such corruption, as they saw it. Others who opposed relaxation on Sundays responded with an intensified campaign denouncing abuse of the rights of kings.

Aware of how far he could push his subjects, King James shrugged this off. His son Charles was not so laid back. James, familiar with separate legislature and parliaments in his main kingdoms, granted to the American colony of the English Virginia Company self-government subject to the Crown. This created the first such legislative Assembly in a British North America colony. Englishmen could not labour well in the Virginian climate. Despite the king's disgust of tobacco, the main export product of the colony, in 1618 the king set aside constraints on alien immigration. He gave permission to the colony to employ Africans as indentured servants – not as slaves. The first Africans in North America arrived the following year. They were free men but for their commitment to their service contract. The colony was nationalised as a Crown Colony when the Virginia Company went bankrupt in 1624. One hundred and seventy years later, Robert Burns would have emigrated to Jamaica on the same terms as those Africans had gone. But Fate altered his path.

King James had a dark side – a fervent belief in the active power of evil. He had an intense fear of witches. He encouraged onto the statute books of England and Scotland extreme forms of punishment against those who, by whatever means, were found guilty of practicing the dark arts. In this he was strongly supported by anti-Catholic factions who found legal models of persecution in the witch-hunting methods of Thomas Cromwell.

American colonies formed by Puritans and Pilgrims were manifestly intolerant of freedom of speech and of religion, where it did not conform to their own. In England their kind viciously criticised King Charles I when in 1632 he banned English newssheets after complaints from the Spanish Ambassador about their seditious libel of Roman Catholics.

In America, 1632 saw the demise of the Scottish settlement at Acadia. A settlement there had been first established by the French pioneer explorers Samuel de Champlain and Pierre de Monts in 1604. It had begun on an island in Passamaquoddy Bay, moving the next year to modern Annapolis, then called Port Royal. When Scots had arrived in 1621 this became the base for the colony of Acadia. As Scots departed Acadia (ironically now in what is called Nova Scotia), adult male heads of households in English colonies on the Eastern Seaboard of America gained the right to select the governor and assistants of the Massachusetts General Court of North America. Amongst their first laws were restrictions on household expenditure on fancy clothes; prohibited were woollen, linen or silk clothes with silver, gold, silk or linen needlepoint lace on them; slashes in clothing were restricted to one on each sleeve and one at the back.

In 1634, economic concern caused by the European Thirty Years War then in train, caused King Charles to demand Ship Money from London and the coastal towns of England. This levy had never before been raised when England was not formally at war. This 'unlawful' tax, though it had precedents as far back as King Alfred, became the pretext for Parliament to deprive the king first of his freedom and later of his life.

That year, facing an increasingly intolerant England, Roman Catholic George Calvert, Lord Baltimore, gained the grant from Charles I to found and manage Maryland. Its constitution embodied the constraint that laws could be made and tax raised only with the consent of the adult male population, thus initiating a modern form of democracy. In 1649, after Cromwell's army had taken absolute control of England, Lord Baltimore directed Maryland to pass a Toleration Act. This granted freedom of worship to all Christians in Maryland. Sectarianism in America meant that in less than five years, this was repealed.

Rigid intolerance of others by those who were Chosen was the hallmark of the religion bequeathed to Agnes Broun by the ministers of the church of her strict male ancestors. Old women in defiance bequeathed household preparations and old remedies, for everything from causing the milk to transform into good cheese to curbing suppurating warts. Charms and spells, these were, the incantation of the words ensuring the right amount of time passed to allow each element of the preparation to blend with the lotion or potion, in proper proportion to ensure maximum efficacy. This was little different from the way amateur photographers in my youth used to count elephants to measure the right passage of time for chemicals to do their work in bringing the picture magically out of the exposed film.

Those excluded from formal education had their own way of learning. Though ministers taught that man must work though women weep, at the heart of the home the necessary application of well-learned women's lore kept her family and their animals in clothing, in warmth and in health. In centuries things changed little for such women.

Robert Burns, that man who actually proudly declared he was brought up by women, is a strange figure. He is a poet who seems a prelude to the 19th century romantic movement while being a throwback to the mediaeval Scottish makars, yet lionised by the intelligentsia of Edinburgh during that prim and proper Age of Reason, the Scottish Enlightenment. This paradox is worth exploring. Historian and musical journalist Bernadette Cahill, steeped in Sixties song, remarks on Burns being an Aquarian. Aquarius symbolises equality of all. Burns was poet author of 'A man's a man for a' that'. This exemplifies equality that should come with the Age of Aquarius which is our modern time. He is like a morning star of the age of the common man. So she dubbed him Morning Star of the Age of Aquarius.

To explain the paradox of Burns requires suggesting that the world in which Burns lived and worked was quite different from the usual academic description of 18th century Scotland. After all, it was not until the end of the 19th century that there began modern investigations that have made folklore an accepted area for academic study. But this study typically presents its results as the finding of surviving quaintness, and not the rediscovery of a body of knowledge worthy of respect in its own right. The world of women, the world of magic, the world of superstition, are equally the world of the simpleton. Thus the presence of such elements in the work of Burns is considered to be usage by an intelligent male poet of readily available elements for creating humour or satire. They are not considered to be there in their own right to capture through the medium of verse remnants of ancient bodies of knowledge. Given the respect in which Burns held the women who influenced his childhood, perhaps this should be reviewed.

Sabine Baring Gould, working in Devon, led modern study of remnants of folk culture. From 1875 onwards he built on earlier work by his colleague Richard John King. These studies were cross-referenced to history, anthropology, sociology and psychology, in an attempt to extract a collective subconscious memory of peoples. Their work inspired Frazer's 'Golden Bough'. Folklore is unofficial, existing alongside any formal or recognised culture. Usually transmitted orally, different versions emerge, although expressed in common patterns. All peoples have folklore, irrespective of background. There is bias in recording it: anecdotal and apocryphal stories from professional groups may be given credence different from that given to groups whom establishment and intelligentsia consider unsophisticated.

The enlargement of academia made more room for such study. It was verified that old stories appeared to have persisted to the 20th century. Thus, investigators were told how rural elderly people would not burn elder wood, because it was the tree that the Holy Cross was made of. Lightning would never strike a holly tree, or those sheltering under one. When holly trees were cut down, locals protested it would cause poltergeist havoc. A rosemary bush growing near the cottage protected from witches – in Scotland this is said of the rowan tree. Mayflower was never brought inside the house because it brought illness and ill fortune. A robin entering the house was a sign of a coming death. Farmers in some areas in the past considered it essential to shoot a robin to bring good luck for the coming year. A croaking raven was a sign of coming bad luck. If a shrew mouse ran over your foot you would go lame and walk with a bad limp all your life. If a dog howled in a sobbing, mournful way during the night, it was a death sign for its owners or a near relation. To be sure of sleeping well, make sure the bed runs the same way as the floorboards; if it is placed across them, you have the Devil against you. It is common to offer a baby a silver spoon; if it grasps it, it will be rich. Never alter the status of a gate you go through; if it was open, leave it open; if it was closed, close it after you. Otherwise bad luck will follow. A table laid with a green cloth, and a white cat in a house are both bad luck.

In the mid 1970s Professor G E Trease, Emeritus Professor of Pharmacognosy, went around local folklore societies lecturing on 'Warts and Wartcunning', dealing with the history of the study of the medicinal uses of plants. The interest in a forgotten past, real or imaginary, is increasing as the world becomes more dislocated from its old social order. In the mainstream this is nostalgic or at best antiquarian, although alternative cultures including homeopathic medicine are giving new credibility to such old ways of thinking.

It is normally presumed that these old ways of thinking passed away only through the onslaught of compulsory general primary education in the late 19th century. But there has been active, deliberate destruction of such old knowledge since the Reformation. Survivals are in spite of fundamental changes in society over many centuries. In lowland Scotland in the time of Burns, most ministers of religion lecturing each Sunday would associate old wives' cures with Romish superstition and evil magic. Burns would have attributed the ridicule of old remedies to Knox's Reformation. In 1560

John Knox gained ascendancy in Scottish religion over Papal power and brought about the Scottish Reformation. For those teaching Burns, that was when modern history began. For the Scotland of Burns, 1560 was what 1776 is for today's United States of America. The Glorious Revolution of 1688 was to that Scotland what the war of 1861-65 is to modern USA.

By the time of Burns, two massive theological questions divided the Scottish church. These questions caused such discussion that it presented a forum every Sunday for the young Burns to sharpen his debating skills, and learn to wield his rapier wit to devastating effect. These were the issues of predestination and the validity in modern times of Divine Revelation. These questions came from the way in which the Protestant Reformation came about. It did not happen spontaneously. Some say it was triggered by the emergence of moveable type for book production. That too must have been triggered by some earlier cause. Exploring those causes helps explain why these two big questions were being asked so earnestly in the Scotland of Robert Burns.

These two questions are as old as Christianity. What makes Scotland so unique is that they were being debated by ordinary people. People were even daring to form their own opinions on the matter, despite the rulings of the General Assembly of the Church of Scotland. Indeed, the questions were dividing the General Assembly.

In earliest Christian times only teachers of the church made rulings on such questions. In due course the first Christian universities were established to enable theology scholars to become adepts in religious mysteries. They studied scripts, they discussed, they prayed, they meditated. By all these processes they learned. Thus were they able to pronounce answers when new questions were raised. These universities produced priests who took the mysteries amongst the people. A throwback to this ancient purpose of universities exists still in the graduation ceremony in England's Cambridge University. The Chancellor takes the prayer-folded hands of the graduate in his own, as in a blessing in priestly ordination. Each new graduate is as a new priest of knowledge.

When you read letters Burns wrote, you find his confidence in Divine Revelation was central to his understanding of the Almighty. And this was contentious. The 16th century Lutheran Reformation had founded itself on the denial of continuing Divine Revelation. In this question Burns took a view that was contrary to that of the founders of his religion.

Calvinists attacked Roman doctrine not just on the Divine Revelation issue but also on the question of the fate of the soul on death. This other question differentiates the hard-line Calvinists from more moderate reformers. Calvin insisted that the fate after death of the soul of every human being was predestined. This denied that Mankind had Free Will. Knox put both those doctrines right at the heart of his Scottish Reformation. That this too was being discussed in Scotland in the 18th century meant that a real rift had appeared in the church that Knox had instituted.

The Roman Church was attacked not only by Calvinists. It was violently attacked at the start of the 17th century, this time within its heartland, Italy. Galileo Galilei opposed Divine Revelation in a manner that at the same time denied Free Will and so justified the doctrine of predestination. Previously the two matters had been disputed independently. Galileo significantly strengthened the arguments of the Reformers. As a child Burns got really interested in that Galilean controversy. His understanding, gained since infancy, of the history of these issues had fundamental influence on him. It enabled the biting humour with which he attacked Scottish Presbyterianism as he found it around him.

Chapter III *Beltane Babe*

I'll come later back to the Galilean controversy, because it contains other significant matters that interested Burns. To follow the mind of Burns we need to follow his understanding of these issues and the history of how Reformation questions came to be important in his Scotland. Burns was aware of their history, because he was required to study it. He learned early that the history in Presbyterian texts was biased.

It is easy to be distracted by the arguments put forward. We can also get annoyed because we don't agree with a position as it is appropriate to represent it if we are to understand what Burns heard of it. We don't need an opinion on the issues, but we do need awareness of the emotion that this discussion can generate. We need to *feel* that emotion in reading the next few pages. People got angry when they thought others seemed to support a ridiculous position. Others felt triumphantly vindicated when argument gave ammunition for positions they defended. Even reviewing these arguments can make us feel strongly today. This is a gut reaction. It is the same gut reaction that enervated even the humblest Scots in the latter part of the 18th century. It is the same gut reaction that causes modern religious sects to be hated or loved for their beliefs and behaviour. It is the gut reaction that causes wars and can generate harmony. And all that gut reaction is totally instinctive. It is seldom ameliorated by facts and logical argument. No matter what the facts seem to demonstrate, there is always that inner defiance. Ah but! So there!

This warning from me that you will react will make you try not to react. The strength of your reaction, despite your effort, shows that there is more to this than just an academic argument. The issue that underlies it is the fundamental question of what constitutes humanity. Are we just mechanical entities whose very feelings will someday be replicated by a programmed automaton designed and made by man? Or is there soul inside us that is the essence of life that no amount of science can ever replicate in a machine?

Or to put it simply, can feelings be explained?

Burns with his whole heart believed they could not. To Alexander Cunningham of Edinburgh he wrote in 1794,

> "I would not quarrel with a man for his irreligion any more than I would for his want of a musical ear."

To understand the significance of his taking this stance in the Scotland of his day, we must review history and argument.

Before the Black Death, study was for the purpose of gaining greater understanding of the Almighty. Before he was allowed to graduate, a student had to demonstrate command of two very different but complementary streams of thought. Theology could be understood only through study of the works of God, and through learning how to think about these works. Before a scholar could think about the works he had to study the works themselves. Thus he had to prove himself master of the Quadrivium. These were the scientific disciplines described as Arithmetic, Geometry, Music and Astronomy. Only then did the scholar learn how to use the tools of discourse. He did this by studying the Trivium of the Arts. This gave him the tools Grammar, Rhetoric and Dialectic which was also called logic. Learning was based substantially on collegiate discussion and verbal examination. The sheer difficulty of acquiring the understanding within the Quadrivium cut down substantially the number of candidates for final graduation. The Quadrivium was the raw material of Theology. The

Trivium was merely the tools for refining understanding. Once they left university many priests did no more than their own prayers, administer the sacraments and give sermons. Others merely formed the professional classes, acting as lawyers, accountants, and clerks.

The Black Death in the mid 14th century, amongst its many curses, seriously damaged the previous education system. So many priests died tending their flocks that it was followed by a need to ordain quickly considerable numbers of new priests. This could only be done with major dilution of priestly education.

After the Black Death, there were so few priests even to service the churches that it made some kind of sense to ordain priests skilled only in prayer, administering the sacraments and giving sermons. To produce enough clerics to serve traumatised communities, the universities were authorised to graduate a lesser stream of scholars. The rigour of the Quadrivium was the bottleneck. Since it wasn't needed in everyday parish work, many argued it should not be imposed on those destined to be parish clerics. Those clerics needed to be versed only in the set of tools, the Trivium. Teaching could be speeded up too by basing learning only on book study and written examination. Without the underpinning of the Quadrivium, the Trivium lost focus. Perforce the average level of education of ordained priests fell sharply. Priests with very limited understanding became commonplace.

Abuses naturally followed. Ritualistic incantation rather than spiritual intonation was too commonly the experience of those who partook of religious celebrations. The Reformation struck hard at this malpractice. John Knox introduced his Reformation on the platform that such canting was an insult to God and to Man, benefiting only rapacious papists. But, two hundred years later, canting had again become too normal in Scotland.

In the 1780s it seemed to Burns that ministers sought not souls to heal but stipends to enjoy. He lashed at this in verse. He spelled out the accusation in 'The Ordination':

> That Stipend is a carnal weed
> > He taks but for the fashion;
> And gie him o'er the flock to feed,
> > And punish each transgression;
> Especial, rams that cross the breed,
> > Gie them sufficient threshin,
> > > Spare them nae day.

The change in the way university students studied had also had an unexpected side effect. By the mid 16th century, many everyday priests were merely book learned. They were not trained through collegiate discussion. A general understanding arose that book learning was more important and better than those older types of learning that included practical observation and experience, meditation and intuition. Reading books came to be thought as good as or better than that reasoned intellectual discourse that had been the province of the great doctors of the mediaeval universities.

The Black Death had also devastated the numbers of clerics manning scriptoria. Private companies filled the production gap. Books were expensive. It became economically worthwhile to find cheaper ways to make books. The movable type printing press first used in Europe in the middle of the 15th century aimed to make books more cheaply than commercial scriptoria. These first printing presses were so inefficient that it was viable to produce books only for the most expensive sector of the market. They couldn't compete with cheap workbooks. So Gutenberg did his Bible. A client could specify what extras he wanted – what quality of illumination, whether or not gold was added, and what quality of leather binding. Thus, each one was different. Amongst those not quite rich enough to afford hand-written books, printed chronicles, such as that of Nuremberg, also found a market. Thus the book printing trade got established in a world that was increasingly seeing books as sufficient – indeed the only – source of real education.

The dilution of education along with wider availability of books set the scene for the Reformation. The Reformation was in essence a concerted combination of individual isolated book readers challenging learned colleges of authorities on key aspects of theology. It was enabled by the expansion of book availability that preceded it. The tyrannical democracy of the printed book was its hallmark. In a way what happened was similar to what the Internet is enabling now. Individuals can now add their input to on-line databases. All positions seem to carry equal weight, despite the one being based on a lifetime of study and another being based on no more than an inspired guess or, what is worse, on rampant prejudice. Statements masquerading as reliable are being generated by averaging all input, however uninformed. In this way, five hundred years ago, printing contributed to Reformation.

Books containing classical knowledge also became widely distributed in the West. The great teachers of Western pre-Reformation Christianity had already had access to and used those classical texts even before 1453. They had known of them through diplomatic exchanges between Rome and Byzantium. They did not become available to a general audience until made available by the printing press. War and developing commerce did bring back more actual books from Eastern libraries, but it was the printing press that distributed the content of them so widely. Increased study of classical knowledge precipitated what is known as the Renaissance. This caused many more in the West to recognise that the West did not have the monopoly of intelligence. All mankind has an innate ability to think and can thus form disparate views of the universe. This re-established respect in the West for learned non-Christian thinkers. This generated a new kind of inter-human respect. This Humanism was the offspring of the Renaissance. Most leading Humanists – Erasmus is an exception – were leading authorities of the Roman church.

The Humanists would have recognised a common spirit in Burns. In one of his letters to Clarinda he wrote,

> "My definition of worth is short: truth and humanity respecting our fellow-creatures; reverence and humility in the presence of that Being, my Creator and Preserver who .. will be my judge."

Humanists respected books, but they had greater respect for informed discourse. Such discourse and reflection could generate revelation.

It is generally claimed that the Enlightenment is the offspring of the Renaissance informed by the Reformation. From long study of the 18th century, I have come to disagree. I suggest that the key difference between Reformation Christians and those of the old school was insistence by the former that in theological discussion only the printed word counted. In my view, the Enlightenment was actually rooted in the Reformation only. Its embryo was that tyranny of book learning. While authorities of the Roman church insisted that through meditation came understanding given directly by God, the Reformed Christians insisted that Divine Revelation ended at the apostolic era.

Theological Reason had been the province only of the Doctors of the Church. A typical righteous Reformer is presented as an idealist who was right when all the doctors of the church were wrong. That requires Revelation. Yet Revelation was denied by these Reformers. As presented by our histories, the Reformer is a paradox.

The followers of these Reformers accepted that when Jesus was on Earth Revelation was an input to the Christian Bible. They also claimed it was vastly outweighed by the written New Testament. They presumed this to be authentic contemporary accounts of the life of Jesus along with letters of those contemporary with him. They added as authentic the collected books of the pre-Christian Jewish period. Reformed Christians rejected Revelation as a continuing experience of Mankind. Reformed Christians rejected the authority of the Pope, and rejected with it those everyday experiences of that authority, in the sanction of places and rituals associated with saints. If things weren't in books, they were empty superstition. They became objects of ridicule. They were not revealed; they were reviled.

It is a strange phenomenon that in 18th century Europe's most theocratic region, the Scotland of Robert Burns, one violently active question amongst intellectuals and common people alike was whether or not Divine Revelation existed there today amongst Scots. This was one of the two questions that brought people to blows in their Holy Fairs. The fiery sword of conflict was double edged. The other reason for blows was that those Righteous Men who believed they were Predestined to Heaven typically also knew that they were absolutely right that Divine Revelation did not exist in their Scotland.

The Justified Christian believed himself in complete armour against those who dared to challenge him. Finding the chinks in that armour, through which he could drive his rapier, became the adolescent sport of Robert Burns. His rapier technique matured to a devastating wit. Flashing at his command, his rapier learned to turn against all manifestations of arrogance and hypocrisy. He also wrote directly without aggression. In that same letter of 1794 to Alexander Cunningham Burns expressed thoughts that he shared with others amongst his correspondents:

> "There are two pillars that bear us up amid the wreck of misfortune and misery. The one is composed of the different modifications of a certain noble, stubborn something in man, known by the names of courage, fortitude, magnanimity. The other is made up of those feelings and sentiments which, however the sceptic may deny them, or the enthusiast may disfigure them, are yet, I am convinced, original and component parts of the human soul; those senses of the mind, if I may be allowed the expression, which connect us with and link us to, those awful, obscure realities – an all-powerful and equally beneficent God, and a world to come, beyond death and the grave. The first gives the nerve of combat, while a ray of hope beams on the field; the last pours the balm of comfort into the wounds which time can never cure."

There had actually existed since earliest Christian times a process for validating supposed new Revelation. This process was not forgotten in Scotland. Burns was taught it by his father within a catechism he had Murdoch prepare.

The process of challenge to Revelation is most visible at the present time in the Roman church in Vatican enquiry into proposed sainthood. The Papal enquiry process demands in the modern day, as in the past, that anything proposed as revelation be subjected to rigorous examination. To be accepted, supposed revelation and miracles must satisfy the reasoned judgement of informed religious experts. The main criteria are that revelation and miracles are never trivial in their impact nor intuitively nor actually Evil in their impact or their final outcome. Revelation and miracles must indeed satisfy the opposite criteria. Their end inherently intuitively Good, they are seen to have substance within a Great Scheme of God, and they must 'make sense' in their implications. Each of these emotional outcomes must stand the test of theological reason. The evolving Roman church had always relied on Revelation – and still does.

History considers the first Protestant Reformers only to be those who denied the authority of Rome. Internal reformers are not Reformers Proper. The Protestant Reformers challenged the power of the leaders of the universities. Often they had themselves not got as far in the extant university system as they thought they should have done. The most successful of them wisely noted that the most effective way to overthrow the control by initiates in mysteries of understanding is to deny the existence of any mystique. This is the academic equivalent of the denial by children of magic by simply uttering the statement "I don't believe in fairies". Refusal to discuss a proposition denies the relevance of the proposition. With no audience a show collapses. With no argument to enable a proponent to defend a proposition, the proposition dies. "We don't believe in Revelation" kills discussion of the matter. In due course this stance could kill belief in the existence of Revelation. Thus increasingly, Reformation teachers denied Revelation. They denied there was such a thing as knowledge influenced from outside that came into being intuitively within a person's mind without conscious thought. They demanded that Reason be founded only on verifiable facts, visible thinking and demonstrated proof.

Facts alone, believed Burns, were insufficient for a human being. Writing to Mrs Dunlop on 9th July 1790 on learning of the death of her son-in-law, he commented on faith in the goodness of God, and consoled her with insistence that:

> "I have no objection to what the Christian system *tells us* of Another world; yet I own I am partial to those proofs & ideas of it which we have wrought out of our own heads & hearts. The first has the demonstration of an authenticated story, the last has the conviction of an intuitive truth."

Denying Revelation enabled Reformers to undermine the authority of Rome. As a by-product it challenged the existence of intuitive understanding by human beings. So this non-Revelation stance rather undermines quite a big chunk of our humanity. While Burns would not have put it this way directly, he certainly in his poems and letters made clear his belief in the importance of intuition. He was a very intuitive person. Facts alone to him were not enough. The most important things in everyday life – the moral sentiments as Adam Smith called them – can be effectively addressed only intuitively. We feel love, fear, hate, horror, excitement, resentment, regret, joy, admiration, sympathy, pity. All the argumentation of the Enlightenment intellectuals could never quite eliminate this irritating reality. We *feel* these emotions. Even in our modern brash consumer world, we *feel*. Increasingly we feel loneliness, worry, concern, dismay, disappointment, disenchantment, boredom, anger. Modern scientists, for all their experiments and machines, can't explain any of these satisfactorily in mechanical terms. The search to do so is like that of modern companies determined to define quality in measures, so they can mass produce this desirable valuable commodity and sell it by weight. Instead, myriad are the fees for 'how to' consultancy by gurus delineating manufacturing processes as worthless as alchemist recipes for transmuting base metal into gold. Dissecting moral sentiments was to Burns the philosophical equivalent of dissecting human bodies in the search for explanation of life. Burns told them not to waste their time trying.

His message was direct. These philosophers were trying to dissect feelings. These feelings are Man's core and Man's life. These are the basis of the Dignity of Man. If you dissect feelings, you destroy the essence of Man. This identified to Burns his core purpose: to defend the Dignity of Man. He defended that Dignity through his writings and his poetry.

Burns was not one just to go along with a majority. He explained to Mrs Dunlop on New Year's Morning 1789 that:

> "However respectable Individuals in all ages have been, I have ever looked on Mankind in the lump to be nothing better than a foolish, head-strong, credulous, unthinking Mob; and their universal belief has ever had extremely little weight with me."

Knowing the intelligentsia of Edinburgh, he was aware that they too indulged in mob-think.

The logic behind the study of the Quadrivium was that God himself was invisible. Study the works of God and God reveals himself to you. Instinct led Burns to return to this ancient way of reaching up to the infinite. Earlier in that letter he told Mrs Dunlop,

> "I have some favourite flowers in Spring, among which are the mountain-daisy, the hare-bell, the foxglove, the wild brier-rose, the budding birk, and the hoary hawthorn, that I view and hang over with particular delight. I never hear the loud, solitary whistle of the curlew in a summer noon, or the wild, mixing cadence of a troop of grey-plover in an Autumnal morning, without feeling an elevation of soul like the enthusiasm of Devotion or Poetry. Tell me, my dear friend, to what can this be owing? Are we a piece of machinery that, like the Aeolian harp, passive, takes the impression of the passing accident? Or do these workings argue something within us above the trodden clod? I own myself partial to these proofs of those awful and important realities – a God that made all things – man's immaterial and immortal nature – and a world of weal or woe beyond death and the grave – these proofs that we deduct by dint of our own powers of observation."

Leaders of the Reformation declared miracles and continuing revelation non-existent. They de facto declared there was no such thing as intuitive reason; reason must be based only on verifiable observable facts. At the outset, curiously, Reformers allowed as 'facts' about Jesus the stories presented in the actual words of the 'correct' printed Bible. Previously education had included meditation leading to insight. In denying intuition Reformed universities' teaching centred on subjecting all thought solely to strict logic. Students must seek facts from which to examine real things and experiences, and reject intuition. Meditation and insight had no place. This was despite the fact that no worthwhile book has ever been written without serious meditation by the author.

Following the 18th century Enlightenment, this process became so dominant that in our modern world many leading teachers accept nothing that cannot to their subjective satisfaction be demonstrably proven with reference to measures. The triumph of the Doubting Thomas was complete.

Or so it seemed. The interesting thing is that intuition has never been completely killed. Indeed, as Kuhn's philosophy demonstrates, scientific development has repeatedly happened only through rejecting apparent 'facts' and invoking intuition.

Burns believed passionately in the Human Right to intuition. He expressed this to Richard Brown on 7th March 1788.

> "Men of grave, geometrical minds, the sons of 'Which was to be demonstrated', may cry up reason as much as they please; but I have always found an honest passion, or native instinct, the trustiest auxiliary in the warfare of this world."

The views set out over the last few pages of the history of educational development can and will be challenged. That intelligent challenge is made to any position however sound, and that challenges always have been and will be made, illustrates the environment Burns too found himself in. As he dutifully attended church each Sunday, he found argument raising the temperature in the discourses of the congregations.

There was far less contention on another matter. Scotland by the second half of the 17th century had, quite independently of all religious discussion, developed a distinct inferiority complex in its relationship with England. Her king went south in 1603. Her nobles followed. They all fouled up and lost control to Oliver Cromwell who in turn subdued Scotland militarily. Scotland's 18th century began badly with the commercial failure of the great national Company of Scotland, now remembered as the Darien misadventure. This was followed quickly in 1707 by the Union whose terms seemed to give protection to two key balanced pillars of Scottish establishment – its independent Law and its Presbyterian church. Reality began to prove a little different once the Scottish Parliament was set aside and that at Westminster took over government.

Even Scottish thinkers were in a backwater. In Britain after the Restoration, thought was identified with the Royal Society's Newtonian scientists and Lockean philosophers or the new breed of journalists like Richard Steele. These all appeared roundly to criticise Scotland as not just economically and intellectually impoverished but also philosophically illiberal, intolerant and backward. Irishmen even came to Edinburgh to lecture on how to speak English properly. The Scots flocked to learn. Burns found himself in the late 18th century in a country that had little national pride.

At least intellectually things were not all bad, it seemed. After the Glorious Revolution of 1688 the bishoprics imposed on Scotland by Charles II were disbanded. Their revenues were redirected to her universities. This returned higher education finances closer to the pre-Reformation position. The new curricula were moderated by Presbyterian committees. Professors approved by the new regime were appointed. The best were excellent thinkers. Their research thought was focused at the outset on ethics and philosophy. Access to studies was expanded by the creation of bursaries. Some believed that the intellectual agenda had got out of hand. It is a well known phenomenon, repeating in our modern era, that rapidly multiplying university posts expands paper output with limited true increase in knowledge. Also, rapidly increasing the numbers graduating can be achieved only by decreased quality of graduate. Thus, in 18th century Scotland the balance of university output shifted from producing graduates with solid grounding in languages and mathematics to those who could use considerable words to debate fine matters of religious dogma. The outcome was increased challenge to the teaching of the established Presbyterian church.

At the same time as the established church began to lose its power, the vacuum left by the absence of the parliament was increasingly filled by pragmatic lawyers and abstract academic thinkers. Within the universities the Darien failure turned attention to economics. Intellectual Scots then began seriously exploring and debating at one and the same time the apparently contradictory issues of ideal spiritual ethics and pragmatic economics and law.

This caused confusion which in turn fuelled scepticism.

Confronting rampant scepticism within himself, by 1730 the prescient Alexander Moncrieff condemned economic growth not tempered by religious ethics as inevitably leading humankind to man-made hell. There was a growing tension in Scotland: Scots desperately desired to become wealthy but their Presbyterian religion demanded that industry and commerce be ethical. This combination seemed well nigh impossible in the real world. Thus arose a question: can a country be rich yet not corrupt? In 1730 Francis Hutcheson was appointed to the Chair of Moral Philosophy in Glasgow University. He had published 'An Inquiry into the Origin of Our Ideas of Beauty and Virtue' following this with 'An Essay on the Nature and Conduct of the Passions and the Affections' in 1728. In 1747 he was to publish 'A Short Introduction to Moral Philosophy'. Instead of accepting that wealth creation must be controlled by religious dogma, he led research on *how* to achieve wealth without corruption. Out of this came the works of Thomas Reid, Adam Smith and David Hume. Their combined thinking has since been greatly corrupted.

Meanwhile work advanced in attempting to establish Reformed consensus on the content of the Bible, helped by such work as the 'Concordance' published by Cruden in Edinburgh in 1737.

The paradox in the Reformers' position had by now been spotted: if there was no Revelation now, what proof is there that there was any then? The Bible itself could be just a made-up story. Hume in his 'Treatise on Human Nature' crystallised the concern amongst thinkers that even the miracles of Jesus Christ might be mere fable.

His logic was that science demonstrated that Nature was subject to mechanistic Laws; miracles contradicted these Laws of Nature; thus miracles are impossible. Thus the Bible is full of impossible stories. It is a very small additional step to say that this is proof that there is no God. In the 19th century, philosophers combined Hume's position with the proposal summarised in the dictum 'I think therefore I am'. That dictum leads to proposing the universe an individual perceives is the product of his imagination. If everything is the product of the thinker, he is god of his own universe. This kind of thinking becomes so mind-boggling that it unhinges some people. At the very least it unhinges any common concept of morality, for it makes each person sole arbiter of right and wrong.

Although Hume's logic is based on the wrong premise that Nature is subject to mechanistic Laws, by the time of Burns, philosophers following Hume's lead were questioning ethics. Much of the ethical framework of philosophy had hitherto been founded on the premise of there being an Almighty God. This raised the spectre of moral degeneration, which so concerned Newton and his followers. It concerned Burns too, although he himself never let go of his belief that there was indeed some Almighty Power.

Hume was one of many prolific writers of quality work. In 1739 he published the first version of the work that became in 1751 his 'Enquiry Concerning Human Understanding'. In 1741 he published the first part of his 'Essays, Moral and Political', completed in 1748. In 1757 he published 'The Natural History of Religion' within his 'Four Dissertations'. In 1779 his 'Dialogues Concerning

Natural Religion' was posthumously published, attacking such arguments for God's existence as had been promoted by Newton, Whiston and Derham.

The dragon of Reformation was beginning to eat its own tail.

In his verse epistle to William Simson, Burns portrayed the previous dominance of the Auld Lichts, as conservative ministers were known, their teaching undisputed by their congregations:

> [in the] past for certain, undisputed;
>
> It ne'er cam i' their heads to doubt it.

But books were too widespread, and those who read them presented challenge. They too were 'weel learn'd upo' the beuk'. The Auld Lichts now felt so threatened that its leaders would use the latest technology – a balloon – to get the facts that would absolutely prove their position. Data was what mattered to 'cowe the louns': full scientific data on the nature of the Moon to prove that each month Earth got a new one that grew and then decayed. Thus,

> Some *auld-light herds* in neebor touns
>
> Are mind't, in things they ca' balloons,
>
> > To tak a flight,
>
> An' stay ae month among the *Moons*
>
> > An' see them right.
>
> Guid observation they will gie them;
>
> An' when the *auld Moon's* gaun to lea'e them,
>
> The hindmost *shaird*, they'll fetch it wi' them,
>
> > Just i' their pouch;
>
> An' when the *new-light* billies see them,
>
> > I think they'll crouch!

The quality of her intellectual contribution to philosophical and scientific debate gained Scotland a reputation for thought leadership. Scotland was also known to have, in theory, widespread education. This had, in fact, been virtually eliminated in the period of extensive civil conflict between 1637 and 1688, which had culminated in the Covenanting times and the Glorious Revolution. Attempts to reinstate it during the 18th century were in many places thwarted by Jacobite disturbances and associated economic disruption. There was a vast gulf between what Enlightened people in universities, professions and aristocracy projected their Scotland as being, and what the totality of the minds of contemporary Scottish ordinary people actually was. We are fortunate in having the contemporary record of a very observant honest Welshman who explored Scotland and published his thorough review, so fulfilling that fervent wish of our poet:

> O wad some po'er the giftie gie us
>
> To see oor'sells as ithers see us.

Thomas Pennant of Whitford was internationally a highly respected Enlightenment biological scientist with early training in ornithology and mineralogy. Pennant intended gathering objective evidence on the state of Scotland. This was, of course, coloured by his own nationality, experiences and education as his observations necessarily must be. But he achieved considerable objectivity. I have gone back to his own editions of his work in preparing this coming section. Actual quotations in the rest of this chapter are from Pennant.

Pennant was a mainstream Enlightenment intellectual. Yet his works published throughout his life show a shift in emphasis. There is visible change between his first published work on Scotland of 1769 and his revision and expansion of it after a second journey. During this period he moved from being the totally rational and sceptical scientific young man who produced 'British Zoology' to the old man who warned that the new generation of academics relied too much on book learning and were careless both in observation and objective thought. Thus increasingly, from his Scottish Journals onward, his work recognises that there is an alternative knowledge in some way embedded in folk practices and folk lore. That there was something 'in there' was evidenced in rural approaches to herbal medicines. As early as 1772 he was recommending these be explored as possible sources for expanding scientific pharmacology.

In the later edition of his tour Pennant presented mostly non-judgemental treatment of folklore and old practices. He thus questioned whether the rejection of old knowledge was in his time so widespread amongst the intelligentsia as modern Enlightenment studies would suggest. His scientific method of observation and his writing style contrast with that of Dr Samuel Johnson. That non-scientist dictionary maker came north to find 'primitives'. He then made scathing report of all his experiences on his tour to the Hebrides. Johnson's visit (in the published diary of which were these dismissive remarks) was in part prompted by the publication of Pennant's record of his first tour of Scotland. Johnson particularly objected to a remark that Pennant came across Gaelic language poetry fragments that clearly underpinned the authenticity of 'Ossian', recently produced by James MacPherson.

Like Pennant implied, Dr John Gregory of Aberdeen in 1772 asserted that Highland society had been superior to that which pertained by the time of Pennant's visit. Gregory argued from this that increasing specialisation of roles meant society had degraded rather than advanced: Fingal and Ossian were each a statesman, soldier, poet and musician in one person; in late 18th century Britain no one person could be all of these. Adam Smith took up this notion as the basis of a key prediction in 'The Wealth of Nations'.

'Ossian' became a very controversial book. It was hailed as evidence of a lost innocence by those who wished to slow down the loss of Scottish identity through the nation's absorption into the United Kingdom. Johnson took the English party line in his aim to prove that Scotland was innately primitive and 'Ossian' was a fraud. MacPherson played into Johnson's fat grabbing hands by not disclosing that he had followed the normal 18th century practice when presenting translated works to a new audience, in correcting the flow of a lot that he had translated.

Pennant's 'A Tour in Scotland 1769' is a book of around 80,000 words. Not much more than one word in a hundred relates to observations on folk customs and belief – but that small amount contains a considerable quantity of detailed observation of a hidden world of thought that was surviving the rationalisation of learning that was sweeping through university circles. After his 1772 tour these sections got expanded. The first section of the first tour describes Pennant's route between his home in Whitford by a sweep south of the Trent to Lincoln, and thence north to Berwick. While in England, his greatest departure from factual observation is the occasional use of the word 'romantic' when describing some view or location. After crossing the Tweed, less 'scientific' expressions repeatedly infiltrated his writing. At Dunbar he noted (the italics are mine) the vast castle dungeon cavern that is:

composed of a black and red stone, which gives it a most infernal appearance, a fit representation of the pit of Acheron, and *wanted only to be peopled with witches* to make the scene complete.

In this first trip he was not aware of Roslyn Chapel, so famous now through its association with 'The Da Vinci Code'. Edinburgh was then enjoying the early phases of the building of George Square (now mostly demolished to make way for modern university tower blocks). It was at the start of the development of its New Town. The Hanoverian cónfidence returned Pennant firmly to down-to-earth factuality. In his evening walk he could ruefully reflect as he

passed by a deep and wide hollow beneath Calton Hill . . the place where those imaginary criminals, witches and sorcerers, in less enlightened times, were burnt.

His scientific mind did not, however, make him immune to a feeling of horror when passing north across the Forth and visiting the one-arched Rumbling Bridge:

flung over a chasm worn by the River Devon, about eighty feet deep, very narrow, and horrible to look down; the bottom, in many parts, gushing between the stones with great violence: the sides, in many places, project, and almost lock in each other; trees shoot out in various spots, and contribute to increase the gloom of the glen, while the ear is filled with the cawing of daws, the cooing of woodpigeons, and the impetuous noise of the waters.

Continuing west towards Stirling, he was reminded that this was once a great forest, with Castle Campbell once called the Castle of Gloom, in the parish of Dolor,

bounded by the Glens of Care, and washed by the Burns of Sorrow.

His readers must have remarked how quaintly Arthurian this was.

Northwards around Loch Tay, he passed through lands confiscated after the defeat of Jacobites in the 1745 uprising. They were by then already in various stages of transformation in attempts to improve financial payback. Thus in Breadalbane, encountering belief in ghosts, he fully reinstated his Enlightened scepticism.

A poor visionary, who had been working in his cabbage garden, imagined that he was raised suddenly into the air, and conveyed over a wall into an adjacent cornfield; that he had found himself surrounded by a crowd of men and women, many of whom he knew to have been dead some years, and who appeared to him skimming over the tops of the unbended corn, and mingling together like bees going to hive: that they spoke an unknown language, and with a hollow sound: that they very roughly pushed him to and fro; but on his uttering the name of God, all vanished but a female spirit, who seizing him by the shoulder, obliged him to promise an assignation, at that very hour, that day seven-night: that he then found that his hair was tied in double knots, and that he had almost lost the use of his speech: that he kept his word with the spectre, whom he soon saw come floating through the air towards him: that he spoke to her, but she told him that at that time she was in too much haste to attend to him, but bid him go away, and no harm should befall him; and so the affair rested when I left the country. But it is incredible the mischief these Aegri Somnia did in the neighbourhood: the friends and relations of the deceased, whom the old dreamer had named, were in the utmost anxiety at finding them in such bad company in the other world: the almost extinct belief of the old idle tales began again to gain ground, and the good minister will have many a weary discourse and exhortation before he can eradicate the absurd ideas this idle story has revived.

Pennant pulled himself together, and added:

In this part of the country the notion of witchcraft is quite lost: it was observed to cease almost immediately on the repeal of the witch act; a proof what a dangerous instrument it was in the hands of the vindictive, or of the credulous.

This introduction to a strange story did, however, give him an opportunity in his later edition to recount superstitions communicated to him in writing by a local gentleman. Pennant added a footnote remarking that similar customs prevailed in Gloucestershire around the feast of the Epiphany, involving twelve fires in a row in a field sown with wheat.

Among the superstitions these are the most singular. A Highlander never begins any thing of consequence on the day of the week on which the 3rd of May falls, which he styles lagh sheachanna na bleanagh, or 'the dismal day'.

On the 1st of May, the herdsmen of every village hold their Beltein, a rural sacrifice: they cut a square trench on the ground, leaving the turf in the middle; on that they make a fire of wood, on which they dress a large caudle of eggs, butter, oatmeal and milk; and bring, besides the ingredients of the caudle, plenty of beer and whisky; for each of the company must contribute something. The rites begin with spilling some of the caudle on the ground, by way of libation: on that, everyone takes a cake of oatmeal, upon which are raised nine square knobs, each dedicated to some particular being, the supposed preserver of their flocks and herds, or to some particular animal, the real destroyer of them: each person then turns his face to the fire, breaks off a knob, and flinging it over his shoulders, says, 'This I give to thee, preserve thou my horses; this to thee, preserve thou my sheep'; and so on. After that, they use the same ceremony to the noxious animals: This I give to thee, O Fox! Spare thou my lambs; this to thee, O hooded Crow! This to thee, O Eagle!

When the ceremony is over they dine on the caudle; and after the feast is finished, what is left is hid by two persons deputed for that purpose; but on the next Sunday they re-assemble, and finish the relics of the first entertainment.

Pennant was incorrect in identifying Beltane so emphatically with May 1st. Beltane is indeed a first day, the end of the first lunar month of Spring. But the actual date in the old business calendar varied as the Moon's phases vary in their timing. Like Easter, Beltane is a Moon feast. Indeed, Beltane, the feast of Bal, is the Moon feast of the coming of summer, as Easter too is the celebration of the strengthening combined light of Sun and Moon. The degree to which Easter and Beltane diverge is simply the difference between different conventions of putting dates on the great calendar of the Sun and Moon. It is the relative positions of Sun and Moon that determine when spring actually arrives in any year. Birds laying their eggs follow the Moon to bring out their young when there is food to nourish them.

Beltane has been conventionalised to May Day. In agricultural societies, Beltane was the day that it was safe to drive into the fields those cattle that had been over-wintered. 'Ne'er cast a cloot till May be oot', says the traditional Scottish saying from my childhood. Never remove your warm underclothes until the Mayflower opens its petals, means the rhyme. When that flower opens it signifies that there is little further danger of severe night frost. Like the timing of the first cuckoo, this is an important signal for all whose livelihood depends entirely on the success of their crops and their animals. The conditions that enable the flowering of the May depend on the warmth of the Sun and the weather impact of the Moon combined.

Pennant was gathering data that would in the following century be combined with observations across Europe. These tell us that across Europe peasant rituals marked the arrival of such important moments in the agricultural calendar. The old Celtic name for the feast of the start of summer is said to derive from a god Beli or Belenus. This appears to be an old god of whom no actual stories remain. But there are Romano-British inscriptions to Apollo Belenus, indicating the deity's close association with the attributes of the Sun god.

Beltane was a great festival of the return of the power of the Sun and Moon. It was thus marked by two great fires and flares. The wood burned represented every type of tree. The flame to light them was struck by rubbing sticks together. These great fires were lit at the same time to signify the combining strength of Sun and Moon working together. All domestic animals and the whole agricultural community passed in ceremony between these two great fires. Passing between these frighteningly hot fires signified purification from all the diseases attracted during the cold of winter. Sweating in the heat of these flames did help purge some intractable winter illnesses. This was akin to the typical child in the early to mid 20th century, who would be ritually held over the pot of melting tar to clear the bronchial cough. Brands lit from the fires were taken to each house to kindle a new fire to bless the young agricultural year of work and growth. The Beltane fire is replicated in modern Christianity in the Paschal fire. Struck from flint to fire the Paschal candle this then kindles the candle held by each participant at the Easter vigil. This represents the resurrected soul of each repentant sinner.

This was a time of exceptional joy; those still alive had survived the horrors of winter. It was accompanied in old Scotland by a great party. This party tended to get rather physical. Even newly-weds could get exceptionally hyped. The more straight-laced, as William Burness seems to have been, at least later in life, could on reflection be more than a bit embarrassed by their Beltane enthusiasm, if only for his wife's sake. The sour-faced Scottish Presbyterians frowned.

Robert Burns was born on 25th January, 1759. Beltane fell on the full moon nearest to 1st May. The phases of the Moon show that in 1758 this occurred at the right time to enable an embryo conceived that day to have the incubation time necessary for a full-term human infant born on Burns's date of birth. Our infant was conceived during the most powerful of old Celtic festivities. He was an infant blessed by all the ancient gods of fertility and creativity. It confused general understanding when Currie published the birth date as 29th January. However, the Register of Births for the Parish of Ayr shows 25th January, as indicated in the poet's own rhyming record of the date. That verse about his birth was not published until 1808.

Death rituals also interested Pennant. He was not involved in such during his first tour in Scotland, but had previously come across them in Ireland. In writing up his Scottish tour, in order to recount Scottish customs, he described his experience of a funeral in Kerry.

> On the death of a Highlander, the corpse being stretched on a board, and covered with a coarse linen wrapper, the friends lay on the breast of the deceased a wooden platter,

containing a small quantity of salt and earth, separate and unmixed; the earth, an emblem of the corruptible body; the salt, an emblem of the immortal spirit. All fire is extinguished where a corpse is kept; and it is reckoned so ominous, for a dog or cat to pass over it, that the poor animal is killed without mercy.

The late wake is a ceremony used at funerals: the evening after the death of any person, the relations and friends of the deceased meet at the house, attended by bagpipe or fiddle; the nearest of kin, be it wife, son, or daughter, open a melancholy ball, dancing and greeting, i.e. crying violently at the same time; and this continues till daylight; but with such gambols and frolics, among the younger part of the company, that the loss which occasioned them is often more than supplied by the consequences of the night. If the corpse remains unburied for two nights the same rites are renewed. Thus, Scythian-like, they rejoice at the deliverance of their friends out of this life of misery.

The coronach, or singing at funerals, is still in use in some places: the songs are generally in praise of the deceased; or a recital of the valiant deeds of him, or ancestors.

When he recounted women's rituals he often appended lists of herbal and natural cures used by people who, living in remote places, lacked Enlightenment treatment of trained medics. In the following quotation he described practices he thought superstitious fancies:

The notion of second sight still prevails in a few places: as does the belief of fairies; and children are watched till the christening is over, lest they should be stolen, or changed. Midwives give new-born babes a small spoonful of earth and whisky, as the first food they taste.

Elf-shots, i.e. the stone arrow heads of the old inhabitants of this island, are supposed to be weapons shot by fairies at cattle, to which are attributed any disorders they have: in order to effect a cure, the cow is to be touched by an elf-shot, or made to drink the water in which one has been dipped. The same virtue is said to be found in the crystal gems, and in the adder-stone, and it is also believed that good fortune must attend the owner.

Before women bake their bannocks, or oatmeal cakes, they make a cross on the last.

He was shown a particularly lucky stone by Captain Archibald Campbell. This was a spheroid set in silver. People would travel a hundred miles for its use. They would bring with them the water it was to be dipped in, to ensure its efficacy in the ultimate place of use.

After leaving Breadalbane, he reached north of Cromarty before he allowed himself again, in his first tour, to be distracted by superstitious practices. His interest was aroused by the story of a woman who, failed by medical men, had been successfully treated by a woman 'skilled in physic'. He learned too that in Thurso a man had chased and cut off the leg of one of three cats that had tormented him. Next day he met an old woman with one leg. This 'proved' she was one of his three tormenting witches. He had already passed Thane's Cross near which in June 1727 a woman was burned for witchcraft.

This was judicial murder, for laws against witchcraft had been repealed only on March 24th 1736. Then, the statute of 1JacI entitled 'An Act against conjuration, witchcraft, and the dealing with evil and wicked spirits' had been removed from the English statute books, as well as removing from Scottish law the act entitled 'Anent Witchcrafts'. England's last judicial murder was as late as 1712. Then Jane Wenham of Walkern, Hertfordshire, had been executed under the English law.

Pennant remarked, though, that Scotland should not be considered credulous for so late a witch burning as 1727. Many in London in 1762 believed in the Cock Lane Ghost. In nearby Tring there had been in 1751 a witch scare with tragic consequences.

Within a few paragraphs, however, Pennant was recounting the possible use of brochs as temples of Picts. Their central atrium he imaginatively explained as designed for capturing blood of human sacrifices, which would then be sprinkled as a blessing over homes and tools.

Reaching the north shore where he got his first view of the Orkney Islands, Pennant was shown the home of a gentleman who, in life, had the second sight. He had a spectral premonition of the drowning of the crew of one of his boats. Pennant had been told of another incidence of second sight by Duncan Forbes of Culloden House. Before the tragedy of 1746 he had declared:

"All these disturbances will be terminated on this spot."

In these northern lands, he found other customs:

On New Year's Day they burn juniper before their cattle, and on the first Monday in every quarter sprinkle them with urine.

He found a different form of Beltane celebration:

A cross is cut on some sticks, which is dipped in pottage, and the Thursday before Easter one of each placed over the sheep-cot, the stable, or the cow-house. On the 1st of May they are carried to the hill where the Beltein is celebrated, all decked with wild flowers, and after the feast is over, replaced over the spots they were taken from.

He noted that these pagan practices were being stamped out by the clergy, but were persisting in secret along with other beliefs and practices.

In certain places, the death of people is supposed to be foretold by the cries and shrieks of the Benshi, or the fairy's wife, uttered along the very path where the funeral is to pass; and what in Wales are called 'corps candles' are often imagined to appear, and foretell mortality.

During the marriage ceremony, great care is taken that dogs do not pass between [the parties] and particular attention is paid to leaving the bridegroom's left shoe without buckle or latchet to prevent witches from depriving him, on the nuptial night, of the power of loosening the virgin zone.

The book of Pennant's Scottish tour with voyage to the Hebrides of 1772, published in two volumes between 1774 and 1776 is four times longer than his first work on Scotland. It has a commensurate amount of esoteric material, although begins more sparsely endowed. This edition seems at first to hint that the tolerance he had built up by the end of his first journey has given way to exasperation. But he soon dispelled that impression. His reportage became more that of the non-judgemental objective historian aware that something important is passing out of existence. He had had in 1769 a personal vision of the devastating effects of the demise of the old social contract of the pre-Culloden Highlands. For his expanded edition, he ended his first volume with this vision.

This near-reversal of attitude might have been caused by what was happening in his own back yard at Whitford in North Wales. Pennant's 'Antiquities of Whitford and Holywell' was published in 1797 in response to the emergence of an immense industrial world, which itself has now vanished. Once there rose a powerful spring in the sacred shrine of St Winifred at nearby Holywell. Its water fell over 200 feet to the Dee estuary. Pennant listed how by the end of the 18th century this drove one mill wheel after another, the outflow from each gathered in an appropriate reservoir for the next. This had become as good a model for Dante's Descent into Hell as the mediaeval industrial complex at the birthplace shrine of St Catherine of Siena.

Mediaeval monks who were custodians of the holy well used just over seven feet of the water's fall to drive a modest corn mill for essential food. It was mainly during Pennant's lifetime from his birth in Whitford in 1716 to the time when he compiled this list in 1797 that full use was first made of the water for industry. Every scrap of the potential energy of that falling water was harnessed by industrial entrepreneurs. By 1797 water-power itself had been substantially overtaken by great smoke-belching furnaces that augmented the pollution of the forges previously water driven. Coal had by then already mostly replaced water pressure in driving hammers and machinery. The water was now used within new filthy factory processes, spilling liquid pollution onto the Dee shore.

Falls of the Holywell Stream, in feet		
Cotton Twist Co	spring to 'corn mill'	7½
Cotton Twist Co	Upper Cotton Mill	20
Cotton Twist Co	Old Cotton Mill	11½
Cotton Twist Co	Crescent Cotton Mill	13½
Greenfield Copper & Brass Co	Brass rolling mill	23¾
Greenfield Copper & Brass Co	Copper rolling mill	21½
Greenfield Copper & Brass Co	Old Copper Forge	21½
Parys Mine Company	Copper wire mill	23
Parys Mine Company	Copper rolling mill	21¾
Cotton Twist Co	Lower cotton mill	28
Parys Mine Company	Copper forge	10¾
	total	202¾

The mediaeval holy well was now dominated by copper production mainly used in armaments and ship enhancement for opposing Britain's commercial enemies. These were Dark Satanic Mills cursing the very heart of ancient Celtic Christianity in an area that by the mid 18th century was already being consumed by considerable expansion of mining for coals and metals.

Before 1733 there had been smelting works but

> the smoke did such injury to the fine woods belonging to Sir George Mostyn of Trelacre, bart. as to occasion many law-suits between Sir George and the company.

Sir George was Pennant's neighbour and friend. He won his Action despite having lost his first suit on a technicality: he wrongly called himself Sir George when his elder brother, a Roman Catholic priest, was still alive in Rome.

Pennant recalled how, in his youth, a white lead and a red lead works were established in Holywell. There had already been a tilting mill and an iron wire mill. There had once been three snuff mills, which had gone out of business. When the cotton company arrived and then expanded, it demolished their buildings. In 1758 the old smelting works was leased by Champion, agent of the

Chapter III *Beltane Babe*

Wormley Company near Bristol,

> who calcined black-jack. He was the first who engaged in such a concern in this country, and probably in Great Britain, which he carried on under the protection of a patent.

In 1764 a pin mill was built on the site of the old abbey corn mill. The pin maker, James Eden, operated it for two years, but his business failed. It subsequently became a paper mill, run by a Mrs Chambers. In 1766 the first battering mill for copper and brass was established, to supply the British navy with sheathing for ships. The digging of the foundation for the brass smelting house uncovered the hypocaust of a Roman bath house. That year in Whitford, with similar foundations in other 'mineral' parishes, was founded a club of 240 members,

> instituted for the support of members in case of illness and accidents.

The club had a celebration each New Year's Day. Pennant came to regard this as a very colourful occasion. He enjoyed the sight of all the miners and their wives and children dressed in their very best. But he also became increasingly aware of industrial tragedies and health risks.

In 1785, in the space of ten weeks in the summer, a great cotton works was constructed. Pennant watched this achievement with astonishment. The mill owners also built two great dormitories, one each for male and female workers. In 1787 a new rolling mill was set up. Industry continued to develop. The population continued to explode. Pollution continued to worsen. Roads began to run through former farmland now devoid of agriculture and crowded with traffic. Birds ceased to sing as they had done of old.

As Pennant watched all these changes they perhaps had a subconscious effect. His perception of the nature of the industrial revolution was altered. This had been spawned by the Enlightenment. It was a movement that could produce much that was clearly not good. Perhaps his consciousness was already affected when he undertook his second journey. He was gradually influenced further during the following years when he edited the correspondence he received from his Scottish contacts and prepared for publication the first and then the second volume of the revised journal.

In 1772 for his second journey through Scotland he travelled north from Whitford through Lancashire and Cumberland. In Keswick the antiquarian in him noted the 'Druid' circle, the first of many comments on prehistoric sites and general antiquities. He observed that until recently Beltane was still celebrated in the area, with locals bringing boughs of mountain ash.

In the borderlands he met active superstition:

> A farmer I met with here told me, that a pebble, naturally perforated, was an infallible cure, hung over a horse that was hag-ridden, or troubled with nocturnal sweats.

Witches had been burned at Langholm in the 17th century. There still remained a belief that midwives could transfer birthing pain from the woman to her child's father.

> I saw the reputed offspring of such a labour; who kindly came into the world without giving her mother the least uneasiness, while the poor husband was roaring with agony in his uncouth and unnatural pains.

Pennant was informed that the brank, the torture for women accused of being scolds, had been used in the month prior to his visit to Langholm. It cut terribly the face of the woman. A contemporary 'expert' considered this instrument preferable to the alternative of the ducking stool. That endangered health without subduing scolding.

Nothing else gave Pennant cause to comment until he reached Paisley. There in 1679 twenty were condemned for witchcraft. Five women were burned. One man died of strangulation while being tortured to extract confession.

At Loch Lomond he visited Buchanan Castle, seat of the Duke of Montrose. There he recalled that detractors of James, Marquis of Montrose, heroic soldier of the 17th century, claimed that witches were consulted at his birth. They predicted he would be trouble for Scotland. They said he had in infancy eaten a venomous toad.

On the Isle of Arran, the tomb of St Maolios had been broken into about six months before Pennant visited it. The treasure hunter found nothing, and soon broke a leg in punishment for his sacrilege. On the island, a curious new superstition had emerged. Pleurisy was common; it was proposed that bleeding would assist cure,

> but it is now performed with the utmost regularity at spring and fall. The Duke of Hamilton keeps a surgeon in pay; who at those seasons makes a tour of the island. On notice of his approach, the inhabitants of each farm assemble in the open air; extend their arms; and are bled into a hole made in the ground, the common receptacle of the vital fluid. In burning fevers a tea of wood sorrel is used with success, to allay the heat. An infusion of ramsons or Allium ursinum in brandy is esteemed here a good remedy for the gravel.

Pennant next encountered superstitions on Jura. Old women kept a stick of the mountain ash, or wicken tree, to ward against elves. They murmured incantations when applying cures. On Isla, Pennant challenged local stories that seeds and even animals and driftwood were borne across the Atlantic from the Caribbean, but had to bow to strong evidence. He found vipers swarming in the heath, and learned that locals considered that a sword on which their poison had fallen would hiss in water as if it were red hot. They believed poultice of human excrement cured the bite. Old customs prevailed:

> The late wakes or funerals, like those of the Romans, were attended with sports, and dramatic entertainments, composed of many parts, and the actors often changed their dresses suitable to their characters. The subject of the drama was historical preserved by memory.

Pennant observed that Columba of Iona is the first on record with the second sight, reported as announcing the victory of Aidan just as in due course it transpired. Since the Reformation, superstition had caused pilgrims to chip off a piece of the white marble altar of the church on Iona, as a piece of it guaranteed success in any undertaking. Naturally, Pennant did not mean his readers to think that it was superstition that caused himself and those with him to break off pieces of the altar for their own future good fortune. He found genuine fear of the evil eye:

> If the good housewife perceives the effect of the malicious on any of her kine, she takes as much milk as she can drain from the enchanted herd, for the witch commonly leaves very little. She then boils it with certain herbs, and adds to them flints and untempered steel: after that she secures the door, and invokes the three sacred persons. This puts the witch in such an agony, that she comes willy-nilly to the house, begs to be admitted, to obtain relief by touching the powerful pot: the good woman then makes her terms; the witch restores the milk to the cattle, and in return is freed from her pains.

But sometimes to save the trouble of those charms (for it may happen that the disorder may arise from other causes than an evil eye), the trial is made by immersing in milk a certain herb, and if the cows are supernaturally affected, it instantly distils blood.

The unsuccessful lover revenges himself on his rival by .. taking three threads of different hues, and ties three knots on each, three times imprecating the most cruel disappointments on the nuptial bed: but the bridegroom to avert the harm, stands at the altar with an untied shoe, and puts a sixpence beneath his foot.

He noted inhabitants of Rum and Cannay believed in the second sight. He gave two examples of local people then alive who were credited with it. It was said that those with the gift would:

fall into trances, foam at the mouth, grow pale, and feign to abstain from food for a month, so overpowered are they by the visions imparted to them during their paroxysms.

On the Isle of Cannay Pennant became aware of a custom for which he could elicit no history or reason. The island had abundance of horses, which seemed to have but one use:

They form an annual cavalcade at Michaelmas. Every man on the island mounts his horse unfurnished with saddle, and takes behind him either some young girl, or his neighbour's wife, and then rides backwards and forwards from the village to a certain cross .. After the procession is over, they alight at some public house, where, strange to say, the females treat the companions of their ride. When they retire to their houses an entertainment is prepared with primeval simplicity: the chief part consists of a great oatcake, called struan Michaeil, or 'St Michael's cake' composed of two pecks of meal, and formed like the quadrant of a circle: it is daubed over with milk and eggs, and then placed to harden before the fire.

Writing of these island experiences in the first volume of his second tour Pennant showed impatience elsewhere controlled. This impatience showed again when describing several gifts of antiquities he was given on Skye. One was a serpent stone. This was a triangular bead engraved with a serpent pattern. It was possibly an Iron Age production. Such were supposed to protect their bearer. He related:

The vulgar of the present age attribute to it virtues; such as curing the bite of the adder and giving ease to women in childbirth, if tied about the knee. So difficult is it to root out follies that have the sanction of antiquity.

On Skye, other superstitions had successfully been suppressed. No-one boasted of the second sight, nor of the help of Robin Goodfellow.

This serviceable sprite was wont to clean the houses, help to churn, thrashed the corn, and would belabour all who pretended to make jest of him. He was represented as stout and blooming, had fine flowing hair, and went about with a wand in his hand.

However, Gruagach, or Grianich, the fair haired Sun god, celebrated on a Roman stone found in Musselborough, still had vestigial following. Formerly he was offered libations of milk.

Milkmaids still retain the custom by pouring some on certain stones that bear his name.

Other superstitions had also been suppressed:

A wild species of magic was practised in the district of Trotterness, that was attended with a horrible solemnity. A family who pretended to oracular knowledge practised these ceremonies. In this country is a vast cataract, whose waters falling from a high rock, jet so far as to form a dry hollow beneath, between them and the precipice. One of these impostors was sewed up in the hide of an ox, and to add terror to the ceremony, was placed in this concavity: the trembling enquirer was brought to the place, where the shade and the roaring of the waters increased the dread of the occasion. The question is put, and the person in the hide delivers his answer, and so ends this species of divination styled taghairm.

He had more respect for the sailors' tale that the presence of a flock of storm petrels following close to a boat meant a storm was gathering. A little later he travelled through the desolate hinterland of Assynt. He was horrified to discover that, a mere three years earlier, a capable woman there had been strangled by children when a rival had put about suspicion that she was a witch.

He travelled by rowing boat to Inchmaree where he found what he considered a Druidical site, reinvented as the shrine of a Christian saint.

A stump of a tree is shown as an altar, probably the memorial of one of stone; but the curiosity of the place is the well of the saint; of power unspeakable in cases of lunacy. The patient is brought into the sacred island, is made to kneel before the altar, where his attendants leave an offering in money: he is then brought to the well, and sips some of the holy water: a second offering is made; that done, he is thrice dipped in the lake; and the same operation is repeated every day for some weeks: and it often happens, by natural causes, the patient receives relief, of which the saint receives the credit. I must add that the visitants draw from the state of the well an omen of the disposition of St Maree: if his well is full, they suppose he will be propitious; if not, they proceed in their operations with fears and doubts: but let the event be what it will, he is held in high esteem; the common oath of the country is by his name: if a traveller passes by any of his resting places, they never neglect to leave an offering; but the saint is so moderate as not to put him to any expense: a stone, a stick, a bit of rag contents him.

Madness was also cured by St Fillan, carer of the insane, as his followers continued to believe in Pennant's day. This too involved offering rags to some Earth spirit, after leading the insane person 'daisil'. This meant turning from east to west thrice round a local cairn, thrice immersing the patient in a holy pool of the river, and then leaving him bound in a local ruined chapel. There, if he survived the night and was found loose in the morning, he was considered cured. A relic of St Fillan was carried before Robert Bruce at Bannockburn.

It was about this stage of his journal that the change began to show in Pennant's writing. He proposed that many of the herbal remedies still in common use by Highlanders would be worth scientifically trialling. Cream was boiled till it became oil and then used for anointing burns. He enumerated a range of natural cures. These were mainly hot toddies of various sorts. One used stale urine and bran poultice for rheumatism. Carrot poultice helped contain cancer. Now began his first comments about the negative effects of the conquest of Scotland by the so-called civilised south: Cromwell's soldiers introduced to the Highlands the hideous venereal diseases called Sivvens. One cure required cold plunge baths followed by a sweat-out. Had he spoken with Burns, Pennant would have learned that this was prescribed to the poet in his childhood when the heavy exertions of excessive farm work first brought on that so called hypochondria. Those plunge baths in youth probably worsened his condition. In due course they would be the death of him.

Chapter III   *Beltane Babe*

Pennant found fevers and colds to be the common diseases. The illness called glacach involved a tightness and fullness of the chest, like incipient consumption. Pennant was scathing of supposed cure through the laying on of hands:

> A family of the name of MacDonald .. touch the part, and mutter certain charms; but, to their credit, never accept a fee on any entreaty.

He ended his first volume clearly affected by the accumulation of all his observations of the Hebrides and Western Highlands, of beginnings of Clearances, the emerging practice of mass exploitation of renewable land and sea natural resources (such as logging, intensive fishing, seashell and seaweed harvesting). He indicated concern for lack of plans for sustainability, increasing poverty caused by rack-renting, ills of absentee landlordism, and firmness of foreign factors who saw land as an economic input and people as dumb labour. Emigration was increasing and becoming extensive. He left his readers awaiting his second volume with his vision of an ancient Highland chieftain, caring father of his clan, mournful of the passing of old ways. At the start of his second volume of this second tour, he thought it worthwhile to enumerate various superstitions so that a record would remain of them:

> After marriage, the bride immediately walks round the church, unattended by the bridegroom. The precaution of loosening every knot about the new-joined pair is strictly observed. . Matrimony is avoided in the month of January, but, what is more singular, the ceremony is avoided even in the enlivening month of May. . After baptism, the first meat that the company tastes is crowdie, a mixture of meal and water, or meal and ale thoroughly mixed. Of this every person takes three spoonfuls.

> The mother never sets about any work until she had been 'kirked'. In the Church of Scotland there is no ceremony on the occasion: but the woman, attended by some of her neighbours, goes into the church, sometimes in service time, but oftener when it is empty; goes out again, surrounds it, refreshes herself at some public house, and then returns home. Before the ceremony she is looked on as unclean, never is permitted to eat with the family; nor will any one eat of the victuals she has dressed.

> It has happened that, after baptism, the father has placed a basket, filled with bread and cheese, on the pot-hook that impended over the fire in the middle of the room, which the company sit around; and the child is thrice handed across the fire, with the design to frustrate all attempts of evil spirits, or evil eyes. This originally seems to have been designed as a purification, and of idolatrous origin, as the Israelites made their children pass through the fire to Moloch.

> The word used for charms in general is colas or 'knowledge', a proof of the high repute they were once held in. Other charms were called paiders, a word taken from the Pater Noster. A necklace was called padreuchain, because on turning every bead they used one of the paiders. Other charms again are called toisgeuls, from the use of particular verses from the Gospel.

> The superstition of making pilgrimages to certain wells or chapels is still preserved. That to St Fillan's is much in vogue: and others again to different places. The object is relief from the disorders mankind labour under. In some places the pilgrims only drink of the water: in others, they undergo immersion.

A Highlander, in order to protect himself from any harms apprehended from the fairy tribe, will draw round himself a circle with a sapling of the oak. This may be a relic of Druidism; and only a continuation of the respect paid to the tree held in such veneration by the priesthood of our ancestors.

They pay great attention to their lucky and unlucky days. The Romans could not be more attentive on similar occasions: and surely the Highlander may be excused the superstition, since Augustus could say, that he never went abroad on the day following the nundinae, nor began any serious undertaking on the nonae, and that, merely to avoid the unluck omen. The Scottish mountaineers esteem the May 14th unfortunate, and the day of the week that it happened to fall on.

They are also very classical in observing what they first meet on the commencement of a journey. They consider the looks, garb and character of the first person they see. If he has a good countenance, is decently clad, and has a fair reputation, they rejoice in the omen. If the contrary, they proceed with fears, or return home, and begin their journey a second time.

The Beltein, or the rural sacrifice, on the first of May, O.S. has been mentioned before. Hallow Eve is also kept sacred: as soon as it is dark, a person sets fire to a bush of broom fastened round a pole: and, attended with a crowd, runs round the village. He then flings it down, heaps great quantities of combustible matters on it, and makes a great bonfire. A whole tract is thus illuminated at the same time, and makes a fine appearance. The carrying of the fiery pole appears to be a relic of Druidism.

The Highlanders form a sort of almanac or presage of the weather of the ensuing year in the following manner. They make observations for twelve days, beginning at the last of December, and hold as an infallible rule, that whatsoever weather happens on each of those days, the same will prove to agree in the corresponding months.

Pennant found all those beliefs active during his journeys. Others were obsolete, such as the fostering out of Highland children. In his travels, Pennant experienced the old hospitality of the Highlands. This was changing – the cause: impoverishment resulting from the hardening attitudes of landlords and the presumption of curious visitors whose numbers had greatly increased. The distinguishing character of Highlanders that persisted, at least in the time he travelled, was fidelity.

His return home took him through Northumberland and Durham and thence west. In compiling his text he was very aware that he had visited a foreign land. It was not simply a land in which the population of a large part spoke a very different language. It was also one in which those speaking English experienced life differently from the Englishmen of his acquaintance. Economic differences alone were sufficient to explain divergence of attitude. Scotland was clearly a very poor country.

A small proportion of Pennant's words on the Scotland of his day relate to superstition or esoteric thought. But he considered this aspect so important that in presenting Scotland to his readers he felt it imperative to list as an appendix original versions and translations of Gaelic proverbs that had been drawn to his attention. Amongst these are:

The eye of a friend is an unerring mirror.

Justice melts in the mouth of the feeble.

Strong is the feeble in the bosom of might.

The luxurious poor will never be rich.

And most relevant to the consideration of old knowledge embodied in the unsophisticated:

Fools often give wise advice.

Perhaps Pennant had noted that, already in 1763, Edmund Stone had described an old wives' treatment of fever using willow bark, from which aspirin was later derived.

The Enlightenment society with whom Pennant mixed in the cities, towns and fine houses in Scotland's richer areas did not give him any awareness of an undercurrent of old beliefs beneath them. True, the ministers of religion ranted on about Satan's Invisible World, and the constant presence of real forces of evil. But witches and magic – that was not part of an Enlightenment man's polite conversation. Old wives' tales had no place in their talk. There was no young ploughman poet then, for him to talk to, who might have put him straight about the reality of the minds of the masses. But it was old wives and his very savvy young mother that raised the infant poet. It was into this ether teeming with stories of a parallel universe interacting with leading-edge developments in science that was born and raised the little baby Robert.

Key life events of Robert Burns

1759   Born 25th January at Alloway eldest child of self-employed gardener father and farm-trained mother. Elderly relative, Betty Davidson, lived with the family.

1765   Attended school at Alloway Mill but when this folded was taught privately, with other local children, by John Murdoch.

1766   Family moved to Mount Oliphant farm.

1768   End of schooling. Education continued from text books, under parents' direction, (mother unable to write). Burns read 'The Life of Hannibal'. Murdoch left him an English grammar and 'The School of Love' translated from French.

1772   At Dalrymple to learn penmanship. Murdoch appointed to Ayr School and gave Burns the works of Pope.

1773   In Ayr for 3 weeks to study English, French and some Latin, boarding with and studying under Murdoch.

1774   Paired with Nellie Kilpatrick at harvest; composed his first song, 'Handsome Nell'.

1775   Dispute with Mount Oliphant landlord. Malnutrition showing its effects on health. Began to borrow 'The Spectator' and read Pope's 'Homer'. He took dancing lessons in defiance of his father.

1777   Family moved to Lochlie Farm. Robert at Kirkoswald for a few weeks at school under Hugh Rodger to study mathematics, particularly mensuration and surveying. Formed friendship with school fellow William Niven. The two debated with each other. In spare moments he skulked under shelves in the local bookshop and managed there to read Thomson's Works, Shenstone's Works, 'A Select Collection of English Songs', Allan Ramsay's Works, Hervey's Meditations, and some of Shakespeare's plays. Got 'collection of letters' from Queen Anne's era. Began imaginary correspondences.

1780   Writing cutting satirical verse as critic of Auld Licht preachers. He met and later proposed to a girl whom biographers generally call Ellison Begbie, servant on a nearby farm on Cessnock Water. She refused him.

1781   Read Sterne's works, Macpherson's Ossian, Mackenzie's 'The Man of the World' and 'The Man of Feeling'. Became a Freemason in Tarbolton.

1782   Ventured into self-employed partnership in flax-dressing in Irvine. Defrauded by partner whose drunken wife also burned down the shop on Hogmanay. Read 'Pamela', 'Ferdinand, Count Fathom' and Fergusson's poems. Severely ill.

1784   Death of his father in February. With brother Gilbert farmed Mossgeil.

1786   Common law marriage with Jean Armour was denied and 'annulled' by her parents. Publication of Kilmarnock Edition on 7th August. Death of the so-called Highland Mary of fever. A myth surrounds an unsubstantiated story that she and Burns had a common law marriage on 14th May 1786. Went to Edinburgh in the autumn.

1787   3,000 copies of the Edinburgh edition published. Toured Borders, western Highlands, north-eastern Highlands and Stirlingshire. Began Clarinda correspondence. Began writing for Johnson's Musical Museum. Visited sites of innovation.

1788   Completed his course of Excise training at his own expense. Rented Ellisland Farm, and formally married Jean Armour. Jean stayed in Mauchline while he built a house on the farm, travelling frequently between Ellisland and Mauchline.

1790   Got his Excise Commission, and moved out of Ellisland into Dumfries. Work involved considerable travel on horseback, irrespective of weather.

1791   The song 'Sweet Afton' supposedly written this year. Managed for Robert Riddell the Monkland Friendly Society subscription book club, buying 150 books, many by leading Enlightenment thinkers.

1792   Writing for Thomson's 'National Songs and Melodies'. Bought for himself Erasmus Darwin's 'Botanic Garden' and 'Loves of the Plants' and Dugald Stewart's 'Elements of the philosophy of the Human Mind'.

1793   Moved in Dumfries to the house in which he died. Took a short tour of Galloway. 'Scots, wha hae' written. Supervised an expanded Creech edition of his poems.

1795   Wrote election ballads and 'A Man's a Man for a' That'. Final illness began showing in last quarter of the year and he died on 21st July 1796.

Chapter IV *Out of the Garden*

How Burns should have been born the son of a rich gardener and instead learned that Galileo caused one-track thinking that enabled cold science to control and enslave people.

It is the modern way for people to be asked to provide their curriculum vitae, appended, as appropriate, with a summary of their key publications. This lets their worth be assessed before they are granted any kind of patronage, whether paid or voluntary employment, or permission to do anything that requires the consent of others. So, for a book written at the start of the 21st century, it is worth summarising Robert's life in such a way. Then we can assess his career on equal terms with the résumé of any other person. Thus we can judge him by the modern criterion that anyone who deviates far from norms or averages is a suspect person.

Suspect persons are automatically up against considerable hurdles when asked to produce a résumé in accepted formats. These documents are, after all, a measure of conformity – will the candidate be fit for a post like a pole hammered into a hole. They are seldom a test of the imagination, capability or other suitability of the person for real human environments they seek to enter. But, since this is the way of the modern world, I have in the table here listed the key events of the career of Burns in the regulation dated table format. It makes sense too to present a short textual summary for Robert Burns, if only to demonstrate how meaningless bald facts can be in assessing any character of outstanding value.

His career can be summarised in a few hundred words. Robert Burns was born poor in Ayrshire. He survived a miserably impoverished childhood. He rose above this through laughter, verse and music, but was disabled throughout life by internal weakness to heart and lungs. This was brought on by childhood exposure and labour and aggravated by toil and further deprivation later in life. He intended emigration in 1786 and published his poems to have something to show for the years of his youth. Their immediate critical acclaim by Edinburgh literati persuaded him to produce a second edition. Its financial success enabled him to provide the capital for the rest of his father's family to achieve a sound income and himself to consider remaining in Scotland. Recognising the economic instability and uncertainty around him, he invested some of his small remaining capital to retrain as an Exciseman. Having applied for an appointment, he allowed himself to be persuaded meanwhile to take a lease on a derelict farm near Dumfries. After another failure at farming, he got a lowly Excise posting. He spent the rest of his short life supporting his wife and children by earning his keep as a very hard working despised civil servant. He spent what free time he could muster writing songs and more poems. These included his famous compositions 'Scots, wha hae wi' Wallace bled', 'Tam o' Shanter' and 'A Man's a man for a' that'. The extreme work involved in his Excise duties aggravated his health defects, which finally killed him when he was merely thirty seven years old. The republication of his poems augmented by his personal letters generated sufficient to ensure that all his dependents had an adequate lifestyle.

Such are the bald facts. The modern typical Human Resources professional would not react positively to them. To judge by those I have had to work alongside too often in business, many would conclude that we have here someone who is shiftless. He has been unsuccessful in real work and had one flash-in-the-pan writing success that he tried to live off, using it as an excuse for not focussing on real work.

To compensate for such dismissal, on this thin skeleton, biographers have over two centuries reconstructed a plastic replica of his visible identity. They have used inferences in his verses, the limited mass of letters that survived the purging of his first biographer Currie, and the enormous heap of hearsay and anecdote that was piled like decaying flowers round the impertinent mausoleum and the vacuous museums that sprouted like weeds as his spirit reunited with the great elemental of the universe.

But what this man really thought and why he is remembered still today in so many disparate corners of the world is not answered for me in any of those so expansive and authoritative tomes of the cohorts of academics who have made careers on the celebration of a ploughman poet. His soul is not there. I found myself searching for his soul.

He had wondered what of a Man survives death:

> "If that part of us called Mind does survive the apparent destruction of the man – away with old-wife prejudices and tales! Every age and every nation had a different set of stories; and as the many are always weak, of consequence they have often, perhaps always been deceived: a man, conscious of having acted an honest part amongst his fellow creatures, even granting that he may have been a sport at times of passions and instincts, he goes to a great unknown Being who could have no other end in giving him existence but to make him happy; who gave him those passions and instincts, and well knows their force."

This he wrote just before he left Mossgeil to go via Galston and Newmilns to Glasgow, and thence to make his second visit to Edinburgh. The second sight he claimed to have had warned him that his contemporary and friend, Robert Muir, lay dying. He wished to console him with his belief that a good man had nothing to fear of the hereafter. Burns got this message very strongly from his father, for all his irascible nature and stubbornness.

William Burness, the father of Robert Burns, is normally thought as being portrayed in the farmer in the poem 'The Cottar's Saturday Night'. This was from its first publication in the Kilmarnock edition considered to be the masterpiece of this heaven-taught poet. It is still one of the most read, because it is in near-English and is in a simple stanza form. That makes it more accessible than most of Burns's poems. It also means that a view of the poet's father is perpetuated – a view that may not conform to how Burns actually saw him. The cottar in that poem is not the man that Burns hinted at in his autobiographical letter.

While there may be misrepresentation of the everyday character of the man, it is certainly the case that the profession in which he was trained was little understood by most biographers. That aspect of his father's influence is thus very thinly considered. To understand the thoughts of Robert Burns it would surely help if we understood more of how those thoughts formed. It is not sufficient to interpret names of professions, or historical incident, merely from the modern perspective; we should surely try to understand these within the context of their contemporary communities.

The poet's father was an odd man in the Ayrshire countryside. He arrived from the northeast via Edinburgh to be Head Gardener of the Doonholm estate, south of Ayr. It is said that there, amongst his tasks, he planted trees and created the roadway alongside the river. He spoke as if he aspired to be a gentleman. He avoided the patois of ordinary labourers. He carried with him always a letter of attestation that he had had no part 'in the recent disturbances'. That last attempt by the senior male Stuart line to regain the British kingdoms was still very recent! It has bequeathed to modern times the continuing legends of Bonnie Prince Charlie's vain march south as far as Derby and of the Duke of Cumberland's brutality at and after Culloden in 1746. In the wake of the failure of the famous '45 there were massive emigrations from Scotland. This was not simply due to desire by many to remove themselves from the yoke of foreign overlords; it was also the result of slash-and-burn tactics by both sides in the conflict. That had destroyed the already fragile Scottish economy. Thus, internally there was also movement. For decades after every stranger was suspect.

Many great estates of Jacobite sympathisers were confiscated by the Hanoverian Crown. Great was the disruption, as land-based workers and professionals discovered that the new owners regarded old ways of land management as weighed down with political baggage quite apart from undesirable uneconomic tenants. Those disciplined in the Scottish professional ways of working land had to rethink themselves to survive.

William Burness was a fully qualified gardener. Born in 1721 and living until 1784, he was one of nine children. He was the third son of Robert Burnes and Isabella Keith. Robert, in the year that William was born, became tenant of the farm of Clochnahill within the Dunottar estate of the Earl Marischal. The Earl was attainted in 1716 for his role in the Jacobite rising of 1715.

In recent years a monument has been raised on the west side of the main Dundee-Aberdeen road near what Robert Burns knew on maps as Stonehive, now called Stonehaven, overlooking the lands of Clochnahill. Dunottar is noted in Scottish history as the hiding place during the Cromwellian conflicts of the Honours of Scotland – the Scottish crown jewels, now displayed in Edinburgh castle. These ancient and, to many, sacred relics were smuggled out of Dunottar castle only hours before Oliver Cromwell's soldiers captured the castle. They were hidden under a floor of the local church. Recovered for the coronation of Charles II, they were in 1707, when Scotland ceased to have an independent Parliament and became mere North Britain, placed in a chest that was sealed behind a wall of Edinburgh castle. They were not rediscovered until Sir Walter Scott, following the trail of old documents, had the wall broken down in 1822. Their saving and disappearance were part of the folklore William Burness carried to Ayrshire and instilled in the childhood mind of the poet.

His father's gardening background is seldom more than mentioned in modern studies of Robert Burns. It was noted at Kilmarnock on the first centenary of publication of the Kilmarnock edition. The great parade that took place that 7th August, during the Trades Holiday, included a large representation of Free Gardeners. These were the most numerous professional contingent in the whole grand parade. In contrast, it was not cultivated flowers that were brought to deck the statue of Robert Burns. Great bunches of large wild daisies were laid in turn by each of 150 young girls.

Robert Burnes was himself one of the five sons of James Burnes of Birness (1655 - 1743) and Margaret Falconer. James was born while those jewels were still hidden near Dunottar. He died at the grand old age of 87. He believed he had left all five sons secure. With the other four each set up on a farm, Robert the eldest starting out on Kinmonth, Robert's brother James continued the tenancy of their father's farm of Brolinmuir. Then came the Rising and those best laid schemes went agley.

The father of James was Walter Burnece, who had been left without means when his father Walter died. James's father trained in gardening, but by putting aside personal savings was able to take on, until his death in 1670, the farm of Bogjorgan in the parish of Glenbervie.

Generation after generation, Robert Burns's paternal ancestors followed the ancient trade of Adam, toiling in the garden. While knowledge and lore was passed on from age to age, by the 17th century in Scotland gardening had become a respected professional activity.

Yet a century after Burns, the Scottish writer Robert Louis Stevenson, in a recollection of his old gardener, illustrated how far respect for that profession had fallen by the second half of the 19th century. The old gardener acted with that gentility which is all that is left when real income has vanished. He spoke of his youth working in the parks of castles. There his army of under-gardeners had treated him with due respect as he surveyed the meres, swanneries, walks, woods, wildernesses, shrubberies, rose beds, kitchen enclosure and herbaria that were his responsibility. Stevenson felt that it was the old man's poverty and not his desire that made him tend the miniature parklands of affluent Edinburgh suburbia. Stevenson felt unwillingly humbled in the realisation that economic reality made this proud professional man its meanest servant.

Today most people think of gardening as something to pass the time, or intrude on free time. This is the small householder's reaction to the passing of any need in him to cultivate for food his allotment of ground or the plot around his tiny domestic castle-home. The modern concept of 'gardening leave', in which an executive, perfunctorily removed from his post, is debarred from the office during the period in which he serves formal notice of dismissal, denigrates the craft of horticulture. This skill is at the heart of the modern craft gardener's mysteries. But even to consider gardening as focused on horticulture is to denigrate substantially the range of skills demanded of the Scots gardener from the 17th century to the early part of the 19th century.

During this period, a gardener was expected to fulfil all the tasks required of land management in an extensive estate. He would be as capable of surveys, land assessment for worth, land improvement, land sculpting, canal-cutting, irrigation (and by the way man-management for the effective fulfilment of the operational completion of all of such responsibilities), as he would be at the design, planting and management of forests, parkland for animal and bird culture, the food and medical herb production such as is now called market gardening (then called kitchen gardening), fruit and orchard design, planting and management, and recreational gardening around the grand houses of the aristocracy and gentry. The true gardener was a master both of the long-term view and detailed day to day undertaking of this extensive scope of work. He would not only require to have those 'green fingers' that we think of today as an instinctive sympathy with the ways of botany translated into hostile environments for the service of man. Equally he must have those mathematical skills of the land and quantity surveyor and the geologist-geographer's feel for topography, land behaviour, weather and soils.

It was in 1683 that the first book was published specifically designed for the gardener in Scottish soil and climate. John Reid, its author, emigrated to New Jersey while it was at his printer. Though New Jersey is called 'the Garden State', it was Reid's surveying skills that were wanted there. These scientific and mathematically oriented aspects of the true gardener of his age caused him to become, from humble beginnings in Scotland, one of the most important and richest men in New Jersey. A century later Scotland was a changed place.

Reid's book was produced by a young man of that first generation that grew to manhood during the Restoration period. Monarchy had been abolished in the middle of the 17th century after Charles I had pushed too far his claim to the Divine Right of Kings. He was beheaded.

Chapter IV *Out of the Garden*

English parliamentarian armies had brought the various kingdoms of the British Isles into the first major modern State, the 'Commonwealth of Great Britain'. This was hammered into existence by Cromwellian armies. This regime of pseudo-republican format was actually a tyranny under 'Lord Protector' Oliver Cromwell. Reid was born before Oliver Cromwell's death. In 1660, Cromwell's dynastic dream was overthrown by the peaceful resignation of his son. Monarchy was reinstated in King Charles II, who had already been recognised king by Scots for many years.

Scotland had dared to declare Charles II king immediately on the death of his father. This accession of Charles II to the Scottish throne during the Commonwealth demonstrated that England's desired supremacy over Scotland would continue to be thwarted as long as Scotland continued to have its own separate crown and government. When James VI of Scotland became James I of England in 1603, both crowns were vested in one person. But England realised that it was easy for this England-dominated single reign to divide, once again, into two separate sovereignties. Thus, the question of unification of the sovereignties to parallel the unification of the sovereign became a burning issue which had hitherto been a mere smouldering academic question.

By 1680 Charles II had no legitimate male heir of his body. The question of succession became a major political issue, because his brother James was a Roman Catholic. As James II of England, he did appear to make a smooth transition to the throne on the death of Charles II. But his personal alliances, while Scotland and the English landed gentry might be indifferent to them, did not suit all the English moneyed and merchant interests. Nor did they suit the interests of the Scottish church. Thus began active campaigns to unseat him, its first manifestation being in the Monmouth rebellion. The second thrust modelled itself on the Scottish Covenant movement that had given rise to the first Civil War in 1639, in the form of objection to James II's blatant religious association with Roman Catholicism.

In 1688 the English crown was unlawfully offered to William, husband of Mary, the eldest child of the king. William soon deposed King James II in England. A new civil war ensued, in which opposition in Scotland and in Ireland was brutally suppressed. William took those crowns too. James's second child Anne got the thrones after William and Mary had no direct successor. This even set aside the traditional rule of primogeniture, or succession by the eldest son, the third child of James.

During the reign of Queen Anne, Scotland in 1707 was commercially bullied and partially bribed into giving up its sovereignty and joining a merged single State of Great Britain. Officially henceforth it would be known as North Britain, while England would be known as South Britain. This arrangement was soon dropped in South Britain and replaced by everyday usage of the word 'England' where 'Great Britain' was correct. (Hence, by the way, the modern confusion in England about its identity, as for three centuries that geographical area has used its own name with two very different meanings.)

Anne died in 1714, leaving no direct heir. The crowns should have reverted to the male Stuart line. Instead George the Hanoverian, another lineal descendent of James VI, was invited by English moneyed interests to accept the crowns. He became King George I. Naturally, Jacobites saw the death of Anne as a propitious time to reclaim their constitutional inheritance. Thus the 1715 rising took place, since styled a 'Rebellion' because it failed. Within four years, another rising also failed. George I held the throne until his death, and was succeeded by his son George II, who in turn was succeeded by his grandson George III. None of these accessions went unchallenged in Scotland. The best known opposition to the Hanoverian regime took place over 1745-46, when Bonnie Prince Charlie, the Young Claimant (the modern meaning of 'Pretender') came very close to successful restoration of the Jacobite direct male line.

Scotland bore the main brunt of every one of these civil wars. They negatively affected all everyday aspects of the economy. During the Cromwellian period, the aristocracy were deprived of their lands. Their gardens were destroyed. John Reid was fortunate that he was apprenticed in one of the first gardens to be re-established after the Restoration. After 1688, aristocrats who supported the Jacobite cause were forced out of Scotland. Subsequent attempts to reinstate the male descendents of King James meant further disruption to the Scottish economy, and further changes of land ownership.

Between the two main Jacobite risings, William Burness, a young man in northeastern Scotland, trained to be a gardener. After the burnt-earth policy of retreating Jacobites in 1746 and the murderous reprisals of the Cumberland-led armies again destroyed the little that was left of the Scottish economy, William had to rebuild a life. He and his brothers went separate ways in search of a living. William's wanderings took him to Edinburgh, where he spent two years on landscaping work. Then he got his first job in the west, working for the Laird of Fairlie. From there, he was appointed gardener to Provost William Fergusson of Ayr, who had retired from his London business and bought a small country estate at Doonholm, beside old Alloway Kirk.

William was soon encouraged to start his own market garden. As like as not, Fergusson in a mere few years got all he needed out of paying for a head gardener. With the garden designed and planted, handymen could keep things going cheaply. Perhaps, like so many young people these days who are encouraged to 'go it alone', William would have done better had he been able to hold on to regularly paid employment, however much he might have fretted at service. But perhaps, like so many people in the modern world, he had no option. The old forms of estate management were changing radically, just as over the last three decades of the 20th century did structures of modern organisations.

Modern outsourcing is merely a mechanism to reduce the fixed costs of organisations. In the kinder cases, organisations transmuted salaried staff into outsourcers through 'encouraging' them by small financial payouts to 'become self-employed'. It is not generally noted that this had the immediate very considerable financial advantage to the organisation of freeing it from the very heavy costs of providing the overheads of healthcare and pensions, and instead paying on a piecework basis at virtually the old salary cost alone. The overheads didn't disappear, but came to be borne directly by the independent worker. This had the effect of greatly reducing the reward of labour, as it must bear this cost itself.

By the way, this was the 18th century rationale that encouraged big commercial interests to appear to take the moral high ground in supporting abolishing slavery.

It greatly increases the dividends to shareholders when an organisation removes to its 'consultant workers' the cost of responsibility for the aged or infirm. This is not just immediate, but into the future too. The parallel in 18th century Scotland was to remove from estates those families who had lived on the land and worked it for centuries. Estates instead bought in labour as needed. Thus, instead of responsibility for welfare being accepted by the landlord, the 'independent' man was left in adversity to fend for himself. This agricultural change had begun in England in the early 16th century with enclosures in the period immediately following the Reformation. It resulted in immediate big windfalls and ongoing bonuses for landlords. At the same time it generated very considerable hardship and poverty for those dispossessed by the new system. It was a mechanism to transfer the wealth of the nation from the populace to a few powerful landowners.

Scotland lagged in the advance of this modern capitalism because its Reformation did not take place until after 1560. Then the form of that Reformation at the outset required continued funding of education and of care for those unable to work. This restrained the excesses of the grabbing of former church lands as happened in England and in continental Europe. Reticence to promote change in the relationship between labourers and land lessened when the Crown relocated to London in 1603. Then funds went south as aristocrats followed. Change was accelerated by the Cromwellian regime.

A man trained in gardening or similar agricultural profession should have been able to hope for a good life through a career based on experience, knowledge and skills. A gardener was an important element in the economic make-up of the area until the days of mass transportation of fresh foodstuffs by canal and, more rapidly still, by railway. He not only supplied the grand house that employed him, but could sell fine produce at the local town. He could indeed hope to make a big mark in the world, and not just for designing landscapes. The notion that 18th century gardening was simply landscaping is a notion generated by the modern tourist impression of historic houses set apart by Capability Brown.

Great lords and minor lairds all needed to employ salaried gardeners, who headed up a team of apprentices and workers. For some, emoluments included their own small holding supplied with manure from the animals of the big estate; for others, there was profit sharing in garden output.

Thus could Walter Burnece, from his gardening capability, become financially independent. Having his own farm, not indebted, and supplying his own family with food, must have been a great boon in that turbulent period between 1639 and the Restoration in 1660. In this period, first Scotland's Bishops' Wars and then the Civil War and subsequent Commonwealth drove big landlords abroad. This undermined the old economic environment, and made big estate gardening posts for the young men much more difficult to get. Yet, in 1653, the Ayrshire Earl of Cassilis was able to offer his gardener the equivalent of one hundred Scots pounds in three years, along with a tied house, enough meal each year to feed his immediate family, as well as two grazing cows and winter fodder for them. The gardener was to supply the big house, whether the household was at Ayr or Teviotdale, with all its needs in turnips, carrots, onions and other roots, cabbage and other greens, light greens and salads, kitchen herbs and even exotic vegetables such as Jerusalem artichokes and soft fruits like strawberries. The orchards were part of the gardener's responsibility, along with the development and care of all trees. He also looked after the bees, an essential source, in their honey and their wax, of sweetness and light.

Even after the disturbances in the early part of the 18th century, gardening could still pay satisfactorily. In 1721 the Earl of Breadalbane kept a Head Gardener and four assistants, who together were paid £Scots216 and provided with the grain they needed. But this was much less than the going rate around 1710. Then gardeners might even expect to be paid in English Sterling – which had been a much more attractive currency even before the Union of 1707. Things did improve when the economy settled down before the second major Jacobite incident: in 1738 the Earl of Cassilis did not just provide his Head Gardener with bed and board within the complex of the Big House. He also paid him £8 Sterling.

Head Gardeners were on an estate a class apart from mere labourers. They were at least on a par with the most senior staff, such as the Housekeeper. Apprentices must in their evenings, after a day of work on the soil, study writing and letters, arithmetic, mensuration, costing and accounting, in addition to botany, horticulture and husbandry. They had practical lessons in the making and improvement of tools and equipment, both for working the land and surveying the land. They were taught to make estate maps and drawings of buildings, and thus must learn relevant aspects of architecture. They had also to be able to behave like gentlemen, because they had to be able to work directly on behalf of and amongst gentlemen. Gardeners were the most educated men amongst those whose work involved physical labour – and indeed were in some ways more widely educated than many in the sedentary professions. It took at least eight years of hard work and intensive study, properly examined, before a man might be recognised as a Journeyman Gardener. William Burness was such a man.

Yet he did not crack it financially. Why, his wife must have asked, were his family so poor? Why did she get nought but grief and pain for promised joy?

One big reason was the Glorious Revolution a century earlier. Demand for traditionally trained gardeners really fell sharply when the government, in the names of King William and Queen Mary, took ownership of estates of aristocrats attainted for supporting James. Then began the real push of capitalist methods into Scotland.

The old order received more deathblows by the additional sequestrations of estates after each Jacobite rising. Trustees and factors of these new Crown estates saw no reason to continue customs of discredited former landlords. From 1746 onwards, 'agricultural improvement' – or treating land as an economic resource for the benefit of landowners rather than as the substrate for the livelihood of the populace – became a commonplace in Scotland. Rural people were redefined as mere units of labour. Absentee landlords began to vie to outdo neighbours in economic performance and monetary productivity. This meant displacement of whole families, sent off the land of their fathers to seek their own future where they might. On few estates was there an occupied Big House that needed the output of a kitchen garden, or the meat supply from managed parkland.

This agricultural improvement in the sequestrated estates of the northeast drove William Burness out of Kincardineshire. In theory as a gardener he at least had a profession. But demand for gardeners was slow to pick up. First he tried Edinburgh and then Ayrshire. William Burness was lucky by the early 1750s to be offered a head gardener's position on the estate of London yuppies who had bought Doonholm. By 1756 he was being urged to 'become self-employed', for he had done all Doonholm had wanted.

William took a lease of the plot of ground at Alloway on which he built the birthplace of the poet. He planned to create a market garden that sold produce to local big houses and the nearby town of Ayr.

When William married on 15th December 1757, he undoubtedly had great hopes that he was going to make his new venture work, and so raise a family that was independent of the vagaries of landlord whim and avarice. His problem, like so many start-up small businesses of the modern world, was that he was severely undercapitalised. He simply didn't have enough reserves to tide him through bad times. Nor did he have what marketing gurus call 'a unique selling point' in what he produced. He was also a long way from a good market. All this meant that the amount he borrowed to get started ensured his repayment commitments were greater than he could afford to pay when times were bad.

When Robert was born in January 1759, such troubles were in the future. There were enough immediate troubles. Within days of Robert's birth, the house William had built was blown down; the 'cruel coulter' of the west wind slashed through his home, leaving them scurrying like mice seeking shelter in a hostile world. So much for his vaunted gardener training in building. This was the beginning of 'nought but grief and pain for promised joy' to his poor wife. Perhaps many a time Robert heard his mother, weary and worn out, in anger voice those words.

William, choosing to take his own farm when it appeared he might have continued as a gardener, was possibly also up against ageism. He was out of date and, if truth be told, over qualified. Already, the quality of young gardeners was being diluted by what Adam Smith would call market forces, and which later generations of economists would redefine as his Law of Supply and Demand. Anyone capable of learning the extent and depth of knowledge necessary to complete a traditional apprenticeship in gardening should expect to achieve far greater financial return than gardening in Scotland offered. Candidates with the right scientific and mathematical bent were not being attracted to gardening. Supply was for a period met by mere labourers, under-qualified. By the end of the 18th century the former profession of gardening had gone the same way as school teaching in Scotland following the Second World War. Then, people were made teachers without such good university degrees as formerly. In both cases, the profession as a consequence lost so much respect and became so badly rewarded that in the following generation few truly capable or well educated people could find it attractive.

Those who had been traditionally trained were the losers. Expansion of demand for teachers failed to bring back anything like the previous degree of skill and professionalism. When salaries were increased to attract people back into the profession, it merely inflated incomes and conceit of the average teacher. Teachers are once again very well paid, but they have nothing like the old attitude or capabilities. There is still memory in Scotland of a time when to be a teacher was to be a truly respected professional in the community. The time is upon us when living memory of those old Scottish teachers will die out.

By the 19th century, although Scotland had so recently been the source of most of the estate gardeners of England, this got forgotten as the old and difficult profession itself fell from favour as a chosen career for young capable Scots. By the mid 19th century people in Scotland had no memory of what it had meant to be a professional gardener before the '45. So biographers and commentators on Robert Burns did not understand that, for William Burness, to be a gardener was to have had a profession that in his youth had had substance.

A lot of water had passed under the Brig O'Doon by 1765 when a prospective gardener at Monymusk could spell out his own conditions of employment: a good well-furnished house for his family, plenty of fuel, sufficient food, his own cow with fodder, a fine salary of £15 Sterling per annum, not to be required to take on more than one apprentice at any time, and the cost of relocation from Edinburgh.

From 1770 to 1776, the Laird of Monymusk, hereditary guardian of that little mediaeval casket reliquary of St Fillan (now in the National Museum of Scotland) that was carried before Robert Bruce into battle at Bannockburn, contracted with his next gardener. He was to be based in Paradise, a property near Benachie. The gardener got half of all the produce, as well as the usual annual supply of food. In return, the Laird and his family alone must, in addition to getting their share of fruit and vegetables, enjoy the pleasure of walking in the garden; thus it must be modelled on its name! Anything that failed that test was a punishable breach of contract. William found no Paradise.

He was realistic, he believed, to come out of the garden business. Passé were sophisticated geometric simplicities of selectively seeded scenes of seclusion behind safe garden walls. Passé were the skills of the old-style journeyman gardener. He had seen the way of the world in an Edinburgh inspired by the regulating poetry of Thomson. It had adopted the blunt mountain-moving muscle style of Capability Brown, who in 1750 laid out the landscape around Warwick Castle.

Even by 1766 few were those landlords who, like the Duke of Gordon, were again employing a gardening team of twelve, under a well-paid Head Gardener. When gardening picked up again as a desirable occupation, it was too late for William. By then he had burned his boats; his first venture in Alloway had seemed insufficient to support his family. The Burness family in 1766 moved up the hill to the rough farm then called Mount Oliphant. There they faced a cruelly cold west wind battering fields of old rigs long drained of fertility. This was another of William's 'great bargains' that did not live up to its promise. He was persuaded to take on considerable bank debt to lease and stock the marginal farm. There, things for William went from bad to worse.

Weather was bad for the decade after his son Robert's birth. Pennant commented in his journal of his tour of Scotland in 1769 that on 20th March that year Loch Tay was frozen over, though folk memory was it could not freeze. Water was not the only thing to freeze: financial credit did too.

There is an anecdote that William once sent a bank-note to his relatives near Stonehaven and that they didn't know what to do with it. This has been interpreted as indicative of the economically backward state of that region. Another possible explanation is that the bank-note was a draft on Douglas, Heron & Company of Ayr, which was known as the Ayr Bank. This bank opened in November 1769 and rapidly expanded. Incidentally, it was started at the time of a transit of Mercury and a few months after the appearance of another great comet, today called Comet Messier. A great comet attracts the attention of a person casually looking at the night sky. This one was first visible to the naked eye on 24th August 1769 and reached its greatest brightness on September 22nd 1769. Many years later, it was discovered that, as it became visible, there was born an infant named Napoleon Bonaparte. Messier did not believe this was a coincidence.

Bad luck followed the founding of the Ayr Bank.

The main shareholders of the Ayr Bank were landed gentry, none of them with any banking experience. It based its business on the land owned by its shareholders. It was profligate with its lending, issuing bank drafts willy-nilly. The Bank of Scotland and Royal Bank of Scotland simply refused to buy what were the 18th century equivalent of toxic credit derivatives. In early 1772 the bank realised it was hitting trouble as London-based bank Neale, James, Fordyce and Doune failed. Soon the Ayr Bank realised that it had hit a serious liquidity problem, and collapsed. Many around Scotland lost their savings. More than likely it took some of William's money with it directly. Indirectly it hit even harder. Its fall put financial pressure on his landlord's factor, who became highly aggressive in demanding due payment of rent and loan instalments. With bad harvests this could be paid only through starving and slave-driving William's children. Oldest child Robert bore the brunt.

Chapter IV *Out of the Garden*

The Ayr Bank had been founded in response to a change in Westminster political management after the removal of the Earl of Bute from leadership after the end of the Seven Years War in 1763. This was a period when domestic Scottish political management was fast reshaping in favour of a legal and mercantile nouveau riche. That year, it was agreed that there was too much paper money in Britain. This was the legacy of a period of credit expansion to fund war. Paper was particularly prevalent in Scotland. With so much paper money around, inflation was getting out of hand. In 1765 Parliament brought in new rules that prevented banks issuing notes of value less than one pound, and required that all notes be repaid in good specie on demand. The purpose of this was to make it more difficult for banks to default on what they owed depositors. It caused the Bank of Scotland, the Royal Bank and the British Linen Bank to tighten their lending criteria. Smaller banks followed.

This didn't suit those who lived their lives on a lively credit card. The Duke of Queensberry had a word with the young Duke of Buccleuch, who had just returned from his Grand Tour with Adam Smith as his tutor. I wonder if Smith noted Buccleuch's enthusiasm for Queensberry's proposal, and feared for the nice pension Buccleuch had granted him. Maybe this persuaded him to begin writing 'The Wealth of Nations', to create the credibility to get a job if his pension dried up. Queensberry proposed that he and Buccleuch form a bank whose lending would be backed by the land of their ducal estates. In November 1769, to the dismay of Adam Smith (or so he claimed later in 'The Wealth of Nations') they formed Douglas, Heron & Company.

The bank rapidly expanded, lending aggressively. Little of the borrowing went into investment in real wealth generating activity. Much of it went to fund the building of fine grand homes. Landlords raised farm rents to fund their interest payments. Land values began to rise, making landlords feel wealthier, and causing them to borrow more. Rents rose again. The bank began taking out small 'rivals' who were perhaps all too keen to sell out for cash. It initiated the 18th century equivalent of the 21st century credit derivatives abuse. Circulating bank notes, not then a phenomenon that economists believed they understood, were in the 18th century equivalent to mortgage credit derivatives in our own time. Soon two thirds of all notes in Scotland were issued by Douglas, Heron & Co. When the crash came, the big banks refused to be party to a bail out. The government had to act.

In 1774 the Bank of Ayr Act created new financial instruments by which the dukedoms of Queensberry and Buccleuch could repay over sixty years what they owed from their borrowings on the Ayr Bank.

Henry Dundas, who became so prominent in Scottish politics, was one of the hundreds who took and lost his share of the equity in this venture. He had in 1766 been given the position of Solicitor General for Scotland. Another loser, by the way, was Archibald, Laird o' Cockpen. His losses forced him to sell that famous estate. In due course many another estate changed hands too, including Doonholm and the estate of Ballochmyle. William Burness proved a loser too. When he got out of the Mount Oliphant lease, William took the lease of Lochlie Farm from landlord McClure. McClure knew that true title to the land which included Lochlie was unclear. He persuaded William not to insist on a written agreement. There was only verbal agreement on the details of the lease. This cost the family dear in ensuing legal battles.

Economic upheaval and the hard times it generated increased landlord pressure on tenants to pay increased rent. Tenants could only pay increased rent by increasing productivity. They could achieve this only by significant investment in labour and money. Such insistence on agricultural improvement continued throughout the poet's life. It was paralleled by industrial innovation. Both were only the immediate expression of the rapidly changing world in which he lived. These were set within a broadening confrontation as political forces contended for the economic benefits of expanding global connections.

The poet's father, seeing how times were changing, perhaps looked back to his own gardening training. From his perspective he might have believed that gardening was reopening as a career. He realised that his eldest son was capable of achieving all the skills needed of a fine gardener. He was excellent at his sums; he was practical in the fields; he had the intellect to study, the dogged determination to work the soil, a natural affinity with nature and an easy ability to remember the names of plants, particularly flowers. Thus he invested in his son's education, sending him to learn geometry, surveying and the creation of sundials accurate to where they would be installed – the nowadays arcane art of dialling.

As Robert Burns is known as a poet, and since most of his biographers and critics are not adepts at advanced mathematics, it is not generally realised that he had a very competent understanding of mathematics and science. This comes through in his letters, is supported by comments from his bosses in the Excise on his outstanding intellectual capability for advancement in the service, and is endorsed by comments from senior academics that he could have excelled in any profession. He was not in jest when he wrote that he found 'The Elements of Euclid' very exciting. Strange though it may seem to those to whom maths is a mystery, many a mathematical mind is entranced by the elegance in Euclid. It was not simply that Burns mastered numbers; his letters show he had that instinctive *feel* for how mathematical concepts work that differentiates a mathematician from a mere bean counter.

That he understood as by instinct was visible to strangers. Dr Moore wrote in 1787,

> I know very well you have a mind capable of attaining knowledge by a shorter process than is commonly used, and I am certain you are capable of making better use of it, when attained, than is generally done.

This strong mathematical bent might have procured him a great future in a professional career, had he not had a greater strength. He was a poet. Thus, when he acquired mathematical skills, his mind used those tools to raise him to a higher plane – that 'other planet' of philosophy, on which the greatest mathematicians live. Thus he was enthralled by his childhood textbooks, for they too rose above mere application of tools.

This poetic ability, challenging him to think philosophically, made him eager to be involved in the debate on 'big issues' that he found going on around him in a Scotland that, though economically poor, was vibrant with thought. That vibrancy even reached the lowliest congregations attending divine service each Sunday. There he heard people arguing about matters that had divided the greatest minds of universities for a thousand years: whether science challenged the Truth of the Bible, and the nature of the destiny of man.

For a mind as capable and eager to learn as his, getting to grips with these debates was irresistible. Equally irresistible temptation was to raise unexpected points so as to undermine the well-versed argument of the most bigoted of every persuasion. He turned out to be really good at it. He made a right nuisance of himself. He put a lot of noses out of joint.

The first of these questions was actively addressed in his science textbooks.

Reading 'Astro-Theology', Robert must have been enthralled when Derham described the various ways that peoples thought about the Earth. This brought his young mind into contact with the mysterious concept of celestial spheres. These were related to the everyday by telling how Pythagoras, in ancient Greek times, taught that the Earth revolved around the Sun. Thus, when Numa built the Temple of Vesta, he built it round, with an eternal fire burning at its centre, to represent the life-giving light of the Sun and the movement of the Earth around it. Derham told him that Copernicus had been the first modern to choose to express his planetary observational data with reference to their centre of orbit, rather than in reference to Earth.

In his poetic mind he could see the great dance of the heavens, like a Scottish eightsome reel. In such reels, all parties are moving. But the dance can be thought of by any one person as herself circling rhythmically round another dancer revolving on a spot, while weaving in a complex pattern in and out of all the others.

"In and out the dusty bluebells, in and out the dusty bluebells, in and out the dusty bluebells", we children sang in our weaving moving ring, till it was time to change the central dancer. In garbled folk memory of some work-inspired movement routine, the communal work long vanished into the mists, the chant of my childhood culminated in "I am the mas-ter". Then the dance began again. Each one of us took our turn in the master role.

In this way, it is as true to say that the Sun burls round the Earth as that the Earth burls round the Sun and that Moon and all planets whirl about too in the wild but highly regulated dance to music of the spheres. Modern scientists know that it is only convention to say that the Earth goes round the Sun. The whole universe is moving, they now say. The Sun and Earth are moving round our galaxy in a co-ordinated movement. Einstein's Relativity shows us that this might be viewed as the Sun, planets and stars making complex movements around the Earth. Copernicus knew fine well that the length of a year is the time it takes for the dancing Earth to burl round the Sun, while the length of a day is the time it takes for burling Sun to dance round the Earth.

In the 16th century days of Copernicus that Derham wrote about, there was no point for those new-fangled newspapers to explain subtleties of spherical geometric calculations to their new-reading vulgar masses who consumed the output of printing presses. Such truth doesn't make headlines. But when Galileo went to print, it was easy for him to grab a crowd by printing 'Earth does move round Sun: Vatican denial'. This sold much more copy.

It also generated a response from big baddie Vatican.

That sold even more copy.

Then the Vatican haters wrote in too.

Then the Vatican responded again.

A good going controversy is just the thing publishers want.

The presses were on a roll. Big baddie Vatican was on a loser.

Copernicus no doubt turned in his grave.

Copernicus warned the Vatican not to publish his refined astronomical observations and his proposed new calculation method based on them. From the 14th century onwards, each scientific theory proposed and examined came to be abused, in the tinderbox philosophical world of Reformation

Europe, as illustrative of Man's relationship with God as either repressive or progressive. Copernicus knew how in every age students – who so commonly take in only half an idea, sufficient merely to pass examination – readily corrupt an idea's implications. He was well aware of the potential for abuse of his new proposals for calculating the calendar. So he suggested that his insight and method be suppressed. The Roman Church chose not to suppress his work on the movements of the planets. The Vatican followed the idealistic route of never hiding well done scientific research. It took the view that it was better to let good honest work be published than later be accused of hiding new insight.

What riled the Vatican was Galileo's faulty logic. The first part of his logic was:

A thing is Truth only if all parts of it are true.

The Bible states that the Earth does not move.

Science shows that the Earth does move.

Therefore there is a falsehood in the Bible.

Therefore the Bible is not Truth.

The second part of his logic was:

A thing is Truth only if all parts of it are true.

The teaching of the Roman Church states each man can affect his own destiny.

Science proves all things obey mechanical laws.

Therefore each man obeys mechanical laws.

Therefore man cannot affect his own destiny.

Therefore the doctrine of Free Will is false.

Therefore the teaching of the Roman Church is not Truth.

There is a lot wrong with both of these apparently logical arguments. One is the matter of the meaning of Truth, as opposed to some item being true or false. This brings to mind the Eastern thought that the Way that can be said is not the True Way. Another is that the so-called Laws of science are actually simplifications of reality. They are made up by scientists. Nor are all those Laws deterministic, even in the very precise circumstances in which they are supposed to hold. We could go on, but this isn't a book about science, or about philosophy. What is relevant in these arguments is that they often get very heated. When apparent conclusions undermine the status quo and threaten the tenure of those in authority and power, they get dangerous.

The everyday reason for calculating the movement of the stars was to be confident about when to sow seed. In the modern post-industrial world this question seems esoteric. In an agricultural world it is fundamental to survival. This question had been addressed in some form or another for aeons. Its answer gave data on when to seek food in returning abundance of wild animals, birds and fish, when to mate domesticated livestock and when to plant cultivated crops. Getting the answer right was a matter of life or death. An 18th century little farming family, like that of William Burness, could survive only if it knew where within the dance tune its world was singing.

Burns was not just interested in knowing when to sow seed. He was interested in the heat of the discourse. In his day, this was argued in the kirkyard with cut-and-thrust of chapter and verse from the printed Bible. The Bible is wonderfully full of apparently contradictory statements. Burns became skilled in bringing to the battle the contrary verse whenever anyone thought he had quoted absolute proof of his position.

At home, his textbooks outlined the history of the questions, showing that much more than Bible quotations had been brought to the arguments. Thus, when he reached Edinburgh, he was able to follow and contribute to the city's heated philosophical discourse.

But first he studied astronomical calculations. These are difficult whatever way you look at them. The way Burns parodied the controversy shows he probably had instinctive feel for this difficulty. The calculations might or might not be slightly easier starting as Copernicus did or as did the 7th century Venerable Bede. The accuracy of Bede's planetary calculations were still in a class of their own seven hundred years after his death. All that had improved by then was the accuracy of input observations. Bede simply calculated directly where everything would be in relation to Earth. Copernicus first worked out where the Sun was in relation to Earth. Then he worked out where all the planets and the Earth itself would be at some future time. He then used an adjustment based on the relationship of Earth and Sun to work out how they looked in the sky from the perspective of Earth.

It is difficult enough either way to calculate the pattern of planets in the sky at a stated future time. But reliable answers were needed to the much more awkward question: at what future times do the skies have the desired pattern that tells you the right time for important festivals?

Easter is a primary date in the sky calendar, but it is only one of many data sources that enabled Mankind to rise from being a wild beast at the mercy of the elements, to become a thinking creature who survived through being in tune with the infinite of the continuing not-quite-regular rhythm of Nature.

The date of Easter is found from the position of the Moon. To an innocent mathematician like me, this looks far easier to calculate from scratch if I use Bede's approach. This is based on what I seem to see, which is that the Moon moves in a sophisticated but definable dance round the Earth, its arc of movement in the sky tipping north or south over the years.

So much for Easter. The equinoxes also matter.

Bede calculated the timing of the equinoxes in much the same way as he calculated Easter. He regarded the Sun and Moon as the main elements moving. He factored in along with the lurching of the Moon, his understanding of the Sun's apparent tipping and lurching as years progressed. Those complex patterns of tipping and lurching are quantified by observing stars and other planets.

Bede, like Islamic scientists who were his contemporaries, learned from the work of all the more ancient astrologers. Their work produced a rigorous science that formed the foundation of modern meteorology. Bede published his work in response to the much-misrepresented ecclesiastical convention known as the Synod of Whitby. Then, the same underlying questions were at stake: whether the calendar in use was correct, and what was the easier way to calculate a correct calendar. By the start of the 17th century there were at least two mathematical ways to calculate the calendar, each with sufficient accuracy, but each increasingly associated with different factions in the evolving schisms within Christianity.

Unlike Bede, Copernicus regarded the Earth, the Moon and the planets as moving elements and had to factor in all their tipping and lurching against a presumed stationary Sun.

All methods of calculating the calendar begin with the same observations of the heavens. Most end with results that for practical purposes are the same. Bede's method was the Ptolemaic-Gregorian. Copernicus proposed another. With new tools for calculation, Danish astronomer, Christian Longomantanus, in 1622 published Astronomia Danica. This argued for using a third model of heavenly movement – the Tycho Brahe approach. This considered planetary movement as heliocentric but then continued the calculations assuming the Sun is geocentric. For agricultural purposes, this works too. Longomantanus did not call the Pope a silly old fool, and so we don't remember Longomantanus.

These were not 'different theories of the universe'. They were different methods of calculation. In other words they were different computer programs that used the same input data to get the same outcome. Each was the legitimate result of academic research sponsored by the Roman Catholic Church. Tycho Brahe, for example, was one of that unique group of intellectuals sponsored in the 16th century by Rudolf II in Prague. This court welcomed and encouraged intellectuals of every branch of Christianity and Islam too. Here worked the most prestigious philosophers, mathematicians, alchemists, artists and astronomers of the day, amongst them John Dee (astrologer to Elizabeth I of England), Francis Bacon and Johannes Kepler.

Burns learned from Derham about fundamental tools for astronomical calculations, and saw them in action at Hugh Rodger's school. He faced these calculations when he attended that school. So he knew from personal experience that they are non trivial. There's much of a muchness in the immensely difficult arithmetical slog whether you use Bede's approach or that of Copernicus. The difference in effort is not enormous, but there is in the old method more of the complex type of step amongst the calculations. Copernicus had invented what seemed to be a calculator that was easier to use. The new way was like using a mechanical calculator instead of an abacus. Those who have seen an abacus used by experts know this is not necessarily much benefit.

Copernicus did great original work. Galileo took the credit.

Galileo's 'Dialogue Concerning the Two Chief World Systems' grasped at the Copernican method and used it to argue for his own view of the universe. The much-misrepresented contents of this treatise are commonly and wrongly believed to demonstrate the triumph of science over slavish superstition, not merely in cosmology but equally in religious affiliation. In fact, the guy was frustrated that he wasn't getting the promotion he imagined he deserved and decided to make a big fuss about it one way or another.

Galileo was an objectionable creature who would go about making it clear that he thought he was right and you were wrong. After he first got his knuckles rapped, he was allowed freely to discuss his cosmology at the University of Florence, provided he did so impartially. He was merely told to stop denigrating other academics, and not mislead students on implications of his method. But he wouldn't stop miscalling other academics and insisted on telling students his approach disproved Church teachings.

Those who have read his 'Dialogue' will be aware that key thought experiments delineated in it are a poor representation of scientific reality. In ridiculing the controversy between the Auld and New Lichts, it was one of the so-called thought experiments of Galileo that Burns used as his model. Burns satirised the key thought experiment that Galileo himself had to admit was a truly big gaffe in his argument. He had said that as you walk along a road when the Moon is behind a row of trees, the changing relative position of the Moon behind the trees demonstrates that the Moon moves.

Galileo's treatise even lacks the entertainment value of 'Solemn Service', Johannes Kepler's story of an imaginary trip to the Moon. This was published posthumously in 1631. That was one of the earliest science fiction novels.

Chapter IV *Out of the Garden*

The key opposition to Galileo by the Roman Catholic Church was not to scientific content of his books but to his persistent seditious libelling of senior Churchmen as ignorant buffoons. The much vaunted opposing 'two world systems' of Galileo versus the Roman Church were not 'flat earth' or geocentric versus 'moving earth' or heliocentric. They instead embodied the 17th century equivalent of the modern clash over operating systems in personal computing. On the one hand there is Microsoft's purported monopoly in having become the de facto standard. Against Microsoft are ranged those who demand 'democracy' in computing. They demand that Microsoft's designers fully publish all their proprietary codes. They argue that this would create better computing because it would enable others freely to develop software that is interoperable with what Microsoft designs and sells.

Galileo wouldn't have been satisfied with enabling others to compete with Microsoft. He would have wanted Microsoft eliminated. Galileo demanded that the Vatican order people to do things the Copernican way. As Bede's approach was so well known to everyone in the time of Galileo, I would have been one of those who opposed changing calculation methods. That does not mean I'm for a Microsoft monopoly. Nor does it make me a flat-earther, though Galileo would have had it so.

The Roman Church did not condemn the new Copernican approach. It was not supportive of a general change in method of calculation. It saw that the benefits of a general change were not significant, while there were very significant costs, in retraining alone, to implement this new operating system. The Vatican said no change was required. Existing methods were sufficiently accurate and tried and tested. Galileo insisted. He accused the Roman Church of ignorance when it endorsed using the old methods. It is obvious, said he, that the Sun does not go round the Earth. It is ignorant to continue making astronomical calculations as if it does.

The simplest way for a modern person to imagine the solar system is to envisage a central sun with all the planets tidily orbiting that massive central point. We envisage it this way not because it is intuitively obvious, but because we are used to seeing pictures of the solar system in this form. But when people actually look up at the sky it is not obvious to think of the Earth going round the Sun. What we see up there is a sun apparently moving across the sky. We know that to state this experience isn't the same as saying it is wrong to think of the Earth as going round the Sun. We also have the benefit of knowing about Relativity. So we know that different mathematical viewpoints are equally good if each gives an equally good answer to the question being addressed. Maths is a tool. But it is only a tool. Maths can be a description, but it cannot be a final explanation.

Galileo did not share this view. He wasn't a philosopher or even a true mathematician. He was a physicist. He intensified his accusations. He insisted this shift in viewpoint from Earth-centric to Sun-centric challenged Roman theology and therefore its philosophical supremacy. He stated that the Copernican method, based as it was on viewing the skies not from the Earth but from the Sun, proved that the Earth moved. This, he said, disproved the teachings of the Roman Church. So that Church was in error. The Vatican strongly opposed this interpretation as illogical. Galileo responded that it was clearly seen by any scientist that the traditional method implied 'flat Earth', and that the new method implied 'the Earth *does* move'. The Vatican said he did not know what he was talking about. It told him to stop teaching such errors.

Galileo said that this new method of calculation proved undeniably that Scripture was at best misleading and in certain passages downright wrong. The Church objected to a science teacher inferring theology from arithmetic. Galileo stated that the Vatican's silencing him proved that Doctors of the Church were silly old fools. The Church came down on him like a ton of bricks. It demanded an apology and retraction of this seditious libel. His manner of challenge became increasingly unacceptable. Pope Urban VIII censured him.

The confrontation is still so easily misrepresented to anyone who does not understand the subtleties of this philosophical debate. It played right into the hands of those who sought to overthrow the old hierarchy of Western Christianity. It was very quickly misrepresented as a group of ignorant reactionary old men in an ivory tower in Rome preventing the young go-ahead academic intellectual from speaking real truth. Thus is it still typically represented.

All this happened around the 1640s. Yet Burns knew all about it. For the anti-Roman perspective was spelled out in Derham's 'Astro-Theology'. Derham repeated that it proved the stupidity and superstition of the Roman Church. But the manner in which Derham presented his argument must have caused the lad's excellent mind to stop and question. The way Derham put things lacked common sense. Surely, Burns must have asked, there was something deeper in here than a crowd of silly old Roman clerics. But the bickering was certainly beneath the dignity of such important office. Around him, Burns saw similar bickering between different parties within the Scottish religious hierarchical structure. It demeaned the office. Whichever side they were on, their bickering insulted the dignity of their role. Thus ministers on both side of this divide could take offence from his 'Holy Fair', 'Address to the Unco Guid' or 'The Ordination'.

Burns studied history at the same time as he studied Derham. So he knew that Galileo made his fuss against the backdrop of the Thirty Years War. Many Scots fought as mercenaries of Gustavus Adolphus in this war. This Protestant army was financed by Catholic gold from France at the instigation of the Pope to contain the unbridled tyranny of an over-ambitious Holy Roman Emperor.

His family folklore held stories of that war. From the land of his father, northeast Scotland, went Gordons under Huntly, Ogilvies, and Urquharts. From the east went Setons and Grahams. They came back trained in the latest military techniques in time to oppose the attempt by Charles I to impose the despotism of the Divine Right of Kings on an unwilling Scottish Presbyterianism. Thus they had inspired the Covenanters, his mother's ancestors. These fine generals taught these labourers the skills that kept them fighting against all tyranny until Scotland was freed at the Glorious Revolution in 1688.

This was not just part of Scotland's history; it was the history of his own ancestors. Interested as he was in all that he could discover about Scotland's past, the war's history was part of his reading. It had broken out across Europe in 1618.

I have extracted much of the following summary from the text book Burns studied. I know he read all about this war. His brother Gilbert wrote of school texts that Robert

> read all these with an avidity and industry scarcely to be equalled; and no book was so voluminous as to slacken his industry, or so antiquated as to damp his researches.

The Thirty Years War began formally in Prague when Protestant rebels threw Catholic councillors out of a window. In response, the Hapsburg Holy Roman Emperor, Matthias II, sent an army into Bohemia to suppress the rebels. The Prince of Transylvania then stood against him, hopeful of gaining the crown of Hungary. War continued under two more Holy Roman Emperors, Ferdinand II and Ferdinand III. This war proved a pyrrhic victory for the Protestant forces which initiated it. During the war the population of the Germanic States fell from around 21 million to less than 14 million, through death in battle and in consequential economic failure, famine and disease.

It is commonly said this was the struggle which successfully opposed absolute monarchy in the Germanic area through preventing the attempts of the Hapsburg Holy Roman Emperors to impose their will on the populace. In fact the chief outcome of the war was the strengthening of absolute monarchy in France. There Cardinal Richelieu was chief minister from 1624 until his death in 1642.

In 1619, a year after the war started, the United Netherlands condemned liberality in religious thought or practice. It embraced the strict Five Points of Calvinism, and expelled liberals from the country. Over the next fifteen years there came madness in the air: Tulipomania reached its height in 1632 as speculators lost sense in their search for quick gains and a 'safe haven' for capital in a world in turmoil. In 1642 was founded the University of Amsterdam in the United Netherlands, born to embrace radical thought. It was established in the heart of a new State whose founding principle was challenge to established authority, particularly that of Spain and Roman Catholic hegemony.

The Thirty Years War quickly became a free-for-all on central mainland Europe, with commercial interests all looking to gain advantage. It took until the autumn of 1622 before the Hapsburg army subdued Bohemia. Soon Austria was conquered, and the army moved into Saxony. In February 1623, Venice and Savoy, between them rulers of north Italy, agreed together to war upon the Hapsburgs. They aimed to gain control of the Valtelline Passes in the Alps, which controlled transalpine trade. The following May, the troops of Pope Gregory XV occupied the passes. After his death that July, his successor, Maffeo Barberini, Pope Urban VIII, concerned about the extent of Hapsburg influence, looked to France to create a balance of power.

By late 1627, Hapsburg armies were triumphantly marching towards the Baltic shore. King Gustavus II Adolphus of Sweden at this stage decided it was prudent to take a stand. Under him learned to fight many a Scot who later applied his skill in the civil wars in Britain. That October of 1627, Adolphus relieved the siege of Danzig. A few months later he was formally at war with the Hapsburgs.

In Germany in 1629 all property which had been alienated from the Church since 1555 was forcibly taken into imperial ownership – not Church ownership – on the orders of Holy Roman Emperor Ferdinand II. The next summer, Adolphus began to advance south from the Baltic. Venice had hoped to get commercial benefits from the war. But its provinces were that year ravaged by bubonic plague. Half a million inhabitants died. The City State never recovered.

In January 1631, France's Cardinal Richelieu agreed with Sweden a financing package to underwrite its war effort. Thus supposedly Roman Catholic capital opposed the so-called Catholic League under the Holy Roman Emperor. Throughout Lent, German princes met in Leipzig and agreed to form an alliance with Adolphus. That May, Magdeburg was sacked by the imperial army. Its 30,000 inhabitants were massacred. Only the stone cathedral remained standing after the firing of the city. In June, Halle was the next city to be destroyed. These events served to harden Protestant hearts, increasing the moral strength of the army under Adolphus. In September he defeated the imperial forces at Breitenfeld, near Leipzig. In May 1632, Adolphus triumphantly entered Munich.

In November 1632 the military ascendancy of King Gustavus II Adolphus of Sweden, supported by many a Scottish soldier, was to culminate in his death. In 1632, Cardinal Richelieu began to consolidate governance in France. France, naturally interested in getting payback for its financial investment in Gustavus Adolphus, then actively took up the running. Soon after despatching an imperial army that had been besieging Heidelberg in 1634, she declared war on Spain. In November 1634, France took over the disputed Alpine passes.

It was in this climate that Galileo took advantage of changing political balance to publish his key treatise. By the time the 17th century was over, the resultant disruption and dislocation of the European universities meant that all that ordinary men remembered of the Galilean controversy was that it had shown that the Pope in Rome was a bigoted fool.

So Galileo won.

Copernicus had nurtured the sown seed of his research in the secret seclusion of his college garden. Out of that garden Galileo stole the seed. He took a handful and broadcast it in the blood-soaked fertile furrows of fields ploughed by war. Galileo had used the power of good black print to broadcast seeds of thought. But he had adulterated the pure seeds of Copernicus with his own rank weeds of personal ambition, intolerance and contempt for alternatives to his stance. His seeds grew on the ruins of Europe like willow herb and nettles on domestic debris.

A small research plot of seed might fail or be discarded. A large handful broadcast wild has more opportunity to take. Broadcasting ideas amplifies their power of growth.

The seeds of this rare plant released from imprisonment inside the garden walls spread like wildfire. But Galileo spread contaminated seed, laced ideologically as with giant hogweed and Japanese bindweed, strangling the Free Will of Europe.

Here was a man whose idea was not original, who not only got splashed across the pages of Derham's little book, but whose name figured amongst the kings, popes, leaders, great events and natural disasters of the chronicles of Europe from which Burns studied his history.

Burns might have reflected how great truths of Pythagoras and Euclid had lived on because their work was so inherently good that it was transmitted down the centuries in quiet cells of scriptoria laboriously supplied with vellum and rare ink. Galileo had the benefit of movable type. His ideas broadcast, they found places to take root. What a power has the printing press! 'Guid black prent' could give even a mediocre man an immortality!

The Thirty Years War had soon become a pan-European conflict between France, United Netherlands and Sweden against the Holy Roman Empire and Spain. In vain did Pope Urban VIII in 1636 invite combatants to Cologne for an October peace conference. No-one came. The only outcome was a backlash war conference the following year in Hamburg which strengthened the Protestant alliance. In due course this brought about a new treaty with Denmark and England, which hitherto had formally stayed out of the conflict.

Protestant forces in 1642 achieved victory at Breitenfeld, but this time did not press home advantage. Over the next six years France did achieve significant territorial enlargement before peace negotiations finally were concluded in the treaty known as the Peace of Westphalia. By the time Spain was again permitted to use the passes, in September 1639, it proved little value. Too much of her former territory in north Italy had been lost.

England was drawn into the conflict, again on the pretext of religion. An intended alliance with Spain, through marriage between the Infanta and Charles, Prince of Wales, was opposed by the

Protestant faction in England. Spain had required that a condition of marriage was the granting of freedom of worship to the future king's Roman Catholic subjects. Thus when James VI and I died in 1625, his son, as Charles I, married Henrietta Maria, sister of King Louis XIII of France. France insisted that England massively subsidize King Christian IV of Denmark and Norway in his campaign against the Hapsburgs in Germany. That year, bubonic plague killed 40,000 inhabitants of London. Those who opposed the subsidy said this was God's sign of disapproval. The English parliament reacted by denying the new king the customary lifetime grant of tonnage and poundage. This crippled Crown finances and helped precipitate the English Civil War. When Charles II suffered similar limitations fifty years later, he repeatedly looked outside England for necessary funds, making a number of secret treaties with France in exchange for subsidies.

Galileo used this era of confrontation to launch his attack. The way he attacked made people believe that science had facts that resolved philosophical questions. Here was another piece of dubious logic:

All Truth is proved by facts.

Scientific method finds facts.

Science can test all supposed Truth.

The Roman Church states that Almighty God is unknowable.

Science can test this supposed Truth.

Therefore Almighty God is not unknowable.

Therefore the Roman Church is wrong.

All this history and his childhood reading about Galileo was there for Burns to draw on in the back of his mind, when as a teenager he realised that the underlying question that so disturbed the Roman Church was still actively discussed by the people around him.

It was the question that faced Adam in the Garden of Eden.

By eating the fruit of the tree of knowledge, could Adam achieve Almighty Power?

He met men of science who thought so. Through the advancement of science men could gain total power over all the universe.

Men were crossing animals to develop new breeds with attributes they thought desirable. They were changing the courses of rivers. They were eliminating habitats of migrating birds to create new expanses of crop land. They were moving plant species across half the world to create new crop types. They were cutting up bodies to discover the secrets of life. They were dissecting thought to discover how the mind worked. They expected to find answers. It was a matter only of improving their measurements, which itself would be achieved over time. His writings show that increasingly Burns questioned the rightness of all the changes men made, and whether Mankind can ever reach such answers.

One question every human being asks at some point in life is whether or not there is meaning in life. This leads to the question: is there some Almighty Power that created the universe? From long before the time of Christ this had led to another question: can we find proof that gives a definitive answer to the question whether or not there is an Almighty Power. This question has divided philosophers since the beginnings of discourse. There are two camps. On the one hand are those who say that any proof is almost certainly beyond the powers of human beings to find. Opposed to this view are those who say that sufficient search for knowledge will inevitably discover evidence to prove or disprove the existence of an Almighty Power. These two camps are mutually incompatible. The first position allows the second position to exist: there might be some future revelation. The second denies the right in the interim to hold the first position. The two positions can never be reconciled.

The first position recognises three possibilities. These are: science can't, science might and science can test the existence of an Almighty. Christianity at its best expects most people to experience doubt during life. But people have free will to seek or reject faith. Galileo taught that science proved that the Church was wrong in one thing. He went further and said this proved that the Church was regularly wrong. He added that science could provide absolute evidence for or against the existence of an Almighty Power. Doing so, he denied human beings that Free Will to choose between belief, doubt or denial.

Denial of Free Will supports the doctrine of predestination.

Derham had produced his book in the early part of the 18th century because leading scientist Isaac Newton was by the late 17th century seriously concerned about abuses of science within theological discourse. The apparent certainties of science were being used to deny alternative explanations of the existence of the universe. They were beginning to be used to deny the existence of God. Newton encouraged the writing and publication of texts to put science in what he deemed its correct relationship to theology. Those two school texts Burns studied in childhood at the behest of his father, 'Astro-Theology' and 'Physico-Theology' by Derham, were simplifications of arguments Newton promoted. The eagerness with which Burns grasped their content encouraged his father to educate him further.

In the 1780s Burns found debate over Free Will and predestination rampant in each Holy Fair he attended. It regularly came to blows. When he reached Edinburgh, he found the same dispute dividing intellectuals of this Enlightened city. There were those who believed that science could merely increase wonder for those with faith in some Almighty Power but that science could not prove or disprove the existence of Almighty Power. Ranked against them were those who believed that the wonderfully increasing accuracy of scientific measurement would inevitably prove or disprove the existence of such a Power. One group maintained the mediaeval view that Theology was by its nature superior to Science; the other maintained that Theology was subservient to Science.

In the first camp were those like Robert Boyle, Isaac Newton, Whiston and Derham. These had insisted that, however apparent accuracy of measurement might improve, it could never give a final answer to the ultimate question of the meaning of life. Anyone who discussed philosophy with Burns, or knew that he had enjoyed Derham in his childhood and studied the lectures of Boyle, would expect him to be aligned with this camp.

David Hume, founding his thinking on the scurrilous texts of Pierre Bayle, championed the latter view. He went further. He implied science proved there was no such thing as a God. Readers of that biography issued by Currie might presume that Burns, having studied Bayle, sided with Hume. One tiny error in transcription of his autobiographical letter implied to those who read that posthumous Currie edition that Burns was an Atheist.

Burns had an unshakable belief that each human being had free will. He saw the insistence of the sceptics that science would prove itself almighty as the denial of the free will of those who had strong faith in their God. He did not take this view out of slavish acceptance of the opinions in the books he studied in childhood. During extremely severe illness as a young man he experienced what tends in the modern world to be called 'an epiphany'. Finding himself in fear of death he instinctively turned to prayer. Thus, the Roman Catholic Bishop Geddes became his very close acquaintance when in Edinburgh, undoubtedly because in him he found a kindred spirit who championed that free will in Mankind, and denied that hegemony of Science.

By the beginning of the 19th century across northern Europe and the United States the number of intellectual followers of sceptic Hume became considerable. Sceptics dominated Western philosophy during the 19th and early 20th century. They out-shouted those who continued to insist that scientific enquiry could necessarily achieve only limited understanding. Non-scientific philosophers built on atheism and produced nihilism. This is denial of innate dignity in Mankind. It encouraged cultural disintegration in the West. The Jewish Holocaust gave extreme manifestation of denial of dignity.

Burns, having in youth studied and internalised Derham and followers of Boyle, took active part in debate against the Hume Atheist camp. His letters are laced with his insistence on the existence of God, the central role of Revelation in Man's relationship with the Almighty, the Free Will that Man enjoyed, and denial of predestination.

In reading in Derham of the Galilean controversy Burns would have realised that Galileo based his denial of Revelation and his refusal to allow others free will on there having been found a new way to calculate the answer to an old problem. Burns had nous. He could understand the big difference between being able to calculate the same thing in two different but equivalent ways, and this meaning Scripture is wrong because it indicates only one way of calculating. He probably liked there being two equivalent methods of calculating the future positions in the sky of heavenly bodies. It is poetic.

We have already seen that Burns remembered the Galilean controversy when he used a poetic analogy of Moon flights to describe the misplaced energies of the 18th century religious confrontation known as the Auld Lichts versus the New Lichts.

In the Western world sceptics so dominated 19th and 20th century science that there is an implicit assumption in Western education that Science is the ultimate arbiter of Truth. One big lobby of modern science holds the paradigm that in multi-dimensional space-time each life can be described as a continuous space-time string. So future experience is described and thus predetermined. This implicitly denies Mankind has free will. That physics paradigm confines us to the barren world of predestination.

There are those who say those strings are at least fuzzy, giving us some leeway.

When Science claims to describe, define and even shape life, it too readily makes itself arbiter of ethics. Those who volubly challenge the supremacy of Science can find themselves denigrated as reactionary, called ignorant, humoured as members of the 'alternative society', laughed at as religious fanatics, or labelled downright mad or at least naïve. Burns was in this camp. He believed that our humanity and not our knowledge of science made us able to judge moral questions. Burns believed our ability to judge what is right and apply free will in acting on our judgement is part of that mix of attributes that constitute the dignity of Man.

This questioned his loyalty to the religion in which he was brought up, for Scottish Knoxian Presbyterianism declared the doctrine of predestination. It claimed that only the Chosen entered heaven. But common sense told Burns that responsible exercise of free will is in the choice of each person. A man's choices surely determine how God judges him. He turned his rapier on the hypocrisy of the Justified Sinner:

> Morality, thou deadly bane,
> Thy tens o' thousands thou hast slain!
> Vain is his hope, whase stay an' trust is
> In *moral* Mercy, Truth, and Justice!
> No – stretch a point to catch a plack:
> Abuse a Brother to his back:
> Steal thro' the *winnock* frae a whore,
> But point the rake that taks the *door*;
> Be to the Poor like onie whunstane,
> And haud their noses to the grunstane:
> Ply ev'ry art o' legal thieving;
> No matter – stick to *sound believing*.
> Learn three-mile pray'rs an' half-mile graces,
> Wi' weel-spread looves, an' lang, wry faces;
> Grunt up a solemn, lengthen'd groan,
> And damn a' Parties but your own:
> I'll warrant then, ye're nae Deceiver,
> A steady, sturdy, staunch *Believer*.

Today, people still ask if there is any meaning in life. People still doubt whether science can answer that fundamental question of life, the universe, everything. Down to earth, some gut feel still causes the ordinary man, with or without the benefit of advanced education, to claim inner capability when faced with a question of ethics. Most believe it is in their own power to decide what truly is right or wrong. But the position taken by Galileo and promoted by Bayle and David Hume is in our modern world raising its head increasingly.

As science advances more and more into realms that everyday human beings regard as the province of ethics, too many scientists are demanding to be taken as authoritative in those ethical arenas. Thus in matters such as genetically modifying foodstuffs, cloning, stem cell research and many others, the debate that took place around Robert Burns when he was in Edinburgh is reopened in our own day. Should Man worship Science?

Should science choose the future nature of Mankind?

Even to pose the question is surely hubris!

This question is implied in more than a few modern scientific research programmes.

In the 1780s there was a separate debate going on about chosen people – the question of who had the right to choose the minister of the parish. Was it the State and landed interests, or was it the congregation? Knox had said it was the congregation. The settlement of 1690 supposedly endorsed this. The Treaty of Union of 1707 supposedly protected this. The Westminster Parliament soon decreed otherwise. This important debate about whether the State or landed interests had the right to impose a minister on a congregation became violent at the start of the 18th century. New Lichts originally consisted of those who compromised on this issue, accepting patronage as a reality. They justified their position by insisting that patronage was irrelevant; people should be arguing about the real theological matter: did men have free will and could they be redeemed by Good Works. Burns held this view, but he also held that continuing bickering by these two parties degraded religion as much as had the Galilean controversy.

The underlying practical question that Copernicus had hoped to simplify was the calculation of an accurate calendar – a matter essential to human life because of its impact on agricultural production. In Christian as in pre-Christian times, the agricultural calendar was anchored by the right timing of planting and by livestock fertility seasons. These were marked by religious festivals in which men prayed for God's blessing on their undertakings. With God's help in the affairs of men, the harmony of Divine Purpose was maintained. Burns learned from his studies that by his time the method of calendar calculation had been refined and refined over at least two millennia.

Mechanical technology was also developing; clockwork and gearing were advancing in accuracy and fineness. In those museums that have not gone entirely touch-screen we can occasionally see clever mechanical models of the solar system. These enable a demonstration of the movement of the planets by turning a handle. They were invented as mechanical computers for estimating past and future relative planetary positions. The new data gathered by Copernicus encouraged improvement in and redesign of such estimating machines.

These machines could be used to illustrate where planets and the Moon were in relation to the Sun and the Earth at different times. Thus, by correlating their appearance with historic data on extreme weather patterns, for example, they could be used for elementary long term weather forecasting. The operator looked for near repetitions of historical known relative positions of the bodies of the solar system.

Others got hold of such machines too. They were useful to all astrologers.

Astrology was by no means dead in the time of Burns. That proto-science along with Alchemy, was alive, if increasingly living in hiding. One place of hiding was within Secret Societies. One such was the Brotherhood of Freemasons, which Burns joined. The recent origins of that Society were, in the time of Burns, certainly associated with the Rosicrucian movement, which itself existed at the time Galileo began creating his rumpus.

In 1633, also in the middle of Europe's Thirty Years War, Robert Fludd, the English physician and mystic, thought it appropriate to publish, in Germany, his 'Key to Philosophy and Alchemy'. This attacked scientific materialism. Robert Fludd (1574-1637) was an alchemist and a philosopher. He published widely. Because he was very good as self-promotion, he did this profitably. He lived in the period that many consider the 'last stand' of alchemy, before what are now seen as its deceptions were replaced by modern scientific chemistry and supposed realism.

Fludd came from a philosophical mindset more in tune with the Counter-Reformation than with Protestants. He actively opposed the harsh constraints of Calvinism. Fludd is closely associated with the emergence of Rosicrucian thinking.

In 1971 Serge Hutin published in French a monograph based on his postdoctoral studies of the role of Fludd in the transition from alchemy to modern science. He introduced this with the observation that alchemy was then not a popular arena of rigorous academic study, despite the number of words that had been written about it. This absence of proper study of the facts and evidence was, he said, because analysis of the evolution from alchemy gave no academic prestige. He determined to begin to address that culpable lacuna in academic research.

To put Fludd in context, Hutin gave a history of the movement that was by Fludd's time called 'Brothers of the Rose Cross'. In 1614 and 1615, published anonymously at Cassel in Germany were three little works which immediately got immense attention throughout Europe. These have become known as the three Rosicrucian manifestos.

The first book, 'Universal and General Reformation', Hutin saw as little more than an amusing satire in which a worshipper of the god Apollo sets out how he would improve the world. Alongside it, however, was published a short piece purporting to describe a secret society called the Order of the Rose Cross. It claimed that the founder of the society was a German nobleman of the 14th century. He had initials CRC. He had travelled to the Middle East where he had communed with sages conversant with the mysteries of ancient civilisation. Returning home, CRC formed a secret society in which each man was dedicated to care of the sick, would seek no payment, would train his own successor in the society, and would never divulge to any others the secrets of the mysteries. It was claimed that, prior to his own death, CRC wrote a great book that was to be buried with him, and would be found again after lying two centuries in the tomb. The two centuries, claimed the publication, ended in 1614 when the tomb had been opened and the book of mysteries indeed found inside. This third book, 'Confession Fraternitatis Rosae Crucis', revealed that the founder of the society was called Christian Rosencreutz, who lived from 1378 to 1414. Rosencreutz thus lived during the supremacy of Rome. These three were followed by the publication in Strasbourg of 'Chemical Rites of Christian Rosencreutz', an allegorical text which described the initiation rites of Rosencreutz. Perhaps Burns used similar allegory in words commonly interpreted merely as a love song:

My love is like a red, red rose that's newly sprung in June.

It was soon claimed that there was probably no such person as Christian Rosencreutz and that the whole series of books was allegorical. But the concept of the Order of the Rose Cross was by then firmly established. Fludd soon identified himself as one of this Order, publishing his alchemical works as representing Rosicrucian alchemy. This was the beginning of a veritable explosion of publications on matters esoteric and occult. Many were those who keenly read these books, eager to make themselves as knowledgeable and competent as the adepts.

The French philosopher René Descartes, one of the founders of modernism in science, declared that he could find absolutely no proof that there was such a person as any member of a secret society of the Rose Cross. But of course, it was secret. What is the use of a secret that can too readily be discovered? Many French churchmen also declared the whole thing to be the work of atheists. It might even be the work of anarchists, known in 17th century France as 'libertines' or proponents of liberty. At the very least it was a hoax. Just as Eric Von Daniken in the 20th century caused many an academic to expend energy denouncing his evidence of life from outer space, so did the serious mainstream academicians of the emerging European Enlightenment try to shoot down in flames a vast deception aimed at capitalising on mass gluttony for things marvellous.

But Reason can't kill a good story. Rosicrucian principles of alchemy were thus retrospectively attributed to many of the seekers of scientific truth of previous centuries.

Chapter IV *Out of the Garden*

A century after their initial publication, Gottfried Arnold in 1729 exposed the man who had published the manifesto in 1615 as Lutheran theologian Jean-Valentin Andreae. Andreae's work had been based on various manuscripts that had been circulating over the previous five years. He had been only 28 when he produced the texts. Andreae, it was said, had himself later claimed that the 'Rites' had been a juvenile prank, initially composed when he was only sixteen years old.

Arnold's claims have not satisfied everyone. Mysteries of alchemy did exist; so might too a secret Order of alchemists. Unscrupulous alchemists could become very rich by pandering to those who wished to find medicines that prevented aging, or methods to turn base metals into gold. Equally, alchemists who invested their fortune in finding such wonders could impoverish themselves and their families. Plus ça change, plus c'est la même chose. At the beginning of the 21st century, many are the adverts for elixirs promising to retard aging; many are the schemes promising to enable investors to get rich quick!

But Rosicrucian thinking, that father of Freemasonry that was an unplanned baby of Counter-Reformation philosophy, strangely very quickly found soul mates amongst natural philosophers of Presbyterian Scotland. There, some key mathematicians had never doubted the existence and inscrutable nature of God. John Napier of Merchiston near Edinburgh had already sought to prove the truth of Revelation through calculating the date of Creation.

His treatise of 1617 known as 'Rabdologiae' or 'Study of Divining Rods' published his methodology for using his numbered sticks, colloquially called 'Napier's bones', to aid complex calculations. Logarithms use in the calculations not the numbers themselves, but the simpler numbers derived from expressing the original number as a power. For example, 'three squared equals nine' translates into 'the logarithm of nine on the base of three is two'. 'Three cubed equals twenty seven' translates into 'the logarithm of twenty seven to the base three is three'. Nine multiplied by twenty seven equals two hundred and forty three. As this also equals three to the power five, it turns out that the logarithm of nine multiplied by twenty seven is exactly the same as the logarithm of nine plus the logarithm of twenty seven. So multiplication becomes addition. Equally, division becomes subtraction. For awkward numbers, addition and subtraction are very much easier than multiplication and division.

Napier marked along the edges of whalebone strips, with extreme accuracy, two parallel rows which related each number directly with its accurate logarithm. Some suggest that what inspired Napier to conceive the concept of logarithms was his awareness of typical approximations used in commerce to assess the impact of compound interest. Napier was a technologist, making such things as Archimedean screw pumps to drain water from mines. Archimedean mechanics, with its gears and pulleys adding together to multiply force, is equally likely to have been inspiration to him. We could now describe 'Napier's bones' as a non-electronic non-automatic analogue computer. The first computers, such as developed by Charles Babbage, were simply semi-automated rods based on these same principles. Understanding how logarithms work also underlies the floating-point arithmetic commonly used to enable the mathematical calculations within digital computing. Logarithms are thus the basis for much of modern technological capability.

In 1622 Englishman William Oughtred created the first circular slide rule, making the 'bones' much easier to use – as anyone who has worked both linear and circular slide rules will know. The down-side is a potential loss of accuracy as the inner rings of the circular rule cannot be marked as accurately as the outer rings, whereas all the linear 'bones' can be equally precise.

Prior to logarithms, people actually did do complex arithmetic on their fingers. How to do sophisticated finger arithmetic is spelled out in the treatise 'De Temporibus' by the Venerable Bede. He published this in the early 8th century. He had used that method to do his astronomical calendar work. Bede's fingers were a ready-to-hand abacus calculating machine. Even a master of the art such as Bede found some calculations daunting using his fingers! Logarithms made such calculations more tractable. This opened up the possibility of developing new ways of cracking difficult arithmetical problems. The most relevant, in this era of increasing global travel, was calculating the movement of the heavenly bodies.

The need for accurate sky maps was then highlighted by the scientific discovery of variation in the Earth's magnetic field, demonstrating that the magnetic compass was not entirely reliable as an aid to navigation.

The advance in tools for calculating the movement of heavenly bodies was amply demonstrated when English curate Jeremiah Horrocks predicted a transit of Venus across the face of the Sun for 24th November 1639. He was the first person knowingly to observe the event since the Greek mathematician and astronomer Theon of Smyrna in AD 128. Another English scientist, William Gascoigne, that year invented the micrometer. This improved on the calliper rule invented by the French engineer Pierre Vernier. Gascoigne put his onto a telescope and used it to measure the angle between stars.

The concept of logarithms, along with the understanding of how they actually work and can be used, is considered to have been a necessary step towards the invention of infinitesimal calculus. Infinitesimal calculus was simultaneously but independently developed by the two mathematicians, Isaac Newton and Gottfried von Leibniz, towards the end of the 17th century. In 1673 Leibniz presented a calculating machine to the Royal Society. This was capable of multiplication, division and extracting roots. Newton devised his mathematics of infinitesimals, his fluxions, around 1666. The next year, dissatisfied with his astronomical equipment, Newton designed and made the first reflecting telescope. He had needed his fluxions to enable him to increase accuracy in calculating the orbit of the Moon. This method of fluxions is the cornerstone of modern mathematics. The calculus notation that came out of it is abused by some economists to much human detriment.

That heavenly bodies were not fixed in solid spheres, but had motions of their own, with planets in particular orbiting the Sun, was scientifically accepted all through this era of machine development. In 1626 the German astronomer Christoph Scheiner published 'Rosa ursine sive sol', setting out his observations of sunspots. From the measurement of their rotation he calculated that the Sun's axis was tilted at 7.5 degrees from the elliptic.

Despite the publicity of Galileo's success, many scientists still accepted that it was beyond the remit of mathematicians or scientists, no matter how senior and capable in their own field, to comment on matters of theology. Despite all the fuss about such matters as investigations of the Turin Shroud and other religious artefacts, there are still those who accept that it remains to this day beyond the capability of mere measurement to address theological questions. Burns recognised the inherent limitations of measurement, in letters and even poems commenting on its limits in aiding understanding of humanity and of the works of God.

Chapter IV *Out of the Garden*

Researchers in general, not merely the scientific, ask the six questions: who, how, what, where, when and why. Mathematicians tend to consider themselves as having a sole focus on the why of things. What mathematics actually does is give descriptions which can then be used to describe phenomena not previously noticed. A mathematical description is called a mathematical model. These models are moving models, in that they can be used to predict things. This predictive nature of mathematical expression makes possible the so-called validation of a proposed model. If the world behaves the way the mathematical model predicts it should, then the mathematical model describes the world in so far as the constraints of the model are relevant in the situation under consideration. The answer to the question 'why does the newly noted phenomenon happen?' is then 'because this system works in the way the mathematical model describes and predicts'.

This is never the answer to the ultimate questions: why is there a universe and why do the universe and life behave as they do? Mathematics can never truly answer *why*, except in the relative sense of describing formulaic relationships between two or more states of things. No mathematics actually tells why a system exists and why it works the way it does. What it *does* do, is suggest why we might expect certain consequences if the system behaves in the way that we think it behaves. So mathematics, no matter how sophisticated and detailed, only confirms that our present answer to the question of *how* the system works is adequate for our present purposes. What mathematicians continue to do is strip that *how* question further and further back towards its simplest form. Thus, when we want to understand the workings of the system in much finer detail we have the tools already available to help us describe it.

Robert Burns had a specific understanding of all this or else, as his writings show, he had an instinct which made him aware of the emptiness of sophistry. The Enlightenment criticised dull mediaeval monks for arguing how many angels could dance on the head of a pin; but the ministers of religion in the time of the Enlightenment seemed to argue matters of little more relevance to everyday questions of moral goodness. They did pin dancing too. So do too many modern academics.

Burns couldn't take life too seriously – life was too important to do such a thing. In verse of apparent immense facility that he must himself have been rather proud of, he wrote that epistle on the religious controversy between the so-called Auld Lichts and New Lichts of his contemporary Scottish Presbyterianism. He sent it to his poet-acquaintance, the Glasgow graduate William Simson who taught at Ochiltree. He compared the disagreement with the Copernican and Galilean controversies. Their arguments were based on using explanations taken far beyond the bounds of their own relevance. As we have seen, he versified that Auld Lichts believed that each month there was a new moon that, over the space of four weeks, wore out like an old shoe. New Lichts said this was nonsense: the Moon simply went round the back of the Earth. Balloons would soon resolve the matter in favour of the Auld Lichts. (Believe that if you like.)

Contemporaries would have understood that, by ridiculing both sides in this argument, Burns was actually saying: except in so far as it of itself augments wonder at the universe, advancing scientific understanding, being material, is irrelevant to understanding God, who is immaterial.

Galileo – and many others – had crossed that line between proving the usefulness of their own mathematical model and extrapolating from that model answers to the ultimate question on the existence and nature of God. The Roman Church pointed out to him that this quantum leap was unjustified. It told him he was not qualified in the theological studies that might give him competence to comment on central issues of religious dogma. They censured him for this academic professional misconduct as well as for seditious libel of senior theologians. That is not how history remembers the confrontation.

And the whole argument came about because Copernicus wanted better calendars.

With the dominance of cities in modern life, the mechanisation of farming, the use of chemical fertilizers and laboratory induced changes in growing things, the relevance of the calendar to food production seems small to the modern mind. Yet increasingly, meteorologists are re-examining the relevance of what might appear to be mere astronomical sophistry. They are building models of global climate change. Equally, biologists are increasingly recognising the role of such as moonlight, starlight and dew in the generation of rare algae and other life forms essential to pharmacology.

In the time of Burns the practical matter at issue remained the accuracy of calculation of calendar dates of the festivals of Christianity. From this came the appropriate timing of agricultural rhythms enabling the continuing supply of foodstuffs and other necessary produce of the land. Everyone then knew that the position relative to Earth of both the Sun and the Moon in the heavens affected weather and seasonal patterns. Thus Sun and Moon together determined right conduct of farming. Work must be regulated not by mere counting of days, but by an understanding of the ebb and flow of the great cycles and forces of nature. The role of other large heavenly bodies was also suspected. Thus their positions mattered too. Gardeners and farmers needed reliable answers to the question of right timing of propagation of plant and animal life. Science had long been grappling with ways to predict future conditions, leading to the widespread study of coincidences in the search for patterns. Predicting future patterns from what happened in the past is what we still do not just for meteorology but to put satellites in space and get astronauts home from space.

Proto-scientific interpretation of such collations of patterns tends nowadays to be dismissed as mere astrology. Certainly, such correlations were abused. One opponent of abuse of astronomical knowledge was English astronomer John Bainbridge. In 1643 he published 'Antiprognosticon' denouncing superstitious interpretation of observations of the heavens. Even an unusual flight of geese that would once have predicted an especially cold winter was dismissed as superstitious augury. Quite another matter was scientific prognostication, such as the discovery by German physicist Otto von Guericke that a sudden fall in measured atmospheric pressure precedes a violent storm. People learned to accept that air existed. Equipment was developed to measure its changing pressure with increasing accuracy. Measure-based weather forecasting began to supersede instinctual awareness of air changes. Those were left as the province of the wild birds and those attuned to nature. Science dismissed those observations of nature that previously had been a commonplace aid amongst those who worked the land or sailed the seas. We came to denigrate rural bird lore. Yet we use sniffer dogs to catch drug traffickers or find lost children.

From the final peace treaty at the end of the Thirty Years War in 1648 even France did not achieve as much as she had hoped. She could not add to her empire the lands of the United Netherlands. Thus she could not control all commerce through the entrance to Europe's main water routes. Between 1648 and 1653, as factions strove for their share of benefits from the peace treaty and to apportion blame for its inadequacies, France was torn by civil war known as the Fronde. Cardinal

Mazarin, who had taken over from Richelieu, went into exile as scapegoat. This enabled King Louis XIV, newly come to his majority, to impose personal absolute rule.

Science went on unabated. In 1651 William Gilbert's posthumous book 'A new philosophy of our sublunar world' proposed that magnetism maintained the relationship between the heavenly bodies. This suggestion was soon scientifically rejected because magnetism would generate too strong a force. Developments in equipment, such as improvement in lenses and length of telescopes, enabled by 1660 (the year that Charles II returned to rule England after the demise of the Commonwealth) such astronomical observations as identification of solar flares, detailed mapping of the surface of the Moon, viewing of comets and measurement of their trajectory, detection of satellites of planets and identification of the presence of a ring system around Saturn.

What took longer was the general acceptance of one name for the non-mechanical process of real inter-influence that clearly did exist between Sun, planets, Moon and Earth. That awaited the physicist Robert Hooke. In 1664 he gave the name 'gravity' to this unseen interconnection and interaction. In 1679 he proposed that his 'gravity' worked on the basis of an inverse square law. Isaac Newton then developed in 1680 the mathematical description of how a gravity following that law would produce the known orbits of the planetary bodies. He showed this in 1684 to Halley. Halley used it to examine known paths of comets.

The end of thirty years of pan-European war had not meant the end of more localised equally destructive conflicts across Europe and the overseas colonies of its States. Commercial conflicts increasingly meant strife wherever European ships sailed. Alliances between States constantly shifted as it suited the mercantilist moment. Thus, the Second Anglo-Dutch War of 1665-67 was only one such global conflict of an ever-recurring pattern. England and United Netherlands were close allies only a year later. England then changed sides and allied with France against the United Netherlands in 1672. Two years later, for the second time, this brought the coveted New York into English ownership.

This Second Anglo-Dutch War is more generally known about than others because it is documented in the Diaries of Samuel Pepys. His over-riding concern, when the Dutch fleet raided Chatham Dock and burned the king's flagship, the *Royal Charles,* was to shift away from himself the blame for the serious breaches of security in his Department of the Navy that encouraged this disaster. This took his attention away from his usual occupation of sizing up the young virgins recently arrived from the country to serve at the inns he frequented, and working out when he would go back to sample the merchandise. Long after the diaries were decoded, explicit detail of the findings of this research of his prevented his diaries being published in full until the present era.

With so much salacious material uncovered in writings by Pepys, it stood to reason that Victorians could presume that Currie destroyed similar material when he sifted through the paperwork collected for his preparation of his life of the poet Burns. Thus are the names of the great sullied by mud spun on the whirling fans of fame! The Victorians reacted to insinuated indelicacies of Burns in shock horror. Perhaps Burns laughed in his grave:

> Hypocrisy, in mercy spare it!
> That *holy robe*, O dinna tear it!
> Spare't for their sakes, wha aften wear it –
> The men in *black*!

Pepys in that war had experienced the Great Plague of London when 70,000 people died of bubonic plague. These numbers were small beer compared with the estimated three to ten million who died of famine in Bengal three years later. London's plague was followed by the Great Fire of London which precipitated the never-executed Wren plans to remodel the city with grand boulevards as in Paris. The strength of vested interests ensured that even today the core of London City is criss-crossed with mediaeval lanes and alleyways forming mysterious pedestrian passages and roadways under the very buildings of the great financial houses and office blocks. They never were replaced by a grand regular scheme mapped out on the basis of geometric allegory of the hidden forces of the universe.

Isaac Newton meanwhile got on with his thinking, considering the distant stars and the nature of light and the unheard music of the universe. Measurement of the stars and interest in mystery thus survived the 17th century and continued into the 18th. In his commentary on Fludd, Hutin considered that, despite the reservations of many academics, the Rosicrucian excitement of the early 17th century did contribute to the Freemasonry which developed in the 18th century. There came into being then men's societies. They were formed symbolically like the guilds of stone masons who had since early mediaeval times employed their skill and knowledge in the building of the major physical environment of churches and cathedrals that remained across Europe after the mysteries of the Christian religion for which they were designed were dishonoured and discontinued.

Burns was born in 1759 in an era when infant modern science was growing to youthful over-confidence. A hundred years of progress of observation and measurement by this arrogant adolescent science had built on mediaeval work of careful record keeping, and the closer observation of individual entities by pioneers in the use of telescopes. Science soon grew to disdain the old-fashioned thought of teachers in an emerging intellectual milieu of sceptical enquiry that challenged all things metaphysical.

But Man needs mystery. It is natural to the human mind to believe there is more to this life than mere hard facts and measurement. The Reformation removed the mysteries of the old Roman Church. The Rosicrucian tracts offered mystery. Speculative Freemasonry built on that mystery to satisfy the soul needs of those who felt increasingly uncomfortable with the growing materialism of the Enlightenment world. In due course, Freemasonry attracted the young inquiring mystery-seeking mind of Robert Burns.

Chapter V *Saturnalia*

How Burns grew up, the many lovers in the battle for his soul and the secret story of the Clarinda affair.

When William Burness bought Derham's 'Astro-Theology' for child Robert to study, it was like a modern father giving his son the gift of a telescope. This was a wealth of wonderful facts for an education-hungry young mind living under the darkness of an Ayrshire night. This book, though it was intended to enhance the boy's understanding of religion, exposed to him all the wonders of the infinite heavens.

The boy could never hope to own one of the fine telescopes that Derham described in the first chapter. One had a glass 'of Campani's grinding'. Another 'of Mr Huygens of above 120 feet' had the limitation that Derham could not lift it high enough to see stars much above the horizon.

Then immediately Derham went on to describe the wonders that he saw through these glasses, turning them on the planets. Of these, Saturn had been the most advantageously placed for observing with the long telescope. He had had hopes of seeing five of its satellites. Derham apologised early in his 1733 edition that his own planetary measurements had not been improved as he had hoped over previous editions. He had also hoped to observe spots on Mars and Venus, and watch those planets revolve. When he finally got the good telescope Mars was too far from Earth and Venus too close to the Sun. Weather and smog interfered too in his observations. So he had had to rely on the observations of others, but of those 'the learned World hath good store'.

But Derham knew from the work of others that the red, red planet Mars was as if like an Earth that had died. It had dried out seas and burnt rocks, eternally revolving, marking a time never ending. It stood in a testimony of the Power of the Almighty until the Second Coming should sweep all away. Burns imagined this eternity:

> Though a' the seas gang dry, my love,
>
> And the rocks melt wi' the sun,
>
> Oh, I will come again my love,
>
> Though the sands of time shall run.

Derham knew that French astronomer, Giovanni Cassini, who had earlier mapped the route of a comet, in 1664 observed that planet Jupiter rotates once every nine hours. At the same time, German philosopher Athanasius Kircher suggested that tides were caused by water moving to and from a subterranean ocean. In 1695 this idea was revived by the English geologist John Woodward in 'An Essay toward a Natural History of the Earth and Terrestrial Bodies'. In 1672, Cassini, by arranging observations of Mars at its nearest approach to Earth simultaneously in Paris, France and Cayenne, French Guyana, calculated its distance at that time. From this he calculated the mean distances from the Sun of the Earth and the planets. John Flamsteed made similar calculations at that time. Flamsteed was Astronomer Royal, appointed by Charles II to work at his Royal Observatory in Greenwich. To the anger of other scientists, Flamsteed took a very proprietorial view of the data he collected over the forty years he worked at Greenwich. This was the 'Dead Sea Scrolls' controversy of the age, as far as England was concerned. Isaac Newton and Halley tried at one stage to pirate the publication of his observations. They got their knuckles wrapped for doing so. Only in 1725 were the

40 years of observations by John Flamsteed using the Royal Observatory finally published. Flamsteed was then dead and Halley was Astronomer Royal.

As a boy Burns read in Derham's book the blunt Copernican facts:

Mercury revolves around the Sun in about 88 days.

Venus takes about 224 days to go round.

Earth takes a year of 365¼ days, and carries its satellite the Moon with it.

Mars orbits in about 687 days.

Jupiter, with four moons in tow, takes about 4333 days.

Lastly, Saturn with five or more moons, takes more than 10,759 days.

In the Firmament beyond, the Fixed Stars were equal distances from the Sun.

From awareness of the wonder of the planets and the patterns within them, Derham soon suggested human imagination could propose not just life on other planets, but an infinity of other planetary systems like our own, in an infinite immeasurable universe. Two decades later Burns could see himself with his love,

"making our remarks on Sirius, the nearest of the fixed stars; or surveying a Comet flaming inoxious by us . . . or in a shady bower of Mercury or Venus, dedicating the hour to love . . . while the most exalted strains of Poesy and Harmony would be the ready spontaneous language of our souls!"

After a great deal of illogical discussion about the relative merits of geocentric and heliocentric explanations of the universe, to outdo my ramblings earlier, Derham quoted Hooke's important inverse square relationship that describes the working of the force of gravitational attraction:

The Squares of their Revolutions are as the Cubes of their Distances.

The true Christian, Derham remarked, should not be concerned that Scripture seemed to favour only one habitable world, one life-supporting sun, and one small finite universe. Scripture was, clearly, full of allegory, quite apart from having been written in a context very different from the enlightened modern world.

The boy learned to believe that he could know God through His works. Thus in later life he wrote in correspondence that in the wonder of this universe were such

"incentives to, and power for, Reverence, Gratitude, Faith and Hope in all the fervours of Adoration and Praise to that Being whose unsearchable Wisdom, Power, and Goodness, so pervades, so inspires every Sense and Feeling!"

Derham brought things down to blunt logical reality that though Chronicles might declare that 'The World shall be stable, that it be not moved', and Psalm 91 might use the words 'The world also is established, that it cannot be moved', along with many other similar instances, these should not be taken literally. Said Derham,

It would be very absurd to take [many Biblical phrases] in a strict literal Sense.

The educated mind thought about the *meaning* of Scripture and was not tied to the face value of its words. Only when face value and meaning coincide should the face value be honoured. Later Burns paraphrased this:

The rank is but the guinea stamp;

The *man's* the gold for a' that!

However, even the Copernican system had become outmoded, went on Derham, to be replaced by the New System, which some men called the True System. This recognised that the stars were not at fixed distances from the Sun, and that the Sun was only one amongst many stars. This True System included for Derham the insight that

> those multitudes of Fixt Stars appear to us of different Magnitudes, the nearest to us large; those farther and farther, less and less.

Derham left open to question whether the Sun was the centre of the universe, stating,

> whether it be really so, whether [the Sun] be in the Centre of the Universe, and whether among all the noble Train of Fixt Stars, there be no System exceeding ours in its magnificent Retinue of Planets, both Primary and Secondary, and other admirable Contrivances, is a difficulty, as out of the reach of our Glasses, so consequently above our ability to fathom, although not at all improbably. But be the various Systems of the Universe as they will as to their Dignity, it is sufficient that in all probability there are many of them, even as many as there are Fixt Stars, which are without number.

What a wonderful concept for a little lad with a big imagination. What a source of great thought in contrast to the lowly life of a ragged starved eldest son of a hardworking but hapless gardener turned would-be farmer. And not simply an infinite number of other worlds of people and places and hopes and dreams, but the Galaxy was known to be a fertile place for the creation of *New Stars*. One had appeared in the constellation Signus, in the neck of the Swan, though in 1733 it was already fading from sight. But the message was clear: God kept on creating. He didn't give up!

How confusing that must have been for the inquiring young mind when he considered alongside it the doctrine of a once-and-for-all Day of Judgement.

He must have asked his dad to explain things that were increasingly confusing. And his dad obliged with answers. It was his dad who had arranged that the young man from Ayr, John Murdoch (1747-1824), be engaged by a consortium of Alloway neighbours as teacher for all their children. Even in the first two years after the Burness family moved from Alloway to the farm up the hill at Mount Oliphant, the youngsters were still sent down to attend Murdoch's classes, until Murdoch himself moved on. Murdoch taught the children to read English and to write fair prose.

He let Robert borrow what books he had, over and above using the school books that William Burness bought. Little Robert borrowed books where he could get them. Robert particularly enjoyed 'The Life of Hannibal'. But he objected strongly when Murdoch read out from Shakespeare's 'Titus Andronicus' that he had proposed as a parting gift. This was unacceptable in its graphic portrayal of man's inhumanities to man. Robert told him to take that video nasty somewhere else or Robert himself would burn it. So Murdoch gifted a tame French comedy instead.

Murdoch later claimed that he also taught his class church music. This did not inspire Robert or Gilbert. This is hardly surprising. Murdoch was teaching the monotonous chant that passed for music inside Scottish Presbyterian kirks. No doubt both lads were instinctively repulsed by its ear-tearing brain-numbing which Robert later ridiculed in 'The Ordination':

> Mak haste an' turn King David owre
> An' lilt wi' holy clangour

Scotland at this time offered, in theory but not in practice, general education through Parish

Schools. That this law was more honoured in the breach gave rise to the need for the families themselves to club together to hire a teacher. There had been depredations of war and economic depression for close on a century. In consequence many of the educated emigrated. This possibly helps to explain the degenerate nature in the 1760s of an education system that had, unusually for countries of Reformed religion, survived dissolution of Church lands and powers. At best, general education came in the form of rabid religiosity from pulpit-bashing clerics. In comparison, at this time, in England education even in religion was in a greater state of decay.

Academic studies of Archbishop of York, Robert Hay Drummond (who wearing another hat owned and enhanced Innerpeffray Library in Crieff, Perthshire, of which more later) have examined his visitation of domains in 1764. This took place within three years of his appointment, following an incumbent considered responsible in his care. His Lordship circulated a questionnaire to all parishes to enable vicars to prepare for his arrival.

One question asked the vicar to state what was done to prepare Christians for confirmation. In other words, the Archbishop wanted detail on additional arrangements made outside church services for religious education of the parishioners, particularly the young and aspirants. He asked which of the books the vicar recommended were read and which ones he made available. Many did nothing more than offer a Sunday school for Catechism. Many others only offered Catechism classes when they knew a confirmational visit of a bishop was soon due. Some did not even do that. Some of the replies exposed that the clergy did not even carry out the full quota of Sunday services. Most clergy were clearly surprised that they might be expected to *explain* the Catechism. Very few prescribed books, though some that parish clergy could well afford were available from contemporary booksellers.

So William Burness was well ahead of his time when, concerned with the constant religious questions from ever-inquiring Robert, he sat down with Murdoch and composed a book of instruction from father to son. This was Robert's own personal Catechism. It is about 1,500 words, in the form of questions and answers. These above all emphasise the loving nature of God. But it added that the intelligent person must not have blind faith. He must use Reason to confirm the Hand of God in any happening. He should apply four tests to prove God's influence in things unexpected. The evidence must first be worthy of a God of wisdom and reason. Second, it must be relevant to humanity in making provision for human weaknesses through offering a source of spiritual help. Third, it must be miraculous and in some way contrary to the normal expectations of the known laws of Nature. Fourth, it must be predicted by prophecy.

But while the Scriptures must be believed, within the Old Testament only the Moral Laws remained binding after the arrival of Jesus. Yet, provided life was always lived with true intention of avoiding breaking Moral Laws, forgiveness for the breach would be granted if repentance was sincere. That striving after goodness meant using the mind to overcome the brute instincts of the body; this put the Godly part of man over the mere physical; this rather than denouncing the physical part of man, as William Burness put it,

> gives to animal life pleasure and joy, that we never have had without it.

This last statement was so contrary to the everyday teaching of the strict Calvinistic Scottish pulpit that William Burness made the child in his dialogue ask him to say more about religion giving pleasure to animal life. In his final extensive response, the father replies that while Jesus warned of the hardship of being a true Christian, not only belief in the final reward, but constant practice of self-control added a relish to every aspect of living.

Who do you believe, as a child? Ministers of the church who bang the pulpit and preach of hell fire? Do you trust them when you hear them hint your father is stranger danger? They murmured that that Burness is not from these parts; he came from Aberdeen way where the rebels were. He would have heard them add: over there are heretical views, tainted with bishopry and papist superstition. Or do you believe the stern father who yet tells you that all the works of God are inherently good? That father had sent you to study in school under that firm demanding teacher whose rod you learned to respect as much as his intelligence. But that father gave you that exciting little book about the planets and the stars that can even fit in the pocket of your pants. And it has all those exciting diagrams of the way the stars work, and the pictures of the face of the Moon and the shadows on Venus.

Before this child was seven years old he was taught that he needed to weigh up alternatives. He was taught to think for himself, and he was hooked for life.

Turning the pages with intense interest he read how God was indeed the great Architect of ingenuity and skill who gave due Proportions to His Works. Derham was awed:

Who can reflect upon these things, and not perceive and admire the Hand that acteth in them, the Contrivance and Power of an infinite Workman!

How he must have wished he had a telescope to reach out to some answers. Instead, all he had was the dark sky, tumbling above him through the turn of the year, with the wild clouds rolling in from the Atlantic or the cold frost biting in the clarity of the light of Sirius in the dead of winter. As the months turned with the seasons, so did the patterns of the sky.

The mediaeval proto-science of astrology, fast on its way to becoming disdained by a core of increasingly self-assured and influential Enlightenment scientists, is based on that natural sky calendar. Matching the twelve months of the ancient Western calendar, created before the days of imperial Rome, were chosen twelve constellations that could usefully mark out into monthly segments the whole of the Milky Way. These form the Western Zodiac or set of star signs. Mathematicians divided the Milky Way into 360 degrees, to match the original number of days in the year of four thousand years ago. One degree indicated one day. These 360 degrees were allocated equally in near equatorial lands to the twelve constellations, making at that latitude 30 degrees in each.

The year in the ancient world started when the Sun was at Aries, the Ram. Only in a total eclipse of the Sun could any part of Aries be seen – but in such few minutes it was clear to the ancients that the Sun was indeed 'in the constellation Aries'. Thus, Aries was, by definition, the first sign of the Western Zodiac. By the end of the first month of the year, adopted in turn by the Roman civilisation, the Sun had moved to the constellation Taurus; it then moved on to Gemini, then Cancer. Thus it moved on, apparently passing round the whole of the Milky Way, at each astrological constellation in turn, until once again, when the new year came, the Sun was in Aries.

Astrology had not yet been totally set aside by scientists in 1759. As it was still vibrant alongside the Enlightenment, it is interesting to consider what astrologers of his day might have made of the new infant. I requested analysis of the horoscope of Burns without disclosing the subject, his biography or his works, but providing the planetary positions for a person born in Alloway at dawn on 25th January 1759. At his birth, baneful star Saturn was positioned at 2 degrees 54 minutes of Pisces, the constellation of the poet. Astrology predicts that such a position would ensure structure and discipline to his focus, but would also have caused delay and restriction in his life.

Today, the word horoscope gets a bad press from those Western newspapers which don't carry them, and a good press from those newspapers which do. The latter like the fact that the presence of horoscopes persuades many, who would not otherwise pick up that newspaper, at least to flick through its pages. This increases eye-fall on advertisements, and thus increases revenue.

Westerners are generally familiar with twelve star signs, relating roughly to the twelve months of the modern Western calendar. Few are aware of the ancient reason that the star signs don't match modern months, but switch to the next one apparently arbitrarily at different points in the month for different signs. This is the result of the evolution and refinement of the calendar over more than two thousand years.

The Earth's orientation relative to the heavens has changed over four millennia, as its axis of rotation is itself rotating. This shifts the pointer of the axis at the spring equinoctial Sun by the extent of a full constellation approximately every two millennia. Thus, the axis appears to have shifted the position to which it points by two full constellations since the time when the first sign of the Zodiac was defined to be Aries. The axis at that old year start now points to Aquarius. Over the last two millennia it has been pointing to the constellation Pisces, the sign of the fish. Some say this pointing towards Pisces coincided with the life and influence of Jesus Christ. They say that this is one reason that the fish was taken as the sign of the New Way indicated by the teachings of Jesus. The pointer has moved on. This is the reason for all that fuss in the flower-power days of the 1960s about the 'dawning of the Age of Aquarius'.

Most Westerners, if asked, give an answer to the question "What's your sign?" Few people know individuals have many signs. What someone usually answers is at best the star sign they were born under. He usually gives the sign allocated by some typical published twelve-sign horoscope to a fixed spread of dates about a month long in which falls his date of birth. An astrologer examining the birth data of that person might name another sign as much more important.

This horoscope of twelve texts, one for each star sign, is very familiar in Western newspapers and magazines. It consists of ambiguous good or bad luck statements. This journalistic invention of the late 19th century was opiate for the people. Such horoscopes form the general public perception of astrology. It has become an industry that has gracefully and profitably translated to telephone service centres and Internet servers.

Naturally, the vast majority of Western educated people, if asked, deny any belief in any prediction set out for them under their so-called 'sign'. On the other hand, research shows that at the end of the period to which any particular vague prediction refers, a majority of people, on reflection, will agree that 'it was relevant'. The same result holds, though, in controlled tests in which people are retrospectively asked to comment on a horoscope reading that has been randomly generated. This confirms the success of the ambiguous wording. So, science generally discounts the existence of meaningful correlation between horoscope predictions and reality.

In 1759 Uranus, Neptune or Pluto had not been identified or named and so were not then included in astrology. Uranus was discovered during the life of Burns. So there is some argument for considering it within an assessment of his horoscope. In 1759 Saturn was the outermost known planet. It was then thought to be the slowest planet. Saturn is to astrologers the planet of the life cycle. Major events on this cycle happen approximately every seven years. Astrologers believe that everyone has a chance to change or grow spiritually at one of these points. But this is not forced on anyone, and in any case, obstacles may block change. If no change happens, the chance or challenge to do so returns about seven years later. Change gets tougher each time you are offered the chance, and if you don't or cannot act. The cycle closes at about age 28 or 29, depending on many factors. This is a major point of closure. The harder a person has fought change at each stage, the tougher this so-called Saturn Return will be. Alternatively, if obstacles have prevented the spiritual growth, this Saturn Return is a big opportunity to achieve the change.

An individual's birth chart is like a snap shot, but the planets are on the move – they continue their journey from the moment of birth. In their movements round an individual's birth chart, all the other planets appear to pass the point where any planet was at the moment of birth. Each does this at its own speed, with greater or lesser regularity. This is called a transit, a word which is also used for movement generally.

Thus, Saturn takes about 28 or 29 years to transit all the constellations of the Zodiac and return to the same point it was at when the person was born. It is thus considered to take this time to transit a birth chart, because at the end of this cycle it transits its natal position. When Saturn meets other planets on its transit, astrologers say events relating to that other planet are likely to occur. The same is true for all the other planets. Thus transits represent one way in which astrologers can predict and interpret events. The Saturn Return is one of the most important transits an individual can experience.

Astrologers also use progressions of planets, in which one day of an individual's life will represent a year in the movement of a given planet. When a planet so progressed conjoins another planet, or an important point in an individual's natal chart, this also gives potential for prediction and interpretation. Many astrologers believe these progressed planetary positions are much more sensitive to human life events than actual transits.

In their actual movements round the Zodiac, every planet appears from Earth to get passed by all those nearer to the Sun. As it happens, during his lifetime Saturn never passed slower moving Uranus. This means that astrologers are doubly relaxed about ignoring any influence of Uranus on the main features of the life of Burns.

Astronomers, just like astrologers, also sometimes describe planets as being retrograde. This is a result of our viewing their movement from Earth and not from somewhere out in space well above the solar system.

We look at the sky as if it is a plane, rather than thinking of it spherically. As they revolve around the Sun the planets appear to us as if they swing out away from the Sun, and then appear to turn and approach the Sun, swing past it, and race off to the other side. Mercury and Venus, being closer than Earth to the Sun are always seen in constellations near to where the Sun is then positioned. Sometimes they are 'above' or 'below' the Sun, visible in such cases during an eclipse. Sometimes they appear to pass in front of the Sun and at other times to pass behind it. When these appear to pass in front of the Sun, they 'cast a shadow' on the face of the Sun. Astronomers call this a transit of Mercury or a transit of Venus. Earth sees a transit of Venus around twice every century, and always within about a decade. Transits of Venus took place on June 6th 1761 and June 3rd 1769. In 1786, on the island of St Helena, despite bad weather hampering attempts to map the Southern Skies, observers achieved the measurement of a transit of Mercury across the Sun.

Planets further out from Earth never transit the Sun's face. They also appear to reach the opposite side of the sky from the position of the Sun. Because of their combined movements as seen from Earth, only the progressed Sun, Venus and Mars appear at the natal Saturn position during the short life of Robert Burns. Mercury and Jupiter did not appear to pass his natal Saturn position during his lifetime.

His progressed Venus on natal Saturn may have been an important time for Burns. Curiously Burns's progressed Venus, planet of love, harmony and beauty, reached natal Saturn position on October 10th 1778. Some biographers think it was as late as this time that he sneaked off to his dancing classes in defiance of his father. Certainly it coincides with his meeting young men of the same age as himself and beginning to debate with them. His progressed Venus had entered Pisces on June 14th 1776 as he absorbed his formal study of mathematics and became entranced with the symmetry and beauty of Euclid's Geometry.

It is incidental that this was about three weeks before the American colonies unilaterally declared their independence from British rule and taxation. It is very important not to correlate personal astrological indicators with wider events. Readings are specific to the subject examined, be this person, institution or nation. What is not incidental to the way we think of Burns is that the young United States took astrology seriously. This shows that astrology was still an active force in his lifetime. So if we want to understand Burns we cannot ignore astrology.

This was the heyday of medic, astrologer and Freemason Ebenezer Sibly. He published a number of books. These include an excellent edition of the herbal works of Culpepper, as well as his own medical text, 'Physick and the Occult Sciences'. One of his beliefs was that when a person's chart has Mars and Venus together, they will take great delight in the opposite sex. This is enhanced further if these two planets are supported by a good aspect with natal Jupiter. At the late January when Burns was born, Mars, Venus and Jupiter appeared very close together. This is considered a good aspect.

Sibly's interest in politics caused him in the summer of 1776 to examine the aspect of the heavens, and contradict the general view that the American colonial rebellion would be crushed. He predicted that the colonies would become fully separated from Britain.

Understanding the American war is itself relevant to understanding Burns for in Scotland it immediately adversely affected the economy, because of the impact on tobacco and cotton. This meant the war was of very immediate interest to ordinary people. Its progress was daily conversation everywhere. The news even penetrated to the remote isolation of Mount Oliphant. When Burns moved to Lochlie in 1777, he was then near enough Tarbolton to walk there and get much more up to date with the gossiping news. For the first time he mixed with friends his own age. He persuaded them to club together to buy newspapers. He read avidly of the unfolding events.

In the early stages of the American War of Independence the British forced the rebels to evacuate Philadelphia. This was a blow to rebel pride. However, after George Washington and his troops survived the winter at Valley Forge, the British under General Clinton began to retreat to consolidate at New York. Clinton was aware of the possible imminent arrival of a French fleet in the Delaware River. He made the decision to abandon Philadelphia.

Clinton had already secured the crossing of the Delaware close to Philadelphia and began making his way northeast through New Jersey. In pursuit, Washington was forced first to head north till he could cross the Delaware and then turn east to chase Clinton. On 24th June 1778, as the royalists retreated, a total eclipse of the Sun, coinciding with this retreat of imperialism, swept across all thirteen American colonies. How must this omen have reached the hearts of the men in the ranks! The opposing forces faced each other near Monmouth Courthouse on 28th June. In numbers involved and in duration, this was the largest encounter that took place in the northern theatre of operations during the Revolutionary War. Though the outcome of the battle was indecisive, the royalists continued their retreat. Though it took several more years to finish, at this eclipse of the Sun the war was won. When another total eclipse blacked out Maine and Quebec on 27th October 1780, it reinforced the message of demise of tyrannical kings.

In 1787 Sibly published his 'New and Complete Illustration of the Celestial Science of Astrology'. This included his prediction of significant turmoil in France within two years. It also included the outcome of work that he claimed had been commissioned from him in 1784 to advise on the appropriate future for the newly independent American colonies. The horoscope he included predicted a very favourable future for the States if they united. (Shortly after 1812, his younger competitor John Worsdale predicted that the United States would in course of time become an empire that gave laws to all nations.)

Sibly strongly promoted belief that the signs of the time of birth were fundamental to the well-being throughout life of the individual or nation. By reversing this equation, it was possible to ascertain the exact time of birth from life events, were the exact time not known. Sibly's horoscope for the United States presumed a birth-time. Sibly presumed 4th July. On 4th July the Sun at 13 degrees in Cancer overlaps the star Sirius – a highly propitious time for beginning war or business. He chose, as the time of beginning, ten past ten in London's evening, which was early evening in Philadelphia. Astrologically, Sibly's exact timing is attractive. In Philadelphia that early evening, Sagittarius is rising and the star Regulus, signifying kingship, is setting. Stars rise and set every day, but a different date requires a different time to get that nice effect.

Philadelphia local time at 5pm on 4th July is historically not substantiated. Official American documents state the timing of independence at "a little past meridian, on the Fourth of July, 1776". While 4th July 1776 is commonly considered an anniversary to be remembered, historians are not agreed that this truly represents even the exact date when the United States was born. President John Adams wrote in his diary that the vote for independence was taken on 2nd July. Adams predicted that 2nd July would become a celebrated date. Historians are on more firm ground in asserting that on 20th June 1782 Congress approved a Great Seal for the United States. This has date 4th July 1776 beneath a pyramid. The pyramid and other elements in the Great Seal reflect the strong Masonic influence in the founding of the United States; George Washington was Grand Master there.

The American war had vicious effect on Scotland's poorest people. Mauchline Friendly Society formed in 1781 helped through stretches of unemployment labourers who could afford its fees. By the end of 1782 Burns took the aggressive step of writing a letter to Sir John Whiteford, Master and thus honorary head of his Masonic Lodge of St James. Burns suggested the Lodge begin to put together a fund for the relief of its more lowly Brothers who suffered the extremes of misfortune. He requested the Master call a meeting to suggest the Lodge "as a matter of high importance" invoke its charitable status to do this. At the very least, he suggested, this fund could draw monies from the many dues unpaid by members of the Lodge. Five years later Burns regretted that he could not be at a meeting called to chase up dues still unpaid. He advocated naming and shaming, hoping this would not cause too much conflict. He appended the prayer:

> Within your dear Mansion may wayward Contention
> Or withered Envy ne'er enter
> May Secrecy round be the mystical bound
> And brotherly Love be the Center!!!

Notice that he did spell like a modern American.

But back to what analysis tells us of the natal horoscope of Burns.

His progressed Mars, planet of sexuality, aggression and energy, entered Pisces on June 12th 1783. That summer, the sensitivity of Burns was heightened when his father's sudden failing health put increasing responsibilities on the young man's shoulders. This is not dissonant with the fiery anger of Mars.

His father's last illness was aggravated by a massive natural disaster. This made 1783 hardly poetic, unless it was the dark poetic justice of the Angel of Death. There was a massive earthquake in Italy. Far more horror began to unroll on 8th June in Iceland and rolled right up and down the hills of Britain, reaching into every corner, until it settled its hideous plague in the damp hollows of Lochlie.

The Icelandic fissures named after the Scandinavian mythical god of hell, Loki or Laki, began to erupt. This continued for eight months. It subsided only in February 1784. Molten lava covered the land. Thick hot vapour filled up Icelandic valleys, causing the sun and moon to appear like heated bricks. In Iceland alone, 9,000 people of its small population died from the combination of fumes, air poison, destroyed crops and the death of most of the island's sheep after they ate grass contaminated with fluorine from the eruptions. This is still remembered in Iceland as a central event in its recent history.

The Laki eruption is now considered to have been the most severe volcanic incident at northern latitudes during the last millennium. The red fire sun was not confined merely to Iceland. Across Europe the eruption caused an environmental disaster that led to human mortality matching an outbreak of plague. A massive dust cloud formed, growing by an amount equal to a major volcanic eruption happening every three days.

This lethal air was spread in a great arc round the European continent. Benjamin Franklin noted that it was observed everywhere. Even in Egypt it caused famine by interfering with weather systems and rainfall. There Frenchman Constantin Volney noted how little grain could be sown in the Nile valley for want of water in the river. Modern analysis can link the eruption to a contemporary weak monsoon over southern Asia. In Japan 300,000 died. When winter arrived, Mt Skaptar in Iceland also erupted.

Normally this poisoned cloud would have moved off to Greenland. That year the weather was unusual. High pressure unusually towards the north caused a wind that took the gas clockwise. The cloud began to roll east and south until it covered the whole of mainland Europe. It then moved up into Britain. The cloud reached Scotland in early July.

Everywhere was blanketed in a cold fog that smelled of the sulphur of hell. The shining of the sun was dimmed. For weeks it was barely seen. At dawn and dusk it glowed like a ball of fire from hell.

Perhaps it was in this period that Burns wrote his ode 'Despondency'.

Chapter V *Saturnalia*

Throughout Europe there are newspaper reports and diary records of this terrible fog arriving. Everywhere, it remained for two months. There were terrible storms. In all Europe in August and September 1783 labourers in their prime collapsed and died in the fields. Outdoor farm workers were the most at risk. There was unusually high incidence recorded of headaches and respiratory discomfort – the kind of cardiovascular diseases associated with heavy smog in modern cities. William Cowper the poet recorded how he daily watched fine men carried in, dying, from the fields. Mortality amongst workers in the fields, being exposed more than others to this poison, increased to three times normal levels.

Modern science explains that massive amounts of sulphur dioxide and other toxic gases were released and carried into the upper atmosphere. In 1783 the dangers of sulphur dioxide were not understood. When inhaled, it reacts with water vapour in the lungs and forms sulphuric acid, so choking the victim from inside. In Burns's era, the farms raised black cattle and kept horses for general work and use. These animals are not immune from such sulphur poison. Livestock was devastated.

Britain that autumn experienced abnormal ferocious rainfall, which ruined harvests by showering acid rain. The winter that followed was the coldest recorded. There was intense precipitation. This meant in due course so much snow melt that soil was washed away in devastating floods. The spring of 1784 was in any case too late for successful crops. The next few years were unusually cold. The ensuing famine caused significantly more loss of life than the sulphur fog itself. Over several years, anyone weakened by exposure to the fog was at increased risk of early death. As this affected most the lowliest and poorest, unlike in Iceland, it is a forgotten tragedy.

This was for Burns the time of "climacterick". English clergyman Gilbert White of Selborne noted the unusual fog in his journal, and the strange weather that followed over the next few years. He kept notes in his detailed natural history diary. He drew attention to this autumn and the following years in the book of his letters to internationally-famed zoologist Thomas Pennant that is known as 'The Natural History of Selborne'. He recorded the abnormal cold, remarking on snow and frost at Selborne on 22nd April 1784.

This was a tragedy that reached right into the home and heart of Robert Burns. The poison fog probably brought on the death of William Burness in February 1784. Soon Burns had lost his youngest brother. The fog may have harmed his own health. Perhaps it inspired him to court the consolation of philosophical rhyme. He addressed the devil:

> Hear me, auld Hangie, for a wee,
> An' let poor damned bodies be;
> I'm sure sma' pleasure it can gie,
> > Ev'n to a diel,
> To skelp an' scaud poor dogs like me
> > An' hear us squeal!

In Britain, the first months of 1784 were amongst the coldest on record. Expecting their father's death, Burns and his brother Gilbert had invested all they could beg or borrow in their newly leased farm of Mossgeil, near Mauchline. Creditors, moving in on their father's estate, accused them of having stolen livestock from Lochlie, as numbers left there were half the inventory of spring in 1783. This rubbed salt in the sulphur wounds of these honest lads.

Mauchline – like Mechelin in Belgium – means the bog where that unusable wild cotton grows. Romantics translate the word as 'field of flax'. It means soil hereabouts is naturally poor, acidic and heavy, when unimproved sprouting that thin wild moss cotton with its ragged useless white beard. This was the heartless farm whose infertile soil drove Burns to think of emigration.

Dr William Auld, minister at Mauchline, writing his submission for the First Statistical Account in 1790, stated that of recent time women had begun wearing silk caps and silk cloaks. Perhaps this was introduced by Robert, home from success in Edinburgh. Then, money at last in the family pocket, he bought fine mourning silk for the widowed mother who had suffered so long.

Previously Burns had spent what little he could scrape together buying farming books. He owned a copy of the 1784 publication by James Small, 'A Treatise on Ploughs and Wheel Carriages'. But study all the agricultural improvement books as he might, Burns found he and his brother were thwarted by bad seed, bad weather and a late harvest. They made a considerable financial loss in their first year. The only consolation to Burns must have been that the planets were not ranged just against him alone.

During that winter of 1783-4 in the employment of the house Lairgieside, there was a plain faced but shapely girl called Lizzie Paton. In the stress following his father's death in February 1784, at the age of twenty-five, Burns longed for a wife in whom he could confide his cares. After he moved to Mossgeil, now head of the family, he released control of his physical impulses to Lizzie Paton who bore him a child on 22nd May 1785. As we have seen, the young people were dissuaded from marrying.

Burns proudly acknowledged the child as his, but was declared a bachelor. When Burns had money available from the sales of the first edition of his poems in 1786, he paid Lizzie £20 in paternity fee. She was satisfied with this, shortly afterwards marrying a farm-servant. Burns had soon after her birth had the child baptised Elizabeth. He delightedly took her into his home, where she was brought up by his mother and lived with her until Burns died. Then she joined her own mother's household. At the age of 21 she received two hundred pounds from the fund built posthumously from Burns's work.

The practice of payment in lieu of marriage is described in a traditional Scottish folk song in which the man addresses the woman who bears his child:

> "I will wed thee wi' a ring,
> Wi' a ring of gold I'll wed wi' thee"
> "Thou may go wed wi' whom thou choose,
> I'm sure ye'll never wed wi' me,"

she replies. Thus, he pays up:

> So he has ta'en a purse of gold,
> And he has placed it on her knee,
> Saying "Give to me my little young son
> And take thee up thy nurse's fee."

The woman repents her haste:

> "I will wed thee wi' a ring,
> Wi' a ring of gold I'll wed wi' thee"
> "Thou may go wed wi' whom thou choose,
> I'm sure ye'll never wed wi' me,"

was now his response. Her chance of marriage with him was gone forever.

Burns was soon being actively courted by Jean Armour who succeeded in seducing him in early 1786. Biographers suggest that since Jean's first twins were born in September 1786 they were conceived by Burns as early as Christmas 1785. This assumes they went full term. After the failure of achieving marriage to Lizzie, he was determined people would not stop him marrying, next time he found a good match. That intention to marry Jean was reversed by her father's behaviour. He viciously thwarted the marriage. Burns again paid paternity but with a bloody-minded intention to look elsewhere for a loyal woman who would partner him as wife.

Yet he continued to fret that Jean too had been stolen from him. After the twins were born, in a letter to John Kennedy, he continued to express his desire for a soul-mate wife and a family around him, frustrated of the right to enjoy partnership:

> "the burning glow when he clasps the Woman of his Soul to his bosom – the tender yearnings of heart for the little Angels to whom he has given existence – These, Nature has pour'd in milky streams about the human heart; and the Man who never rouses them into action by the inspiring influences of their proper objects, loses by far the most pleasurable part of his existence."

Some modern biographers criticise Burns that at the end of June 1787 he wrote to James Smith that he had still no intention then of marrying Jean Armour. "Clearly", say such critics, "this is against the rules! He had already two weeks earlier made her pregnant again." Ferguson proposed that this letter cited in evidence against him had been written around 1st August 1786. Let us suppose the 1787 date correct, and Burns is not here stating his reaction to Jean's father's refusal to recognise their common law marriage. Biographers still tend to quote the poet's statement that under no consideration will he marry Jean, yet choose to ignore his further statement about himself. This statement surely denies heartlessness:

> "I have scarcely any vestige of the image of God left me, except a pretty large portion of honour and an enthusiastic, incoherent Benevolence. If you see Jean, tell her I will meet her, So help me Heaven in my hour of need!"

Also men always assume that twins naturally go full term. They do not. Perhaps he had not yet made her pregnant in August 1787. Jean's second twins were buried on 10th March and 22nd March 1788. Suppose they were born prematurely about 6 or 7 months with one stillborn. This is a typical timing and outcome for early birth when the womb is strained by a dual burden.

Equally, men dispute whether it is possible – irrespective of whether it is appropriate – for a fair-minded man to have intercourse with a woman in the advanced stages of bearing twins. I tell you from personal experience that it emphatically is not possible. A woman at that stage will certainly not let a man get physically that close, simply because of pain. Only a brute would force his way and penetrate. An infamous letter of 3rd March 1788 is cited to prove Robert was a brute. It was written to adolescent-minded Bob Ainslie, fair-weather cronie from the Crochallan Fencibles, that infamous bawdy men's drinking club that was de rigueur for those with hopes of literary success in the entertainment world of 18th century Edinburgh. I guess that what Robert and Jean did together was paraphrased in male terms when Burns used horseplay analogy and said Jean in their intercourse

> "rejoiced with joy unspeakable and full of glory".

There are other manifestations of intense sexuality that can give great pleasure that a woman at that advanced stage can greatly appreciate. It needs a creative mind, such as that of a poet, to have the necessary imagination. Women will generally attest that few men have the imagination to do other than fuck. But Burns had imagination in love. In 1788 he wrote:

"What a strange, mysterious faculty is that thing called Imagination! We have no ideas almost at all, of another world; but I have often amused myself with visionary schemes of what happiness might be enjoyed by small alteration, alterations that we can fully enter to, in this present state of existence. . . .Imagine our bodies free from pain and the necessary supplies for the wants of nature, at all times and easily within our reach: imagine further that we were set free from the laws of gravitation which bind us to this globe, and could at pleasure fly free, without inconvenience, through all the yet unconjectur'd bounds of Creation. What a life of bliss would we lead, in our mutual pursuit of virtue and knowledge, and our mutual enjoyment of friendship and love!"

The start of 1787 was a propitious time for Burns to present outward macho show. Progressed Mars for Burns conjoined Burns's natal Saturn on February 15th 1787, following his winter in Edinburgh and when he was exulting in the prospect of a second edition of his poems.

At this stage you will think I am going too far identifying correlations between life events of Burns and notional progressed conjunctions in his putative horoscope. But I am illustrating the way a fair proportion of his contemporaries would have thought. It is by no means too fanciful to consider astrology in reassessing Burns. It is not considered by biographers because of modern perspective that the late 18th century was the Age of Reason.

Pennant found all kind of omens in his journeys far into the mountains, where belief in their meaning was still strong. Returning to the Lowland areas of Scotland meant for Pennant a return to ordered scientific reporting of facts, interspersed with extracts from quaint historians. Yet at Melvil House at St Andrews, once a summer retreat of the Archbishop, he was shown Cardan's Well. St Andrews was the site of the reputed arrival in 370 of Christianity into Pictland, brought by shipwrecked St Regulus, who brought with him Culdees, the Cultores Dei, worshippers of God. Cardan was a physician who came from Milan in 1552 to cure Archbishop Hamilton of asthma. Hamilton was convinced he would die of choking. Cardan drew up his horoscope and predicted that he would not die of asthma. Neither he did. As it transpired, he did die of choking – a result of his being lynched at Stirling, an early atrocity in the Scottish Reformation. Seven years later, in a single day, John Knox achieved the demolition of the cathedral at St Andrews.

Burns too heard stories of relevant horoscopes told in Scotland, if only to amuse tourists. There were tales of omens. In 'Hallowe'en' he made the old woman retell her experience of a terrifying omen that happened just before the 1715 horror of the Battle of Sheriffmuir. Thus spoke she:

"Ae Hairst afore the *Sherra-moor*,
I mind't as weel's yestreen,
I was a gilpey then, I'm sure
I was na past fifteen:
The Simmer had been cauld an' wat,
An' *Stuff* was unco green;
An' ay a rantan Kirn we gat,
An' just on *Hallowe'en*
It fell that night.

Our *Stibble-rig* was *Rab M'Graen*,
          A clever, sturdy fallow;
His Sin gat *Eppie Sim* wi' wean,
          That lived in Achmachalla:
He gat *hemp-seed*, I mind it weel,
          An' he made unco light o't;
But money a day was by *himsel,*
          He was sae sairly frighted
                    That vera night."

The word 'astrology' simply means 'the reading of the stars'. Without astrology, there would have been no meteorology and no man-made Earth satellites. Astrology was one of the disciplines studied by the great names of modern scientific history – Robert Boyle the father of modern chemistry and Isaac Newton the father of modern physics amongst them. Both were adepts at the casting of horoscopes. Much earlier than both in being an astrological adept was the great mathematician and historian the Venerable Bede. He created sky charts in tabular form – each one what astrologers would call an Ephemeris. These enabled users to read off as from ready-reckoners accurate allocation of the date of Easter from the time he wrote his 'De Temporibus' in 707 until 1066. We have seen that this dating was no simple ecclesiastical nicety but in agricultural communities vitally important for choosing when to plant seed, and when to mate cattle, sheep and pigs. The right timing for these annual functions needs to be chosen to fit the rhythm of the seasons. Astronomical relationships affect the fecundity of the Earth.

Thus if a child was born in an agricultural community as the cycle of the heavens was moving into an adverse phase, in terms of weather and agricultural productivity, it could be predicted that that child would probably face hardship in early life. Such a prediction was no less meaningful than modern weather forecasting. There are very subtle variations in seasons caused by wobble in the orbit of the Moon and the fact that the Moon's orbit round the Earth is not an exact fraction of the Earth's orbit round the Sun. With regular variation over a very long timescale, the position of the rising of the full moon is seen to change each year. In one part of this long cycle its rising moves northwards. Then it turns back on reaching its maximum northerly rising. These long cycles were understood by Bede and Newton.

As civilisations developed, records of measurement of stars and of planetary positions became more extensive. Correlations were able to be accumulated, allowing adepts to increase the detail of their navigational charts and agricultural and general long-term weather predictions. Adepts naturally came under pressure to extend the scope of their predictions. Many obliged, though they learned to hedge their own bets by voicing these more spurious predictions in increasingly vague terms. Thus astrology, having been one of the most useful of proto-sciences, came to be discredited.

The casting of a horoscope increasingly went out of favour once clocks became standard equipment and calendars became increasingly standardised. The latter was not technologically feasible until John Harrison perfected his chronometer in the third quartile of the 18th century. Even so, calendars are not standard around the world today: Chinese, Jewish and Islamic calendars are the main major 21st century time-markers alongside the Western everyday calendar. All are superseded in modern science by the atomic clock.

The everyday modern Western calendar is based on the Gregorian calendar. This was introduced when it was finally accepted that the calendar then in use was too out of line with the seasons. It was not adopted by Russia until after its Revolution of 1917. It had not been adopted by England until 1752. England had defiantly held out against this Romish plot to vaporise nearly two weeks of one particular year. Major calendar reform followed analysis by astronomers of Pope Gregory III. These leading research mathematicians of the day recalibrated the dating system. The Pope announced the removal of ten days in October 1582 to set the year right. Reformed Scotland had quickly abandoned the Julian calendar and followed this wisdom of Europe's greatest scientists.

Two different calendars operated under the one crown when James VI of Scotland followed Elizabeth of England as ruler of the southern kingdom too. This caused a fair bit of initial confusion, until lawyers and businessmen simply got into the habit of writing both dates on their letters to each other. The problem was compounded by the fact that England still did not change the year number until the Spring equinox. Finally, fed up with the inconvenience and the outright silliness of being out of line with key trading partners, England adopted the Gregorian calendar.

The man who thus kept English calendars firmly rooted in the Middle Ages was Elizabeth's personal astrologer, John Dee (1527-1608). Son of Henry VIII's kitchen manager, this Cambridge mathematician edited Euclid, and was an expert on navigational instrumentation. He studied extensively at European universities and was a popular public lecturer while at Rheims. He turned down job offers from Ivan the Terrible and from the king of France to return to England and the court of Queen Mary. He found his real strength as Elizabeth's personal confidant. He was tasked with casting her horoscope to determine the right date for her coronation.

A true horoscope is neither more nor less than a star-date. Since it is easier to identify the moment of birth than the moment of conception, personal horoscopes are normally calculated relative to time of birth. This can be extended to the birth of States and the birth of enterprises.

By describing exactly what would be visible to an observer within the hemispherical vault of the sky above the birthing woman, were all the stars and planets and other bodies in the sky fully visible at the point of birth in time and place whether it is day or night, that time-place moment of birth is uniquely identified. There is no need to rely on transient human calendars when stars and planets are up there providing an unquestionably reliable record of the passage of time.

During a birth, people on the spot tend to be preoccupied with more immediate things than planets. So convention has arisen to note local time of birth in calendar date and hour. At a convenient time, provided good tables of planetary positions are available, it is not too difficult to work out by arithmetic the star-date description of the birth. This kind of birth-dating is very useful because it is independent of calendars, clocks and even boundaries of states and names of places. It relates to things natural and extraterrestrial with measurable patterns of regular change. Horoscopes have thus been drawn up for political and religious leaders of all past civilisations which have developed sufficient record-keeping to build up enough time-related astronomical data to make possible suitable annotation of birth star-date. Interpreting a horoscope requires much more data than merely drawing one up. It requires very extensive correlation of planetary patterns with human experience and then extrapolating what this implies for similar patterns. This is a complex model akin to those mathematical tools meteorologists use.

Chapter V *Saturnalia*

Because star-dates are composed of the co-ordinates of the Sun, Moon and planets against the backdrop of the stars, they typically were written as an extensive table, like a spreadsheet. Alongside a symbol in this table for each moving heavenly body are its spherical co-ordinates in relation to Earth's north-south polar line and the equatorial plane of the Earth. Alternatively, because the planets are helpfully more or less on the same plane, which happens to coincide roughly with that galactic plane that we see as the band of stars of the Milky Way, a horoscope can be drawn as points on a circle. This, though, simplifies the horoscope, losing its three-dimensional nature. The horoscope given in Appendix IV of this book is of the simplified two-dimensional circular one except that it is written as a table.

Each person has a totally unique true horoscope. Equally the evolution over that person's lifetime of the heavenly positions of the Sun, Moon and planets, is also totally unique. So the use of horoscopes for predictive purposes is always at best limited to using comparison with similar situations experienced in the past by people with different star-date profiles. The best that can be done, as in meteorology, is to gather together all star-date profiles that are mostly similar and look at how the skies then evolved and what happened to the people. This is how the ancients built up their arcane dossiers from which they made statements about experiences a person might encounter in his future life.

In the great whirl of the heavens, the fastest moving dancers that clearly follow a regular pattern are the Sun, the Moon and the visible planets. Their movements are against a narrow band of sky in the fuzzy limits of the dense circle of stars called the Milky Way. The ancients considered the Sun as the main dancer, and Moon as lady partner who burled separately in a pretty step, sometimes showing Earth the full light of her face, sometimes turning her dark back on observers, often dancing so that her orb fell under a red shadow.

Copernicus proposed we consider the Sun fixed in space with Earth and Moon dancing together, with all the other planets dancing round the Sun too.

The Moon is substantially bigger relative to Earth than any other satellite of our solar system is to its host. Scientists now believe that this causes the daily revolution of the Earth to be stabilized. The Moon-Earth dance is like a dance in which the lady, always facing her partner, makes a stately circle of 29 steps, holding the hand of the man in the centre who twirls right round once for thirteen stately steps round the Sun. Together, they are able to maintain this dance with regularity and stability. A single dancer burling round could become dizzy and tumble about. A single dancer moving too slowly in a circle can, like a comet, lose the steady count of time.

The Moon and Earth dancers revolve around the Sun, steadily maintaining time and count. They dance together within an amazingly narrow band at precisely that distance from the Sun where surface temperatures on Earth allow water to be liquid and so maintain life. Because the Earth turns, the gravitational effect of the Moon on the surface of that liquid creates tides. The littoral so created, the space between low and high tide, proved a benign and supportive environment for complex life to form. It is now realised that the chance is extremely small that, anywhere else in the known universe, there exists any planet with these and other supportive conditions for the creation of the complex life form known as Man. We appear to be an incredibly unique consequence of a large number of unlikely coincidences.

The ancients observed that about these main dancers – Earth, Sun and Moon – burl first of all darting Mercury and then stately feminine Venus. Mars dances more slowly. Jupiter, a great lumbering soul, moves very slowly, taking many Earth years to complete his assigned steps around the sky. For long periods he will appear near the Sun before moving away to the furthest end of the Milky Way. Saturn moves slower still, taking half a long human lifetime to complete his circuit. The ancients thought there might be other dancers.

Resurrecting ancient myths, Immanuel Kant in 1756 predicted the existence of the planet Uranus. On 15th March 1781, William Herschel, through his telescope, spotted Uranus – its first sighting. Uranus was at the birth of Burns at 24 degrees 25 minutes of Pisces, the sign of the poet.

While Uranus was of no interest to the ordinary man in the fields in the days of Burns, he clearly kept abreast of developments in astronomy and was aware of its existence. Herschel named the planet the Georgian Star, or Georgium Sidus. In his extant writings Burns made several references to it. In 1786, before he left for Edinburgh, Mrs Dunlop warned Burns to beware of the transience of fashion. To her he had replied that he had no misconception of there being permanent honour in the academy of fame. In 1788, home from his season of being pop idol in Edinburgh, he had occasion to write to her son Andrew:

> "Do you know that, except from your Mother and the good family, my existence or non-existence is now of as little importance to that Great World I lately left, as the satellites of the Georgium Sidus is to a parcel of your Ditchers. I foresaw this from the beginning. Ambition could not form a higher wish than to be wedded to Novelty, but I retired to my shades, with a little comfortable pride, and a few comfortable pounds."

Uranus is again in Pisces at the start of the 21st century. This planet is associated by modern astrologers with opportunities for sudden awareness of higher realms, and thus with the mystical.

Immediately before Kant proposed another planet, in his treatise that suggested that the solar system was formed from dust, watchers of the skies knew that in 1755-6 they were experiencing in Europe an extremely cold winter. It would be one of the coldest for which records were made. The Golden Horn around Constantinople froze over. This is considered to mark the beginning of another severe 'mini Ice Age' that lasted several decades. Henry Fielding died in Lisbon in 1754, a year before its disastrous earthquake, but Voltaire wrote a poem on the earthquake in 1756. It prompted Kant to publish a treatise proposing a cause for earthquakes. Coincidentally, that day in early November 1755 when Lisbon was destroyed, luckless Marie Antoinette was born.

Since 1970 the considerable advance in the power of computational technology has enabled a substantial improvement in the predictive capabilities of the science of meteorology. General scientific knowledge of the structure of the Earth's atmosphere has also expanded and deepened. It is now recognised that severe cold in European winters can be caused by changes in the location on the surface of the Earth of an air movement known as the Jet Stream. This phenomenon, like a continuous river winding round the Earth, is instrumental in forming weather patterns. In its most common position in the 20th century this Jet Stream caused British winters to be relatively warm and dry. Whenever the Jet Stream has passed north of Britain in winter, British winters have been bitterly cold, with extremely heavy falls of snow that then would not thaw. What causes movement of the Jet Stream is not yet understood. Lack of understanding makes reliable very long range meteorological predictions impossible.

Chapter V *Saturnalia*

It goes without saying that five thousand years ago electronic computers were not available. But long term meteorological predictions were no less desirable to the civilisations of Mesopotamia, Egypt, China and Central America than they are to our modern civilisations. Scientists thus sought correlations between astronomical observation and actual experience. This built up a body of lore.

From the earliest known times there have been charlatans offering predictive services without sufficient arcane knowledge and without communicating to clients the severe limitations inherent in the reliability of predictions. Even during the time that academics call the Enlightenment there were not a few who claimed they could use astronomical observations not merely to provide long-term guidance on likely weather patterns based on experience, but predictions on the outcome of individual human lives. Abuse of the methods of astrology could cause serious social problems. Political and religious powers constantly opposed the unauthorised provision of arcane services. The Roman Church also opposed the abuse of astrological methodologies to promulgate unorthodox and misleading teachings.

The Roman Church could not deny relevance of astronomical knowledge. After all, its mysteries were, and are, based on scientific astronomical principles, properly applied. Christmas is the festival of the growing light of the Sun following the winter solstice; Easter is the beginning of spring and is associated with the Vernal Equinox. These in the sight of the Church are both God-given material blessings to Mankind. The Church uses the changing seasons allegorically to represent the spiritual blessings of the coming of the Light of Christ and the Resurrection from physical death of Jesus himself and of Christians at the Last Judgement. Easter is also historically justified annual remembrance of the Passover timing of the Crucifixion.

It was not astrology per se that secular governments and the Roman Church were at one in opposing. What both opposed were: first, the assumption that correlation between past observations of stellar and planetary movements and past human experience proved that positions and movements of the stars and planets *caused* human experience; second, the claim that natal position of stars and planets *therefore predicted* the fate of that human life. The objection to the first was both scientific and theological: correlation is not causation, quite apart from the dogma that the primary cause is God. The objection to the second is the same with the added specific aspect that prediction of the outcome for even a single human life denies free will.

Hard line Calvinists, of course, did not believe in free will. They believed in predestination. In 18th century Scotland, one of the most voluble philosophical battles was fought out in the kirks of the ordinary people between those ministers who taught that humankind was divided by God at birth into the Justified and the Damned, and those who believed that each person could, through his own striving for goodness, achieve the reward of paradise. This is the issue behind the fracas that Burns described in 'The Ordination'.

Burns got really stuck into this battle of philosophical difference between the Auld Lichts and the New Lichts. As we have seen, he believed in free will and opposing the Unco Guid, or the self-professed Justified Sinners of his Holy Willie type.

But it is not intrinsic contradiction to believe in free will and also to believe that there is correlation (though not causation) between planetary positions and human life. What Burns clearly seems to have believed was that the universe was a great and magnificent place, worthy of an incredible Godly presence.

During the Enlightenment, those who desired the demise of predictive astrology were delighted with the finding of Uranus. They claimed that this showed that the old tabulations of the meanings of horoscopes were clearly, by its discovery, 'proved' to be incomplete and therefore false. Others brought Uranus into the canon of astrological prediction. Neptune was similarly naturalised. Pluto was later added, following the discovery of this little irregularly-orbiting entity. Pluto is in the process of being re-evaluated, having been, in some scientific circles, denounced as a fraudster. It is a bit too small to merit true planetary status.

Astrologers consider the position of the planets at the point of birth and their changing positions throughout life to be fundamental to the destiny and spiritual role of the individual. Planets do not appear to move uniformly, and this needs to be taken into account in interpreting a person's horoscope. Variation arises because the steps in the sky-dance appear not simply to be burling in a forward direction round the Sun, but to have little on-the-spot steps like the Scottish pas-de-bas and backward steps as in the dance called the Gay Gordons. So planets, as observed from Earth, can appear stationary or retrograde.

This appearance of pas-de-bas steps and burling backwards is because, when we observe planets, they are projected onto the backdrop of the stars. Because the Earth and the planets all orbit, relative positions with respect to the backdrop are constantly shifting. Sometimes a planet seems to 'get ahead' against this backdrop, and sometimes it seems to 'fall behind'. It is the period in which it is 'falling behind' that a planet seems to be going back over its own previous position in the sky.

The frequency with which a planet 'falls behind', relatively speaking, depends on how fast the planet moves. So Mercury quite often 'falls behind', while the planets that orbit more slowly appear to have a less jerky dance but all go retrograde. When planets go retrograde there is a comparable reversal in the change that is constantly taking place in their gravitational relationship with the Earth. Small though that be in relation to the gravitational interaction of the Earth with the Sun and even with the Moon, it is non zero. Astrologers came to link retrograde movement with reversals in the 'influence' of planets. In this context it is worth noting the scientific experience of developing supersonic flight. Aeronautical engineers discovered that to fly supersonic successfully aeroplanes need to change the way they fly if they are to avoid being destroyed by impact with their own sound waves. This impact causes the immensely powerful sonic boom. Wing and tail aerofoil controls must be reversed as the plane accelerates through the speed of sound.

Saturn is considered to have particular astrological influence in dividing a person's life into phases of around 28 to 30 years in length. The end of the period is the Saturn Return. This is identified by astrologers as the time at which Saturn achieves its same position with respect to the Earth as it had at the outset, against the backcloth of the Milky Way. The Saturn co-ordinates in the star-date of the birth of Robert Burns were 2 degrees 55 minutes of the constellation Pisces. Burns had only one Saturn Return. It centred on March 3rd 1788.

It was at that time that Robert Burns left Edinburgh, abandoned the hopeless nonsense of the association with his Clarinda, Agnes McLehose, and began the serious process of concluding his previously aborted marriage with Jean Armour, qualifying for an Excise post, setting up home as a married man and focussing his creative energy on song.

By the way, on Thursday 13th September 2007, when this Saturn Return was calculated for me, Saturn was positioned at 1 degree 22 minutes of Virgo, at 180 degrees, or directly opposite, or in opposition to, Burns's natal Saturn. The 180 degree point from a natal planet is considered by astrologers to be the high point of a cycle, the point of maximum growth. It means maximum involvement. I asked what astrology would make of this. This opposition to natal Saturn suggests his message can now achieve greatly increased outreach.

This position relative to the constellation Virgo is what is called 'within orb', or directly overlapping. Thus Virgo, relative to the spirit of Robert Burns, or what Robert Burns stood for, is having maximum effect. Virgo is the sign of analysis, details, exactness and determination to achieve perfection. This point in time, two hundred and fifty years after his birth, is not merely his centenary. It is also astrologically a most significant moment to broadcast to the world his message: that man to man, through all the world, shall brothers be.

Not that he had been thinking much of that during his meetings with Agnes McLehose. He was more interested in intimate love and music. Writing to Clarinda on 24th January 1788 he remarked with delight that he had just had a session with Johann Georg Schetky who had created a fine tune for his song 'Clarinda, mistress of my soul'. This musician born in Darmstadt had become an excellent cellist. In 1773 he was engaged for the St Cecilia Concerts in Edinburgh. He settled in the city as a music teacher.

The curious Clarinda-Sylvander affair apparently of unconsummated love on his part and probably, in my view, no more than toy-boy game-playing that turned nasty on her part, has at least left us with one of the finest of love songs, 'Ae fond kiss and then we sever, ae farewell, alas forever', with at its painful heart:

> Had we never loved sae kindly,
> Had we never loved sae blindly
> Never met, and never parted,
> We had ne'er been broken-hearted.

And the ultimate love blessing:

> Fare thee well, thou first and fairest,
> Fare thee well, thou best and dearest,
> Thine be ilka joy and treasure,
> Peace, enjoyment, love and pleasure.

At its outset when he was in Edinburgh the correspondence between the two was extremely frequent, with more than one letter in some days when they saw each other. This indicates to me that he saw the correspondence as a creative exercise. He signed himself 'Sylvander' in the early phase. When Agnes found out she did not possess him she virtually stopped writing except for offensive letters. His letters to her then became rare, but outnumbered hers. They were not of the same type as his 'Sylvander' letters.

Read in the context of the letters that Burns was writing to others at this time – particularly the juxtaposition of the first few letters to Clarinda with those to the young ladies at Harvieston, with whom he began to exchange letters in early November 1787, the Clarinda correspondence acquires a different colour from the fine story of mutual love that it has been made out to represent.

Burns compliments the young Harvieston ladies that, unlike so many of their sex, they had the intellectual confidence not to need the prop of a lover to make them whole rounded persons. He described Margaret Chalmers and her friend Charlotte as:

> "two favourite resting-places for my soul in her wanderings through the weary, thorny wilderness of this world"

in the struggle in which,

> "I glory in being a Poet, and I want to be thought a wise man – I would fondly be generous, and I wish to be rich".

But he knew the last to be a vain hope.

It happened that within a month he was laid up with a hideous knee injury that affected his walking ever after. He was stuck in Edinburgh and being pursued by Agnes McLehose. She, behind protestations that he must not talk of love, wanted to do nothing but talk of love. He wrote to her politely on 8th December, and instead of taking the hint to back off, she took encouragement. He wrote again on 12th December, but again was too polite to get her off his back. She responded that his letter was tantamount to paying addresses to a married woman. This he roundly refuted on 20th December. But he couldn't shake her off. Then came her Clarinda invention. He must have decided to make the best of this business as her imaginary country eunuch swain Sylvander – a too pure lover for a frustrated prudish Lady Chatterley.

It was not through the delicacy and propriety of flirty Agnes that nothing untoward came to this respectable lady of Edinburgh's fine society. It was not through her exertions that her virtue, as a separated mother living alone, was not in any way impaired by the association. The fact that for a chunk of their affair Burns had that damaged leg merely allows the imagination to exercise more interestingly on how they might have had it off together. But they didn't. Clarinda, in one of her later letters to him, though it had been she who had instigated and insisted on the affair, congratulated herself for being the one who had maintained and preserved her 'chastity' against his advances despite their close encounters. This made him very angry.

> "When you call over the scenes that have passed between us, you will survey the conduct of an honest man, struggling successfully with temptations the most powerful that ever beset humanity, and preserving untainted honour in situations where the austerest Virtue would have forgiven a fall. Situations that I will dare to say, not a single individual of his kind, even with half his sensibility and passion, could have encountered without ruin; and I leave you to guess, Madam, how such a man is likely to digest an accusation of perfidious treachery!"

This was a lovers' tiff in spades after a falling out that was never repaired. A few more letters were exchanged. They did meet again, on 6th December 1791, shortly before he sent her a copy of 'Ae fond kiss'. But it was formal, and strained. In January 1792 Agnes McLehose sailed to Jamaica, to attempt reconciliation with her husband. She sailed on the *Roselle*. Burns himself might have sailed on that boat six years earlier. By 1792 it was captained by his friend Richard Brown of Irvine. It had been he who first suggested to Burns that he print his poems. Burns asked Brown to take care of Clarinda on her voyage.

Clarinda soon returned to Edinburgh. She had found her place as mistress of her Jamaica plantation taken by a black woman. She tried to resuscitate correspondence with Burns, but he had risen above her ebullient bosom.

Chapter V *Saturnalia*

Clarinda was no soul-mate, but she was an inspiration. It is not unlikely that Burns had initially responded to her suggestion of an affair of love-letters for its harmless value to his creative development. In all ages there are two kinds of literature, which sometimes overlap. There is the kind that is found entertaining by a very wide audience, and there is the kind that transcends the everyday and is true art. The vast majority of those who aspire to writing success try to create the first type. After all, it is the only type that can bring considerable financial reward. The true worth of the second type tends to be recognised when its author is already old or even dead. Few are those authors whose work is financially successful in their own lifetime and then continues to be considered great by later generations. More commonly for the real artist – and this was where the balance lay for Burns – he is recognised only after he is gone.

The big Scottish literary success of Burns's day was Henry Mackenzie, author of 'The Man of Feeling'. This book probably inspired Goethe to write his 'Young Werther' about a young man with so much melodrama in his makeup that he commits suicide. Goethe's book caused a stir in Germany because it precipitated a number of copycat deaths amongst young people. Robert had his own copy of the English translation.

An earlier book of similar 'emotion', Henry Fielding's 'Amelia', had been the 18th century equivalent of the modern romantic novelette. It had gained a large audience of swooning females, including Agnes McLehose.

Burns wanted a literary income. He had practiced letter writing since childhood. Letter-centred romantic novels were very popular. Her suggestion that she and Burns correspond offered this young man – who had been trained in such polite letter writing – an opportunity. Here was a woman offering to collaborate in generating a whole series of those artificial letters that tell a heart-throb of a sentimental story. He could work out, through a harmless real-life encounter, a whole frivolous intercourse of hopeless love, with a pre-defined tear-jerking conclusion of inevitable separation. This was a big chance to get into creating a real money-spinner of a novel.

What better way to compose the book than exchanging letters with a woman who was way above any risk of that sexuality that most women were trying to foist on him. Or so he probably thought. Except it turned out she wasn't thinking that way. She wanted him for herself. Perhaps Burns didn't realise that Mrs McLehose, being a married woman, could actually intend to take the whole thing seriously – if platonically. She had, after all, chosen not to divorce her husband. She wasn't amused when he continued to hanker after his bonnie Jean. When Burns realised she had taken their correspondence too seriously, he backed off quickly. Her response, while he lived, was nastiness and hatred. In due course she was inflamed with rage when he was finally able to formalise his marriage with *that woman*, Jean Armour. He accepted that Clarinda had turned against him only after his pain when she joined the Edinburgh elite in foisting on him paternity of the child of her maid Jenny Clow.

Had Burns been able to publish during his lifetime a novelette based on the Clarinda-Sylvander letters, Burns might now be remembered as a writer of the same calibre as Henry Mackenzie. The letters would have made a cleaner version of Henry Fielding's 'Tom Jones'. In novels, the society hostess gets herself a rustic toyboy. Unlike Clarinda, who kept declaring her poverty, she kept her toyboy in fine clothes and plenty of pocket money. He was paid handsomely as her gigolo. Since

Clarinda wasn't getting the goods, she never offered any to Burns – who would in any case have been disgusted with the suggestion.

So instead of writing soppy or risqué novels, Burns transcended his era as the producer of hundreds of songs building on the ancient musical heritage of Scotland.

But he might have preferred to have earned the comfortable living.

Experience of Clarinda, though, did impress on him that, as she couldn't manage on *her* allowance, no way could he ever afford a wife, however intellectual, if her sole aim in life was to be a society hostess. Jean, town girl though she was, had the guts to knuckle down for a whole summer living with mother-in-law to learn dairying and care of animals.

In the event, at a suitable period after his death, it was Clarinda who turned the correspondence into the money-spinner, entirely for her own benefit. She got good social payback from association with his name. Many years later, Walter Scott met old Agnes, now a self-made legend after selectively publishing Burns's letters to her. He found her 'old, charmless and devout'.

Where the heart of Burns really lay at the time of this correspondence may be assessed from a pair of white kid gloves that lies today in a case in the museum in Lady Stair's House in Edinburgh's Royal Mile. Tolstoy describes a Masonic ritual, strongly honoured in the late 18th century. A true Mason must seek the woman who would be his soul mate, and to her and her alone he would give a pair of white kid gloves in token of his dedication and commitment. The families of neither Highland Mary nor Clarinda produced such gloves in evidence of the poet's affection. But throughout her life Jean on dress occasions proudly wore on those stubby hands, fattened with milking cows and coarsened with farm work, those gloves that were the gift from her Masonic husband.

That one and only Saturn Return in Burns's lifetime was also marked by a slight wobble in his relationship with his lady mentor Mrs Dunlop, although she indeed stood by him until 1795. Then he insensitively wrote to her so positively supporting the French revolutionaries only a short while after her daughter Susan died in Muges, Aigullion near Bordeaux, leaving an infant son. Her husband James Henri, who was from Bernaldean, died in Scotland in June 1790. She had gone to France to claim his inheritance. A few years later she fell victim to the disruption and famine then sweeping the French countryside in the wake of Revolution.

Near the Saturn Return, on 21st January 1788, Mrs Dunlop took offence from a letter he wrote her from Edinburgh. He was seriously depressed, that smashed knee having confined him in a room all winter in a hostile dirty city.

> "After six weeks confinement, I am beginning to walk across the room. They have been six horrible weeks, anguish and low spirits made me unfit to read, write, or think.
>
> I have a hundred times wished that one could resign life as an officer resigns a commission; for I would not take in any poor, ignorant wretch, by selling out. Lately I was a sixpenny private, and, God knows, a miserable soldier enough; now I march the campaign, a starving cadet; a little more conspicuously wretched.
>
> I am ashamed of all this; for though I do want bravery for the warfare of life, I could wish, like some other soldiers, to have as much fortitude or cunning as to dissemble or conceal my cowardice.
>
> As soon as I can bear the journey, which will be, I suppose, about the middle of next

week, I leave Edinburgh, and soon after I shall pay my grateful duty at Dunlop House."

Mrs Dunlop was not amused; she read this letter as impious, and accused him of lacking true faith in God. On 12th February he defended his belief in God, writing:

> "Some things in your letters hurt me: not that you say them, but that you mistake me. Religion, my honoured Madam, has not only been all my life my chief dependence, but my dearest enjoyment. I have indeed been the luckless victim of wayward follies: but alas, I have ever been 'more fool than knave'."

Mrs Dunlop wrote back unconvinced, accusing him of using his wit and poetical ability to hurt. More importantly she focussed on a comment he had made in praise of the character that Milton had given to Satan. She took this as indicating that he honoured Satan, implying he was a Devil Worshipper.

Burns never had any of those modern motivational posters that tell you 'when you are stuck in a hole, stop digging'. He used even more of the costly paper, ink and pen, and the valuable time to try to explain himself to Mrs Dunlop. On 7th March 1788, back in the farm at Mossgeil, he replied in his defence:

> "That I am often a sinner with any little wit I have, I do confess: but I have taxed my recollection to no purpose to find out when it was employed against you. I hate an ungenerous sarcasm a great deal worse than I do the devil; at least, as Milton depicts him; and though I may be rascally enough to be sometimes guilty of it myself, I cannot endure it in others. You, my honoured friend, who cannot appear in any light but you are sure of being respectable – you can afford to pass by an occasion to display your wit, because you may depend for fame on your sense; or if you choose to be silent, you know you can rely on the gratitude of many and the esteem of all; but, God help us who are wits or writers by profession, if we stand not for fame there, we sink unsupported."

That wobble was over. But he realised how easy it could be to lose even his most sympathetic patron in a world that increasingly saw a bogeyman round every corner.

Aware of how unsupported he was, and how precarious was the self-employed life of a smallholder farmer, Burns had already sought paid employment. The Saturn Return marked his turning away from reliance on the plough to seek security for his family in a Civil Service job in the Excise. But most significant of all, it was at this turning point of his life that he finally decided he would reach out to song as the means through which he could create for his Scottish homeland that legacy he dreamed of.

For dear old Scotland's sake he would make a useful book worthy of the spirits of the ancient nameless poets and bards from whose works he drew his inspiration.

Coila

"All hail! my own inspired Bard!
In me thy native Muse regard!
I marked thy embryo-tuneful flame
    Thy natal hour."
Her eye, ev'n turned on empty space
    Beam'd keen with Honor.

"I saw thy pulse's maddening play
Wild send thee Pleasure's devious way,
Misled by Fancy's meteor-ray,
    By Passion driven;
But yet the light that led astray
    Was light from Heaven."

"To give my counsels all in one:
Thy tuneful flame still careful fan:
Preserve the Dignity of Man,
    With Soul erect;
And trust the Universal Plan
    Will all protect."

"And wear thou this." – She solemn said,
And bound the Holly round my head.
The polish'd leaves and berries red
    Did rustling play;
And, like a passing thought, she fled
    In light away.

Chapter VI *Magic*

How Burns discovered power brokers used witch hunts and superstition to usurp power, make fortunes and deprive people of freedom, but that ancient ideas could release the mind.

While Covenanting stories laced with witchcraft were the stuff of childhood fireside tales, the growing boy Robert had available to him a hefty history tome that his father brought home one night in 1767, on returning from market in Kilmarnock. It was the newly published up-to-the-minute 'Geographical Grammar' by Thomas Salmon. Salmon never lived to enjoy the royalties of this completely rewritten text, produced at the press of James Meuros in Kilmarnock for Sands, Murray and Cochrane.

When teacher Murdoch moved on there was no proper schooling available for the children. Their father became dominie. William, though, had to work each day on those hard fields of Mount Oliphant farm. This left little time for teaching. Of course, if any of the children was working alongside him – and Burns did the work of a galley-slave – there might be times when there was sufficient attention left over from the actual work to discuss some point of learning. But the imagination balks at this being sufficient to achieve the education Burns accumulated. After his death, his mother recounted how exhausted her husband invariably was in the evenings after working in the fields. He was not farm-trained. He is unlikely to have been as efficient as a true farm-trained person, for he constantly must have come up against challenges whose solution had not been instilled in him in youth. She was born a farmer's daughter. Already stretched in the hard role of farmer's wife, she used her reserves of stamina to support this gardener husband. She frequently took on tasks normally allotted to the farmer. This suggests William had little energy to be the active teacher.

If he was not teacher, who was? There is only one contender. Agnes Broun could read. It is often commented in our modern world that women can naturally multitask while men can't. This may well be more a result of generations of training leading to expectation, than any inherent differences between men and women. Since the beginning of time it has been a commonplace for women to multitask – they do their woman's work while at the same time actively watching a clutch of children. In itself the role of farmer's wife demands multitasking. Children on a farm do some heavy field work but also assist 'woman's work'.

Whenever tasks allotted to the children of William's household were in house or barn, this farmer's wife could add reading and discussion to her multitasking. I suggest that it is more than likely that Agnes supervised a great deal of young Robert's formal reading – and was able to challenge him when he got words wrong.

As she did her own work, Agnes sang. She had a lovely voice. From her Burns first heard not a few Gaelic songs amongst those in the Scots language. There also lived with the family Betty Davidson, the widow of a cousin of his mother. This was the woman whom Burns recalled in his autobiographical letter to Dr Moore. Whether or not she was a believer in the stories she told, she had a fund of tales. Betty Davidson perhaps joined in too in an exciting harmonised chorus. In later life he pressed his mother to sing again those songs so that he could record their music and their words.

Betty Davidson and Agnes Broun both also instilled wonder stories into the cranium of the young poet. These were entertaining and an exciting release from the tedium of dull everyday oppressive work. Agnes may well have augmented her store of stories heard at gatherings by reading prophecies of Thomas the Rhymer, got in a well-used book from a passing chapman. The 19ᵗʰ century Chambers Biographical Dictionary remarks disdainfully that these had been published regularly from 1615 and were still actively circulating in Scotland in the late 18ᵗʰ century. In the same article the contributor criticised Burns for using complex archaic Scots verse forms, particularly that from the ancient song called 'The Cherry and the Slae'. With such a climate in the 19ᵗʰ century, it is hardly surprising that the influences on the works of Burns from women such as his mother, old Betty and other old wives, were ignored by his early biographers.

In April 1793 Bob Ainslie demanded Burns answer his previous letter. Burns was "damnably out of humour". His pen was now driven onward by the flight of his mind:

> "I will not at this time, nor at any other time, answer [your letter]. Answer a letter? I never could answer a letter in my life! I have written many a letter in return for letters I have received; but then – they were original matter – spurt – away! zig, here, zag, there; as if the Devil that, my grannie (an old woman *indeed*!) often told me, rode on Will-o'-wisp, or, in her more classic phrase SPUNKIE, were looking over my elbow. A happy thought that idea has engendered in my head! SPUNKIE – thou shalt henceforth be my Symbol, Signature, & Tutelary Genius! Like thee, hap-step-&-lowp, here-awa-there-awa, higglety-pigglety, pell-mell, hither-&-yon, ram-stam, happy-go-lucky, up-tails-a'-by-the-light-of-the-moon, has been, is, & shall be, my progress through the mosses & moors of this vile, bleak, barren wilderness of a life of ours.
>
> Come, then, my guardian Spirit! Like thee, may I skip away, amusing myself by & at my own light: and if any opaque-souled lubber of mankind complain that my elfine, lambent, glimmerous wanderings have misled his stupid steps over precipices, or into bogs; let the thick-headed blunderbuss recollect, that he is not SPUNKIE – that
>
> 'SPUNKIE's wanderings could not copied be;
> Amid these perils none durst walk but he'."

The letter turns to other matters after his adaptation from Dryden. At the end he signed off as SPUNKIE.

There is more, though, than devil-inspired humour in this letter. Clow and Mrs McLehose had become matters of contention between the two former friends. Burns was the very devil, Ainslie insinuated. Well, if they thought him the Devil Incarnate, he would damn'd well respond like the Devil Incarnate! Having come to admire Milton's Satan during his stay in Edinburgh, Burns now accepted the accolade of being identified with him. He drew on his childhood learning to make this clear.

The education of the children was not only augmented by stories of the supernatural, but would have been enhanced in another way too. There was an old Scots tradition that was finally formally driven out from schools only within the last century. Robert would have been expected not merely to study for his own advancement but also so that, as oldest child, he could be pupil-teacher to his brothers and sisters. Often, the most capable in a modern school class informally help least able colleagues. Such people soon know that to do so they must themselves do far more than just read the lesson over. It is essential to understand the lesson. You need to develop several ways of explaining the difficult points if you are really to help another learn. Otherwise, you get caught out when the person you are trying to help learn asks a question because they have not understood your way of explaining the lesson.

I am writing this from experience, not as someone who has been through teacher training college. I in childhood actively acted pupil-teacher for a formative period of three years in my final stages at junior school. Discovering that I was a challenge within the normal teaching system, the everyday but somehow enlightened school that I attended took a novel approach. There was in the school a Mrs Murphy, war widow of a medical doctor in Burma. This very well educated woman had of necessity become a teacher on getting back to Britain. To dissipate my over-activity she challenged me intellectually. She gave me the responsibility to teach arithmetic and mathematics to my classmates. Each evening she gave me special study in addition to class homework. Each morning we had a session together in which she confirmed I had understood the lesson. For subjects such as history and geography I was a pupil like everyone else. But for part of each day Mrs Murphy divided her class into two. She gave me one half. I taught them maths, while at the same time listening to her giving her lesson in English to the other half. Then we each took over the part of the class that the other had been teaching. I now gave them the maths lesson, half listening a second time to her lesson in English.

(I allow any critic of this book gleefully to pounce on this disclosure as proof that I clearly can know nothing whatsoever about English literature nor hence of the life and work of Robert Burns. By the way, the school inspectors did know this was happening. They took more than usual interest in Mrs Murphy's class. So in retrospect I know that this illegal behaviour was being closely monitored and she was taking a degree of professional risk.)

Far from being ostracised by my classmates for this special treatment, during these three years I enjoyed my greatest rapport with my peers; I was never subjected to abuse of any sort. They recognised that I was in some way intellectually different and was actually being given more school work than they were required to do. When they thought I was too modest about my abilities, they roundly criticised me for insulting their best attempts through doing myself down. In the playground they wanted me to be part of their games. They begged me to come to their parties. They appreciated the increased individual attention they were able to get in maths and English because there were two teachers in the class instead of one. They thanked me.

In 18th century Scotland, in the home such as that of William Burness, a capable older child would, without a second thought, have been expected to take on responsibility as pupil-teacher. Robert's brother Gilbert stated that Robert read every book from cover to cover and virtually memorised the text within every one of them. Certainly, it would have appeared so if Robert was the dedicated teacher that his stern and demanding father no doubt expected him to be. It probably made the task a great deal easier for Robert that he enjoyed learning.

He gathered into his head a lot more than book-learning. The fairy stories stuck.

In early September 1792, still awake at the "witching time of night", he "scrawled a page or two" to Alexander Cunningham in Edinburgh, after

> "all the hurry of business, grinding the faces of the Publican & Sinner on the merciless wheels of the Excise".

He apologised for not having had time or appropriate inspiration to thank in proper poetic form the Royal Company of Archers in Edinburgh. That august body had, five months earlier, on 10th April, honoured him with membership. Nor had he congratulated Cunningham on his marriage. Now he wished Cunningham health, for as a nightcap he had:

"a nipperkin of Toddy by me, just by way of Spell to keep away the meikle horned Deil, or any of his subaltern Imps who may be on their nightly rounds.

But what shall I write to you? - 'The Voice said, Cry: & I said, What shall I cry!' – O thou Spirit! whatever thou art, or wherever thou makest thyself visible. Be thou a Bogle by the eerie side of the auld thorn, in the dreary glen through which the herd-callan maun bicker in his gloaming route frae the fauld! – Be thou a Brownie, set, at dead of night, to thy task by the blazing ingle, or in the solitary barn, where the repercussions of thy iron flail half affright thyself, as thou performest the work of twenty of the sons of men ere the cock-crowing summon thee to thy ample cog of substantial brose! – Be thou a Kelpie, haunting the ford, or ferry, in the starless night, mixing thy laughing yell with the howling of the storm, & the roaring of the flood, as thou viewest the perils & miseries of Man on the foundering horse, or in the tumbling boat! – Or, lastly, be thou a Ghost, paying thy nocturnal visits to the hoary ruins of decayed Grandeur; or performing thy mystic rites in the shadow of the time-worn Church, while the Moon looks, without a cloud, on the silent, ghastly dwellings of the dead around thee; or, taking thy stand by the bed-side of the Villain, or the Murderer, pourtraying on his dreaming fancy, pictures, dreadful as the horrors of unveiled Hell, & terrible as the wrath of incensed Deity!!! – Come, thou Spirit, but not in these horrid forms; come though with the milder, gentle, easy inspirations thou breathest around the wig of a prating Advocate, or the tête of a tea-bibing Gossip, while their tongues run at the light-horse gallop of clishmaclaiver for ever & ever – come, & assist a poor devil who is quite jaded in the attempt to share half an idea among half a hundred words; to fill up four quarto pages, while he had not got one single sentence of recollection, information, or remark, worth putting pen to paper for. –

I feel, I feel the presence of Supernatural assistance!"

Agnes and old Betty would also have known the old wives' tale that 'all work and no play makes Jack a dull boy', and surely interspersed Robert's formal study with stories and songs from their own repertoire of women's lore.

But Burns took care how he wrote, in polite company couching in humour his awareness of the more ridiculed of such old beliefs. In mid October 1789 he had assisted in the parliamentary campaign of the son of his neighbour Robert Riddell. He wrote in anticipation of victory:

"I have watched the elements and skies in the full persuasion that they would announce it to the astonished world by some phenomena of terrific portent. – Yester night until a very late hour did I wait with anxious horror, for the appearance of some Comet firing half the sky; or aerial armies of sanguinary Scandinavians, darting athwart the startled heavens rapid as the ragged lightnings, and horrid as those convulsions of Nature that bury nations.

The elements, however, seem to take the matter very quietly: they did not even usher in this morning with triple suns and a shower of blood, symbolical of the three potent heroes and the mighty claret-shed of the day."

In his childhood, on moonlit nights and on Sundays, his dad no doubt would, book in hand, have cross-examined all his children. He tested them on the facts of history. But that history would in the imagination of this child come alive because it was interlaced with legend. He recalled to Mrs Dunlop one song his mother sang, that she as a child had been required to sing for an aged blind uncle. It had brought tears to the eyes of the old man. This was the old Scots Ballad, 'The life & age of Man'. It related events of 1653.

Thus, Burns from the books became thoroughly familiar with the year on year events that made up the previous two centuries before his birth. He desired to know them so as not to fail his father's tests. But they also gave the context of his mother's songs and folk memories.

Where the story abruptly ended in his text books he turned to contemporary material to make himself just as familiar with the course of events up to his present moment. From the books he was familiar with detail of history of Europe's warring States from the Thirty Years War to the Seven Years War. By finding out about more recent and unfolding events, by the time of his father's death in 1784 he knew every published detail of the course of the American War of Independence. He kept himself on top of current affairs until his death, always rounding out his understanding by seeking to relate events in some way to real people and places. Thus, that one textbook by Salmon was thumbed over again and again to give context to the world as conflict and hardship rolled on their devastating ways. So too would have been the copy of Guthrie that he was required to study.

Some familiarity with all that background knowledge within the head of Robert Burns is surely necessary to understanding how he felt about life, the universe, everything. For this reason, in this book I have given summaries so far of some of the history that he is likely to have known. This is not to pad out my word count, which you probably think is too great already for other reasons. But everything I have in this book is here with the aim of amplifying awareness of how he felt.

So I am not going to excuse giving you more history detail now. It is part of the makeup of the mind of Robert Burns that has been too much ignored over two centuries.

I also have tried to understand how he might have felt when he was studying. To help myself in this, I have gone back to the tomes his father insisted he understand so that he could help his brothers and sisters learn. In the National Library of Scotland I requested Salmon's 'Geographical Grammar'.

The Library offered me two copies. One with reference RBS.2454 had been gifted to the National Library on 5th October 1949. The book, bigger than octavo size and about two inches thick, had been bound in firm dark leather probably in the 19th century. Inside in copperplate were words to the effect that it had previously been the property of Mrs Burns at Dalkeith. I felt a thrill in the realisation that these pages were quite possibly the very ones first turned by the child poet himself. As I leaved through its six hundred or so pages and pored at the maps bound amongst them, I felt a tingle on the paper as of the touch of the poet's hand.

This was the 1766 edition of Salmon. That new edition of Salmon's work included ten new copper-plates, not in previous editions. Facing the title page is a beautiful engraving with in the sky at the top a winged goddess, lying back blowing a trumpet, accompanied by a cherub struggling to hold a sextant. Below, surmounted by a single crown are portraits of Queen Charlotte and King George III. In the lower third of the picture, two cherubs clamber over a globe with a map laid on it. The map drapes over a cannon pointing outwards to two ships that are in a fire-fight. Cannon balls are lying nearby. Also on that shore lie a broken cannon and an anchor. The Seven Years War had not long ended when this edition was published. The book proclaimed that

this tract presents the youth of Britain with the world in miniature.

On page vii, the third page of the preface, the young Robert would have read:

As I am a citizen of the world, I look upon all men as my brethren; and have long endeavoured to set them right in their notions of one another. I am extremely concerned to see almost every people representing the inhabitants of distant nations as barbarians, and treating them as such. For my part, I have met with people as polite, ingenious, and humane, whom we have been taught to look upon as cannibals, as ever I conversed with in Europe, and, from my own experience, am convinced, that human nature is everywhere the same, allowances being made for unavoidable prejudices, occasioned by custom, education, and savage principle, instilled into many in their infancy by ignorant, superstitious, or designing men about them: and as I have observed on other occasions, nothing has contributed more to render the world barbarous, than their having been taught from their cradles, that every other nation almost, but their own, are barbarous.

Salmon then explained further:

Two things we see contribute greatly to make men rapacious and cruel; namely, covetousness, and mistaken notions of religion. Some make gold their god, and then everything must bow to that, others think they do God good service, by murdering and extirpating nations of a different faith. They imagine this furious and mistaken zeal will infallibly procure them seats in paradise. Thus religion, which is the best thing in the world, and designed to improve and meliorate mankind, is converted to the very worst purposes, by ignorant or designing men.

Through this book Robert was supplied with a chronicle of history. Naturally, the child probably first turned to the historical chronicle for his homeland, Scotland. No doubt he was dismayed when he found that the entry for 1603 merely stated that James VI had gone south to London. It then added that readers should thus turn to the section on England to get any history that had occurred since. It had been promised that this edition would have considerably more about Scotland than previous editions. Instead Salmon apologised in his introduction that this would have taken too much paper. In lieu of the additional data – and he suggested this would make up for the lack – he included the brand new maps, prepared by the engineer Smeaton, of the proposed canal that would link the rivers Forth and Clyde.

Bound in beside page 329 in the Mrs Burns volume is a map of Scotland. The book would not have been acquired bound, for it came with binding instructions. It would have been bought as a collection of its various sections, perhaps each already sewn, perhaps only folded and not even cut.

The maps came in a separate pile of sheets – a great delight to a boy. No doubt he would have unfolded and spread on the board that served as the household table the map of Scotland. Perhaps he traced out with his finger the word 'Aireshire', and had seen on the wavy line that marked a river, the town name 'Aire'. He would have seen the town name Sanquhar in the adjacent county Dumfries. East of Scotland was marked the German Ocean, which we now know as the North Sea.

With the size of the print, distances looked small. The map projection gives modern readers the impression of distances north of Inverness being relatively shortened, as if Inverness is as far north as Scotland in reality extends. No doubt his father pointed out on the map the town of 'Stonehive', the Stonehaven near to where his father had been born. There was 'Montross', or modern Montrose, 'Irvin' that we now spell Irvine, and the town of 'Jedburg' that we associate with Jedburgh Abbey.

On the map too is marked the Roman Wall of Antonine, and the proposed Forth and Clyde Canal, ending on the Clyde at a spot called Dummuir – the Dalmuir where I myself was born.

The book was issued at a time of emerging great intellectual and scientific development, during the early years of the reign of George III. He had succeeded at the age of 22 on 17th October 1760 to the throne of his grandfather, George II.

An era was ended and a new one beginning. On 7th January 1758 there died in Edinburgh the poet Allan Ramsay, the father of the painter. Later that year, John Wilkinson had installed his first blast furnace at Bilston, Staffordshire and Jedediah Strutt invented a machine for knitting hosiery with ribbed or ridged weave. That year too, Captain James Cook began surveying and charting for the Royal Navy the St Lawrence River, Nova Scotia and Newfoundland. The year Robert Burns was born, Samuel Johnson published 'The History of Rasselas, Prince of Abyssinia'. Voltaire published 'Candide', satirising thinkers and institutions as reactionary. Adam Smith published his 'Theory of Moral Sentiments'. William Robertson published 'History of Scotland, 1542-1603'. The British Museum opened, based on the collection of Hans Sloane. Arthur Guinness opened a brewery in Dublin and the Duke of Bridgewater commissioned James Brindley to build a canal completed in 1761 between Worsley and Manchester, innovatively incorporating tunnels and aqueducts.

The year George III succeeded, Kew Botanical Gardens was inaugurated. John Smeaton devised a cylindrical cast-iron bellows for smelting iron. Josiah Wedgwood opened his new factory at Burslem, Staffordshire. In literature, Lawrence Sterne published the first parts of 'The Life and Adventures of Tristram Shandy, Gentleman'. James Macpherson published 'Fragments of Ancient Poetry Collected in the Highlands of Scotland and translated from the Gaelic or Erse Language'. Macpherson followed this by 'Fingal' in 1762. In 1762, Jean Jacques Rousseau wrote opposing independence in women's thoughts or deeds. Work such as Macpherson's began to be disparaged. From 1762 Samuel Johnson was granted a civil list pension of £300 a year, and began his campaign to deny that so rude an environment as Gaelic Scotland could possibly give rise to such tales as Macpherson retold.

But what did Johnson know of Scotland or her ways? He even scoffed at the word 'pony'. His 1755 'Dictionary' had the comment

I know not the original of this word, unless it be corrupted from *puny*.

In the posthumous 1660 edition of Gervase Markham's 'The Horseman's Honour or the Beautie of Horsemanship' is noted a breed of small horse of

fine shape, easie pace, pure metal and infinit toughness.

He did not call this a pony. He named it the Galloway nag, a creature resilient to unremitting travelling. Those could even run for fifteen miles without slowing. Burns learned to be thankful for this ability in his Excise work. 'Nag' usually means a small saddle horse that neither pulls a plough nor goes in harness, but Galloways also pulled ploughs. The Galloway nag was mentioned as a small horse by Shakespeare. These were typical mounts of Border rievers because they were particularly sturdy and resilient for the terrain of marsh and mountain. Within two years of ascending the throne of England, James VI and I enacted in both his kingdoms that Borderers were not permitted to own anything but a poor-grade riding horse. This deprived rievers of their most important martial advantage.

Johnson never accepted that Scots words were as real words as any in England. He ridiculed Scotticisms. So he never could have accepted that the word 'pony' probably came to England with

James VI. It had been in common use in Lowland Scotland before the Union of the Crowns. Allan Ramsay, born on a farm at Leadhills at the headwaters of the Clyde, regularly used the word 'pownies' in 'The Gentle Shepherd'. He meant his local West Lowland small horse. Burns used the word on an everyday basis. It appears casually in such writings as his letter of November 1786 to George Reid of Barquharie, thanking him for providing him with his transport to Edinburgh. The couplet,

> A blessing on your frosty pow,
>
> John Anderson my jo,

shows that the word is reminiscent of the Scots word 'pow', or forehead – a feature that breeders use to distinguish ponies from horses. The word may have been derived from mediaeval French usage of the word poulenet, meaning foal. The French picked up the Scottish form of humour, using poulenet to infer they did not believe these were fully-grown horses. Scots, emulating the light French manner of pronunciation, began to talk of the 'powny'. Equally, the dedicated plough horse, such as a Clydesdale, might be called a hobby, or dobbin. Both were mediaeval words, shortening of the name Robert, to liken the powerful worker to their hero king's battle horse.

A leader in battle in the early 14th century would commonly have been heavily armed and ridden high above the ground on a great warrior steed. But the legend of Bruce emphasises that in 1314 he used a small horse before battle at Bannockburn. Anthony Dent and Daphne Machin Goodall in their 'A History of British Native Ponies' of 1962 suggested that Bruce deliberately chose to ride a small horse when he reviewed his troops at Bannockburn because it gave him a better understanding of the land.

To Scots, who know so little of their history, it is yet a well-known story that when Robert Bruce reviewed those troops he was not in full armour and not on the great horse. He was probably alert to a common mistake: riding a tall horse you get a very different view of landscape than riding a small horse. He needed to get around his troops, but he also realised that he would get a better idea of what they would see confronting them if he rode a small horse for this task. The small horse also had another advantage: typically, it would stand still to be mounted. So the leader could get off to see the land from his men's eyes. Then he could remount without assistance. He couldn't have done this with a war horse. A snorting destrier might need three men to hold it still before a man could mount. Thus, the poet Barbour related that Bruce

> rode on a grey palfrey, small and good looking.

Sir Henry de Bohun, high on his charger, got a wrong impression of their relative advantages. Old Scots tells us that Bohun

> thought that he suld weill lichtly
>
> win him, and haf hym at his will,
>
> sen he him horsit saw so ill.

But Bohun had been deceived by his own superior viewpoint. This cost him his life.

Martin Martin, who reported on his travels around Scotland in the early 18th century, recorded that Scottish Highland horses had the second sight, as might cows, but no other animals. Perhaps such instinct also added to the luck of Robert the Bruce, aware through the horse of the advancing evil.

Robert Burns rode over the site of the battle on his own little grey mare. He saw the land with the same eyes as his hero. When in 1787 Burns rode out at Bannockburn, looking at the lie of the land through the eyes of that brave victor king, perhaps it was not just he but equally his horse that felt the presence of the ghost of Bruce.

Such crazy tangential thoughts would have tantalised the mind of our poet, the hero's namesake. In his verse epistles as a young man he would let his rambling muse wander where she may, riding with her on his Pegasus, proving his prowess in always reining the winged horse in to a well-rounded conclusion that demonstrated clearly who had, all the time, really been master.

He did not ride so wildly as a child under teacher Murdoch and stern father William. He worked hard physically, and they worked him hard intellectually. They created in him an ability to concentrate on books. Despite the tyranny of the word he learned to love learning.

There would be so much to learn. When in Dumfries he ran the circulating library called the Monkland Friendly Society for Robert Riddell he had a ready list of desirable books for the subscribers to purchase. He arranged the purchase of suitable books for the edification of the circle around him. After four years this society owned one hundred and fifty worthy books. But he knew that not everyone shared his passion for knowledge nor had learned how to study.

Over a twenty year period from May 1763 Catharine Macaulay published the 8-volume 'History of England from the Accession of James I to That of the Brunswick Line'. Her writing embodied strong republican sympathies. Scottish theologian George Campbell in 1763 published 'Dissertation on Miracles' contesting David Hume's attack on miracles, but de facto supporting country belief in the supernatural and thus giving ammunition to those who would mock his writings.

These works were not then available to the lad. But he was gaining from Salmon a solid framework of what happened when, to which he could add such facts as they came to his attention in the hours spent reading in bookshops. He also had Guthrie's great tome, with corresponding material to confirm what Salmon presented. After the success of his first edition, he learned more during conversation at dinner or soirées in grand company. Private libraries were opened to him.

He learned facts and history, but through these he learned pride in his nationality.

To the young boy reading Salmon's great tome, its open-minded author must have seemed to understand the inner Scotsman and recommended Scots be admired and emulated.

> As to their genius and temper, they have certainly more command of themselves in the beginning of life, and commit fewer extravagances in their youth, than the English do: their frugality and temperance deserve our imitation, which is, indeed, the foundation of that discretion we observe in them, at a time of life when our gentlemen are half mad.

On the down side, he stated that they were easily distinguished from South Britons by the tone and roughness of their accent, and were a race tyrannised by their ministers of religion. The power of the Scottish Kirk had greatly increased when King James VII was driven out. King William was easily persuaded to abolish episcopacy in Scotland because the bishops had sided with their anointed king. Queen Anne had been only slightly more tolerant of episcopacy. Thus, learned the young poet, Kirk Sessions had acquired

> power enough to make any gentleman uneasy, if they happen not to like him. A man that is subject to these petty jurisdictions, can hardly be denominated a freeman.

In childhood, his father warned him sternly about his dreaming, joining a dominie's authority with pulpit-thumping ministers in railing against the Sin of Rhyme. So the child tried to keep his imagination in rein as he read Salmon's great ordered tome of carefully listed facts, while around him a black magic was transforming the world as knowledge advanced.

At his Carron ironworks in 1762 chemist John Roebuck developed a method for converting cast iron into malleable iron. He used coke instead of charcoal. At the gaming tables Earl John Montague found a way to have his food delivered so as not to interrupt his squandering money on chance events. Thus he could fill his time with the meat of his passion and so bequeathed the ubiquitous sandwich of 21st century office slaves. Games of chance occupied the thoughts of mathematician Thomas Bayes, who in 1763 published his probability theory. Hopes of reducing risk of loss at sea caused English astronomer Nevil Maskelyne to publish that year his 'The British Mariner's Guide'. This enabled mariners to assess longitude by making observations of the Moon.

Over the years, as the boy studied, the industrial revolution gathered momentum. In 1764 James Hargreaves invented the spinning jenny, allowing several threads to be spun simultaneously by one operator. James Watt invented the separate condenser, vastly improving the Newcomen steam engine. In 1769 Richard Arkwright patented the water frame, capable of mechanically spinning cotton suitable for warp threads – the base threads, necessarily strong, on which cloth is woven. Over the next few years he established several factories and began manufacturing calico. In 1769 Nicolas-Joseph Cugnot built a steam carriage that transported four people, very slowly. 1770 saw the invention of a screw-cutting lathe, and the endless chain-drive for transmitting power. Benjamin Franklin charted the Gulf Stream. Richard Lovell Edgeworth invented an elementary caterpillar track for vehicles.

Art, literature and philosophy moved forward. The Adam brothers and John Wood were active architects around this time. In 1769 William Robertson published his 'History of Charles V'. In 1770 Oliver Goldsmith published his 'Deserted Village'. Immanuel Kant published 'On the World of Sensible and Intelligible Forms and Principles'. Edmund Burke published 'Thoughts on the Cause of the Present Discontents'. As Henry Mackenzie published 'The Man of Feeling', in 1771 Tobias Smollett published 'The Expedition of Humphry Clinker'. The first edition of the Encyclopaedia Britannica was completed. This was the magnum opus of polymath Smellie, the man who would later print the poet's first Edinburgh edition. In 1772 James Cook circumnavigated the globe, testing John Harrison's newly invented naval chronometer, intended to aid the calculation of longitude. In October that year Mount Papandayan on Java exploded.

Though Salmon's chronicle perforce ended in 1766, chapman gossip and pub conversation would have informed the family of emerging events, however isolated they were in Mount Oliphant. In 1761 the first 'Whiteboy' societies of agricultural labourers had been formed in Ireland to protest against the sharp increase in the cost of pasturage. Two years later they launched their terror campaign in Ireland. The underside of life was churning. Technological change was not all good; people were finding that old ways of work no longer brought in the expected earnings; people were being forced to change what they did and even where they lived. It was causing pain and hardship. This was aggravated by economic deprivations from weather and war. In response to changes in labour conditions, on November 9th 1769, the Weavers' Society of Fenwick, Ayrshire, became the world's first co-operative society, organising non-profit distribution of foodstuffs.

After 1777 messages filtering through the ether were confirmed in newspapers that Burns read in the Bachelors' Club he formed at Tarbolton. Even then, studying his Geography as much in the sheer desire for knowledge as in his search for explanations of his mother's curious Covenanting stories, young man Robert kept reading Salmon and Guthrie.

Undoubtedly he sought through listings of events after 1603 for the sparse references to any Scottish matters, pouncing on any that lit up the pages. His mum had sung about 1653. His ancestors had fought at Bothwell Bridge. The Glorious Revolution took place in 1688. What had all this struggle and pain been about? It must have been important, because it had imprinted strong emotions in his mother's breast.

Thus he learned from Salmon that in June 1673 James, Duke of York, was forced by the Test Act to resign his post of Lord High Admiral, because he was a Roman Catholic. The Test Act had been enacted by Charles II, under financial pressure due to the Anglo-Dutch War. To satisfy the moneyed interest, he had found it inevitable that he must withdraw his Declaration of Indulgence of March 1672. This had suspended the execution of the penal laws against non-conformists, and in particular, Roman Catholics. During 1678 rumours were put about that James, Duke of York, intended to murder Charles II and himself take the throne. In response to the ensuing panic, in November the Test Act was tightened to exclude Roman Catholics from both Houses of Parliament. Only the Duke of York was exempted. In March the next year he was persuaded by Charles II to leave England to calm the anti-Catholic mood of the House of Commons. Those moneyed interests denied people freedom of worship.

In May 1679 Anthony Ashley Cooper, Earl of Shaftsbury, attempted through an Act of Parliament to exclude James, as a Roman Catholic, from the line of succession to the throne. His Habeas Corpus Act was also passed. In November 1680 the Exclusion Bill was thrown out after George Savile, Lord Halifax, threw the weight of his excellent debating skills against the Whig pro-Exclusion party.

Then Covenanters began to rise, in response to increasing fear of interference in Scotland's divine right to Presbyterian monopoly of religion.

It was probably more than rabid religious fervour that caused the uprisings. This was a time of intense cold. Famine stalked abroad. People died of deprivation and hypothermia. The Thames froze in the coldest winter in living memory. In May 1684, James, after having been excluded for eleven years, was brought back into the Privy Council. On 6th February 1685, Charles II died and his brother succeeded as James II of England.

The moneyed interests did not like this turn of events. They looked for some way to change the status quo. They turned to Charles II's illegitimate son, James Scott, Duke of Monmouth. He was personally dischuffed when James II succeeded. He had earlier gained the favour and support of William of Orange. On 11th June Monmouth landed in Dorset and proclaimed James a usurper. Archibald Campbell, Duke of Argyll, invaded Scotland in support of the Duke of Monmouth. Defeated, Campbell was executed for treason on 30th June. The Duke of Monmouth was then defeated in Somerset. After being found guilty of treason, he was executed on July 15th at Tower Hill in London.

A few months later, just as James II was trying to get himself fully accepted, Roman Catholic King Louis XIV of France, after suffering years of insurrection by his Protestant subjects, revoked the tolerant Edict of Nantes of 1598. This caused emigration of hordes of Huguenots to Britain, the United Netherlands and to Brandenburg. The latter two responded by turning against France. James II instead embarked on his policy of general religious tolerance throughout his domains, culminating in his Declaration of Indulgence on 4th April 1687, allowing general freedom of worship.

But three months later, he publicly received the newly created Papal Nuncio, or Ambassador of the Pope to England, Ferdinando d'Adda. This caused consternation. It raised general fear amongst the wealthy and England's established church that there would follow a revocation of rights to land and livings sold by the Crown from the reign of Henry VIII onwards as a consequence of England's Reformation.

Since public auction in England of old church lands took place mainly in the 1540s, it is hard for modern readers to believe that in the late 1680s there should be such panic. But there are enough extant papers and tracts to show real fear amongst landowners that they would lose their valuable property. Thus landed gentry joined the moneyed to protect their interests. They looked for some way to oust James. They turned their eyes to Europe.

In 1641 Mary, eldest daughter of King Charles I, had married William, son of Frederick Henry, Prince of Orange. She subsequently gave birth to William of Orange. It was he who was invited to become King William III of Great Britain and Ireland.

On 14th March 1647, William II, Prince of Orange, succeeded as hereditary stadtholder in the United Netherlands on the death of his father, Frederick Henry. Mary's husband died of smallpox in 1650, a few days before the birth of her son. The United Netherlands took the opportunity to become a Republic. This is why Mary's son is not called Prince of Orange, but simply William of Orange.

In 1674 the most senior executive office of hereditary stadtholder was granted to William of Orange. In November 1677 he married his first cousin Mary, daughter of James, Duke of York. So just to confuse things, there are two Marys in this story – the daughters of Charles I and James II. These were aunt and niece.

In May 1688, James II required his Declaration of Indulgence to be read out in churches. Senior bishops refused. James found himself unable to use judicial process against them. At that point senior aristocrats invited William of Orange to 'intervene' on behalf of the Protestants of England. On 5th November, William landed with an army and marched into Exeter. London rallied to William of Orange. King James was captured in Kent, but later escaped to France.

William assumed control of England, Scotland, Ireland and the colonies. On 28th January 1689 a newly formed Parliament declared that James had de facto abdicated. It offered the throne of England jointly to William and his wife Mary. This Parliament also issued a Declaration of Rights, claiming for Parliament the sovereign powers of making or suspending laws, levying taxes and maintaining a standing army. On March 14th, the Scottish Parliament offered William and Mary the crown of Scotland. Though royal blood might purportedly run in their veins, William and Mary had had it spelled out to them by both England and Scotland that these were constitutional monarchies and they had no Divine Right to wear these crowns.

There was no doctrine of Divine Right of Kings within Roman dogma, but the concept was by ordinary men identified with papal authority. The concept of Divine Right of Kings had been introduced to Christendom by Charlemagne after he had forced the Pope to crown him. Widespread belief in it was amplified by subsequent papal anointing of European monarchs in endorsement by the spiritual head of Western Christendom of their temporal power in their lands. Reason could argue against Divine Right of Kings, as George Buchanan had shown when instructing young James VI. Realpolitik was a stronger argument, for acceptance of it suggested subservience to papal authority.

France gave King James support against these rebels. Thus Britain found itself a key party in Europe's Nine Years War. All this time, there was fighting across Europe as France slugged it out with northern enemies. That October, Bonn was recaptured from the French by Brandenburg and Hanoverian forces. In the British Isles, a resistance movement began with James landing at Kinsale in southwest Ireland on 12th March. On the mainland there was a rising of loyal forces in Scotland. The Scottish resistance was seriously weakened with the death of its military leader John Graham of Claverhouse, Viscount 'Bonnie' Dundee, though his army defeated the forces of William at Killiecrankie.

> I met the Devil and Dundee
> On the braes o' Killiecrankie, O.

William soon took an army to drive James and his supporters out of Ireland, meeting failure only at Limerick, where the heavy rain got the better of him.

A muddy mixture of controversy, mundane and philosophical, began the Jacobite romance. For the manner of removal of King James was linked not merely to the question of Divine Right of Kings but directly to the question of freedom of worship. On 16th December 1689 the Bill of Rights had removed all political rights from Roman Catholics in England and prohibited any Roman Catholic succeeding to the throne of England. In different form this was the same philosophical question behind the Galilean controversy. Here was a variant of the question of free will: has the individual a right to freedom of conscience?

John Locke in 'Two Treatises on Civil Government' argued against the Divine Right of Kings. In the face of the 'Glorious Revolution', as William's usurpation came to be called, he published his first 'Letter Concerning Toleration', arguing for religious tolerance. His 'Essay Concerning Human Understanding' came out in 1690 by which time William and Mary were consolidating a firm grip over British affairs. Locke continued to beat the tolerance drum until King William clearly demonstrated his intolerant resolve to subdue Scottish hearts and minds by ordering the incident at Glencoe of 13th February 1692. Forty MacDonald men, women and children were massacred by a force led by Captain Robert Campbell of Glenlyon. Lord Advocate Dalrymple of Stair and the deputy governor of Fort William were made scapegoats.

The 'Glorious Revolution' was quick to spread across the Atlantic. Activists in the English colonies in 1689 successfully drove Roman Catholics out of positions of influence. Those supporting William attacked the French in neighbouring colonies. William's forces seized Port Royal in Acadia on 11th May 1690. The tried and tested great guns of inciting superstition against supposed public enemies were rolled out directing North American credulity about witchcraft against those who opposed the new regime. Preacher Cotton Mather published 'Memorable Providences, Relating to Witchcraft and Possessions'. Soon, at Salem in Massachusetts, a major witch hunt began. Nineteen women were hanged. In 1693, Mather published 'Wonders of the Invisible World', recounting the evil forces he envisaged at work around him. Robert Calef responded with publication that year of 'More Wonders of the Invisible World' which denounced the Salem executions. Around 1700 the North American merchant Thomas Brattles wrote exposing the Salem witch hunt in his book 'A Full and Candid Account of the Delusion Called Witchcraft'. Unfortunately, this was not published until 1798.

Major landlords were immediate gainers from the 'Glorious Revolution'. A key part of England's deal with William was that the Crown would give up its monopoly on mineral extraction. Robert

Boyle and other leading scientists persuaded Parliament to repeal the statute of Henry III against 'the multiplication of gold and silver'. This to Boyle's dismay led to a considerable upsurge of misplaced interest in alchemy and metallurgy. Many a charlatan worked on intensive new searches for that Philosopher's Stone that made base metal precious. In 1693 financiers began to reap dividends when King William took loans to finance his wars and had them guaranteed by taxes raised by Parliament. Thus was initiated National Debt, with interest on some loans to be paid in perpetuity. In July 1694 the Bank of England was founded to lend money for war. That December, Queen Mary died, leaving William III as sole ruler. He was quick to make up to his sister-in-law Anne, second daughter of James II, to ensure that she would not rally support against him to restore her father.

France formally acknowledged William's kingship in September 1697 as part of the Treaty that ended the Nine Years War.

With peace promised at the end of the 17th century, Scotland placed its economic hopes in its Darien adventure. King William actively undermined any hope of its success when on 2nd January 1699 he ordered English colonies to boycott the Scottish enterprise. On 8th March 1702 William died after a fall from his horse. Anne succeeded him in Britain, though she had no claim to the United Netherlands. Her repeated failure to bear children that could survive to adulthood prompted immediate discussions on uniting Scotland and England into one State, to eliminate dispute on succession. By 1706, riots were taking place in Scotland in response to how these discussions were progressing. On 1st May 1707 came into force the Act of Union. Parliament's manner of its acceptance was abhorred by many Scots.

> Fareweel to a' our Scottish fame,
>> Fareweel our ancient glory;
> Fareweel even to the Scottish name,
>> Sae famed in martial story!
> Now Sark rins o'er the Solway sands,
>> And Tweed rins to the ocean,
> To mark where England's province stands,
>> Such a parcel of rogues in the nation!
>
> What force or guile could not subdue,
>> Thro' many warlike ages,
> Is wrought now by a coward few,
>> For hireling traitors' wages.
> The English steel we could disdain,
>> Secure in valour's station;
> But English gold has been our bane,
>> Such a parcel of rogues in a nation!

The martial adventures leading up to the Glorious Revolution and Scotland's inglorious Union so soon after were paralleled by an ongoing battle for hearts and minds. Condemnation of witches proved a crowd-pleaser. Fear of accusation of witchcraft was a formidable force to ensure conformity. There is great power in maintaining fear of witches amongst the ignorant classes. James VI had set the tone of attack in trumpeting the evil of witchcraft. In 1631 the German Jesuit poet Friedrich Spee von Langenfeld published 'Cautio Criminalis' or 'Criminal Warranty', the first effective modern argument against the persecution of supposed witches. In contrast, in 1666 the English philosopher Joseph Glanvill published 'Philosophical Consideration Concerning Witches and Witchcraft' arguing witchcraft is real.

It is said that there was a book published in 1691. No-one has a printed copy of this book. Perhaps it never was printed. Perhaps every copy was consigned to the flames as each in turn was found by some Enlightened minister. An incomplete manuscript is said to have survived in the Advocates' Library. Longman & Co issued one hundred copies of this supposed book in 1815, under the title 'The Secret Commonwealth of Elves, Fauns and Fairies'. It embodies that kind of superstition that Robert Burns would have heard as an infant, intermingled indiscriminately with those legendary anecdotes of Covenanting fervour.

This book is purported to have been written by Robert Kirk, graduate of St Andrews University and ultimately minister of Aberfoyle in the Trossachs area of the southern Scottish Highlands. He had removed there from Balquidder, the place famous in the annals of the outlaw Rob Roy. Robert Kirk was a seventh son, born about 1640. He claimed the mystic privileges of such a birth. Told as a child that as a seventh son he would have psychic powers – if indeed he did not naturally become aware of them – he made a special study of the unexplained. He was a Gaelic scholar, and thus had immediate access to stories current in the Highlands. Whether his parishioners spun yarns for his credulous ears, whether he heard the true confessions of honest people around him who knew things not revealed to the sceptic, or whether indeed he madly conceived all the contents of his book himself, is not for us to judge. Some say he did not die, but in 1692 was carried away by the fairies, perhaps in immediate punishment for setting down the contents of his book.

The recumbent tombstone of Robert Kirk lies in the southeast corner of the old cemetery at Aberfoyle. It is said that the grave is empty, because the fairies took old man Kirk away to fairyland. The tombstone is one of the sites for those who seek out the mystical places of Scotland. When I visited in May 2008 I found that some visitor had placed at the head end of the stone a tiny model of a fairy. The inscription on the stone, cut firmly and still legible because so many fingers have traced out each letter over the intervening centuries, praises Kirk as scholar of the Gaelic language who told the true story of fairyland.

Magic and associated mischief was recognised in Kirk's time and for some time after as an ever present reality. In 1679 was recorded a crop circle in an English field of corn waiting to be harvested. We know of it because it reached the courts. It caused an argument between the farmer and his mower. It was attributed by the judge to supernatural causes – an early example of the 'Act of God' judgement, so disliked by modern insurance claimants, and turned into comedy by that modern Scottish entertainer from the labouring classes, Billy Connolly, in the film 'The Man Who Sued God'. Crop circles persist – and they do not all seem to be hoaxes. And who does not remember a childhood fable and shudder when a mirror breaks or a pin drops? Something of the primeval persists in each of us.

Out of Edinburgh in 1684 came 'Satan's Invisible World Discovered: or a Choice Collection of Modern Relations, proving evidently, against the Atheists of this present age, that there are Devils, Spirits, Witches, and Apparitions, from authentic Records, and Attestations of Witnesses of undoubted veracity'. This was compiled by Mr George Sinclair, 'late Professor of Philosophy in the College of Glasgow', no less. The title of this book reflected preoccupations of Scottish Presbyterian ministers whose sermons gave idiom to the language. Burns wrote to William Dunbar in Edinburgh in late September 1788 who had sent him Cowper's poems. He sent his regards to Dunbar's two little nieces, warning that he was

> "positively of the opinion that there is more bewitching destructive mischief in one of their GLANCES, than in the worst half of 'Satan's invisible world discovered': now witchcraft can never make a part in the character at least of a GOOD Angel. – I am sorry for the young Ladies' sakes that I am forced to bear this witness against them; but however I may deal in fiction, under my Poetic Licence, I sacredly stick to truth in Prose. – To say no more on this unlucky business I give the young Ladies notice, that, married man as I am, & consequently out of the field of Danger, still I have so much regard for the welfare of the world I lately left, that I have half a thought to advertise them in RHYME, to put mankind on their guard against such a dangerous & still growing Mischief."

(By the way, the subtext is: not everything in poetry is factual.)

Now, a hundred human years passed between the deaths of Kirk and of Sinclair and the death of Robert Burns. To our modern eyes, a century seems to cause the passing of infinite change. It is surely the case that beliefs current at the end of the 17th century were mere gothic fantasy in the eyes of those of the late 18th century. Indeed, that were then true – were you a sceptical university man. Burns was not alone amongst the educated in Scotland who would look over his shoulder when forced to travel on a wild moonless night lest there be supernatural evil lurking in shadows. He was alone in admitting that he would.

Today, there are not a few who enjoy not just collecting but actually reading books printed at the start of the 20th century. In past centuries, books were considered to be so valuable that they had an even longer shelf life. That great tome of history that Robert Burns used as a child was kept in the family and used well into the 20th century when it was presented to the National Library of Scotland.

People, taught to read in those days by perusing the Bible, came to believe that to be 'there in black and white' meant Truth. Thus, when a Professor of what is now known as Glasgow University put his name to stories of witchcraft, as a king had done before him, few were the ordinary people who would disdain the truth of such evidence. His book had a very long shelf life. Thus too, tales of a minister of religion, fulminating against evils of witchcraft and insisting on the reality of sprites and goblins, told with authority of the pulpit, endorsed the fear of darkness. That fear was rightly based on the wildness of wind in the woods, of wolves in the forest, or foxes in the undergrowth, of rushing streams that grab at the ankles of the unwary. These fears are based on bogs that sucked daring cavaliers in Covenanting times, horse and all, into the mire, to be found still on the saddle of terrified steeds, reaching up with terrified eyes gaping in attempt to escape the morass. Such was the poor horseman whose mummified body was found in the bog when they began to cut through that channel for the Forth and Clyde Canal.

It was in the poet's time still commonly put about that the Epworth home of John Wesley, founder of Methodism, became invaded by evil spirits in 1715; it was in John's brother Samuel's own journal to prove their ongoing presence for decades. In 1724, the same year Defoe began publishing his 'Tour of Britain', William Stukeley published 'Stonehenge: A Temple Restored to the British Druids'. In 1743 Stukeley published 'Abury: A Temple of the British Druids'. As late as 1751 there was a lynching in England of a man accused of being a wizard. Jean Markland, one of the girls Burns danced with, was called along with her mother and sisters before Mauchline Presbytery charged with accusing another woman of witchcraft. They were found not guilty. Mind you, Mauchline Presbytery described strong drink as 'bewitching', when in 1790 they found guilty of drunkenness the church elder William Fisher – known to us as 'Holy Willie'. In 1818 Sir Walter Scott and a servant man fruitlessly investigated frightening invisible hammering and banging noises in his Abbotsford house at what turned out to be the very time when its builder was dying in London.

By 1790 disdain of the old beliefs had not infiltrated the masses. Very frequently in his poetry can be found influences of this milieu of other-world belief in which Burns was raised and which surrounded him in the labouring classes in Scotland. It would underplay the degree of such influence to select even a few verses. In verse he reflected a current credulity around him, rather than merely anticipating the quaintness of 19th century romanticism. Four decades after the death of Robert Burns it was more widely true that witchcraft was just considered a quaint historic curiosity. By 1830 Sir Walter Scott had completed his 'Demonology and Witchcraft'. By then such tales were for many mere stories and the stuff of romantic horror fiction and the stage sets of gothic novels.

Yet in the 20th century, one of the duties of Royal Canadian Mounted Police was to punish Native Americans who murdered people accused of witchcraft. The most recent conviction for witchcraft in Scotland was in 1944. A medium, Helen Duncan, was convicted because she had announced in a séance the sinking of a battleship before there had been any public intimation of the actual event. In 2007 a female vicar in Boscastle, Devon, was censured by her Parish Council for visiting the local witchcraft museum.

There is a degree of belief in the fairy world still alive in our own scientific era. I supped with an officer of the Bank of England a few days before I drafted this chapter. I noticed her touching wood to ward off evil after describing some good fortune. She is by no means alone, for many of us avoid walking under ladders, or note the movement of a black cat across our path, or throw salt over our shoulder if some be spilt. Superstition is so often represented as the mark of the retrograde papist. Yet on 28th February 2008 a petition was presented to the Scottish Parliament asking for Pardon for the four thousand or so people, mostly women, who, over the four centuries since the Reformation, had been convicted in Scotland of witchcraft.

Surviving practices that were once connected with spirits and witchcraft have mostly now been turned into folklore festivals, particularly in areas with Celtic associations. Like Scotland's Hallowe'en, in Somerset the last Tuesday in October is Punkie Night. The punkie is a mangold carved into a mask with a candle inside to make a lantern, like the turnip or tumshie lanterns of Scotland and the pumpkin lanterns of America. Children in Somerset parade these around their village, singing, and asking for donations for their fireworks on 5th November. On Twelfth Night villagers ran to their apple trees, danced round them, and poured cider on their roots to ensure a good harvest. On Shrove Tuesday a silver ball was hurled by teams representing country and town in a beating of the bounds. It was good luck to touch the ball as it passed. In one village, eggs were brought to school, scrambled, and given to the Vicar as his Lenten meat. On Hallowe'en in one Somerset village the church bells are rung twice, once in tune and once out of tune, to discourage the Devil. The ringers then warn him off by rolling over outside the church gate the Devil's Stone, said to have been dropped there by him as he fell to hell from heaven. The Glastonbury Thorn blossoms on Christmas Day, apparently having conveniently changed its behaviour when the calendar was changed in 1752. A week before Christmas the Mayor and the head boy of the local school would each cut a sprig and both were sent to be placed on the Queen Mother's Christmas table. At Sherbourne on Christmas Day the owner of the castle distributes one coin to every comer. Mummers and Mystery Plays have been generally revived with a hobby horse going amongst spectators sniffing out evil.

Most modern academic effort in collecting folklore is in the form of audio and audio-visual recording of the elderly and their tales. I became aware of this when Glasgow Museums requested input for its researches on the 20th century in Glasgow. I volunteered to contribute stories relating to my deceased mother and her siblings and parents. My input was rejected because I was reckoned too young, having been born in 1951, to add value to their project. Such a narrow view precludes the recording of considerable inner knowledge owned by any community, and limits its value by enshrining it in archives. Often the freshest awareness of old understanding is in those younger people who have become aware that time is running out to appreciate persons whom they will soon lose; at the last stages of life of their parents or older acquaintances for the first time they truly listen to tales they previously considered old and irrelevant. Their interpretation of what they have heard, and its relation to their own memories, is then community knowledge in transition. Knowledge transmitted and in transition is knowledge that is alive and interacting with creative imagination. Thus it is at its greatest power to influence attitude and action. The folklore and scraps of music collected by Robert Burns from the old people around him were immediately transformed by his creative application into his own poetry and new songs. He thus uniquely captured power from the ancient bodies of knowledge entrusted to him.

Burns was fortunate in that his mother lived to a grand old age, so that when he came to appreciate the importance of gathering old songs and stories, she was still around. Others had already passed away. Then he had to rely on his own recollections and the collected memories of contemporaries. It is a commonplace to describe his 'Tam o' Shanter' as a rip-roaring ghost story. Indeed it is, but it by no means ridicules credulity any more than his repeated reference to sprites of the land and the air ridicules the everyday awareness around him of some spirit abroad within Nature.

In mid July 1789 a Captain Grose came to stay with Robert Riddell, who was next-door-neighbour to Burns when he lived at Ellisland. Riddell was an antiquarian, who was surely enthralled when he discovered how knowledgeable Burns had already made himself about the origins of Scottish folk song. He was also impressed with the critical faculty that Burns had developed since those childhood days. Then, demanding but influential Murdoch had trained him to critique everything, songs not excepted. Around May 1789 Robert Riddell had given Burns two blank quarto volumes into which he could transcribe chosen examples of his prose, letters and poems. Robert himself arranged to have bound the volumes that have become known as the Interleaved Museum. In these he wrote summaries of his background knowledge of songs. (Robert Riddell died on 21st April 1794, shortly after an unresolved quarrel with Burns. The cause of the quarrel is not known.)

Grose had first travelled to Scotland in the party with Thomas Pennant in 1772. That visit created the revised journal in which Pennant first paid considerable attention to the stories of the supernatural. Grose was aware of how these were discovered amongst the lairds and lower classes in the Highlands.

Chapter VI *Magic*

Grose had taken up this interest. He was looking for more examples of ancient beliefs that might still be extant in the Lowlands. Burns and Grose perhaps first met in Edinburgh, where Grose may have been present that night when Burns was hailed as Caledonia's Bard. Burns was clearly delighted to meet such a man as Captain Grose. The poet was more than willing to provide him with tales of the supernatural. Burns also had a vested interest in preserving the derelict churchyard in which he had five years earlier buried his father. This prompted him to create the magnificent verse-tale of witches and the supernatural, 'Tam o' Shanter'. Its raison d être was to persuade Grose to include an illustration of this otherwise irrelevant Alloway ruined kirk in the forthcoming volume of his 'Antiquities of Scotland'.

It is an interesting comment on the dumbed-down nature of modern thinking that of all the work that Grose produced the only example readily available today is his 'The Vulgar Tongue'. This is a slang dictionary that is a take-off of Johnson's English Dictionary. The introduction to the 2004 edition belittles the reality that here was the man chosen by Pennant to ensure proper visual record be made of relevant scenes on the itinerary. Grose was no mean 'champion drinker'. He was a dedicated antiquarian in his own right, though undoubtedly with a very keen sense of humour too. Before his death from fever in 1791 he produced eight illustrated volumes of antiquities of England plus two on Scotland and had already prepared, for posthumous publication, two more on Ireland. He prepared a history of Dover Castle, wrote on military antiquities and wrote essays on Gothic architecture.

Burns no doubt was particularly interested that here was a man who had, in his journeying, collected many local proverbs and details of popular superstitions. Their conversation in the congenial home of Robert Riddell at Friar's Carse must have been animated with their exchanges. Riddell would have contributed too to talk of all those fascinating beliefs that still permeated the rural world from which Burns had emerged. Few scholars yet realised this lore was too fast being eliminated by the march of Enlightened progress. If they did, they attributed little value to its preservation.

The story of the supernatural achieved the poet's purpose. Alloway Kirk became an important landmark. The Auld Brig o' Doon at Alloway was rescued from demolition in 1812 and again in 1831 by Burns enthusiasts intent on preserving its magical associations. In the second half of the 19th century harbour deepening caused the river Doon to flow more violently under the bridge. By 1868 it was reported that the piers of the bridge were in a very dilapidated condition. In 1903, the piers of the bridge were thickened in an effort to strengthen them. This, by narrowing the channels through which storm water could rush, actually brought more pressure to bear on the piers. By 1905 the Burgh of Ayr was seriously considering demolishing the bridge. This caused uproar. Even the alternative of dismantling the bridge, creating deeper foundations for the piers, and rebuilding the bridge in its previous form was met with horror by senior members of the Burns Federation. A world-wide appeal was organised. By July 1910 the bridge had once again been totally restored. In 1923 it was scheduled as an Ancient Monument.

In his 'The Brigs o' Ayr', first published in the first Edinburgh edition of his poems, Burns in an aside stated:

> That Bards are second-sighted is nae joke,
> And ken the lingo of the sp'ritual folk;
> Fays, spunkies, kelpies, a', they can explain them,
> And ev'n the vera deils they brawly ken them.

When he related in verse encounters with the Devil and conversation with Death, his light-hearted familiarity greatly offended the powers of the reactionary Scottish churchmen who ruled their congregations with the arrogant hand of divine right and predestined righteousness. Burns was familiar with Death, defying him more than once. And when he first circulated 'Death and Dr Hornbook', Death was all too familiar to his audience. He wrote it in the wake of that terrible plague from the miasma of the Icelandic eruption. So horrific was the incidence of death that Burns was one of those who overcame the trauma with laughter. This old Celtic way, which Burns inherited from his mother's ancestry, even in modern times does not go down well with stern Calvinism.

Burns was born into a time when the countryside of Scotland still held many indications of old Celtic ways, and memorials of the presence of Death through all ages. It was a land unrecognisably different from that of today. Those whose only aim was to increase agricultural returns had not yet devastated ancient landscapes of tree, moor and heath, nor yet dug for treasure in every mound of ancient graves, nor pulled to destruction the alignments and circles of timeless stones. The rigs of barley were indeed rigs: soil heaped in narrow lines, with drainage ditches between each line, meandered across each tilled field. Forests were fearful. Roads in rain were mud tracks, unfit for wheels. Such bridges as existed were narrow and rose in great arches across rivers that fought resentfully against the intrusion of their piers. Wild with the noise of animals were the nights. Dark were they when the Moon was not full or when hid in the menacing clouds. When in the soil a plough turned up a stone, napped carefully to the shape of an arrow or a spearhead, easy it was to believe that it had been flung there by one of those creatures who grasped for the cloak flying in the wind as the horse pushed a route through thorn-grown heath. When the wild storm crashed, and the lightning struck, tumbling the house gable, easy it was to see in the blasted tree the work of an evil force whose weapons could strike death yet leave no visible mark.

Kirk's 'Secret Commonwealth' purported to examine those invisible people that those with second sight call elves, fauns or fairies. Of these, the fairies were subterranean inhabitants, called in Gaelic the Sleagh Maith or Good People – so called in the attempt to contain their mischief. Thus, the name of the Clava Cairns near Inverness translates as 'the good stones' to avert any evil influence that might surround these ancient sites. Though protected by modern Ancient Monument legislation, they are frequently found to have been used by a range of different kinds of modern people for their particular ritual purpose. Fairies, said Kirk, particularly moved about the country on Quarter Days, when those with second sight would be most likely to see them. Kirk insisted that those with second sight did not have the freedom to see when they wished it. They could see only when they passed into a different state of awareness, at which moment they were inspired with some genius. Those of creative bent will recognise the feeling of the urge from somewhere unknown inside them to express understanding they never previously were aware they knew. It is as if from within some external spirit speaks.

Those who in the modern world attest to experiencing such feelings know they can arise in any environment. Some find them most encouraged when the mind is surrounded by influences that dispel the everyday. Thus, the wanderer out of the ordinary, perhaps alighting on one of those mounds even nowadays called fairy hills, letting imagination roam to the vastness of unknown history and distant futures, might see figures of a different universe, hear them talk and laugh, and as the wind breathes gently on their cheek or a gale howls in their ears, learn through the wavering intangible ether the secret messages of other realities.

Chapter VI *Magic*

Kirk discussed whether having the second sight was witchcraft. He concluded it was not. To be a witch is to choose magic. The person with the dubious gift of second sight never chose to have it. It therefore was not punishable under any witchcraft laws. In trance persons could find themselves in a different place for a period of time, though the body was seen not to move from the spot, and the length of the trance might be only a few minutes.

The currency of such a belief was useful to Burns, for it enabled him without fear of legal retribution or writs for seditious libel to recount that out of body experience that enabled him on 4th June 1786 to be transported to the birthday levee of King George III. In the dream he added his good morning wishes to those of the Poet Laureate. He published this newly-written poem in his Kilmarnock edition. In this he took the considerable risk that he be immediately branded a radical for refusing to add another mere 'cuckoo song' of 'God Save the King' to the sycophantic throng. Instead he let his Muse express his birthday advice to King, Queen, royals and counsellors, in his own blunt if ingenious terms.

He followed this rampage in the Royal Court with a very bleak description of his own smoke-filled black-house home reality. There he was visited, darkly consoled, and given his mission in life by Coila, the spirit of his poetic Muse.

In his misery his Muse consoled him. His imagination was vivid. His ability to transport himself out of the horror of reality to a better world was a constant saving grace. He had need of it when he was suppressed by his recurring illness or trodden underfoot by financial cares worsened by the knowledge of forthcoming bad harvest and the increasing needs of those who relied on him as head of an impoverished extended family.

In the background of his mind the cluck of fowl, the lowing of cattle, the crackle of the stick burning on the fire and the wind whistling viciously through the gaps in the rubble wall and thinning thatch mingled with echoes of his mother's rough songs, the scratch of the fiddle announcing a wedding dance, or the ring of the piper's tune coming over the hill. The strings of his heart reverberated in harmony that reached to the depths of the dark cold Earth, to the outer edges of the visible universe and beyond to the great Unknown to mingle with the music of the spheres.

The era of the Enlightenment is commonly presented as having relegated the classical and mediaeval concept of music of the spheres to the dustbin of redundant philosophy. As modern physics has it that matter can take the form of physical substance or of energy waves, and is best thought of as both together, there are again emerging those who see the value of musical allegory to describe the nature and functioning of the universe. While the science of the Enlightenment world might have been more prosaic, there were still at that time those who valued the concept of music of the spheres, if only for its allegorical strength. Few were those who still heard its harmonies.

The nobleman, composer and churchman Johann Friedrich Hugo Freiherr von Dalberg (1760-1812), contemporary with Burns, held the post of Domkapitular at Trier Cathedral. He not only composed conventional European music but also devised settings for Indian songs. He was a scholar and translator, who wrote about Islamic and Indian matters and on the ancient Meteor cult. He was a Pythagorean music theorist and wrote a treatise on the monochord. He reminded his readers that this instrument of single string and soundbox can be used to explore the inter-relationship of musical keys, the complexity of musical harmonies, the nature of dissonance, and the progression of chords.

Through measurement it emphasises the parallels with mathematical progressions. Equally it shows the relationship between sound and scientific wave theory.

In 1787 von Dalberg wrote an essay in German which described the vision he experienced of the various Spirits that watched over music. An illness of depression had taken hold of him when the sound of Pergolesi's 'Salve Regina' reached his ears. This brought to his bedside the Genius of Harmony, who whispered to him secrets of higher levels of understanding not granted to ordinary mortals. His soul left his helpless body. He was transported beyond the material universe. Soon he was floating amongst suns, planets and stars of indescribable beauty. In observing them he became intricately aware of the different music contribution of each to the great harmony that surrounded the throne of God and intermingled in the Almighty.

Though there was little published in English on the theme at that time, von Dalberg was by no means alone in extolling the music of the spheres. The Evangelical pastor Ludwig Theobald Kosegarten (1758-1818) who became Rector of Greifswald University, was a prolific poet inspired by 'Ossian'. After reading Macpherson, he put into verse the deeds of mythological Teutonic heroes. He surrounded them with a harmony of spheres far removed from the now over-familiar planets of our solar system, singing eternally in the distant stars. Composer Andreas Romberg (1767-1821) set to music for soloists, chorus and orchestra his poem 'Harmony of the Spheres'. It was published in 1797, when Burns was recently dead. It came out in several English versions during the 19th century.

The constellation Lyra wrought music that was carried to the heavens by the flight of Cygnus, balance ensuring harmony, sound mingling with waters pouring from the urn of Aquarius, while the rattle of the shield of Orion caused the distant tiny stars to tinkle melodiously. On Earth the sound echoed in the voices of the trees and rustle of leaves, and the gentle rippling of the streams.

In Revolutionary France, François René Vicomte de Chateaubriand (1768-1848) came to prominence when Napoleon and he reinstated Christianity after he had come back from a seven-month exile in America. There, he had pondered on how Satan had taken up residence. From 1794 he began to describe his thoughts in his allegorical novel 'Les Natchez' centred on the lives of one Native American tribe. The music of the spheres surrounds French saints who come from heaven to aid the young American nation. Thus amid Enlightenment rationality continued a tradition that went back to classical Greece and re-emerged in the Romantic era, though by then the concept was merely used allegorically, stripped of any semblance of belief in ultimate reality of astral harmony that was a higher form of music.

Burns insisted that no poet could find his Muse until by himself he learned to wander by meandering streams and clear his mind of preconceptions. Lulled in reverie by the song of birds and music of the water babbling over pebbles, his mind would see the air open and at those brief times he grasped the corner of eternity and nestled in it beneath the boughs of peace. This was vibrant exciting soul peace pregnant with poetry.

Chapter VII Mystery

How Burns learned from the rituals of Freemasonry how to infiltrate and subvert opinion through being a laughing poet, and the tales of the curious coincidence of his marriage with Bonnie Jean and the mystery of Highland Mary.

It is said of self-educated people that their hallmark, the one thing they never learn, is the ability to forget anything they study. But the most significant thing about the capable mind that achieves such a high level of self-education as did Burns is that such minds are not tied by preconceptions of teachers and text-books. They never stop challenging; they keep on asking why. They are never satisfied with answers until they are convinced by them that it is as much of an answer that is currently possible to achieve. They remain seekers after truth.

This characteristic is one of the public descriptions of themselves given by those who are privy to the mysteries of Freemasonry. It is therefore not surprising that Burns involved himself in this movement when opportunity arose.

Very many books have been written on Masonic matters, most of them ill-informed. I have no intention of swelling their numbers. I merely note that secret societies invariably believe or at least project the belief that they have things secret only to their own members. Otherwise, what is the point of secrecy?

When any group projects itself as having secrets, people speculate about what those secrets are. Thus rumour grows.

What is certain about Freemasonry is that there are mysteries. But without being pedantic, let's consider what the word 'mystery' means. Most people are very happy to concur with the statement "mathematics is a mystery to me". Most people would be happy to replace the word 'mathematics' with many another obscure or arcane area of study. Indeed, most people would be only honest were they to state that most things outside their own specialist work activity are a mystery to them: "the law is a mystery to me"; "medicine is a mystery to me"; "technology is a mystery to me"; "finance is a mystery to me" are all common statements. Wherever there is need for a profession there is an expectation amongst non-adepts that the knowledge needed to serve in that profession forms a mystery.

This use of the word shows the best modern translation of the meaning of the Latin word from which 'mystery' is derived: it means 'professional knowledge'. While 'de-mystify' is commonly taken to mean 'take away the obscurity and wonder', it might be better translated as 'de-professionalise'. It really means 'dumb-down'. So it is a peculiar and worrying thing in the modern world that we don't often hear people say that "teaching is a mystery to me". Teaching was, in my own early life, one of the honoured professions. In our modern dumbed-down world where mystery is decried except for its entertainment value, professionalism may have been most undermined just at the moment when awareness of its true past meaning is increasingly relevant.

One of the very positive things that the entertainment industry can achieve, in passing, is to illustrate that arcana of science and mathematics often have very practical uses for general everyday benefit. In murder mysteries, 'mystery' has the different meaning of things deliberately obscured for the purpose of deception, in this case to deceive justice. Since the days of Sherlock Holmes these have been made much more exciting by using science in the process of discovery. This does not mean discovery of obscure aspects of science. Those stories usually bore people. But discovery of criminals uses obscure science knowledge to bring about justice.

After considerable reading, I have come to suspect that Masonic mysteries can never be exposed by writers of books. The reason is the same as that which caused the ancient Chinese Taoist compilers of I Ching, The Way, to say, "the Way that can be said is not the True Way".

Written words are by their nature incomplete representation of Ideas. Those who by writing books would expose arcana are tilting at windmills: they ignore the reality that human beings learn not merely through words in a book but through some internal transmutation of those words into understanding. They do this against the background of their own general experience and knowledge.

To be a true adept of mysteries, be these Masonic or Mathematic, two things are needed: dedicated study and instinctive internalisation. There can be those who might remember everything that is written, and yet lack that extra professional dimension of inner understanding, the instinctive revelation of the greater meaning. There can be those who are denied the opportunity or the academic gift to learn anything from written form, and yet, through some osmosis from a great ether that invisibly surrounds us, can be the greatest of adepts through revelation. So there are people classified as mentally retarded who are also brilliant mathematicians. Such are limited in their ability to communicate their insight and need to be supported by equally brilliant mathematicians with the book-learned skill to translate their thoughts and ideas into generally readable formats.

There are many members of Masonic Lodges. How many of those, I wonder, are truly party even to the more elementary Masonic Mysteries? Yes, there is the social club of comradely brotherhood. Vastly different is transformation of personal belief, commitment and behaviour through full acceptance of those revelations that, apparently, leaders of movements that subscribe to the Ancient and Accepted Scottish Rite of Freemasonry would have its adepts internalise.

Albert Pike, Grand Commander from 1859 to 1891, on behalf of the Supreme Court of the Thirty Third Degree for the Southern Jurisdiction of the United States compiled a major tome on the 'Morals and Dogma' pertinent to each of the 32 degrees leading up to that Degree 33 that is the highest level of office. This book can hardly be called a vade mecum. It is a massive reference text for those who instruct their fellows in each step as they learn the mysteries. That this is readily available to general readers is proven by the fact that the copy I used was found in an American thrift store. Other copies readily come to light in such places.

Pike's input to discussion on Freemasonry can be controversial, even amongst Freemasons. What I have interpreted from him must be read in that context. Do not take this chapter as definitive about Freemasonry now or in the time of Burns, but merely as indicative. There are authorities who can expand on the mysteries of Freemasonry. Purely to indicate how his own thought could have developed in his discussions with fellow Freemasons a century earlier than Pike was writing, I juxtapose how Burns himself might have thought with what I have interpreted from Pike. Do not take this as meaning that in the time of Burns either that Pike's philosophies or that his structure of Freemasonry held good in Scotland.

Perhaps in reading paraphrases I have made from what Pike wrote you may feel they are gibberish. Remember that what you are dealing with here is mysterious stuff. Any jargon you are not familiar with may sound like gibberish. The kind of language used by those who involve themselves in esoterica is strange to other ears. That does not mean that it does not mean something to initiates. Bear with me, and you'll get to the end of the chapter.

The book proposes that the Mysteries at their simplest are ways of approaching life so as to live a better life. They appear to the outsider such as myself as being similar in form to, for example, mysteries of Roman Catholicism in that symbol gives substance to Idea. In both, clothing, headgear, accessories, ritual, images, elements, words and allegorical stories contribute to the totality of the symbolism. Despite attempts to prove ancient lineage, Masonic brotherhoods appear to have arisen not much earlier than the 16th century. Freemasonry provided camaraderie which, as with the old religion, for many was its most important attribute. I have shown earlier that it probably arose from the Rosicrucian movement that paralleled the Counter Reformation. In Reformed communities Freemasonry by the end of the 17th century filled the gap opened up by their loss of the theatricality of the Roman Church. As pomp and circumstance have so often been abused, so has Masonic camaraderie at times been abused to further personal interest at the expense of others. I suspect it is unlikely that such is sanctioned by sincere adepts of true Freemasonry.

Travelling through Scotland in August 1787, Burns commented in his notebook on the grandeur of the position of the old Gothic church outside Linlithgow Palace, inside which he was shown the room where Mary, Queen of Scots was born.

> "What a poor, pimping business is a Presbyterian place of worship, dirty, narrow and squalid, stuck in a corner of old Popish grandeur such as Linlithgow and, much more, Melrose! Ceremony and show, if judiciously thrown in, absolutely necessary for the bulk of mankind, both in religious and civil matters."

Presbyterian Robert Burns was a Mason from 1781 until his death. In the last years before his father's death he had walked the lonely wild miles home from his first meetings, down the hill, over the bridge, up the long haul on the other side to where, beyond the brow, the farm of Lochlie seemed to be sucked inexorably into the morass of its miasmic hollow. All the while he wrapped his russet cloak tight around him against the howling wind and bent double like the bending trees that even in the calmest days of summer never ventured to stand tall and straight for fear of the wild westerlies. In the light of the myriad stars he entered the farmhouse. There increasingly often he saw in the corner his father, crouching like a caged bear, his eyes reflecting anger red from the last of the smouldering peat. Then he knew that another of those lawyer letters had arrived, and the bottle in the medicine cupboard was once again mysteriously empty, and his mother had crouched the children round herself in the shelter of the bed, staunching tears. Then he turned his mind for strength to ancient stories of Holy Grail and Templar Knights and secrets that he dare not speak, whispered to him by welcoming strength in Tarbolton, who shared with him their firm grip.

He joined their numbers when he lived at Lochlie, being initiated on 4th July 1781 in St David's Lodge, No 174. at Tarbolton St David's Lodge had been an amalgam of two others. Within Burns's first year of association with it, members who had previously belonged to one constituent, Kilwinning St James's Lodge, once again broke away. Burns went over to Kilwinning St James's Lodge with Sir John Whitefoord as Master. There Burns on 17th July 1784 was elected Depute Master, a post he held for four years.

His Masonic studies made him more aware, than had his father's instruction, of accretions that had attached themselves to the simple Bible stories of Jesus who died horribly after a loving gentle life, and returned in glory to live on. Accretions to the Jesus story have continued to expand: in the early 19th century after the Napoleonic Wars, the German Augustinian nun, Anne Catherine Emmerich, assigned to print her horrific imaginings of the detail of that Passion, as 'The Dolorous Passion of Our Lord Jesus Christ'. She bore the stigmata, these being replicas of the wounds of Jesus endured during his Passion and death. She had possibly been a victim of the kinds of brutality too common in warfare. Her take on the very sparse Gospel stories added considerable violent embellishments from imagination or personal experience. Her writings became the script for Mel Gibson's controversial and undeniably nasty film 'The Passion of the Christ'.

The Scots have always enjoyed a good discussion. They like getting their teeth into a good meaty bone of philosophical contention. So around Aberdeen, Burns's father would have heard discussion on the work of the academics. They had taken much time and trouble to compare and contrast all the different versions of the Jesus story. They dissected not only the four Evangelists in translation, but also in the different languages in which their earliest versions were extant. The Concordances they produced were stripping off accretions and even challenging the trade that Jesus was trained to. After all, did the Greek word 'tekton' not mean craft maker rather than carpenter? A 'tekton' could be a craftsman not just in wood, as a carpenter is. He could be a metal worker. More fundamentally, he could work in stone. Surely the son of the Great Architect of the Universe, the Almighty God whose Name is too great to speak, must himself have been trained in the Craft of the Builder.

While studying the mysteries of the Order, Burns was building up a network of local dignitaries and influential people. Claud Alexander and Professor Dugald Stewart were admitted as members of his Lodge on the same day in 1787. Depute Master Burns was present. Alexander had bought Ballochmyle House from Sir John Whitefoord. Professor Stewart had become a keen patron of Burns as soon as he read the Kilmarnock edition. He had invited Burns to dinner in 1786. There, impoverished farmer Burns dined with Lord Daer. This first time he "dinner'd wi' a lord!" fired Burns with excitement.

It was Stewart who took Burns to Professor Ferguson's soirée in Edinburgh.

When Burns met him Stewart was professor at Glasgow University. He later succeeded to Adam Ferguson's post. He is remembered for the result of his editing the 1805 edition of Adam Smith's 'Wealth of Nations'. He drew readers' attention to the 'invisible hand' of market forces. Stewart discovered this well hidden in a footnote to the philosopher's text. He ignored Smith's main text warnings about abuse of mathematics. He told readers that the 'invisible hand' of market forces guided a commercial and industrial world. Concern about ethics was unnecessary. The 'invisible hand' automatically stabilised economies. He identified this as the core of Smith's theories. Stewart propounded the dogma that unregulated industry could cause no irreversible devastation. Thus Stewart gave 19th century industrialisation and 20th century consumerism belief in the moral rectitude of its unbridled entrepreneurialism. He obviated the ethics-based Smith model and opened the gates of the hell of 19th century industrial exploitation of human cattle that in terrible form in Manchester so incensed Frederick Engels.

Of course, Stewart ignored physical experiment that showed that oscillations are not all naturally damped. The modern world had a very dramatic visual incidence of this in the collapse of the Tacoma Narrows Bridge in 1940. Then an invisible hand in the form of a wind of very specific direction and speed shook back and forth a bridge engineers had believed would never oscillate out of control. The seemingly solid bridge was smashed to pieces in minutes. The same can happen in economies. Boom-bust cycles don't naturally level out. Nor does seemingly clever mathematics of monetarists contain reliable ways to stop every non-damped oscillation. This was shown when in 1998 Long Term Capital Management collapsed. There has now been a much more devastating example in the failures that led up to the present day Credit Crunch. Yet many still believe the 'invisible hand' is always benign.

Any ploughman driving a ploughshare knew not all oscillations are damped. If a wobble isn't actively controlled, the plough coups. This can injure horse and ploughman.

The 'invisible hand' socked Stewart in the jaw. When war ended in America, Banker David Dale in 1785 opened innovative mills at New Lanark. He combined revival of cotton imports with glut of available labour. He shipped orphan children and unemployed adults from Glasgow to a remote Clyde gully near Lanark. He brought in Irish refugees too. In their new state of the art cotton mill imprisonment they earned Dale profits. He went into partnership with Alexander to replicate his business model on the powerful Ayr waters rushing through the gorge above Stewart's Catrine house next to Ballochmyle. The noise, the smog, the crowds of slavish labourers, over the years encroached on Stewart's peace. He abandoned his home and built again downstream. Pollution followed him. He sold up.

When Burns returned to Mauchline in 1787 he found his favourite river walk threatened by newly-begun Catrine industrial town. Perhaps this encouraged Coila to relocate to the Afton and himself to move south to Dumfries.

Dale cashed in his investment in New Lanark by selling to son-in-law Robert Owen. After the Napoleonic Wars, Owen saw more opportunity for turning destitute to good industrial use. In 1817 he commissioned architectural plans for self-supporting factory communities of 2,000 people of all ages. Contemporaries described these plans as proposals for 'parallelograms of paupers'. It puts in context the exploitation Engels recorded when we remember that the institutional slavery of Dale and of Owen was enlightened.

At the time of Burns there were already those who were only too pleased to think that whatever they did in business some invisible hand would set things right in the world. Thus Burns told Robert Graham of Fintry on 31st July 1789 that too many

> "generally grow so attentive to ourselves, and so regardless of others, that I have often in Poetic frenzy looked on this world as one vast ocean, occupied and commoved by innumerable vortices, each whirling round its centre, which vortices are the children of men; and that the great design, & merit if I may say so, of every particular vortex consists, in how wide it can extend the influence of its circle, and how much floating trash it can suck in and absorb. . . . I shall return your books very soon: I only wish to give Dr Smith one other perusal."

Graham had to wait a few weeks more to retrieve his copy of 'Wealth of Nations'.

In the summer of 1783 Burns had studied Smith's 'Theory of Moral Sentiments', perhaps introduced to this reading as part of his training in Masonic thought. The work impressed him. He translated at least one passage of the text into verse. It is not unlikely that he asked his Masonic colleagues to listen to his personal verse readings of its concepts. Those who were particularly important or intellectual people amongst them could thus test his understanding of the philosopher's ideas.

Poetry is peculiarly capable of capturing the essence of mystery. This would not go unnoticed by his fellow Masons. Perhaps he was thus encouraged to use his native ability in verse as the means to crystallize his understanding of each of the stages of Masonic instruction. Thus surely it is not surprising that many of the liberal ideas within his verses parallel the morals of Masonry. Astrologers would say that he began this at the time, crystallising on August 17th 1783, that his progressed Sun indicated that the constellation Pisces, sign of the poet, would increase its influence on his life.

The fundamental allegory of the Masonic movement is the work of the stonemason. The apprentice needs to learn how to wield a gavel and a twenty four inch gauge. In this he must learn to regulate the force he uses and direct it exactly where he measures it should go. Rough ashlar – hewn stone – needs to be shaped to the perfect ashlar or finished cubic stone, delineated by straight lines, right angles and smooth square surfaces. The Lodge is where the apprentice lives and meets his Master and Wardens – who are represented by the Sun and the Moon. Thus, Wardens reflect the direction of the Master as the Moon does the light of the Sun. Each apprentice must obey Lodge discipline, which Pike expressed like Mosaic Ten Commandments.

Allegory can be a powerful teacher, but allegory is not always understood. Once I was an honorary man at a conference attended by around one hundred of the most senior men in global finance. Guest speaker after the second lunch was Douglas Adams, author of the science fiction story 'The Hitchhikers' Guide to the Galaxy'. Those who are aware of that cult book know that it centres on a quest for The Answer, the question at stake being the meaning of life, the universe, everything. This Answer is the goal in most religious quests. In Adams's story, massive number crunching computer Deep Thought had been set to find the Answer. When it came to the moment of disclosure it shockingly announced: "The Answer is Forty Two". Asked to be a bit more explicit, the computer explained that the Answer boiled down to nine multiplied by six. Immediately, hearers knew something was drastically wrong. The chant of the times table from school days spells out that nine sixes are fifty four. Not only had the great computer given a meaningless result, it had given a wrong result.

Adams did not explain in his book that, of course, further thought would have disclosed that the result of the final bit of arithmetic is 'wrong' only when the numbers are in a system based on ten. There are other commonly used number systems, even in our decimalised computer world. The best known is the binary system, in which every number is expressed as powers of two.

But it is a more unusual number system that makes Deep Thought correct. Adams was using numbers expressed with a base of thirteen. Thirteen is so mystical that there are many Western people today who consider it so unlucky that they will neither live nor work on a skyscraper floor numbered thirteen. The number is considered even more unlucky when it is linked to Friday, the day of the week on which Christ was crucified. The ill luck is thought by some to relate to there having been thirteen people in the group made up of Christ and his twelve apostles. One of those proved to be a traitor. But if that sum, nine times six, is actually within a number system of base thirteen, the correct answer is indeed forty two. Thus, the hearers had been too narrow minded in jumping to the conclusion that the answer they had been given was arithmetically wrong.

Chapter VII *Mystery*

Using a base of thirteen may seem very odd even in modern science fiction. There are other number bases that seem more reasonable because they have for centuries been used regularly in everyday life. For example, there are sixteen ounces in a pound, so that ounces are counted in base sixteen. There are fourteen pounds in a stone, meaning that pounds are counted in base fourteen. The old systems of land measurement are equally to unusual bases.

But the prime number thirteen is surely, one might think, a strange choice of base. Well, at regular intervals there are thirteen full moons in a solar year. Thirteen has long been the standard base for counting that mystical combination, loaves and fishes. The baker counts: one, two, three, four, five, six, seven, eight, nine, ten, eleven, dozen, baker's dozen. When a barrel was sold as containing twelve hundred of herring it contained thirteen hundred fish. In both cases, the number base thirteen ensured good measure.

The choice of different numbers as the base of counting systems means that two plus two can only be said to equal four if the number base used is five or more. In base 3 the sum is written $2 + 2 = 11$; in base 4 it is written $2 + 2 = 10$. But the quantity produced when two items of one thing are added to another two items of that thing is not changed. Only the words for the numbers and their representations are shape-shifters. The underlying numbers mysteriously defy the change of words.

The magic of shape-shifting, with the underlying essence never changing, was a commonplace in stories of fairies and the supernatural. In his long ballad 'Tam Lin', Burns used this familiarity to enhance the telling:

> They'll turn me in your arms, Lady,
> > Into an asp and adder,
> But hold me fast and fear me not,
> > I am your bairn's father.

> They'll turn me to a bear sae grim,
> > And then a lion bold;
> But hold me fast and fear me not,
> > As ye shall love your child.

> Again they'll turn me in your arms
> > To a red het gaud of airn;
> But hold me fast and fear me not,
> > I'll do to you nae harm.

> And last they'll turn me, in your arms,
> > Into the burning lead;
> Then throw me into well-water,
> > O throw me in wi' speed.

> And then I'll be your ain true love,
> > I'll turn a naked knight:
> Then cover me wi' your green mantle,
> > And cover me out o' sight.

This underlying consistency of numbers added to their magic and mystery and gave rise to the study of numerology. Like astrology and alchemy, this was all too soon extrapolated far beyond what true adepts knew to be its relevance. One particular intriguing outcome of numerology was the discovery of what are known as Magic Squares. These are marked out like a chequer board and filled with integers in order from one upwards. If numbers are set out in a particular 'magic' way, a very special thing happens. The sum of the numbers in every line, whether it is taken horizontally or vertically, becomes the same. A magic square was allotted to each planet.

One magic square that fascinates adepts is called the Magic Square of the Sun. Of side length six, the numbers one to thirty six are set out as shown. The summation of each row or of each column in this six square equals 111. In this case, if that number is multiplied by the length of the square it produces 666, the Number of the Beast. Apart from the representation 666 being dependent on writing these numbers to a base ten, no inherent values of any Magic Square calculation change when the number base is changed. This makes these squares an interesting curiosity. The sum of numbers in opposite corners is always equal, in this case 6 + 31 = 1 + 36 = 37, which happens by the way to equal the number of whole years in the life of Robert Burns.

6	32	3	34	35	1
7	11	27	28	8	30
19	14	16	15	23	24
18	20	22	21	17	13
25	29	10	9	26	12
36	5	33	4	2	31

But whatever the number base, in 'The Hitchhikers' Guide' the fact remained that the Answer as given by computer Deep Thought was meaningless. When probed, Deep Thought announced that a greater would come after him. He would help them build this much more powerful computer. The new computer was the analogue type. It was the Earth. It was just about to deliver its Answer when it was bulldozed to make way for a new bypass on the interstellar highway. Later it turned out that it too would have given a meaningless answer. Its thinking mechanism, centred on evolved humankind, had been contaminated in past aeons. On Earth had crash landed a spaceship full of management consultants. Their leader stayed in his bath to ensure a constant supply of bright ideas. Amongst other bright ideas, he decided leaves should be legal currency. To contain the ensuing inflation, he ordered all forests be burned. Ecological balance was upset. Real people died out.

The session chairman who introduced Adams clearly expected Adams to give an extremely humorous presentation matching the hilarity of 'The Hitchhikers' Guide'. This being an international audience not everyone had heard of him. Those who had, equally expected light relief in the midst of a technically very heavy conference. Adams gave a very serious speech. Thus, in looking around I saw first a growing perplexity in the faces of the audience and then the glazing over of eyes as they one by one turned their minds off.

I spoke to Adams afterwards, because I found his presentation very interesting. He confirmed that indeed his story had arisen out of allegory: number crunching computers can never answer those questions in life that really matter to the human soul. Nor even can the far greater capabilities of as yet undesigned highly sophisticated analogue artificial intelligence machines that science promises for the future. Those who find a meaning in life do so through their experiences and insight generated from something outside themselves. The laughter his book had provoked had obscured his allegory. He was a disappointed man.

Adams's allegory implied that understanding of the meaning of life is beyond the scope of science. Adams shared the position taken by Pope Urban VIII against Galileo Galilei. It was the position taken by those who opposed Pierre Bayle and his follower David Hume. It was a position discredited by the success of science by the middle of the 19th century. It is a position that will not die; it remains stubbornly alive in the modern world, though it may hide in the protection of science fiction. It remains a fundamental issue: are the deep questions of the meaning and purpose of life within or beyond the scope of science? Masonic philosophy aligns with those who believe these questions are beyond the scope of science. Robert Burns took this position, his opinion repeated frequently in his letters.

Pike instructed that, no matter how straightforward and mainstream Masonic teaching might seem, the Mason must demonstrate his respect for the mysteries by curbing any careless talk. This gave reason for the vow of secrecy. A vow of secrecy naturally caused – and still causes – ignorant gossip amongst those who don't share the secret. Where there is ignorance, and a belief that there is something hidden, there is invention about what is hidden. Thus tales have been told about Masons and Masonry since its inception. It was early on in its existence even linked with devil-worship.

> When MASONS' mystic *word* an' *grip*
> In storms an' tempests raise you up,
> Some cock or cat your rage maun stop,
>   Or, strange to tell!
> The *youngest Brother* ye wad whip
>   Aff straight to *Hell.*

An insider, Burns could joke about this in his 'Address to the De'il', which it is said he wrote in the winter of 1785-6. Killing a cock was an uncommon treat for making the good old Scottish celebration winter soup called cock-a-leekie. Killing one to ward off the power of the devil was rather more of a cock-and-bull story.

South of the border in England, though, cockfighting increasingly became associated with devilry. It had formerly been tolerated at religious festivals, particularly Shrove Tuesday. In southwest England church bells might announce the winning of 'a long main' or a contest of several pairs on this festival before Lent. The sport was widespread, with cockpits in inns throughout England. Some places held fights at Christmas, others on Good Friday or Easter Monday. It was also common at hiring fairs. All fights became the occasion of heavy betting.

Some people took rather too big a gamble. On 1st October 1788, the notorious Deacon Brodie received justice in Edinburgh. His crimes were discovered. He escaped. It was generally thought he had gone to the United States, which would not then have extradited him. He made the mistake of writing home to Edinburgh to enquire on the outcome of a main of cockfighting. His handwriting was recognised at the Post Office. The letter was opened. When it was found he had actually gone to Holland, extradition processes began immediately. He was executed by the improved hanging machine that he had himself developed.

When in the early 19th century cockfighting was outlawed, it was argued that it was in the nature of cocks to fight. If a cock did not wish to fight it would raise its hackle and show the white feather. This is the origin of the expression denoting a coward. Once it was driven underground by law, and became more of a sport for gentlemen's secret gambling societies, savagery grew; cocks were 'improved' by being fitted with deadly artificial talons.

Pike stated that the Second Degree taught that a fundamental disagreement between pre-Reformation Christianity and Masonry hung on the question of the Rights of the Individual Man. In the 4th century Emperor Constantine established Christianity as the religion of the Roman Empire. This status was conditional on acceptance of the existing political order. It is seldom accepted in the modern world that this constraint on the Roman Church ended with the end of the Roman Empire. Then, the Roman Church *became* the political power in the West. This was a reversal of what had been the case since Constantine. Thereafter, temporal authority required formal sanction of Rome. This complete reversal of the Constantinian agreement began to be overthrown by the secular Reformations that again subjugated religion to temporal authority.

But the Constantinian arrangement had for some centuries held the Pope of Rome in thrall. This out of date fact enabled Masonic teaching to claim that, while Roman Christianity might teach Fraternity, it was limited by its subjugation to temporal authority in how far it could teach Equality of Man. Only in its monastic houses was there true fraternity and equality, said Pike.

I suspect 19th century backfill, because Pike then denied that Christianity hitherto recognised free will. He thus claimed that Masonry added the concept of liberty to create the famous Revolutionary Triad.

Every man, said Pike, has a primary duty not to his country but to himself. That duty involved gaining and exercising freedom in government, thought, conscience and speech. This duty came with inalienable Rights which for many centuries individuals had been denied. But great truths are frequently disguised as falsehoods: thus right to liberty had been turned into an almost universal fear of anarchy. The removal of such pervasive falsehoods could be achieved by progress in science. Such progress should go hand in hand with philosophy. He defined philosophy as knowledge of God and the soul. Through science men could know God better. On the other hand, liberty is a curse to the ignorant and the brutal. Pike warned that it is worse than ignorance to have too much pride to realise that the best sounding of theories might be wrong.

Men might hold power through money or weapons, but a man of true intellect could never be enchained. His intellect would be an invincible force. Before any mind can justly lead another, that mind must be master of itself. But mastery of mind over mind was uniquely a conquest well worth achieving.

The Compasses and the Scale represented intellectual power. This power is most potent in the science of numbers: through their use even the distance of Jupiter and the much more vast distance of the star Sirius can be calculated. No tool has true value until it is put to use. Thus, religion serves to create ethic; political theory serves to create action for change for the better.

To be master of one's own mind means rejecting selfish ambition and recognising the limitations of the human condition, but also the power inherent in the mind. Consider the rich, and their pleasures and their advantages, and see how hollow these are in the great scheme of things, advises the Masonic teaching.

> Young stranger, whither wand'rest thou?
>
> Began the rev'rend Sage:
>
> Does thirst of wealth thy step constrain,
>
> Or youthful Pleasure's rage?

That old sage had a sombre message for the impatient youth. Wisdom must be sought and listened to. Unmanaged ambition is the enemy of personal success. Thus, anticipating Coleridge's 'Ancient Mariner', Burns wrote the poem 'Man Was Made to Mourn: A Dirge', to be sung to an old Scottish tune called 'Peggy Bawn'.

In this early stage in his studies, Pike would have the Mason realise that amongst French Freemasons before 1789, each member had to work out for himself what he should understand by these strange new concepts, Equality and Liberty. Such personal interpretation of these concepts was thought by the Westminster government to have been curbed since 1717. Masonry had been regulated. Pike believed that there had in Britain remained many adepts who refused to give up freedom of thought. Pike stated that ongoing concern that thought within Lodges could destabilise established government caused the States of Holland to proscribe Masonry in 1735, France to enact laws against Masonry in 1737, and Pope Clement XII to issue against Masons a Bull of Excommunication in 1738, which was renewed by Pope Benedict XIV. Pike then, with the morality of a true son of the 19th century, made the illogical jump to say that this led to such 'evils' as the regulation of labour and its wages.

At the third stage, the seeker after truth must realise that even language is only a symbol of thought. Thus, to show symbols is not the same as giving away their hidden meaning. Interpretation of apparent evidence, such as is taught in history, may be the opposite of the true meaning. Things should never be presumed to be how they appear. This might be true of Pike's book, for in claiming that his Masonic fraternity championed open-mindedness, dispassionate thought and anti-sectarianism, he repeatedly uttered invective without evidence against the Church of Rome.

The mathematics studied at this stage is the rule commonly known as the Theorem of Pythagoras: in every right angled triangle the square on the hypotenuse is equal to the sum of the squares on the other two sides. Pythagoras used his hands for calculations. As clasped hands were the symbol for the number ten, it suggests he usually did his arithmetic on a ten-based number system. His science included the notion of the Music of the Spheres. Perhaps it was the Masonic ideal and not ideal human love that Burns eternalised in his love song:

> My love is like a melody that's sweetly played in tune.

Numerical relationships amongst Sun's orbiting planets, reflecting musical harmonies, were being confirmed by the mid 18th century by advances in astronomical calculations. From this came the symbolic meaning that Morality is a force which, as if like magnetism, attracted the heart towards Truth and Virtue. Like the compass needle to the pole star, Masons should be attracted to Honour and Duty. Pike ignored the work of Halley who was commissioned by Charles II to travel the Earth to map out the variations, some very wide, between magnetic and true north.

Electricity is like sympathy, said Pike, sending messages and impulses in instants. All the forces of science have, said Pike, their counterpart in the emotions of human beings and the changes in nations. Thus Public Opinion is an immense force, which can be overwhelmingly powerful. Each manifestation of intellectual capability can thus, through understanding of these great forces, add to the strength of the people who are the nation.

It must have meant a great deal to the young Robert Burns to learn, through such discussion of the nature of force, that even music and song could have incalculable value. That value is counted more in lives improved that in money accumulated. Thus he continued to versify, and embody in his verses the rules he was integrating into his life. In this way he could pass the wisdom on to more junior Masons, as occasion arose.

> Where ye feel your Honour grip,
>   Let that ay be your border:
> Its slightest touches, instant pause –
>   Debar a' side-pretences
> And resolutely keep its laws,
>   Uncaring consequences.

The next level of allegory, symbolised by a key, allowed pause to consider what had been learned so far. Many a man at this stage indeed commonly would wonder whether anything he had been taught were really new. Not surprising that those who were genuine seekers of truth would now demand a bit more meat with their morals. Thus, apparently contrary to the emphasis in the first three degrees on freedom of thought, Pike stated that the fourth degree, that of Secret Master, focused on obedience to the Law of God. The Ten Commandments, as adjusted to Masonic Code, were thus reiterated. Then, with his foot inside the inner temple, the Mason could advance to the fifth degree. This Pike symbolised by a coffin surmounted by a burning candle, emblematic that the curse of idleness is for the thinking man like being buried alive.

Pike superscribed his chapter on the sixth level with three glyphs set out in a triangle drawn round by three triangles connected at a single corner in the centre. Masonry, he summarises for this degree, is the great Peace Society of the world.

In what is known as his First Commonplace Book, Robert Burns wrote:

> "The grand end of Human being is to cultivate an intercourse with that Being to whom we owe life, with every enjoyment that renders life delightful; and to maintain an integritive [sic] conduct towards our fellow-creatures; that by so forming Piety and Virtue into a habit, we may be fit members for that society of the Pious, and the Good, which reason and revelation teach us to expect beyond the grave."

It was during his early years of learning the Craft that Burns wrote his First Commonplace Book – a collection of his essays in the craft of writing both prose and verse, embracing not just completed poems but also philosophy and self-criticism. The last entry in this short workbook is dated October 1785. Its abrupt ending seems unexplained. I have read no commentary relating its ending to a natural step in creative learning process. After all, Burns started the notes with a clear statement that the purpose of the book was to fill the gap present because he had no peer to review his essays. He ended with the comment that the book had served its purpose as far as he himself was concerned

– but might have use to other young aspiring writers:

"If ever any young man, on the vestibule of the world, chance to throw his eye over these pages, let him pay a warm attention to the following observations; as I assure him they are the fruit of a poor devil's dear bought experience. I have, literally like that great poet and great gallant, and by consequence, that great fool, Solomon, 'turned my eye to behold madness and folly'; nay I have, with all the ardour of a lively, fanciful, and whimsical imagination, accompanied with a warm, feeling, poetic heart, shaken hands with their intoxicating friendship. In the first place, let my Pupil, as he tenders his own peace, keep up a regular, warm intercourse with the Deity."

By October 1785 Robert Burns had not only advanced through the early degrees of Freemasonry, but through expressing what he learned in verse to his colleagues, had gained the beginnings of the critical circle he had desired.

The Seventh Degree, symbolised by scales and a key, taught that Justice must guide all aspects of the conduct of a Mason's life. Predating modern Chaos Theory, the Mysteries taught that even a breath of air, once breathed, sets up motions that affect forever the movements of the atoms of the universe. This applies to speech as well as action, making the air a vast library. Written within its motions are every word spoken, however softly. Equally, the movement of the waters of the ocean have recorded in them forever the impressions of all the ships that have ever sailed. These affect the subsequent movements of all the particles of the universe, particularly those that pass through the same space.

The Mason must act to achieve justice and act to prevent injustice. Injustice can never be undone. Even God cannot uncommit a deed. No man can know another's heart, yet each tends to judge fellow men. Yet often the judge is more guilty than the judged. Robert Burns in 1786 took these lessons sincerely on board. He penned his 'Address to the Unco Guid', publishing in his first Edinburgh edition of poems those lines so often quoted:

Then gently scan your brother Man,
　　Still gentler sister Woman;
Tho' they may gang a kenning wrang,
　　To step aside is human:
One point must still be greatly dark,
　　The moving *Why* they do it;
And just as lamely can ye mark,
　　How far perhaps they rue it.

Who made the heart, 'tis *He* alone
　　Decidedly can try us,
He knows each chord its various tone,
　　Each spring, its various bias:
Then at the balance let's be mute,
　　We never can adjust it:
What's *done* we partly may compute,
　　But know not what's *resisted*.

177

Pike emphasised that the Eighth Degree was not for those who simply wanted ritual; it was for those who wished sincerely to understand and embody the Mysteries. His symbol for the eighth degree is scales alongside something that looks somewhat like a sprig of mistletoe berries – actually the ancient Hebrew symbol for the un-named God – inside the Jewish pointed star. This degree demanded more than rote learning of rules, symbols and ceremonies; it required actual study of jurisprudence and Masonic learning. The seeker was advancing towards a star that was the emblem of divine Truth. This representation of star and symbol is placed at the east end of many Masonic lodges.

Life and Earth were made out of nothingness, most religions teach, and Freemasonry is no exception. The great Zero, the Emptiness and the Void pre-empted all material reality. A curious by-product of this Masonic thinking is the numbering of the affiliated clubs in the original Burns Federation. This was formed in 1892 to give common focus to the many societies that had arisen all around the world to celebrate the poet and extend his messages.

The Federation was proposed by the Kilmarnock club. The head of the London Burns Club, Colin Rae-Brown, insisted that the idea of a Federation had actually originated in London. He insisted that the London Robert Burns Club should be called No.1 on the Roll of Honour. Provost Mackay, representing Kilmarnock, demurred. Captain David Sneddon, past president of the Kilmarnock Club, persuaded Provost Mackay to let Colin Rae-Brown have his way. Captain Sneddon was then senior within Masonic circles. He took responsibility for compiling the numbered list of affiliated clubs. He described London's club as Club One, but allocated to Kilmarnock the number Zero.

Pike stated that what distinguishes Man from the brute animals is that he searches for Truth. This requires the diffidence of true Humility. From the search in Moderation and Temperance come love of God and love of neighbour. The great body of Masons were like the bees of a hive, each contributing his little bit to the great sweetness of the whole. No true Mason disparages any aspect of world condition, for God made the world as the place of Man's work; rather than disparage, the Mason must strive to improve what he finds around him. Adversity is an opportunity to focus our strength. The stars indicate what a man might be, but the wise man can over-rule anything that is predicted. A man's will can exert greater power than all the influences of all the constellations and planets in the skies.

These intermediate Degrees of Masonry required the student to accept that understanding involved reflection. Truth discloses itself slowly and in many ways. Truth is not a single ray of light, but like the rainbow separates into many different colours. All the rays are part of one whole, whether in the guise of moral truth, political truth, philosophical truth, religious truth, or scientific truth. What appears to be truth can be mirage,

> Like the snow falls on the river,
> A moment white, then melts forever,
> Or like the borealis race
> That flits ere you can point its place.
> Or like the rainbow's lovely form,
> Evanishing amidst the storm.

To reach Truth the student must recognise Truth has many enemies. He must learn how to overcome them. Thus the Ninth, Tenth and Eleventh Degrees focus on fidelity, obedience and devotion, these dedicated to bravery, devotedness and patriotism, tempered by toleration, and directed to honesty and justice in the service of fellow human beings.

Justice seemed elusive to Burns. He wrote to his Excise superiors warning that mercy to a thief is injustice to a victim. He had watched his father escape debtor's prison only by the timely intervention of death. Yet his father had on 27th January 1784 actually won in the Court of Session, the highest civil court of Scotland, the legal case brought against him by his unscrupulous landlord. But winning at law is a Pyrrhic victory when the costs awarded you are never recoverable, or if they are, are swallowed up by the avarice of legal practice.

Burns, deeply upset by his father's anger at him even unto death, was wary and suspicious. Dr John McKenzie of Mauchline, remembering the family thirty years after the death of William Burness, said Robert took after his mother. He described what he remembered of his first impression of the poet and his brother:

> Gilbert, in the first interview I had with him at Lochlie, was frank, modest, well-informed, and communicative. The poet seemed distant, suspicious, and without any wish to interest or please. He kept himself very silent in a dark corner of the room; and before he took any part in the conversation, I frequently detected him scrutinising me during my conversation with his father and brother. But afterwards, when the conversation, which was on a medical subject, had taken the turn he wished, he began to engage in it, displaying a dexterity of reasoning, and ingenuity of reflection, and a familiarity with topics apparently beyond his reach, by which his visitor was no less gratified than astonished.

'Common Sense' in 'The Holy Fair' is identified with this doctor. Burns lived with Jean Armour next door to Dr McKenzie when first legally married. Burns addressed a Masonic poem to him.

Burns and Jean were an unexpected couple. In April 1785, his father a year in the grave, very shy Robert Burns was a non-participating attendant at a dance during Race Week. His over-active still-puppy collie dog burst into the room. It sought him out with such attention and affection that it disrupted the whole proceedings. Burns, recently prevented from marrying Lizzie Paton, remarked that he wished he could find a girl who would pay him as much attention as that dog. Some while later, as he crossed Mauchline's green, a girl loudly accosted him. The girl was Jean Armour. She demanded to know if he yet had found the girl he needed. They got to know each other. By the end of 1785 Robert Burns was again under severe emotional pressure. His youngest brother, for reasons not now known – possibly some fever aggravated by malnutrition in these years of plague and famine – died when he was merely sixteen years old. He was buried in Mauchline in November. The family was able to afford only a second rate mort cloth.

Jean ministered to the grief of young head of the family, Robert. Burns wanted to marry her. She got pregnant. In the Scottish church, following Calvin, marriage is only blessed by a priest and does not require a priest to make it sacred. It was commonplace for ordinary people to regard marriage as a natural sacrament. The celebrants were the two parties coming together in the blessing of God. This had been the way in the times of the old religion, before the Reformation. The Roman Church changed the rule only at the Council of Trent. Burns had lost Lizzie as his bride. He would not be thwarted a second time. In accordance with old Scottish custom, Robert and Jean married each other by mutual consent. To protect Jean's interests in civil law, in line with evolved practice, Burns committed the event to paper record for Jean's benefit.

When Jean's pregnancy began to show in early 1786 and her parents found out, all hell broke loose. But there was excellent precedent to show tyrannical James Armour, successful stonemason and pillar of the church, what to do. The papers in London and the chapman gossips throughout the whole length and breadth of Britain had, for the previous year, been full of rumour. Against the wishes of his father King George III, the young Prince of Wales had enacted a common law marriage with the widow Mrs Maria Fitzherbert. The young prince had given the lady a paper proving they were man and wife. The lady was a Roman Catholic. Such a marriage to a commoner and one of the outlawed religion potentially precipitated a constitutional crisis. The Powers That Be had made up their minds to disprove the marriage. The gossips related that the paper proving its existence had been destroyed or mutilated, and the marriage so denied.

The cartoons in the newspapers were full of the whole incident. Undoubtedly, Armour's Ayr lawyer proposed that what was good enough to deny the marriage of the Prince of Wales was good enough for Robert Burns. Jean's father demanded that she hand over the paper. He had it mutilated. He attempted thereby to deny that the marriage had taken place. The marriage in fact was totally proper in Scots law, though irregular (but not illegal) in the eyes of the authorities of the Presbyterian Church. Lawyer Aiken cut out the names of Jean and Robert and returned the mutilated paper to James Armour. Removing the names did nothing in law: the marriage stood. But Burns was convinced that Jean had deserted him, treasonously. He thought himself divorced. Later that year, having subjected him to public punishment for fornication, Mauchline Presbytery gave Burns a certificate of bachelorhood. In recognition that the actual legal position had been over-ruled, Burns accepted the humiliation standing in his own pew and not on the infamous degrading cutty stool.

The two incidents, though contemporary, were in fact not comparable. In response to the various politically unhelpful marriages of the king's brothers, King George III in 1772, then sane, caused to be enacted a law for the regulation of royal marriages. The future George IV was then ten years old. Under this law, any person who might be in line of succession to the crown must, until the age of 25, gain permission of the monarch before marriage. In any event, royals were expected to marry dynastically. Commoners were infra dig. Marriage to a Roman Catholic in any event meant giving up any chance of succession.

Maria Anne Smythe was born on July 26th 1756 of an ancient line from Durham. That old papal palatinate had become de facto part of England when it was annexed by Henry VIII in the throes of his Reformation. The Smythes, like many Durham families, were staunch Roman Catholics, intermarrying with such Roman Catholic families as Lambton of Lambton, Eshe of Eshe, and Gage of Sussex. Fines reduced their ancient aristocratic wealth. Such families survived the penal fines through judicious marriage. Maria's first marriage to Thomas Weld was no exception. He was much older, and intended that she inherit his possessions. He died so soon after their marriage that his will in her favour was not signed. (One of his properties was Stonyhurst, which was later granted to the Jesuits as a base for their school.) Three years later she married Thomas Fitzherbert of Synnerton, near Stone. He was descended of that Fitzherbert who in 1125 had been granted the Lordship of the Manor of Norbury by the Prior of Tutbury. This young, tall and powerful man died at Nice on May 7th 1781, reputedly from over-exertion. That over-exertion may have been trying to prevent the trashing of homes of London Roman Catholic friends during the anti-Catholic Gordon Riots in 1780. In the fighting he may have sustained internal injuries.

In 1783, the twice-widowed young Maria was spotted in London by the over-actively sentimentally romantic young Prince George. He persuaded himself that he had fallen violently in love – in the exquisitely over-dramatised sentimental manner of Henry Mackenzie's fashionable

'Man of Feeling'. When he failed to get her to become his mistress, in the summer of 1784 he fell on his sword, undangerously. He had Maria dragged to his presence. There, covered in his own blood, he threatened he would fall on his sword properly this time, if she did not immediately accept him as her husband. Maria had had the good sense to drag with her Georgina, Duchess of Devonshire, who witnessed the whole business. She was present when Maria acquiesced to having one of Georgina's rings thrust onto her hand by the heir to the throne. Later that evening, reflecting on the implications of the incident, Maria and Georgina wrote a minute of the day's events. They signed it, and carefully locked it away in the Devonshire strong box. In the wake of another constitutional crisis in 1936, this document was found still to be held safe at Chatsworth.

Such a marriage was treason not only by both parties but by any witnesses. Maria denied any marriage had taken place. For safety, she fled the country. For the next eighteen months, the prince, prevented by his father's orders from leaving Britain, pursued her in letters and gifts. At the end of 1785 he wrote her an extensive letter – 42 pages – telling her his father would now condone the marriage. He insisted it was safe for her to return to England and have their marriage legally formalised by an Anglican clergyman, in a manner that would satisfy her Roman Catholic scruples. She agreed to this. A private marriage was conducted. A proper marriage certificate was written out and signed by the two parties and their witnesses. When King George III found out, all hell broke loose.

To protect from the horrific punishment for treason all parties involved in the ceremony, the evidence of their presence was destroyed by cutting their names from the papers. But meanwhile, Maria had the good sense to put into the vault of Coutts Bank the 42 page letter, to which was added the mutilated marriage certificate.

These two marriage incidents were different in another way: Robert Burns wanted seriously to commit his life to Jean; the Prince of Wales, an inveterate gambler, probably hoped he could get from Maria what he wanted and then when it suited him be able to discard her. Divorce was, after all, the foundation of Anglicanism. He was the son of a young king; he could expect his father to live for many years yet. At some later stage the question of succession to the throne could be renegotiated. (George III lived until 1820. He was incurably mad in the last eleven years of life.) Moreover, in those days, female mortality was high. So the future George IV could actually expect to outlive Maria. (In fact, he did not.) Maria considered herself his wife until his death; romantics suggest this was reciprocated, but the behaviour of the prince suggests other interpretations.

In the backlash of rejection and the apparent annulment of his own marriage, Burns is said to have turned for emotional support to an attractive young lassie. She was then a nursemaid in the home of Burns's landlord, Gavin Hamilton. To him Burns had turned for help against the attack of Jean's parents. The story goes that this Mary Campbell, born in the West Highlands, in the loving manner of her kind, consoled him not just emotionally, but physically. On the first Sunday in May 1786, Burns and Mary are said to have exchanged Bibles. The little two-volume Bible that Burns gave to Mary has survived. The one she purportedly gave him has never been found. They are said to have mutually promised marriage. She agreed, goes the myth, returning home to Dunoon to make her preparations. They were to meet in Greenock where they would take ship for Jamaica. There Burns would indenture himself – in other words sell himself as a slave for a period of years – to pay for their passage. He had asked her (they quote his song in proof) to emigrate with him across the wild Atlantic:

Will ye go to the Indies my Mary,

And leave auld Scotia's shore?

It is accepted as fact that a girl of a different name but identified as Mary reached Greenock and there found her brother in a fever. In nursing him she caught the fever. She died in Greenock. Her grave was dug up. An infant was in the same grave. This caused speculation that she was vulnerable to fever through being in the early stages of pregnancy. Burns is said to have found himself suddenly in the most vicious way relieved of the potential embarrassment of unwitting bigamy. He is said to have remained all his life riven with guilt. If this is true, perhaps those academics are wrong who regard as mere pastoral, 'To a Mountain Daisy, On Turning One Down, with the Plough, in April 1786'.

Wee, modest, crimson-tipped flow'r,

Thou's met me in an evil hour;

For I maun crush amang the stoure

Thy slender stem:

To spare thee now is past my pow'r,

Thou bonie gem.

It has always seemed to me that a poem of such intensity as this ode is no mere exercise in sentiment. Perhaps the sprightly slim red-head took Burns to her bosom, consoling him with generous loving when he felt so rejected by his faithless Jean. Her death does indeed seem to have pierced him to the heart. The poem would thus be no pastoral fancy, but allegory of grief, smeared with guilt. It tells of despair, loneliness, possibly heightened by realisation that he would pay full price for the evil in having to face slavery in Jamaica alone.

The billows rage, and gales blow hard,

And whelm him o'er!

A virgin 'Highland Mary' became central to the Burns myth during the 19th century. Thus Greenock shipbuilding company Messrs Caird & Co, after it purchased the old West Parish Church, had a four years' struggle begun in 1917 to resolve the matter of moving her supposed grave. The Corporation of Greenock supported the demolition of the church as part of its slum clearance programme. The British Parliament passed an Act providing that Mary Campbell's monument must stand forever over her actual grave, where it had always stood. It was later moved after permission was granted.

Then at the beginning of the 20th century it was suggested that the supposed virgin love of Burns had died in childbirth. Today there is even dispute about the woman's name. She is supposed to have been a dairy maid at Coilsfield, but for this house there are no surviving 18th century servant records. The one surviving list of Gavin Hamilton's servants in 1785 includes no mention of a suitably named woman.

John Richmond then in Sorn, a clerk in Gavin Hamilton's office, claimed in 1817 that Highland Mary had been kept for some time by a brother of Lord Eglinton. Richmond was a pal Burns went about with in youth. He said Burns had denied Mary was that man's mistress. Richmond and James Smith, the third of the 'lads', demonstrated to Burns that it was true by discovering the pair together in a private room in an inn. The lover was identified as Captain James Montgomerie of the 93rd Regiment, younger brother of Hugh Montgomerie of Coilsfield. Hugh became twelfth Earl of Eglinton on the death in 1796 of his cousin Alexander, who had succeeded his brother Archibald as Earl of Eglinton in 1769.

There is another suggestion that no-one has yet made. Perhaps Burns found out that a lovely girl he had seen in Tarbolton church had, on innocent arrival from her Highland home to be a dairy maid, found she was expected to give service of a different kind. Perhaps, like a 'Tess of the Durbervilles', Burns sought to rescue her. He believed he had persuaded her she was better to go home. If he subsequently found that she was still being imposed upon by Montgomerie, he would indeed have been as morose as Richmond described. This perhaps is why he got this Highland girl to swear an oath on his Bible, writing on the flyleaf dire words of warning on the breaking of a holy oath. In this explanation Burns himself would have taken no oath. So we have here good reason no reciprocal Bible has been found. There would have been none.

Under this Bible signature is a water-damaged copy of the Mason mark of Robert Burns in his own hand. Some Masonic texts say all Masons should always subscribe their signature with their mark. Clearly this is a rule more honoured in the breach. That Burns should in this Bible have subscribed his Mason mark emphasises the solemnity of the oath. It suggests he considered Mary had taken a terrible oath to which he was witness before God.

Thus he parted with Highland Mary, never again to see her in life. Her death in such loss of innocence would have angered him.

I wonder whether this experience caused him during his first winter in Edinburgh, when seeking support for a second edition of his poems, to attend the Court of Session to hear the case of another Campbell versus Montgomerie. The wife of Charles Maxwell Campbell of Skerrington, Cumnock, had borne a child to Captain James Montgomerie in 1784. The case was continued in March 1787. He wrote to Gavin Hamilton on 8th March on the ruling that Campbell need not divorce his wife before proceeding for damages against the lover. He was free to deal with his wife as he would. Burns lamented:

> "O all ye Powers of love unfortunate and friendless woe, pour the balm of sympathising pity on the grief-torn tender heart of the hapless Fair One!"

Burns and the Captain were both Brothers in Tarbolton Lodge. Their very different attitudes, about personal conduct and towards women, demonstrate the vast differences there can be in moral response to the ethical training supposedly received within Freemasonry.

Captain Montgomerie went abroad with his regiment. A continuing hearing by the Court of Session in 1790 and again in 1792 ruled whether an Action of Meditatio Fugae could be raised against an officer going abroad on service, as well as whether significant expenses for recovery of debt were also due to the creditor. Montgomerie appealed, claiming the writ and expenses were unfounded; it was improper to consider him as running from justice when military service had called him away before he had paid the damages awarded to Charles Maxwell Campbell. Such a writ issued in those circumstances could only have the intention of maligning his character, and for the creditor to gratify revenge, he claimed. The ruling went against Montgomerie, citing a precedent of the arrest of a Scottish merchant in America similarly to recover debt. Campbell didn't even then get his money, as witnessed by records of further Actions in Court over ensuing years.

Burns had no patience with wilful evil, in man or woman. When a prostitute set up business in 1785 in Poosie Nancy's tavern at Mauchline, he did not approve. Teenager Adam Armour, the poet's future brother-in-law, and Adam's pals took things rather further. On 6th March 1786 the group of lads was hauled before the Kirk Session for 'stanging' out of town the thieving serving woman Agnes Wilson, Mauchline's resident harlot. Stanging is the cruel lynch-punishment of forcing persons to ride astride the roughest pole available, with the intention that it lacerates them. Wilson's employer accused the boys of assault. Adam hid out at Mossgeil to avoid physical retribution. Robert's poem on this event, 'Adam Armour's Prayer' illustrates disgust of criminality, theft and harlotry.

He even more detested hypocrisy, which he considered a far greater sin than harlotry. When he could not fail to notice who customers of Mauchline's thief-harlot were, he used the knowledge when relevant in penning satires against hypocrisy.

In Edinburgh, John McLaurin, Lord Dreghorn, Senator of the College of Justice, who published tracts on law, religion and poetry, was cousin to Clarinda. She described him to Burns as a detestable character who:

> enjoys more pleasure in the mercenary embrace of a courtesan than in relieving the unfortunate.

Of course, by 'the unfortunate' she meant herself. In leaving her husband, she had unfortunately lost all the financial benefits of her Jamaican estates. She was complaining that the allowance Dreghorn generously provided to her wasn't big enough. Dreghorn did not increase her allowance; he expressed his view that her behaviour with respect to Burns – and possibly others – was scandalous. She should behave with the decorum of the married woman she was. He later came to hate prostitutes. In 1789 he closed Edinburgh's brothels and banished the inmates. The manner of it angered Burns. In his letter to Peter Hill on 2nd February 1790 he railed against

> "those flinty-bosomed, puritanical Prosecutors of Female Frailty & Persecutors of Female Charms"

who closed the brothels of Edinburgh, adding,

> "May Woman curse them! May Woman blast them! May Woman damn them! May her lovely hand inexorably shut the Portal of Rapture to their most earnest Prayers and fondest essays for entrance! And when many years, and much port and great business have delivered them over to Vulture Gouts and Aspen Palsies, *then* may the dear, bewitching Charmer in derision throw open the blissful Gate to tantalise their impotent desires which like ghosts haunt their bosoms when all their powers to give or receive enjoyment are for ever asleep in the sepulchre of their fathers!!!"

He had been shocked with what he saw as a naïve youth in Irvine. There for the first time he was exposed, perhaps by his friend Richard Brown, to a house of ill repute. Currie certainly identified as illicit sex the "fashionable failing" that he was introduced to. We have no evidence to believe Burns used prostitutes. Whether or not he did, he was right in saying Irvine "did him a mischief", for seeing seedy life sullies innocence.

Burns was too aware that brothels had been massively swelled by the economic change that had swept Scotland since the end of the '45 Rising. 'Highland Mary' was one of many thousands who had come south in search of work because there was no longer a living in the mountains. Many such young innocent girls soon came to be abused whether as household servants or having fallen under the control of whore masters. In notes on changes in Edinburgh during his lifetime, publisher Creech commented how much morals and social conditions had deteriorated in the twenty years between 1763 and 1783. Fines for bastard children increased four-fold; the five or six brothels and a few night-walkers of 1763 were contrasted with a hundred brothels, and hundreds of women offering sex for sale, in a town become thick with robbers, pick-pockets and criminality. The same kind of statistical change is too visible in the 21st century as economic disruption alters the previous social balance.

Chapter VII *Mystery*

In this world of uncertainty, Burns needed a spiritual anchor which the Presbyterian Kirk did not provide. What the Craft might teach him was how he might come to terms with all this darkness and suffering and rise above it. He turned to the Mauchline lawyer and friend Gavin Hamilton. Burns had strongly defended him in verse against the attacks of church authorities. Hamilton perhaps encouraged him to seek consolation and emotional support in more fervent study of the Craft.

Masonry is not, said Pike, a speculative exercise, for thought alone; it is about doing right and opposing those who deceptively pay lip service to right form. Thus, the Mason must guard against those who display sentiments but lack underlying principles of conduct. Those who achieve greater things do so not by dint of being more greatly gifted (though that can help) but by making greater effort. Pike says a severe limitation of being *inside* the physical Lodge is that there is no opportunity therein actually to *act* on principle; the most anyone can do therein is *talk* about action. So, in modern consultant's parlance, many a Mason may talk the talk, but how many walk the walk?

On 27th March 1786 Burns was introduced by Hamilton to another Lodge. They rode east from Mauchline, climbing the escarpment. Pausing to let their horses draw breath at the top, they could look back on the town. There it nestles still amidst the great cloak of Coila, spread wide north and south between the escarpment and the sea, with grand houses set like jewels here and there in a tartan of farm, moor and marsh. They turned north before they reached Sorn, to go over high moors and past Galston to the village of Newmilns beyond Loudon Castle. They arrived at what is now the Loudoun Arms Inn. This fine building was adapted in 1742 by extending an old farmhouse with outbuildings that clustered round a mediaeval fortified tower-house, once home to the Campbells of Loudoun. Here met the Loudoun, Kilwinning, Newmilns Lodge. It recorded in its Minutes that night their considerable satisfaction to admit as one of their number, in honorary membership, this farmer of Mossgeil.

Burns stayed overnight at St Margaret's Hill, home of Rev George Lawrie (1727-1799), Minister of Loudoun. (Lawrie was granted a doctorate in Divinity from Glasgow University in 1791.) Lawrie was impressed on meeting Burns. That night in Lawrie's house Burns experienced a revelation. He heard a spinet played. Seventeen year old Louisa Lawrie played and his heart thereafter never stopped reverberating to the sound of music. His childhood, full as it was with country song, had been deprived of fine music. The young lady's excellent singing, exactly on pitch, raised his soul to wondrous awareness of a music beyond the power of man's ears to hear. He heard an echo of the Music of the Spheres.

The Twelfth Degree, or Grand Master Architect, was where the dedicated Mason could truly begin to reach for the stars. Pike symbolised this with five columns of the Greek orders of architecture: the Tuscan, the Doric, the Ionic, the Corinthian and the Composite. These in turn represented five stages of passing through Degrees of Masonry. The Tuscan represented the first three Degrees. The Doric represented those from the fourth to the fourteenth. The Ionic represented the fifteenth and sixteenth, also known as the second temple Degrees. The Corinthian represented the seventeenth and eighteenth Degrees, known as those of the new law. The Composite represented the philosophical and chivalric Degrees, or those from the nineteenth to the thirty second.

Stars were allegories of the Masonic quest. The North Star represented God in the centre of the Universe. Jupiter rising in the east represented the dawning of Masonic light. That light showed that true Divine Right to govern is vested in those who are wisest, most able and have greatest integrity.

The Twelfth Degree acknowledged the dark night of the soul passing through the loneliness of the depths of sorrow. Understanding required awareness of the meaning of nothing – the meaning of the loss of those things that are only truly appreciated when they have been taken away forever. In Pike is the observation:

> We never know the full significance of the words 'property', 'ease', and 'health'; the wealth of meaning in the fond epithets, 'parent', 'child', 'beloved', and 'friend', until the thing or the person is taken away; until, in the place of the bright, visible being, comes the awful and desolate shadow, where *nothing* is: where we stretch out our hands in vain, and strain our eyes upon dark and dismal vacuity. Yet, in that vacuity, we do not *lose* the object that we loved. It becomes only the more real to us.

Burns had already experienced loss: the loss of his father, the loss of his brother, the loss of 'Highland Mary', the loss of Jean Armour. Perhaps he knew inside himself that he had suffered even the loss of his health through his life in unrelenting toil. But he was not alone; he was part of Mankind. As the Universe was held together by the great forces of gravitation, so Mankind was held together by the mutual bond of Society. Remove the gravitation, and the Universe crashes to chaos; remove the social bond, and Mankind falls into the helpless destructive vortex of despair. The social bond is the interlocking of every human soul, past and present, within and part of the infinity of God. Only the pomp and follies of the physical and intellectual world prevent us each from feeling that magnificent worth of our own spiritual soul. The inner Dignity of Man exceeds all worldly power, wealth and glory, whose paths lead but to the grave.

The Twelfth Degree teaches that the most significant difference amongst men is in their power to communicate the deepest feelings that all men share. Eloquence and poetry express those feelings and so make all hearts glow with joy.

That summer Burns published his first edition of poems. Lawrie eagerly read the new book. He sent a copy of the book to Dr Blacklock of Edinburgh. On 4th September, Blacklock wrote back enthusing about the poems. Lawrie passed the letter to Hamilton. Hamilton passed the letter to Burns. Burns was overwhelmed by praise from such an unexpected source as Edinburgh. He resolved to go to Scotland's capital to seek the necessary support to enable him to remain in Scotland and renew his efforts. For he already knew that he wished he:

> For dear old Scotland's sake
> Some usefu' plan or book could make
> Or sing a sang at least.

On 26th October Kilmarnock's St John's Kilwinning Lodge also granted Burns honorary membership. He was, by this time, advancing well through his studies. On reaching Edinburgh he was made a member of Canongate Kilwinning Lodge No 2. Here, colleagues included his 'near neighbour' in Ayrshire, the Earl of Eglinton. Other members were the Earl of Glencairn (whom he considered his real patron), the judge Lord Elcho, Lord Torphichen, banker-innovator Patrick Miller of Dalswinton, Lord Pitsligo, the lawyer Alexander Cunningham, schoolmaster William Nicol, publisher William Creech, painter Alexander Nasmyth, and lawyer Henry Mackenzie, whose novel 'The Man of Feeling' had been one of Burns's favourite teenage books.

The lessons for the Thirteenth Degree are allegorically woven round the earliest Biblical stories, plus the building of Solomon's temple, and the myth of Enoch the Initiator. Its core practical lesson is that to gain freedom is worthless if freedom is not then secured. Any leaning towards weakness brings its due consequence. Thus, an arch will fall unless the keystone is fixed in place. In human society, particularly the Nation State, the keystone of the Royal Arch of the great Temple of Liberty is its written or unwritten constitution. This, built up over ages by the accumulated wisdom of the people, should never be changed unless after due consideration.

Many books on Masonry acknowledge only three Degrees – Entered Apprentice, Fellowcraft and Master. Sangeet Duchane produced one of the very many publications that surfaced in the wake of the success of the novel 'The Da Vinci Code'. His little booklet entitled 'Freemasonry' remarked that some recognise higher degrees, of which the best known is Royal Arch. This appears to have its origin in France around 1750 or in Ireland.

In Pike it is explained that to reach Royal Arch, the Master dies to the past and is reborn into the highest, most magnificent level of awareness of the meaning of life. This level of renewed consciousness he symbolised by an equilateral triangle with a point in the centre, allegorical of spiritual, physic and physical elements of the person all equally balanced and centred on life.

Burns received the Royal Arch degree on 19th May 1787 from St Ebbe's Lodge in Eyemouth. Above the side door of this building is a Masonic sign identifying this as Lodge No 70. It is claimed that this is the third oldest purpose-built Masonic Lodge in the world. The interior was embellished in 1918 with a mural of the coastline from Coldingham Priory to Burnmouth. With its foundation stone laid in 1757, this Lodge held a rededication ceremony in 2007 to celebrate its quarter millennium. This was led by The Grand Master Mason of the Grand Lodge of Scotland, Sir Archibald Orr Ewing.

On 30th November 1786, two days after Burns arrived in Edinburgh, there had been a Grand Visitation of the Freemasons to mark St Andrew's Day. They assembled at New Church at midday for the election of the Grand Master. Six weeks later Burns attended the meeting of St Andrew's Lodge on Friday 12th January 1787. Grand Master Francis Charteris of Amisfield was present. To the poet's consternation the Grand Master made a toast to Scotland's Bard, Brother Burns. Burns rose and gave a totally impromptu response – the very greatest challenge an entertainer can face. This was greeted with a loud "Bravo!".

The Masonic camaraderie of such occasions undoubtedly led him to know that the Eyemouth building would reach an important milestone in the coming summer. Here, on the 30th anniversary of the laying of the foundation stone, came the newly famous poet, Burns, for this highly important moment during his tour of the Scottish Borders. He was raised to the Degree of Royal Arch in a tiny building exactly aligned to the four compass points, the Master's seat against the east wall.

When the Lodge was founded, Eyemouth was a grain port, but by the time Burns arrived its modern industry of fishing had begun. Burns, ever keen on seeing new technology and economic development at first hand, went out by boat to view the fishing fleet in action.

On 27th December 1791, by then living in Dumfries, Burns joined St Andrew's Lodge No 179. He was elected Senior Warden there on 30th November 1792 two months before the French guillotined their king. Burns remained an active participant in its meetings until his last illness. By then, in Bavaria, a secret society called the Illuminati, formed in 1776, had been exposed as having plotted insurgence. Freemasonry, though denounced by the French revolutionaries, was clearly associated with the concept of Liberty. It was now sullied with blood lust. The movement was looked on with increasing suspicion.

Hanoverian King George III was already succumbing to the weaknesses due to the illness that ultimately caused his irrecoverable madness. In London, the Establishment were determined to wipe from any record of history the thought of alternatives to the Hanoverian line. The Old Pretender, who would have been James VIII of Scots and III of England, had died in 1766. He had been succeeded on his death by his son, Charles, Count of Albany, Bonnie Prince Charlie, the Young Pretender. It was recognised on his death in 1788 that his heir was his brother Cardinal Henry Benedict, rightful Duke of York, Henry I of Scots and IX of England. It was rumoured that he would be succeeded by Bonnie Prince Charlie's son, James. Down to the present time it is claimed the line continues, represented today by Prince Michael of Albany, recognised by some as King Alexander IV of Scots. By others he is declared an impostor.

It is said that after 1307 Scotland's king, Robert the Bruce, welcomed the remnant of the Knights Templar who were fleeing from the pogrom initiated by the avarice of the King of France. Those knights had fought with Bruce at Bannockburn, went the story. When Scotland gained her victory, and gained the support of the Pope in her recovered freedom, a new secret Order was formed from the remnant of the Templars. This was called the Elder Brothers of the Order of the Rosy Cross. Their constitution was aligned with the Declaration of Arbroath of 1320. That was the first modern Declaration of Independence and became the model for that of the United States of America. This Order was centred in a Lodge founded by King David II at Kilwinning, Ayrshire. James Steward, Fifth High Steward and ancestor of the Stuart line, became its Grand Master. It is said of Prince Michael of Albany – as retrospectively of all monarchs of Scots since Bruce – that he is hereditary Grand Master of the successors of the Templars.

It is said that this Freemasonry was brought to London in 1603 when James VI succeeded to the English throne after the death of Elizabeth I. Initially this formed a body of Scottish counsellors around the isolated king, but by the 1640s English thinkers, led by such as Ashmole of Oxford, were joining Masonic ranks. Prince Michael of Albany, in his book 'The Forgotten Monarchy of Scotland', states that the Kilwinning Lodge worked Templar ritual. Its Minutes record that a charter to work Templary and Royal Arch was granted to the Kilwinning Lodge in Ireland. This ended only in 1799 when the Hanoverian government passed the Secret Society Act. Thereafter, Scottish Rite Freemasonry was exiled from its homeland.

As he was a member of several daughter houses of Kilwinning Lodge, eyebrows might well have been raised when, not for the first time, Burns was in late 1792 accused of disloyalty to the Hanoverian line. He was threatened with loss of his lowly civil service post. Poorly paid though it was, it was all that stood between the poet's family and starvation.

Burns wrote on 5th January 1793 to his boss Graham of Fintry denying disloyalty. Yes, he had been in the pit amongst the crowd in the Dumfries theatre in early December 1792. Then the very aggressive British patriot song 'God Save the King' had been demanded of the orchestra by a group of rowdy right-wing rich lads, who formed the vigilantes self-styled the Loyal Natives. No, he had not joined the rabble response of chanting the French revolutionary song, 'Ça ira'. He had pulled his hat firmly over his head trying to keep out of the likely ensuing punch-up.

So many enemies had this man whose stinging verse had dared to raise him above the ploughshare that at this time John Francis Erskine, who in 1824 was restored to his hereditary lands as twenty seventh Earl of Mar, offered to lead a subscription to create a fund to make him financially independent. The poet, perhaps too quickly, gracefully turned down the offer as being unnecessary.

Chapter VII *Mystery*

Perhaps Graham, meanwhile, took another look at the letter Burns had sent him during 1792, declaring his loyalty:

> "I never uttered any invectives against the King. His private worth it is altogether impossible that such a man as I can appreciate; but in his public capacity I always revered, and always will, with the soundest loyalty, revere the Monarch of Great Britain as (to speak in Masonic terms) the sacred Keystone of our Royal Arch Constitution."

His Masonic connection with the Kilwinning Lodge, a central pillar of Jacobite support, marked him out. Burns had named no king. So which King did he mean? Again he named no king when in January 1793 he begged Graham of Fintry to reflect on the welfare of his helpless family before pronouncing judgement on his inquiry into the loyalty of this too romantic poet. He did not in those letters explicitly say he supported Hanoverian and opposed Stuart monarchy. He had only added in that first letter to Graham of Fintry:

> "I look upon the British Constitution, as settled at the Revolution, to be the most glorious Constitution on earth, or that perhaps the wit of man can frame."

Masonry taught him much. Masonic brothers helped him to his successes. Masonic circles may have protected him now. Careless he had been with wit until a growing reign of terror spread through Britain that winter, silencing free speech.

Then he turned to other skills learned in childhood. From Salmon's 'Geographical Grammar', massive though the tome was, Burns no doubt learned how not to waste words, how to put his own maximum meaning into the smallest space. From extensive experience of the Law he knew the difference between lies and careful truth. Thus, a man who was fully independent, he could truly write,

> "I never dictated to, corresponded with, or had the least connection with, any political association whatever – except that when the magistrates and principal inhabitants of Dumfries met to declare their attachment to the Constitution, and the abhorrence of riot".

After all, to write to newspapers is not political association.

His Masonic studies would have resonated with what he had learned about the universe in Salmon's microcosm of the world. Salmon, describing on page 9 the place of Earth in the universe, had found it appropriate to quote the words of Whiston, whose teachings Derham made available to children. Thus Salmon amplified lessons of 'Astro-Theology'. On page 10 Salmon defined Zodiac and Ecliptic, and a few pages further on defined 'climate' as

> a space on the globe between two supposed parallel lines, where the day is increased half an hour in the lesser parallel.

There is not always an absolute Truth to find, learned Burns. Salmon warned the reader to be aware that not all peoples thought of time and dates in the same way. In 1767 Italians and Jews still began their day at sunset, just as Ancient Babylonians had begun theirs at sunrise. British seamen had their own peculiar way of doing things:

> Our seamen begin their day at noon, that being the time when they correct their reckoning, by taking the height of the sun with their quadrants.

Many curious observations in Salmon, along with indications that paradox was the source of question and hence enlightenment, came alongside instructions on how to use a globe as an analogue computer. From it could be found the length of the longest days and nights at any place on Earth, as well as when twilight begins and ends. The lad would have noted in the chronicle on page 327 an entry for a mere two years before publication of the edition of Salmon he was reading, on October 28th 1765. The much sought after technical advance required by the Navy was recognised as having been achieved: an accurate and reliable clock had been invented suited to measuring longitude during sea voyages. A certificate had been signed and issued by the Commissioners of Longitude, confirming that the Harrison time-keeper actually achieved the intended maritime purpose. Thus, after years of controversy, Harrison had become entitled to the reward of £10,000 Sterling for solving the problem of being able to use clockwork to measure accurately using time the passage of distance at sea.

Burns never saw a globe until he was invited into the homes and palaces of the intelligentsia and aristocracy. I can imagine him being drawn to them, his fingers itching out to touch them and turn them, his excitement growing as he found himself illustrating to the bemused owner of these mysterious orbs their real purposes in navigation and understanding of the changing seasons of the evolving year. Thus he incidentally measured against the greatest in the land of Scotland his own intellect and his ability to learn and truly understand. His knowledge of using globes, gained purely in imagination, he found to apply to these real things in great homes amongst privileged men in positions of power. Important and wealthy though they were, they clearly knew so little of the true meaning of what they casually owned. This must have emphasised those deeper questions about each man's true worth that had been planted in his mind in childhood and emphasised by his Masonic studies.

For all that he had reached the mystical Thirteenth Degree, the Degree of Royal Arch, though he had spent his lifetime in pursuit of learning, reaching for understanding, yet, even when he returned to Mauchline in the summer of 1787, he still felt he lacked an aim. True, he had had that Vision. True, Coila had come to him in his hovel, in wondrous light, through the choking Delphic smoke of the aromatic peat. True, she had told him to proudly write his verse. But then she had charged him: "Preserve the Dignity of Man!" and crowned him with a crown of thorns.

Preserve the Dignity of Man! What kind of an aim was that? A man needed something concrete. Even a poet needs something concrete. On this first return from Edinburgh he still did not have that something concrete.

But Edinburgh surely held the key. That letter from Dr Blacklock had been a sign. Of this he was certain. It had come to him through Rev. Lawrie of Newmilns. There for the first time he had heard what he knew could only be an echo of the Music of the Spheres.

Chapter VIII *Enlightenment*

How modern history misleads about the Age of Reason and why Burns opposed its narrow-mindedness.

When a person is remembered two hundred and fifty years after his birth, it begs some explanation. This is even more the case when that person was simply a poet, or so it appears. It is especially relevant to ask it when the poet is in the minds of most people not even amongst the 'greats' like Shakespeare. Why he is not dismissed is a mystery worth exploring. Why many do dismiss his poetry almost certainly lies in the timing of his death – in the throes of the major world war in the wake of the French Revolution.

This love surely is not because, one of the lowliest of labourers, he intellectually impressed in his day. He did write well; he worked hard at it. But that is still not enough. Nor is it that he was seen then as a natural genius, a phenomenon that philosophers then fashionably spoke of but seldom encountered. He would have been a mere flash in the pan, forgotten as quickly as intellectuals forgot him. Even James Boswell would not deign, once his meteor flash of fame was over, to grant Burns a meeting with his august self. No, there is something else. In some way he transcended his time. It cannot simply be because his biographers made him out to be a drunken anarchist, and so was taken up as mascot of Socialism.

He lives on, though the Russian Communist experiment is over.

The degree to which Burns was unusual in his day not only as a labourer of exceptional gifts and high education can be understood by comparing him directly with the norms of his time. Even a college-taught lone young writer, faced with a bound book of blank pages, fears his inadequacy to fill it worthily.

The First Commonplace Book of Burns shows that he actively taught himself to write well. Instinctively he felt he had something to say and wanted to say it. The extreme case of the untaught is beautifully portrayed in the film 'Il Postino'. In that story, the uneducated near illiterate postman is given the present of the blank book by his friend the Nobel Prize winning poet, Pablo Neruda. The aspiring postman poet sits at his desk, pen poised. He faces that daunting first blank page, the infinite expanse of all the empty pages of the book ahead of him like an unstarted uncharted journey. Searching his mind for the proper words worthy of this front page he gazes out of his little window at the great blank face of the full moon. He begins to seek in his heart to express the feelings of his soul. His pen reaches down to the paper and carefully draws a circle.

Robert Burns was less daunted by actual paper, because he had since childhood been required to fulfil the farming routine of keeping the ledger. But in his home paper was a luxury. Cash was a rarity. He stole the indulgence of spending hard won cash on an actual book to contain his own written thoughts. He no doubt considered very carefully what he would put on that first page. In his lowly world paper was neither cheap nor easily got. So the drafting of those first words would have been carried out substantially in his head, over long reflection. Perhaps too he might have sketched out a few phrases on the family slate – the erasable notebook of the day. This was so commonplace as the normal writing medium that the phrase 'to slate it up' has come into modern language meaning 'making a note', usually of credit taken in an inn. The single high quality piece of good slate was a necessary tool in the farmhouse. On it, the family kept note of such important matters as financially-related comings and goings, in advance of their formal writing into the ledger. The same slate was used for children's lessons in writing and arithmetic. In the absence of books, teachers wrote on a slate for pupils to read.

Sheffield University excavated a blackhouse on the island of Barra, in the Outer Hebrides. This hovel was contemporary with and probably not much different from the home of the child Robert Burns. They found, to their surprise, an excellent piece of black slate. This, the archaeologists noted, was a house that would have been roofed with thatch or turf. What, they asked, could explain the presence of this slate? To me, who in childhood used a slate for school exercises, the explanation is obvious. But to the modern world of easy paper and electronic notebooks the presence in a mud and rubble thatched hovel of a thin rectangle of fine stone is a mystery.

Books in the impoverished home of William Burness were an astonishingly expensive luxury that the poet's father refused to forgo. Before print became so commonplace as being simply a precursor to its own pulping, in any homes thirsty for learning, books were typically used as long as they lasted. They thus in the 18th century had what magazine editors today call a 'long shelf-life'. They were not, like yesterday's freebie paper, being today put in the recycle bin. When they had been read they were carefully put on a shelf so that another reader could derive the benefit from them. Thus, text-books were passed down from grandfather to father to son. Though our world treats all writing as disposable, good books can still have a shelf-life of many years. In Burns's day, it was quite normal to have as school text a book written nearly forty years before the pupil's birth.

The actual physical books were eked out to last for generations. The actual content of books could last even longer; Robert Burns used the standard geometry textbook of the era – the 'Elements' of Euclid. This is still read today by those who want the best introduction to geometry. It was written two and a half millennia ago. That is quite a shelf-life. This text remained a standard geometry school text until after the Second World War. Then the lack of trained teachers – since teaching pupils, let alone training teachers for the future, was not a high priority in wartime – meant a need for simplified textbooks. There were not enough of the old educated people around who could understand Euclid, never mind explain it to all the new young minds entering schools in the post-war baby boom. Thus dumbing-down education was encouraged in the latter half of the 20th century.

But amongst the literati of late 18th century Scotland, the modern idea that old books are old hat was already growing. While this attitude did not reach the homes of labourers while Burns lived, we can only understand how Burns might have felt about book knowledge if we have some view of how far Enlightenment thinking had reached homes such as his.

That the 18th century was the era of the Scottish Enlightenment is a commonplace. Edinburgh then gained the nickname 'Athens of the North' not merely from its considerable physical expansion and building investment in the latter half of the century.

Scotland in the 21st century still vaunts the era's faded laurels. These are particularly those attributed, inappropriately, to Adam Smith for creating modern capitalism. Smith, with ethics in the core of his economics, promoted division of labour, free trade and enlightened self interest. Hume argued that economic growth was *promoted* by law and order but *generated* only by allowing free rein to the human profit motive – otherwise known as selfish greed. Smith opposed him. Their contemporary, Thomas Reid, also had ethics at the centre of his economics, but argued against extensive division of labour. But subtlety of argument is hardly likely to have been the commonplace form of discussion on commerce and industry in the gentlemen's clubs. There the central question was how to get rich quick.

These subtle differences, which Burns understood, matter now to our crisis ridden modern world. Smith, Hume and Reid each claimed to found his argument on Newtonian reasoning. Hume demanded that all philosophical positions be based on actual measurement. In this he ignored Newton's warnings that measurement can never be so fine as to be truly exact. Reid and Smith, in different ways, used their mathematical ability to oppose such limitations they saw in Hume's argument. Measure by human beings was not enough to explain their totality of experience.

Reid showed that different contemporaneous descriptions of the universe explained different perceptions of the same underlying reality. Smith showed how historical development of theories of the universe, rather than contradicting each other, simply reflected mankind's developing and deepening understanding of everyday experience. Thus even more so in economics – a far less precise science than astronomy – it was not against reason to allow common sense and instinct to be right when they opposed what seemed irrefutable on the basis of measures.

Reid and Smith differed on the practical route forward. Reid sought a way in which society could develop the full potential of each of its members and at the same time grow materially wealthy. Smith argued that material wealth could be rapidly developed only by individual specialisation. He thus compromised on realising individual potential. In recompense, he argued that the wealth so generated could then enable the nation as a whole to achieve "that full complement of riches" normally embodied only in full individual realisation. But since the human beings were paramount, he argued against exploitation of people. Humanity demanded that entrepreneurs temper their greed with consideration for others. This last bit of his thinking got dropped by the start of the 19th century. By 1800 the balance of intellectual opinion had already settled closer to Hume's position. Thus in 1805 Dugald Stewart met little intellectual opposition when he cavalierly described as sole instrument of Smith's economic model the 'invisible hand'.

Realpolitik decided the intellectual argument; war with France in the 1790s made Britain move fast forward its industrialisation. Development was through the superficially Smithian specialisation by division of labour. It was implemented with the pragmatic sanction of Hume's freedom from the restraint of religious ethics. Rational thinking based on measure is paramount. There is probably no God, argued Hume. This life is real. Go for it! This sceptical rationalism increasingly coloured Western culture as industrialisation appeared ever to advance towards its intended objective of creation of wealth in monetised form.

How a person thinks is built on what he learns in childhood. Burns came from the poorest classes. We can only understand how his thinking developed if we know how far the discussion in the universities, town or country salons and gentlemen's clubs percolated down to the poorest classrooms. We need to know how deep and wide was the impact of enlightened thinking beyond these for a. I found no ready answer to this query within academic literature. There is no direct evidence of how the lowest classes thought; the best we have are commentaries. These give what others thought the lowest classes thought. Nor is there in the academic literature much evidence of pointers to available data sources to address the query. Indeed, there seemed a paucity of locations or documents which might prove to be sources of data suited to testing the question. Great libraries existed in Scotland during the 18th century, but many were private. When private users use a private library, they seldom keep a list of what books they pick off the shelves, even to study in depth. So such libraries may have been well used, but the extent of their true usage will forever remain a mystery. What I needed was to find a library where readers could not simply sit down and read books 'off the shelf'. It must have the books they could read and those they did read properly listed.

I drew this challenge to the attention of Cairns Mason, Fellow of the Society of Antiquaries of Scotland. He suggested he do something that no-one had tried before: he would try to examine usage, in the light of this question, of one library whose books had all been read off-site and that had actually been open to the general public throughout the second half of the 18th century. This is the Innerpeffray Library near Crieff. If this library did indeed prove to be an Enlightenment library, its usage could answer whether Enlightenment thought was penetrating to the ordinary people of Scotland.

In the days of Burns, books were a luxury to the common man. When they had them, they shared them round, passing them to each other but somehow keeping track of where they were. So difficulties Mason encountered in interpreting book usage from examining Innerpeffray Library serendipitously throw light on how books circulated amongst those in the lowest classes who wished to read them. So, it is worthwhile not only looking at his results but also sharing in some of his research experiences. As this may seem an elliptical flight with real chance of flying off into the void, most comment is in Appendix II.

Innerpeffray Library was set up by David, Lord Maddertie in the late 17th century. He established it as a free study resource for any local person, male or female, who aspired to learn. It was initially stocked from his personal library. Books got added over time. There exists a fragile and very illegible borrowers' register.

Interpreting the register showed Mason when sons borrowed under the surety of their fathers, or servants came to get books for their masters, or a male relative or minister borrowed a book for a widow. He could see when a borrower came back to get his loan extended for a second or even a third period. From about 1780 Mason found a new style of behaviour: he concluded that groups of people might together journey to the library on its open days and borrow a set of books. They became jointly responsible for their return, as if they were sharing a pile of books, circulating them amongst themselves in mutual study. The presence of the signature of each against the total bundle showed that they were all present together. Perhaps this made more of a social event of coming the long distances across the fields to the library, and increased their reading enjoyment by encouraging them to discuss amongst themselves what they read.

Many books taken out were great big tomes. In Dumfries Burns helped to found and then managed the subscription library known as the Monkland Friendly Society, so called because it was located on the old lands of the monks of Lincluden near Ellisland. Thus was established on ancient academic soil a new college of readers, guided by a man of genius. Burns kept a record of what books the library owned, who had what book, listing those out on circulation and noting those brought back. He observed that books taken out did not always get read – or if read, understood – by the readers. He made a facetious remark to one plodding reader that wisdom could pass by osmosis from the book to the brain. It was sufficient to carry the book always with you. A great lumbering man took this to heart. He took out daunting heavy tomes and tied them to his back under his coat. Thus he walked about, day by day, until in due time he brought the book back. He became never the wiser that Burns had been pulling his leg.

Over a summer of working on the defaced borrowers' register in the small main room of Innerpeffray Library, in its quiet collegiate space beside an ancient church, Mason learned to recognise the hand and the meanings of the cryptic scripts of long forgotten readers. He came to imagine them arriving from every direction on a Thursday, sometime between 10am and 2pm when the librarian had opened the doors, to bring back previous borrowings and seek another, to fill the precious evenings in the search for enlightenment by the glimmer of candle, wick, farthing tapers and homely hearth, to expand their understanding of life, the universe, and everything under God's heaven. And indeed, religious texts proved particularly popular to this homely group of quiet forgotten readers in the long cold winters of the later 18th century. Much did they value this gift of the Library. Surprisingly few volumes disappeared from the library shelves – indeed one of the very few wayward volumes turned up one quiet day, in an envelope, through the post, discovered and recognised a century after being mislaid in a forgotten dusty attic after the delinquent borrower's untimely death.

Enlightenment had begun with a dawn that some academics date in the Renaissance era and others in the mid 17th century. In 1648 clergyman John Wilkins published 'Mathematical Magic'. He was a member of the Invisible College, which became the Royal Society at the Restoration. Economist William Petty is credited with forming the Royal Society in 1660. It was granted its Royal Charter on 15th July 1662. That year Petty published his 'Treatise of Taxes and Contributions' in which one theme is how division of labour reduces production costs.

Following the end of Cromwell's Commonwealth, with new peace and personal freedom returning with monarchy, expanding freedom of speech avidly employed the increasingly available publication technology. Entrepreneurs installed printing presses to meet a growing demand for news. Despite apparently restrictive Restoration laws, books suppressed during the repressive Commonwealth could now be published. The economist Thomas Mun had begun 'England's Treasure by Foreign Trade' in the 1630s; it was published in 1664. The new freedom of the press caused an explosion of printed material. Agitators increasingly used this access to technology as a means to destabilise the new Restoration Establishment. So in England in May 1662 the Licensing Act was passed, requiring all published works be licensed and registered with the Stationers' Company. This Act prohibited the publication of seditious books. As any book published in England had to be registered, this has bequeathed modern students a body of helpful data on what was published.

The Act was never intended to limit the spread of such knowledge as was in Robert Boyle's 'The Sceptical Chymist'. Published in 1661 this proposed 'corpuscular' or atomic matter, and introduced the modern concept of chemical elements. This book began a train of focussed study that over years made considerable advances in chemistry. Soon, many elements and compounds were isolated. In 1757 Italian astronomer and mathematician Roger Boscovich revived the ancient Greek concept of atoms in his 'Theory of Natural Philosophy Reduced to a Single Law of the Strength Existing in Nature'. In 1787 Antoine-Laurent Lavoisier edited 'Method of Chemical Nomenclature', the first modern chemical textbook.

While the term 'Enlightenment' itself is a Victorian construct, modern academic studies of Enlightenment texts typically group them into subsections using late Victorian labels. These subsections came to be separate disciplines: moral philosophy, natural philosophy, economics, husbandry, politics, law, medicine, and perhaps historiography. This of itself distorts how 18th century thinkers thought about their studies. It is just a modern starting point for looking backwards. It is limiting because the leading thinkers of the era were polymaths, by no means restricting themselves to work within even a few of these labels. Such specialisation is one of the negative modern outcomes of the division of labour that, even in thought, Victorians championed to intensify the fire of their all-consuming industrial revolution.

Despite such limitations of labels, Mason made a list of what he would hope to find within a good Enlightenment library. First of all, he wanted earlier thought-advancing texts, particularly a strong grounding in the works of René Descartes, of Francis Bacon and perhaps Hugo Grotius. On the shelves at Innerpeffray he found enough. The library owns Descartes' 'Opera Philosophica' and 'Opera Omnia Theologicala' and 'The Rights of War and Peace' and 'The Truth of Christian Religion' by Grotius. Mason found two sets of 'Works of Francis Bacon', as well as Bacon's 'Confession of Faith', 'Essays or Counsels, civil and moral', 'History of the Reign of King Henry VII', 'Wisdom of the Ancients' and 'Sylva Sylvarum'. During the Golden Age of the Enlightenment, the era of Robert Burns, borrowers were very seldom taking out any of these volumes. 'The Truth of Christian Religion' was borrowed merely three times, 'Sylva Sylvarum' got borrowed twice, 'History of the Reign of Henry VII' got borrowed once and 'Works of Bacon' got borrowed once. Yet this was a time when borrowers were actively taking out books.

Perhaps readers already considered these books 'old hat', thought Mason. So he looked also for more up-to-date Enlightenment texts, such as Robert Boyle's chemistry. Lord Maddertie's own copy of Boyle's key text, 'The Origine of Formes and Qualities', published in Oxford in 1667, was there, available to be borrowed. But in all the sixty years from 1747 onwards, it never was. Neither Newton's 'Principia Mathematica' nor other writings by Newton on natural philosophy were able to be borrowed as the library did not own copies. It did have a copy of Colin Maclaurin's 1750 exposition of Newton's mathematics: 'An account of Sir Isaac Newton's philosophical discoveries'. This was first borrowed in 1774, and got taken out a mere further 7 times before 1800.

What the library did have were six volumes up to 1732 of 'Philosophical Transactions (Abridged)'. These were selections from the output of the Royal Society. Some people did borrow these between 1747 and 1757, but they all designated themselves 'students of philosophy'. No borrower designated himself this way in the later part of the 18th century register. No-one borrowed these in that later period.

Interestingly, on the shelves is a 1740 edition of Bayle's 'Dictionarie historique and critique', first published half a century earlier. There is no record of Bayle having been borrowed from Innerpeffray Library during the late 18th century. Despite, or perhaps because of its extensive scurrilous 'footnotes' that take up most of every page, this was a very influential book in its era. David Hume came across it when he was studying in Paris. The train of thought it began in him encouraged him to write his 'Treatise on Human Nature'. Bayle's is the book whose name appeared erroneously in the list given in the autobiographical letter of Burns as transcribed in the edition of Burns's works edited by

Currie. Thus readers got the impression that Burns was in sympathy with the scepticism of Hume. This justified labelling Burns an atheist.

Readers at Innerpeffray regularly took out volumes of periodicals, such as the *Critical Review*, the *Monthly Review*. After 1784 the Library got a set of the past issues of the *Scots Magazine*. This got actively borrowed. In those days the *Scots Magazine* was a vibrant mouthpiece of ideas emanating from the salons, clubs and lecture rooms of Edinburgh. Mason assessed from its contents that it was a major channel of written communication in Scotland in the later 18th century. Ordinary people thus read journalistic reports of Enlightened ideas but only long after they had been current conversation.

Robert Burns was a dedicated student of folk memories, old songs and country tales, particularly of the invisible world. Burns could well have been defiantly alone in treating the recording of such matters with seriousness, but others might also have been studying these areas. Perhaps ordinary people were denied access to books that would support such study, despite the growing number of antiquarians amongst the gentry from the last quartile of the 18th century onwards. Mason wondered whether the library's hereditary patron at the time of Burns, Robert Hay Drummond Archbishop of York, had given the librarian instructions to discourage reading of such work. In other words, perhaps there was some form of censorship pushing readers in certain directions of study. Mason looked for books that today would be classified as esoterica or arcana - in other words, books focussing on ancient customs, witchcraft, the supernatural and even homeopathy. If in the library there were such books, Mason could expect these to be accessed unless they were prohibited reading.

Mason found in the library only three books, all 17th century texts, that might be classed as esoterica. These were 'A Treatise of Specters', 'The Discovery of Witchcraft' and 'Physiognomie & Chiromancie'. All indicate that the founder of the library was opposed to witch hunters, rather than being interested in matters magical, extra-sensory or supernatural. None was taken out to be read.

On mythology, the library had three works by Jacob Bryant. There was a two volume work bound as one book. It had been published in 1768. Its success had enabled Bryant to expand to three volumes between 1774 and 1776. This three volume set was also on the shelves. These books aimed to codify ancient mythology, making an attempt to separate true tradition from mere fable, from the time of the Biblical flood. Finding a Deluge in all the mythologies he studied, Bryant postulated that these mythologies, if correlated, could corroborate Biblical stories as being founded in historical fact. He dismissed Greek myths as mere tales. The library also had Blackwell's 'Letters on Mythology', published in London in 1748. As the books bore indications that meant they had been introduced to the library by the main patron, Mason saw no reason to believe that borrowers would be prevented from reading them, had they wished. None did.

Mason reasoned that if study of the esoteric were acceptable in mainstream circles he would find relevant articles in the *Scots Magazine*. The January edition for 1777 opened with an obituary notice for David Hume, written by himself, followed by a letter in appreciation of his life written from Kirkcaldy by Adam Smith. The book reviews for that month included Beattie's 'Essays'. In June 1777 the magazine published a beautiful, detailed description of the process in which the Grand Master Mason for Scotland laid the foundation stone for the new High School of Edinburgh. Burns would have come across this magazine rarely in youth. After he moved to Lochlie he would have seen copies more frequently. There his increasing circle of Masonic friends would have included subscribers.

In the whole of 1777 the *Scots Magazine* carried only one article that Mason could consider to be on an esoteric theme: in March there was a note on a young woman who suffered from fits. She was encouraged to wear around her waist the skin of a slow worm, wrapped in a linen girdle. She wore this for nine months and was clear of fits. Then one day she discovered that there were five or six live worms within the linen girdle. The discovery induced three fits, but thereafter she was free from fits for more than a year.

It is hardly surprising that she had those three fits.

Throughout that year the magazine was very fully each month reporting on the rebellion in the American colonies. It seems that reports from the commanders in the field were made far more available to the public than we would expect in a modern war. The magazine also contained extensive political reports both for Britain and for many other European States. But there was little discussion on esoteric or even antiquarian subjects. Herein was general access to current affairs and reports on emerging practical technology.

By the time that Robert Burns was born, scientists had for a full century focused on increasingly precise scientific measurement. This approach was a commonplace amongst those men of science who came to be called natural philosophers. It was as far back as 1675 that the Danish astronomer Ole Römer calculated the speed of light from the delay in the expected eclipses of Jupiter's satellites when the planet is furthest from Earth. He estimated that the Sun's rays reach Earth in eleven minutes. These men sought to combine the new accuracy in scientific thinking with traditional religious belief. Western man was spreading into every corner of the Earth, and the advance of what was known as civilisation was making its mark abroad and at home. In 1681 the dodo, the giant pigeon of Mauritius, became extinct. In 1683 the last wild boars in Britain were hunted to extinction. In 1682 French philosopher Pierre Bayle published 'Thoughts on the Comet of 1680' arguing against superstitious beliefs in comets as ill omens. In 1691 naturalist John Ray published 'The Wisdom of God Manifested in the Works of Creation', an exposition of natural theology. In 1698 Halley took command of the naval sloop *Paramour Park* on a voyage to chart magnetic variations at sea, in order to aid navigation. His results were published in 1700. The industrial revolution had already begun: in 1698, Thomas Savery patented a pumping machine powered by steam, and Thomas Newcomen and John Calley built a prototype of their atmospheric engine.

In 1677 Dutch philosopher Baruch Spinoza's book 'Ethics Demonstrated According to the Geometrical Order' had been posthumously published. It argued that mathematical formulae could describe how people behave. It attempted to construct a comprehensive world view in which there was one substance, God, with infinite attributes that ultimately could be delineated by measurement. The rabbis of his Jewish religion had already in 1656 excommunicated Spinoza for perceived heresy in his 'The Philosophical Principles of Descartes'. Thus he anonymously published his 'Treatise on Religious and Political Philosophy'. This contained the first modern historical interpretation of the Bible.

I have earlier quoted the letter Burns wrote in 1787 to his school friend Candlish, then a student at Glasgow, demonstrating that, unusually for contemporaries let alone those of his lowly status, he knew of Spinoza's theories. Burns instinctively recognised that Spinoza was one of those who dangerously abused mathematical symbolism. Burns thought those teachings damaging. No Innerpeffray reader had access to Spinoza's writings.

Spinoza's 'Ethics' was found to propose that free will is an illusion – endorsing predestination in Calvinist extremists. Those rabid types drew forth Burns's ridicule in such poems as 'Holy Willie's Prayer' and 'Address to the Unco Guid'. He railed against bad or unfounded logic used to substantiate religious dogma. In his letter of September 1792 to Alexander Cunningham in Edinburgh, he wrote that he was:

"Circled in the embrace of my elbow-chair, my breast labors like the bloated Sybil on her three-footed stool, & like her too, labors with Nonsense. – Nonsense, auspicious name!!! Tutor, Friend, & Finger-post in the mystic mazes of Law; the cadaverous paths of Physic; & particularly in the sightless roarings of School Divinity, who, leaving Common Sense confounded at his strength of pinion, Reason delirious with eyeing his giddy flight & Truth creeping back into the bottom of her well, cursing the hour that ever she offered her scorned alliance to the wizard Power of Theologic Vision – raves abroad on all the winds, 'On Earth, Discord! A gloomy Heaven above, opening her jealous gazes to the nineteen thousandth part of the tithe of mankind! And below, an inescapable & inexorable Hell, expanding its leviathan jaws for the vast residue of Mortals!!!' – O doctrine comfortable & healing to the weary, wounded soul of man! – Ye sons & daughters of affliction, ye pauvres Miserables, to whom day brings no pleasure, & night yields no rest, be comforted! – 'Tis but one, to nineteen hundred thousand, that your situation will mend in this world; so, alas, the experience of the Poor and the Needy truly affirms; & tis nineteen hundred thousand to one, by the dogmas of Theology, that you will be damned eternally in the World to come!'

But of all the Nonsense, Religious Nonsense is the most nonsensical."

There is very little on the shelves of Innerpeffray Library that Mason, whose honours degree is in Mathematics and Natural Philosophy, would describe as Natural Philosophy. The mathematician Colin Maclaurin is represented only in his text on Newton's developments. Geologist James Hutton and chemist Joseph Black were not on the shelves. Mason found on the shelves three books from the early 1770s by James Ferguson. These were 'Astronomy explained upon Sir Isaac Newton's Principles', 'Select Mechanical Exercises' and 'Lectures on select subjects in mechanics, hydrostatics etc.' Between 1779 and 1800, 'Astronomy' got borrowed 11 times, and each of the two mechanics books got borrowed seven times.

Mason hoped to find Joseph Priestley's work on oxygen, and didn't. He did not find Priestley's 'Disquisition Relating to Matter and Spirit' of 1777. This was written to show that despite being a scientist he believed in Revelation as a fundamental in religion. In 1783 Joseph Priestley published 'A History of the Corruptions of Christianity', also not in Innerpeffray. Instead, Priestley was represented only by his book criticising Thomas Reid's 'An Enquiry into the human mind on the principles of common sense'. There was the 1733 'Introduction to Natural Philosophy' by Keill, which offered access to the work of Huygens. There was also an English translation of Gravesande's 1726 work. But none of these was borrowed. This surprised Mason, because one local potential reader was Thomas Thomson. Thomson in the early 19th century became Regius Professor of Chemistry at Glasgow University. When he borrowed from Innerpeffray Library in the late 1780s it appears to have been for light relief.

Mason hoped to find moral philosophy well represented in the library, because this is often viewed as a staple contribution of Scottish thinkers of the era. The library held the 1767 text 'An inquiry into the principles of political economy being an essay on the science of domestic policy in free nations' by Adam Smith's opponent Sir James Steuart of Coltness. Alexander Gerard's 'Essay on Genius' and James Beattie's 'Essays on truth, on poetry, on music, etc.' were on the shelves. So was Adam Ferguson's 'An essay on the history of civil society'. That book is now considered to have founded the study of sociology. There were books by the legal leaders Lord Kames and Lord Monboddo. Kames was represented by his 'Principles of Equity' and 'Sketches of Man'. Monboddo's 'Of the origin and progress of language' was on the shelves. Available though all these were, they were hardly borrowed, with the exception of a little interest in Kames's 'Sketches' and Beattie's 'Essays'. Voltaire was represented by his essay on 'Toleration'. It was taken out twice.

There was not on the shelves the seminal work of Francis Hutcheson, his 1724 'Inquiry into the Originals of our Ideas of Beauty and Virtue'. Mason looked for Locke's 'Works', Hume's 'Treatise on Human Nature' and 'Essays Moral and Political', and Smith's 'Theory of Moral Sentiments' and 'Inquiry into the Wealth of Nations'. A multi-volume set of Locke's 'Works' was available. Mason found 21 instances of one volume of this being borrowed. The data never specified which volume was borrowed. Each time it was by one of a number of readers describing himself as 'student of philosophy' or 'student of divinity'. No general reader borrowed Locke. Mason concluded from the evidence he encountered that Hume's 'Treatise on Human Nature' and 'Essays' were probably not on the shelves before the 1790s. He found no evidence that any of Smith's works had been available in the library.

Mason hoped to find 'Leviathan' by Thomas Hobbes, 'Two Treatises on Government' by John Locke, 'Du contrat social' that Jean-Jacques Rousseau published in 1762, and Thomas Paine's 'Common Sense' of 1776 and 'Rights of Man' of 1791. None of these was on the shelves. Mason mused that perhaps the library trustees thought these texts too explosive in a part of Scotland that had been sorely divided a generation earlier by Jacobite uprising.

The absences caused Mason to question the value of Innerpeffray Library in promoting Enlightenment thought, whatever its importance in disseminating knowledge and understanding locally.

Law, Scottish and English, was well represented. Medicine was represented only by second-rank texts, but these were borrowed by the Crieff surgeon. Mason concluded that the uptake of the history books on the shelves was more in the nature of the search for a good story for long evenings, rather than for the studious application of true Enlightenment readers. Edward Gibbon's 'Decline and Fall of the Roman Empire' was popular. So were Robertson's 'History of Emperor Charles V' and his 'History of America'.

Mason found enough typical Enlightenment texts to consider Innerpeffray to have been not a leading but a modest Enlightenment library. There were some important omissions, normally considered to be core Enlightenment texts. With this proviso, on the basis of books on shelves, assuming they were there during the 18th century and not added before the existing catalogue was drawn up in 1813, the library could be viewed as having been a potential centre for ordinary people to study at least some up-to-the-minute Enlightenment thought. But that is not how these ordinary people used this local library. They were more down-to-earth if not to say parochial. The library got a copy of the 1776 edition of Pennant's 'Tour of Scotland' apparently in the mid 1780s – and the locals avidly took it out to read. They also borrowed books on husbandry when they came available. 'Farmer's Letters' published in 1768 and 'Six Week Tour' published in 1769 soon got borrowed. Arthur Young's 'A Dictionary of Husbandry' of 1769 and 'Experimental Husbandry' of 1770 got borrowed early on. His 'Political Arithmetic' of 1774 was quickly taken out. Anderson's 'Agriculture' of 1777 and 'Present State of Husbandry in Scotland' of 1778 both found a ready audience.

His data collection confirmed what the rules stated – that there were no restrictions on what could be taken out, even if the books had already become rare and valuable. Hector Boece's 'History of Scotland' was permitted to be taken off to be read at home, as was 'Holinshed's Chronicle'. Of course, smaller books, easy to slip into a pocket, were popular, but the massive 'History of the Emperor Charles V' by Robertson was no less popular than tiny 'Natural History' by Buffon. But in analysis of the borrowers' register up to 1800 Mason found minimal interest from the users of the library in the new-fangled thinking of such leading-edge books as it had. It was not until the start of the 19th century that readers began to borrow these texts in any number – and this coincided with a general considerable upsurge in use of the library.

Mason concluded that Enlightenment thinking was very slow to penetrate beneath the crust of academia. His evidence showed this to be so amongst people around Crieff, whom he also proved can reasonably be considered as having been fairly typical of the Scots of their day. Out of all the many borrowers, nine students borrowed 67 Enlightenment texts, two ministers borrowed eight Enlightenment texts, and forty others each hardly read more than one such text. Of the students, it was three only who dominated usage of these texts.

In contrast with those of his class who lived around Crieff and had the benefit of this tremendous library, Robert Burns was, even in comparison with many a man who had been through college, a well-educated man. He kept himself up to date in the latest Enlightenment discussion. Few had read as intensely as he had. Though he might have read fewer books, he read them cover to cover and repeatedly, absorbing what he gleaned from them, and relating it to his experience and understanding of the underlying principles.

Nor is the list Burns gave in his autobiographical letter anything like complete. I have already shown that in 1783 he studied Adam Smith's 'Theory of Moral Sentiments', and was so impressed that he began to transcribe passages of it into verse. It is albeit rather heavy classical verse, but then he was still learning verse-craft. His letters repeatedly refer to his latest reading or to books he recommends to others. All his life he read widely and deeply as his verses and correspondence show.

Out of this reading he formed ideas – and those ideas were his own. Burns had been trained in childhood to think deeply about important issues. He kept aware of the happenings of the world and not just of his own immediate surroundings. In youth he learned the science of debate. On Burns's arrival in Edinburgh in 1786 the greatest minds of his day were astounded with the extent of his knowledge on a great range of matter. They were impressed with the quality of his understanding and his argument. From then until his death he remained an active contributor to discussion on matters that were even then forming the modern industrialised world and its political format. He may not have said or written much on any of them, but his input was right to the heart of the matter.

It is unlikely that Burns would have taken the side of Karl Marx; Burns would have been more understanding of human frailty and so accommodate it more. He would have realised that while the idealist might demand from each according to his ability, the common man can face so many barriers to realising anything close to what another can objectively think him capable of. Morale so readily falters. Nor would Burns so blatantly redistribute material wealth according purely to apparent need: he believed in meritocracy and fair payment for individual effort and contribution. Burns, I suspect, would have described himself politically using a word that since the start of the 21st century is deemed offensive in the bending-over-backwards-for-political-correctness modern days: he would probably have found the word 'Christian' useful: in the Biblical sense of a follower of that person who announced that the key commandment was "Love one another as I have loved you".

Such benign belief was a far cry from the rabid hell-fire sermonising that Burns met in Sunday service in Mauchline. The laws of the Roman Church, like its rituals, were set aside almost in their entirety by the Geneva Calvinist reformers. The exceptions were those against invoking the power of the Devil. Those were emphasised. Previously, legal punishment was in the main prayer and penance. The exception was when the crime extended to civil treason. In Reformed churches, punishment for invoking magic was death.

The horrors of extreme Reformation came to Scotland with John Knox who forced the abdication of Mary, Queen of Scots. She had been lectured by Knox on the evil of regiment of women. At last she was driven from her throne to be replaced by an infant son, James VI. He was brought up fearing the darkness around him. Thus, he developed a phobia of the supernatural. By adulthood he was convinced that he was surrounded by witches trying to overthrow him. He published his 'Daemonology' in 1597. His laws against supernatural evil encouraged similar fear amongst his subjects. When he succeeded to the throne of England in 1603, all the British kingdoms and domains came under the sway of the hysterical murderous witch hunt.

In England in 1603, laws against witchcraft with capital punishment had long been part of the armoury of government repression. They were created to assist Henry VIII against his opponents. Such crimes were readily 'proved' by purchased perjury or through torture. A physical deformity was sufficient to justify the judicial murder of Anne Boleyn. Elizabeth augmented those laws when she was joined in the late 16th century by many who had spent the reign of her sister Queen Mary in Geneva, and there learned the power of the witch hunt to eliminate opposition to their reforms.

As in a garden, for every year that weeds are allowed to seed there come seven years of pain to clean them out, so the spreading of fear and hatred, once set loose upon a land, takes generations to eradicate.

Enlightenment was marked in Britain by the Act of George II of 1736 that removed the extreme penalties for witchcraft, while maintaining penalties for fraudulent use of forms pretending to be "Witchcraft, Sorcery, Inchantment, or Conjuration" or for "undertaking to tell Fortunes, or pretend [to] his or her Skill or Knowledge in any occult or crafty Science". In other words, the law did not deny such skills existed – it made it an offence to claim to be an adept without having the necessary training.

Science advanced. In 1733 Swedish astronomer Anders Celsius published a scientific description of the aurora borealis. In 1739 simultaneous measurement in Lapland and in France indicated the Earth is flattened at the poles. In 1740, Scottish natural philosopher Colin Maclaurin published his acclaimed gravitational theory to explain tides. Two years later he published 'Treatise on Fluxions' which expressed Newton's calculus along the lines of Greek geometry. In 1743 French astronomer J N Delisle proposed an improved methodology for measuring transits of planets across the face of the Sun. His method was used to achieve improved accuracy in observing the transits of Venus in 1761 and 1769. In 1746 the mathematical theory of complex numbers was developed by Frenchman Jean d'Alembert – an essential tool in modern space science. That year Benjamin Franklin began to concentrate on research into electricity. He developed an improved Leyden Jar, known as the Franklin pane. This was a piece of glass coated on each side with conducting foil. In 1748 Leonard Euler published 'Analysis Infinitorum', his exposition of analytical mathematics. He also put forward a formula linking the circle to complex numbers by relating π to the square root of -1, the primal imaginary number. British Astronomer Royal James Bradley completed a 19-year study of the effect of the Moon's orbit on the Earth. He causally linked the Moon to a wobble in Earth's orbit, called nutation.

This period saw considerable advances in the mapping of stars and nebulae and in astronomical tables. From about this time, Jean d'Alembert, Euler, Lagrange and Laplace worked together on the highly intractable 'three body problem' of the gravitational interaction of celestial bodies. Getting acceptable answers to this problem is essential for getting satellites into stable orbits around the Earth, quite apart from getting astronauts back from their space stations. In the modern world it usually gets tackled using great number-crunching computer models. The ether itself was no longer able to be considered real. It was replaced with mere emptiness and void – an approach now being re-evaluated within research physics.

Some things clearly went wrong. In 1753 in St Petersburg, Russia, German scientist George Wilhelm Richmann attempted to replicate Benjamin Franklin's experiment of bringing electricity out of a storm. He was killed by the lightning strike he brought down.

That year Swedish botanist Carolus Linnaeus published 'Species Plantarum', using his system to classify thousands of plants. In 1754, Jean d'Alembert explained using calculus how the precession of the equinoxes arises, along with explanations of perturbations of the Earth's orbit. Another Frenchman, Pierre Louis de Maupertuis, outlined a theory of evolution in his 'Essai sur la Formation des Corps Organises'.

Natural philosophy had been championed by Isaac Newton when in 1703 he took his place as President of the Royal Society – but it was changing. In this climate of advancing science in 1713 William Derham published his 'Physico-Theology'. He soon followed this with 'Astro-Theology'. Both were early text-books for Burns. In 1721, the year the Brandenburg Concertos were completed, Scotsman Alexander Malcolm published 'A Treatise of Musik, Speculative, Practical and Historical'. In 1730 Mathew Tindal published 'Christianity as Old as the Creation'. This defended the emerging Deist belief that God can be understood directly from Nature, without intervention of Bibles, Revelation or priests. In 1746 Princeton University was founded as the College of New Jersey, but its role was to train clergymen, although they studied natural philosophy. The emergence of many books in defence of God shows that God was under attack. In 1750 Thomas Wright described the modern perception of the Sun's place in the galaxy but in a universe divinely designed and controlled. In 1751 Henry Home, Lord Kames, published 'Essays on the Principles of Morality and Natural Religion'.

In retrospect scientific enquiry may appear to have advanced in the 18th century steadily to well-earned modern objective confidence.

Burns might have thought modern science guilty of hubris.

Burns watched as he listened and contributed to the discussions of the university at Edinburgh. He became more fully aware that already, battle had been formally joined between two increasingly entrenched parties. There were those who wanted to free all thought from religion. They claimed that their modern science disproved the existence of God. They wanted to cast God out of the intellect of Man. Ranked against them were those who, like mathematician and philosopher, Gottfried Wilhelm von Leibniz, argued like Newton that there is no contradiction between a loving God and the existence of both good and evil. In 1710 Leibniz published 'Theodicy'. Voltaire ridiculed his argument in 'Candide' in 1759.

Burns was right out of tune with atheist thinking when, towards the end of his life, in 1794, he wrote to Alexander Cunningham of Edinburgh of how he hoped that any child of his would in

> "the blooming youth of life [look] abroad on all Nature, and thro' Nature up to Nature's God; his soul, by swift delighting degrees, is rapt above this sublunary sphere, until he can be silent no longer, and bursts out into glorious enthusiasm".

Alongside his intellectual involvement in the Age of Reason, Burns did not allow himself to get out of touch with inner feelings and life around him. Indeed, his childhood text-books enabled him to understand the context of such little chapbooks that circulated in his lifetime to help the farmer plan the year ahead. But though the academic man might understand the need for a farmer to know the dates of quarters of the moon, the average peasant would not take a purely detached view of the movements of the heavens that so greatly influenced lives and daily happiness. The era of the omen continued even as science increased the accuracy of astronomical observation and could teach that the planets held their courses strictly regular because they were subject to mechanical laws.

Despite their teaching, despite all the advancement of science and the Enlightened thinking of the intellectuals, what general readers really wanted was to read almanacs – and they read these in great numbers. Those told them what the weather would be like. And increasingly, as the Enlightenment wore on, they speculated on the future. Like the science books with all their god-killing theories, almanacs increasingly promised to take the uncertainty out of life.

The Aberdeen Almanack had been, according to Chambers Encyclopaedia of 1860, published since the beginning of the 16th century. By the Glorious Revolution it had in Scotland a circulation of about 50,000 each year, by which time there was another being published in Edinburgh.

The British Library holds a copy of the 16 page pamphlet entitled 'Aberdeen Almanack or New Prognostication for the Year of Our Lord 1759, being the third year after Bislectile or Leap-year, and from the creation according to Holy Writ, 5762, but according to the best of prophane history, 5718'. This harmless pamphlet was aimed at farmers and seamen. It provided key astronomical events for each month of the year, and a prediction of likely weather, supposedly based on past experience of astronomical configuration. Its weather forecast was mainly a very broad description of typical Scottish weather on a month by month basis. It also listed for each month the main fairs that took place then. It was declared to be by Merry Andrew, Professor of Prediction by Stargazing at Tamtallan – which the reader could, if he wished, treat with humour. The book gave a list of key dates for Scotland's history, real and mythological, and a perennial tide ready reckoner table, with a fair splattering of typographical errors. The publication became greatly enlarged towards the end of the century, but its core market continued to be farmers and seamen because of the relevance of its core data.

For 1759, it stated that there would be frost and snow until January 5th, then wind and rain until the 15th, with variable weather until the end of the month, followed by wind and rain in early February. The new moon would be on 28th January, and the full moon on 13th January would set eclipsed. It listed the quarter days, identifying the beginning of the second quarter as 19th March, being in that year the true equinox. This reflected the general knowledge in those days that the equinox did not occur on a fixed date. This is a consequence of that wobbly movement of the Earth as it goes round the Sun. It identified the fourth quarter, Martinmas, as beginning on All Hallow's Day, or All Saints Day, but dating this as 12th November. Our modern date for Hallowe'en, the night before All Hallow's Day, is 31st October – not reflecting changes in the definition of the calendar, but realignment.

In Scotland in the 18th century, Hallowe'en parties appeared timed to the redundant Julian calendar. But it was defined as 31st October. A great party, though, was held on the eve of Martinmas at the end of the feeing year. This happened to coincide with the old calendar date of Hallowe'en. The two celebrations got merged. (By the way, that was more profitable; it saved time and money.) In the early 20th century this former annual great party had become a children's festival. It was removed from what was now Remembrance Day. This was the anniversary of the Great War Armistice. Fighting was timed to end on the eve of Martinmas, the end of the third legal quarter of 1918.

In the 18th century, the big party for Hallowe'en took place at the end of the Scottish feeing year. This was after the end of the harvest. Just like modern office parties, since earliest times this had been a day of great jollification. Rolled in with Hallowe'en, many an ancient ritual of prognostication got associated with the party at the end of feeing. There was a night of stories of ghosts and fairies and doings of the supernatural world. Burns described one such party in his poem 'Hallowe'en'.

With the launch of 'Edinburgh's True Almanack, or a New Prognostication' from 1683 onwards, there was competition in the Scottish almanac market. This really began to heat up only a century later, with the number of pages increasing significantly. By the end of the 18th century, these almanacs were substantial books. In this, Scotland came into line with England, France, Hungary, and the main centres in Europe. These were a reality of popular culture that outlasted the era of rational enquiry that we call the Enlightenment.

Almanacs took off with the invention of movable type and multiplied with the Reformation. Then publishers broke away from what they saw as the interfering supervision of bishops, who had insisted that content of almanacs be approved before their publication. Predictive almanacs then began to flourish. Of these, the Almanach Liégeois got the widest circulation. Its predictions were treated seriously in the later 18th century. In 1774 it predicted, for example, that in April a royal favourite would play her last part. In France, the king's mistress Madame Dubarry fussed through the whole of April, wishing the month at an end. No sooner was it over than Louis XV died. Thus Dubarry's role at court ended, adding weight to the prophetic reputation of this almanac.

In Britain, the almost equally spurious publication, 'Poor Robin's Almanack', produced by the 'prophet' Partridge for the Stationers' Company of London, was sanctioned by the Archbishop of Canterbury. Daniel Defoe said later of 1665 that superstitious beliefs promoted by 'Poor Robin' were widespread in that plague year:

the people, from what principle I cannot imagine, were more addicted to prophecies and astrological conjurations, dreams, and old wives tales than ever they were before or since. Whether this unhappy temper was originally raised by the follies of some people who got money by it – that is to say, by printing predictions and prognostications – I know not; but certain it is, books frighted them terribly, such as Lilly's Almanack, Gadbury's Astrological Predictions, Poor Robin's Almanack, and the like; also several pretended religious books, one entitled, Come out of her, my People, lest you be Partaker of her Plagues; another called, Fair Warning; another, Britain's Remembrancer; and many such, all, or most part of which, foretold, directly or covertly, the ruin of the city.

The Stationers' Company gave licenses for printing 'Poor Robin' outside England. It was first printed in Belfast in 1753. In England this almanac had a monopoly which was overturned in 1775, but in 1779 Prime Minister Frederick Guilford, Lord North, moved that this monopoly be reinstated. This was vigorously opposed by Henry Erskine on the grounds of the pernicious influence of the publication, and the widespread superstition which such publications promoted. Their monopoly denied, the Stationers' Company continued to dominate the market by dint of buying up all their competitors. Jonathan Pearson, mathematician and schoolmaster of Nottingham, edited 'Poor Robin' for many years until his death in 1791. The monopoly was finally de facto abolished only in 1828, a year before Catholic Emancipation. 'Poor Robin' continued to be published for another decade.

In Rhode Island, America, James Franklin published 'Rhode Island Almanack', perhaps plagiarising 'Poor Robin'. His brother Benjamin Franklin did one better: he produced 'Poor Richard's Almanack' from 1733 to 1758, making a real success out of a combination of reliable astronomical data and good humour. He reached a circulation of 10,000 a year. Burns rejected the fortune telling of such books, not just because they misled, but because he was aware they caricatured and belittled some deep instinctive understanding in the human psyche. Superstition he detested, but respected true value within old knowledge. Almanacs denigrated that value. Chambers attested that by 1860 predictive almanacs were still extremely popular. Today, of course, their counterparts are the widespread daily horoscope, yearly books of day-to-day predictions by star sign, and drawn-down messages on personal computer Internet home pages.

Even at the end of the 18th century, the Almanach Liégeois was, according to Chambers, particularly useful to those who had difficulty reading. It used symbols against dates to identify such matters as the most appropriate phase of the moon for taking draughts of medicine, the best days for taking pills, and good days for letting blood.

Had Burns's Dr Hornbook had a copy, perhaps the poet would not have had that entertaining conversation with Death, who was frustrated that this local quack doctor was putting him out of business by carrying so many to an early grave. We now know from the chance discovery of the notebook of an Irvine doctor that when the poet was ill during his time there, the treatment he got probably damaged a heart already weakened by childhood malnutrition and excessive exertion in damp, cold, smoky living conditions.

For many villages in Europe, medicine such as Dr Hornbook's was the best they still had. The Reformation had destroyed the pharmacies of the religious houses and eliminated these local medical centres. When the inmates had been dispersed, they had been deprived of their herb gardens, their laboratories and their medical research records. They had to rely on what they had in their heads. Thus old wise women, witches, became through dire community need the only health service. So de facto they represented the banished Roman Catholicism. They were evil, hunted down and burned or drowned to obviate their influence.

Pelican in 1965 republished Pennethorne Hughes's scientifically well-balanced 1952 book, 'Witchcraft'. He stated that, while the existence of those who actively invoked the forces of evil against those whom they hated was actively opposed by the Roman Church from its earliest days, it was only in the wake of the Reformation that intensive witch hunts began – and then only in regions of Protestant influence.

From study of history and philosophy it becomes clear that canon law is centred on moral and emotional law and secular law is centred on material law. The Reformation, by removing canon law, removed controls of and sanctions on ethical and emotional behaviour. Replacing these sanctions is only now being addressed, and crudely, in the development of regulations on Human Rights. Removal of moral sanction against ill behaviour towards others in due course gave rise to the scepticism of such as David Hume. It ultimately generated the 20th century nihilism that created the environment not just for the Jewish Holocaust in World War II. On the simple suspect reasoning that they cannot be imagined within constraints of modern intellectual paradigms, it equally is used to justify that modern claim that there are no fundamental laws of universal life that dictate pause for consideration of consequences in economic or scientific endeavours and developments. I echo Burns in saying,

> An atheist's laugh is small exchange
> for Deity offended.

The Roman Church had opposed abuse of astronomical data for another reason: belief in accuracy of predictions about a person's life was contrary to its doctrine of free will. The Roman Church had long had, through its mathematicians, a keen grasp of the inadequacies of mathematical modelling for accurate calculation of astronomical data, even if it could be presumed that the mechanical 'laws of physics' were as precise as scientists might claim. With arrogance that they claimed was justified by their newly acquired scientifically measured 'knowledge', Calvinist reformers claimed in analogy to astronomical 'reality' that for each person the full course of his journey through life is by immutable law unchangeable and fate after death predestined.

Burns made it clear that he could find no way to square the circle that separated the sceptical scientists from his instinctive belief in an Almighty. He spelled out his opposition to the sceptics in his letters. He warned against them in his verse. He wrote directly and in analogy. He learned this from his study of the Bible, a book with which he was intimate.

As Jesus had used parables, the Roman church knew the strength of analogy; through long experience of dealing with heresy it had become very aware of the danger of analogy taken too far. From the emergence of its earliest centres of study, such as that in Jarrow on the Tyne where the Venerable Bede had proved himself such an able Chief Scientist, that church had promoted those studies of mathematics. This clarified the fact that, despite visible intuitive geometric realities of square and circle, there is no rational arithmetical relationship between square and circle. The numbers we use for counting and calculation are all based on integers. There is absolutely no ratio of integers that gives the relationship between the length of the circumference of a circle and the radius of that circle. This means that it is impossible using numerical arithmetic to calculate with absolute accuracy the movements in space of heavenly bodies. There is always fuzziness in every prediction of their future positions, even were there no wobbles in their elliptical movements. Using this as an analogy for human moral decisions, though choices may be restricted, there is always room for choice; mankind enjoys free will. Burns did not argue in so many words; he argued from the feelings of his soul. He treated Truth by its conformity to Common Sense.

Burns believed that only when intuition and reason are both permitted their place can there be understanding. But extreme promoters of the so-called Enlightenment challenged this. Of course, many had previously held 'truths' to be self evident, despite assumptions behind their beliefs not standing up to real hard common sense thinking. They gave common sense a bad press. This abandonment by advocates of pure Reason of former 'common sense' assumptions about religion, politics and society, was initially challenged by French philosophers. That opposition was eliminated by France's own bloody revolution. Responsibility to humanity thus gave place to the clamour for individual Rights.

It was not until the start of the 20th century that science began again to recognise fuzziness, through creating what it calls the Uncertainty Principle. This has hardly yet influenced modern philosophy. The humanities of our time remain too tied to the deterministic understanding of science that had become the norm in universities by the start of the 19th century. The new economic dogma of division of human labour was accepted by those who followed the Enlightenment. In our modern world, we see the most extreme applications of that dogma in industry and commerce. This results in terrible wastage of human beings, discarded when their over-specialised training is made irrelevant through technological development or market changes. People are thrown on the scrap heap, worthless, and face alone the horrors of the hell of believing that life has no meaning.

The dogma infected academia just as badly. By the end of the 19th century, academia had already split into what C P Snow called 'the two cultures'. Those who studied humanities no longer understood science; those who studied science could no longer explain to philosophers the relevance of their new understanding of the fuzziness of reality.

Burns educated himself to span the sciences and the humanities. He was a true polymath. He could talk as a peer with any professor. He was a natural philosopher in the old-fashioned sense of one who studied nature to understand the meaning of life. But division of academic labour has ensured that he is now considered merely a poet. His knowledge and understanding of the natural world is by too many considered merely to reach to an exceptional mental catalogue of the common names in botany and zoology, and rural lore of the ways of nature. He was much deeper than this, and broader. This is a whole massive part of his brain that has seldom been tapped when considering his legacy.

Chapter IX   *Wha sae Base as be a Slave*

How Burns, born enslaved, could never escape slavery but in the American War of Independence learned to use his mind to establish his true freedom and so fight for human rights.

On 19th February 2008, I was lying on a hospital bed having been diagnosed with an invisible illness. In heightened awareness of intimations of mortality I re-read the autobiographical letter of Robert Burns. I suddenly had the disturbing thought that the apparently couthie 'The Cottar's Saturday Night', far from describing benign days of the poet's own childhood, was perhaps instead the articulation of a dream – a dream of what might have been, not what was. The first verse muses on "what Aiken in a cottage might have been". Perhaps, imagining an admired man, Burns mused how such a personality would have behaved in the poet's childhood home. Thus this poem may tell what the poet would have liked to have experienced in his childhood. Instead, the reality was that he had been a slave, his father his slave-master. He wore the heavy chains of his religion, clamped to him in the form of filial piety and the moral suasion of his father's paternal right, insufficiently tempered with responsibility to his growing child. These forced Burns as a child to accept familial responsibility that ruined his health as he worked harder than the dog under a man with a quick temper and unforgiving nature.

The harshness of these days of youth initiated in the poet that invisible disability that stalked his life and eventually killed him so young. His one dream in youth was to be the head of a contented family – no more – and Fate denied him this. Hence, in his dream of his muse, Coila, she presents him as poet laureate of the Land of Kyle with not a laurel wreath, but with a crown of holly. I had, in the preceding December, gone into my garden to prune for the first time holly bushes that had grown there from seeds scattered by birds over the previous quarter century from a neighbour's rampant hedge. I had let the little slow-growing bushes grow with nature. But now a few of them had reached the age when they were ready to be shaped and controlled. I had intended to combine the cuttings with ivy that I annually trimmed, so that for Christmas I could deck the halls with the holly and the ivy. But in cutting the holly for the first time – a gardening task so few commentators on Burns are ever exposed to doing – I realised that the holly leaf is no benign Christmas decoration. It is a tough leaf, not easily swept aside, and with hard sharp points that are able viciously to tear the hand that touches it. If near the head, these leaves would be treacherous. Their many spikes would each be able to rip out an eye. I realised how careful I needed to be deploying holly in decorations. I significantly cut down on the quantity to use, so as not to create serious risks for those who would enter my home over Christmas. The wreath of holly Coila in his dream pressed on the head of Robert Burns was a crown of thorns, red berried, like drops of blood.

Defiance towards a father caused the boy to wander. Through an inner consciousness, he must surely have identified an enemy. When the family moved to Lochlie, he walked out over the hill to the village of Tarbolton. There he sought alternative company to home tyranny. He passed a tree, naked in winter, young but bent backed and gnarled from the whipping of western winds. There today trees are bent double against constant barrage. This puts in harsher context his remark to Mrs Dunlop that he identified with the naked tree standing against the freezing wild winter storm. When still a teenager he had written:

Thou grim Pow'r, by Life abhorr'd,
While Life a *pleasure* can afford,
   Oh! hear a wretch's pray'r!
No more I shrink appall'd, afraid;
I court, I beg thy friendly aid,
   To close this scene of care!
When shall my soul, in silent peace,
   Resign Life's *joyless day*?
My weary heart its throbbings cease,
   Cold-mould'ring in the clay?
    No fear more, no tear more,
     To stain my lifeless face,
    Enclasped and grasped
     Within thy cold embrace!

He kicked over the traces and stayed alive. He had no doubt seen the normally docile overworked dog thus suddenly turn and snap the hand of a bullying handler. Yet his fear of retribution, seemingly overcome, came back to haunt him in the form of guilt. For had he not, in defying his father, wilfully broken the Mosaic Holy Commandment? Undoubtedly there were words between them. But this was behind closed doors in the privacy of Lochlie. It was normal social practice, then, not to wash dirty linen in public. I distrust the protestations in later life of his brother Gilbert that his father was never angry with Robert. In such confrontation, I wonder what would have been the role of their mother. Indeed I wonder, how much when William Burness died was it a release for her from wife-battering. Perhaps he never hit her physically. His bullying may have taken 'only' the invisible form of mental cruelty. But that can destroy the very soul, leaving the body apparently unscathed.

It is not uncommon that when spouses are emotionally truly close the one does not long outlive the other. It is not so hard a rule, but when one party is released from a bond too devastating, he or she often lives a long, long life thereafter – as Agnes did.

His father died. Perhaps it seemed release. He then was twice prevented in his choice of marriage. Perhaps it was not simply the legal proceedings against him by the parents of Jean Armour that Robert Burns wished to escape. Perhaps he wanted to put behind him a life too constrained. His past was truly hideous. He planned emigration to Jamaica. The worst outcome of work in Jamaica could not be worse than being the galley-slave.

He had the moral strength to turn adversity to laughter when others would have cried. He had survived through his ability to joke. This had enabled him to live through the impositions of childhood work. In due course it helped him overcome their potentially mortally devastating impact. He constantly relied on his humour to carry him through. He put his massive intellect in harness with his humour. Together these gave him determination to love life. He knew how often it is in life that if you don't laugh, you cry.

   My name is FUN – your cronie dear,
    The nearest friend ye hae.

Chapter IX   *Wha sae Base as be a Slave*

So she greeted him on his way to the Holy Fair. With her as invisible companion, he could meet Death in the lane as he walked home from Tarbolton, and have a conversation with him, as a fearless equal. With her egging him on, he could exchange curses with the Devil, and with Fun outdo the Powers of Darkness. Fun wasn't Coila; Coila took Fun's mischief and transformed it into great art in words and music. Humour in the poems of Burns may be enjoyed, but few enjoying the performance of a comedian seldom consider the pathos that generated it, and that its creation may often require.

Virtually all those who had met him, who commented, described his poetry and writings as pale reflection of the man. This suggests to me that he talked with a dry sense of humour that put a coating of sugar round the unpalatable truth of life, whether his own reality or that of the world around him. A modern example might be in the autobiographical novel 'Angela's Ashes' by Frank McCourt. Many people, without personal exposure to the kinds of social horror that it describes, find that book humorous. They cannot relate to the fact that it contains little exaggeration. Rather it glosses grim reality with an airbrush of defiant laughter. It is a technique as old as time itself: to laugh at misery and evil as the best intellectual antidote to their oppression.

Few people talk of their own miseries with humour. Most, indeed, are only too ready to talk of their own miseries. On top of slavery, Burns contended with an extra misery. There is no sympathy – as I learned in my youth – for those with invisible disability. While the modern world may make a cult of visible or labelled disability, the unlabelled disability is seldom given credibility. If one should to a companion mention an inner unseen medical obstacle, one is all too likely to get in response a torrent of history from childhood to the present of the companion's every cut and bruise, with extra colour and detail added for a tooth extraction or a sprained ankle. So, unless the cause of irritation is visible, or the disability emphatically obvious, the real sufferer is best not to mention obstacles or pain, unless as the basis for a joke and a prelude to laughter. Speak reality only to such few true professionals as actually are prepared to listen, are in a position to alleviate the pain or hardship, and are willing to try to do so.

Many are the studies that explore the source of the vigorous radical principles that fired the heart and eyes of Robert Burns, and inspired so many words. These typically attribute his strong principles to his studies of English literature forms. I wonder how many people acquire genuine depth of commitment to principles purely from such study. Why, I ask, should Burns have done so?

I suggest that personal experience of poverty, misery, slavery, oppression and unseen illness gave birth to his revolutionary humanitarian ideals. He knew what was and defiantly dreamed of what could be. The ideals born within, his education gave him the tools and his intellect gave him the ability to express them. The strength of his experience gave him the power to speak out forcefully. He discovered he could talk as an intellectual equal with professors of the universities. He learned that his thought, fed into their processes of debate, enriched their discussions, and flowed into the mainstream of philosophical dissemination.

Talking was the thing: the spreading of ideas, the fertilisation of latent thought. It would spring like wild flowers in the fields and its seed be borne on the wind. He knew from his education that once a great idea is released into the ether it takes immense effort to kill it. Powerful ideas, their ability once fledged to rise on the wind, multiply and indestructibly populate the airy skies, as did the ideas of the great philosophers of ancient times. Of course he also wrote letters in addition to his poems, but instinctive understanding of the reality of how thoughts propagate would have made him unafraid if his mere papers did not survive.

The environment of the quarter century after his death was not fertile for the growth of ideas of true equality. This did not kill his input. If it had, he would not still be a focus of cult entertainment and academic study. Nor would his works be as vital as they now are to emerging republics and developing states. I believe too that his experience is relevant again in today's post-industrial world.

The copy of Salmon's 'Geographical Grammar' that I studied in the National Library of Scotland had bound in beside page 541 a map of Central America and the Islands. This particular map shows signs of having been repeatedly opened and folded before it was finally bound into the volume. When the book was then trimmed the paper lost its original rectangular shape. On the map is indicated the island of Jamaica. This is a little mark on this map like a long thin natural pearl. The island is well south of the Tropic of Cancer. Numbers show dawn comes there five hours after it crosses Greenwich meridian.

There is a little picture in the top right corner of this map. It shows a man at a desk, clearly important in his context. He is writing. A respectful white man is talking to him, while an equally respectful, and clearly more subservient black man shows him a tied cuboid bundle that appears heavy. Behind this stooped black man is a great barrel of cut canes and a few other bundles, each inscribed with numbers. I wondered how Robert Burns felt when he looked at that picture. Perhaps he imagined what the role would really be like being in Jamaica overseer of labourers, but indentured servant. Did he imagine himself as that important man writing at the desk, legs spread out in confidence? Or, having sold himself to pay for passage, would he be a head-bowed white of status little better and perhaps worse than that of the strong-armed black man?

In early 1786 Robert Burns could not afford the cost of the sea journey to Jamaica. Thus he opted to accept a status legally no different from that of slave for the period of years needed to work the passage. He had no illusions about what giving up freedom meant. Across the county boundary in Dumfries was the mining town, Sanquhar. There, while workers might enjoy good earnings, they were bound to their jobs. They were at the mercy of their master, with the legal status of mere serf. They were bought and sold with the land. Burns elected to accept that status in Jamaica in order to escape the grinding poverty of Ayrshire and the persecution by those who despised him, who hated him, or even claimed to love him.

> 'Tis not the surging billows' roar,
> 'Tis not that fatal, deadly shore;
> Tho' Death in ev'ry shape appear,
> The Wretched have no more to fear:
> But round my heart the ties are bound,
> That heart transpierc'd with many a wound;
> These bleed afresh, those ties I tear,
> To leave the bonie banks of *Ayr*.

On page 583 began Salmon's article on Jamaica. Robert Burns would have read this thoughtfully. He was considering joining the multitudes of Scots who had already emigrated from a land increasingly failing to offer its agricultural youth any realistic future. Jamaica was the first listed of what Salmon called the British American Islands. Bound into the volume in the National Library of Scotland, facing page 583, is a well-worn map of Jamaica. The legend on the map states that the island is 140 miles in length and 60 across. This suggests a place much like a Scotland set in the American sea. The legend said it was about one hundred miles south of Cuba and seventy west of Hispaniola.

Salmon gave a benign description of its seasons:

> Frost and snow are never seen here, but sometimes large hail. The chief rainy seasons are in May and October, when it rains violently night and day for a fortnight.

Anyone used to the seemingly incessant rainfall of the Ayrshire coast, where wild westerlies can drive the rain horizontally in what the Scots describe as stair rods, is unlikely to have realised that this was a serious understatement for hurricanes.

Salmon went on to describe the topography:

> The valleys or savannahs are exceedingly level, and without stones.

Wow, what a blessing, must have thought any Scot reading this.

> Fit for pasture, when cleared of wood.

Another massive understatement of the work involved.

> They are green and pleasant after the rains, or seasons (as they are called) but parched and burnt up by dry weather.

No imagination of one who had never by that time travelled outside the harsh bounds of Ayrshire could have understood the reality behind such diplomatic summaries.

Jamaica had in the latter part of the 18th century become a good place for merchants to get established, since

> In June 1766 certain Jamaican ports were declared to be free, after considerable representation about trade losing out to international competition because of high British taxation.

Kingston, the main town of Jamaica, grew, said Salmon, after Port Royal was destroyed by earthquake on 17th June 1692. Before then, he noted, rents in Port Royal had been as high as those in London. The town had survived, but was severely damaged by fire on 9th January 1703. This storm was part of a long spell of violent weather. Another storm in that sequence crossed the Atlantic, destroyed the Eddystone lighthouse on the south shore of England, and felled many a steeple. The extensive damage caused is recorded in old country churches on wall-affixed painted boards in remembrance of considerable donations for rebuilding. What was left of Port Royal was finally destroyed by a tidal wave on 20th August 1722. This was at the height of what is well known in the modern world as the hurricane season. It is around the time of year of the destruction of New Orleans in 2005. In 2004 extreme hurricanes had submerged the Cayman Islands causing the bodies of the dead to be raised from their graves. I was then working in Jamaica. It was also extremely badly hit. I can only admire the resilience, coolness and good humour of the population in the way they picked up the shattered pieces. Similar severe batterings suffered by Jamaica and all other Caribbean islands are too often by global newscasters simply ignored as being normal.

The one warning that Robert Burns might have taken from Salmon could also, in the unnaturally freezing weather of the Scotland in which he had grown up, be taken as a benefit:

> The air of this country is rather too hot for European constitutions, and generally unhealthful, especially near the sea-coast.

Bred poor in Scotland he had known starvation. Porridge gruel was the staple (though it could often not be got for love or money) and meat a very rare luxury. A struggling farmer would envy an exotic island where the poor could expect to feast on sea turtle. Not only that, along with a regular supply of bread, yams and potatoes, an indentured servant, unfree though he might be for the term of his contract, would be entitled to get meat. His master should give all servants, white and black, three pounds of salt beef, pork or fish every week. A more disturbing thought was that rats were sold by the dozen as food; if bred amongst the sugar canes they were considered particularly delicious. But that would be better than Scottish grain-fed rats. Salmon implied they were washed down with Madeira wine that kept well in the warmth.

Yet this was not entirely paradise, as Burns might infer from Salmon's advice:

> It were to be willed, that the English would forbear to treat their negroes with that cruelty they have formerly done, which, no doubt, occasioned many of them to defect; for though torture be abolished in England, it was exercised upon the negroes here with the greatest barbarity. They were almost whipt to death, without any trial, on the arbitrary commands of a private planter, for the smallest offences, and for greater crimes were fastened to the ground, and burnt by degrees, till they expired in torments. The crime, perhaps, was no more than an attempt to regain that freedom they had been injuriously deprived of, which would be looked upon as an heroic action in a Christian slave taken captive by the Turks.

In his youthful bouts of terrifying illness in which he lay so near to death, Burns had learned to pray. He faced the terrible choice of remaining impoverished and hunted in Scotland or debasing himself as a slave in Jamaica. As he looked around him he no doubt sought signs from God, from Nature or from his flighty muse Coila to assist him to deciding what he should do. Portents, his rational mind told him, were a will o' the wisp deception for the superstitious. But perhaps they were not; Derham could declare comets avenging angels.

The modern world ridicules mediaeval man for his awe of portents and omens. We ridicule chronicles compiled in the ecclesiastical establishments as peppered with tales of solar and lunar eclipses, comets and unusual meteorological and ecological events. When Robert Burns got his big geography book in 1767, this kind of ridicule was certainly not as commonplace as it is now made out to have been.

As he reflected on Jamaica, holding Salmon in his hands, Burns would surely have been tempted to turn over the pages of the familiar book, and let his eyes be seduced into reading again the many and varied stories it contained. Perhaps his eyes lighted on entries in its intensive chronicles, and he remembered how as a child he had used them to trace the history of Scotland. He remembered how he was forced, after the peremptory instruction Salmon gave for Scotland's era after 1603, to look to the chronicle for England to find what happened next. How exciting, after his reading of Derham, to find for 24th December 1664 the entry that "a comet or blazing star appeared". Remembering Derham's judgement of comets, he must surely have thought how curious this timing. It might have been a warning for the Stuart dynasty so recently restored to the British thrones.

In tracing the history of the many states of Europe, he had found that the time of the early Restoration had been a general period of economic optimism. Alongside scientific advances, there was investment in infrastructure and manufactures. Demand for luxury goods was picking up. In 1662 this caused the founding in France of the Gobelins factory as Manufacture Royale des Meubles de la Couronne or Royal Manufactory of Furnishings for the Crown. Expectation of trade increases encouraged England to pass its first Turnpike Act in 1663. In 1664 France's finance minister Jean-Baptiste Colbert abolished internal tolls to promote internal commerce of agriculture and manufactures. This was much resisted by vested interests. In 1668 Josiah Child, a director of the East India Company and an economist, published 'Brief Observations Concerning Trade and the Interest', including suggestions for tackling poverty. In 1671 William Carter published 'England's Interest by Trade Asserted', his focus being on improving speculative profits.

At the same time as economic theory was being explored, science was once again challenging preconceptions. In 1669, Danish scientist Nicolaus Steno proposed how fossils could be formed from living matter. He outlined the basic principles of geological stratigraphy. In Aberdeen University in 1663, James Gregory had worked on improving the telescope. This led in 1672 to an improvement attributed to Cassegrain of France, who manufactured a compact telescope.

In 1674 George Ravenscroft incorporated black flint and lead oxide into glass, inventing lead crystal. In 1675, glassmakers in Normandy rediscovered how to cast glass in sheets, enabling the manufacture of very large mirrors, in due course leading to the creation of that candle-reflecting shimmering fairy world of the Hall of Mirrors in the Palace of Versailles. Change and economic pressures threatened established industries. From 8th to 12th August 1675, silk weavers in London rioted against the use of engine looms. They destroyed at least 85 looms belonging to two dozen different owners.

As he read Salmon, Burns must have wondered at repeated references to religious contention. In the early 1680s, James, Duke of York, was excluded from the throne because of allegiance to the Roman faith. By the Regency Bill, the duke's daughter Anne and her husband were expected to be regents on the death of Charles II. The question then was what would happen if the Duke of York had a son who was brought up a Protestant. In 1682 there was the Rye House plot and a fire at Newmarket. Both were linked to concerns that the Regency Bill would in that case lapse. Then on February 5th 1685 Charles II died. James in fact succeeded to the throne. His public attendance at Mass only three days after his accession was sufficiently newsworthy nearly a century later for Salmon to record the event in his chronicle. James threw oil on the fires of religious bigotry by publishing two papers that appeared to prove that Charles II had on his deathbed embraced the Roman Catholic faith. Soon there was revolt, quickly put down. On 30th June 1685 the Duke of Argyle was beheaded in Edinburgh for treason to King James VII. But within three years, Roman Catholicism had been put to flight and the Glorious Revolution triumphed.

Omens continued, the young man must have observed. Salmon listed many. Of course, in such listings neither mediaeval chroniclers nor Salmon considered themselves judgemental of these events. They were simply giving natural cross-references to enable future historians to confirm the calendar dates of the human events chronicled.

On January 4th 1698 Whitehall Palace, centre of constitutional government, caught fire. Within three years there was raging war in Europe. On the death of King James II, France recognised his son as James III of Britain. British historians call him the 'Old Pretender'. Already, in 1701, war had broken out between Austria and France when each claimed they were heir to Spain's vast lands. This conflict became known as the War of the Spanish Succession. Two families, the Hapsburgs and the Bourbons, martially slugged it out over that lucrative inheritance, the Spanish crown. While the War of the Spanish Succession was waged in south Europe, the Great Northern War was simultaneously fought. Sweden was attacked on all sides by a coalition of Denmark, north German States, Saxony-Poland (then under one ruler) and Russia.

Britain and United Netherlands sided with Austria. Immediately they persuaded Frederick III, Elector of Brandenburg to support Hapsburg claims against France by elevating him as King Frederick I of Prussia. The war was soon fought globally. France won that war. England withdrew from European conflicts when Philip V, grandson of Louis XIV, was secured as King of Spain in 1713. He had renounced any future claim to the French crown. At the same time his cousins, the dukes of Berry and of Orleans, renounced any future claim to the throne of Spain. Of course, they all later reneged on this agreement.

England – excluding Scotland before 1707 – was meanwhile fighting its own wars to establish economic control in the Americas, in India and wherever else across the globe that opportunities appeared. Scotland's young men had often, for lack of other economic opportunity, hired themselves out as mercenary soldiers. Merely half a page in Salmon's chronicle relates to the Union of Scotland's and England's parliaments. As this drew Scotland directly into global war, the very short coverage surely disappointed Burns. He must have read between the lines that Scotland was reduced through the Union to a source of conscripted cannon fodder for England's aggression. One month before the Act of Union, the French army of James FitzJames, Duke of Berwick, decisively defeated English, Portuguese and Spanish forces in Spain at Almanza. This forced those allies to evacuate Aragon. A month after, June 1707, the French community of Port Royal on the American mainland was unsuccessfully attacked by English colonial forces.

Queen Anne died on 1st August 1714. England acted unilaterally, inviting the Elector of Hanover, George Ludwig, great-grandson of James I, to succeed to the throne as George I. Scotland then found herself embroiled in the unfinished Great Northern War as well as England's worldwide trade wars. At London on 22nd April 1715 no doubt the rude classes, those that would in Burns's adult life be called the swinish multitude, whispered amongst themselves and wondered in the darkness of

> a total eclipse of the sun, about nine in the morning. The darkness was such, for about three minutes, that the stars appeared, and the birds and fowls retired to their nests, as if it had been night.

Even financiers of the City must have become concerned about the impact on business confidence of such an unusual spectacle.

France was now under the child king Louis XV. Henry St John, Lord Bolingbroke, dismissed from his political offices on the accession of George I, went to France to join James Francis Edward Stuart, Chevalier of St George. This Old Pretender made him his Secretary of State. Robert Harley, Earl of Oxford, accused of Jacobitism, was imprisoned in the Tower of London on 9th July. He was not released until 1717. On that 9th July, the British Parliament, fearing Jacobites were potential terrorists, passed the Riot Act. Three days later it suspended the Act of Habeas Corpus, enabling arbitrary imprisonment of suspected Jacobites. On 6th September, John Erskine, Earl of Mar, raised at Braemar the standard in the cause of King James, who landed a few days later at Peterhead. After the failure of his campaign and his return to France, James dismissed Bolingbroke. By the end of

1716, France had given up any interest in James in favour of a treaty with Britain and the United Netherlands against Spain and Sweden. Financial confidence in London recovered after the crisis. Following this rising began mass emigration of Scots and Irish to the Americas.

On March 19th 1718

> a surprising meteor was seen about nine at night, being a globe of fire, equal, in dimensions and brightness, to the sun, and illuminating the whole region. It disappeared in half a minute, but the streams of light which issued from it continued a quarter of an hour.

Data on political events elsewhere in Europe implied criticism of the Hanoverian cause. Burns would have had to search elsewhere in Salmon to find it. Burns was a voracious reader, and probably did find at least some. In 1718 Spain seized Sicily, which formerly had been a Spanish island, but had been given in the 16th century to Savoy. Holy Roman Emperor Charles VI joined forces with Britain and the United Netherlands to oppose Spain. On 25th March 1719 James Francis Edward Stuart was acknowledged in Madrid by King Philip V of Spain as king of Great Britain and Ireland. In the ensuing two year war, Spain between April and June 1719 sent two frigates to Scotland, landing four hundred men. These in vain awaited the arrival in support of the Stuart cause of a major Spanish invasion force. This was led by James Butler, Duke of Ormonde. His fleet left Cadiz but was dispersed by storms. In June 1719 the few Spanish soldiers who had arrived were with some Highlanders defeated at Glenshiel Pass. They surrendered, ending this second and now commonly forgotten Jacobite rising.

The next year, on 6th February, a peace treaty was agreed between Spain and the Quadruple Alliance of France, the Holy Roman Empire, Britain and the United Netherlands. France had invested heavily in this war, without payback. On 24th March 1720 banks in France closed in the financial crisis caused by speculation and war debt. On 12th December, John Law fled from France in the wake of its national bankruptcy following the collapse of his equally spurious Mississippi Company. On 10th September 1720, the English 'South Sea Bubble' burst after frenzied financial speculation that peaked in August. That year had seen the last wave in Europe of Black Death epidemic. This had recurred at intervals since its first appearance in the mid 14th century. In Marseilles, 50,000 died. (In 1722 Defoe published his 'Journal of the Plague Year'.) By December 1720, thousands in London were ruined. In 1721 there was a smallpox outbreak in London, prompting the first smallpox inoculations.

The Hanoverian regime was shaken by all these events. Francis Atterbury, Bishop of Rochester, was arrested on 24th September 1722 accused of having contacted the Old Pretender. The Habeas Corpus Act was again suspended on 'discovering' this Atterbury 'plot'. Imprisoning political opponents made no headway in addressing fundamental economic problems. So the Westminster parliament decided to up tax on Scotland. This swept away the fiscal protection secured to Scotland by the Treaty of Union. Tax was levied on malt. On 24th June 1725,

> a tumult happened at Glasgow on account of the malt-act; and the rioters being encouraged by the magistrates, they were apprehended, and sent prisoners to Edinburgh by General Wade; where the magistrates were met by the citizens of Edinburgh, and caressed as so many patriots, and the government thought fit to release them after a short confinement.

Westminster feared another rising. There was no easy access for government troops into the Scottish Highlands to enable fast subjugation in areas of unrest. General George Wade was sent north in 1726 to begin his road building campaign. Wade oversaw the building of very few roads, but the work was significantly expanded when handed over to General Caulfield. These military roads enabled Burns to consider in 1787 hiring a coach for his tour of the Highlands with the older man Nicol, who refused a long journey on horseback.

On 11th June 1727, George I died while in Hanover, not long after Spain began a fight with Britain to regain Gibraltar, which had been ceded to England in 1704. Constantly embattled aggressive England wanted a docile Scotland. It irked Westminster that it could not blatantly ride roughshod over Scotland without appearing to use proper process in bullying her. So those in power tried similar strong-arm tactics to those that had helped secure the Union. Government forces decided to take control of Scotland's representative peers. Overseen by Colonel Handafide's regiment, troops intimidated voters. In June 1734 the Earl of Stair found himself driven to lead formal protest that the election of Scottish peers to the Westminster House of Lords had been rigged.

All this time, political uncertainty had been paralleled by industrial advances. In 1708 in England Abraham Darby developed a method of casting iron in sand only. This significantly lowered production cost – incidentally a great benefit in arms manufacture. Facing high prices for raw wood, the following year he achieved the use of coke instead of charcoal in iron smelting. This further lowered his cost structure. In 1717 Thomas and John Lombe established the world's first power-driven textile mill near Derby. In 1718, Thomas patented a machine to make thrown silk. In 1725 French weaver Basile Bouchen invented the punched card system for operating looms. This was the first step towards automated production machinery and modern computing. Scottish printer William Ged invented the stereoscope, a cast of laid-out movable type used in printing. This released the type itself from use in actual printing, vastly reducing the amount of typeface needed by a printer. This increased the capacity of a printworks. In 1730 Charles 'Turnip' Townshend over-wintered a herd of cattle by feeding them turnips. This in due course made fresh beef generally available all year round. On May 26th 1733 John Kay patented his flying shuttle. This reduced loom manpower input by one third. Despite such advances in labour saving and increases in productivity, in 1731 Britain had initiated emigration restriction to stop factory workers going to America.

Labourers looked abroad in the face of agricultural as well as industrial difficulty. Weather was extreme. With no Thames Barrier in those days to protect low-lying London riverside properties, on February 16th 1736

> this being the day after the last full moon before the equinox, there was a spring-tide, which exceeded near a foot and a half all that had been before: in Westminster-hall the council was carried out in boats to their coaches.

Would that they had been washed away, must have wished many a technology-threatened hard-pressed English labourer and starving Scottish patriot.

Only a few months later there took place in Edinburgh the incident called the Porteous Riots. Some smugglers had been arrested. The crowd rioted, objecting to the taxation that they deemed unlawful and which they felt made smuggling necessary. John Porteous ordered troops to fire on the crowd. There were fatalities. On 22nd June he was due to be executed for murder. On a reprieve arriving from Queen Charlotte, he was released. He immediately got lynched by the angry mob. His grave in Edinburgh's eerie Greyfriars' Kirkyard is even in modern times said to be a haunted spot.

On 31st July 1737, Frederick Prince of Wales quarrelled with George II and with his wife left the Royal Household at Hampton Court. He thus became de facto leader of Parliamentary opposition during hard times, with exceptionally harsh weather. Salmon's chronicle, London-centric though his history is, noted for December 25th 1740 that:

> as severe a frost as has been known began on Christmas day this year; some people were frozen to death upon the Thames, and in the streets and fields; several ships were sunk by the driving of ice on the Thames. Great want ensued, with people unable to work because of the cold. There was a demonstration in London of the cold and starving.

Such weather ushered in the War of the Austrian Succession, fought until 1748. It was triggered by the death of Holy Roman Emperor Charles VI on October 20th 1740. The agreed succession of his daughter Maria Theresa, known as the Pragmatic Sanction, was widely challenged. King Frederick II, the Great, of Prussia had succeeded his father Frederick William I of Prussia on 31st May 1739. He struck the first blow, intent on proving his manhood through adding the rich province of Silesia to his domains. Bourbon France always opposed Hapsburgs of whom Maria Theresa was one. France supported other enemies of Maria Theresa, while beginning her own land grab. Britain was already fighting Spain over colonial rights in the so-called War of Jenkins' Ear. After failing to stop the free-for-all multi-faceted war on mainland Europe, she first attempted to persuade France to accept her neutrality. When this proved impractical she in 1742 entered the fray. Hanoverian interest in mainland territorial power meant Britain went against France, at first as ally of Prussia. Then in another twist of allegiance, by 1744 France was fighting alongside Prussia. By 1745 the war had spread to North America, where France and Britain slugged it out.

On June 14th that year Admiral Lord George Anson arrived home from his round the world voyage after four years. He had lost most of his men and most of his ships, but he brought booty. This delighted those moneyed interests; his return was a good omen.

On 30th April 1745 the French forces defeated at Fontenoy, near Tournai, the army of Britain, Hanover and the United Netherlands. This army had been led by William Augustus, Duke of Cumberland. The Duke was dismissed as incompetent. This may well have put his nose out of joint and made him determined that he would get his own back on someone, somehow, in some very bloody way. His chance came the following year, in that barbarian land, Scotland, on dreadful Culloden Moor.

With the Hanoverians confused and preoccupied, the Young Pretender saw his chance. He persuaded France to support an invasion of Britain through Scotland. Three months after Cumberland's defeat, Bonnie Prince Charlie was marching south through Scotland. He had landed on 14th July on Eriskay and crossed to Moidart on July 25th. British troops were rapidly recalled from Europe. On 2nd September, Hanoverian forces under General George Cope were defeated at Prestonpans.

In nice contrast, on 9th September 1745, Madame de Pompadour was installed in Versailles as official mistress of King Louis XV. She died young, in mid August, 1764.

On 17th September 1745, Charles Edward Stuart entered Edinburgh. There his father was proclaimed King James VIII of Scotland. By early December, the Jacobite army had reached Derby. 'God Save the King' was at this point first performed in Drury Lane Theatre, begging God to scatter the Hanoverian king's enemies. To the delight of London, Bonnie Prince Charlie began returning north. The Duke of Cumberland did his best to catch up with him. The Jacobites defeated Hanoverians at Penrith and again at Falkirk. On 16th April 1746, at Culloden, their luck ran out. The Duke of Cumberland resoundingly earned his nickname of Butcher. Two days later, Lord Kilmarnock, imprisoned earlier in the conflict, was beheaded. On 18th August at Tower Hill in London, Arthur Elphinstone, Lord Balmerino, captured at Culloden, met the same fate. Before capture, he gave his dirk in payment for army supplies. Burns was given the dirk as a gift, for Balmerino was one of his heroes.

> Bold Balmerino's undying name,
> Whose soul of fire, lighted at Heaven's high flame,
> Deserves the brightest wreath departed heroes claim.

Repressive laws on Scotland's clans were enacted. These included outlawing the tartan and the bagpipes as being liveries and weapons of war. In 1748, heritable jurisdiction in the Highlands was abolished. This eliminated the former powers of clan chiefs. It also undermined traditional familial loyalty, mutual responsibility, community and culture.

On 7th July 1745, the French fleet had arrived in Pondicherry. This took war to India. That December young Robert Clive came too as a clerk of the British East India Company. On September 10th 1746 the French captured Madras. Days later, Bonnie Prince Charlie escaped from Scotland to France. Burns lived in a Britain that had increasingly been pushing out the boundaries of freedom of speech but suddenly found itself in 1793 under the Damoclean fear of near-tyrannical oppression in the name of anti-terrorism. Burns then drew from the chronicles inspiration for historical and Jacobite songs. He placed words into the mouth of the war-failed Young Pretender:

> His right are these hills, and his right are these valleys,
> Where the wild beasts find shelter but I can find none.

In 1749 Britain set up the fortress of Halifax, Nova Scotia, initiating in North America a new confrontation with France over mutual boundaries. With so many war fronts, England was determined to keep a firm grip on its northern flank. The ensuing more intrusive involvement of the English government in Scottish affairs actually caused England to bring itself a bit more into the modern world. Since 1582 England had been living, astronomically, in the Middle Ages. She had consistently rejected the considerable improvements that had caused the Gregorian calendar to be adopted widely.

On May 22nd 1751 the Westminster parliament enacted that from that year onwards the Gregorian calendar be adopted in England and the year should begin on 1st January, not on 25th March as formerly. Thus its 1751 moved directly from 2nd September to 14th September. (In this book I have corrected all year numbers to the modern format throughout.)

At the end of August that year, Robert Clive in India captured Arcot, capital of Carnatic, an ally of France. Two weeks later at Arni he defeated Joseph, marquis de Dupleix, the French governor-general of India. In June 1752, France surrendered to Clive and Major Stringer Lawrence of Britain's East India Company. Success in India increased opportunities for unemployed Scots.

Britain's advantage in access to leading-edge armaments improved further in 1754 when the first iron-rolling mill was opened at Fareham. In 1755 Vice Admiral Edward Boscawen, who earned the nickname Old Dreadnought, engaged the French at the mouth of the St Lawrence River. This caused France to recall its ambassador from London. That year, Britain agreed to pay Russia to defend Hanover. Britain also agreed to pay Prussia to defend Hanover and abandoned its former alliance with Austria. William Pitt the Elder objected to the payments and was dismissed from his office of Paymaster General. In April 1756, Russia proposed to Austria that Prussia be partitioned, returning to Austria its hereditary possession of Silesia and returning to Russia the Polish province of Courland. Austria had also been talking with France. A treaty was signed at Versailles on 1ˢᵗ May 1756. This became known as the Diplomatic Revolution, when former enemies France and Austria formally combined against Britain. Britain responded by declaring war on France. That June took place the incident in India that became known as The Black Hole of Calcutta.

At the end of August 1756, Prussia invaded Saxony, formally starting what came to be called the Seven Years War. This was fought across Europe until 1763, expanding the confrontations taking place in respective colonies. On the European continent, in 1757 Prussia, under King Frederick II, the Great, first captured Saxony. France was promised territory in the Austrian Netherlands on formally accepting Prussia be partitioned. Austria and Russia made war on Prussia. Prussia won at Prague, but was then defeated at Kolin. In Hanover, William Augustus, Duke of Cumberland, was defeated by the French. William Pitt the Elder was brought back into power. The French meanwhile made headway in North America. Their Indian allies slaughtered British and colonial prisoners. George II refused to accept the surrender terms agreed by the Duke of Cumberland who was replaced as general.

In his last years Burns was denied freedom of speech to write of current politics. Salmon's and other chronicles gave him the facts on the rumble-tumble world of commercial and political greed and grab that he remarked became the province of the poet, once the politicians had done with it. All the facts were before him ready to line up into clever, biting, incisive contemporarily-relevant verse that purported to relate only to history.

Russia captured East Prussia, after its ally Sweden had preoccupied Prussian forces. Prussia managed to hold its own in Silesia, from where in the spring of 1758 it invaded Moravia, but Austria drove it back. A British army defeated the French at Krefeld, and began having successes in North America. At Zomdorf, Prussia bloodily fought off the Russians, but was then defeated by the Austrians in Saxony. A month later, on November 24ᵗʰ 1758, the French abandoned Fort Du Quesne on the Ohio River and General Forbes took possession of it the same day, putting under British control a considerable tract of rich land. Britain called the place Pittsburgh after the prime minister.

Burns must have been particularly interested in reading of these events, for it was in the midst of this war that he was born. Reading of the year of his own birth, Robert must have been intrigued to learn that on January 12ᵗʰ there died at The Hague Her Royal Highness the Princess Royal of Great Britain, Governante of the United Provinces. Britain began six months of mourning. No doubt that did no good for the sale of produce from a run of the mill market garden some distance from the town of Ayr.

Four days after his birth, the island of Goree off the coast of Africa was captured by Commodore Keppel, who made the French garrison prisoners of war. In India, French troops laid siege to Madras, where the British fleet arrived on 2ⁿᵈ February 1759. British troops then drove the French from the Deccan, southeast India. Back in Europe, Russia again invaded Prussia, and the British continued to drive back the French. Austria recaptured Saxony in mid August, but the British fleet under Boscawen then defeated the French off Cape St Vincent. On 13ᵗʰ September, James Wolfe got round the back of the French defences at Quebec, Canada, but was killed in the ensuing action. So was the French commander, Louis-Joseph, Marquis de Montcalm. Thus French Canada came under British control. On November 21st, Prussia capitulated in Saxony and was defeated in the passes guarding Silesia, but in mid-1760 was fighting back. Also in 1760, in January, the British made further advances in India. In Canada, Montreal was captured in September. Two months later, Prussia got success against Austria, recapturing Saxony. On October 25th 1760, George II died but war continued. By January 1761, Britain was dominant in southern India while Austrian troops were blockading Prussia's armies in Silesia. At the start of 1762, Britain extended the war by attacking Spanish territories in Italy, while its navy captured West Indian islands from France and Spain. When Portugal refused to prevent British ships using its ports, she was invaded by Spain.

This fast-paced chronicle of events in Salmon surely inspired his racy poems on political history. It gave him the ready raw material for that soldier song that he attributed to that discarded maimed mercenary veteran he observed in the inn at Mauchline.

> My Prenticeship I past, where my LEADER breath'd his last
> > When the bloody die was cast on the heights of ABRAM;
> And I served out my TRADE when the gallant game was play'd,
> > And the MORO low was laid at the sound of the drum.
> I lastly was with Curtis among the *floating batt'ries,*
> > And there I left for witness, an arm and a limb;
> Yet let my Country need me, with ELLIOT to lead me,
> > I'd clatter on my stumps at the sound of the drum.

In keeping up to date with current affairs it is more than likely that Burns appreciated the strength of setting out events in the form of chronicle as found in Salmon. He became aware of the emerging events of the war that raged in North America between 1775 and 1783. He needed to lift his mind from that war's impoverishing impact on Scotland's economy. He might well have memorised lists of dates to distract himself from the increasing destitution of his own home life. This approach provided structure to emerging events. In due course it would provide him with content for other poems on political history.

In his infancy, in a strange turn of Fate in Europe, on 5th January 1762 died Elizabeth, Empress of Russia, daughter of Peter the Great. She was succeeded by her nephew, pro-Prussian Peter, Duke of Holstein-Gottorp. As Czar Peter III of Russia he quickly ended all hostilities with Prussia, instead agreeing alliance and returning all conquered territories. Russia persuaded its ally Sweden to do the same. All of them turned on Austria, which was soon driven out first of Silesia and then Saxony. Success was despite the murder on 17th July of the Czar with the connivance of his wife, Grand Duchess Catherine Alexeevna. She succeeded him as Catherine II, the Great. She filled her coffers by confiscating church lands, and then joined Prussia and Britain in pushing France back across the Rhine. A peace treaty was signed by all contestants on 10th February 1763.

Britain now controlled Canada including Nova Scotia and Cape Breton, St Vincent, Tobago, Dominica, Grenada, Senegal and Minorca, all previously French holdings. In India, France re-established its settlements. Spain was given Louisiana, formerly French. Britain got Florida in exchange for returning Cuba and the Philippines to Spain. On mainland Europe, the pre-war borders of Prussia and Austria were reinstated. Across France in April 1764 marched a partial eclipse of the Sun, perhaps signalling to many the partial eclipse of French global power.

The ending of hostilities with France in North America signalled the start of the guerrilla war of Ottawa chief Pontiac. This was not suppressed until 1766. On 5th August 1766 across the Canadian homelands of the first people swept the broad swathe of another partial eclipse of the Sun. These, said Salmon, were truly free peoples. Strange it must have seemed to the young Burns that Salmon described the lands of the American Indians as having no European monarch as their superior lord. Now as he looked again at this familiar text, and drew his fingers across the map of Jamaica, he knew that once Britain left North America to an expanding young united nation of independent republic States, the native peoples had found their proud freedom torn away.

In those former colonies, in 1764, Britain passed a Colonial Currency Act forbidding payments from the American colonies to Britain in certain currencies thought unsound. That year, Adam Smith began that long pensioned sabbatical at whose end he wrote what is now called 'The Wealth of Nations'. The Act caused a currency shortage in the colonies. This bred a great deal of resentment there. The government then passed the Sugar Act enabling Britain to take levies on sugar and other products to defray the cost of defending the colonies. Boston lawyer James Otis, in response, described this Act as 'taxation without representation'. Boston merchants began to boycott British luxury items named in the Act. In 1765, Britain passed the Stamp Act, levying direct taxes on all colonial legal documents and a wide range of printed material. This aggravated colonial protests. The Virginia assembly in May adopted a resolution defining 'British freedom' as 'taxation of the people by themselves', thus joining the 'no taxation without representation' bandwagon. In October, delegates from nine American colonies in the so-called Stamp Act Congress together created the 'Declaration of Rights and Grievances'. On 1st November there were riots in New York following that Congress. Homes of British officials were attacked. In March 1766 Britain repealed the Stamp Act but passed another declaring its supreme authority in the colonies.

Britain's next gambit was in midsummer 1767, as Charles Mason and Jeremiah Dixon completed their demarcation of the Pennsylvania-Maryland border, initiating the Mason-Dixon line. King George III gave his signature to the Townshend Acts, taxing a range of imports to the American colonies and establishing a Board of Customs at notoriously recalcitrant Boston, to ensure compliance. In September, leaders of the Boston citizens agreed to boycott imports. The customs officials arrived on 5th November. In June 1768 the officials seized John Hancock's sloop *Liberty* in Boston harbour for alleged smuggling. A riot followed. Britain sent troops. When they began to arrive in October, their billeting aggravated resentment. In February 1769, the British Parliament reactivated an old statute of Henry VIII, sanctioning the removal of treason trials from the colonies to England. In May, the Privy Council affirmed the tax on tea in the colonies. On 5th March 1770, British troops, faced with a mob, fired on them causing fatalities. The incident is now called the Boston Massacre. On 12th April, to reduce tension, the British Parliament repealed the Townshend duties on all items except tea, diffusing the American boycott on imports.

Things were sufficiently calm until 16th December 1773. Then, in the incident known as the Boston Tea Party, activists dumped into the harbour a cargo of tea. On 31st March 1774 Britain passed the Boston Port Act, closing the port. This was the first of the so-called Intolerable Acts.

A second forbad public meetings of Massachusetts citizens. A third removed elsewhere all trials of British officials accused of capital crimes. The Quartering Act, ordering Boston citizens to house and feed British soldiers, was soon passed as a fourth Intolerable Act.

The Quebec Act then extended Quebec's boundary south and granted privileges to the Catholic Church in former French Canada to persuade Canadian Catholics to enter British armed forces. This alienated anti-Catholic colonists. That year, Thomas Jefferson published 'A Summary View of the Rights of British America', arguing that the British Parliament had no sovereignty in the colonies.

The first military action of the American War of Independence broke out on 19th April 1775. In May 1776 the colonists went to France to seek a loan to support their ongoing military opposition to Britain. With cash in hand, the unilateral American Declaration of Independence was approved and has since been celebrated annually on 4th July.

Since 1663, when the Company of Royal Adventurers Trading to Africa was started in competition with the existing Dutch company for trade in slaves, ivory and gold, England had been in the slave trade on her own account. In 1711 England's South Sea Company had been formed initially to trade in slaves with South America. The commercial promises it made precipitated the South Sea Bubble. That made it all the more imperative that Britain get payback from her overseas interests to recover from that financial disaster that crippled the infant Bank of England. England built up massive commercial interests in slave trading. In 1778 Thomas Jefferson signed treaties of trade and defence with France. He then aimed a direct attack on British trading interests. He achieved the passing of an Act in the new independent States prohibiting the import of slaves. Britain then approached its rebelling American colonies with peace overtures, which were rejected.

The French sent their fleet across the Atlantic having first barely escaped from a fight with the English fleet in the Channel. Expecting their arrival, British forces evacuated from Philadelphia. Their retreat was interrupted by the former British officer George Washington.

The wars between colonists and British authorities that ended in the creation of the United States were fought between 1775 and 1783. In this conflict there arose in Britain a man who would become castigated by biographers of Burns for denying the poet a government pension. This was the powerful Henry Dundas, by some nicknamed King Henry of Scotland. Over the last two centuries he has been roundly blamed for not granting Burns a pension or sinecure that would have enabled such a genius to create even more and perhaps greater verse. Wordsworth got the sinecure of Distributor of Stamps for Westmorland worth £300 per annum. Samuel Johnson got a State pension of £300 per annum. Burns had to fend for himself toiling as a farmer and then as one of the lowliest of hard-working Excisemen.

Burns might first have heard the name Henry Dundas in 1769, the year the Ayr Bank was formed. Dundas then presided at the trial for murder of Mungo Campbell, a customs officer on the Ayrshire coast. The tenth Earl of Eglinton, riding on the sands at Saltcoats, found Campbell poaching. The earl demanded he hand over his gun. Campbell refused, began to back off, and tripped over a rock. The gun went off and killed the earl. Campbell escaped hanging by suicide. Henry Dundas became Lord Advocate. He is not, by the way, the person who built Dundas House, the grand private residence at the east end of Edinburgh's New Town and now nominal headquarters of the Royal Bank of Scotland; that had been his early arch-rival, the nouveau riche Edinburgh

Chapter IX *Wha sae Base as be a Slave*

entrepreneur Lawrence Dundas. As Lord Advocate he had considerable patronage to bestow as well
as being in a position of influence with his own superiors in government. He gained promotion for
Robert Macqueen, who as Judge Lord Braxfield gave in 1783 the final judgement on the purported
debts of William Burness of Lochlie and presided at the sedition trials of 93/94. In 1777 Dundas
got Adam Smith the well-paid job of Commissioner of Customs. On Smith's advice, he promoted
the removal of trade barriers between Scotland and Ireland. Partial success by 1780 increased trade
between the two regions, partly offsetting the loss of commerce due to the American war. Smith
moved into Panmure House, a comfortably-sized townhouse. This still stands east of the Canongate
Church in Edinburgh, in which the burial place of this reputed architect of capitalism is marked by
a single brick in the cobbled path.

Henry Dundas was continuously approached for jobs and patronage. One bundle of around six
hundred papers in the National Library of Scotland suggests he was probably rejecting each week
around two requests received in writing. He had the influence to get people military and navy jobs,
church livings and university posts. He also was able to farm out government financial business
to the banking system. A very small proportion of such patronage as he did grant went to literary
persons. He persuaded the Prince of Wales to put his name to a Literary Fund to give some aid to
widows or orphans of literary men.

Nepotism was a different matter. With his own son Robert away on his grand tour to finish his
education, Henry turned his attention to fostering the interest of his young Arniston nephew and
son-in-law, also named Robert. He had influenced his nephew's appointment as Solicitor General in
1784 when aged 26, and by 1789 the young man was raised to Lord Advocate, a post he held until
1801. He was also an MP from 1790.

By that time, alongside Prime Minister, William Pitt the Younger, Henry Dundas, Treasurer of
the Navy, was the most powerful man in Britain. The entire Dundas dynasty is described in detail
in Chambers 'Biographical Dictionary of Eminent Scotsmen'. Michael Fry in 1992 published under
the title 'The Dundas Despotism' a thorough discourse on the role in British politics of the Dundas
families of Arniston and Melville in the late 18th and early 19th centuries. Fry gives a perspective of
the Scotland in which Robert Burns lived the second half of his life.

Henry Dundas is indicted that his miserliness condemned Burns to his last decade of all-
consuming hard labour. Creating a pension for Burns should have needed no intervention by him.
But Mrs Dunlop was the only one who really worked hard to get a decent income for Burns. He
repeatedly thanked her for her efforts. She helped him improve his Excise position. She even tried to
get Burns a professorship – though he told her that he wouldn't stand a chance because of academic
prejudice against someone of his lowly origin, who lacked a university degree. The future Earl of
Mar would have led a subscription, had Burns been in dire straits in January 1793, but he had no
influence. There were plenty of other people in Scotland who could have put their hands into their
own pockets to make life comfortable for Burns. Burns was already seen to consort in Edinburgh
with the opposition party. Even if his satirical skills had not been so sharp politically, this association
would have caused coolness in government circles. Burns in Edinburgh moved in the circle of James
Cunningham, fourteenth Earl of Glencairn (1749-91) and the Erskine phalanx. Dundas was not of
the same political bent as those men.

Dundas could not have known that music, not politics, attracted Burns to this circle. Elizabeth Macrae, Glencairn's mother, had been a commoner. She was one of three nieces of a millionaire nabob bachelor who had been looked after in youth by itinerant musician, Hew McQuyre. The nabob's brother had married the musician's daughter. The bachelor left this musician's granddaughters good dowries. Elizabeth was given the Barony of Ochiltree. Before then, she had been servant to farmer John Tennant of Laigh Corton. She appointed his son factor to the Glencairn estates. Her sister Margaret inherited the estate of Alva and married James Erskine, later Lord Alva. The third sister, inheriting Orangefield, in 1750 married Charles Dalrymple of Ayr. From Hew McQuyre were descended James, Earl of Glencairn, James Dalrymple of Orangefield and Captain James Macrae of Houston and Holmains. The 14th Earl's younger brother Rev John Cunningham married Lady Isabella Erskine, sister of the Earl of Buchan and of Hon. Henry Erskine, Dean of the Faculty of Advocates.

Burns gets blamed for not making opportunities to get on the right side of this very important man. Dundas came to Blair Castle as Burns toured the Highlands. Yet Burns did not wait one more day to be there when Dundas arrived. But it is unlikely that the presence of Burns would have been welcomed by the Duke of Atholl when Dundas arrived. Atholl had quite enough quibble of his own with a man who wielded so much power. There was an ongoing business to attend to – the matter of the value of the independent Lordship of Man, inherited since the reign of Henry VII until it was subject to compulsory purchase by the government in 1765.

The Isle of Man lies in the middle of the Irish Sea, conveniently placed offshore to Ireland, Scotland, England and Wales. It is now an offshore financial centre that also took over Cayman Islands business when hurricanes in 2004 swamped installations there. Man is still not even part of the European Union. On Man in 1682 England had a spy who sent a report to Customs and Excise. In 1689, when England went to war with France she imposed massive duties on French wine and brandy. Man took over the wine business to Scotland and began what the English called smuggling. Three years later, to the rightful indignation of Atholl's ancestor, Lord Derby, Lord of Man, England placed a customs officer on Man. Derby proposed that England guard its own shores, rather than invade his.

But, as Earl of Derby and subject to the English crown, he was cautioned to do something about the 'smuggling'. He ordered his own officers on Man to be more stringent in gathering Manx import dues. Since these were negligible in comparison with England's, the revenues of Man increased, but the 'smuggling' continued to thrive. When the Scottish Parliament was dissolved after some arm twisting in 1707, Man got seriously scared that its days of freedom were numbered too.

England's Navigation Acts encouraged smuggling. These allowed goods to be imported only in English-built and English-manned ships. Tariffs were increased greatly after 1689 to pay the debts incurred in overthrowing the Stuart dynasty. The 'running trade' became a tempting enterprise and a thrilling adventure.

The crux of the matter was that Man was an independent country. It was doing nothing illegal. After all, merchants imported goods to Man and paid port and customs dues. Then they exported the goods. It wasn't up to Man to police where those goods went. Goods were brought to Man from France, Spain, Portugal, Norway and Sweden, but then run into England, Scotland and Ireland into little coves and havens around the shores of the Irish Sea, boats offloading goods liable to high English and Scottish Excise duties. This smuggling into Britain was so profitable that Manxmen largely lost interest in fishing and farming. Every haven of Britain was a potential landing spot.

In 1736, after the tenth Earl of Derby died without children, the Lordship of Man passed through the female line to James Murray, second Duke of Atholl. His maternal grandmother was Amelia Sophie Stanley, third daughter of the seventh Derby earl. (The Derby title went to a cousin.) James had got the Atholl estates and honours in 1715 after the attainder of his eldest brother William, Marquis of Tullibardine. (In the Jacobite rebellion as in the Civil War, aristocratic families often hedged bets by brothers taking different sides.) He ruled Man till his death in 1764. By then, Westminster considered Man the centre of a vast network of smugglers who deprived the British government of considerable revenues.

James was succeeded by his only surviving child Charlotte. She carried the Man inheritance, and her husband and first cousin John Murray became Lord of Man. John also happened to be the nearest male heir to the Atholl dukedom. However, his father had also been on the wrong side in the 1745 Jacobite rising, and had been forfeited. John asked the Hanoverian king nicely, and got the dukedom. Then came the crunch. The very next year they got a 'nice letter' from Prime Minister George Grenville, offering to 'buy the island of Man' to curb the 'smuggling'. There appears to have been an unspecified 'or else'. When the new duke was dilatory in replying, the letters got stronger. So 'negotiations' started. John committed suicide ten years later. This is never officially connected with his being forced in the Revestment Act of 1765 to sell to the British Crown rights to all duties taken in the island while being left with all his costs, effectively bankrupting him.

The immediate effects on Man of the changes following the Revestment Act were bad. Their Lord was replaced by officers of Britain's Treasury. On Man, poverty became widespread, prices increased rapidly, and many were forced to emigrate. But the island became a nest of entrepreneurial smugglers. Merchants from England and Scotland invested their capital in the business. Douglas was especially full of it. Thus Edmund Burke described Man as 'the very citadel of smuggling' in 1774. Yet Burke compared what had happened in Man to what was happening in America: people were being taxed without representation. Today, the behaviour of Westminster in the 18th century vis a vis the Isle of Man and the Lord of Man might be viewed as a breach of international trade convention and subversion of the independence of another country.

In our modern times, while we might have sympathy for the poor people of Man, it is unfashionable to have much sympathy for rich people who get done out of their wealth and have to fight in the courts for it. But the reality is that if governments are allowed to steal from rich people then there is little hope for the little people.

The Duke of Atholl's position would have found little sympathy amongst the general British public during the hundred years of strong socialism that only really began to abate recently. That era culminated in the growth of widespread home ownership with an appearance of widespread share ownership through the demutualisation of building societies. More people today might appreciate what happened to him if we compare what was taken from him – albeit on larger scale - with some everyday ideas of the modern world.

He owned an independent island, which he mostly rented out. He didn't interfere with what the people did otherwise. This is similar to owning outright, without mortgage, a few freehold houses, renting all but one out, and not bothering what the occupants do, as long as the tenants keep the terms of their leases. Britain forced him to sell his island, without arbitration, for a sum decreed by Britain. That is like having all your freehold houses compulsorily purchased by a hostile property company who had no rights over you, for a low price set by that company. This new company now sets new high rents for everyone, including yourself, and interferes with what you all do.

What Atholl had left was, in effect, one house to live in. But he found that more and more, Britain was depriving him of old rights. It was like our former homeowner finding he was getting charged for parking a car on the road, then having his old garden built on, then leylandia trees planted and let grow wild in thick rows close to all his windows, then massive buildings erected all round to cut out light, then pylons strutting across his lawn, and then mobile aerials erected on his one remaining roof. And all his own former tenants were blaming him.

The Revestment Act, while depriving the Duke of the Lordship of Man, left him with other rights and privileges which he enjoyed as manorial lord – in other words, as a landowner. The problem was defining which rights were manorial and which regal. Westminster arbitrarily paid Atholl a paltry sum for the value to him of his regal rights on Man, on the basis that these were minimal. It then restricted his manorial rights.

Atholl objected – as any home owner today would object. But who was he, one man with no sympathisers, against the might of Britain? He had no higher authority to appeal to, whereas today he might even go to the United Nations. In our hypothetical rental property case, we would go to the High Court to retrieve our property or get damages. From 1774, the fourth Duke took up a fight abandoned by his parents, and began to attempt proper enforcement of manorial dues – to the great resentment of the Manx. There followed many years of legal wrangling between the Atholls and the British government. Surprisingly, he managed to make enough of a nuisance of himself that he was made Governor of his old island in 1793. The island gave an undertaking that its parliament known as the Keys would become democratic. From 1793, the story of the fourth Duke of Atholl was a fight with the British government on the one hand and the Manx people on the other, to retrieve his hereditary rights. In due course Atholl got an improved offer from Britain to buy him out entirely. It took him till 1826 to get final settlement, and he didn't get all the money for several years after that.

Henry Dundas had become an MP in 1775. The Scottish electoral system was then actively being abused by those with land or money. He made active efforts to achieve reform. This was so contentious that after a few years he dropped the subject. In any event, government energies were focused on the conflict with the American colonies.

In the government of 'Guilford Good' Lord North he was made Lord Advocate of Scotland, a post which he retained until 1783. Henry acted for the black man Joseph Knight, brought as a slave from the West Indies to Scotland by his Perthshire master, gaining the judgement that slavery was unlawful in Scotland. Thus Knight could give his master notice to quit his job. Henry is credited with the Act of 1775 to emancipate serfs in Scotland. Previously, coal miners and salt panners were born bound to those occupations. This appears like a stroke for human liberty. But the convincing argument, embodied in the preamble to the law, is the capitalist one quoted by Adam Smith in 'The Wealth of Nations'. Serfdom had been instituted because coal masters had thought it was the only way to ensure a workforce. But serfs had no competition for their jobs. So masters increasingly found they must improve their working conditions to get productivity. The only way to keep up the supply of labour was through encouraging their fertility. This brought its own costs. The Act of 1775 meant that in Scotland thereafter no-one could become a serf, and provision was made for gradual freeing of existing serfs. Serfdom continued to exist in Scotland until the last serf died in 1844, long after full liberation of slaves throughout all other British lands.

When war began in the American colonies Henry Dundas was adamant that the rebels should be taught their lesson. The first major engagement of this conflict was the Battle of Bunker Hill on June 17th 1775. There regulars finally ousted militiamen from entrenchments overlooking Boston. Six months later, George Washington's Continental Army drove British regulars out of Boston, but the British cleared Canada of opposition. On September 9th 1776 by declaration the rebels renamed the colonies as the United States of America. For a while, Britain held the field. Then George Washington, taking his army across the frozen Delaware River on Christmas night, defeated a group of Hessian mercenaries at Trenton. Soon French support arrived for the rebels. It came in the forms of arms, ammunition, men and money. In October 1777, Britain's General John Burgoyne surrendered to the rebels near Saratoga, New York. More French military support arrived at the end of the winter, mainly in the form of a fleet to harass British interests. Spain declared war on Britain on June 16th 1779, France having promised to help her get hold of Gibraltar and Florida. The Dutch Republic then offered support against Britain. This allowed John Paul Jones a place of refuge when in September 1779 his squadron captured two British vessels.

In March 1780, Russia inaugurated the League of Armed Neutrality, to prevent British ships searching neutral vessels for weapons of war intended for the American rebels. Austria, Prussia, Denmark and Sweden joined this league.

Britain was at that time solidly in control of Georgia, but in the summer of 1780, 6,000 French troops arrived to add their weight to the rebels, while the French fleet blockaded the British force. By the end of 1780 Dundas had privately faced the reality that Britain was going to lose this war. He began privately suggesting that Lord North should resign the government, and the colonies should be given independence. George III was a problem, for that king would not readily give up sovereignty over so large an empire. On 5th September 1781, as the crucial turning point in British war fortunes, the French fleet prevented a British fleet from relieving their land force. Two weeks later at Yorktown, Charles, Lord Cornwallis, surrendered to the besieging French and American army. On 27th February 1782, the British Parliament called a halt to its military opposition to the independence of the American colonies. A year later, on 14th February 1783, the war formally ended. Lord North resigned as Prime Minister, in recognition of the failure of his policy with regard to America. The Peace of Paris, signed on 3rd September 1783, ended the western war between France, Spain and America on the one hand, and on the other a Britain that had been fighting on too many fronts.

Already, slee Dundas, as Burns labelled him, had actively begun looking for a way forward. He sought a new regime with new leaders and new attitudes. He publicly supported the concept of a coalition between North and Henry Fox. This lost him his job as Lord Advocate. Henry Erskine got the post in 1783. When the coalition quickly fell, Dundas put his weight behind the young unknown, the younger William Pitt. At the end of 1783 he was Pitt's main supporter and was duly rewarded when Pitt took power.

There are few better short summaries of the progress of this war from the perspective of its disruption of British politics than Burns's poem known as 'When Guilford Good'. In nine eight-line rollicking stanzas he summarised the key events of the confrontation and the impact on political power within Westminster. So good is this verse chronicle that many a Scots academic writing on the American War of Independence can only with difficulty refrain from quoting from it.

As Burns had matured, he would have been unable to listen without interest to emerging data on the rapid flow of developments, political and economic. He was so concerned about this poem being taken badly by the Powers That Be that he did not publish it in the Kilmarnock edition, and sought the reassurance of Henry Erskine before he included it in the Edinburgh edition. Perhaps Erskine was not against the printing of a poem that included criticism of Henry Dundas.

In a brand new government, headed up by Pitt, Dundas in time became more powerful than he had ever been. He used his influence to cause the restoration in Scotland in 1784 of those estates confiscated in 1752 from Jacobite supporters. He encouraged the formation of the Highland Society that year, led by the Duke of Argyll and with Henry Mackenzie as secretary. Its stated aim was to promote Highland culture and economy. Study of Gaelic again became kosher. Coastal trade was encouraged through enhancing ports by building harbours and roads. Economic analysis drew attention to the opinion that salt taxation discouraged fisheries. This explained why the wealth of herring in Scottish waters was being taken by the Dutch. Thus tax laws were changed.

These changes had given Burns no personal benefit. There seemed no future for him in Scotland. He considered emigration to Jamaica as a slave for as many years as it took to work the cost of his passage, knowing he would be making an irrevocable choice. He wanted one last throw of the dice. So he published his poems. Only weeks before he was scheduled to sail he was passed a letter in praise of his poems from Dr Blacklock of Edinburgh to the Rev. Lawrie of Loudon. This was the sign he had hoped for, for the letter had come through that place where he first reached the Music of the Spheres.

In late 1786 he went to Edinburgh to seek sponsorship of a second edition of his poems. There he gained the support of the city's Establishment in the form of the members of the Caledonian Hunt. These all subscribed, though at very reduced price, to that second expanded edition of poems. This enabled Burns to remain in Scotland.

These people represented all the landed and capital interests of Scotland. Why did such people, to a man, purchase the right to get one or more copies of a poetry book? The poems in the Kilmarnock edition exposed the thoughts of a man who strongly desired equality of opportunity for all men and individual freedom. Such thinking was at odds with a group of people who individually had enormous privileges that they were loath to share. Yet they backed this poet's second edition. Commentators have long praised the magnanimity and open-mindedness of these representatives of the emerging capitalist order. Surely they were a breed apart from today's grasping capitalists. Yet Mammon seldom sides solicitously with Idealism. When the immediate aims of these two great forces coincide, it is almost certainly because the immediate forms proposed by Idealists are the best pragmatic match for those necessary to fill the immediate desires of Mammon. Their mutual interests served, Mammon abandons Idealists to the inevitable fate of those who try to stand firm against the roaring in-rushing tide of greed.

These men of the Caledonian Hunt had recently watched the great disturbances in the Americas. Their trading interests were still disrupted. They expected more bumpy weather ahead. At home, particularly in Scotland, they were aware of emergent labour troubles. Yet they backed a venture that would give Robert Burns the possibility of staying in Scotland and continuing to write poetry rather than emigrating to obscurity in Jamaica.

Some commentators have suggested that these men with their remaining colonial interests feared that if this man was installed amongst their plantations his rising voice of righteous indignation would flail up such a hurricane as would destroy all their endeavours. No plantation owner wanted to go through the trauma observed in the Spanish colonies, where all invested capital in equipment and training was wiped out overnight by insurgency of disgruntled slaves. They had noted the words of Adam Smith who had pointed out that slavery was not a cost effective way to manage labour in comparison with waged labour – but there was no magic overnight formula for replacing slave labour gangs with paid employees. They noted that they could make more profit if they replaced slavery as it then existed with hired hands, but they needed time to achieve such a change. It would also be attractive if, after due preparation, they might receive government subsidy to implement the final change from expensive slave labour to cheap wage labour. Better get others to pay. That was what taxation was for.

Robert Burns posed a threat: capitalist planters knew that should that man get to Jamaica he was out of their immediate sights. It could take time for them to silence him. He could do much damage before they even knew he had rampaged. Best give him the means to stay in Scotland. To stay in Scotland, but not to shout his thoughts.

Perhaps it was for this reason that the Caledonian Hunt, these pillars of the Establishment, to a man signed their names to a covenant that in fact muzzled this radical poet. Though he stayed in Scotland, he was not made free. For the rest of his life he struggled, unable to find enough time to write because of his constant, health-grinding need to earn. Yet a government or private pension, so inexpensive and so easily given, would have enabled his words to shout and his ideas to soar. As with young-dead poet Robert Fergusson, a tenth of what one rich merchant or aristocrat lost at cards would have stowed the pantry for Burns and his family.

They gave pensions, after all, to those younger men, Coleridge and Wordsworth. Both grew old, and both grew to love the Establishment. But pensioned though they were, was it because their imaginations were limited, or was it through frustration of any possibility of fighting against impossible odds that denied freedom of speech, that caused such and other contemporary poets of England, radical when young, to grasp after creativity through turning – as Burns never did – to hallucinatory drugs?

When that apparently vibrant, attractive young Burns arrived in Edinburgh, he was already dying of the malnutrition and degeneration of his galley-slave childhood. The Establishment did not know this. Had they let him go to Jamaica he might have died sooner. That would have saved them the years of constantly watching him and containing his influence. But they did not know, and it is not certain that the climate would have not done him good. Jamaica, when Jamaica is kind, is a beautiful, loving place. He might well have become the National Poet of Jamaica, and re-strung his lyre to the wild notes of the Afro-American. But the Caledonian Hunt sponsored the Edinburgh edition. He remained in Scotland. There, they encouraged him to prettily sing like a caged enslaved linnet.

And he prettily sang, but like no caged linnet.

Burns appears, in seeking sponsorship for his Edinburgh edition amongst the aristocratic and academic elite in Edinburgh, to have kow-towed to the Establishment. Yet Henry Mackenzie noted in his observations on the Edinburgh of his day that this young man from Ayrshire opposed the tyranny of elitist intelligentsia. His self-taught independent mind and his down-to-earth common sense constantly challenged their sophistry.

We could for a lifetime – and many do – study the words left by a person, and still not understand the person who distilled them from his mind, in the hope of leaving something of his insight. For all human words are mere words, however much men might pretend that words are great because in the beginning was the Great Word. Thus, in studying all he left us bound in books, we can at best see only a shadow of his thoughts.

To reach through to more than just that shadow needs more than such analysis. It needs insight into how he related to his world. It needs that human instinctive understanding so often denied as mere fanciful imagination in our mechanistic modern mundanity. Had Burns lived in our day, he no doubt would have had something to say in all the debates of our time whether this be in social engineering, environment experimentation, nuclear physics, or genetic engineering. He undoubtedly would have looked askance at such arrogance of science that claims to sufficient understanding to dare to rush on like unfearing avenging angels to challenge and rearrange the very building blocks of created life. He would have brought the naïve questioning mind of innocence to bear upon the great ethical questions of unfettered science. He would have challenged the right of a numerical majority, however democratic, to dictate its self-interested opinion of right and wrong to the outnumbered quiet voices of justified instinctive concern. He would have spoken out – with dark humour, naturally. Down by Tarbolton mill, in conversation with his scrawny companion, scythe-bearing Death frustrated of his designated role by an arrogant murdering medic, he would have wondered at the book-engineered devastation of our weary planet, its worst yet to come.

To ensure food for his family, he became a civil servant. What time he had free from toil he could hardly call his own for he must take care of every word he wrote or said, or fear to suffer consequences.

> Searching old wives' barrels! Oh, what a day
> That clarty barm should stain my laurels.
>> But what'll ye say?
> Those moving things, ca'd wives and weans
> Wad move the very hearts o' stains.

Burns knew he was chained – not chained as a slave, but chained as Prometheus to the rock, punished by his vital organs daily being eaten by the savage ravens of poverty, bodily degeneration and fear for the future of his family, for daring to fire up his vivid imagination and show others how to follow, for spreading the light of freedom of thought, for showing even to the common man the light that fired the soul.

Chapter X   *Warring Sighs and Groans*

How the French Revolution showed Burns the machinations of politicians and money men, and confirmed his opposition to all forms of arbitrary government.

Scotland suffered hard from the American War of Independence. It virtually eliminated the tobacco and cotton trades. Trade resumed slowly, reinstated by a new wave of entrepreneurs. Self-employed hand loom weavers were hit by other economic down-turns that plagued Scotland during the 18th century. After apparent resumption of normal hand weaving work at the end of the war, in 1787 cotton cloth sales faced a slump. With sales devastated, merchants challenged the piece work rates paid to hand loom weavers.

In 1785, upstream from Glasgow, David Dale founded his mills of New Lanark presaging fundamental change in the way cotton would be processed. Not merely eliminating hand spinners, this was the beginning of the end of hand loom weaving. The power loom was enhanced in Glasgow in 1793, although hand looms continued to be used for another century.

By the summer of 1787, Burns was finding himself subjected to strongly-worded advice to return to his former role of Scottish farmer. Though unhappy with this, he had reviewed his plan of emigrating. Now he found himself watching the unfolding events of the strike of weavers of Glasgow. What he saw, he saw in the light of having heard discussion in Edinburgh of new theories of economics. These treated labour as a mere unit of production.

The slump in cotton cloth prices was due to competition. In part this was caused by a change in taxation in 1779, resulting from Britain wanting more return from its Indian holdings during the American conflict. The government of Lord North removed the import tax on French cambrics. This taxation change had been inspired by ideas presented in the first edition of 'The Wealth of Nations', published in 1776. Smith suggested removal of import dues was the first stage in transforming overall management of the British economy from mercantilist to free market economics. This change precipitated adjustment pain that starved many of Smith's fellow Scots. On feeling the impact of the tax change, hundreds of weavers in the Anderston area of west Glasgow marched in protest. They were joined in the city centre by weavers from all surrounding districts. They hung an effigy of Lord North from a French rope and then exploded it.

Since the end of the American wars, the Westminster government had encouraged cheap cloth imports from India as a way to get Britain more payback for the considerable cost of defending her interests there. In the summer of 1786, the government under William Pitt wanted to generate further profits from the Indian colonies. Importing cheap Indian muslins was expanded. This further threatened weavers and fuelled new protest. That November, the standard wage for a British weaver was cut substantially.

In May 1787 Edmund Burke in Parliament moved for the impeachment of former Governor General Warren Hastings for mismanagement in India. Hastings had been sent there a few years earlier to clean up the affairs of the self-interested and warmongering East India Company. Henry Dundas took over the management of India.

In June 1787 further success importing Indian muslin caused more wage cuts. The cuts in weavers' wages precipitated a mass meeting of journeymen weavers on 30th June 1787 on Glasgow Green. Some weavers accepted a lower piece work rate. Protestors resolved not to work for the new wage rates, but to hold a protest, non-violent even when seizing any locally woven cloth being sold for the new low piece work price. That whole summer, without support, without income, the workers held out.

Such behaviour was illegal. In 'The Wealth of Nations', Smith contrasted the contemporary legality of combinations of capitalists for the sake of fixing prices and wages with the illegality of combinations of workers for the sake of negotiating better wages or conditions. Workers combined, noted Smith, out of desperation; capitalists combined out of mutual self-interest. His observation that this seemed unfair cut no ice with capitalists or government.

Whatever the hardship of workers, businessmen couldn't take a long period without production. The *Scots Magazine* published an account of the final confrontation that took place on 3rd September 1787. Then, a large crowd of weavers assembled to prevent cheap work being produced. The Lord Provost authorised the use of military force. The army was called out. It at first attempted to intimidate the starving protestors. This failed. That evening, full riot broke out. Stones and bricks were thrown by people in the crowd. The army responded with gunfire. Three men died that day, and three others were wounded.

The affair was not yet over. When the rioting continued the next day, so did the shooting. Three of those who died in this confrontation were amongst the first to be laid to rest in the Calton Burying Ground in Blackfauld or Calton just north of Glasgow Green. That burying ground had been purchased by the Master Weavers only in May 1787. The walls were not then completely built round this cemetery that lay to the east of the mediaeval ecclesiastical centre of Glasgow. It is said that six thousand people attended the funerals, their numbers stretching out far beyond the bounds of the cemetery.

Glasgow University that November elected Adam Smith as Rector. That year Jeremy Bentham published 'Defence of Usury'. The trial of Warren Hastings on the charge of corruption began on 13th February 1788.

After the calm of desolate defeat came the roundup of ringleaders, the trials, the punishments, the deportations. In March 1788 John Stewart was accused and later tried in Edinburgh. After he had been imprisoned for eight months it was concluded that he had been an innocent bystander in the affray and was set free. In April 1788 five men were sentenced with exile. In July 1788, it was decided to make an example of the weaver James Granger. This man was sentenced to be whipped through the streets of Edinburgh and exiled for seven years. Scotland was not yet automatically using the new penal colony in Australia founded on 18th January 1788. Its first fleet of prisoners landed at Australia's Botany Bay and soon moved to the site of modern Sydney. Only six years later, Australia would receive a due quota of high profile Scottish political prisoners.

Many weavers, put out of business by economic change, found themselves with no recourse but to enlist in the very regiment that had fired on them and killed their colleagues.

Britain's decision to remove the tax on French imports needs to be considered within the wider political climate of the time. After conceding defeat in America, Britain had continued to make headway against the Dutch in the east, where confrontation with France continued. While the British navy made headway, France got into financial deep water.

Since the 17th century the French government had not collected taxes directly. It had instead accepted sums in lieu from capitalists who then gathered taxes to get payback. This approach is called a tax farm. In its imperialist wars, France had got into the habit of not only taking the annual sum but also borrowing heavily on future taxes. This created a national debt. (Britain had begun doing this after 1688. It was a key aspect of King William's revolutionary approach that was so glorious for capitalists and bankers and ultimately so inglorious for the ordinary British person, every one of whom too soon became a taxpayer.)

The main taxes collected by France's tax farmers were on salt, alcohol, tobacco and various goods entering Paris from elsewhere in France. In 1774, France's newly appointed controller-general of finance, Anne-Robert-Jacques Turgot, ordered a report on the General Farm. Turgot was a follower of the so-called Physiocrats. Comparable to modern monetarists, these believed that economics could be reduced to deterministic mathematical models. Having got his report, Turgot then set up the Caisse d'Escompte, or Discount Bank. This was a private institution for lending money to the Royal Treasury.

His report had been prepared by the chemist Antoine Lavoisier. He is best known for inventing the Periodic Table of the Elements. Lavoisier was also asked to investigate the saltpetre industry, which was a key input to the supply of gunpowder. This investigation was not before time, because France had been obliged to give up the fight in the Seven Years War because of a saltpetre shortage. Lavoisier proposed production process improvements. One result of this was excess production that in due course made supply to the American revolutionaries appear a very attractive proposition.

Turgot did not get finances on an even keel fast enough for his bosses; he was removed from his post when French finances were stretched in 1776. The Swiss banker Jacques Necker succeeded Turgot. Necker began supplying America with ammunition, getting, for each delivery, another big i-o-u from the revolutionaries. Thus he was actually heavily financing them against Britain. Lavoisier could rightly claim that the United States owed its existence to French gunpowder. Necker borrowed heavily to create the support he was providing. In 1781 Queen Marie Antoinette opposed this policy of raising loans to finance France's support of American rebels. Necker was forced to resign. Her intervention did not change the view that she was ill-omened. She had been born on 2nd November 1755, as a massive earthquake followed by a tidal wave destroyed Lisbon. Her wedding in 1770 had been marked by vicious storms. Its Parisian celebrations occasioned a massive catastrophe when fireworks exploded and in the ensuing panic hundreds were killed and thousands seriously maimed or disfigured.

Economic mismanagement in France had already gone too far. France never got paid for supplying the American rebel forces. The government of the newly independent States proved unable to raise common taxes to begin repaying the massive debts taken on to fight their war of independence. Over the next few years, to raise money, the American Congress agreed to expand United States territory by grabbing the land of the indigenous populations and selling it. France got neither territorial nor economic gain from the American war.

Meanwhile, the default by the newly independent American States of their common sovereign debt compounded France's financial problems. By October 1783, Charles-Alexandre de Chalonne, France's new controller-general of finance, to address the financial crisis, could think of no idea other than raising more loans. The Discount Bank started to lend very heavily to the Treasury.

Austria at this time decided to demand improved access through the waters of the Dutch lowlands to the seas. This by October 1784 caused a diplomatic crisis, which France managed to calm.

The Dutch paid dearly. For three years the Stadtholder, William V of Orange, was ousted by anti-aristocrats. Those were not overcome until Prussia captured Amsterdam for William V in 1787. This threatened the Bank of Amsterdam which sent a destabilising economic ripple through Europe.

In France, increasing anger about the state of national finance put nobles in opposition to King Louis XVI. They voiced this through the Paris Parlement. They demanded that a so-called 'Estates General' be summoned. To silence opposition, on 14th August 1787 the king banished the Paris Parlement to Troyes. When this proved ineffective, he allowed it to return to Paris on 24th September and called the Estates General for the following May.

By now France was suffering from general economic decline, manifest in labourers flocking to towns in hope of work. This aggravated urban food shortages. Large numbers from the countryside had arrived in Paris. Bonds issued by the Discount Bank began to lose credibility. The Treasury began on its own account issuing paper money, called Assignats. This raised general suspicion of the viability of the financial institutions. Trust began to fail, further aggravating economic difficulties. This raised food prices, hitting ordinary people.

The declining economy hit revenues of tax farmers. As food prices in cities rose, relatives sent in private food parcels. Tax farmers decided this was tax evasion. They decided to tighten tax on everything entering Paris. It had in any case got increasingly difficult to tax produce entering Paris. So in 1787 they commissioned architect Claude-Nicolas Ledoux to enclose Paris with a wall with sixty six toll gates. Not just regular imports but all food parcels from the countryside for those who had gone to the city to seek work would be stopped at these gates. If not actually purloined, they would be taxed.

When Burns began to study the theory of taxation in preparation for becoming an officer of the Excise, he would have come to understand this evolution of events in France. In 1787, Burns had thought long and hard about his future. As flash-in-the-pan pop idol, he knew he could expect no patron to give him a role in which he could focus on writing. He feared farming for himself; he knew his own physical weaknesses. He also feared the changes he knew were underway. He could not afford to buy a farm. An improved farm was beyond his means. He had seen what investment was needed, in effort and money, to transform an unimproved farm. He wanted some job that would give him a reliable income. He was already considering applying to become a member of the most despised of all occupations – an Exciseman. Each time he talked of this, he saw the disdain it involuntarily raised on people's faces. But it was a reasonable income, and a steady job. But even Mrs Dunlop was pushing him to go back to the plough.

The horoscope of Burns points to March 1788 as the beginning of a major new phase in his life. This was when Saturn again held the spot in the sky that it had occupied at birth. It is interesting that it was at that time that Burns put into effect his big decision to put his own money behind his instinct. He began the exacting training to enable him to get the necessary examination passes to be considered for a post in the Excise.

At Blair Atholl he had met Graham of Fintry. He no doubt had been there at that time to go over figures with the Duke's man in preparation for the arrival of Henry Dundas and those hard negotiations. Burns was unashamed to lobby Graham of Fintry to be considered for training, and even to be given an Excise post ahead of others already trained. In due course, he lobbied to be promoted ahead of others. In this, he recruited the active support of Mrs Dunlop, having persuaded that good friend that with the best will, farming might not work out. She pulled out all the stops she could to get Burns into the system.

One of the first people whom he told of his decision to enter the Excise was Peggy Chalmers. He thought very highly of her intellectually. He had met her at Harvieston, near Alloa. Back in Edinburgh from his Highland Tour of 1787 he had made a second trip up the Forth. He got caught at Harvieston when the river broke its banks that October. It is said he there asked Peggy Chalmers to marry him. I find this not supported in any reading of his letters to her. He would have known her wedding to Lewis Hay was already planned. He also knew that he was not in her social class. He wrote bluntly to correspondents that he could not support a wife of superior class, for he needed a wife prepared to knuckle down and carry her own economic weight. He wrote to Peggy on 17th February 1788 to tell her he was about to enter on his period of instruction to enable him to be appointed to the Excise. He began his studies around 7th April 1788. This involved expensive personal investment undertaken after "mature deliberation" and considering:

"not at what door of fortune's palace shall we enter in; but what doors does she open to us".

Burns trained under James Findlay at Tarbolton. The dedication required to complete the training satisfactorily put paid to writing any good poetry in this period. The Powers That Be had intended he be trained in Edinburgh, but this was too costly for Burns. Again he had strings pulled to get this changed. As it was, as well as paying for the tuition, he also had to clear all other incidental expenses of the training period of six weeks. At the end of training, the quality of his work was examined. He got the certificate that made him eligible for an appointment. In due course, the Excise provided the necessary income for his immediate family, but the strenuous work seriously restricted energy and time for literary effort.

Meanwhile, he took the farm of Ellisland, on the Nith. This was unimproved. There was not even a house on it. Though the rent was initially low, he was required to build a farmhouse and improve the lands. In his first winter there, his only home was a ruined rubble hovel where he had a choice between freezing in the draughts that wailed through the crevices, and choking in the fumes of a peat fire. Any modern City financier would spend long evenings in his club rather than return to a small pad. Small wonder that Burns rested after physical labour in a convenient howff. There he got warmth and a table on which to place paper and ink. He could try to be creatively productive. Small wonder not much work came out of this period, and small wonder his health deteriorated further. Then in the Spring he was let down badly by his builders. Altogether, the investment was a mistake. At the start of January 1789 he wrote to Dr Moore telling him that he was married and had a farm. From the first he was very much the better. The farm was already proving a wrong move. It needed far more money dug into it than he had been led to believe. He wrote to Graham of Fintry requesting an immediate Excise appointment, telling him he could not keep on the farm without having Excise income to invest in it. He petitioned a post whose work he could do while working the farm.

That spring, *The Star*, London's first daily evening paper, offered Burns a salaried post that would match the earnings of any low-grade Excise post he might get. Burns discovered that a few days before the letter was written, another paper had published four lines attributed to him. The lines criticised the Duchess of Gordon, who had lionised him at Edinburgh, and implied Burns consorted with prostitutes. Burns was doubly incensed, for an insult on his friend the Duchess, and for a libellous slur on himself. The lines were traced back to having originated in *The Star* of 27th March.

The Star had then printed additional lines. The mainstream London papers repeated them. They were said to have been submitted through Dr Theodore Theobald Theophilus Tripe who had got the manuscript a short while earlier from the poet in Mauchline. On 10th April Burns complained directly to the papers. *The London Gazetteer* published a full apology after discovering that it was Henry Dundas who had written the verses and ascribed them to Burns.

Burns thus felt the first sting of being associated with bad press. It made him aware that, though Dundas had instigated this attack on him, such as Dundas would soon react very strongly if personally riled. The previous year had been the anniversary of the Glorious Revolution of 1688. Burns knew his history and the power of the press. Revolutionaries of England in the reign of Charles II had worked a propaganda machine to ensure that the monarchy was chained. They defined Roman Catholics as 'public enemy number one', threatening that a Catholic Stuart succession would cause old Church lands to be returned to the control of Rome. This got a great number of people on side for a Revolution in 1688 – noticeably on the actual anniversary of England's great victory over the Armada in 1588. The Glorious Revolution, despite the Risings that followed it, was itself comparatively bloodless. But once in power, the new regime muzzled the media.

By 1789 the British media had become free again – too free in the eyes of some. Burns had reason to be apprehensive. He had enjoyed being part of the free media. But he knew already that his use of that freedom had brought him powerful enemies. He was constantly under threat of being muzzled. He had not a few times already been criticised for exercising a bit too much freedom of speech, in criticism of government actions and attitudes, and in contrasting the present ruling dynasty with the deposed Stuarts.

Burns declined the newspaper salary, though did allow the newspaper, along with others, to publish work he would submit from time to time.

That year he had domestic matters on his mind too. His oldest son was now the age when he himself had been performing so well on Murdoch's teaching. So the down-to-earth poet ordered up a copy of William Halbert's brand-new 'The Practical Figurer or An Improved System of Arithmetic', published in Paisley. Alongside grand names of Ayrshire schoolmasters, merchants and tradesmen, he gave his address as 'Parnassus'.

On 7th August 1789 Burns was unofficially told that he was soon to be appointed to the First Dumfries Itinerary responsible for Upper Nithsdale. Again Burns studied Smith's 'Wealth of Nations'. This was not simply because it contained the most detailed and best explained account of the history and contemporary state of British taxes, customs and excise duties, but because the work impressed him. Burns began work on 7th September. He took his Oath of Allegiance as an Officer of the Excise on 27th October during the Dumfries Quarter Sessions.

By then in France the riots had started. They began with hunger, but they were aggravated by those actions of the tax farmers to tighten their hold on their income, dwindling in the economic crisis. Inside Paris, economic problems threatened job losses for those lucky enough to have paid jobs. On 27th and 28th April 1789, around 5,000 workers rioted in the Faubourg St-Antoine in Paris. They feared a cut in wages for their work for the printer and wallpaper manufacturer Réveillon, as had happened with the weavers in Glasgow two years previously. Guards killed about 300 workers.

When on 5th May the Estates General – Clergy (representing the Church), Nobles (representing the land), and Burghers (representing the towns and cities) – met again in Versailles, the Burghers insisted, against all precedent, on sitting in the same chamber as the Clergy and Nobles. When this was refused, they declared themselves a National Assembly. Most representatives of Clergy and Nobles decided to join them. King Louis XVI regarded this grouping as unconstitutional. He continued to take steps to address the financial crisis. The National Assembly published its objections to his doing this. Meanwhile, the ring of steel around Paris that the tax farmers were building could only mean one thing: more hardship for the starving mob. A massive increase in taxation, landing on the poorest people, was inevitable. The ring of steel was due to be closed around 14th July 1789.

Lavoisier had established a new gunpowder administration centre in the grounds of the Paris Arsenal. In the Arsenal was stored gunpowder for the Bastille fortress nearby. It had direct communication with the Arsenal. On 12th and 13th July, concerned that the Arsenal would be attacked, the commander of the Bastille ordered his gunpowder to be moved into his fort. On 14th July, seeking arms, the mob stormed the Bastille.

On 15th July the Commune de Paris formed itself. It set up a 'National Guard'. But it couldn't resolve the financial crisis. Nobles began to flee France. On 5th October, the women amongst the starving mob that had gathered in Paris marched on the palace of Versailles, protesting against the price of bread. The Bishop of Autun, Charles-Maurice de Talleyrand-Périgord, responded by offering the National Assembly all Church property to assist in addressing the crisis. This offer was quickly accepted. The sale of Church lands began. The National Assembly outlawed any to take offices offered by Louis XVI. On 12th November, the Assembly divided France into 80 administrative zones and began to try to sort things.

At the end of that year Burns was asked by George Sutherland, who ran the old Dumfries Theatre, to compose a prologue for his wife to say before the performance on the evening of New Year's Day. Burns dutifully sought clearance for his piece, writing to David Staig as the appropriate authority amongst the Dumfries gentlemen. He expected Staig would find no difficulty allowing it to be performed, despite drawing his attention to "a dark stroke of Politics in the piece". His jocular treatment of the important process of due censorship might well in retrospect have been deemed disrespectful of authority of government. He promised that:

> "if the said Poem be found to contain any Treason, or words of treasonable construction, or any Fama clamosa or Scandalum magnatum, against our Sovereign lord the King, or any of his liege Subjects, the said Prologue may not see the light."

On 8th March 1790, the National Assembly granted self-government to all French colonies. On 14th July 1790, King Louis XVI accepted the authority of the National Assembly and the Constitution they had drawn up. This initiated a Constitutional Monarchy.

In July 1790 Burns, now an Exciseman, was transferred to Dumfries Third Division. Once his Excise work was based in the town he took advantage of his landlord's desire to sell Ellisland with less loss than he might have expected of another bad bargain. Much he regretted, though, selling the fine cow that Mrs Dunlop had given him as a house-warming present. Much he regretted the loss of another fine cow from Mrs Dunlop's son. At first he had found the patronage of her family awkward, but she had put him at his ease, and he learned to accept her support in the spirit in which it was intended. There was nothing patronising in her demeanour. She insisted, and he accepted, that she had and he did not. So as she valued him, so she would insist he accept first a generous wedding present, and the other gifts that followed.

Both watched what was happening in France, he from his interest in current affairs, she from having a French son-in-law. France's governance appeared to Burns to have done a fast-track upgrade to the British 1688 model of governance by constitutional monarchy. But not everyone saw it so. Edmund Burke published 'Reflections on the Revolution in France', striking fear into the heart of British moneyed interests. In 1790 Catharine Macaulay responded with 'Observations on the Reflections of the Right Honourable Edmund Burke on the Revolution in France'. This influenced Mary Wollstonecraft to produce her 'Vindication of the Rights of Man'. Intellectual discussion was paralleled by fear amongst the people. Joseph Priestley spoke in favour of the Revolution in France. On 14th July 1791, his home in Birmingham was attacked and destroyed by a mob.

What had offended Burke was not that France had changed her constitution. She had not, at the outset, declared herself a republic. What bothered him was that property rights were challenged. This threatened the wealthy.

Even the question of republicanism might not have offended the privileged, if property rights had been secured. Republics were from classical time an accepted political form. In the mediaeval period, the form was commonplace in Italy. There, increasingly by the post-mediaeval period, leadership of States centred on merchant cities. These became semi-dynastic or oligarchic. But risks to property holdings were known too, and were associated with emerging republics. In 1645 English republican agitator John Lilburne issued 'England's Birthright Justified'. His pamphlet outlined the main ideas of the recently founded Leveller movement which he led. Alongside the formation of a republic with annual parliaments based on manhood suffrage (though excluding servants and day labourers), he advocated electoral and legal reform and religious toleration (except for Roman Catholics). But he also proposed the abolition of established churches, opposition to monopolies, and the provision of free medical care. In 1688 the so-called Glorious Revolution in Britain was trumpeted as having replaced Divine Right of Kings with constitutional monarchy – but it maintained existing property rights for those who accepted the new dynasty.

Such discussion did not centre, as it would now, on one-person-one-vote democracy and individual human rights. Those are more modern concepts. So, to understand the position of Burns in debates on Democracy, we need to start with knowing how he understood the conflicts around him. Burns's continuing contribution based on what he left to us must be seen in the context of thought in his era. His memory was hijacked by the most extreme of radicals. It is time now, in my view, to reconsider where he would have stood in the big issues of our own day – for it is my belief that in his legacy is indeed true value in resolving modern dilemmas.

The Scottish Enlightenment was the time when Reason held sway, we are told. Reason was then keenly concerned with answering a political question: what is the nature of appropriate human government? The human being as an individual was also a concept that was gaining ground. Thus, those considering the nature of government asked deeper questions directly related to human beings as individuals: what is equality, what is freedom, are these desirable, and if so, how should these be manifest in the best human society?

In contrast, the French Revolution was seen by many, in its early days, as the chance for France to catch up with constitutional progress pioneered in Britain. British politics was not then democratic in any modern sense. William Robertson, Principal of Edinburgh University, and leader of the General Assembly, had in 1788 on the anniversary of the Glorious Revolution, preached – presciently – on his hope that France would soon see constitutional change. In his view its millions needed to be delivered from the follies of arbitrary government. Burns in his poetry repeatedly pointed out that the average person in the United Kingdom was then equally subject to the follies of arbitrary government. It was simply a different sort of arbitrary government.

Other letters of Burns indicate that he looked on what was happening in France as a belated replay of what had happened in Britain a century and a half earlier. Burns had written to the *Edinburgh Evening Courant* in November 1788 complaining that a sermon in his parish church did not focus on the principle behind the 1688 Revolution, but denigrated personalities of the former Stuart line. Look to present times, he argued, for the American revolt mirrored that overthrow of tyranny. He saw France as the same again.

The principle behind revolution is simple: the main object is for one party to grab the privileges they perceive enjoyed by another party. Once revolution is achieved, the media has to be muzzled to protect the new regime. Truth, in so far as it survives, goes underground.

Oliver Cromwell had wanted the privileges of the aristocracy. His Civil War showed England that violent revolution was inefficient economically. The French were to discover the same. Thus, England in 1660 decided to revert to its previous format.

After a generation of reflection, England again tried revolution. This time, rather than copying Oliver Cromwell, revolutionaries turned their minds to Thomas Cromwell, who had been far more efficient in the revolution he achieved for Henry VIII. That king wanted the power and privileges that belonged to the Catholic Church. Thomas Cromwell realised that the best way for the king to undermine the Roman Church in England so as to get its lands was to get the people to do it. So he instituted a regime of propaganda against the Church, making out priests were the enemies of the people. This model worked splendidly. The land grab was done with apparently minimum initial economic disruption. The effects of the removal of the benefits to the people of the care, spiritually and materially, by the former Church were not truly evident for several decades. But first Mary and then Elizabeth did have to reinstate such routine things as upkeep of roads, education, health services, and care of the destitute and elderly. But creating an enemy through propaganda definitely got the people to 'do' the revolution.

Too soon affairs in France began to go awry. On 3rd May 1791, the mob prevented King Louis XVI moving from Versailles to St Cloud. At the end of June he tried to flee France but was captured. The Holy Roman Emperor Leopold II then invited others to join him to support Louis XVI against the National Assembly. Thus began a European war against France's new regime. Britain refused to join other European powers against the National Assembly. Seeing French success, on 14th October 1791 the Irish Protestant, Wolfe Tone, founded the Society of United Irishmen, with the aim of promoting Irish reform.

The mob in France demanded the abdication of Louis XVI. Fifty people were killed or wounded in the suppression of the ensuing riot when troops fired on the crowd. The National Assembly dissolved itself on 30th September 1791, giving over the power it had taken to the new Legislative Assembly. It rashly insisted that no-one who had served on the National Assembly could be part of this new government. Those who now took control at the start of October 1791 urged war on the European powers who opposed their existence. They drew up a decree demanding the return of those nobles who had fled France. Louis XVI vetoed its enactment, as he later vetoed another that attacked the clergy.

Burns kept his attention on his work. On 29th December 1791 Alexander Findlater, Burns's boss, wrote his appraisal in fulsome terms, declaring him:

> capable of achieving a more arduous task than any difficulty that the theory or practice of our business can exhibit.

Whether he wished it or not, a magnet drew Burns across the ether into politics. At the start of 1792, former bishop, Talleyrand, visited England. He came as ambassador of the Legislative Assembly that was then protecting King Louis XVI and unhappy that the Austrian Emperor was aggressively planning invasion of France in the name of restoring the status quo ante. Talleyrand was well received by Pitt. Their discussions caused Pitt to make a 'peace in our time' speech a short while later. While in London, Talleyrand took English conversational lessons from that same man Murdoch, Burns's childhood teacher. Perhaps a letter speeded its way to the radical poet with such a piece of gossip.

On 27th February 1792 Burns was responsible for the seizure of the smuggling craft *Rosamond* – a great derring-do exploit of guns blazing and wading shoulder high into the retreating waters of the Solway estuary after crossing quicksands in pursuit of criminals. The pincer movement from the shore attacked fore, aft and broadside as she lay in the channel. Exciseman Burns headed the three attacking groups of Excise backed up by the militia. He led the broadside attack. As Excise officer he must be the first to board the ship. He drew up the full inventory of contents and cargo. In the ensuing sale, he bought the boat's four carronades. He dispatched them to France. This was to assist the moderate Legislative Assembly supported by Pitt.

In France in March 1792 the republican Girondists took power. Talleyrand's aims were frustrated. In July France declared war on Prussia in response to its promise to defend the French royal family. When Prussia invaded France in August, it was driven back by the French army. The mob stormed the Tuileries Palace and imprisoned the royal family. Then war began between France and Austria. France became increasingly radical. The guns sent by Burns, then in transit, were seized at Dover. In mid September, the now radical Legislative Assembly dissolved all religious orders and instituted a Civil State. It then dissolved itself and called a new National Assembly. There, radicals took power. In November they issued a statement offering to help all peoples who wished to overthrow their governments. Within two weeks, such a coup had taken place in Geneva. That same day the National Assembly put Louis XVI on trial.

Britain became increasingly tense as that year progressed. Not least, this was caused by disruption of food prices and supply. Corn Laws had long before been enacted in Britain, initially to prevent export of grain. Rising domestic corn prices caused exports to decline, though the high price of corn caused starvation. When Burns was born, imports had become the norm. That being the case, the Corn Laws were suspended all through the 1760s. After troubles began in the Americas, in 1773 the Corn Laws were reshaped to reflect the new situation. The market outcome was erratic. So in 1777 a new Corn Bill included the provision that the price of oats in Scotland would be raised by one fifth. Oats were the staple grain of Scotland. Such a price increase would have meant cost of living increases across the board. While landowners supported the bill, Glasgow merchants had objected to it, because it would force a rise in wages. In spite of this history of erratic impact, in 1791 Britain intensified its Corn Laws. This encouraged exports but caused hardship in Scotland. On June 4th 1792, the King's birthday, the home in Edinburgh's George Square of the mother of Prime Minister Pitt's right-hand man Henry

Dundas was attacked by the mob and Dundas was burned in effigy. When things soured further, the army were called out and fired on the mob, killing one man and wounding six others. Scotland that autumn experienced riots against enclosures, against turnpikes and against the Corn Laws.

In Scotland a Society of Friends of the People was set up in 1792. Leading radical aristocrats were amongst its several hundred members. Lord Daer, second son of the Fourth Earl of Selkirk, actively led this drive for a democratic voice. This was the same man with whom Burns had dined when he was first invited to the home of Professor Dugald Stewart at Catrine. With the number of such societies rapidly growing, it was decided to hold a convention. Of the 160 delegates who turned up, the most vociferous was the young advocate, Thomas Muir. What the delegates demanded, though, was not general or even manhood suffrage. In vague terms, they demanded improvements in equity and honesty of government. They gave a cool reception to a radical Address sent to the convention by the United Irishmen.

The bigger new Theatre Royal in Dumfries, promoted by Robert Riddell, opened on 29th September 1792. Riddell gave Burns a silver ticket giving free entry to all performances. The leading lady of the theatre company was Louisa Fontenelle. For her benefit night on 26th November Burns had written the prologue 'The Rights of Woman'. Before this was recited, Burns went through due censorship process to have its content and import authorised by a Justice of the Peace. That prologue ended with the words 'Ça ira', the key words of the song of the French revolutionaries. The content of the prologue reflected Mary Wollstonecraft's recently written letter to Talleyrand known as 'Vindication of the Rights of Woman'. She had written this because France had removed all freedoms women had formerly enjoyed. In France women were denied all rights and freedoms. When Claire Lacombe and Pauline Léon led women against the restrictions placed on them, they were imprisoned.

When Burns took three days of leave that Christmas, he returned to work to find that enemies had taken that absence to begin stabbing him in the back. They accused him to his superiors of seditious behaviour. They said a mob in the theatre had shouted for 'Ça ira' to be sung in response to the vigilante Loyal Natives demanding 'God Save the King' and Burns had joined in. Burns wriggled off this hook, but the incident damaged his immediate promotion prospects. By May 1792 the quality of his work had got Burns onto the list of Excise officers eligible for promotion, but he did not live long enough. Otherwise, says wishful thinkers who desire firmer local Burns connection, he might in 1797 have become Supervisor at Dunblane.

France executed Louis XVI on 21st January 1793. Burns saw the executions of the French king and queen as merely a copy of what the English had done in executing Charles I. He did not feel in it any personal threat. France was simply woefully behind the times in her manner of revolution. This was, after all, the Age of Reason. The manner of political change could have been more modern. Mrs Dunlop felt differently. She felt her own children were directly threatened. She later lost her daughter to the French troubles.

When Britain immediately backed the enemies of France, in February 1793 France declared war on Britain. Westminster was only too happy to take up the gauntlet. This was a new opportunity to assert commercial dominance over its ancient rival and for rich merchants to recover from a recession heightened by the French Revolution. On 11th March, Pitt issued Exchequer bills to raise funds for defence and for subsidies to Britain's allies in the pending war. He caused British armies to seize all French colonies in India.

On 15th March, The Traitorous Correspondence Act was passed and Habeas Corpus was suspended to contain any pro-French action within the British Isles. Burns was not alone in considering Britain unjustified in entering the conflict. But when such as Henry Erskine could be censured and demoted for voicing protest, Burns knew he needed to take care. Henry Dundas suggested to the new Lord Advocate that he publish in Scotland a ban on seditious writings. George Washington, starting his second term as President, declared the United States neutral in the European war.

The previous autumn, the highly voluble James Tytler (1747-1805) had been arrested. He was tried in Edinburgh in January 1793. This was the man who made the first balloon flight in Britain in 1784. Burns in a letter to Mrs Dunlop of 13th November 1788 had described him as:

> "an obscure tippling but extraordinary body: a mortal, who though he drudges about Edinburgh as a common Printer, with leaky shoes, a sky-lighted hat, & knee-buckles as unlike as George-by-the-Grace-of-God & Solomon-the-son-David, yet that same unknown drunken Mortal is Author & compiler of three fourths of Elliot's pompous Encyclopedia Britannica."

Burns had little time for him. He later described him to Peter Hill as "that odd being, Balloon Tytler", considering his verses very poor stuff.

At this time, Burns was remitting letters regarding music from Dumfries post office to Alexander Fraser Tytler, Professor of Universal History at Edinburgh University. Burns had in Edinburgh got to know the musicologist, William Tytler of Woodhouselea, Alexander's father. From the old man, Burns had taken down notes about the background to a number of Scottish songs, but he himself had built up a far greater knowledge than William, recently dead, had ever commanded. Few in Dumfries would know that there was absolutely no connection between these Tytlers and James Tytler. It undoubtedly caused a few malicious tongues to wag that there was correspondence going on between Burns and a man who answered to the same name as the notorious revolutionary.

Thomas Muir was on the way to observe Tytler's trial when he was arrested on a charge of sedition. Released on bail pending a hearing in February, he went to France. While there, war broke out. Stranded, he missed the hearing, and thus became de facto a fugitive criminal. He was declared an outlaw. In France he met Wolfe Tone, who was not impressed.

A second convention of Scotland's Friends of the People was called for April 1793. Fewer came, though still in excess of a hundred. The balance of feeling was more extreme. They demanded manhood suffrage and opposed the war. The groups had already been infiltrated with well-paid government spies. These were only too ready to finger the most dangerous ringleaders.

On 13th July 1793 Girondist Charlotte Corday assassinated the Girondist leader Jean-Paul Marat. The image of his death is famous in modern times through the painting by Jacques-Louis David. On 27th July Maximilien François Robespierre became effective leader of the so-called Committee of Public Safety. Muir was by then on his way back to Britain on board an American ship. This dropped him off at Dublin from whence he sailed to Stranraer. There he was recognised and arrested. He was taken to trial in Edinburgh. At this time Burns was in the midst of a summer tour of Galloway with John Syme, Distributor of Stamps for Dumfries and Galloway. They made a second very short tour the following year. Burns got to know Syme because the stamp office was on the ground floor of the building in The Vennel in which Burns had his first apartment in Dumfries.

The journey was for Burns full of bad omen. On a river trip from Kenmure Castle to Airds, former home of the minor poet John Lowe, the boat got stuck in the reeds that still grow thick there. Robert's splendid new top boots were soaked wading through water. On his back he carried a clergyman who had refused to get his feet wet. For this Burns was ridiculed. Following the soaking, Burns suffered nausea and headache. The boots dried so badly that they tore when he tried to put them on the next day. They went on to St Mary's Isle, home of the Earl of Selkirk, father of Lord Daer. Burns said his 'Selkirk Grace' to bless the food at dinner. The Earl took the boots into Dumfries in his carriage, determined that they could be mended.

Not long after, the two men were thoroughly soaked again by the first of the heavy penetrating rains typical in Scotland as August arrives. In this wild storm Burns is reputed to have composed 'Scots Wha Hae', his defiant song in defence of freedom. There are extant a number of his letters with which he enclosed copies of this poem. He identified it to his intimate readers as relating to immediately current events. They would have understood it as allegory of his detestation of the draconian anti-terrorist measures and the forthcoming sedition trials. The song became Scotland's national anthem until modern wimpishness replaced it with the sentimental 'Flower of Scotland'.

Of all songs by Burns, it illustrates most clearly today what he himself repeated often: that music first and foremost inspired his verses. Old music ringing in his head demanded he join words to free it from mere memory, or pages of old books, or even the fingering of practiced instrumentalists, and give it active life force through the power of the human voice. This martial theme was in his head, and the spirit of the ancient music inspired the content. The martial theme carries the meaning, even shorn of words.

This came forcefully home to me one evening on a contentious tourist boat sailing down the Yangste River. When we reached the quay at Qongqing, our tour guide had discovered that four parties were all allocated places on a boat that had room for only three. We were British, American, Japanese and Taiwanese. None would give way. All of us crammed on board, all crowded, all resenting all the others. This was the stuff of international incidents. That night we all had dined. Around the tables sat angry people. Bowls came round. Chinese hosts explained that these were luck cookies. Whoever got a cherry won a prize. No-one played. I took a bowl, and with a knife cut through each cookie. Our guide looked on dismayed. I found a cherry. With a shout I claimed my prize. Then the truth came out. It was not prizes, but forfeits. I was to do a turn!

Our guide gave me a look: I must not lose face.

Boldly I went to the microphone, I took a breath, and loudly intoned the song:

"Scots wha hae wi' Wallace bled,
Scots wham Bruce has often led,
Welcome to yer gory bed,
Or to victory!"

The room was ringing with clapping, cheers, banging feet. As I sang on, they marked the time of the music. They egged on my martial song, for one brief moment hatred gone. Even my British companions understood not a word, but all hearts on that boat understood the music. Its strength made us one, all factions nought, united against some common threat.

Burns and Syme travelled on to Gatehouse, where they possibly saw the captured Thomas Muir being escorted to Edinburgh to stand trial. Muir was tried on 30th August before Lords Braxfield,

Henderland, Swinton, Dunsinnan and Abercromby. He was found guilty of seditious speeches, of circulating 'The Rights of Man' and of having promoted the treasonable Address of the United Irishmen. Lord Braxfield sentenced him to fourteen years' transportation. He handed down the same sentence two weeks later to Rev Thomas Fyshe Palmer of Dundee.

That August, in a letter to music publisher George Thomson, Burns wrote of his having difficulty getting musician Stephen Clarke, who was with him, to concentrate on transcribing music that Burns had taken down from country singers:

"I hold the pen for our Friend, Clarke, who at present is studying the Music of the Spheres at my elbow. The Georgium Sidus he thinks is rather out of tune."

On 16th October, Marie Antoinette was guillotined. On 31st October twenty-one leading Girondists were guillotined and soon others followed. On 10th November took place the first French so-called Feast of Reason, an atheistic event celebrated in the church of St Eustace, Paris. The idea was not strictly French. In a letter to Mrs Dunlop in November 1788, Burns promised to celebrate his established correspondence with her. He would thus

"indulge myself in a festive day of 'The Feast of Reason & the flow of soul'".

A week after France's Feast of Reason, an obscure French soldier, Napoleon Bonaparte, led a group that recaptured the French naval base of Toulon which had been taken by royalists, supported by the British. Many royalists were executed.

France also outlawed Christianity. In Britain, while freedom of political thought was increasingly curtailed, intellectual battle was joined against those radicals who denied the very existence of God. In 1793 William Blake published 'Marriage of Heaven and Hell'. This satire on conventional religion and morality was accompanied with his own illustrations. Immanuel Kant published his 'Religion within the Boundaries of Reason' in which he argued that, although Reason cannot prove the existence of God, this does not mean that God does not exist. He followed this in 1795 with 'On Perpetual Peace'. Samuel Taylor Coleridge and Robert Southey together wrote the verse-drama 'The Fall of Robespierre'. William Paley published 'A View of the Evidences of Christianity', defending religious belief.

The most radical members of the Societies of Friends decided to defy the government with yet a third convention, which met in Edinburgh at the end of 1793, with some United Irishmen present. One of the Irishmen, during his speech, challenged the Lord Advocate to a duel. This was deemed sufficient cause to send officers to disband the convention and arrest three leaders, William Skirving, Maurice Margarot and Joseph Gerrald. In 1794 they were also brought before Lord Braxfield. They were each also handed down sentences of transportation for fourteen years. (William Creech, who had served on the jury that convicted Deacon Brodie in 1788, was with Peter Hill amongst the members of the jury.)

With war in train, soldiers were needed. To bring a potentially dangerous religious minority on side, and reduce the attractiveness to its members of joining radical groups, in Scotland Roman Catholics were given some freedom of worship in 1793.

Throughout the life of Burns, ever since the end of the Seven Years War there had been increasing emigration to America of Scots particularly from the Highlands where there was great disenchantment with post-Culloden conditions. The beginning of hostilities in America in 1776 meant that such emigrants were lost as potential recruits to the British army and could swell foreign forces. Emigration was legally restricted. The lowlands, already thick with Highlanders as seasonal workers, were inundated with vastly increased numbers looking for employment. The ranks of the underclass of the towns swelled. Men amongst such might be persuaded to become soldiers. They would of course need training. Since 1747 Highland Scots were not permitted to bear arms. The government had persisted in the 1770s in refusing to allow the forming of militia in any part of Scotland.

Many Highlanders were also Roman Catholic who would on signing up as soldiers have had to renounce their faith in taking the oath to the king. In Canada in 1774 Catholics had been granted toleration to maintain the loyalty of the French Canadians. Ireland had had some relief in 1778. There were discussions ongoing in England about removing constraints on Catholics. Thus in the parliamentary session of 1778-9 the Lord Advocate introduced a Bill for the relief of Scots Roman Catholics, his agenda being to encourage Highlanders to sign up for the army. In doing so he lit a tinder cask which exploded violently.

In the gift of Henry Dundas, when he had been Lord Advocate, had been a number of church benefices. He had used these to bolster his party's support within the Scottish church. Dundas realised that the reaction against his Catholic Relief Bill threatened to undo this work, as senior members of his own packed General Assembly of the Church of Scotland preached against the Bill. Pamphlets were circulated. Local Synods of the Presbyterian Church opposed any freedom to a religion which dare claim to be the one true holy apostolic church. That church, they claimed, was the common enemy of the liberties of mankind and of the British constitution. There were riots in Glasgow. Premises of Catholics and sympathisers were burned and looted. On January 30th 1779 a large crowd gathered in front of the home in Edinburgh of Bishop George Hay, Vicar Apostolic. Over the next few days they broke all the windows with showers of stones. On 2nd February, as Hay returned home from discussions in London, he arrived in time to see the building set alight. He was lucky to escape with his life. It was now Edinburgh's turn for a general burning and looting. The magistrates did nothing to stop it, despite the personal exhortations of Henry Dundas. The next year, when the Gordon Riots broke out in London, people pointed the finger at him for unsettling the populace. Dundas withdrew his Bill. From that time he was a political pragmatist, never again fully trusting even those whom he himself had promoted.

There was an old law in Scotland that permitted the forming of fencible regiments which could be raised only for the duration of a war. These were not allowed to fight outside Scotland. Their membership could not be drawn on to swell the regular army. When American vessels began attacking Scottish ports in 1778, locals had reacted by forming themselves into such fencible regiments. This was a precedent for the widespread formation of fencible regiments when after 1793 a real fear emerged that France would invade Britain. Such regiments had been the model for the way in which that drinking club, the Crochallan Fencibles, organised itself.

In 1794 the French were trouncing their enemies, but they lost political sympathy when they announced their no quarter policy and guillotined a group of British cavalry prisoners. On 5th April 1794, as conditions in France worsened, the Jacobin leaders Georges Danton and Camille Desmoulins were executed. Antoine Lavoisier was one of those who lost his life in the carnage, guillotined on 8th May 1794. On June 2nd, the extreme Jacobins overthrew the last of the Girondists. Then the Reign of Terror began. From June onwards, there were mass executions. On 28th July, Robespierre and Louis St-Just became victims of their own terror.

Taken up with a more dangerous war centred on France, Britain relinquished to the United States its remaining authority over the Old Northwest. The United States army was already in Ohio brutally driving out the indigenous peoples to make way for colonial expansion. France began making headway in its war on the European mainland. By December both Prussia and Spain had separately opened peace negotiations with the revolutionary government. Paper money had been issued by the revolutionary government when it first came to power. In December 1794 more of their Assignats were issued, further devaluing French money. The French ended the year by capturing the Dutch fleet frozen in at Texel, after the Grand Old Duke of York had been driven out of Flanders.

In Scotland that year, one man was executed. Robert Watt was a government spy who submitted such a high expenses claim that the government sacked him. He joined the radicals and began gathering weapons to arm an uprising. He was accidentally caught. He was hanged in September 1794. The Lord Advocate then suspended the Act against Wrongous Imprisonment, which is the Scots equivalent of Habeas Corpus.

At the start of 1795, Austria, Prussia and Spain sued for peace with France. Then Britain stood alone. Pitt gave Winston Churchill his cue with a call to arms of all able-bodied British men. It became de rigueur to be seen to be one of the Volunteers. Just in case the various severe punishments for sedition had indeed, as some claimed, been unlawful, in 1795 were enacted the Treason and Sedition Bills. Dean of the Faculty of Advocates Henry Erskine objected. He was removed from that position which the Lord Advocate himself took over. Spies were everywhere. Everyone came to distrust even his closest friends. There were no more radical incidents of any note in Scotland for a generation.

Burns was in the forefront in being a founder member on 31st January 1795 of the 18th century local Home Guard, the Dumfries Volunteers. Burns was diligent in his attendance and also supplied the regimental song that was taken up by other Volunteer units across Scotland. The patriotic song, published in the *Edinburgh Evening Courant* on 4th May 1795, ended with a sentiment that by some was considered too democratic:

> The wretch that would a *Tyrant* own,
> And the wretch, his true-sworn brother,
> Who would set the Mob above the *Throne*,
> May they be damn'd together!
> Who will not sing God Save The KING
> Shall hang as high's the steeple:
> But while we sing God Save The KING,
> We'll ne'er forget THE PEOPLE!

It was at this time that his letter to Mrs Dunlop spoke too much in favour of the principles being fought for in France. Mrs Dunlop could take no more of it. He wrote thereafter to her repeatedly, and got no answer. On January 31st 1796 he told her that he had been unable to buy bread for his family, for there was none to be found in Dumfries. But no answer came.

In Dumfries, despite ostentatious loyalty, Burns remained taunted as a radical by the disruptive local Loyal Natives. Despite his high profile and active role in the Volunteers, people avoided socialising with him. But perhaps they had a point. A recent new acquaintance for Burns was Dr William Maxwell (1760-1834) of Kirkconnel near New Abbey. His father had fought for Bonnie Prince Charlie. He himself was a medic, graduate of Edinburgh. He had been so much in support of the French Revolution that he had been one of the National Guard present at the execution of Louis XVI. In September 1792, well before war was declared, he had openly advertised for funds to support the French. In the House of Commons on 10th September, waving a dagger above his head, Edmund Burke had falsely announced that Maxwell had in Birmingham ordered two or three thousand daggers for the French to kill honest men. Extolling this man's virtues to Mrs Dunlop did nothing to bring them back together.

In 1788 Birmingham gunsmith David Blair had presented Burns with a pair of pistols. When Dr Maxwell gave Burns the dirk that had belonged to Lord Balmerino, who had been executed for his part in the '45 Rising, Burns gave the dirk to Blair. Just before his death he presented Maxwell with the pistols.

Burns's letter to Blair of 23rd January 1789, addressed to Mr David Blair, Gun maker, St Paul's Square, Birmingham, thanking him for the pistols, was put up for auction on 7th May 2008 as part of the sale of certain contents of Fasque House, a home of the Gladstone family. When he wrote the letter Burns had had the pistols for two months. He had been at a loss how to give proper thanks. Finally he sent a copy of his recent poem written in meditation at Robert Riddell's Hermitage at Friar's Carse. He remarked that the tools, being so beautifully made and finished, did honour to their maker – and thus did

"more than half mankind".

They were too good to sully with use, continued Burns, but he anticipated often bringing them out to admire them. He added that he very much hoped he would meet Blair again, though it seems he never did.

On 1st April 1795 a mob invaded the National Convention in Paris, demanding bread. Riots spread through France. This led, by end May, to further purges. On July 14th 1795, in a curious historic irony, the royalist rallying song 'La Marseillaise' was adopted as the French national anthem. On 22nd August France tried yet another new form of government, giving power to the five members of its new Directory. The French army meanwhile got on with fighting and advancing into surrounding lands. On 1st October 1795, she formally annexed modern Belgium, then the Austrian Netherlands. On 5th October, Napoleon Bonaparte, now a general, overcame royalist insurgents who were marching against the National Convention. He thus earned the status of France's national saviour. His military successes in early 1796 were therefore newsworthy. In November 1795, an attempt was made to assassinate George III of Great Britain, prompting the passing of Acts against Treasonable Practices and Seditious Meetings. The latter forbad meetings of more than fifty persons without prior notice to a magistrate. In March 1796 Britain began peace overtures with France.

Modern left-wing writers, viewing the poet's life from the comfort of their armchairs, find it unacceptable that his recognised corpus of self-acknowledged work should contain so little from this last period that can truly be considered critical of the war. They ask why he did not 'stand up and be counted'.

We have already seen that he took seriously family commitments – what others might call his hostages to fortune. Apart from Lizzie Paton's child, he had a full complement from his fertile Jean plus, in Jean's care, his child by Anna Park. Jean bore a child on 21st November 1792 and another on 2nd August 1794. He made Jean pregnant again. Why should he put his head literally in a noose by literary output when men less vulnerable than he realised that this was no time for false courage? But his socialist apologists are not satisfied with this. They must seek out works to set against his name. Thus there has been a search in radical newspapers, such as *The Star*, for Burnsesque verse which might be rammed into the canon of his collected works. Each proposed addition rekindles the fire of dispute.

I search instead within the writings to which he put his name and find that many of his songs, verses and letters were alive with protest, if carefully worded. It is in this period that he wrote those songs that are most vibrant with demand for human rights.

He seldom put his name to the songs he published in those last few years of life. He intended compiling them in one book, but died too soon. Through those songs he managed more than once to bypass the spy network that the Dundas regime engaged in Scotland.

In my view it is irrelevant whether or not particular anti-establishment verses of this period were written by Burns. The issue is whether his spirit had reached out into the ether and inspired those words to be written. It is not the labourer who creates a cathedral. He merely builds. It is the mind who designed and commanded the edifice who is its author. An idea once spoken ripples into the waves that permeate the universe of human thought. The powerful idea reverberates and grows in volume and strength until it sings its message through the minds of all mankind. Thus is the work of Robert Burns in advancing the Rights of Man in his later years: the seeds of this thought were sown in his early writings; it needed only disciples then to pick up that tune. He himself tuned a different key – freedom of mind, and love not war.

> I murder hate by field or flood,
>> Tho' glory's name may screen us:
> In wars at hame I'll spend my blood –
>> Life-giving wars of Venus.
> The deities that I adore
>> Are social Peace and Plenty;
> I'm better pleas'd to make one more,
>> Than be the death of twenty.

If XI is one symbol within his Masonic mark, it was well chosen, for Eleven is the number of transcendence over earthly conflict to the higher realm of spirituality. Burns may have used such poetic freedom in designing his mark.

Robert Burns was born during a war. He died as Britain sought peace after the first major engagements with France in a war that historians consider only to have ended with Waterloo in 1815. At the end of his life Burns was labelled a Jacobin – an extreme agitator for those elusive things, liberty, equality and fraternity. These words are so debauched in their meaning in the way they were promoted, particularly in the suppression of women's rights, in the century after 1789.

This is to some degree unfair. When Currie was compiling his four volume edition of the Works of Robert Burns he focussed on fairly antiseptic poetry, and excluded and destroyed political writings in poetry and prose alike. Currie was working in a time of highest security alert: in Ireland there was a major uprising in the name of Home Rule in 1798. In south Wales at Fishguard, the French actually landed in invasion – the last recognised hostile incursion onto British soil of an enemy army. Currie was aware that he ran a personal risk if he published Burns's more 'subversive' writings.

The aim of Currie and those who had persuaded him to take up this potentially dangerous task of editing the Burns papers was simple. It was to provide the maximum future income stream for the destitute widow and orphans of the poet. Robert Burns would no doubt have wished him strength to his hand. The downside of this approach is that a veil of mystery was laid over a man who in his lifetime stunned the most senior university professors with the strength and breadth of his intellect. Contemporaries were insistent that his poetry was a very bland shadow of his mind. Academics sought his company to get his input to their thinking – and this was a peasant, virtually self-educated.

James Currie edited the papers he found in the home of the poet and papers sent to him from many interested parties. What was deemed likely to be taken as truly offensive in such papers were political writings. The picture Currie painted was empty of depth. Forgetting the climate of those times, prudish Victorians concluded that the offensive stuff that had been suppressed must surely be pornography. So Burns gained a reputation as a sexual libertine. This is almost certainly unjustified. No woman made love with Robert Burns without wishing to. Many a woman wished to, but was prevented by his constraint or the mores of the society in which they lived.

With his aim being to raise money for the poet's family, Currie was sensitive to the need to present this 'ploughman poet' in the best possible literary light, and protect him from the ridicule of any who chose to pretend intellectual superiority. Currie was not of a kind with the modern editor – whether sensationalist or academic – who desires to 'uncover the truth'. He had no wish to rake out to the eye of the gawking public all the cinders of the burning creative process. He had no agenda to prove that the purported great person was only human after all, burning mere dross or even dung to fire the creative furnace.

He knew as Burns did that every learner must go through a learning phase. In that learning phase it is inevitable that even the best of us produce stuff that we would rather not remember. Only the most warped writer wants to parade stuff that would be better consigned to the shredder or even the incinerator. It is perhaps because in our modern day there is so little real understanding of creativity that academics pay attention to the detritus of the creative process to try, as from its excreta, to determine its food. But it is also perhaps human nature that the general audience so often prefers to exploit the findings of the dung heap to pull the idol of genius from its pedestal and dash it in pieces in the gutter to prove its frailty is merely human too, or even detestably subhuman.

Thus the scrabbling hacks of the 19th century did find lots of juicy things to say about Robert Burns. The academic establishment, aware that 'Burns studies' make a good basis for comfortable tenured posts, in the 20th century elevated those exposures to the stuff of biography. So this poor man, poor in material wealth and poor in true friends, has been presented to the world as a spineless drunkard, a sexual libertine, and a pornographic writer.

So be it, perhaps his soul says, as long as his children benefited.

Rather that than that they be reduced to the squalor, struggle and indignity of his life.

It is said that in the last minutes of his life he voiced his anger at the tailor who for a paltry outstanding bill had in the previous days terrorised him and his family with threats of the debtor's prison. That tailor who had made his Volunteer's uniform sent a lawyer's letter demanding £7 – a debt paltry in comparison to what any tailor would allow a normal gentleman client to let lie over as a mere trifle.

But as his soul at last was released from the chains of a shattered body like a quiet wind that moves through the woods and gently rustles the leaves of the trees in passing, his thoughts turned too on how his works would be viewed by the Great Judge. The will o' the wisp fairy lights had led him astray and enchanted him with the beauty of the finely turned phrase and enthralled him in the magic of the crafted verse gem set in the gold of music. So he had broken loose from the chains of his predestined role of insignificant mindless poor plough hand. He had been led astray from his born place of submissive brow-beaten slave to a domineering father, tyrannical religion and humiliating class system. But Coila had reassured him:

> The light that led astray
> Was light from heaven.

He had fashioned fire darts from the brilliance of that light and fired them willy-nilly at hypocritical clergy, and at kings, lords and ministers of government, daring to advise them on how better to run their state. He had objected and been cast down when Britain began fighting a cold new war against a Terror that flew the flag of Liberty. But in that final moment of heightened awareness, he would have seen another terrible darkening front of battle lour. He had challenged the greatest academic minds in their insistence that progress could be achieved only by ensuring labourers were production units of input to a New World Order. Chains of slavery might have been cast aside by men of France demanding dignity, but physical chains were nothing to chains to clamp minds already being forged in the repetitive monotony of sweating industrial furnaces. The warring sighs and groans of even the best of poets perhaps might not prevail against them.

Chapter XI   *The Dignity of Man*

How Burns realised the Industrial Revolution would undo Mankind's partnership with Earth and threaten global ecology – and the antidote he developed.

We do not know when Coila first showed herself to her poet. Perhaps it was in that terrible winter of 83/4 as his father lay dying. She announced to him his aim: preserve the Dignity of Man! In the Kilmarnock edition he published that mystical experience of the visitation of Coila. But even when he wrote his autobiographical letter to Dr Moore he still felt he had no clear aim in life. Still by mid 1787, the import of Coila's command had not yet crystallised in his mind. Only then, after his exposure to thought-leaders in Edinburgh, and his disgust with their patronising attitude to their intellectual equal, himself, was he beginning to understand that he *must* fulfil it. He did not know *how* to fulfil it.

Burns died young. He still gets labelled as that genius who failed to achieve his potential because he whored and drank himself to death. But how many could fulfil potential to preserve the Dignity of Man?

The truth of his life makes it clear how difficult was this task. But he did not balk it. It took until the 20th century for medical science to vindicate his cries for help against his invisible hypochondria. The illnesses that constantly beset him, and increasingly grew worse in his last decade, were the product of malnutrition, exposure and excessive labour from the days of infancy. From late 1787 onwards he also suffered from long-term knee damage in an incident caused by a thoughtless uncaring coachman.

As a child labourer on his father's farm, Burns worked far harder, was more deprived, and had far fewer legal rights than the meanest black slave in the colonial plantations. For this reason he so strongly favoured improving human rights. He was no mere Abolitionist. That smacked too much of positive discrimination of one readily identified sector. It merely pushed other persons to the bottom of the heap of those exploited. Abolitionism did not tackle the issue of man's inhumanity to man. It sidetracked it.

But he expected no handouts. The key human right he demanded was the right not to be subjected to another man's disdain for asking work from him. He demanded freedom from being despised for having to beg gracious permission to make honest effort to earn the means to support himself. He did not demand 'the right to work' as many commentators say; he demanded to be respected for wishing to work.

> See yonder poor, o'erlabour'd wight,
> So abject, mean, and vile,
> Who begs a brother of the earth
> To give him leave to toil;
> And see his lordly *fellow-worm*
> The poor petition spurn.

He developed this ideal through his own bitter experience of addressing change in the face of economic disruption in an era of rapidly developing technology. He sympathised with workers made redundant but was no Luddite. He was keenly interested in technological progress. This could be of

253

great benefit, if well directed. As an adult, he was constantly showing his interest in how things were changing around him. He knew from his personal experience the impact on individuals of economic disruption. In youth he had been personally deeply scarred by fall-out of the Ayr Bank failure. In his youth there were food riots. All change causes hardship somewhere. Specific causes of change may be different, but the typical outcome in each badly affected community is comparably devastating – general economic dislocation and hardship. This is because those in the most directly affected activities normally lack alternative skills or education for other jobs, or are simply in the wrong place for new work. They face real difficulty finding ways of replacing livelihood. Burns was fully aware of the atmosphere of rioting when he was in Glasgow.

All developments that precipitated such disturbances did not go unnoticed by Robert Burns. All this puts into different perspective Burns's response to the events of the era he lived in. He faced the facts, and evaded its worst devastation through using his imagination.

With his invisible pain tearing at his chest, did those around him when a child see devil's work in those raving fevers of near-death that he suffered? At this time it was still commonly thought that mental dismay was a form of demonic possession. There would have been eyebrows raised in wonder when in 1778 Austrian Franz Mesmer first practiced 'mesmerism' in Paris. He was thought to be using magic fluids in his hypnotism. It was not until 1792 that chains were first removed from mental patients, when Philippe Pinel began his revolutionary treatment in Paris. In 1817 James Braid, the Scottish surgeon, successfully used hypnosis in improving the condition of mental sufferers. This also demonstrated that hypnosis was a physiological state.

So Burns needed to take care in whose company he exercised imagination. But those with access to such publications as the *Scots Magazine* could in imagination escape the hardships of Scottish economic reality by reading of contemporary journeys of global exploration. They might have been dismayed at the death on 13th February 1779 of Captain James Cook in Hawaii. Later that year, German astronomer Heinrich Olbers developed a method to calculate the orbits of comets, while Samuel Crompton invented the spinning mule. This combined a spinning jenny and a water frame spinning machine, making possible large scale thread production.

There was widespread discussion in 1778 when Henry Dundas brought in the Catholic Relief Bill. In early June 1780 Lord George Gordon led a mob to Parliament to petition against it. Rioting resulted. There were then about 70,000 Roman Catholics in England. Scottish labourers discussed such things, as Luath in 'The Twa Dogs' described:

> An' whyles twalpennie worth o' *nappy*
> Can mak the bodies unco happy:
> They lay aside their private cares,
> To mind the Kirk an' State affairs;
> They'll talk o' *patronage* an' *priests*,
> Wi' kindling fury i' their breasts,
> Or tell what new taxation's comin,
> An ferlie at the folk in LON'ON.

Thus it would have amused village howffs' gossips as much as conversationalists in grand salons when in 1778 Joseph Bramah began manufacturing and selling his improved valve-and-syphon flushing toilets. Much more central to the 19th century industrial revolution was his invention in 1795 of a hydraulic press. This was capable of delivering a force of thousands of metric tons. In 1781 James Watt worked out how to translate the up-and-down motion of the piston of steam engines into circular motion able to turn a shaft. The following year he developed the double-acting engine that took power from both the up and the down stroke. Meanwhile, Jethro Tull improved his seed-planting machine by adding gears. In 1783 the Marquis Jouffroy d'Abbans sailed a pioneering paddle-wheel steamboat *Pyroscaphe* on the River Sâone near Lyons. That 21st November in Paris Joseph and Etienne Montgolfier, Jean-François Pilâtre de Rozier and the Marquis d'Arlandes made the first human flight, using a hot-air balloon. This brought in a brand new fashion in hair-styles that gave occasion to Burns's poem 'To a Louse'. It was a time of passing too, for on 30th March 1783 William Hunter died in London. On 18th September Leonard Euler died. On 28th October Jean d'Alembert died. On 13th December 1784 Samuel Johnson died in London. The scourge of Ossian returned to dust.

Little attention is paid to the fact that Burns was actively involved as participant in economic change, often unsuccessfully, but determinedly facing reality. Burns was never afraid to try new ways. His life embodied practical experience of what today is called change management at the micro and macro level. In this respect alone, a quarter of a millennium after his birth, Robert Burns is perhaps more relevant now than ever in the past. Lochlie gave inadequate agricultural output. Realising his father's new farm was a water-logged disaster, he and his brother Gilbert sub-rented a parcel of the land and worked by moonlight planting and growing flax. This damp and back-breaking work is not unlike the processes required to grow rice in paddy fields. In July 1780 Burns planted three acres. Finding that flax growing was not of itself sufficiently profitable, he then in 1781 set out to learn flax dressing, which had effects on his lungs akin to the industrial damage normal to long hours of work within any dust-laden environment.

The Commissioners and Trustees of Fisheries, Manufactures and Improvements in Scotland in 1783 awarded £3 – about half a year's wages for a farm labourer – to Robert Burns of Lochlie for linseed for sowing. With most such awards going to Dunbartonshire and Lanarkshire, Burns was unusual being one of those growing flax successfully in Ayrshire. But his attempt to adapt to changing circumstances did not lift him out of poverty. It instead exposed him to greater health risks.

He was wilfully financially ripped off severely more than once. A Dumfries acquaintance persuaded him to go guarantor for £20 and then laughed in his face when Burns had to pay up. Creech screwed his publication commission to the minimum and even then would not pay. Papers and publishers elsewhere reprinted his poems without rewarding him.

Burns was entrepreneurial in that he put his own money and time behind his own attempts to improve his family's financial position. Biographers do not consider him an entrepreneur because he never had that great luck to become a millionaire. Too often the luck that creates a millionaire is of a type Burns would not accept. It is the luck that your contractor seriously undercharges you. Most shrug if their contractor's quoted price proves less than his actual cost; it is *his* loss. Those of us denied salary who have been forced to work on contract know how real such loss is. He who takes excess value from contract work gets windfall profit. Some entrepreneurs actively seek and make profit from replaceable people who undercharge. Burns would not take such 'luck'.

When he undertook to improve Ellisland, this required a long drain be dug in partnership with David Newal of Bushy Bank. Drain cutting proved harder than expected. Burns acted overseer and noted that the men worked hard long hours. His quick mind could do the arithmetic. It was clear to him that the price they had agreed would not pay them a living daily wage, let alone reward their backbreaking effort. In November 1789 he wrote to Newal putting the figures on paper. He proposed they pay the men more. The men had not asked for this. They expected the asked-for 17d or 1/5d per rood amounting for the whole drain to £6.0.5. Burns got Newal to compromise and with him pay 20d or 1/8d per rood.

> "Even at that, they have not the wages they ought to have had, and I cannot for the soul of me see a poor devil a loser at my hand."

When this work was underway, Burns was already having a general falling out with his Ellisland landlord, Patrick Miller. The poet's refusal to take his side in party politics miffed that Edinburgh banker, who had thought Burns was his man. Had he not, after all, started his relationship with Burns with an anonymous gift of £10 on the poet's arrival in Edinburgh? This made Burns all the more amazed that he had one stroke of luck – just when he desperately needed out of Ellisland, Miller got a good offer for the farm and desired Burns to quit. So Burns was able to break his lease on better terms than he expected.

Luck was not usually on the side of this young man who tried against the odds to improve financial results on each farm. 1781, 2 and 3 were years of exceptionally long and hard frosts, and 84 and 5 were also unusually frosty. In 1783 snow still lay in April. There was heavy continuous rain in May and June. That was even before the Loki eruption. We have seen that August was as cold as February. A hurricane struck central Scotland on 24th August, devastating standing crops, such as they were. Hard frosts started that October.

Fifth Earl of Loudoun, James Mure-Campbell, was ultimate feu superior at Mossgeil. He in 1782 succeeded the fourth earl, his cousin, who had been a noted improver. The fifth earl's wife had died in childbirth in 1780. A soldier by trade, in April 1786, finding himself not up to the task of improving the performance of his lands, he shot himself. If such was the experience of the great, what hope for the poor widow's son?

If he did not think Burns had a head for business, Gavin Hamilton would not have asked him, on his arrival in Edinburgh in 1786, to attend to note outcomes at the Loudoun estate auction on 5th December. Burns got to the auction, though in his first week in Edinburgh he got a tummy bug and had a continuous headache. I can sympathise with him: once, walking through a thriving town in an underdeveloped country I turned a corner directly into the fumes of the town's open sewer. My instinct was to retch. I got away quickly to cleaner air. Such was hardly possible in the tenement closes of gardy-loo Edinburgh.

Even after the success of his poems Burns was not sure where he should seek his future. Around 11th June 1787 at Mauchline he wrote that he was unsettled in his mind, still considering whether he might yet go to Jamaica, and concerned that he fritter away the benefit of the success of his book. It was in this frame of mind that he made his journey to the West Highlands about which so little is known.

Of one incident we do have the story. He wrote to James Smith on 30th June 1787 announcing he would soon call on him at Linlithgow. He told Smith of dancing all night in the home of a

Highland gentleman. This is one of many times when Burns admitted how natural awe, ancient graves, mounds and stone circles drew him to themselves as cause for pagan prayer. Next morning Burns as priest led prayers to the Sun:

"We went out to pay our devotions to the glorious lamp of day peering over the towering top of Ben Lomond. We all kneeled; our worthy landlord's son held the bowl; each man a full glass in his hand."

This spontaneous prayer on the rising of the solstice Sun is unlikely to have been mere poetic-inspired whim. That Icelandic eruption of 1783 had ever since in Scotland caused overcast skies and foul weather that had thrust famine on the populace. Farmer Burns blessed the Sun, not just Poet Burns. This was the first time in years that Scotland could celebrate the summer solstice under a clear sky. This marked the end of the famine. Emotion ran high. When the Sun was seen rising over Ben Lomond, it provoked prayers of thanksgiving.

Ancient instinct of pagani, people of the soil, praised the Light.

The claim is made that this prayer service was conducted in the grounds of the present Cameron House Hotel. When I visited this Victorian Gothic hotel at midsummer 2008 I was fortunate to arrive during extensive renovations of the basement. This enabled the manager to show me that, behind dust sheets and rubble, was stonework from a much older building. While the 18th century laird's castle was further up the hill to the west, there had indeed in earlier times been a fortified house on the shore of the loch.

Out in the grounds I looked for Ben Lomond looming above the loch. I found the mountain in the north. Burns implied he watched the Sun rising over Ben Lomond. At Cameron House the Sun cannot rise over Ben Lomond even around the summer solstice, although sunrise is then at its most northerly. This Sun praise surely took place further up the loch. I suggest near the pass from Loch Long, beyond Inverbeg.

Next day Burns ran a mad horse race along the side of Loch Lomond against a Highlandman riding bareback. He overtook. The Highlandman zigzagged towards him but his horse tripped and threw him into a hedge. Burns and his horse toppled over them both. He admitted a week later to John Richmond that his cuts and bruises would keep him off horseback for a month. This forced on him that opportunity to write to Dr Moore.

Room for speculation on this trip gave so much scope for mythmaking about his relationship with Highland Mary. Had he indeed married her by ancient pagan rite, at the same time that he was already legally bound to Jean Armour?

Less speculative are developments he would have witnessed. Innovation fascinated the poet. He missed few chances to get to know about innovations, though it was coincidence that he reached Edinburgh on the evening of 28th November 1786 when the town was celebrating the arrival of the first of John Palmer's mailcoaches from London. In 1785, Commissioners of Northern Lighthouses were appointed for the first time. He knew fishing was being encouraged. Over the next ten years the number of barrels of herring landed in Scottish ports increased fifteen-fold. On west and east coasts, Burns would have noted the beginnings of this expansion of fisheries.

In 1784 William Herschel believed he discovered clouds on Mars. In 1785 he proposed that the Galaxy is made up of individual stars rather than being a luminous fluid. That January 7th Jean

Blanchard and American John Jeffries crossed the English Channel in a balloon. On 15ᵗʰ June de Rozier and P A Romain were both killed trying to copy the attempt. In the Netherlands a radical political manifesto declared that 'the sovereign is the vote of the people'. In London there began to be published the *Daily Universal Register* which was renamed *The Times* in 1788.

There is no record of Burns visiting his friend Smith in Linlithgow. There his friend no doubt showed him round the shawl printworks, for Burns later praised their quality. He ordered one for Jean as a wedding present. As he travelled he saw and experienced many changes in train. A loan had just been issued by the government so that work could begin again on the Forth and Clyde Canal. This had been started in 1768, but its promoters had run out of capital three miles short of Glasgow. He could have seen evidence of this work. He would have remembered reading in Salmon of its beginning – the cause of those intriguing maps in that big geography text that Burns enjoyed so much. It was completed by 1790, enabling water transport between Edinburgh and the expanding industrialising city on the west coast. In 1793 the Crinan Canal began to be dug to provide safe sea passage avoiding the rounding of the dangerous waters of the Mull of Kintyre. This enabled fresh fish to be brought from the Western Isles to the Clyde shores. Adam Smith had warned that increasing trade also increases prices. The increasing coastal trade soon exposed an anomaly in Scottish taxation arrangements: any goods that crossed any water were taxable. This aggravated inflationary pressures.

In 1784 Henry Raeburn painted 'The Reverend Robert Walker Skating on Duddingston Loch'. This was innovative portraiture, with the subject in movement – but it was also unusual because that cold year froze the loch. That year, Henry Cort developed the 'puddling process' through which, by stirring when molten and thus burning off impurities, pig iron can be converted to wrought iron. Over the next two decades the quantity of iron produced increased fourfold. At Carron a great luminous fluid was churning out carronades, invented by Patrick Miller, a director of the Ironworks.

The story is commonly told of the time Burns failed to get inside Carron Ironworks because he arrived on a Sunday in 1787. People quote the verse he penned when he found the gate locked. It voiced the hope he would find the same when he reached the gates of hell. Few take notice that he made a special trip back to Stirlingshire so that he could get inside and be shown the full process.

Miller became Deputy Governor of the Bank of Scotland. He bought Dalswinton Estate in 1785 and in 1786 added Ellisland on the opposite bank of the Nith. He learned that Burns was looking for a farm into which to sink his book royalties, just at the time when he was looking for a tenant likely to take lease of a severely run-down place. He sold the idea to Burns as a great bargain the poet could afford. Miller was an inventor and innovator who had arranged to have sailed to Sweden in 1787 a twin-hulled boat driven by hand-operated paddles. The King of Sweden presented Miller with a rich gold box containing turnip seeds. Thus was the little white turnip, known as the Swede, introduced to Scotland and by the end of the 18ᵗʰ century was a staple in the diet. His paddle boat having worked in crossing the German Ocean, he ordered James Taylor and William Symington to build another with a steam engine added to drive the paddles. When Burns moved to Ellisland farm in 1788, he was delighted to rearrange his workload so that he could observe a milestone event on Dalswinton Loch. This was the new paddle steam boat's pioneering run. It outmatched John Fitch who had launched a steam boat on the Delaware River on 22ⁿᵈ August 1787.

Chapter XI   *Dignity of Man*

In 1788 Joseph Louis Lagrange published 'Analytical Mechanics', making Newton's work (slightly) easier to understand. In 1789 Edmund Cartwright patented a wool-combing machine. The US industrialist Samuel Slater, defying patent law, memorized the plans of Richard Arkwright's spinning machine and installed the technology in America. James Watt invented a governor for the steam engine, to control its speed, and the next year added a pressure gauge.

Around this same time, James Hutton was actively proposing that geological forces are long acting and continue. He found proof in the rocks themselves. Hutton had played a leading role in promoting the Forth and Clyde Canal. He was born in 1726 and educated in Edinburgh, Paris and Leiden. He qualified as a medical doctor and chemist. Though living in Edinburgh since 1768, he thought of himself as the farmer who had imported agricultural innovation from his own experience gained in Europe and in Norfolk. In Edinburgh he was a close friend of Adam Smith and chemist Joseph Black. Together they founded the Oyster Club to enjoy eating.

In 1777, faced with a question from his pal Smith on the right way to assess duty due on the coastal trade, Hutton published the pamphlet 'Nature, Quality and Distinctions of Coal and Culm'. The result of this paper was that small coal taken on short coastal journeys in Scotland was exempted from duty. He was even then working on his 'Theory of the Earth', on which he presented a paper to Edinburgh's Philosophical Society, precursor of the Royal Society of Edinburgh.

Hutton took holidays in the Highlands collecting geological and fossil specimens. There is no record of any written correspondence with Burns, but they met in early 1787 in the house of Professor Adam Ferguson in the weekly conversazione of its extensive intellectual circle. Once Dugald Stewart overcame the young man's diffidence, Burns no doubt exchanged words, and probably a lot more than a few, with these gathered men of wisdom. Hutton was asking questions on the rock strata he observed. He mused how they might have come about, concluding that rocks were 'God's books, wrote upon by God's own finger', telling the story of the Earth. Hutton strongly supported the Deist concept of Natural Religion, that God was fully visible through His Works.

How might this thought have inspired the poet to look with wider eyes as, for that summer of 1787, he travelled as if a leisured man. He was searching for song, but he was equally searching for deeper knowledge and particularly seeking out the key examples of innovation. In Ayr he had watched the building of a wide bridge of modern design alongside the resilient but narrow mediaeval multi-arched bridge. Old men murmured. They said these new-fangled techniques from those foreign engineers would not stand up to the rush of the winter currents. So he composed that poem in which the spirits of the two bridges disputed their merits, with the wizened old soul prophetically declaring:

"I'll be a brig when ye're a shapeless cairn!"

In Edinburgh perhaps the poet's jaw dropped at the great span of the North Bridge, completed twenty years before his arrival. His new lawyer pal Ainslie would perhaps have scoffed and told him how – though Edinburgh tried to forget it – there had been a terrible tragedy. It was in that summer of 1769 as the populace tried to observe the transit of Venus and wondered at its ominous meaning. Five people died when the short section nearest old Edinburgh collapsed on itself. They were carried down in the rubble. Of course, this story didn't even get into either of Pennant's celebrated editions of his 'Tour of Scotland'. Burns was to have the truth confirmed at Ochtertyre farm near Blair Drummond west of Stirling.

Burns travelled there to witness Scotland's showcase agricultural improvement, funded by Lord Kames. An arched bridge crossed the Forth and reached the ridge of gravel between the rivers Forth and Teith. On this ridge a long straight road was built. North from this led narrower causeways through former peat bog, by then drained. On the banks of the Teith, gardener and keen farmer John Ramsay had leased the improved estate of Ochtertyre. Ramsay remained all his life a bachelor. He lost his betrothed in that Venus-transit disaster.

Perhaps Ainslie boasted of an even better long wide bridge. A fine five-arched sandstone wonder had only ten years earlier finally replaced the small boat ferry across the Tweed at Coldstream. This was a mere day's horse ride from Ainslie's family home at Duns. Young Burns decided that with money in his pocket for the first time in his life it was only reasonable that a bit should go on travel. Where better to start than in the company of someone who might show him leading-edge technology while he searched for the roots and evidence of Scottish song.

Thus in May 1787 Burns made what is now called his Borders Tour. The unthinking gentry had suggested he travel to broaden his mind. They meant, of course, he make the Grand Tour, then so natural a part of the young gentleman's education. With little money really, Burns settled for a mini-grand tour of Scotland. No doubt in Edinburgh he had seen a copy of the fine 1776 road map. Possibly he borrowed a copy to use on his travels. Perhaps he bought one. He would not have had to pay the full cover price of twelve shillings, for half the production run of 3,000 had got remaindered. The producers, Taylor and Skinner, couldn't sell enough quickly enough to cover the expenses of all that surveying, map drawing, accurate engraving and production. Gone bankrupt, they headed to America to start again.

In the libraries that were opened up to him in Edinburgh he would have been able to take off the shelves the very popular 'A Tour in Scotland'. Pennant's guide book, enlarged and partly revised after his second tour in 1772, was reissued between 1774 and 1776. From this he could readily plan a route to Newcastle, thence across to Carlisle, and hence back to Mauchline. This would take in Melrose, Dryburgh and Jedburgh abbeys. At the same time he could learn about all the agricultural innovation that had spread up from Norfolk to Northumberland and the Lothians.

He needed this knowledge if he was to farm. No man those days could make a living if he were not prepared to use the latest technology and put his back into improving the land. For rents were being racked up on the presumption farms would be improved.

Burns as he travelled had his eyes wide open with wonder, looking, asking questions and listening. On 22nd May he breakfasted at Skateraw farm alongside the modern nuclear power station at Torness. He was so entranced that whole day by the conversation of the eminent farmer, Mr Lee, that it was the next morning before he moved on. They would hardly have stopped around the farmhouse all day. They would have looked at animals and discussed their merits and their breeding; they would have walked fields to examine the new drainage and the innovative patterns of sowing seed; they would have gone to the shore to see the burning of lime.

There on the shore Burns might have gazed out at a quiet sea beneath a blue slightly hazy sky, the horizon a misty line where water and air merged as if one. Above seabirds wheeled and cawed. Waves, breaking slightly, lapped over the ridges of stone that fanned out from the kelp-rimmed sand into the rounded bay. He had heard it said in Edinburgh that Hutton had found some curious eroded cliff in which red sandstone lay horizontally over folded and compressed vertical strata of greywacke. Hutton sought a particularly marked example. On that Skateraw beach, Burns saw that north and south the crescent of the bay was edged with low cliffs. Perhaps he asked Lee if somewhere near here there might be such strange layers that were Hutton's quest. In the summer of 1788 Hutton went purposely to the Berwickshire coast on the lookout for his special rocks. Perhaps Burns had been first to feel that excitement and delight that enveloped Hutton when he followed the poet's journey to this spot where Earth seemed to merge into the heavens. South he went to Eyemouth. There the strata proved even more amazing. Here was the proof. God indeed was great that He could shape and carve the very rocks to patterns of His own choosing.

In his Border Tour Burns deliberately visited places associated with Scottish songs. He went out of his way to meet people connected with poetry and song. At the same time he arranged discussions with people on the latest developments and viewed installations. On the day that he visited the castle of Thomas the Rhymer he dined with Andrew Meikle (1719-1811) of Houston Mill. He had just invented a new threshing machine for separating grain from straw. He got the patent that same year. Burns inspected cutting edge technology on this tour. At Berwick he dined with John Clunie, partner in a timber and iron company – though in this case he was not impressed. At Eyemouth, he went out on a boat a few days later to view the fishing fleet.

Into northeast England, after Ainslie returned to Edinburgh, Burns travelled on in the company of farmers. He will have been told how turnips had been introduced as early as 1727: Mr Proctor deliberately brought to Rock on Tyneside the gardener Andrew Willey, who sowed turnips on horseback for the surrounding farmers. In 1770 over at Hawkhill, Mr Ilderton had begun teaching boys and girls to how turnips, leaving only a certain number growing in each square. This was before drill culture was introduced, which was as recently as 1782. Mr Gregson had made a flax threshing machine in 1765. This enhanced the design of a small mill that some Scotsman had carted around the farmhouses, to help them swingle the flax they had been growing for their own use. Applied to wheat, that first machine required a man to work like an ox all day to thresh twelve bushels. But Mr Oxley of Flodden soon made a horse machine. The fields were first limed in 1757, when James Hall of Thornington first brought a cartload onto his fields. Maybe the liming had gone too far, thought one of the company, for the fish were failing in the streams.

Look around Akeld, north of Wooler, he would have heard them say, to see how things were moving forward yet again. They were beginning to make useful new types of cattle by cross-breeding to combine the toughness of the Scottish black with the fat of English breeds. These fine rich English farmers even joked that they were making machines now to cut the thistles from the pastures.

What becomes of the people who used to work the old ways, Burns may well have asked aloud. If so, he gained those looks that made him write to Ainslie that he could in this company say nothing out of the ordinary without being considered a naïve ignorant fool. The answer, of course, was obvious; they were removed from the land and went to work in the factories. On 1st June at Carlisle, he got Mitchell, senior partner, to show him round the calico print works of Mitchell, Ellwood and Company. There were nearly five hundred people employed there.

He stood in great factory halls. He heard the constant drumming, banging, clashing, screeching of great machines. He heard the raucous whiplash of the tyrant foreman's shouts. He saw the sweated brows and bent backs of wage slaves. In spinning and weaving mills he saw infants crawling beneath rapid rhythmic hammers of machine rods, scavenging threads, bobbins, fibres. He breathed what passed for air: a constant agitated thick cloud of motes and fibres. He coughed and remembered the dust of the flax dressing. There he had choked. His breast had heaved. He had gasped for air and gasped for life as sweating, burning, churning, for weeks he had lain, spitting out in blood his inner life.

From infancy he had been a galley-slave. It perhaps could have been even worse.

The products in the factory shop were impressive. Such style, such colour, such variety, so inexpensive!

But yet, perhaps he pondered: for all their deafening noise, there was no music here. Where was the firm rhythmic voice of women fullers as their feet worked back and forth across the soaking cloth? What had happened to the gentle murmur of the spinning song as the wheel rolled round? Where were the songs of the reapers in the fields, those songs that gave them rhythm to their work? What had happened to those harmonies of the rowers on the seas whose sound had entranced Boswell and disgusted Johnson? There was rhythm, heavy rhythm, in those pounding factory machines, but there were no voices murmuring in song. Just heavy metal.

He reached Mauchline and heard the talk. Upstream the surveyors had marked out the land. Digging had begun. Buildings would soon rise apace. Stonemasons were excited at the prospect of orders. No more mere bridges over paltry streams. These mills were going to be big. No mere five hundred would they master. No, thousands would they rule. Three years later, he saw the changes wrought by the strength of David Dale's bank capital. His favourite riverside walk through Ballochmyle had vanished evermore.

> The Catrine woods were yellow seen,
> > The flowers decay'd on Catrine lea;
> Nae lav'rock sang on hillock green,
> > But Nature sicken'd on the e'e;
> Thro' faded groves Maria sang,
> > Hersel' in beauty's bloom the while;
> And ay the wild-wood echoes rang; –
> > 'Fareweel the braes o' Ballochmyle!'
>
> Low in your wintry beds, ye flowers,
> > Again ye'll flourish fresh and fair;
> Ye birdies, dumb in with'ring bowers,
> > Again ye'll charm the vocal air;
> But *here*, alas! for *me* nae mair
> > Shall birdie charm, or floweret smile;
> Fareweel the bonie banks of Ayr,
> > Fareweel! fareweel sweet Ballochmyle!

He felt eerie at encroaching industry devastating Nature's social union. Often he wrote of feeling eerie or of places eerie – that dreaded closeness to another world wherein dwells evil power. In the 1950s, travelling to and from New Cumnock, my mother was aware of an eerie feeling as we drove down that winding darkening road to old Howford Bridge below Catrine Banks. The feeling in her was strong of something evil, for she would insist that we say prayers to avert an evil as my father drove down in our Morris 10. She said she feared the brakes of the pre-war car would give way and plunge us over the gully into the torrent. But there must have been more to it than that; it was not normally she, but my father, who was the one for prayers. Down to Howford Bridge my father drove as he drove confident on many roads as bad. But my mother felt it eerie, and with her we children prayed.

Catrine became, for its massive water wheels, grandest in the industry of its day, the great tourist attraction in Ayrshire's 19th century. But the braes of Ballochmyle were gone, never to return. Catrine's mills decayed, bequeathing devastation. In the 1960s, they spanned the Howford gorge with a grand new viaduct. Beneath today is dark and eerie.

If this be the fate of Nature, what of puny Man?

Burns saw the fields laid bare and waste and a dreary winter coming fast.

How could Mankind preserve Dignity against such darkening industrial blasts?

What is the Dignity of Man?

All his life Burns had been poor. He knew that even in poverty there could be dignity. But he knew too that poverty threatened dignity. Honesty in poverty averted that threat. Thus Burns wrote of 'honest poverty'. He wrote not as those misguided levellers who decry all wealth and would destroy all aspiration. He wrote that even in poverty a person could remain a Man. But the person must first retain dignity. Retaining dignity in the face of adversity is difficult. In the face of great adversity and massive change, a lonely person may feel the task impossible.

In the time of Burns great political and economic change was underway. Old social norms were being ploughed up, discarded and destroyed. Those who had based their dignity on the old ways found themselves undermined. Around him Burns saw multitudes of desperate, destitute, dismayed, who knew no way to hold up self-respecting heads. Such people fast descended to life's filthy gutter. For any person who bases personal dignity on role and not on self-respect loses that dignity when the role is withdrawn.

Our modern world experiences as great change as Burns saw in his time. We see multitudes whose roles are torn from them. Too many based their dignity on roles that have vanished. Deprived of their role, they find no meaning left in life. Some are offered new roles, and feel that lesser role degrading, for it lacks the adulation they formerly enjoyed.

There are too many, young or displaced persons, in our modern world who have not yet had a role that seems to give dignity. Denied a dignified role they act undignified. Those have never learned to discover and nurture their self-respect.

Burns knew that dignity does not arise from role. A dignified person elevates even the lowliest station in life, even if that person has no recognised social role. Burns respected all who created their own true dignity. He only gave rank to those who dignified their role through having the integrity and thus the self-respect that made them worthy of the role assigned them. How he addressed his letters to the great and to the poor shows his respect for all who dignified their role, whatever that role was.

Burns despised those who debased role and rank. No role gives dignity where there is none in the person. True worth is in a person, not in rank. An unworthy man debases the role most dignified, just as false metal debases the guinea stamp impressed on it.

Burns said all this in poetry far better than I can in words. But I must, for we have let the meaning of his poetry slip away, not realising he speaks to us of our time now.

No role can debase true dignity. Dignity comes from self-respect. No-one can give us self-respect. Self-respect comes from within. Self-respect comes from an honest soul. Self-respect comes from effort to maintain integrity, honesty and humanity. The seed of self-respect is in each one of us. But each must find that seed inside and nurture it, each one of us.

Knowing that dignity came from within, Burns was not ashamed to take the greatly despised role of gauger, for he knew he would carry it out honestly, and lend it dignity.

Coila tasked Burns to build a bulwark to protect the Dignity of Man – but first, Man must make that Dignity.

Burns mused on the changing world around him and his own prospects. As one of those little people who could not afford to own his own farm, he must accept a lease if he had the means. He must continue to find the way to finance all the new equipment necessary to keep his own production apace with the continuously falling costs of better capitalised farms. Only thus could he meet the landlord's expectations of continually rising rent. His father had abandoned gardening, and failed in farming. He himself had tried flax, and found it no way forward. He realised that his main asset was not such skill as he had gained in farming, but the knowledge that he had gathered in his head. His strength was his innate intellectual ability and as yet untapped skill potential, and his preparedness to adapt – to apply himself to any work that would earn the necessary income. The one proviso always – that what he did must never conflict with his own strict ethical code. Those words of that strange vision of Coila came to him to have new meaning:

Preserve the Dignity of Man!

The voice of his demanding Muse remonstrated, reverberating in a mind that would the following summer more clearly understand than so many of his contemporaries and so many readers since, those concerns expressed by Adam Smith in the fifth book of his 'The Wealth of Nations'.

People, asserted Smith in that volume, usually learn their core true understanding not from *books* but from what they *do*. As division of labour advanced, people would do fewer things. Those things they did would be increasingly repetitive and predictable. This would reduce their need

> to exert understanding or exercise invention in finding out expedients for removing difficulties.

As division of labour advanced, the typical worker that would evolve would be a person who had lost the habit of making the effort to *think*. This mass of the population would become

> generally as stupid and ignorant as it is possible for a human creature to become . . . . The torpor of his mind [would] render him not only incapable of relishing or bearing a part in conversation, but of conceiving any generous, noble, or tender sentiment and consequently of forming any just judgment concerning many, even, of the ordinary duties of private life.

Smith expressed his concern that such a person could not make reasoned judgment on great political issues nor even defend his own country in war. Worker dexterity is

> acquired at the expense of intellectual, social and martial virtues

because the narrowness of thinking enforced by industrial work would destroy mental courage and an increasingly limited range of physical exertion would destroy strength and vigour. Increasing industrialisation destroys the humanity of the working population unless government acts to redress it. Forcing people into regimentation of cities, in other words 'civilising them', said Smith

benumbed the understanding of almost all of the inferior ranks of people.

Gathering people into cities, so-called civilisation, allows great increases in collected knowledge, great collective widening of tasks, and certain great opportunities for exceptional people, but at the cost of impoverishing the minds of the great majority. Very few whose minds are sharpened by the challenges of increased knowledge and tasks have opportunity – if they have the will – to contribute to the increased happiness of the rest. General education specifically designed not merely for vocational skills but to counteract narrowness of experience and dumbing-down of roles is imperative to prevent the nation succumbing to this

sort of mental mutilation.

Capitalists understand readily that individual efforts need to be recombined to release intended profit. They also understand too readily that keeping workers separated while they themselves combine increases profit further. Adam Smith did not voice concern for what would happen to the world of thought, of letters and of education. It too would equally split and splinter in the great advance of division of labour. Medicine has realised how dangerous this can be and is now actively drawing together its many disparate threads. But too many in academia have no incentive to recombine thinking; they live not by profit but on public funding. Thus advancing knowledge has fragmented into ever increasing specialisations, that each burrows its narrow well into research depths, each separate, each different, each unconnected and each resenting the voice of the community requesting interdisciplinary co-operation to seek to achieve common good.

Governments are responsible for protecting the nation as far as possible from epidemics and pernicious diseases. But they are as much responsible for preserving in individuals a healthy attitude and health in knowledge. Good governments, suggested Smith, benefit very directly from such broader general education, since a population of educated active minds rarely capriciously throws out good government.

"That man Smith writes a lot of good sense!" scribbled Burns in his notes.

Robert Burns never met Adam Smith. Burns was reticent about calling on Panmure House without formal letter of introduction. In early April 1787 he finally got sent one by Mrs Dunlop. It arrived the day after Smith went to London to seek medical attention for that abdominal illness that marked the beginning of his end. Henry Dundas had bought a pretty house west of Wimbledon Common. There his principal guest was newly arrived Adam Smith, given precedence over all the company, including young Prime Minister Pitt. The previous year, Henry Dundas had begun enhancing his own Melville Castle as a gothic fort with landscaped park suited to his high station.

Dundas was not an ancient aristocratic family. James Dundas (1620-79) had been one of the very many radicals who signed the Scottish National Covenant which precipitated the Bishops' War. After the Restoration, appointed judge in the Court of Session, he stepped down rather than renounce the Covenant in the tightened Oath of Allegiance. When his eldest son James showed himself to be a Jacobite and a pamphleteer, he disinherited him. His other son Robert had been abroad. In 1689 he returned in the train of William of Orange.

Back in Scotland Robert Dundas wanted to put behind him every trace of the discomfort he had experienced while abroad in the tight brick closes of the Netherlands. He tore down Arniston's

Jacobean walls, opened up the garden and built a cascade. This idea caught on in south England, beginning a new fashion in gardening that was hailed as allegorical of the new freedom brought by the Revolution. In Buckinghamshire, the old Saxon boundary marker, the ha-ha, was given a new lease of life as a key part of the new garden style. A garden ha-ha made a great house seem to be integrated with the active lowly farms around it. In fact, this deep ditch created an invisible impenetrable new barrier between rulers and ruled. Soon, estates began to clear villages from around great houses to make parkland. Landscapes began to be redesigned. So soon after Scotland's first gardening book had been published, this anti-Jacobite laird of Arniston began a trend that would eliminate the old Scottish gardener. He was appointed as a judge, which he remained until his death in 1726. He was one of those Whigs who, as a member of the old Scottish Parliament, strongly supported the Act of Union in 1707. Robert succeeded as Lord Arniston. So did his son, another Robert who had been born in 1685 and lived until 1754.

This Lord Arniston was a senior member of the Scottish legal system. He found himself part of the local body, a de facto surrogate local 'parliament', for refining Scotland's independent system of laws whose survival was guaranteed by the Treaty of Union. He actively objected to Prime Minister Walpole's imposition on Scotland of a malt tax in 1725, since the terms of the Treaty of Union explicitly exempted Scotland from such a tax. While the tax generated riots, the far greater issue that generated unrest amongst Scots was the principle of setting aside elements of the Treaty. The Patronage Act in 1712 was an earlier example, undoing agreements of 1690. Scots had been told the Treaty was inviolable. Such alterations suggested that in 1707 English business interests had simply achieved a successful takeover of the small northern competitor. This was rather different from opening up English markets to Scottish interests, as Scots had been led to believe Union implied. Ending heritable jurisdictions in 1747 also set aside provisions guaranteed and enshrined at Union.

The Patronage Act ultimately caused the creation of the Original Secession Church after Ebenezer Erskine, minister of Stirling, was deposed by the General Assembly in 1733 for preaching against such lay patronage. The rumbling on of the patronage question gave Burns a powerful source of inspiration for satire.

Arniston is credited with giving Scottish juries the option to return a verdict of Not Guilty, when previously the only options were Proven or Not Proven, leaving the judge to make the final decision. His oldest son was Robert (1713-1787) who himself by his second wife had another Robert (1758-1819) as his heir. In 1734 Arniston wrote to Robert then studying in Utrecht, that private letters were being opened by agents of the government which increasingly suspected that it was surrounded by conspirators. On 28th April 1742, Arniston had by his second wife another son, Henry, who by marriage became Viscount Melville. He lived until 1811.

With his background, Henry was a reliable Hanoverian man. He was born in a house called Bishop's Land in Edinburgh, east of the present North Bridge. This apartment block was a grander version of the present National Trust of Scotland's property known as Gladstone's Land on the Lawnmarket. It had had a ground floor that was a piazza of deeply arched pillars, springing from massive stones. One of the apartments was then occupied by Sir Stuart Threipland of Fingask, who is credited with having been helped by the fairies to enable the escape of Bonnie Prince Charlie after Culloden. An oil painting illustrating this moment hangs in Duff House near Banff. Fingask

Castle in Perthshire, still in the hands of the Threipland family, has in its grounds large statues of key characters in Burns's great poem of the supernatural, 'Tam o' Shanter'.

Burns regretted not meeting Adam Smith, for here was a man brave enough to put in print his belief that farming was so complex and subtle that it could never be captured in so trivial a form as was even the most sophisticated and intellectual book. Despite all their book learning, scholars were typically much less knowledgeable than the farmers they despised.

In August 1788 Burns had tried to get his brother William, training as a saddler, into an appropriate position in Edinburgh. That failed. Ainslie even refused help. This exposed the emptiness of the superficial goodwill of all those fine contacts. William lived in Ellisland for a while before getting work at Longtown, and then Newcastle upon Tyne, and finally moving to William Barber on the Strand, London. There he died on 24th July 1790 of a fever.

There are parallels between present global human experience of the trauma of achieving change and the experiences of Robert Burns. He repeatedly tried to retrain to become marketable. He had failed to gain the qualifications in land management that his father desired of him in sending him to study surveying and dialling. But this mathematical training served him in good stead when he acted on his determination to become re-skilled to be appointed to an Excise post. In his life are perhaps lessons for those who manage economies today, of how the individual is affected by change. This might give understanding that could ease current transitions in global economics with their attendant cultural change. His interest in technological development extended – as it did for Adam Smith – to the impact on individuals and on communities of technological and economic change.

Change in ordinary life in Scotland became so pervasive that John Sinclair in 1791 began supervising the collection of data for the first Statistical Account of Scotland. This added numerical rigour to the observations of travellers such as Thomas Pennant. It qualified the general observations of those, such as Arthur Young, who made a living out of writing texts promoting uniform approaches to agricultural improvement that took no account of local conditions. Like a true journalist who can produce words on anything that pays, Young in 1792, like Moore, published his 'Travels in France'.

Scotland was castigated – and as always gained an inferiority complex – for her tardiness in adopting methods of farming improvement that suited only English conditions. Yet she was actually at the forefront of invention. When he reached Aberdeen in the autumn of 1787, Burns no doubt heard how a new bleaching process using chlorine was being used there commercially. At that time, the entrepreneur Gordon got lichens from the west Highlands to make a violet dye. Human urine was used for fulling cloth. Urine was gathered in cottage buckets and collectors went round to buy it. Some cottagers added water to increase their payment. This brought the invention of the hydrometer, which urine gatherers carried with them to test the quality of every bucket load they bought.

At Ellisland, Burns became known locally as a farming innovator, for example recommending in raising horned cattle to blunt the stud's horns before putting it to the cow. He introduced Ayrshire breeds to the Dumfries region because of their better milk yield.

On 24th January 1792 he visited, with a party including Maria Riddell, the lead mines at Wanlockhead. He found himself unable to cope with the oppressive airlessness of the mines. The exploration required first a strenuous climb to the adits, and then walking through low tunnels, in water more than knee-deep with a constant drip from the roof. His health again affected, he had to struggle on earning a living and at the same time keep up to date with all relevant changes in excise duty. In early 1793 Henry Dundas achieved the removal of the Scottish coastal trade tax anomaly. By 1796 Dundas had reason to be concerned at the degree to which the rise in Scottish commerce was accompanied by growing discontent in the main towns. There, congestion and poverty were aggravated as country people, deprived of their livelihood through agricultural improvement, sought paid work in a world of increasingly mechanising capitalism.

Early in 1795, Burns would have been pleased to note that the Irish Parliament, following the English acceptance in 1794 of the rehabilitation of Roman Catholic education on British soil, had established the Roman Catholic seminary at Maynooth College. This was approved because of the vested interest of the government to ensure that persons wishing to become priests need not go to any college on the continent of Europe. There they might pick up revolutionary ideas. Whatever the political purpose, such toleration was not readily achieved in Scotland. Full religious toleration in Scotland, that freedom of conscience for all that Burns championed, a central pillar of human dignity in his eyes, was denied during the poet's lifetime.

In September 1795, Burns's daughter Elizabeth Riddell Burns died at Mauchline after a long illness. He himself was subsequently ill for a very considerable time. He still continued his work on the 8-man organising committee of the Volunteers. That September, after the assassination attempt on King George III, Burns wrote their loyal address of thanks for his deliverance.

Poetic and very spiritual though his mind was, he had a keen business head, as his supervisors in the Excise testified. What he did not have were business mentors who could guide him safely amongst the jackals that devoured his meat at every turn. Few are the biographers that have had the experience of being a self-employed person rising from the labouring classes to move amongst those who are most elevated in the powers of the land. Thus few can understand how alone was this failed gardener's son trying to navigate the treacherous waters of the business world of the hostile big city with his stock in trade being that ephemeral substance, intellectual property, which even today laws try to grapple, like a crane grab trying to lift jelly.

Burns detailed his intellectual property in the Deed of Assignment of 22nd July 1786 to Gilbert of his property for the care of his child by Elizabeth Paton about to emigrate and when faced with potential legal action by James Armour, after that man had obviated his marriage to Jean. Knowing his priorities, over the next ten days he hid at Old Rome Ford, a farmhouse outside Kilmarnock, enabling him to get into town to proof read the typesetting of his poems.

From the start of his business correspondence with respect to his publications, he used humour to impart firm messages – a necessary business skill that few develop. In a letter to Peter Hill telling him to supply books ordered, he stated

> "This I write to you when I am miserably fou, consequently it must be the sentiments of my heart"

– in other words, "I am writing this in vino veritas so I really mean it! Get the finger out!" One biographer, James Mackay, considers being drunk while writing business letters 'a curious feature'. Burns did not get himself drunk to write such a letter. It is a lucky man who never has to chivvy people with humour when all else fails.

Creech was tardy in making payments and paid a lot less than Burns had been led to expect. In April 1792 he proposed a second edition with a derisory offer to Burns if he contributed more poems.

Burns had been persuaded to sell the copyright of the works in the first Edinburgh edition to Creech. He wrote back making clear he would be involved but that the new poems would absolutely remain his own copyright. He knew asking Creech for money was a waste of paper. So he stipulated that he should get as many copies of the new edition as he should request.

In 1792 he was approached by George Thomson who intended a new musical publication. Burns agreed to provide new songs, but at his own pace, for the first call on his time was his paid employment. George Thomson (1757-1851) was trained as a lawyer's clerk. From 1780 he worked with the Board of Trustees for the Encouragement of Art and Manufacture in Scotland, where he became Chief Clerk. Following the publication in 1792 of Pietro Urbani's 'Selection of Scots Songs', he decided there was a market for a quality production. When Thomson tried making changes to his songs, Burns objected that if he didn't like a song as provided he must leave the song out. At a time when there was yet no general intellectual property law, concerned at Thomson's behaviour, he required Thomson to print in his volumes that he published with the author's authority and that this authority did not extend to others making copies. Some biographers thus state Burns gave his copyright gratis to Thomson. It surprises me that such writers, so keen to protect their own intellectual property, seem not to be aware of the difference between granting an authority to print and transfer of copyright.

Thomson hired Joseph Ignaz Pleyel (1757-1831), Haydn's best pupil, as chief musical collaborator. He put a proper contract in place and paid him well. He made a profit from the music of Burns and insulted him with minor tips. Burns, misguided by Henry Mackenzie in the drafting of his contract with Creech, found himself with no mentor to draft a proper contract with Thomson. He got ripped off. On publication, Thomson sent Burns a 'free' copy of his first volume. This contained a considerable input from the poet. He patronisingly enclosed a derisory tip of £5. This raised the poet's ire. There are not a few occasions when people have tried to drain my brain for a bottle of champagne. Though I learned early to tell them to go and stuff themselves, I still got ripped off too often, for too much. I can sympathise with a misplaced gardener's son who never had a mentor who cared to fight his corner. Burns stated

> "the profits of the labours of a Man of genius are at least as honourable as any other profits whatever".

It was some consolation in May 1795 on coming home one day to find that Jean and a delivery lad had had so much pleasure on opening George Thomson's gift in a flat crate that had suddenly arrived. It contained a painting by David Allan of Alloa of 'The Cottar's Saturday Night' with Burns centre stage. That painter had been paid well to produce illustrations to garnish the book of songs that could never have existed had the poet not penned them. As the poet died, very grudging Thomson condescendingly sent £5 the poet had begged as essential to unblock cash-flow difficulties caused because his Excise pay was docked for his illness absences.

> O Life! Thou art a galling load,
> Along a rough, a weary road,
> To wretches such as I!

Thomson always persuaded himself righteously that, since Burns got enjoyment out of writing songs well, he needed no other payment. Many a time I've had the same song from those who would use my mind; "You enjoy your work, Catherine", they say as they try to bargain down my fee. "I work, and I enjoy", I reply. "They are two different activities that I put effort into at the same time."

Burns seems never to have learned such a reply. Instead, to emphasise that he would not be hurried to create good work, he wrote that much misunderstood letter which states that a price per line was 'Sodomy of Soul'; his work was "either above price or below price". Any self-employed consultant knows that this means: pay the respectable fee; I won't insult you with trash. Of course, I am not aware of any biographer of the poet, from the first to the present day, who has himself been in any situation to understand these inferences from various letters that appear to decline payment. What these letters decline is cheap tips, peanuts and dirt payment.

His relationship with James Johnson (1742-1811) was totally different. Here were together two enthusiasts making good songs cheaply and widely available to the Scottish and wider general public. Burns never sought and never wished payment from a man who, had he been able to pay, would have done so gladly. Burns rejoiced at the many copies of the 'Musical Museum' that he was able to distribute to his friends. He valued the armorial watch fob that Johnson had made for him.

Burns never produced that romantic novel that could have come out of that Clarinda correspondence. He never wrote that stage play that people deem necessary if they are to contrast him with Shakespeare. He never produced a musical opera. But these last ten years of his life, between the Kilmarnock edition and his death, his literary freedom marred by his sterling service in the Excise, were marked by an unrivalled output of song. He raised Scotland from its misery and spiritual deprivation to become the leading land of song.

In this he built on the legacy he knew was there – the ancient music of Scotland. He, alone amongst modern poets, began his writing not from words, but from the music. He wrote his songs to preserve and expand the ancient heritage that sang the soul of his country.

When in Edinburgh he met Johnson, his soul was drawn to the dream that Johnson had of music for the multitudes. Johnson had invented a process for reproducing sheet music on pewter plates. By the end of April 1787 Burns was already enthusing about his intention to gather and publish an extensive collection of Scottish songs. Johnson took out no patent. Thus he made no money from the invention. The invention was overtaken by lithography at the end of the century. In the short window that Johnson's process was used, it enabled substantially cheaper production of correct sheet music – for pewter could readily be spot-softened while copper etching is unforgiving of mistakes. This enabled much more widespread availability of new songs. This was the pop-music revolution of the era, comparable with the invention of the gramophone for the 20th century, and the invention of mobile phone downloads for the 21st. Burns was more than keen to be at the forefront of this musical technological revolution.

The people might not sing in the drudgery of the factories, but they could sing in their hearts and their homes, the music carried to them on cheap printed sheets.

In Dumfries an irony of music associated him directly with the fortunes of Patrick Heron, onetime partner of the failed Ayr Bank that had so devastated his youth. John Syme was friendly with Heron, now living near Dumfries. He had after the crash married the daughter of the 8th Earl of Dundonald. This brought him the estate of Kirroughtree near Newton Stewart. Lady Elizabeth was interested in song. In 1794 she provided some music so Burns could add lyrics. Thomson discarded the music but kept the words. The by-election in which Heron gained his seat in Parliament took place in the summer of 1795. Burns wrote the persuasive electioneering songs and the triumphal odes.

On 6th May 1794 David McCulloch of Ardwall was admitted to the Masonic Lodge of St Andrew that Burns attended. McCulloch had been in France to learn French when the Bastille fell. He stayed in France until after the death of Louis XVI, but came home in late 1793 because his father was dying. David loved Scottish song. Having a fine voice, he enabled Burns to hear some of his own songs sung well.

Music attracted him in 1794 to Jean Lorimer, daughter of a farmer neighbour when Burns was at Ellisland. In 1793 she had been abducted to Gretna Green and forcibly married. She was then abandoned by the cad and went home to keep house for her father. It was after this that Burns and Jean from time to time over a summer enjoyed tea together at her father's house. Sometimes she came to take tea with Burns's wife. Jean Lorimer became Chloris in song. She inspired more songs from Burns than did any other woman.

In this last decade he created that amazing corpus of work that set Scotland singing eternally of freedom, peace, joy and love. So it is ironic that it is said that in due course Burns was buried in his Volunteer uniform – the cost of which tormented his last days with fear of debtor's prison. In early 1795, during winter weather horrendous by Scottish standards, Burns was acting Supervisor during the illness of the incumbent. One four-day blizzard covered southwest Scotland in worse snow than living memory. Burns was trapped at Ecclefechan. From that May his health deteriorated rapidly. From the beginning of the 20th century biographers of Burns, such as James Barke and Sir James Chrichton-Browne, have observed how the horrific exposure that Burns suffered at various points in his life must surely have contributed to his early death. Effects of the strenuous work forced on him as a child worsened with unremitting farming and Excise work. In his letters he remarked how he feared being promoted to Supervisor if this constant all-hours-of-the-day commitment was what it implied; it would be death to his literary output, if not to himself.

Chrichton-Browne identified disease to the substance and lining membrane of the poet's heart. He cited the first evidence in the illnesses the poet recounted at Mount Oliphant in his early teenage years. From December 1781 onwards, Burns wrote of illness. That terrible sulphur cloud of 1783-4 brought a worsening. Thereafter his decline was marked by feverish attacks, quickened pulse, feelings of being weak and squeamish, and symptoms of being highly strung, easily agitated, and nervous – the visible 'hypochondriac' symptoms of his invisible disability. On 13th September 1784 he was recovering from illness, and was still in a slow fever – a letter to John Tennant junior tells us – apparently a recurrence of illness throughout that year. It affected his heart. He had fainting fits – most visible to others when they happened in the night. In 1789 his symptoms were dismissed. They were mere 'farmer's lung' caused by dust. Perhaps brucellosis was the final straw. After his illness of the winter of 1795-6, his birthday in 1796 saw the peak of violent gales that lashed southwest Scotland. Though there was neither snow nor frost, the lead roof of the Coffee House in Dumfries was carried away in one gust. A few days later he braved the elements to attend his Masonic Lodge. He collapsed on the way home.

Brow Well is a chalybeate spring near the Solway shore east of the Raffles Burn. Maria Riddell, at Brow for the waters while Burns was getting this final treatment prescribed by his doctors, sent her carriage to bring him to dine with her on 5th July. She was shocked at his appearance. He knew he was slowly, painfully, dying. All he could eat was thin porridge with a medicinal touch of his own port. In three weeks he used only two bottles. The second was forced on him as a gift by the innkeeper's brother, because Burns had not a penny left in his purse and offered the valued fob from his watch.

Before it became a spa, Brow was a staging post for drovers driving cattle to England. So there was a tiny inn. Its location was cut through in 1863 by the modern road. Burns lodged during the three weeks in which he daily took the waters and went down to the sea to bathe up to his armpits in the cold water. 'Domestic Medicine' of 1769 by Dr William Buchan, the Bible of Burns's murderous 'Dr Hornbook', advised cold plunges for his symptoms. In youth a barrel of water had been placed beside his bed.

In the last year of his life, concerned with his own illness and the future livelihood of his family, Burns could be forgiven if he was not aware that Edward Jenner was carrying out the first smallpox vaccination, replacing the inoculation process of deliberate infection. Burns had had all his own children inoculated – that life-threatening approach to generating immunisation. Despite his life-long interest in astronomy, he probably did not know that, as he lay dying, Pierre-Simon Laplace published 'Account of the System of the World', suggesting that the solar system was formed from a cloud of gas. Nor would he have learned that Spanish inventor Francisco Salva linked Madrid to Aranjuez (around 40 miles) with an electric telegraph. Its electric signal created by electrostatic machines was detected by people holding the ends of the wires. A method for extracting the sediment from champagne, enabling the production of clear sparkling wines and pink champagnes was developed by Nicole-Barbe Cliquot. He would undoubtedly have applauded them all, including the last, for the added frothy dimension it would have given to such satirical political poems as his 'Fête Champêtre'.

As you approach the end of my book you might be saying to yourself that I have failed to bring Robert Burns to life. Indeed! Robert Burns is dead. Dead as a doornail. Or perhaps we should say as dead as a dodo, for by the time the last dodo was killed in 1681 the early Enlightenment scientists had collected and stuffed a few. So there might be some dodo DNA around to shoot into the egg of a modern pigeon and, like a Jurassic Park, reconstruct the bird. Just as arguably there must be some DNA around that correlates to Robert Burns. But we can never reconstruct the man.

The news of his death spread quickly. Soon Dumfries was filled like a London crowded out with the mass commiserating mob for Princess Diana, mock-mourning with a bombastic military funeral the man they had refused to honour in those ten years since the Kilmarnock edition made some small noise in the country. Well, at least in death he fulfilled that childhood Hannibal-inspired soldier dream of being part of the big parade. But those had been his idiot days, of idiot piety, in mindless youth when he had not yet learned to think. Jean and the women were not part of the grand party; domestic matters of infants and care took their minds. Etiquette anyway excluded them from graveside pomp.

The husband of Peggy Chalmers, now a director of the Bank of Scotland, opened a book for subscriptions for the benefit of his widow and children. Little was donated. Twenty years later a far greater sum was readily collected to erect a mausoleum in the cemetery in Dumfries and over the next century considerable donations enabled the building of substantial monuments to his immortal memory in Edinburgh, Kilmarnock, Mauchline and Alloway. The first Burns Supper was held in 1801 and his Immortal Memory has been toasted since, to the sound of pipes and violin, reciting of poems, singing of songs, long speeches, and toasts for every conceivable reason.

But what of the man? When the mausoleum was ready for his rotted carcase, they opened the grave in which he had been laid. When they reached his coffin the wood broke and inside the watchers saw a spectre. There he lay, as if on the day he died, his eyes closed, his face calmed after that final despair of poverty, wearing the uniform of the Dumfries Volunteers, whose price demanded by threatening legal letters had precipitated that final financial terror of debtor's prison. The watchers stood in awe, as if before them they must be seeing the mediaeval miracle of non-corruption. But then one moved to begin lifting the coffin. The face vanished in a scatter of dust. The curious phrenologist bent down and lifted the skull, blowing off the last remnants of what had been the flesh of the man. He began pawing at its shapes and hollows to interpret what had been the nature of this genius they had decreed was clearly flawed. Then they laid the bones in the mausoleum to more pomp and ceremony, and held a great party to toast his memory.

But if not the man, what of his so-called Immortal Memory? The memory today is typically an annual get-together in the form of a dinner with recitations, song, speeches and toasts. They are still usually all male, though increasingly women's lib means the lassies come along too. That tends to preclude performances deemed risqué or downright lewd. An Immortal Memory is given by some brave soul who typically will talk about Burns the Radical, Burns the Lover, Burns the Religious Man, or just safely tell a story of his life. But it is all getting a bit passé and perhaps the memory is not so immortal after all, particularly in Scotland. Few of the Burns monuments that were once places to be visited are regularly open to the public. Even the birthplace in Alloway was in a dire state and only given attention when the Scottish Executive realised it could cause some embarrassment if from abroad on the 250th anniversary of his birth there should come pilgrims to seek the meaning of the man.

If the soul of Burns observes, it will hardly be with surprise. In Stirling he saw in the castle the great hall that James IV had built to welcome his Tudor bride Margaret, for the celebrations of that wedding that would take the Stuarts to the English throne. It was a hollow shell. He had just come from Edinburgh, where he had become disgusted with the vacuity of the wealthy, the legal fraternity, the aristocracy, and even most of the academics. He saw around him the culture of Scotland vanishing, few seeming to care, and many actively seeking its demise. But he saw and heard many other things too that were even more hurtful to his humanity: he saw hereditary rank insultingly demanding authority; he saw money masquerading as wealth; he saw intolerance masquerading as loyalty and he saw hubris masquerading as knowledge and understanding. In this city that would be called the Athens of the North, the mind of an old Scotland that he had come in childhood to admire seemed replaced by vacuous arrogance. Mindless! All this flooded over him as he looked up at the empty sky from inside the hollow hall. Lines flooded into his head that in anger he wrote with a diamond stylus on a window pane. A foreign race, an idiot race, without honour, was that society he had come to know in Edinburgh.

> An idiot race, to honour lost;
> who know them best, despise them most.

The words came back to haunt him. The madness of George III was soon a frightening reality to a nation that had recently lost the American war, and that had no constitutional mechanism to create a regent, should the king be unable to fulfil his duties. Bonnie Prince Charlie, old and decrepit though he was, still lived. Later, Burns destroyed the pane of glass. But the words had been written; they had been read; they had been noted, and the idea was out there flying fast through the ether, wider and wider, condemning him a traitor – but yet also giving him a new message.

Ideas, set free, can live and keep on living.

He had learned that Pythagoras and Euclid were long, long dead, but their ideas lived!

Thus in adversity he gained an insight. Speak the idea, let it out, set it free, and that idea if great will be immortal.

He spoke of human responsibilities; he spoke of justice; he spoke of liberty. He defied hypocrisy. He spoke of them all in laughter, yes, so he would be heard, but with sincerity. He was told he must stop speaking his ideas, or his Excise job was on the line. Thus he is accused of having in his latter years dropped out from actively working for the better world he craved. But he was not silent. He wrote defiantly, privately to friends. Sending letters to newspapers he used pseudonyms unless only the most twisted could take offence. Yet they did take offence and hounded him. In his verse, he changed his tune. Rather, he now sang more than he had ever done before and sang as much as he could to pre-existing familiar tunes. His instinct knew the Music of the Spheres carried the Almighty Idea through all creation. A simple song, sung by a simple voice, could carry a great idea nestled within it safely through the hostile world of men. In song he infiltrated homes of the humble and salons of the mighty with those great messages that fought to get out of his heart.

His memory may not be immortal, but the messages have stood the test of time and are as relevant today as they were when he put his name to their manuscripts.

Amongst all the parlour songs of love, he slipped in not a few that told directly of the deep emotions that fired his eyes. He drew attention to the injustice of aggressively warring on France in 'Scots Wha Hae wi' Wallace Bled'; he objected to corruption in the elections he observed in 'Such a Parcel of Rogues in the Nation'; in 'A man's a man for a' that' he insisted that a man's humanity and not his money measured true value.

Despised for daring to say the thoughts of his heart, he died impoverished.

The inventory of his effects at his death showed that he had nothing except a library valued at £90. Ainslie was quick to point out that Burns had given Gilbert money out of his Edinburgh edition earnings. To support Jean and Burns's children, the poet's executors hounded Gilbert to repay support that Burns had declined to recall. The normally placid Jean vigorously opposed forcing Gilbert to sell up at Mossgeil. It would have made Burns's mother and Gilbert's family homeless. Accommodations were made, mainly thanks to that small general subscription. But that raised a mere couple of hundred pounds. This tided Jean over until profits came in from Currie's editing and publishing of her husband's works.

The financial problems that beset Burns on his deathbed were entirely a result of his last illness. The Excise docked his pay for absences. He fulfilled all his work commitments until the end of February 1796, but then had half his pay docked for the next two months. From mid April to end May he struggled back to work, but in June he was finally unable to go on. Thus, he was deprived of cash flow equal to three months' pay.

Chapter XI *Dignity of Man*

He came home from Brow on schedule on 16th July and died begging for a pittance from the miserly George Thomson who commercially owed him so much. In contrast, his pal James Clarke, the Moffat schoolmaster who had by then moved to Forfar, whom Burns had helped financially through legal harassment in 1791-92, speeded up his loan repayments to help the dying man. Amateur music enthusiast James Johnson wasted no time to send yet another free copy of the Scots Musical Museum so that Burns could present it to Jessie Lawers, who nursed him in his last illness. He died at 5 o'clock in the morning of Thursday 21st July 1796. For Jessie he had written his very last verse:

> O wert thou in the cauld blast
> On yonder lea, on yonder lea,
> My plaidie to the angry airt
> I'd shelter thee, I'd shelter thee.
> And did misfortune's bitter storms
> Around thee blaw, around thee blaw,
> Thy bield would be my bosom
> To share it a'.

He had had no bodily dignity left as he lay on that bed. He had begged the loan of a coach to bring him back from Brow Well because he could not stand on his legs. He certainly could not ride a horse. Curious bystanders watched as the women met the coach and carried his emaciated death-body up the lane to the steps of his home. Yet even then in his heart he knew that his human dignity was unimpaired, for he had nurtured it through all adversity. True dignity of man sprang not from wealth and worldly power, but from that inner spark that lit a glimmer in the soul that burst to fire to light up the air and raise him above the clouds so that he could look down on the vast ruffled carpet of the Earth, as he had seen displayed on Coila's coat of many colours.

As he lay dying, his many enemies began to swarm like bees when herd boys raid their comb. His Pegasus rallied, but he could ride no more. The market place filled to gape around his corpse. "Whoring drunk!" a voice cried out. The mob, as one, started and raced in chase to catch his fleeing soul. Then was the tale of the poet mangled in the dust beneath their crowding feet, his fragile reputation torn and shredded by devil-hordes.

His wit, the silver sword, shivered to the stones. Coila leaned, lifting the shattered shards. She caressed them and, head proud, bore them loving to that moonlit woodland pool, Imagination. There she cast them to a waiting white-wreathed hand, which bore them back to the Queen of Fairyland.

His self-righteous enemies carved his epitaph in stone: to drink he was inclined; cutty sarks ran in his mind. Thus the story has been told, again and again, so that the legend stands. And who would publish truth where legend makes more profit?

Thus was the human mind, fired with the power of imagination, set free to realise its full dignity, soaring above human misery to the wonder of the heavens, free flying to infinity and beyond. Thus Mankind could enjoy and employ the mind to find the way to obviate that primeval curse that man was made to mourn. In thus realising the worth of the imagination, that great gift of Almighty Power, lay the true Dignity of Man. He had preserved his own dignity. But he had also heeded Coila's command. Through his legacy of poetry and song he saved Scotland's music. He had given the best efforts of his soul to preserve for future generations that pillar of dignity.

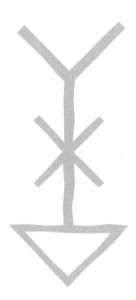

Epilogue   *Squaring the Circle*

How the 18th century Enlightenment ripped humanity out of modern life and ushered in our era of Big Brother – and how Robert Burns bequeathed us the means to retrieve freedom.

Burns left Brow Well because the tides had become too low for bathing. Tides are Moon-driven. The Moon had waned. Burns waned with it. With his passing also passed the last era before Modern Man severed his umbilical cord to the rhythms of Nature.

In these last years, Burns was aware of change. He would have read the obituary for Edward Gibbon who died on 16th January 1794. Some forms of modern delegated sovereign authority had come into being. On 6th May 1791 Britain divided Canada into two regions, Upper and Lower, giving each its own legislative assembly. Lord North, Tory Prime Minister during the American War of Independence, died on 5th August 1792, two weeks after John Paul Jones died in Paris. By then the powdering of men's hair was right out of fashion. People had caught up with that outlandish hairstyle of the poet's youth when he had been marked out as a rebel because he let his hair grow long. He then had had the only tied hair in the parish. Now every man had his own hair tied in a stylish pigtail.

Though in 1792 William Bligh successfully transported breadfruit to the Caribbean (where in modern Jamaica it is still an everyday food), the anti-slave trading lobby was growing in power. Science advanced. It was a world pushing forward scientific development. Pioneering surgeon-medic John Hunter had improved understanding of disorders. He died on 16th October 1793 leaving much work to successors. For this was a world of human misery. In 1792 bubonic plague killed 800,000 in Egypt. In 1793 the volcano Miyi-Yama erupted in Java, Indonesia, killing over 50,000 people. In Japan an earthquake killed as many. The last entry that Burns had read when he studied the history notes in Salmon's 'Geographical Grammar' recorded food riots in 1766. In December 1766 a number of men were tried. Some were executed. In January 1796 his own children starved in Dumfries while from his sickbed he could hear outside the noise of food rioting.

In part the shortage was caused by exports having been encouraged by the Corn Laws, leaving insufficient in domestic markets to feed the population. Partly it was a build up from the war, with farm labourers having found work as soldiers. Partly it was the weather that had been an underlying factor in causing many political struggles during the lifetime of the poet. With food plentiful in our western world, we are apt to forget our dependence on natural things. Seasonal rhythm depends on the Earth's movement round the Sun, but like the movement of the tides, there is a secondary big variation from the movement of the Moon. The Moon circles the Earth around thirteen times each year – but not exactly thirteen times. Thus the position of the Moon relative to the Sun is different at each point in each year. This affects weather patterns. In our modern world of mechanised farming, controlled seed production, artificial insemination and heated stabling and barns, we are apt to forget this astronomical relationship. It was not yet forgotten in the late 18th century.

"Is Fortune's fickle Luna waning?" Burns had asked in a verse epistle to James Smith. As if in answer, the industrial era was gathering pace. Humphrey Davy, credited with inventing the miner's safety lamp – disputed by railway man George Stephenson – had been born on 17th December

1778. The first industrial heroes, such as Richard Arkwright, had already passed away. In December 1753 was born Samuel Crompton, inventor of the spinning mule. This was not long after John Kay, inventor of the flying shuttle, was forced into exile in France, after his home and workshop were attacked by a mob. In Ayr on 21st September 1756 had been born John Loudon McAdam, inventor of the macadam road surface. He lived until 1836 dreaming that one day surfaced roads would cover all the world. On 9th August 1757 Thomas Telford was born near Westerkirk, Dumfries. He lived until 1834, driving those roads and the new railways too across grand bridges, building the Caledonian and other canals, and installing harbours and docks to develop commerce.

In 1754 on 21st August William Murdock was born at Cumnock. In 1792 he used coal gas to light his home. Men prophesied a day of ubiquitous artificial light. Then farm workers need no longer stop because the sun had closed the winter-day.

None too soon in the eyes of science did the neon light split the night stopping men's ears to the sound of Nature and blinding men's eyes to the power and the glory of the mere Moon. Then science split the atom too and threatened to blot out the light of the Sun.

Development was being led by men called lunatics. The word did not then imply insanity. This entrepreneurial science-minded group got their name from their meeting arrangements. Benjamin Franklin named them so, for they met at the full moon. Their minds 'danced by the light of the moon', as Edward Lear might later have put it. Contemporary with Burns, they like him knew the phases of the moon. The waxing crescent moon is seen near the sun after sunset. The waning crescent passes below the horizon before sunrise. But the full moon rises in the east as the sun sets, and sets in the west as the sun rises. When the moon is full and the sky is clear Mankind has all night a God given brilliant though cold lantern to guide his path.

> Oh thou pale Orb, that silent shines
> While care-untroubled mortals sleep!
> Thou seest a *wretch* who inly pines,
> And wanders here to wail and weep!
> With Woe I nightly vigils keep,
> Beneath thy wan, unwarming beam;
> And mourn, in lamentation deep,
> How *life* and *love* are all a dream!

For a short period each month the thinking man of good eyesight can read and write 24/7 without the expense of a taper. When writing opportunity exists only after the end of a full day's labour, this matters. It is particularly important at northern latitudes where long winter nights devastate this limited reading and writing opportunity. Thus even in his infant studies, Burns learned to work along with the rhythm of the natural light not just of the sun but equally of the moon. His mind attuned this into lifetime instinctive ability. His creativity became rhythmic. All year it swelled with the growing moon, and it faded as the moon faded. Thus he explained in letters to Johnson and Thomson that his song output waxed and waned with the moonlight. They must be patient in awaiting the input to their music collections demanded of him. Within the year, his written output swelled with the growing length of the summer days, culminated in the autumn and subsided with shortening daylight hours.

In his youth he did not burn the candle at both ends; the cost of candles was too great an expense. When nights were dark, his thoughts were sobered. He would plan to be an ordinary mortal and do sensible everyday things. Then the moonlight gave him opportunity and his Muse found her way to the hand that held the quill. In his letter to Richard Brown on 30th December 1787 he remarked that he was

> "the will-o'-wisp being I used to be. About the first, and fourth quarters of the moon, I generally set in for the trade-winds of wisdom; but about the full, and change, I am the luckless victim of mad tornadoes, which blow me into chaos. Almighty Love 'reigns and revels' in my bosom."

His heart burned with the lights of the night sky. His creativity was inseparable from his source of light. As he gazed up from his page seeking inspiration, the movements of the heavens impressed themselves on his inner mind. Everywhere he used metaphor of and reference to Sun, Moon, planets, meteors, comets, stars, and the power of Nature. In this book I have explored if this impregnation of natural rhythms in his work has for our modern world, so dissociated from Nature, a message as yet unread.

Many ways of thinking have changed over two and a half centuries. I have ranged wide over matters that many readers might think irrelevant to enjoying the poems of Burns – indeed, these are matters discarded by many an intelligent modern mind. I am not proposing we reinstate all the old ways of thinking. In reviewing them, I try to show that Burns was in his work focussing on big underlying human issues as alive today as they were in his time. These remain big issues today, despite our ways of thinking having changed. Burns was addressing these deep big issues. He wrote about them. I suggest that how he thought about them is perhaps even more relevant today than it was in his own time. So I have explored how he became aware of these big issues, to help explain the language in which he expressed his response to them. He has left a legacy that can be enjoyed as art, but the works of Burns contain even more than that wealth. They contain understanding of modern fundamental human concerns.

The life of Robert Burns has been told in many ways. Undoubtedly there are those who will pounce on the astrology in this book. They may remark that to examine how far selected aspects of his life are in concordance or not with one interpretation of a putative horoscope is simply yet another gimmick attempting to grab attention for an old and worked out tale. Either that, or its author is a lunatic.

There is a story told about the man who was repeatedly told he was mad. When he went to his doctor for advice, the doctor mused and said: "If I say you are mad, and you say you are not mad, then perhaps I am right, and perhaps you are right, though we surely can't both be right at the same time. If some people sometimes say you are mad, and others sometimes say you are not, perhaps you are mad. But if everyone always says you are mad, then you are certainly not mad, since everyone cannot be right all the time."

Undoubtedly, modern psychiatrists have their opinion of this apocryphal story. But it has relevance to the life of Burns, the nature of the Enlightenment and the relevance of both to the modern world. For it says that differences of opinion are the sure sign of intelligent life. As it is not given to Mankind to have absolute knowledge, where there are differences of opinion there remain questions worthy of exploration. It is my interest in the relevance to the modern world of the general thoughts of Burns that primarily has motivated me to undertake the study necessary and the effort required to write this book, and to present it, warts and all, as a contribution to a debate that is by its nature necessarily unfinished and evolving. I propose astrology must be part of this study because in his time it was still promoted as relevant by some academics.

In the days of Robert Burns, astrology was not yet the archaic idea it seems in the modern world. Indeed, some would say that in the modern world it is still not a spent force. In March 2008, release of British Government papers under the 60-year rule disclosed that during the Second World War the Hungarian Louis de Wohl was hired to replicate the astrological input supplied to Adolf Hitler by Karl Ernest Frafft. De Wohl was also sent on a lecture tour of the United States to help bring them into that war on the side of the Allies. The British Government treated access to astrological data as relevant, if requiring due caution.

Thus in this study of Burns I have considered astrology amongst the other matters normally missing from the biographies. In particular, I have considered belief in the fairy world, which Burns declared was part of the milieu in which he lived. In each of these areas I have presented a starting point for others to consider all of them further.

Of course, some readers will automatically ridicule the forms of thought, rather than looking at how they help us to learn from Robert Burns. But in the face of ridicule there are always those who will defend a form of thought.

One of the objections to astrology is that there are many systems which surely can't all be right, so contradictory they are in form and thus inevitably in interpretation. Challengers of astrology naturally demand there be, for example, correlation between interpretation of Western and Chinese astrological readings. The Chinese system was not generally familiar even to the most international of academics at the time of Robert Burns. Today Westerners are increasingly aware that it exists. The Olympics in Beijing, for example, in 2008, took place during the Year of the Rat, which began at the new moon on 7th February by the Western calendar.

The lunar calendar has been in use in what is now China for over three millennia. This consists of heavenly stems and earthly branches. The ten heavenly stems are, in Western pronunciation, Jia, Yi, Bin, Ding, Wu, Ji, Geng, Xin, Ren and Gui. There are twelve earthly branches, which Westerners pronounce Zi, Chou, Yin, Mao, Chen, Si, Wu, Wei, Shen, You, Xu and Hai. Years are named by combining a heavenly stem with an earthly branch in sequence: thus year Jia Zi is followed by year Yi Chou, and then Bin Yin and so on. Because there are ten of the one and twelve of the other, these cycle round over sixty years. Similarly, months and days each have a heavenly stem and an earthly branch. Thus is each day in each year given a name.

As in Western astrology, in ancient Chinese philosophy the heavens and Mankind formed a unity with all life. Twelve animal types were identified to match each of the earthly branches. These are the animal year symbols. Thus Zi is associated with the Rat, Chou with Ox, followed by Tiger, Rabbit, Dragon, Snake, Horse, Goat, Monkey, Chicken, Dog and Pig. The Chinese talk of people being Shen Xiao or having birth resemblance to one of these animals, tempered by the heavenly stem of the year of their birth and the characteristics of the day of birth.

For example, those born in a Chicken year would be expected, in general terms, to be firm, quick-minded people, up to date with thought. Honoured people would help them. They would be excellent with language, and be original. They would speak their minds, holding back nothing of their thoughts. They would challenge authority and accepted ways and modes. People would find them frank and witty, and at the same time brave. They would be expected to be enthusiastic and generous, and to care for those whom they loved.

The Chinese New Year begins at that new moon which in Western terms falls on or after 22nd January. Naturally, generating a true Chinese horoscope is an esoteric art, but is as much based on astronomical data as Western astrology. So it is possible to calculate retrospectively its simplest features for a child of known birthdate and thus illustrate its expected character within this mode of thought.

Robert Burns lived in what the Chinese would undoubtedly have described as interesting times. The ebb and flow of his own life was against the backdrop of global turmoil and change as European nations and the fledgling American United States fought to carve out their territories and identity. The era in which he lived had fundamental impact on the shape, activities and attitudes of the modern world. His own legacy was formed in that same cauldron. Surprisingly, when poetry is no longer a fashionable commodity, and the words and works of so many others described as poets are no longer read or recited, from his era his alone still has a worldwide active audience, annually regenerating. That such should be means surely that there is some intrinsic worth to our modern age of what, on the surface, appears to be a mere collection of poems chiefly in an out of date obscure Scottish dialect.

That Scottish dialect found itself sung throughout the entire world on the night of the start of the Western millennium year 2000. At every great show of Chinese-inspired fireworks around the Earth, people joined hands and sang 'Auld Lang Syne'. This perennial song of friendship was written to pre-existing Scottish music by Robert Burns.

Three hundred and sixty six days before Robert Burns was born, on 24th January 1758, the full moon over Ayrshire was fully eclipsed during the second quarter of the day, the eclipse beginning about two hours before dawn. This tells us that the Chinese Year in which 25th January 1759 fell began approximately two weeks later on 7th or 8th February 1758, ending about 26th January 1759. This suggests that Robert Burns was born at the very end of a Chinese yang Tiger Earth year, in a yin wood ox month, at the dragon hour. Chinese astrology suggests that a person with personality of a Tiger year would outwardly be daring, entertaining, exhausting, passionate, dangerous and hasty. He would inwardly, from his birth month be moderate, have a sense of loyalty, like to belong, like company, need to be needed, would pay attention to detail, would seek harmony but could be stubborn. Tigers are charismatic and excellent with language and able to be spontaneous with words. Male tigers are passionate lovers but rebellious spirits. An Earth Tiger understands the feelings and needs of others. Born in the last month of the lunar year, these elemental traits would be transformed into purposeful activity by the ox characteristics of patience, courage, reliability and intelligence, with these tempered with respect for tradition. However, such a person would in addition have the very definite incorrigible trait of not suffering fools gladly. He would tell people, whoever they were, exactly what he thought of them. The Chinese view the ox as relentless in the pursuit of truth, integrity and what is right. The tiger-ox combination produces a person who would live dedicated to results but probably die young.

From Burns's birth hour around dawn, the Chinese astrologer would have expected him deep down to have the characteristics of the dragon – enthusiastic, daring, inspiring, successful in what he did, aware of the real world, and fiercely independent. A Dragon constantly seeks to gather wisdom and aims to travel so as to learn. The Chinese astrologer would not be surprised that a person of Burns's horoscope would show the intense attachment in his creativity to the very soil of his homeland, and would find it harmonious that he expressed in his poetry his close relationship not just with ploughed fields and landscapes, but with the clay to which all Men ultimately return. These together would suggest Burns had as Earth element what the Chinese astrologer calls the Palace of the Bright Moon. An interesting point is that the Chinese would recommend someone with such a strong Earth element in his makeup to avoid damp. No Chinese physician would have recommended to Burns that he seek cure to his terminal illness through immersion treatment in the chilly exposed Solway while drinking the freezing waters of Brow Well.

In so far as there are fundamental similarities between Western and Chinese horoscopes, surely this is because both are centred on great movements that enable the counting of time: the revolutions of Earth, Moon and planets, refined by observation against changing seasons. The concept of twelve earthly branches surely does not arise from the Moon, as the Moon, in one cycle of seasons, circles the Earth about thirteen times, not twelve. But there are twelve year cycles in nature: the behaviour of sun spots, which correlates to some degree with weather patterns, appears to have something like a twelve year cycle. As sun spots can be observed in a projection such as through the pinhole of a camera obscura – the room-sized equivalent of an old pinhole camera – it is possible that ancient Chinese astronomers noted a weather correlation with sun spot activity.

Sun spot activity in any day or month is not a reliable indicator of location on a twelve year cycle. Thus astronomers might look around for some other time measure with a reliable twelve year cycle. In the sky they found Jupiter, conveniently cycling the Sun in approximately twelve years. Thus the position of Jupiter in the heavens could be read, provided the stars were mapped in the visual memory of observers.

Our brains like organising things. Humans find stars are most easily mentally mapped if they are deliberately grouped into patterns, or constellations. The night sky can be divided into twelve parts by defining groupings so that each one roughly fits one twelfth of the circle of the sky. Thus, in order to use Jupiter to mark the twelve year cycle of the Sun, Chinese astronomers and Western astronomers might independently have defined twelve constellations of stars to mark out their night sky.

When Robert Burns was born, Jupiter was against the backdrop of the Western constellation Capricorn. Jupiter went through just over three Sun orbits during his short life, from the perspective of Earth completing each of these on January 8th 1771, December 23rd 1782 and December 6th 1795. As this last gap is 13 years, not 12, I remind you that planetary periods do not appear consistent in length when viewed from Earth.

Western astrologers associate Jupiter with physical well-being and material success. When it influences strongly, it creates an optimistic outlook. But they consider that when Jupiter is in Capricorn, its normal expansive and positive influences are seriously restricted. Mercury was also in Capricorn when Burns was born, and in addition was doing one of those backward whirls in the sky dance; Mercury was retrograde. Mercury is the planet of communication; retrograde indicates that this communication is particularly strong with respect to traditional forms. When someone is born with Jupiter and Mercury in the same constellation the communicative ability of Mercury is considerably strengthened in this person.

Birth positions of planets for Burns suggest to astrologers that this Mercury influence would be particularly strong in his twenty seventh year. This would develop in the next two to three years to emphasise the importance of past things. Robert Burns was in his twenty seventh year in 1785, when poetically he was very productive. This led to the publication in 1786 of the first edition of his poems. In his thirtieth year Jupiter was in the constellation Gemini which emphasises the importance of things historic. Saturn's return marked the beginning of the second phase of his life. It was then that he confirmed in his own mind the task allotted to him by his Muse: he was to apply his poetic abilities to the very challenging task of rescuing the fast vanishing old tunes of Scotland. He set about collecting scraps of music and fragments of verse. He dedicated the remainder of his life to producing his magnificent legacy of song.

Basic parallels between two very different astrological systems would not of themselves imply any correlation in the interpretation of fortune based on horoscope. Where such a correlation is shown to exist, it weighs in favour of those who believe that the star-date of birth of a person or institution and subsequent fortune in life are linked.

The use of the word, parallels, highlights a subtle issue of the modern mind that emerged during the later Enlightenment period: the vast majority of ordinary people think digitally in a world that is not digital. Digitally numbered time has become the norm. There has been international agreement to replace astronomical time with atomic time. Our Earth is orbited by numerous digital satellites. It has become an everyday matter that the conventional change in the numbering of the hours of the day around the vernal equinox, called moving 'forward' from winter time to summer time, is now accompanied by satellites sending out digital signals. These are picked up by receiving electronic chips in hundreds of millions of digital clocks from cars to computers. Thus we need no longer fear that we forget to 'change the clock'. Big Brother does it for us.

Big Brother is digital – indeed, normally either binary or decimal digital. Computers are ubiquitous in modern life. Digital numbering, to some base or other, accounts for the vast majority of computer operations, whether data is numerical, verbal, linguistic, image or sound. As a mathematician and philosopher, this causes me to muse. It has intriguing implications at the abstract level and has already had massively disruptive impact at economic level, despite the smoothness with which the modern world appeared to move through the dangerous territory of the so-called Millennium Bug.

Digital numbers by their very nature can represent only a small component of reality. There is, for example, no such thing as a true finite decimal or a true finite binary number which accurately represents the extremely ordinary everyday fraction, one-third. This can only be accurately represented in tertiary or tertially-multiple systems. These are rarely employed, because they fit so badly with everything else. Fractions used to be taught in schools. They have gone out of fashion, because they are in the too difficult category for many modern teachers. That doesn't mean they don't occur in real life; at the trivial level, we often need to divide a cake or a pizza into six parts – each one simply one half of one third. We usually do this 'by eye'. It becomes more fractious if the matter to be divided so equally is a plot of land fought over by three antagonistic nations.

Fractions are rational things – they are the ratio of integers, which themselves are based on the fingers on our hands on which we all as children first learned to count. Yet this rational set of numbers – of which decimals form a tiny fraction – is itself by no means all the numbers there are. The ancient

Greek mathematician Pythagoras was aware of this. He noted that there was no rational number that gave the length of the hypotenuse of an isosceles right angled triangle. This needed a number we call the square root of 2. He found he could produce another, by making his right angled triangle have sides of length 1 and 2. The hypotenuse was then of length the square root of 5. He continued and found an infinite number of similar numbers that are not rational. Then he thought about the numbers that multiplied up produced the volume of cubes. Reversing this, he got more irrational numbers out of thinking of cube roots of volumes that were prime numbers. He possibly thought into four and more dimensions and discovered more and more and more irrational numbers. He would have found an infinite number of infinite groups of irrational numbers that weren't there on the real line when all the rational numbers were marked on it.

Pythagoras was aware of even more numbers still, because he tried to solve a problem that kept turning up in land surveying: what is the area of a circular plot of land? Burns needed to be able to calculate areas and volumes based on circles, cylinders and cones, as an everyday part of his Excise duties.

Nowhere does 'The Elements of Euclid', as published since the start of the 18th century, deal with the area of a circle, or the question of identifying circles and squares of equal area, reasonable though the question remains. Compasses for drawing circles are constantly used in teaching Euclid's thinking – but as a tool for generating lines, squares and angles. Nowhere in Pike's 'Morals and Dogma' of Freemasonry is there any consideration of the circle, except as a symbol in the early Degrees and within the 28th Degree of Knight of the Sun, or Prince Adept. For this high Degree it is stated that "the Square, turning on itself, produces the circle equal to itself", which mathematically is very misleading.

It is misleading because it does not say in what way there is any equality. Mathematics needs that to be defined. There is a circle of area equal to the *area* of the square, if you can find it. There's a fun way to start looking for it. Get yourself a bright yellow square and put a hole through its middle. Put a spindle into the hole and spin the square fast as smoothly as you can. This is the square turning on itself. Your brain sees a circle, but it is a circle with a broad very fuzzy rim. The inner edge of this rim is a circle of diameter equal to the side of the square. The outer edge is a circle of diameter equal to the diagonal of the square. Between these two, at an indeterminable spot, lies the circle whose area is equal to the area of the square.

We can calculate the area of a rectangle rationally by multiplying the lengths of its sides. But if I want to exchange a circular field for a rectangular one, how am I sure I get fair value? There is no rational answer, in the sense of being able to state the area of a circle accurately. Although the area depends on the radius in a very real way, it is not rational dependency.

Pythagoras conveniently noticed for the circle that both the area and the length of the circumference bore similar dependencies to the length of the radius – but to express this as a number he had to invoke an approximate multiplier, which he found had an indeterminate value close to the ratio of 22 to 7. Over centuries, mathematicians sought to get more accurate about what this ratio actually was. Eventually, they realised that, no matter how many digits they might invoke, there was no answer. The number is real enough, but it cannot be written using any true fractions. So as there are no ratios of integers that can express it, it isn't rational. Thus was invented the symbol π to represent the dependency. This is the same as the Greek letter pronounced pi. This became only the first of a set of vitally important numbers none of which is rational – and they are vital in the sense that they keep recurring in life in nature.

Mathematicians long ago noted that they could use a straight line to set out all their integers, and added zero and negative numbers. In the gaps between the integers they had put the fractional or rational numbers. Only with the discovery of the irrational numbers and those strange ones like π was all the space filled in. As we have seen, mathematicians discovered there had been an infinite amount of such space filling to do. The rational numbers had merely been like dots on the line.

Accountants discovered they often needed negative numbers. Declarations of losses and bankruptcies are very much real numbers too. Mathematicians began to ask whether the properties of positive integers extended to negative integers.

And can real areas also be negative? The simplest way to express this question in maths is to ask if there is a number which multiplied by itself, gives negative 1. In other words, has minus one a square root? Or another way: can a negative number represent a square? This seemingly preposterous question caused the invention of imaginary numbers. These are very useful things that let mathematicians make Complex Numbers.

A very good way to represent complex numbers is to map them out on a circle. This drew attention of mathematicians to the fact that the behaviour of complex numbers included the behaviour of the sines and cosines already used by surveyors. These complex numbers can do very real things. Remember that Tacoma Narrows Bridge. Mathematicians have now worked out ways to make formulae that describe the behaviour of bridges in winds. When complex numbers fit those formulae it can mean that, in certain winds, the bridge will shake itself to pieces. Such understanding is part of the standard design toolkit nowadays when designing aircraft, or oil rigs capable of operating in violent or deep oceans.

Thus rational numbers by no means represent all reality. Imaginary numbers do represent reality. Insisting on rationality that leaves out the non-rational and imagination leaves out just about everything there is. Burns had to do accounts for his farming and so learned a lot about negative numbers. He was master of circular-based volumes for his Excise work. He had become very familiar with sines and cosines from his studies under Rodger in Kirkoswald. So at every stage of his life, non-rational numbers were part of the everyday reality of Burns. He was very proud of mastering the use of his slide rule to do the sophisticated calculations needed in certain Excise assessments.

As a poet, Burns knew the difference between handling elaborate formulae and actually understanding what the formulae ultimately mean for real life. He was aware of the enormous gulf between a true mathematician with intuition and someone who calls himself a mathematician because he can do more clever sums than others can. Unfortunately for our own times, even senior professionals can often not tell the difference. Thus in charge of some banks have been put persons thought to be mathematical but who lack intuitive insight. Such people cannot understand the true import of complex mathematical tools they authorise their staff to use. In ignorance they can blithely steer their bank irretrievably into a whirlpool. The world has recently seen how such people express surprise when assets are sucked down into black holes such as sour money market deals or credit derivatives. Burns was quite familiar with this kind of naive yet highly respected character. Typically he so enthrals those around him with his dexterity that he easily gets another top job. These are of a kind with those who in the poet's day called themselves mathematicians and claimed they could prove with science that there was no God. A true mathematician knows that his maths is only valid within the limits which he himself has defined for it. Definite absolute claims of any sort are anathema to true mathematical discipline. Lacking that intuition, pseudo-mathematicians of the 18th century denied any God could exist. These were the Sceptics. They carried out that lobotomy which severed Natural Philosophy from Nature. Thus on 12th February 1788 Burns could remark to Mrs Dunlop of the Edinburgh he had come to know:

"A mathematician without religion is a probable character; an irreligious poet is a monster."

We are still living with the consequences.

Modern science calls itself rational science. It is interesting that modern Physics – the poor thin child of Natural Philosophy – *needs* to invent parallel universes and a Void in order to comprehend its realities. This may be because the totality of the truth of Creation slips through the thin net of rational thinking, which cannot by its very nature comprehend all reality. Modern thinking demands rationality and calls it Reason. This abuse of the word 'Reason' was already happening during the life of Burns, causing him to remark:

"In vain do we talk of reason; we are the offspring of Caprice, and the nurslings of Habitude. The most pleasurable part of our existence, the strings that tie heart to heart, are the manufacture of some hitherto undescribed and unknown Power within us."

It is amusing to reflect that perhaps the Enlightenment was not so much the Age of Reason, as the age when amongst the educated, knowledge became rationed.

I will take a leaf out of our philosopher-poet's book. I will try to put the non-rational back into Reason and invent a new word. Let's start talking about things being *Reasonal*. Of course, rational spellchecking softwares object to this word, as being unreal. Were it not Rational science but instead *Reasonal* science, there might be more humility. Humility leads to acceptance that even with such a science that could comprehend the irrational as a true part of Reason – and indeed one of the greater parts – not everything can ever be understood by any human mind, and certainly not fully discussed through the limited articulation of human communication mechanisms.

The 19th century saw the burgeoning of our modern era of Rational Science and that departure from the totality of Reason that was capable so readily of including dreams, imagination, inspiration and Common Sense. My new concept, Reasonal Science, had it developed, would not have *needed* parallel universes and a Void to explain the paradoxical complexity of totality. Reasonal Science would instead accept that such are amongst the many options that present themselves to the mind as possibilities for mathematical models to help describe an infinitely varied Creation. *Which* model is most relevant to address any challenge facing humanity is *then* the choice of intelligent and informed decision.

With the initial invention of complex numbers, the circle of rational and imaginary rational numbers was beginning to be squared with the down-to-earth reality of land-surveying and building. But not quite. This set of complex numbers still wasn't everything – until the irrational and imaginary irrational numbers were added to this circle, all that had been created was a fine lace net instead of an impenetrable covering of the so-called complex plain. It is a finer net than the

snaw white seventeen hunder linen

that would have impressed the poet had the withered beldams of Alloway Kirk's satanic dance been wearing it. But such fine smooth cloth is net none the less, and it won't hold water. Paradoxically, the finer the linen, the more holes it has! So all the rational numbers make a very fine net, but yet it is only a net, with true reality able to slip right through it. This is what all modern digital representations do – they pretend to represent reality, when all they do is cover over reality with a very fine mesh of numbers.

This is the point at which, in my view, the modern study of humanities departed from reality, for philosophy began to focus on the net and not the intuitive humanity that slipped so quietly through it. Enlightenment scholars, without being aware of what they were doing, divided into those who believed that everything could be expressed accurately by numbers, and those, like Newton and the increasingly esoteric mathematicians, who knew this was impossible.

Mathematics became too much for non-mathematicians to follow when Isaac Newton invented a whole new way of using his discipline in order to work out the motions of the planets. In his demonstration of the impact of an inverse square law force of gravity to form elliptical orbits he abandoned numbers altogether. He invented those fluxions that are the basis of calculus, and generated modern abstract analysis and geometry that seldom have a number in them, yet can get us to the Moon and back and put a satellite in stable orbit. Ever since then, mathematicians – who had long been very comfortable using abstract symbols – virtually gave up using actual numbers. Mathematics, from being a central discipline as it was in ancient times, has become the ultimate arcane discipline of modern universities.

Burns understood that Newton never meant that number could describe and explain all creation and humanity, but the exact opposite. He wrote to Nicol that Man is:

> "an erring wretch, of whom the zig-zag wanderings defy all the powers of calculation, from the simple computation of units up to the hidden mysteries of fluxions!"

This mathematics of fluxions, which was the beginning of modern very advanced mathematical studies, was a bridge too far for the vast majority even of the polymaths of the Enlightenment. With fluxions began the ragged rift between such Natural Philosophers as could embrace understanding of mathematics, and the majority of academics who were already unable to comprehend that irrational numbers were at the heart of Reason. In a letter to Mrs Dunlop on 21st June 1789, Burns challenged the Enlightenment philosophers for their narrow application to the question of moral sentiments of the very limited mathematics they were able to understand:

> "What a poor, blighted, rickety breed are the Virtues & charities when they take their birth from geometrical hypothesis and mathematical demonstration. And what a vigorous Offspring are they when they owe their origin to, and are nursed with the vital blood of a heart glowing with the noble enthusiasm of Generosity, Benevolence and Greatness of Soul. The first may do well for those philosophers who look on the world of man as one vast ocean, and each individual as a little vortex whose sole business and merit is to absorb as much as it can in its own center; but the last is absolutely & essentially necessary when you would make a Leonidas, a Hannibal, an Alfred or a Wallace."

From that time on, the words Rational and Reasonable (not Reasonal, note) have, in ordinary discourse, increasingly converged in meaning. Before then, Reason embraced all activities of the mind, both factual and intuitive. The architecture of the Enlightenment, with its mere squares, cubes and right angles, reflected the beginning of a narrow dogmatic view that Reason was represented by the line, the square, the level and the right angle. The circle was banished as representing the evil darkness of Mediaeval Unreason – but lived on in Freemasonry.

Instinctively, Robert Burns rebelled against the denigration of the circle. As a surveyor and gardener, he had in youth learned its importance in the creation of what mankind felt was beauty. As an Exciseman he knew how imperative it was to recognise the volumes of barrels and to be able to estimate quantities of non-rectangular form. In his poetry he rejoiced in the rounding verses he learned from the old Scots bards. In his song he revelled in the sound of the reel.

Burns may not have used the stars to guide his life decisions, but the intelligentsia amongst whom his own genius enabled him to move were by no means indifferent to the stars. Nor did they all despise the legacy, thousands of years old, of those who had studied the stars and sought to make sense of their meaning in the great scheme of things. No longer was there any room for simplistic views of life and the universe; Man had been truly challenged to use his mind, that organ most godlike, to search out the meaning of life. Not even the distant stars were affixed to some static firmament, however they might be held in the great ether. In 1718 Halley, having spent several years studying the works of the classical astronomer Ptolemy, concluded that certain so-called 'fixed' stars had over fifteen hundred years moved relative to other 'fixed' stars. Those stars did not simply move on notional spherical surfaces: in 1728 James Bradley discovered the aberration of twilight, this being the difference in the angle at which starlight arrives, depending on whether the Earth is moving away from or towards it.

New ways are often needed to express new discoveries. Isaac Newton had shown the way; but his work was too obscure for most people. In 1730 Scottish mathematician James Stirling published 'Differential Method or Treatise on the Summation and Interpolation of Infinite Series'. While this explained Newton's new language to some, for many others it only emphasised that mathematicians had orbited off into an imaginary world of their own making. Today, anyone who claims in general company to be a mathematician is typically ignored as a geek of no social relevance.

Out of this world of mathematics have come many great very real things, amongst them the ubiquitous electronic technology that equally allows the most uneducated at their personal computers to pretend to be authors and delicate dedicated surgeons to perform what in the 18th century would have been considered miracle cures. It also makes it easy for a lot of supposedly highly educated people to abuse elaborate tools that they do not fully understand. Thus, some latter day leading actuaries – the profession invented to gain understanding of risks in life – abandoned the old discipline of testing theories against common sense. Instead they began to use massive number crunchers to 'prove' their ideas. Some of these were endorsed by Nobel Prizes. Some modellers offered the promise that applying their ideas guaranteed big quick bucks to money market traders. Along with the big bucks, these models generated big risks.

An early result of this use of those too limited digital rational numbers was the crisis generated by the crash of the company known as Long Term Capital Management. As I write the world is working itself through the global economic trauma of a credit crunch generated by even greater abuse of derivative financial vehicles multiplied as a result of similar absence of understanding of the inadequacies of mathematical modelling when applied to real human beings. Adam Smith warned about the dangers of such abuse.

Some say that bank leaders are culpable if they employ tools whose components were never appropriate for the purpose to which they are applied. It is taking enough public money to fix the immediate consequences of the credit crunch. But it will take considerable investment and strong action by governments and universities to redress that absence of understanding of the deep implications of mathematics that began as the Enlightenment entered what is called its Golden Age.

At that Golden Age, Aberdeen printer James Chalmers and his son from 1771 took over production of the 'Aberdeen Almanack'. This was a practical publication for farmers, fleshed out with general information. When Burns made his tour of the Highlands, he met one of these men, probably the son. Perhaps the poet asked about that curious prediction made by that old woman at his birth. The old witch had said there had been an invisible eclipse of the Sun the day before Burns was born. Burns knew his astronomy: the moon was not new until 28th January that year. So how might the old woman have thought that this baby, conceived at Beltane, was born under a comet after an eclipse of the Sun?

Chalmers undoubtedly shook his head and remarked that this was one reason that his printing company now were the ones to do the 'Merry Andrew'. The previous printers had been so keen to get the copy out that they were lax on the proof-reading. That 1759 copy was notorious: right up front it stated that there were three eclipses in 1759. Chalmers could even quote the words to show how foolish was any reader that failed to spot the error.

> Three eclipses this year, one of the moon and two of the sun. The first is of the moon, Jan 13, sets eclipsed. The second is of the sun, Jan 24 invisible. The third is of the sun, Dec 19 invisible.

How could anyone not spot the error? If January 13th were a full moon, January 24th could not be a new moon, necessary for an eclipse of the Sun. The next page confirmed there was an error: the new moon was on 28th January. So when the page read 'Jan 24' this was clearly 'Jun 24' misprinted. NASA confirms that there were two eclipses of the Sun that year, both invisible in Scotland – indeed, visible to few of European origin, for the shadow on June 24th was a very narrow path across the Pacific Ocean, northern South America and the southern Atlantic. The second, annular, on 19th December drew a shadow across South America, across the Atlantic, and into Africa from Angola to Kenya.

But the old woman could not read. As she came through Ayr the previous night, she had perhaps heard read out in some howff the words of Merry Andrew – an eclipse of the Sun has just happened, on January 24th. No doubt this had met with a laugh from those who realised how preposterous this was. Not so the old woman. With so many strange things happening in the sky she thus watched out for an amazing birth. Like an impoverished Magi, she lavished her prophecies on a boy child who would so soon need to be laid in a manger. Perhaps the enlightened gentlemen in Aberdeen, well versed in their astronomy, musing when he told the story of the prophecy at his birth, responded with a chuckle:

"Mr Burness" – they would have called him by his old Aberdonian name – "Indeed you must be a man of remarkable parts, were you born out of an eclipse of the Sun just as Halley's comet was seen to be rising in the sky too. All but one of the planets and the Moon were then gathered around the Sun. The ancients would have said that you were blessed with all their strengths. But with Saturn sending its energies square across their path as it did at the day of your birth you would have great struggle to realise any benefit from it."

Another, looking at the Ephemeris table again, might have added. "It is my view they would have said the one big blessing was that you had Jupiter on your side, pointing out the Path of the Great Architect. So you have been right, Mr Burness, to use the Brotherhood so keenly to support your cause."

Amid a round of light laughter at this solemn discussion of these so very unfashionable matters, the first perhaps looked at the poet keenly. "The ancients would have said you are a Man of Destiny. Do you know yet what that Destiny is?"

This would have drawn from Rabbie a sad laugh. This was the one great fear that he had kept so well hidden even from his closest friends: the want of an aim but the desperate need to have an aim worthy of the talents he knew he possessed.

The men looked at each other, exchanging glances of knowing and understanding.

Then one of them quietly said: "Saturn approaches the same position as we speak, and its return there will be in spring in this coming year."

"Does this mean anything, gentlemen?" Robert might have asked.

They would have looked at each other, again musing, smiles playing on their lips.

"The body of opinion amongst the learned is undecided", one might have answered. "But perhaps Shakespeare has a word for it: 'There are more things in heaven and Earth than are dreamt of in our philosophies.' There let the matter rest."

A few months earlier, at the height of his social success in Edinburgh, Burns had penned a song to celebrate his 28th birthday. It was not published in his lifetime, and was brought to public attention in 1808. 'There was a lad' spelled out the original prophecy. It also reflected an experience mirrored by the innocent young modern Scotsman who, having pushed his friend with moral and technical support through to becoming 'Fame Academy' winner, found himself living with his mate in a very posh London flat. They were invited to all the media events and parties. They found themselves surrounded by that type of gold-digger women who respond to the smell of the power inherent in emerging financial success, and offer their naked siren bodies as bait.

> There was a lad was born in Kyle
>   But what na day o' what na style,
> I doubt it's hardly worth the while
>   To be sae nice wi' Robin.
>
> Robin was a rovin' Boy,
>   Rantin', rovin', rantin; rovin':
> Robin was a rovin' Boy,
>   Rantin' rovin' Robin.
>
> Our monarch's hindmost year but ane
>   Was five-and-twenty days begun
> 'Twar then a blast o' Janwar' Win'
>   Blew hansel in on Robin.

The Gossip Keekit in his loof,
      Quo' scho wha lives will see the proof,
This waly boy will be nae coof.
      I think we'll ca' him Robin.

He'll hae misfortunes great an' sma',
      But ay a heart aboon them a';
He'll be a credit 'till us a',
      We'll a' be proud o' Robin

But sure as three times three mak nine,
      I see by ilka score and line,
This chap will dearly like our kin',
      So leeze me on thee, Robin.

Guid faith quo' scho I doubt you Stir,
      Ye'll gar the lassies lie aspar;
But twenty faus ye may hae waur –
      So blessin's on thee, Robin.

The poem was probably not printed because the final verse, prophesying that women would throw themselves at him, is still often deemed too risqué for polite society.

John Cairney in 2000 produced 'On the Trail of Robert Burns' (by the way, a summary not only of the life of Burns but also a first-rate commentary on many places associated with him) in passing remarking on a repetition of 'three times three' in the life of Burns. He was born 1759; he died in 1796; nine Freemasons of Kilmarnock Kilwinning Lodge were largely responsible for the publication of his first edition of poems, and were the first to describe him officially as 'Poet'; nine men helped cause the Edinburgh edition to be published; nine attended the first Burns Supper in Alloway; he had nine children by his wife Jean Armour; and to round it off he was five feet nine inches tall. Of course, of any life we might seek out and find a range of incidents which have some number in common. I can add that he begins "in the name of the NINE" – the Muses in this case – a letter to pals, William Chalmers and John McAdam, whom he describes as,

      "Students and Practitioners in the ancient and mysterious Science of Confounding Right
      and Wrong".

Cairney in my childhood was an actor who made a name for his one-man shows portraying the life of Robert Burns. I was fortunate to be taken by my mother to one of the first presentations of his first show that was entitled 'There was a man'. Cairney tells in an autobiographical note how he used the character he had created to earn a living. He also visited people confined to elderly homes or hospitals. There he learned about perceptions of reality.

He visited a psychiatric ward in one hospital. He talked to men in beds and on wheelchairs. On his way to the car park he overheard two old men sitting on a bench in the sun, chatting. Said one:

"They've taken away the man who thinks he's Rabbie Burns."

Each person who meets the work of Burns or studies his legacy creates in his mind a different character. I have sought to understand the nature of his humanity.

During his tour of the Highlands in 1787, an esoteric discussion on Monday, 10th September with the printer Mr Chalmers, the 'facetious fellow' as Burns called him in his journal, undoubtedly would have reinforced his instinct that the academy of fame in which he had been so celebrated such a short time earlier was as diaphanous as the fairies. But the encounter was propitious. Amongst the others at the 'lazy town' of Aberdeen, were Thomas Gordon, Professor of Humanity and Philosophy at King's College, the poet Andrew Shirrefs whose father had been a builder and Rev. John Skinner, the senior Episcopalian whose father had written the song 'Tullochgorum' that Burns so much admired. Bishop Skinner wrote to his father – the author of 'Tullochgorum' – after meeting Burns, and told him that the poet was enthusiastically working on a Scottish song project. He also met a Mr Marshall. This Mr Marshall might have been William Marshall (1745-1818), the experimental agriculturist who wrote 'Rural Economy of England'. But he was probably the factor of the Duke of Gordon, the William Marshall (1748-1833) who is remembered for song and music.

Burns described William Marshall as the greatest writer of Strathspeys then alive. His song 'Of a' the Airts the Wind can Blaw' is written to a tune by Marshall, as is 'My luve is like a red, red rose'. Born in Fochabers, the house demolished when the new planned village was established to improve the grounds around Gordon Castle in 1776, Marshall had had no more formal education than Burns. Working in the household of Alexander, 4th Duke of Gordon, he found himself in an environment where his natural musical ability was encouraged to flourish. That Duke, a man of Enlightenment interests, keenly promoted music and played the fiddle. Burns admitted to being able to scratch a tune on the fiddle, which was probably modesty to prevent him exposing his insufficient skill to play the violin as formal entertainment. The Duchess of Gordon was the fashionable Edinburgh hostess with whom Burns was already on good terms. Before the notorious estrangement of duke and duchess – she was rather too vivacious and he was very fond of the girls – they together had in 1781 encouraged Marshall to publish music he had written.

Marshall's musical understanding complemented his other skill of numbering time: he is known to have constructed at least three clocks, one being a long-case built before 1770. He later made an astronomical clock that gave in addition to the time of day: the months of the year, the difference for each day that the time on the clock differs in minutes and seconds from the time by the Sun and from the time by a clock regulated to exact equatorial time, the phases of the moon and the length of the interval between present time and the moon phases, the time of the Sun's rising, the length of the day, the date of that year's Spring and Autumn equinoxes, the length of the longest and shortest days with their date, timings of high water at various locations, the relation of present time to the twelve signs of the zodiac, and for each day the degrees and minutes of the Sun's position within the zodiac, and the Sun's declination north or south of the equator for each two days. This clock, which needed winding once a month and then carefully recalibrated, was in Gordon Castle and in working order until it was sold in 1938. Marshall, in the castle library, could have studied the works of the scientist James Ferguson. He in 1775 published 'The Description and use of Astronomical Ritual', having in 1756 published 'Astronomy Explained upon Sir Isaac Newton's Principles'. Ferguson in 1768 produced 'Easy Introduction to Astronomy for Gentlemen and Ladies', and later 'An Introduction to electricity and an Astronomical lecture on Eclipses'. Ferguson had designed his own orrery and other astronomical instruments, which would have been available as models for Marshall's own mechanical constructions.

An orrery was only the most up to date of a long line of astronomical instruments. It is now known that even in the Bronze Age there existed portable mechanical devices to tell when the moon phases had got too out of line with the Sun's timings for seasons. These were used by the guardian of the community's calendar for identifying, from stellar observations, when he needed to direct that the end of this Sun cycle of seasons was after thirteen moons, this time, and not twelve. In Halle Museum in Germany is one such device, known as the Nebra Sky Disc, recently found by illegal metal detectorists who were caught extracting finds from known historic sites.

Burns had visited Gordon Castle in Fochabers on 7th September, but the musical factor might then have been in Aberdeen on business and so he caught up with him there. Burns himself was, to his immense anger, whisked away from that meeting in Gordon Castle by his selfish travelling companion, Nicol. It is consistently presumed that the subsequent row between Burns and Nicol was because Nicol had once too often imposed his general impatience on Burns. It is similarly suggested that Nicol's impatience was earlier the cause that Burns did not meet Henry Dundas at Blair Atholl – which as we have seen is by no means a clear-cut assertion.

There was another real reason, other than feeling abandoned at the inn, that Nicol would have felt very uncomfortable in Fochabers: this region was a hotbed of Roman Catholicism. Very close is Tynet Chapel that illegally operated before Catholic Emancipation. It enabled Catholicism to stay vibrant in the face of persecution. It is more than likely that Nicol wanted out of a place where he felt threatened by the Whore of Babylon. Burns, on the other hand, was actively consorting with this evil – for there was nothing sectarian about the poet's makeup; indeed he detested sectarianism along with all other forms of discrimination. Nicol no doubt was dismayed but not surprised at his companion's behaviour, having observed that in Edinburgh he actively courted that detestable Bishop Geddes. Burns would have been doubly angry with Nicol – first for depriving him of good musical company, but on top of that for demonstrating that deep in his soul was an implacable hatred of the innermost belief of other fellow men. His good friend the Latin scholar denied his fellow man the basic human right – freedom of conscience with its attendant freedom of worship. Burns would blame no man for his religion any more than he would for not having an ear for music.

At Fochabers or Aberdeen, Marshall may well have had access to at least three important historic musical manuscripts. One was that of Sir William Mure of Rowallan, dated to 1612-28, another was that of John Skene of Hallhills, dated to 1615-20, and the third was that of 1627 compiled by Robert Gordon of Straloch. Straloch is just outside Newmachar, but there is no record that Burns visited Robert Gordon's successors during that tour, despite possibly becoming aware of that family in discussion with Marshall, three days later. The Straloch manuscript is lost, but first half of it was transcribed in 1839. Dr George Skene, perhaps a descendent of John Skene of Hallhills, and Professor of Humanity and Philosophy at Marischal College, had it in 1781 when it came into the possession of a Dr Charles Burney, who sold it to a James Chalmers, who died in London, after lending out the manuscript and not recovering it. Out of these manuscripts came many tunes for which Burns later wrote words that have saved them for posterity. Skene's manuscript included the tune 'Kilt Thy Coat Maggie', said to have been played prior to 1659 by piper John Douglas to enable eight witches to dance for the devil.

In meeting these custodians of Scotland's ancient music Burns found the way forward for the change of life that faced him when the glitz of 'fickle Fortune's Luna' was dimmed by the re-asserting dismal reality of his baneful star.

The men in Scotland's north were concerned for the future of Scottish music. Their compatriots were increasingly looking to England for cultural leadership. They no doubt brought to the poet's mind the works of Robert Fergusson. Fergusson had written an elegy for music. He had prefixed it by the Shakespearean quotation "Mark it, Caesario; it is old and plain; the spinsters and the knitters in the sun, and the free maids that weave their thread with bones, do use to chant it". Fergusson hoped that music, the voice of the threatened soul of Scotland, the basis of her self-respect, would find a champion.

> O Scotland! That could ance afford
> To bang the pith o' Roman sword,
> Winna your sons, wi' joint accord,
>   To battle speed,
> And fight till Music be restor'd
>   Whilk now lies dead?

There indeed was the gauntlet thrown down by Fergusson before the greater young man who had come after him. Burns knew within his heart that, for old Scotia's sake, he had his destiny to fulfil. He had already, deliberately or subconsciously spelled it out in his dedication to the Caledonian Hunt – that his highest ambition was to sing in his country's service. Before he left Edinburgh he had met James Johnson. He had looked with interest at the emerging first volume of Johnson's 'Scots Musical Museum'. Johnson had asked Burns if he would contribute a song or two. No sooner was he back south than he began to write to everyone he could think of to join in helping him support the creation of Johnson's collection. Johnson had intended a modest collection when the first volume was published in early 1787. Once under the guiding hand of Robert Burns, his project became the main focus of Burns's creative energies until his very last breath. Nothing so specifically mundane, of course, was explicitly predicted in any horoscope or almanac.

Before their conversations ended, those wise men in Aberdeen who knew their astronomy possibly asked Burns further questions: so you know the date of your birth, you say, but do you know the hour? Burns had already mused on those starting lines of his poem: the year was five and twenty days begun. That, of course, can be interpreted two ways – it was day 25, or day 25 was already over or virtually over.

Here we encounter another of those 'chiels that claim they winna ding'. Burns is said to have had his baptismal certificate, also said to have been transcribed into the register of Ayr. Records state he was born 25th January and baptised 26th January. But the hour of his birth is a different matter. It was not until the last quarter of the 19th century that Scotland first insisted that birth registrations must give the time of birth along with the other legally useful data of mother, father if known, indications of ancestry and place of birth. Scotland is one of the few nations which insist on registration of time of birth – an interesting awareness of the niceties of the star-date in the heartland of Freemasonry.

"What time of day were you born?" asked the wise men.

"They tell me it was very late into the night", he might have replied. "It was the minister Dalrymple, the one who has since been honoured with a doctorate, who baptised me. My father instructed him to write down my birthday as 25th January."

What happened on that birthday? The biographies of Burns are almost exclusively written by men. While fathers today are permitted into the room while a baby is born, they were certainly not wanted in the cramped dirty space of a blackhouse. Any birthing, even in the modern world, is a time of danger for mother and child. The midwife would have sent every man out. She let the father kick his heels in the barn, or vent hysteria by walking in the snow under glowering storm clouds that sometimes separated to show stars in the blackness.

Inside, the midwife was aware that this was the first child of this little woman. A first child is particularly difficult to birth – the body has never before loosened up the bones of the pelvis to allow the infant to slip through. Even if the baby has properly turned (and it is not uncommon that it does not) those pelvic bones sometimes don't loosen sufficiently. Sometimes the pelvic gap is too small, necessitating drastic action – the origin of the Caesarian section. Sometimes this is necessary simply because the baby has a large head. Burns may have been a big baby. Five foot nine was a big man for those days. His head was big. Phrenologists who examined the skull of Burns when he was exhumed in the 19th century tell us that he had an unusually large head. That birth must have been difficult.

The mental processes of birth are also unrecognised by most men, with the father too often only aware of his own prowess in producing his child. Anyone who has dislocated a joint knows it is painful. The pelvic separation, albeit a natural process, sends to the brain the same pain messages. As the chemical that causes the pelvic separation also affects the rest of the body, the whole body feels pain. Add to this the actual stress of the processes of contraction, which pain the whole internal structure of the body by intense squeezing, and any real pain caused by tearing of the flesh as the baby's head forces itself out of the body, and it is no surprise that women scream. Indeed, midwives encouraged them to scream because it allows the brain to convince itself that the pain is being dealt with.

There are other measures that the old midwives used to take: they put a knife under the bed on which the woman lay. Any children around, asking why a knife was put under the bed, were told that this iron knife kept away the evil fairies. In fact, it did something much more practical: akin to acupuncture, it adjusted the magnetic field around the woman, thus diverting the pain messages. So, in the old saying, 'it cut the pain in half'.

Thus, the midwife got on with supporting the woman until that final scream of relief when the child slipped out. Then she did her job of cleaning the baby's air passage and getting it to give its first cry, then easing the afterbirth out of the woman, tying the umbilical cord, cleansing the woman, and cleansing the child. Then she wrapped the child in sympathetic linen that gently swaddled its new skin, and laid it to the breast of the mother to take its first suck of milk. Then could mother sleep and father be called in to see his child.

Outside, as all this was going on, sheltered in the lea of his cottage from the full force of the howling wind of the storm, William Burness paced up and down, looking at the passing hours marked in the stars that glinted through the fleeting flying gaps of the wild night. In the darkening sky he watched to the east. He was a knowledgeable man. As a gardener, trained in dialling and surveying, he knew the constellations. As he glimpsed a star here and two there, he imagined the great mechanical device he had studied in those now so far off days before the Prince's war devastated once again the lands above Dunottar that he had loved. He saw the revolution of the stars around the pole – the slow Great Bear, the hanging Cassiopeia, and from his memory of their relation to the circle of the Sun, though in Scotland's winter he could not see far south, he counted the passing hours in the names of their constellations: Virgo, Libra, Scorpio.

The hours passed, and his heart was torn by the continuing screams that increasingly loudly came from inside his little home. But put his head through the door and he was shouted at to shut that opening and leave the warmth in or he would kill his poor wife. This is woman's work! Sagittarius rising soon; the hours wore on. Then it would be Capricorn, he mused. The wind roared and the deep thick clouds scuttled across the freezing sky. In that tiny gap he saw the stars again, and the glint of light – the horns of the Moon.

His mind became suffused with the old tales, the ancient stories, told round the excitement of the dying embers of a heath fire, by an old man of wisdom, who knew the meaning of the circles of stones that were being torn from the fields. Capricorn, the goat, the horned one, the cloven footed, the memory in the stars of the great nature Pan-god of the unchristian times; the progenitor of the Christian Satan: the Grand Master of the witches' coven; the Devil – the ancient Celtic Cernunnos. In that dark stormy sky he glimpsed the silver shining crescent of the Moon and in his mind's eye he saw it as the horns of Cernunnos. Just then he heard that tiny cry of the new born child. He looked back nine months to that orgy of Beltane when this child was conceived. A Beltane child born in the darkness under the horns of Pan-Cernunnos! How he must have prayed to his Christian God that this child was made in his own image! As he looked down at his faintly smiling exhausted wife and the helpless infant child with the big head, the dawn began to break.

No wonder that the story goes that he mounted his horse and sped to get the minister to baptise such a child born under the sign of Capricorn. He looked no more at the sky. Behind the dying storm clouds, behind the glory of the Sun, the constellation Lyra, sign of the spirit of Orpheus, began to ascend the great arc of the Scottish sky. When he came back, that old witch was cradling his child! He was a rational man, a professional man, but a man born in the northeast of Scotland who had travelled across the land and knew the stories. His rational heart could yet be gripped by the fear of an unknown noise in the stormy night. The minister asked him when the child was born. He hesitated.

"At the darkest hour of the night", quoth the witch.

Those of us who lived through the music of the 1960s know, from the song requesting the loved one to say a night prayer to all the stars above, that the darkest hour is just before dawn.

William Burness perhaps reflected how in that dreary early hour after that wild night of howling wind he had mounted his beast to ride to Ayr. A keen wind still whistled as he rounded that well surmounted by the thorn bush, where Mungo's old mother had finally put an end to her life's misery. On through that whin-strewn gully past the cairn he had raced, his mind recalling another infant, that hunters found dead there. Not long after he passed the clump of fine birch trees, his horse had drawn back and neighed sharply as it approached that great rock. There carousing Charlie, after a few too many, had convinced himself he could fly. He had dashed himself to the ground, breaking his neck. As he approached the ford, his imagination was racing at the evil that had been in the night. His horse had paused at the rush of water. On the other side he had seen that old crone, toeing the dark clutching surface of the swollen stream. He remembered the story that, in the snow-driven waters of the ford, they had found the chapman, drowned. "Away with your superstition!" he had thought to himself. Once on the other side he lifted the old woman behind him onto the horse and had ridden back to carry her across the dangerous waters. He had watched her begin to wend her way onward to the old kirk at Alloway. There she could cross the swollen Doon by the great hump-backed bridge.

But now he saw her here, rocking back and forth at his own hearth, cradling his child, and telling the minister that the child was born at the darkest hour of the night. Dalrymple would not just accept the word of an old woman who had not herself been present when the child was born. He would have looked at William for confirmation of the time and thus date of birth. Burness would have hesitated a moment, dark superstition tugging at his heart. Another formula for the dark of the night might have rushed to his brain:

> that hour o' night's black arch the key-stane.

A child born before the winter midnight would be blessed by Libra, sign of Balance, of the cool even-tempered man of equity and justice.

"He was born just before midnight", perhaps he stammered. Thus might it have been enshrined in memory that Robert Burns was born on 25th January, leaving future biographers – once they had agreed that 25th January was correct and Currie's initial date of 29th January was wrong – to contend with a confusion of myth about the exact time of the poet's birth.

Certain it is that tradition goes that the child was born 'late into the night' and that the father rushed off at the earliest opportunity to get the minister. This tradition was first related by the purported midwife long after the poet's death. In the days before chemical induction, first births after long labour often happened just before dawn – the mother tires and the birthing slows during the hours of night. The new energy of waking is needed before the final push can release the baby. Thus, in the agricultural world in which women's bodies were attuned to rising before the family to prepare food, many a child was born in that darkest hour just before dawn.

What, then do we make of the official fact that he was born on 25th January, and baptised on 26th? Carelessness in recording the time of birth is commonplace. After all, the exact time of birth is not the thing the matters: what matters is that the child is alert and well formed and that the mother is well enough to return to full strength. In addition, fathers are usually so taken up with asserting or denying their own fatherhood that the time is hardly relevant to them. So, even when times are given on birth certificates, they are not always accurate. In the case of Burns, we have two dates, one purporting to be date of birth, the other as date of baptism.

We must question the meaning of dates. We know from Salmon that there were many conventions existing in different cultures for the Sun-time of the changing of a day number. In Britain alone, there were different conventions in different places, ranging from midnight to noon. Even in the modern song 'Memories' from the musical show 'Cats' we get the association of dawn with the arrival of the new day. In Britain, a general standard in time came only with regular railway trains a century after the birth of Burns. A sundial can divide the daytime into hours but can do nothing for the night. There was no attempt at general standardisation before the chronometer was invented and a zero meridian agreed. It then took time to be generally accepted. Before our modern standardisation of time the night and the day were considered to be identical with the hours of darkness and light respectively. Each of these two periods was originally itself divided into twelve sections – although the 1759 Aberdeen Almanack does state that sunrise at end January was 7am, showing that this publication considered the whole midnight to midnight period as divided into twenty four equal sections. That, though, does not make us conclude that a clerk in Ayr, a seaport, did not consider the date as changing, not at midnight but at dawn. Thus, it is possible that he would write the birth date of Robert Burns as 25th January when he was actually born before dawn on what today we would number 26th January. This would mean five and twenty days had been completed since the beginning of the year.

At various places throughout this work are computed planetary aspects of the putative Burns horoscope as if he was born just before dawn, but on what we now number 25th January. This starts with an Ephemeris that, as with all mathematical models however 'accurate', cannot actually precisely reflect all the wobbles of the gyrations of the Earth, Moon and planets as they burl and dance their great reel in the music of the eternal heavens. If he had actually been born just before dawn on 26th January, those computer models give a horoscope reading that according to astrology could equally be interpreted as of someone born to hardship, fighting against the odds and seeming to fail, loved intensely and sometimes aggressively loving, recognising the responsibility of Mankind to each other as brothers and to the world around in which we live, and fighting to the end to preserve the Dignity of Man through being a great poet transcending his own time.

Perhaps Burness had been mistaken, were he indeed afraid for his newborn son of omens in the stars. Perhaps in the storm he did not see Capricorn coming over the horizon as his child was born. Perhaps it was not Capricorn in which he saw those Moon horns. Celebrants at the table raising their goblet in praise of the Immortal Memory on 25th January can relax: astrologers admit the possibility that, rather than being born with a Capricorn ascendant, his life suggests both a Sagittarian Moon with Sagittarius rising at the moment of his birth. This would explain those stories of how visible in his eyes was the fire that burned with so much passion inside him.

But there's another wobbly. This can now be examined readily by all the world because in 2006 the register of births for the Parish of Ayr was imaged onto a publicly available database, accessible by Internet. Search 'Robert Burns' and there it is, not in guid black prent, but in fine copperplate handwriting: Robert Burns a son born on 25th January to William Burns and Agnes Brown. Yes, I did write William Burns and Agnes Brown. So what of those stories that Robert was the first to spell the surname this way, and what of his mother's name actually being Broun? The record demands a closer look.

The record is at the bottom of a page – almost falling off the bottom of the page, in fact. The record is out of order. Six February births are listed before that of the poet – the last of these baptised on 25th February. The record for Robert is written in a very fine hand. The hand is similar to the writing on the rest of the page, but is much more even than the rest of the records on that page. The record states that the child was baptised by Wm Dalrymple – but does not give a date for the baptism. Dalrymple had baptised the previously registered birth, where his name had been written as William Dalrymple. A suspicious person would wonder whether this record was backfilled into an empty space at the bottom of the page some time – a long time – after the poet was baptised. This questions birth date.

Undisputable is that Robert Burns was born in a thatched cottage in Ayrshire, in Scotland in late January 1759 during a violent storm which later blew down the gable of the house. This is taken by many as a sign of the impact he was later to have throughout the world with his proudly and freely spoken egalitarian views – 'A man's a man for a' that'. He died in July 1796. He was remembered ever after because of his poems, songs and letters, and the pop-star legend that had grown up around him in his lifetime – though he lived and died without financial success. He gained a reputation during the Victorian era of having been a libertine and a drunkard. He was a pretty normal working class man of his day in having to sterilise drinking water with alcohol, and being direct in his sexuality. His death in Dumfries is now attributed to some degenerative illness, perhaps endocarditis, initiated by damp and excessive work during a harsh childhood.

Of those who are remembered beyond their own time, some are remembered for their births, some for their deaths, many for their mistakes, but few for their legacy. Of those remembered for their legacy, few are in our own day celebrated in every corner of the globe, and credited with influencing Humankind's happiness. Of those, such a one is Robert Burns. In his day, though the scientific era was already gathering steam, many men would have said it was in his stars. Robert Burns lived in the last age in which credibility was commonly given to astrology. Today, few acknowledge this. His legacy – such as the fact that to celebrate not only the new millennium, but many a new year, hands are joined around the world in singing his 'Auld Lang Syne' in every current language – is picked over now by armies of academics and laymen, trying to understand what made his contribution so timely in his own day, and since so influential in the politics and everyday mind of Man.

Some who read this rambling record of the ramifications of the writings of Robert Burns will criticise me for unscientific lack of objectivity. Despite immediate appearance, this work is the result of academic examination. It has been done through a form of academic examination that I will call post-modern. My approach recognises, as does the Uncertainty Principle of Natural Philosophy, that complete knowledge is impossible, and that the best understanding is gained through recognising the unavoidable impact between observer and observed.

Mankind is granted no power to 'see ourselves as others see us'. But surely, as did Robert Burns, we can grasp the power to recognise that each one of us has a different view of every aspect of truth. To understand the legacy of Robert Burns, we need to understand the man. I have dealt in this book with the recent history of the world as Burns saw it, and with what he knew of its changing politics, economics and technology. I have also brought into the picture esoterica, superstition, folklore and astrology because they were part of the everyday and intellectual milieu in which Robert Burns lived.

In writing this book I have deliberately not constrained myself within that straightjacket which is so often championed as equating to rigour of scientific thought. Instead, as a result of my early training as a mathematician and natural philosopher, I have done what I have learned to do – allow my own instinct the necessary rein to unravel the threads whose loose ends and apparent contradictions pose unanswered questions and entice the imagination. In so doing, I deliberately present a challenge to sole use of objectivity, because I believe that in all areas of knowledge and understanding objectivity excludes too much of what is truth. Robert Burns gave me the lead in this stance, for he was the true man of independent mind. Through this he came to oppose equally the tyranny of monarchs and the anarchy of democratic majorities. It was true in his day as in ours that to be a man of independent mind is to live dangerously. In January 1776, Thomas Paine published his 'Common Sense', denouncing monarchy and declaring the American position the 'cause of all mankind'. Burns saw how, a mere fifteen years later, men could be transported to the new penal colony in Botany Bay or even hung for daring to lend a friend a copy of Paine's works.

You may have felt nettled, reading this book. If my argument stings, perhaps my rhetoric grazed the thin skin of inner-held convictions. I have not been argumentative for the sake of it. Only through this stance could I, with my limited skills, hope to make you feel an echo of how each person felt, at least one time, who met in life the man called Robert Burns.

Burns was aware of the Void. He was alarmed that the rationalism of the Enlightenment, by enabling what we now know as the Big Brother society of digitalisation, was casting into a new Void all that truly mattered in human life. This is all the inexpressible things: quality, virtue, integrity, trust, empathy, care and, most importantly, love. But it left untouched opposition and confrontation. An entirely digital world is expressed only in yes or no, white or black, friend or enemy. This he learned from his studies and his devotion to the ideals he found expressed in Freemasonry. He focused on song, that expression of inexpressible emotions, as the true weapon to defend Humanity. He built his armoury while combating the rational opposition that even after death tried to destroy him.

His so fine silver rapier wit burned with dragon fun. Its playing touch left but a tiny stinging scratch, met by happy scorching laughter of amazed onlookers. But they say no-one can create true laughter unless his heart is full of tears. His keenest rapier strokes could kill. Victims lay devastated. Time and again he was told his wit caused pain. He meant no pain. But he was driven. No self-deception, no hubris, no manner of hypocrisy could he leave alone, for all defiled the Dignity of Man. No-one was safe; for each of us has some unfounded shibboleth, hurtful to our brother man. Though gently did he scold his sister woman, the time of all would come. His best friends, in time, in anger riled.

I have tried in mimic show, in weave and thrust, to tell some of the wonder of that fire mind, whom all who met him said was merely shadowed in his written words. My wit holds not a candle to his mid-day sun. My puny hand wields but a plastic toy, when he, with skill and art and strength, startled audiences as air-cutting display and precision thrust slipped in ease through finest-crafted intellectual armour, in chinks unseen but to his piercing eyes.

My skills can show so little of the man. Such flights as his are far beyond my power, to tell how his wit leapt and sprang, so supple was his muse, and strong too. His audiences stood bewitched, knowing themselves enriched by this sight. He drew daggers from the eyes of his enemies; their ire fired. They spluttered and lambasted in every manner. But his wit heightened, and rose. His rapier flashed. His effort stretched. At last he could lift his rapier no more, for his heart burst. Coila helped him onto snorting Pegasus, but he could barely ride. One spring brought his master over that bourne whence no traveller returns. Thus Burns safely crossed that bridge, but left behind his tale. Carlin hordes clutched it. They shredded and sullied and crushed it in the stour.

I have focused on that one greatest command that stands above all the others he voiced in his description of Coila's fateful visitation. I propose that if the life of Robert Burns had a role, that role was to preserve the Dignity of Man. He spent most of his life trying to work out what in that context 'dignity' might mean, and thus how he might strive to preserve it. He finally realised that at the heart of the Dignity of Man is the beautiful combination of emotion with reason. He held the view that this combination within the Almighty was expressed through the Music of the Spheres. So he applied his gift of poetry to describing the potential beauty of humanity with emotion and reason in harness. Music he chose as the vehicle of his poetry, with the deliberate objective in so choosing, to preserve a vanishing remnant of the armour of Scotland's own dignity. His words rang with defence for human dignity, while at the same time he preserved the central threatened cultural heritage of Scotland, by transmuting base chants of bothies into the gold of memorable song.

The Enlightenment era of the eighteenth century was followed by the industrial behemoth of the nineteenth and the materialism of the twentieth. Throughout all this time, when the inner worth of humanity has constantly been battered by the dehumanising march of so-called progress, against the odds, in spite of literary fashion and micro-dissection by critics, the true legacy of Robert Burns has survived through the strength of his song and laughter. Robert Burns has been a solid anchor of imagination through an era of rational insanity. His legacy is to teach present and future generations to be guided not just by what appears to be factual but to temper this with their inner feeling of what is right and good.

The strength of Robert Burns and his gift to humanity is that, in the face of the fullest force of the rationality of the Enlightenment, he championed, fought for, and gave back to Western Man his right to dream – and to dream so much that it could give rise to such radical unthinkable visions as that man to man the world o'er shall brothers be, for a' that!

FINIS

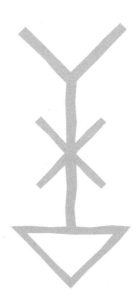

Mind and the Internet
By Graham A C Smith

Many things reduce to a simple question of numbers. The human population of the Earth is today roughly 6 billion. This is an unimaginable quantity. One may estimate that roughly one $30,000^{th}$ of that number (so, approximately 200,000 people) are born every day, and roughly as many die. This is also impossible to imagine. It is as if a fair sized town is wiped out every day, and another springs up somewhere else to take its place. More people die every day than there are members of certain endangered species, and the number of people born every day is comparable to the number of generations since the first ancestor of humanity stared into the flames, and is about three orders of magnitude greater than the number of generations since the beginning of civilisations, the discovery of wine, and the writing of what would later become Genesis.

All of these people are living, observing, feeling and thinking. Many, like me, are writing, and most are writing roughly the same thing: there is very little originality in the world. However, all these people are communicating with one another, and many are communicating over the internet, taking part in a global discussion of incomprehensible scale which is getting bigger all the time. Even in such narrow fields as my own line of work (a relatively specialised form of mathematics), certain Google searches will return over a billion hits. One imagines here something like the feverish activity of the trading floor of an international bank, where hundreds of voices heatedly shout over each other like gamblers at a dogfight. However, this could only evoke the quieter corners of this immense cacophony.

The internet is the most effective medium of democratisation of opinion, certainly more effective than the 'roving reporters' or the letters pages of newspapers. In the internet, everybody can speak, and everyone's voice is almost equally loud. Through their blogs, everyone may enjoy a brief taste of international celebrity, from the New York prostitute to the great grandmother in Catalonia. Every single voice is completely overwhelmed within this current where they merge like the whisperings of leaves when the wind sweeps a forest. Meaning is almost completely lost.

The internet is also the reification of nightmares. The world is so large that all perversions must be practised somewhere. Once again it is merely a question of numbers. Every perversion that we would previously occasionally have imagined, caricatured and even have rendered bearable by our minds' own censor is now carried out by sordid creatures who are today able to find enough kindred spirits in the darker holes of cyberspace to create their own communities which return to poison reality. The darker side of the soul has found a powerful new means of conscious expression: the floodgates of hell will soon be opened.

The internet is humanity: it is the closest thing to an expression of the experience of modern day mankind. It is the world as seen through the billion-faceted compound eye of a giant, schizophrenic fly. This seething, senseless mass of information is continually evolving as, every day, 200,000 cells suddenly freeze, another 200,000 spring into existence and yet another 200,000 are accidentally forgotten, relegated to eternity by a power cut or a faulty transistor.

But in all this chaos, what is lacking is intention, or mind: mind which binds ideas and feelings together in a way that might never be understood. Regardless of what one does, one needs mind to unite thought towards any action or any creation.

For example, in a game of chess, one can learn the possible movements of every single piece, but no-one can play well without being able to sense the forms of two opposing sides wrestling against each other, like black and white amoeba in accelerated film eating each other across the surface of the chequered board. Computers nowadays are capable of beating most humans, but it should not be forgotten that, whereas the *arithmetic* abilities of even the machine that I am typing on right now are orders of magnitude greater than that of the greatest human mind, it requires one of the most powerful supercomputers to even equal the greatest chess players: what the computer achieves through brute force, the mind achieves through much more subtle means.

The activity of mind is present in every act of creation. When mind is lacking, thoughts are not bound together. One recognises this in bad art where the artist is clearly not feeling what he's creating, or in bad writing, where the writer lets feelings be distracted from what he really wants to say. One recognises this absence of mind more clearly in the strange poems written by computers. Words are placed together according to rules of association and grammar. The effect is stunning: each line conveys a vivid and pregnant image, but there is nothing to relate successive lines. There is merely a stream of meaningless, powerful images, and one recognises within it the sound and the fury of a tale told by a madman.

In the internet, in this entire cacophony of actively competing information, where segments of knowledge creep and fight and devour each other like billions of black, crawling insects, there is no mind. There is nothing uniting the seething abyss of thought, and one imagines that any single consciousness simultaneously aware of all these visions must suffer the elations and horrors of the worst schizophrenic delirium.

Because this is the soul of humanity, and here and in the films we see, the music we hear and the books we read, we find the prophecies and frightened psychoses of a super-consciousness that has yet to open its eyes, because humanity is lost within the unconscious horror of a dark and troubled sleep.

One day, however, humanity will awaken.

Appendix II

Usage of Innerpeffray Library

Cairns Mason BSc FSA(Scot) carried out intensive research in Innerpeffray Library to address the question: did those of the lower classes with ready access to books study current Enlightenment issues and therefore how typical of his class in his era was the education of Robert Burns?

Innerpeffray Library, near Crieff, was founded in the 17th century as a public lending library. It is now open to the public as a charitable museum. Within it is held the original borrowers' register. Fragile, and extremely difficult to read, Mason hoped that this would throw valuable light on this question. The register is particularly difficult to read because as each book was brought back to the library the entire entry for the loan was scored out in black ink. Many entries referred to several books loaned and brought back at different times, further confusing interpretation. Thus, the register's contents needed to be deciphered in spite of heavy multiple scoring. It then needed to be interpreted. This meant comparing usage with what books were made available. Mason also needed to study any available lists or directories of people who lived locally and might have used the library in the context of local contemporary topography. Basic data collection took months of daily work in the library and elsewhere. Full analysis took longer.

To analyse the usage of any lending library over a specific period there must be reliable lists of what books the library held and when each book was acquired and made available to users. There must also be reliable lists of who might borrow and who did borrow, along with lists of what they borrowed, under what rules and constraints. None of these data sets was fulfilled by Innerpeffray Library. Mason sought appropriate ways to substitute for their absence, or otherwise fully make up for the limitations this placed on his analysis.

Defaced borrowers' registers do exist, initially for the period 1747 to 1757 and then there is an actual gap in the register which starts again in 1763 and runs to 1968. There is no listing of the date of acquisition of volumes. There are no written rules surviving of the operation of the library prior to 1813. The oldest extant rules were on a handwritten sheet attached to a catalogue of books created in 1813.

Once Mason had sufficiently examined the register, and worked out how to read through the scores to the handwriting underneath, he discovered that in the majority of cases the borrower himself or herself had completed the initial entry. Each had an idiosyncratic way of describing the book or books borrowed. So Mason had to match book names, as written by readers, with book titles as found on the library shelves. As many books published before the 19th century had extremely long titles, various shorthand descriptions were used. In those days there was no such thing as the English Short Title Catalogue, listing all volumes published in English before 1800 – which of course would not in any case have included the books in other languages. But the writer of the 1813 catalogue, who had written in a beautiful copperplate hand, had also given typical short titles. Mason later discovered (by cross-checking entries) that sometimes the same short title was used by different readers actually to refer to different books. It was not always clear when someone had taken away 'volume 4', meaning the fourth volume of a set, or 'volume 4' meaning all four volumes of the set. That these two interpretations were possible came clear from some marks indicating the return of part sets.

Despite the challenges, Mason reconstructed for the period 1763 to 1811 virtually all borrowing records, the data within them of the name of the book or books borrowed, who borrowed, their address, what their occupation was, when they borrowed, and any other data he could deduce from what he saw on the written register. He forensically reconstructed the borrowers' register. Not every register entry contained a complete set of such data. It turned out that of all the many books available on the library shelves, very few were actually taken out to be read.

In seeking to assess whether ordinary people were discussing Enlightenment thinking, Mason found there was no existing academic definition of what constituted an Enlightenment library. So there was no yardstick of whether what was being read by any group matched what an Enlightenment teacher would have prescribed. This presented its own challenges. Mason constructed a measure of Enlightenment reading. He focused on the period immediately surrounding 1760 to 1790, which is the Scottish Enlightenment's Golden Age as defined by historian David Daiches. Mason created a yardstick by carrying out desk research to define an ideal Enlightenment library, taking into account books published during that Golden Age and those considered seminal that had been published in the previous century. This formed a measure that can be used to assess of any library whether its usage promoted Enlightenment thought.

Though books were being taken out, in so far as ideas were being taken on board, Mason explored whether this was merely by certain types within the community, or if uptake was broadly based. He examined whether users were representative of the local population. This meant more desk research, from which he concluded that, as far as the males were concerned, readers were indeed representative of the community. Not so the women readers. Mason deduced that during the 18th century women were not encouraged to be borrowers – and if anything, things got worse as the century progressed. Though Mason identified over four hundred separate male borrowers, only seventeen women received books from the library between 1747 and 1800, and the books they got were typically religious or otherwise 'improving'.

As his transcription of data for borrowings during the 18th century rolled on, Mason began also to get the feeling that, as time wore on, the range of borrowers changed. Those in trade were falling away as readers. Numbers were being kept up by the addition of men who called themselves students or scholars. This was an intuitive feel only, for the data was too thin to carry out any decisive statistical test.

Despite data limitations, Mason was able to draw valuable conclusions. He was forced, by his data collection and its analysis, to conclude that during the later 18th century itself, Innerpeffray Library, enlightened as was its concept, played only a minor role in promoting Enlightenment thought in its locality. Its role in this direction became much more positive during the early years of the 19th century.

Appendix III

The Burns Supper

It is claimed that at Greenock on 21st July 1801 the first Burns Club was formed. The early Minutes were kept in an unused Excise notebook said to have been found by an Excise colleague, Adam Pearson, in the Dumfries house of Robert Burns after his death. The members in 1803 travelled by coach to Alloway to dine at the birthplace, then an inn. The registered birthday, 25th January, is by Scots throughout the world celebrated as Burns Night. Core activity is cutting the traditional peasant food of the 18th century, the oatmeal haggis.

In addition to a genuine reputation for progressive thinking, Burns is an annual excuse for revelry, and the 'Burns Supper' on or around 25th January around the entire world, each year, follows what is now a standard formula. It is centred on the **Ceremony of the Haggis.**

With everyone standing, the Haggis is brought in on a silver platter, accompanied by a piper in full ceremonial dress and often also by a master of ceremonies. Those around the table, usually also wearing full dinner dress, stand. Each has a glass of whisky. The Haggis is placed in front of the Chairman or before the Master of Ceremonies after it has been shown to the Chairman. One or other of these (almost always men) will then address the Haggis, using the 'Address To the Haggis', written by Robert Burns. This poem was written for the Edinburgh drinking club, the Crochallan Fencibles, which included many leading lights and most of the rich rakes of the Edinburgh that celebrated Burns in the winter of 1786-7. The haggis was developed to sink the drink. The satirical Address praises the haggis as greater than the best Edinburgh Nouvelle Cuisine of the day. However, the Address and the haggis, from the perspective of Burns, also embody for the initiates far deeper revolutionary meaning. During the Address, the Haggis is knifed and its guts spew out. When called for by the host, the Haggis and the piper are then toasted with the whisky. The piper downs his glass in one. Each guest is then served with a ceremonial plate containing a spoonful of the Haggis and spoonfuls each of mashed potatoes and mashed turnip (champit tatties and neeps). The proper Haggis is a sausage-like pudding, enclosed in a sheep's stomach. When properly cooked the contents should dramatically spurt out during the ceremony. For it to do so is the sign of a well-heated Haggis. Despite the general sobriety of Robert Burns himself (no good entertainer dare get drunk as it spoils his act) in men-only Burns Suppers heavy drinking has traditionally been non-optional. Vegetarian and alcohol-free Burns Suppers are now becoming quite fashionable.

The main meal follows. After dinner speeches follow a set pattern, the first four in the following list being obligatory, as is the singing of 'Auld Lang Syne'. The number of speeches depends on the appetite of the audience.

> The Immortal Memory - a eulogy on Robert Burns.
>
> The Toast to the Lassies.
>
> The Reply to the toast.
>
> The Recitation of the poem 'Tam o' Shanter'.
>
> The Recitation of the poem 'Holy Willie's Prayer'.
>
> Songs by Robert Burns, usually including 'Ae fond kiss'.
>
> The optional toast to the King Over the Water, and/or the Loyal Toast.

The evening ends with hands held crosswise, and singing of the Robert Burns version of the ancient Scots parting song, 'Auld Lang Syne'.

Morning Star of the Age of Aquarius

Natal Chart and Interpretation for Robert Burns

The paradigm of a reasonable proportion of the learned men in the latter half of the 18th century reflected continuing belief in astrology. Modern understanding of the man in his context is thus improved through exploring how such people could have perceived him. This commentary was prepared independently of the writing of this book. It represents how adepts contemporary with Robert Burns would have perceived him through their knowledge of the positions relative to his birthplace of the Sun, Moon and known planets at the time of his birth, additionally taking into account the discovery of Uranus in 1781.

In creating a birth chart the first step after discovering the time and place of birth is to find the position in the sky of the Sun, Moon and planets. This requires having a listing of observed or calculated positions at midnight on the day in question and the next day. Such a listing is known as an Ephemeris. These were produced at Greenwich Observatory from the time of its foundation, and circulated from early in the 18th century primarily for navigational use. With an Ephemeris, the planetary positions for the time and location of birth can be calculated and Robert Burns would have been expected to do so as an elementary exercise when he was studying Dialling. From these measurements a horoscope can readily be drawn out. This is a trivial task. Interpreting the horoscope so produced requires an adept.

Planetary readings for birth at Alloway, Ayr, Scotland
06.00am Greenwich Observatory Time
January 25th 1759 in the reign of King George II

Sun	Aquarius	05deg 05min	First house
Moon	Sagittarius	18deg 57min	Twelfth house
Mercury	Capricorn	23deg 36min	First house
Venus	Aquarius	08deg 07min	First house
Mars	Aquarius	10deg 41min	First house
Jupiter	Capricorn	08deg 34min	First house
Saturn	Pisces	02deg 54min	Second house
Uranus	Pisces	24deg 26min	Second house
Midheaven	Scorpio	06deg 35min	
Ascendant	Sagittarius	25deg 40min	

At this time also it is retrospectively known that: Neptune was in Leo at 16deg 30min in the eighth house. Pluto was in Sagittarius at 24deg 17min in the first house.

An astrological adept views a birth chart as a means, from the experience of those who have lived before, of identifying what would be the most fulfilling life for that soul on Earth. The interpretation points out ways to avoid inappropriate routines, bad choices, and unproductive effort. It identifies spiritual resources. It indicates what can go wrong when resources are abused. Some adepts believe that consciousness and cosmos follow the same laws because they have the same underlying structure and patterns. The stars, the place of dreams, are the source of those dreams which, if realised, bring happiness and if thwarted, bring grief – but happiness and grief that may not be of this world. Being in tune with natal forces enables the person to call into play the spiritual powers of the universe, and reach higher levels of consciousness and existence. Each horoscope is individual to a particular person and so is its meaning. The house in a person's birth chart which Sun, Moon or planet occupies defines the personal influence on the person of that entity.

Analysis of the primal triad of Sun, Moon and Ascendant indicates that this person is a genius who speaks truth but is ostracised by society. He is constantly seeking to expand his experiences, develop his mind, and seek philosophical understanding. He will have a charismatic presence that can appear in the various guises of wandering gypsy, scholar and philosopher. Saturn in Pisces alters this balance, by bringing the influence of the mystical sign Pisces down to earth. This enables form to be brought to philosophical thought, because Pisces is the sign of the poet. The poet is the philosopher putting the inexpressible into words.

The primary influence on any person is the Sun. The Sun represents the process of becoming self. This is opposed by pressure to conform with preconceived norms.

Aquarius is the sign of geniuses and criminals. Those with Sun in this sign do not readily fit their predetermined place in society without betraying inner self. As this person becomes more himself, the more outlandish he will appear to the world into which he was born. This would carry a high price, but less high than the price of self negation. Those things that fire this spirit will seem strange to the world at large, as they emerge from the fringes of existing culture and social norms. Every figure of authority will be discomfited by him. Society will work against this person, pushing him back into his 'proper place'. He can expect to be put under every pressure from flattery and bribery to downright intimidation to go back to the level and role in society in which he was born. Well-meaning friends in his life will actually be spies who monitor his behaviour, discover his thoughts, and seek ways to assist society to coerce him to submit to its will. To be himself he will have to hurt people.

Adepts consider Aquarius to be the night house of the Sun. The Sun in Aquarius thus influences a person to be etherial and electric, with open forthcoming personality, natural refinement, and humanity. He will prefer quietness, but have intense independence and idealism, tempered with practicality. He will be very strong and forceful, although nervous and highly strung, but will tend to hide all this behind a façade of frivolity. He will be quick and active, and will find enormous temporary resistance to fatigue, but will tend to injure his health by devoting himself to over-demanding work.

The first house represents the development of character. Those with the Sun in the first house tend to act out their character visibly and dramatically. Such persons are leaders with a lot of charisma and presence. People who meet this person will be impressed and will remember him – though they would too easily find him overpowering. This outward show of confidence hides an inner awareness of a need to find an aim in life, a worthy destiny, because this person is born with no pre-determined goal set for him by Fate! He was born to Freedom, and must make of that Freedom what he will!

The second influence on any person is the Moon.

Sagittarius is the sign of gypsies, scholars and philosophers. There is fire in this sign. There is rebellion but trustworthiness. There is strong loyalty but it is independent. There is fierce optimism. Sagittarius represents the urge to break out from apparent boundaries, to set aside imprisoning routines. There are three general ways to do this: dropping out, or formally educating yourself and developing your intellect, or seeking the meaning of life intuitively through meditation and reflection. Whichever of these routes is taken, this person needs frequent stimulation of new experience for he is spiritually fed by amazement. The gravest mistake for a person influenced by Sagittarius is consciously and willingly to let himself become bored.

A Moon in Sagittarius makes the instinct daring, open and innocent, fascinated by the universe and the whole world in which to seek understanding. This person will have a very positive sense of humour. The Moon in Sagittarius influences a person to be a moral reformer, a missionary for better ways of living. Being stuck in predictable routines will devastate this person. But pleasure will come from the company of those who like to explore new ideas and who seek themselves to be amazed by new discoveries.

The twelfth house is the passageway from mere self to unity with the universe. Not everyone has an astronomical entity in their twelfth house. A person with a planet in the twelfth house can learn to be in tune with the infinite, but that learning is not easy. A person is well warned not to ignore an opportunity to reach higher consciousness. The twelfth house is known as the House of Troubles, because failing to take up its professed enlightenment in the manner in which it is offered incurs cosmic punishment.

For this person, the Moon is alone in this house, and acts as his bridge to eternal concepts. The Moon makes a person feel, from infancy and through life, a strong instinctive pull towards some world different from the real world he sees around him. The Moon draws at the heart in subjective and emotional ways, insisting on intuitive trust in inner feelings and understanding of what it is the senses experience. Reflection is essential or the power of the rush of impressions can overwhelm self-confidence! This person might find himself, before he knows it, drawn deeply into relationships with others that greatly undermine his self-esteem. He might even just want to seek oblivion because he can endure no more feeling.

The so-called Nodes of the Moon are not listed in the table of the natal chart. The Moon is considered to have two nodes that are always in directly opposing astrological signs. Astrologers consider the South Node of the Moon to refer to events before birth, while the North Node relates to things in the future – the cosmic reason that the child has been born. Whichever of these influences dominates will have a major influence on the life lived. Some adepts consider the North Node of the Moon the most significant point in a birth chart because it represents the potential of the life, the ultimate reason it came into being.

The South Node of the Moon is in Capricorn, representing the Great Father and regression to the primeval era of mankind. Aeons of authority culminate in this infant newly born. This child is tough and resourceful, as if coming into the world already rich in the guile of self-preservation. This means reticence to show emotion, to be spontaneous, and to recognise inner feelings.

The South Node also falls in the first house. This child came from a long line of ancestors who had had to stand alone, without help, and yet succeed. While this bred independence, it also meant isolation.

The North Node of the Moon is in Cancer and in the seventh house. Cancer is the sign of the Great Mother. Cancer is also the House of the Moon. Moon in Cancer influences a person to be deeply emotional with an intense love of home and family. With this influence a person will also love the theatre and excitement of spectacle, and have obstinate tenaciousness. To achieve the potential of the North Node in this sign this person must break out of an instinct to remain defiantly independent of others. He must develop emotional self-expression, accepting against his natural inclination that only with the help of others can he realise his visions. He also needs one person to stand by him through thick and thin, in spite of all he is driven to be and do.

Had this child been born 24 hours later, the Moon would have moved into Capricorn and been in the first house, but there would have been only minor changes in all other measures. Thus the influence of the Moon Nodes is the only change in the interpretation of this horoscope. In Chinese astrology, it would imply a similar difference.

Capricorn promotes integrity, character, morality and a sense of personal honour. These together make for a strong will able to dominate all other aspects of personality, including emotion. Moon in Capricorn implies a person of visible natural authority. It requires a person to identify the one big principle that matters to him, and live his life accordingly. Moon in Capricorn means vivid emotions, and deep desires that seek fulfilment, but often these are dangerous inclinations. This person needs to apply his energy to a Great Work that with firm self-discipline involves concentration, excellence and commitment. This will make this hard-working person at risk of nervous disorders.

This following morning, the Moon is in the first house. This person would have very strong instinct to provide for those reliant on him. He would have a vast capacity for creativity. People would see this person as imaginative and sensitive. But they would also see him as having the means to fulfil their needs but needing no help to achieve his own ends – so he would be used and taken for granted. He would be leaned on more than he could take.

The third influence on a person is the rising sign or Ascendant. This is the sign that was rising over the horizon at the moment of birth. Adepts consider it to define the external image that a person best projects in company to be able to remain true to himself. If a person adopts their Ascendant image, they are drawn to people with whom they are happy and to experiences that will contribute to their happiness. This endows life and grace.

Ascendant Sagittarius represents a desire to experiment, independence and the curiosity of a philosopher. This person will appear to be bright, sociable and self-confident. He will appear alert and very interested in and involved in what is around him. He will constantly be inquiring and looking for explanations. He will project himself as a straightforward direct man with strong independent spirit. Such a person will be ill at ease tied down to responsibilities, which will make him appear to ignore those around him and care nothing for them. He needs variety; he needs to get out, to get around, to find the surprising.

The first house, or House of the Self is defined by the first hours of life but duration at any location is determined by latitude and time of year. On this star chart it embraces part of Sagittarius, Capricorn and part of Aquarius. Planets in the first house modify the influence of the Ascendant. Mercury, Venus, Mars, Jupiter and Pluto are in this house on this chart.

Mercury is in the first house in Capricorn and thus people's first impression of this person is of someone very quick witted. On the other hand, this person can be seized by an urge to an outbreak of irresponsible flippancy. Preventing this needs exercising strongest self-control.

Mercury represents thinking, speaking, learning and wondering. It is associated with observation and curiosity and the raw intake of all the senses. Capricorn affects Mercury by transforming a mischief into a focused power, enabling crystal clear logic and instant insight into the meaning of what is observed. It enables instinctive awareness of pattern and reason in apparent chaos. It promotes precision and clarity. Mercury in Capricorn creates a shrewd mind capable of long concentration that will produce practical and well-organised ideas. Equally, it can produce wild ideas and impractical schemes while having instinctive understanding of things mathematical. Boredom for this person is dangerous.

Mercury was retrograde at the time of birth. (All planetary revolutions are in the same direction round the Sun. Because Earth moves round as the other planets move round, sometimes it looks as if a planet goes back on itself. When this appears to happen, adepts consider that it alters the influence of the planet.) This retrograde movement would add a 'spice' to the influence of Mercury on communication, making a person much more quiet than he might be, but giving a rapier wit, adding a streak of obstinacy and exposing the person to a risk of fouling up through saying the wrong thing. The retrograde movement causes this person to consider and review his words before he commits his name to them.

Venus is in the first house in Aquarius. Venus promotes serenity, harmony, peace and the aesthetic functions. Venus in the first house gives a person intense animal magnetism, but also makes people instantly trust the person. Venus in the first house makes a peacemaker and an artist. Aquarius affects Venus by focusing the aesthetic sensibility on the unexpected, whether in the works of nature or of man and promoting instinctive courtesy, diplomacy, friendship and romance. Aquarius encourages this person to seek relationships with others who have got spirit and look on life in new ways but requires for harmony that relationship towards this person is tolerant and uncritical. But this person will not allow anyone to possess him; his freedom is too important. Because of its position within Aquarius, Venus is in this star chart aligned with the Sun. This brings the influence of Venus into the centre of this person's being. The presence of Venus and Sun in the first house means that this person, if he makes the utmost of his abilities and opportunities, will achieve his destiny and spiritual purpose. Modern astrologers, noting Venus in this chart is directly opposite Neptune, consider this would greatly increase this person's attractiveness to the opposite sex.

Mars is in the first house in Aquarius. Mars represents courage, will power and assertiveness. In the first house this signifies a spiritual warrior who carves out his own right path and sticks to it. Mars in the first house makes a person give an impression of being one you don't trifle with, a daunting person of strong will. This person will exude passion and intensity. He will be happiest if he faces up to those things of which he is instinctively frightened. Aquarius affects Mars by causing this person to question and challenge authority and be passionate about truth. This inevitably causes the person to become ostracised and alone. Mars is also aligned with the Sun, strengthening the impact of this person's independent spirit.

Jupiter is in the first house in Capricorn. Jupiter represents the Great Architect. In the first house, Jupiter will make a person radiate a positive brightness, even when he is down. Indeed, to overcome depression, this person should adopt the Jupiter approach of choosing a grand goal and working hard to achieve it. Adepts considered Jupiter in the first house to be good luck, but the luck that Jupiter gives is often not what this world calls luck! Moreover, the influence of Jupiter is considerably restricted when in Capricorn – but on the other hand, when Jupiter is in Capricorn it influences a person to accept responsibility, to value what has been proven to be of worth, and to be of high integrity and good judgement. Note parallels with the influence of Moon in Capricorn.

Had Pluto been discovered by the end of the 18th century, according to modern astrologers, adepts would have considered its presence in Sagittarius and possibly interpreted this as enabling the person to face honestly and squarely those things that cause fear. Such might include sexuality, or disease and death-fear, or guilt. The Plutonian way to face the fear is to see meaning in it beyond self. Pluto moves so slowly that its position would at this general level influence a whole generation. In the first house, Pluto makes it imperative that this person find an aim in life or all the intensity with which he was born would be dissipated worthlessly. He would in any event constantly be plagued with fear of his tendency to irresponsible behaviour. Pluto was close to the Moon at the moment of this birth. Modern astrologers propose that Pluto would thus have been considered a key influence in the person represented by this star chart.

The second house is crudely described as the House of Money, but is more correctly considered the House of Resources. This house represents other people's opinion of our worth. Its message is proving our self-worth to self as failure to do so causes self-doubt that can paralyse.

Saturn had just moved into Pisces. Saturn in Pisces influences a person to look for life guidance in the past, and to feel excessive regret. Saturn undermines effort. It makes building self-confidence a painstakingly slow step-at-a-time process, without help being offered by others – not even the ready pat on the back for achievement. It insists that a feeling of personal success comes only by taking on and slowly working to conclusion solitary projects that absorb the spirit and which require the person to develop real skills and take active steps to reach a result. Pisces dominates the second house in this birth chart. With Saturn in this position this child was born with little belief in his own worth, but with great ability to develop it. From the perspective of Earth, Saturn was at this time moving against the sky backdrop quite rapidly, which adepts consider would mitigate its power. Were this child born ninety minutes later, and thus had Capricorn Ascendant, Saturn would be in the first house and its negative influence would be considerably increased. In any event, the strength and position of Saturn indicate a life of intense struggle.

Uranus, in 1759 not yet discovered, was quite far through Pisces at this birth. Uranus when in Pisces is now considered to influence a person to draw on memory and on the past for creativity, invoking dreams and subconscious thought to create beauty. Uranus moves much more slowly than Saturn. Uranus in Pisces proposes the Path of the Mystic. This person would find his identity through radically and independently exploring his own awareness. This philosophical process can be described as religious, but is not tied to formalised religions. Uranus in the second house gives the message that what matters is not other people's opinion of this person, but what he knows of his own true worth. All the social approval of the world is worth nothing if a person does not try to be the man he could be.

314

Appendix IV

Uranus would not have appeared in a natal chart drawn up at this time of this birth. However, this planet has been designated the ruler of Aquarius, the Sun sign of this birth. The Age of Aquarius is the time of equality of all.

Some astrologers will consider in their interpretations such planets as Uranus, Neptune and Pluto despite the chart being erected for a time before their discoveries. Some prefer to interpret older charts based only on the traditional planets. Even if using this approach, it would in this case be valid to include Uranus in analyses for after 1781. Certain of the progressed planets in this chart do conjoin Uranus during the person's life.

The eighth house is the house of mysticism in the instinctive levels of consciousness.

Neptune in 1759 was not yet discovered. Neptune moves so slowly that it remains in one sign for over thirteen years. Neptune is the planet of dreams and meditation – the doorway to what we are not. Neptune was in Leo at the time of this birth. Leo is the Performer. Neptune in Leo requires conscious and deliberate efforts to achieve purest expression of creativity. Leo corresponded with the eighth house of this birth chart. Modern astrologers propose that, had Neptune been recognised, in this house adepts would have expected it to demand unreserved self-expression. True relationships would be deep. Neptune's presence in the eighth house of this chart would have suggested that here was a man instinctively capable of arcane healing crafts, of working with powerful symbols, of interpreting dreams; a man attuned to other worlds and the supernatural.

Halley's Comet was sighted approaching the Sun shortly before this birth.

With so many planets grouped so close to the Sun, the return to visible realms of Halley's Comet days before this birth intensifies planetary influences. This increases challenges, makes emotions stronger, but also enriches resources.

Selected Astronomical Events 1758 - 1797

Later 18th century Solar eclipses in Europe or North America

Total Eclipses

Year	Date	Where visible
1760	13th Jun	Crete and Turkey
1769	4th Jun	Labrador
1778	24th Jun	Mexico City to Virginia
1780	27th Oct	Quebec and Maine
1788	4th Jun	Crete, Cyprus, Turkey

Annular or Hybrid Eclipses

Year	Date	
1764	1st Apr	Portugal, Spain, France, Kent, Netherlands, Denmark, Sweden
1766	5th Aug	Nova Scotia, Alaska
1768	19th Jan	Mexico, East America, Labrador
1771	6th Nov	Mexico, Central America
1773	23rd Mar	Crete, Cyprus and Palestine
1777	9th Jan	Kansas, Texas and Florida
1781	23rd Apr	Dominican Republic and Panama
1782	12th Apr	California to Hudson Bay
1791	3rd Apr	Ohio to Newfoundland
1793	5th Sep	Southern Scandinavia, Poland and Ukraine

No solar eclipses visible in Scotland during this period.

Transits of Venus took place on 6th June 1761 and 3rd June 1769.

Transits of Mercury took place on 9th November 1769, 2nd November 1776, 12th November 1782, 4th May 1786 and 5th November 1789.

Visible Comets 1759-96: In addition to the appearance of Halley's Comet in January 1759, the comet Messier – considered 'great' in that it would attract attention of a person casually looking at the night sky – was first visible to the naked eye on 24th August 1769, and reached its greatest brightness on 22nd September 1769.

Total Lunar eclipses visible in Ayrshire from start 1758 to end 1797
Western modern calendar, GMT.

Year	Date	Start time of totality
1758	24th January	05.42
1761	18th May	21.25
1768	30th June	03.22
1776	30th July	23.14
1779	23rd November	18.55
1783	18th March	20.40
1783	10th September	22.43
1787	3rd January	23.04
1790	28th April	23.05
1790	22nd October	23.50
1794	14th February	21.29
1797	4th December	03.28

Listings created from data sourced in NASA website.